BLOODY BUNA
THE BATTLE FOR THE BEACHHEAD NEW GUINEA 1942-43

Copyright © David W. Cameron

First published 2023

This book is copyright. Apart from any fair dealing for the purposes of private study, research, criticism or review as permitted under the Copyright Act, no part may be reproduced, stored in a retrieval system or transmitted in any form or by any means, electronic, mechanical, photocopying, recording or otherwise, without written permission.

All inquiries should be made to the publishers.

Big Sky Publishing Pty Ltd
PO Box 303, Newport, NSW 2106, Australia
Phone: 1300 364 611
Email: info@bigskypublishing.com.au
Web: www.bigskypublishing.com.au

Cover design and typesetting: Think Productions

A catalogue record for this book is available from the National Library of Australia

BLOODY BUNA
THE BATTLE FOR THE BEACHHEAD NEW GUINEA 1942-43

DAVID W. CAMERON

OTHER BOOKS BY DAVID CAMERON

Assassination of the Butcher of Prague, Reinhard Heydrich – Hitler's Protégé.

Gona's Gone: The Battle for the Beachhead New Guina, 1942.

Retaking Kokoda: The Battles for Templeton's Crossing, Eora Creek and the Oivi-Gorari positions.

Saving Port Moresby: Fighting at the end of the Kokoda Track.

The Battle for Isurava: Fighting on the Kokoda Track in the heart of the Owen Stanleys.

The Battles for Kokoda Plateau: Three Weeks of Hell Defending the Gateway to the Owen Stanleys.

Macquarie Harbour: Convict Hell.

Convict era Port Arthur — 'Misery of the deepest dye'.

Australians on the Western Front 1918 Vol 1: Resisting the Great German Offensive.

Australians on the Western Front 1918 Vol 2: Spearheading the Great British Offensive.

The Charge: The Australian Light Horse Victory at Beersheba.

The Battle of Long Tan Plantation: 18 August 1966 – Australia's four hours of Hell in Vietnam.

Our Friend the Enemy: Anzac from both sides of the wire.

Shadows of Anzac: An Intimate History of Gallipoli.

Gallipoli: The Final Battles and the Evacuation of Anzac.

'Sorry lads the order is to go' The August Offensive at Anzac Gallipoli, 1915.

The Battle for Lone Pine: Four Days of Hell in the Heart of Gallipoli.

25 April 1915: The Day the Anzac Legend was Born.

Hominid Adaptations and Extinctions.

Bones, Stones & Molecules: 'Out of Africa' and Human origins (with Colin Groves).

MAP LEGEND

Military Symbols

III	Brigade/Regiment
II	Battalion
I	Company
...	Platoon
⊠	Infantry Unit
▭	Headquarters
▣	Artillery
	Medium/Heavy Machine-gun
	Mortars
⊠	Defensive Position

Natural Features

	Jungle
	Palm Trees
	River
	Track
	Wetland
	Kunai Grass

ACKNOWLEDGEMENTS

I am indebted to those mentioned in this book who wrote down and/or recorded their experiences. Without these critical historical records this narrative could never have been told in any meaningful detail. It has always been important for this author to tell the story using the words of those that were there – it brings the narrative into a whole new light as many voices are heard as opposed to the monotone of a single writer. Like all researchers, I am also indebted to these individuals for unselfishly donating their precious documents, writings and 'curios' to numerous research institutions for others to study. This also applies to relatives who have provided similar valuable records. For those copyright holders I was unable to locate or who did not reply to my request to use quoted material in this book, I trust that the material quoted meets with your approval.

I would like to thank Dr Gregory Blake for supplying the primary source material relating to the 32nd Division and the Australian 2/6th Independent Company, in their efforts to take Buna as part of his doctoral research while at the Dwight D. Eisenhower Library, Abilene Kansas, and the National Archives and Records Administration, Washington, D.C., USA. Gratitude to the Department of Veterans Affairs and the University of New South Wales for enabling me to quote from the extensive collection of interviews of Australian veterans of the campaign as part of the *Australians at War Film Archive (AWFA)*.

At Big Skey I would like to thank my publisher Denny Neave for believing in this book, when all too often others incorrectly stated there was nothing more to be said about the Papuan Campaigns – we still have much to learn. A similar thanks to Michele Perry who took on the manuscript and quickly and efficiently had it ready for publication; similarly, to Eric Olason for drafting the maps. It goes without saying any remaining errors are those of the author alone.

My biggest thanks are to Helen, and my three wonderful and special children, Emma, Anita and Lloyd, and my precious little granddaughter Naomi.

CONTENTS

Prologue 1

PART 1. The Early Fighting to take Buna 4

1. 'I don't think it would be too much trouble to take Buna …' 5
2. 'The Ghost Mountain Boys' 14
3. 'Worse yet, we didn't understand the Japanese' 27
4. 'Naturally, the strips gave the enemy fields of fire' 35
5. '… deprive the Allies of any room for a counter-offensive' 43
6. 'It is imperative that our forces push forward at the greatest speed …' 49
7. '… first defeat and clean up the Australian force' 52
8. '… all columns will be driven through to objectives regardless of losses' 56
9. '… charging an enemy machinegun post, submachine gun in hand' 65
10. 'The parade of injured GIs was heartbreaking to watch …' 68
11. 'Stirring up the Japs' 83
12. 'I am beginning to wonder who will reach zero first' 89
13. 'At this rate, we can't hold out' 97

14	'Our unit daily becomes weaker'	106
15	'… the Japs had hurriedly withdrawn'	112
16	'This is the MDS, or what's f…g left of it!'	120
17	'The Emperor … has asked that Buna be defended to the last man!'	125
18	'To a girl I Love'	133
19	'Buna is gradually falling into a state of danger'	137
20	'Want you to take Buna, or not come back alive'	150

PART 2. Stalemate 159

21	'At the break of dawn, the enemy charged'	160
22	'Have you taken out the Triangle yet?'	167
23	'… watched parachute troops making a safe landing'	181
24	'… these are NOT tanks'	188
25	'We have hit them and bounced off'	196
26	'… much to be proud of during the day's operations'	208
27	'… there is always enemy mortar fire'	216
28	'During the day, considerable Jap movement was observed …'	222
29	'… may start a general attack in revenge of Hawaii'	229
30	'… we have bullets of flesh'	238

31	'Four tanks had just arrived at Hariko'	246
32	'They fire rifles a lot'	254

PART 3. Taking New and Old Strips and Buna Village ... 259

33	'Buna will not be reinforced but should eventually be evacuated'	260
34	'A guardian angel was watching over me'	266
35	'Captain Honda graciously died in action'	270
36	'Borrowed clippers at night and all had haircuts'	275
37	'The sergeant commanding the carrier platoon and I concocted a plan …'	279
38	'You are expendable, we must take the objective at whatever cost'	286
39	'We knew the bastards were there, but you couldn't actually see them'	295
40	'… the capacity of seasoned AIF troops'	329
41	'I am going to bring Tomlinson in here for a day or so …'	336
42	'That's what we're trying to do sarge'	350
43	'I won't send my men over that creek …'	359
44	'Maybe I can get a toehold there'	369
45	'… circled around the turret like a tin opener'	378
46	'… get on with your job, my boy'	394
47	'I nominate that bloke for the next round'	403

48	'The shit hit the fan as usual'	414
49	'Withdraw for Buna, assemble at north Giruwa'	422

PART 4. Buna Beachhead Falls 435

50	'… fairly traumatic experience to see the dead and decaying bodies'	436
51	'Enemy tanks have already penetrated near unit headquarters'	448
52	'Today, we are moving on Buna Mission from both directions …'	452
53	'… easy picking with my Tommy gun and hand grenades'	461
54	'"… Oh, those two," said the CO and seemed quite amused'	475
55	'… here we were, thoroughly defeated'	488
56	'Ensign Suzuki entered the sea at 2.30 am'	492
57	'Now that the battle for Buna is over and won …'	504

Epilogue 511

End Notes 514

Bibliography 546

Index 553

PROLOGUE

The crossing of the Kumusi River by the Australian 16th and 25th brigades by mid-November 1942 signalled the end of the four-month-long Kokoda Campaign. Within days, the battles for the Japanese beachheads would commence.

Four months earlier, the beginning of the Kokoda Campaign had begun with the Japanese invasion by the *South Seas Force* at Gona and Buna on 21 July. From there they began their advance south along the Kokoda Track across the Owen Stanley Range. Just before reaching their objective, which was Port Moresby, in late September, the Japanese high command ordered them to withdraw. The attack against the township was on hold until the fighting on Guadalcanal in the Solomon Islands had been decided.

During the Japanese advance and withdrawal, the troops of the *144th* and *41st regiments* suffered appalling casualties inflicted upon them initially by the Australian fighting withdrawal conducted by the militiamen of the 39th Battalion, the 1st Papuan Infantry Battalion, and soon after, by the men of the 2nd AIF, 21st Brigade (2/14th, 2/16th and 2/27th battalions), with the fighting at Oivi, Kokoda Plateau, Deniki, Isurava, Brigade Hill, and Ioribaiwa Ridge.

The Australian advance by the militiamen of the 3rd Battalion, and the veterans of the 2nd AIF 16th Brigade (2/1st, 2/2nd and 3/3rd infantry battalions) and the 25th Brigade (2/25th, 2/31st and 2/33rd infantry battalions) would encounter stubborn Japanese resistance, first during their defence of Ioribaiwa Ridge and later in the fighting to retake Templeton's Crossing and at Eora Creek in October. With the fighting below the northern slopes of the Owen Stanleys, to take Oivi and Gorari in early to mid-November, the Japanese *South Seas Force* basically ceased to exist as an effective fighting force, with its

PROLOGUE

commander Major General Tomitarô Horii drowning a few days later in his attempts to reach the coast.[i]

Generals Douglas MacArthur and Thomas Blamey now planned for the Australian 7th Infantry Division, commanded by Major General George Vasey and the American 32nd Infantry Division commanded by Major General Edwin Harding, to take the three Japanese beachheads. It would represent the first time in the war that Australian and American land forces would conduct large-scale joint operations against the Japanese. The 25th Brigade would approach from the south-west with the militiamen of the 3rd Battalion and Chaforce (elements of the battle-weary survivors of the 21st Brigade) to take Gona, while the Australians of the 16th Brigade would take Sanananda. The line of approach for the 25th Brigade was Awala – Jumbora – Gona, while that of the 16th Brigade was Popondetta – Soputa – Sanananda.

From 19 November, the Australians of the 25th Brigade, supported by the 3rd Battalion, later reinforced with the remaining troops of the 21st Brigade and the militiamen of the 39th Battalion, did battle with the Japanese to take Gona and Haddy's Village representing the western flank of the Japanese, beachheads. The Gona beachhead would finally fall to the Australians on 9 December, while the Haddy's Village area would not be taken until 18 December. As the fighting to take Gona raged, the battles to take Buna and Sanananda[ii] continued into January 1943.

The Americans of the 128th and 126th infantry regiments were assigned – along with the Australian commandos of the 2/6th Independent Company, supported by Australian artillery – the task of capturing Buna beachhead from the east and south respectively. By mid-December, however, the Americans and Japanese there had

---

i   For a detailed account of the Kokoda Campaign (22 July to 16 November 1942) see Cameron (2020) *The Battles for Kokoda Plateau*; Cameron (2022), *The Battle for Isurava*; Cameron (2022), *Saving Port Moresby*; and Cameron (2022) *Retaking Kokoda*.

ii   For a detailed account of the fighting to take Gona, see Cameron (2023) *Gona's Gone: The Battle for the Beachhead, New Guinea, 1942*.

fought to a standstill, and it was now that the newly arrived Australians of the 18th Brigade, who had earlier repulsed the Japanese invasion at Milne Bay in late August, were committed to the battle. Assisted by Australian artillery, Bren gun carriers, tanks, and Allied airmen, the Australian and American infantrymen would finally take Buna on 3 January 1943.

Collectively, the fighting to take the three Japanese beachheads represents some of the most horrific fighting to take place during the entire Pacific War.

PART 1

THE EARLY FIGHTING TO TAKE BUNA

1
'I DON'T THINK IT WOULD BE TOO MUCH TROUBLE TO TAKE BUNA ...'

With the Japanese withdrawal from Ioribaiwa Ridge just north of Port Moresby in late September 1942, the tide had finally turned in the Kokoda Campaign, and the Australians were now on the offensive, rapidly driving the Japanese north along the track. By early November 1942, they had retaken Kokoda Plateau and its airstrip just below the northern slopes of the Owen Stanley Range, and by mid-November, they had fought the Japanese just east of Kokoda to retake Oivi and Gorari and were crossing the Kumusi River further east.[1]

American warlord, General Douglas MacArthur – the Supreme Commander of Allied Forces in the South West Pacific Area (SWPA) – and Australian General Thomas Blamey, commanding the Allied SWPA Land Forces, were now determined that their forces would command the mountain range between Milne Bay at the eastern tip of New Guinea through to Wau; around 350 kilometres as the crow flies further west. Additional attacks would be undertaken to take the three Japanese beachheads at Gona, Sanananda and Buna, directly north of Kokoda Plateau.[2]

On 2 November, MacArthur and Blamey decided that they would immediately drive through with a three-column advance against these beachheads, provided that New Guinea Force (NGF) – representing the command of all Allied forces in New Guinea – could offer ten days supplies behind each advancing column. The columns would unite on

CHAPTER 1

or about 15 November, east of the Kumusi River. The following day, NGF would order the American 32nd Infantry Division[iii] to patrol up to, but to make no move beyond, the Oro Bay-Bofu-Wairopi line just south and east of Buna until ordered. Earlier, on 6 November, MacArthur and an advance echelon left Australia, arriving at Port Moresby to establish his forward headquarters.[3]

***

With the outbreak of war in September 1939, Australia had two military systems in place –the militia and the 2nd AIF – the 1st AIF refers to the men who fought in the First World War. By law, the militia could not serve outside Australia, its territories, or protectorates; only members of the 2nd AIF could serve overseas. The south-eastern part of New Guinea –Papua – became an Australian protectorate in 1906. And with the defeat of Germany in the Great War, north-east New Guinea and the islands of New Britain, New Ireland, and Bougainville, which had been German colonies, were in 1920 ceded by the League of Nations to be administered by Australia. With the outbreak of war with Japan in December 1941, the former German territories were incorporated by Australian authorities into Papua, to be governed by the Australian New Guinea Administrative Unit (ANGAU).[4]

Sergeant Victor Austin, a 22-year-old from Prahran in Victoria, who was with the militia 39th Battalion, succinctly recorded the rivalry between the men of the 2nd AIF and militia: 'Since the men of the AIF had enlisted for overseas service and were thus fairly assured of seeing active service in one or other theatres of the war, they understandably felt "martially superior" to the men serving in the militia, referring to them disparagingly as "chockos"'.[5] This was a derisive term implying they were chocolate soldiers who would melt in the heat of battle. It

---

[iii] An American Division consisted of three regiments, each with three battalions – similar to an Australian division, which consisted of three brigades, each with three battalions – with each battalion numbering around 500 fighting men at full strength in four rifle companies.

was also suggested, by some, that the militiamen should 'get some weight on their shoulders', referring to the brass 'AUSTRALIA' shoulder flashes worn by the men of the 2nd AIF.[6] The courage and ongoing fighting abilities of the militia – especially those of the 39th Battalion during the fighting withdrawal along the Kokoda Track and later at Gona and Sanananda, as well as those of the 3rd Battalion during the later defence of the track around Ioribaiwa Ridge and the advance to Kokoda and Oivi and the fighting around Gona – would put to rest the 'chocko" myth.[7]

* * *

The American 32nd Infantry Division, commanded by Major General Edwin Harding, would initially be committed to the fighting to take the Japanese beachhead at Buna. Two of his units, the 126th and 128th regiments, which consisted of men trained as part of a National Guard formation from Michigan and Wisconsin respectively, would be involved in the fighting. The national guardsmen were essentially like the Australian militia in terms of training and status.[8]

On arriving in Australia, Lieutenant General Robert Eichelberger, commanding the American I Corps, had instituted a rapid increase in training for the men of the division, but the infantrymen of the 126th and 128th regiments were already preparing for transportation to New Guinea, and so their training schedule was seriously disrupted. These men were described at the time as not being in top physical shape, and they had received little training in scouting, night patrolling, or jungle warfare. Looking back, Harding recorded: 'I have no quarrel with the general thesis that the 32nd was by no means adequately trained for combat – particularly jungle combat. A Third Army (Krueger) training inspection team gave it a thoroughgoing inspection about a month before I joined it and found it deficient on many counts. I got a copy of this report from Krueger, and it was plenty bad .... On the other hand, I found the division well disciplined, well behaved, and well-grounded in certain elements of training .... My estimate

CHAPTER 1

of training when I took over is that it was about on a par with other National Guard divisions at that time'.[9]

Harding wrote to his wife Eleanor, concerned that he and men might be sent to New Guinea before they were ready: 'I prefer to get a crack at them [Japanese] when the time comes .... When I go, I hope it will be with plenty of power – air, land and sea – enough to make sure that none of those I am taking along with me will be sacrificed needlessly'. He also wrote to his mother at the time: 'I want to bring back as many of the Red Arrow lads with me as I can. That ambition won't be furthered if we move before we are good and ready to go'.[10] Events would prove he had a right to be concerned.

The official American historian of the campaign, Samuel Milner, recoded in *Victory in Papua – the War in the Pacific*:

> Not only were the troops inadequately trained, equipped and supported for the task in hand, but many of the difficulties they were to meet at Buna had been neither foreseen nor provided for.
>
> The division, whose insignia is a Red Arrow with a crosspiece on the shaft, was a former Michigan and Wisconsin National Guard unit. It had a record of outstanding service in World War I, having fought with great distinction on the Aisne-Marne, the Oise-Aisne, and in the Meuse-Argonne drive. The division was inducted into the federal service on 15 October 1940 as a square division. The following April, some 8000 Michigan and Wisconsin selectees were added to its strength. After participating in the Louisiana manoeuvres, the division was triangularine into the 126th, 127th, and 128th infantry regiments ....
>
> Ordered at the last moment to the Pacific, the division took on more than 3000 replacements at San Francisco and reached Adelaide, Australia, on 14 May. Training had scarcely got under

way when the division was again ordered to move – this time to Brisbane. The move was completed in mid-August, and training had just got into its stride at Camp Cable, the division's camp near Brisbane, when the first troops started moving to New Guinea.[11]

Although the troops had the standard equipment of the day, not all of it was to prove suitable for service in the South Pacific. The Australian militia were very much in the same position when they first arrived at Port Moresby in 1941–42. Much of the American (and Australian) radio equipment failed to function in the rough jungle-covered mountains and ravines, and most American infantrymen did not have the M1 carbine that would have been an ideal weapon in the tangled, overgrown vegetation dominating the beachhead area.

Although the M1 was available elsewhere, it was to be months before they would reach the South West Pacific Area in any numbers. These troops, like the Australian militia before them, had none of the specialised clothing and equipment that later became routine for jungle fighting. While their uniforms were dyed to aid concealment in the jungle, they caused great discomfort because the dye ran, and the fabric was mostly nonporous. As a result, they became unbearable in the tropical heat, resulting in hideous jungle ulcers.[12]

Eichelberger recalled after the war: 'No one could remember when he had been dry. The feet, arms, bellies, chests, armpits of my soldiers were hideous with jungle rot …. The soldiers themselves steamed and sweated in their heavy jungle suits. These suits were supposedly porous. Back in Australia, before the New Guinea expedition, it was I who had ordered them dyed a mottled green to aid troop concealment. This was well meant but a serious error. The dye closed the "breathing spaces" in the cloth'.[13]

Though they were about to enter a jungle area overgrown with vines and teeming with insects, the men were short of machetes and had no insect repellents. Nor had anyone thought to issue them

CHAPTER 1

with waterproof pouches for the protection of their personal effects and medical supplies from the extreme heat and wet. Cigarettes and matches became sodden and unusable, and quinine pills, vitamin pills and salt tablets began to disintegrate almost as soon as the men put them in their pockets or packs, and often the same thing happened to the water chlorination tablets.[14] Lieutenant Colonel Alexander MacNab, executive officer of the 128th Regiment, also recorded on 15 December: 'We dug wells to get drinkable water. There was a scarcity of chlorinating chemical, but water was generally chlorinated. I always chlorinated my own water, but I suffered from dysentery as much as any of the troops. There was a scarcity of quinine. Troops were eating Australian rations. Razors were not shipped. They had been requested but not sent'.[15]

Various means were employed to lighten the weight each man carried in the jungle. Where possible, the troops were equipped with Thompson submachine guns, and the heavier weapons, including most of the 81 mm mortars, would be sent forward later by boat or aircraft. Medical units used gas stoves or kerosene burners to sterilise their instruments and provide the casualties with hot food and drink.

The frontline troops, however, had none of these things. Without their normal mess equipment, they had no choice but to use tin containers of all kinds to heat their rations, prepare their coffee (when available) and wash their mess gear. Since it rained almost continually, and there was very little dry fuel available, it was usually impossible to heat water sufficiently to sterilise the tins and mess gear from which the troops ate – contributing to diarrhea and dysentery.[16]

American officers failed to appreciate the toll that the jungle and terrain would take on their men. They also badly underestimated the fighting abilities of the Japanese. On 14 October, Harding wrote to Major General Richard Sutherland, MacArthur's chief of staff: 'My idea is that we should push towards Buna with all speed, while the Japs are heavily occupied with the Guadalcanal business. Also, we have complete supremacy in the air here, and the air people could do a lot to help in the taking of Buna, even should it be fairly strongly defended, which I doubt. I think it quite possible that we might find it easy pickings, with only a shell of sacrifice troops left to defend it and Kokoda. This may be a bum guess, but even if it proves to be incorrect, I don't think it would be too much trouble to take Buna with the forces we can put against it'.[17]

Two weeks later, Harding wrote that even though he previously assessed his men as being largely untrained and not in great physically shape: 'All information we have to date indicates that the Japanese forces in the Buna-Popondetta-Gona triangle are relatively light. Unless he gets reinforcements, I believe we will be fighting him on at least a three to one basis. Imbued as I am with considerable confidence in the fighting qualities of the American soldier, I am not at all pessimistic about the outcome of the scrap .... The health of the troops has been remarkably good. The sick rate is very low. If our luck holds in this respect, we should go into the operation with our effective strength reduced very little by sickness – less than four per cent, I would say'.[18] The Americans would soon realise that the evacuation of their sick would far outstrip battle casualties.

Colonel Handy, with the 32nd Divisional staff, noted in early November that many believed, 'Buna could be had by walking in and taking over', while Colonel Harry Knight, also with the headquarters staff, assessed:

> The lid really blew off, when the order was received on 3 November that American troops were not to move forward from Mendaropu and Bofu until further instructed. The reason for the order was, of course, to gain time in which to stockpile supplies for the impending advance, but the division, restive and eager to be 'up and at 'em' did not see it that way .... Opinions were freely expressed by officers of all ranks ... that the only reason for the order was a political one. GHQ was afraid to turn the Americans loose and let them capture Buna

CHAPTER 1

because it would be a blow to the prestige of the Australians who had fought the long hard battle all through the Owen Stanley Mountains, and who therefore should be the ones to capture Buna. The belief was prevalent that the Japanese had no intention of holding Buna; that he had no troops there; that he was delaying the Australians with a small force so as to evacuate as many as possible.[19]

This, of course, was nonsense, as the Americans alone were then tasked with capturing the Buna beachhead, not the Australians, although the Australian infantrymen within a month would be called on to help do so, and they would capture most what would become known as Warren Front, aided by Australian artillery and armour regiments, and the fighting here would be directly commanded by an Australian Brigadier.

On 6 November, American Intelligence Officer Major Hawkins, who was with the divisional headquarters, noted that both ground and air reconnaissance reports indicated that Buna, Simemi and Sanananda each held perhaps 200 to 300 Japanese, with only 'a small number' of enemy troops at Gona. This assessment would prove to be spectacularly inaccurate. The Japanese at these beachheads numbered in the thousands, entrenched in strong defensive positions, including strong reinforced earthen bunkers, criss-crossed with trenches and machinegun, mortar and mountaingun positions. Hawkins went on to incorrectly assess that the Japanese were already reconciled to the loss of Buna and were likely evacuating the position by way of the Mambare River mouth to avoid a 'Dunkirk', as the beach was open to heavy air attack.[20]

These optimistic assessments of an early Japanese withdrawal were not initially shared by Major General Charles Willoughby (MacArthur's intelligence chief). Willoughby estimated Japanese strength on 10 November to be two depleted regiments, a battalion of mountain artillery, and 'normal' reinforcing and service elements – about 4000 men in all. However, by mid-November, Buna and Sanananda each had around 3000 troops dug-in and waiting, while at Gona, another 800 troops were also dug-in. With Japanese reinforcements from Rabaul during November and December 1942 this number would swell to around 10,000 Japanese distributed between Buna, Sanananda, Gona, and the area just west of Gona Creek (considering around 2000 sick and wounded were likely evacuated to Rabaul from mid-November and December 1942). Willoughby believed an enemy withdrawal from Buna was improbable, at least until the issue was decided at Guadalcanal. He was aware that Major General Tomitarô Horii, commanding the Japanese *South Seas Force*, had been ordered to hold Buna until operations in the Solomons were successfully completed.[21] These orders, along with the Japanese expectations of success in the Solomons, and what was known of the Japanese commander's character, indicated to Willoughby that it was unlikely there would be 'a withdrawal at this time'.[22]

2
'THE GHOST MOUNTAIN BOYS'

The task of the 32nd Division was formally defined by NGF on 8 October: 'The role of 32 Div is to attack the enemy at Buna from the east and south-east'.[1] They were to approach the Japanese beachheads, using overland routes through the Owen Stanleys, just as the Australian 16th and 25th brigades had done using the Kokoda Track. They would advance well east of the track. Unlike the American troops, however, the Australians and Japanese not only had to cross the range on foot, but along the way, they fought several significant battles as the Australians at first withdrew south, including those for Deniki, Isurava, Abuari, Mission Ridge, and Ioribaiwa Ridge, then more battles as they advanced north, including those at Templeton's Crossing, and Eora Creek.[2] The route to be taken by the American troops would be well clear of any Japanese troops.

East of the Kokoda Track, and roughly running parallel with it, troops of the American division were to reconnoitre and develop overland routes leading to Jaure from Rigo, and Abau to Wanigela by way of the Musa River. A system of supply by small watercraft through Abau was also to be established. At Jaure, it was to locate and maintain a force no greater than two battalions and leave one regiment at Port Moresby, as a reserve. Brigadier Hanford MacNider, commanding the 128th Regiment, was appointed to command the Wanigela force and was ordered to consolidate Wanigela as a sea and air base, to exploit forward movement to Buna by land and sea and to develop small craft supply routes from Wanigela to Pongani, which was located about 40 kilometres east of Buna.[3]

Meanwhile, a difficult overland movement, by the men of the 126th Regiment, through the mountains of eastern central Papua was already underway. An advanced detachment of its 2nd Battalion, led by the unit's intelligence officer, Captain William Boice, had followed the reconnaissance party over the Jaure Track, arriving at Jaure on 4 October. He reported back by radio to Major General Harding, commanding the 32nd Division, that while the going was difficult, it was passable.

On 6 October, an advanced guard of the battalion was on the move, with troops of the regimental Anti-tank and Cannon companies serving as riflemen, commanded by Captain Alfred Medendorp, leading the advance. Medendorp moved forward with 45 men from 'E' Company, along with a five-man radio detachment commanded by Lieutenant James Downer, and a 40-man rifle platoon under Lieutenant Harold Chandler.[4]

Medendorp recalled the first day's journey through the jungle-covered mountains: 'The troops had no trail discipline. The hills were steeper. Footing was insecure. Leeches and insects began to be a nuisance. The trail was strewn with cast-off articles. Leather toilet sets, soap, socks, and extra underwear told a tale of exhaustion and misery. Upon reaching streams, the men would rush to them and drink, although upstream some soldier might be washing his feet. The trail was filled with struggling individuals, many lying on one side panting for breath. The officer bringing up the rear, reached the bivouac that night with a platoon of limping and dazed men. There were no stragglers, however, for it was feared all through the march that stragglers might be killed by a Jap patrol'.[5] Medendorp and a small advance party reached Jaure on 20 October, representing the halfway point across the Owen Stanleys.[6]

On 14 October, the remaining men of the 2nd Battalion, 126th Regiment (II/126th Regiment) led by the battalion commander, Lieutenant Colonel Henry Geerds, began to advance into the mountains, leaving Kalikodobu. Attached were the men of the 19th

CHAPTER 2

Portable Hospital and a platoon of the 114th Engineer Battalion, a force totalling 900 men. The march was more difficult for these men compared to the advance guard, as the rainy season had set in, with a daily and nightly downpour.[7] Among these men trudging along the narrow track through the cloud-covered Owen Stanleys was Sergeant Paul Lutjens with 'E' Company, who recorded in his diary:

> It was one green hell to Jaure. We went up and down continuously; the company would be stretched over two or three miles [5 kilometres]. We'd start at six every morning by cooking rice or trying to. Two guys would work together. If they could start a fire, which was hard because the wood was wet even when you cut deep into the center of the log, they'd mix a little bully beef into a canteen cup with rice, to get the starchy taste out of it. Sometimes we'd take turns blowing on sparks, trying to start a fire. I could hardly describe the country. It would take five or six hours to go a mile, edging along cliff walks, hanging on to vines, up and down, up and down. The men got weaker; guys began to lag back .... An officer stayed at the end of the line to keep driving the stragglers. There wasn't any way of evacuating to the rear. Men with sprained ankles hobbled along as well as they could, driven on by fear of being left behind .... Our strength is about gone. Most of us have dysentery. Boys are falling out and dropping back with fever. Continual downpour of rain. It's hard to cook our rice and tea. Bully beef makes us sick. We seem to climb straight up for hours, then down again. God, will it never end.[8]

These men were accompanied by 200 Papuan carriers, led by Sergeant Russell Smith, a 37-year-old trader from Wainapune, Papua, with ANGAU, who later wrote: 'The natives in my team across the ranges deserve the credit for the arrival of the US troops we convoyed .... There is a point which should not be forgotten regarding these boys. They felt instinctively that the US soldier did not possess the hardihood of the Aussie and so knew that with them they did not have the protection their fellow carriers with the CMF [Citizen Military Force] enjoyed. This being so made their effort in crossing the range and their frontline work at Buna all the more meritorious'.[9]

The American troops of the II/126th Regiment finally stumbled into Jaure on 28 October, two weeks after starting their trek. By 2 November, they were passing through Natunga (about 30 kilometres inland from Pongani), and soon after Bofu (about 20 kilometres inland from Oro Bay), in the steep foothills of the range north-east of Jaure heading for Buna. These men would be the only US troops to march across the Owen Stanleys. The men of this battalion would forever after become known as 'The Ghost Mountain Boys'. The difficulties of the Jaure Track were so bad that the overland route had been abandoned two weeks before. The men of the regiment's 1st and 3rd battalions were now to be transported by C-47 air transports to the northern side of the Owen Stanleys.[10]

* * *

Two weeks before, on 14 October, Colonel Tracy Hale and his men of the 128th Regiment, along with the Australian commandos of the 2/6th Independent Company (less patrol detachments still operating in the vicinity of the Kokoda Track) were flown from Port Moresby directly to Wanigela, rather than taking the difficult overland route. Within two days, the transfer of these men to the northern side of the range had been completed.[11]

Twenty-one-year-old Commando Barrie Dexter, from Kilsyth in Victoria, with the 2/6th Independent Company, recalled the flight to Wanigela; he was one of about 100 commandos initially flown into the newly occupied position along the north coast: 'But for all of us I think, it was pretty terrifying. Very few of us had flown before. We were packed in like sardines and couldn't help wondering whether the planes were not over-loaded; they certainly circled a lot to gain

CHAPTER 2

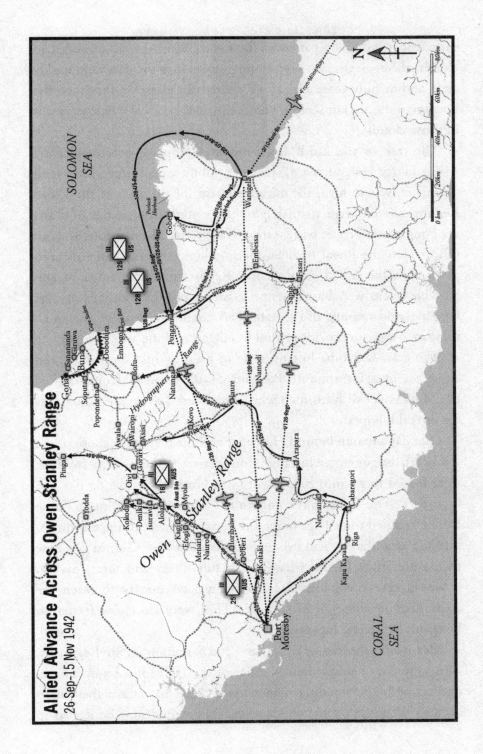

sufficient height. The pass over the Owen Stanleys was shrouded in clouds, although the two sides sloping down into the pass were starkly clear and awfully close and as we cleared the pass, we imagined the bottom of the aircraft scraping on the trees or rocks or whatever it was in those clouds'.[12]

The task of the 2/6th Independent Company, commanded by Major Harry Harcourt, a 47-year-old public servant from Hobert in Tasmania, was to form the advance guard for the men of the 128th Regiment, who were to march to the eastern approaches of Buna via Pongani. Harcourt was a Great War veteran, having fought as an officer with the Royal Irish Fusiliers, going on to fight in Russia in 1919 with the Allied contingent.[13] Reports on the conditions and passable tracks were basically non-existent, and the locations of river crossings and swamps also remained an unknown quantity; therefore, these men were to provide critical intelligence of the area. On arriving at Wanigela, Harcourt lost no time in pushing his commandos out along the overland route to Pongani. Scarcely had Harcourt crossed the Musa River with his men when it flooded, submerging the tracks for several kilometres.[14]

One day's march behind Harcourt and his men were those of the III/128th Regiment, who after floundering in knee-deep swamps, were forced to go into bivouac at Guri Guri the following day (16 October). The battalion commander, Lieutenant Colonel Kelsie Miller, recalled the village being the 'most filthy, swampy, mosquito-infested area' that he had ever encountered in New Guinea'.[15] These men were stuck in the village for a full week, and after leaving, it would take them four days to cut across country to reach the coast, arriving there on 27 October. They were soon after ferried to Pongani, by several luggers.[16]

Meanwhile, the men of the 1st and 2nd battalions, 128th Regiment, who were days behind their buddies of the III/128th Regiment still dealing with the flooding, had been ordered to retrace their steps back to Wanigela on the coast, where they would now be ferried to

CHAPTER 2

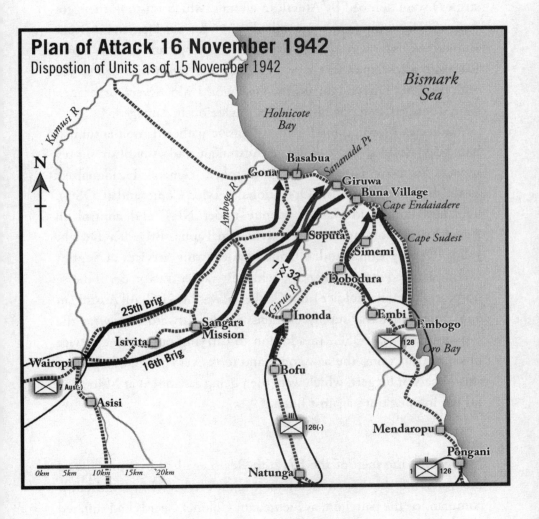

Pongani in 20-ton supply luggers, which had only recently arrived from Milne Bay. The two leading luggers, captained and manned by Australian and American crews, arrived off Pongani on the morning of 18 October. The *King John* and *Timoshenko* (both flying the 'stars and stripes') were bombed by American aircraft, which mistook them for Japanese. Two Americans were killed – 31-year-old Lieutenant Bruce Fahnestock, who was in charge of small boat operations, and Byron Darnton, a correspondent with *The New York Times* who had served with the 32nd Division during the First World War. Several other men were wounded, and one of the boats was seriously damaged.[17]

Earlier as preparations for the offensive gathered momentum, it had been decided to consolidate Australian and American supply services in New Guinea. On 5 October, General Headquarters established the Combined Operational Service Command (COSC). The new command was to operate under NGF and control all Allied line of communication activities in Papua. Brigadier Dwight Johns, Deputy Commander, United States Army Services of Supply, was designated its commander, while Brigadier Victor Secombe, a 45-year-old regular soldier from Canberra, was his 2i/C. All Australian and American naval supply elements in the forward area were the responsibility of COSC. In addition to carrying out routine service of supply functions, the new command took over control of a pool of small boats or luggers, which were then being assembled at Milne Bay for use in operations against Buna.[18]

* * *

Meanwhile, the men of the II/126th Regiment had by now crossed the worst of the Owen Stanleys. Major Herbert M. Smith now commanded the battalion, as Lieutenant Colonel Geerds had suffered a heart attack during the trek and was evacuated back to Port Moresby. These men left Jaure on 28 October, and they were closing in on Natunga by 2 November, after a comparatively easy march. They spent more than a week in the area, no doubt recovering from their

CHAPTER 2

hard trek through the mountain, drawing rations, helmets, boots and other equipment from a nearby drop zone. They then pushed on to Bofu, reaching the village on 12 November.[19]

On 5 November, Colonel Lawrence Quinn, the commander of the regiment, was on board a 'biscuit bomber', determined to improve dropping techniques, which would get more food to his men. The regimental war diary records: 'Because of the difficulties in supplying the forward marching units and because the troops had been without sufficient food for several days, Col. Quinn, accompanied by Capt. Andrews, attempted to correct the situation by riding in the plane that dropped the supplies and observing the results. The trip of Nov. 5 was ill-fated; the plane carrying the Regimental Commander, Capt. Andrews, and five of the enlisted personnel, crashed, killing all on board'.[20] A cargo parachute caught on the tail assembly, sending his plane out of control. Quinn's loss was a blow to the division. Harding, in a letter to Lieutenant General Eichelberger, described Quinn as 'my best regimental commander, and that by a wide margin'.[21] Harding chose Lieutenant Colonel Clarence Tomlinson, commanding officer of the III/126th Regiment, to take over command of the regiment. He was soon after promoted to full colonel. Major George Bond took over command of the III/126th Regiment.[22]

The airlift of the remainder of the 126th Regiment commenced on 8 November, with the men of the I/126th Regiment leading the way. Because heavy rains had made the airfield at Pongani temporarily unsafe for the landing, Lieutenant Colonel Edmund Carrier, along with 590 men of the battalion, flew to Abel's Field. Upon arrival, they began marching to their original destination: Pongani. Within hours, however, the remaining 218 men of the regiment, led by Major Richard Boerem, flew directly into Pongani and at once began marching to Natunga.[23]

Three days later, on 11 November, Colonel Tomlinson and his staff, along with the men of the III/126th Regiment, flew into Pongani. On landing, all elements moved out for Natunga. By 14 November,

Major Boerem and his 218 men of the I/126th Regiment were approaching Natunga, with the Regimental Headquarters and men of the III/126th Regiment moving rapidly behind them. At this time, Lieutenant Colonel Edmund Carrier and 590 men of the I/126th Regiment, who had been forced to land at Abel's Field, were a few days behind. At this point, Major Smith and his men of the II/126th Regiment had passed through Natunga almost two weeks before and had reached Bofu.[24]

* * *

On the coastal flank, Brigadier Hanford MacNider, commanding the 128th Regiment, was consolidating in the Oro Bay–Embogo–Embi area. Patrols were operating inland as far as Borio and up the coast to Cape Sudest, just below the Japanese eastern defences at Buna. The last two companies of the I/128th Regiment, commanded by Lieutenant Colonel Robert McCoy, had flown into Wanigela from Port Moresby on 8 November and had been brought forward by boat. The battalion (except for 'A' Company, which had been left at Pongani to guard the supply dumps) was now at Embogo, about five kilometres south of Cape Sudest. The II/128th Regiment, under Lieutenant Colonel Herbert A Smith, was at Eroro Mission, while the III/128th Regiment, under Miller, was near Embi.[25]

There was now a supply depot at Embogo, but American quartermaster Lieutenant Colonel Lawrence McKenny was planning on establishing an advanced depot at Hariko, a small, narrow spit of land running parallel with the coast about three kilometres south of Cape Endaiadere, occupied in strength by the enemy. The northern tip of the spit of land defining Hariko was joined to the main beach by a bridge, about 1.5 kilometres south of Duropa Plantation (also held by the Japanese). MacNider, in turn, planned to move his headquarters to Hariko as soon as boats were available.[26]

On 12 November, Major Harcourt and his Australian commandos were still in the Pongani area conducting patrols. Harcourt now

CHAPTER 2

received orders to bring in his patrols and concentrate at Pongani. From there they would move by sea to Oro Bay, which was to be the advance base for the Buna Task Force Headquarters. All stores were to be packed in preparation for the move, and information of tracks and general type of country in and around Buna was to be obtained from interviewing local missionaries (they would find that all missionaries, but one, in this area had been murdered by the Japanese months before) and troops of the Papuan Infantry Battalion recently relocated in the area who were seeking out Japanese infiltration parties. The role that the Australian commandos were to play in the assault against Buna remained unspecified.[27]

The next day, the Australian gunners of 'F' Troop, 55th Battery, 2/5th Field Regiment, and four of their 25-pounder field guns, arrived at Wanigela on board the SS *Kooraki* from Milne Bay. The unit war diary records that the corvette arrived at Wanigela just before dusk at around 5.30 pm and the officers and gunners proceeded to their bivouac area about 1.5 kilometres from the beach close to the Australians of 'A' Company, 2/10th Battalion. 'Unloading of guns and stores not commenced, as light prohibited'.[28]

* * *

By mid-November, Australian and American forces were converging on the Japanese beachheads along three main lines of advance. The Australians of the 25th and 16th brigades were crossing the Kumusi River, advancing towards Gona and Sanananda, respectively. To the east, the American concentration was almost complete. The men of the 126th Regiment had approached Buna from the south, using inland tracks, while the men of the 128th Regiment had advanced along the coastal strip and by sea just east of Buna.[29]

On 14 November, NGF published its orders for the attacks against the Japanese northern beachheads by the Australian 7th and the American 32nd divisions. The area of operations was defined by the Kumusi River (west), Holnicote Bay (north), and Cape Sudest (south). The boundary between the two forces was to be a line running from the mouth of the Girua River to Hihonda in a south-westerly line along a stream hallway between Inonda and Popondetta. Each division, however, was to be prepared to strike across the boundary against Japanese flank or rear positions, should the opportunity arise. The Australians were to operate west of the river, and the Americans to the east. The advance was to start on 16 November, with the 32nd Division against Buna and the 7th Division against Gona and Sanananda.[30]

* * *

Meanwhile, on 11 November, an unknown Japanese soldier [A] [iv] at Buna recorded the following document, which was later captured and translated and is now preserved in the 18th Brigade war diary. He wrote of the American troops landing just east of the Buna beachhead:

> From morning the enemy bombers and fighters came and went, bombing above my tent, but I have not been injured. The number of bombs dropped by the enemy till about 4.40 PM I was unable to count. At about 3.30, an order came down for us all to fall out. We immediately carried two shells per individual to the AA positions. It seems that the AA shells ran out and for a while firing had ceased. During this time several enemy planes came over and bombed us. On this day, from about 2.30 PM until about 5.00 at approximately 2½ miles from where we stay, an enemy unit of about 1000 landed. That is, about 2½ miles in front of the Buna airfields on the beach, five enemy ships appeared and landed troops, so it seems. Furthermore, at about 6.00, two more ships followed the others and appeared.

[iv] Several diaries that were recovered after the fighting have been attributed to unnamed Japanese soldiers; in order for the reader to gain some idea of each soldier's experience, unnamed individuals will each be attributed a prefix [A], [B] etc., so that each soldier's experiences can be appreciated and placed in overall context.

CHAPTER 2

The time for which we had been waiting for some time had finally come. Soldiers were all given ammunition and set out for the front to beat back the enemy. Loud explosions were heard around 5.30.[31]

3

'WORSE YET, WE DIDN'T UNDERSTAND THE JAPANESE'

By mid-November, Lieutenant General Edmund Herring, a 52-year-old barrister from Melbourne, who had been sent to Port Moresby to replace Lieutenant General Sydney Rowell commanding Advanced New Guinea Force, informed General 'Bloody' George Vasey, a 47-year-old professional soldier from Victoria commanding the Australian 7th Division, that the Australian 21st Brigade was to be sent to him. These veterans had been involved in extensive operations along the Kokoda Track and were still battle-scared and weary. They would soon be flown in from Port Moresby and represent the 7th Division reserve to be based near Wairopi. Their final assignment to support the 25th Brigade at Gona or the 16th Brigade at Sanananda would depend on events.[1]

* * *

With the onset of the rainy season, the Girua River was in full flood. After losing itself in a broad swampy delta stretching from Sanananda Point to Buna Village, the river emptied into the sea via several channels. One of these, Entrance Creek, opened into the lagoon between Buna Village and Buna Mission[v]. Between Entrance Creek and Simemi Creek to the east was a huge swamp. This was formed when the overflow from the river backed up into the low-lying ground

---

[v] Note: Bunia Mission and Buna Government Station are the same position, they are used interchangeably in both primary and secondary sources.

CHAPTER 3

just south of Buna Mission Station, reaching as far inland as Simemi and Ango. It was assessed to be largely impassable, and it effectively cut the area east of the river in two, making the transfer of troops from one area to the other a difficult process.[2]

Because of the swamp, there were only three good approaches to the Japanese positions east of the river. The first led from Soputa and Ango Corner, along the western edge of the swamp, to a track junction about one kilometre south of Buna Mission Station, which was to become known as the 'Triangle'. From this junction, one track led to Buna Village and the other to the Buna Mission Station. A second route was from Dobodura and Simemi, along the eastern end of the swamp and along the northern edge of the 'Old Strip' to the Buna Mission Station. The third approach lay along the eastern coastal track from Cape Sudest to Cape Endaiadere, where it back-tracked diagonally through Duropa Plantation to the 'New Strip', and then it ran from there to the Buna Mission Station.[3]

On 15 November, Major General Harding issued his divisional plan of attack. Brigadier Hanford MacNider, who commanded the three battalions of the 128th Regiment, with the Australian commandos of the 2/6th Independent Company attached, were collectively designated 'Warren Force' – named after the county in Ohio, which was the birthplace of Harding.

The following day, MacNider was to send one of his battalions to march along the coast via Embogo and Cape Sudest to take Cape Endaiadere. A second battalion was to occupy Buna's New Strip via Simemi Village from the south. The remaining battalion, acting as the division reserve, was to proceed to the Dobodura area to prepare a landing strip for transports. Each battalion was to have an engineer platoon and a body of Papuan carriers from ANGAU attached.[4]

Meanwhile, Colonel Clarence Tomlinson and his men of the 126th Regiment (less the elements of the I/126th Regiment arriving at Pongani) were to head for Inonda and from there on to Buna by a route yet to be specified. His force, which was approaching from

BLOODY BUNA

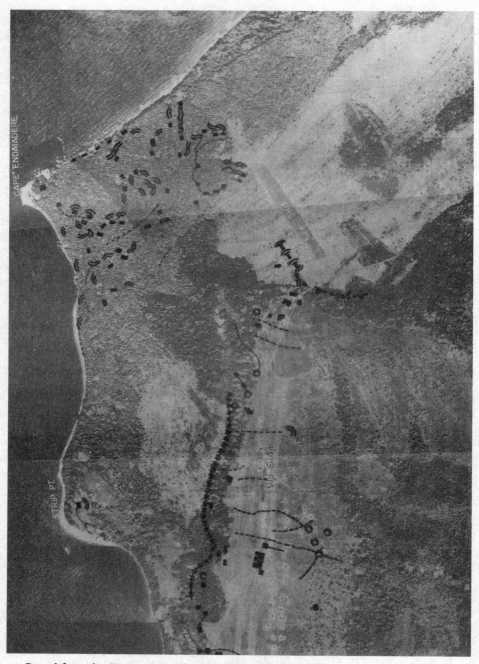

Buna defense plan (Japanese). As compiled at the end of the campaign.
⌒ Breastworks   ■ Bunkers   ------ Fire trenches   ✖✖✖✖ Barbed wire   ◉ Anti airecraft positions

CHAPTER 3

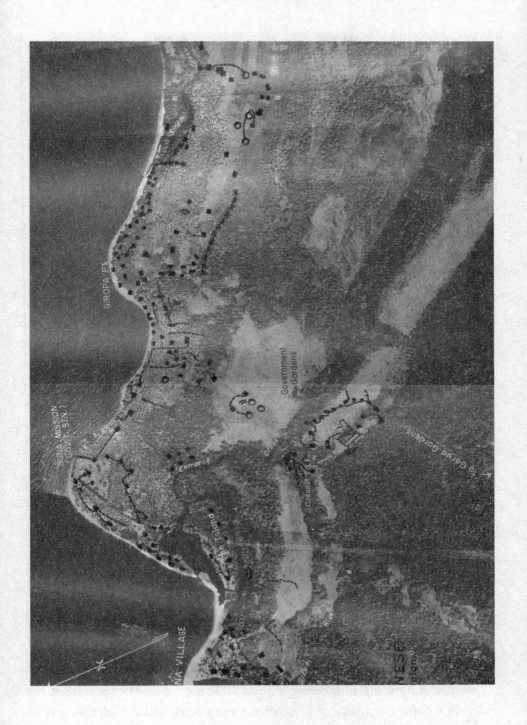

the south-west of Buna, was designated 'Urbana Force' – named after the Ohio city that was the birthplace of Lieutenant General Eichelberger.[5]

While Urbana Force would be supplied by airdrops until the airstrip at Dobodura was in operation, Warren Force was to be supplied principally by sea. A deep-water harbour was being established at Oro Bay. Colonel John Carew, the divisional engineer, reported its completion would make it possible for large ships to anchor. He also assessed that the airstrip and associated roadworks at Dobodura would make this area a significant airbase, not only for fighters and transports, but also for all types of bombers.[6]

That day, 15 November, Harding attempted to get information on the location of his battalions, but the radio equipment was found to be faulty. He sent a note to be passed onto NGF in Port Moresby by telephone: 'No sitreps from 14 November due to failure W/T equipment. Unable to contact elements 32d Div. Resulted in no info to be fwded'.[7] Tomlinson, in a similar vein, wrote a note to the divisional headquarters staff, stating: 'Present state radio communications unsatisfactory. Take more care in encoding. No correctly coded message has been received so far'.[8]

* * *

The condition of the Australians by mid-November was of concern. The 16th and 25th brigades, which had chased the Japanese all the way across the Owen Stanleys, had been in continuous action under the most arduous conditions for almost two months. The battalions of these brigades had received significant casualties, and those men that remained were mostly sick and exhausted. The 21st Brigade, Major General Vasey's reserve, though rested and regrouped, was also far below strength, having fought the costly delaying actions south along the Kokoda Track throughout August and September. Only the untried Americans, numbering around 7000 men, could be considered fresh troops, but many of these men were already sick.[9] Eichelberger

CHAPTER 3

succinctly recorded the situation, even before the division had its baptism of fire, saying that the troops were covered with jungle ulcers and 'riddled with malaria, dengue fever, and tropical dysentery'.[10]

Medical supplies remained in critically short supply, even as the troops marched out for the attack. There was not enough quinine sulphate, which was the malaria suppressive in use at the time, for regular distribution to the troops. Harding had arranged to have his medical supplies go forward by boat, only to find at the last minute that the boats could not take them, as they were already overloaded. Harding contacted Brigadier Ennis Whitehead, with the US Fifth Air Force, stating that the medical supply situation was 'snafu' ('situation normal – all fucked up') and asked him to fly in the most urgently needed items 'to take care of things until we can get the boat supply inaugurated'.[11]

Meanwhile, the men of the II/126th Regiment, who had crossed the mountains on foot were severely affected by the ordeal. Major Smith, commanding the battalion, recalled the situation. The men had been on short rations since mid-October, and they had made extremely exhausting marches through the jungle 'on a diet of one-third of a C-ration and a couple of spoonfuls of rice a day' and many already had 'fever, dysentery, and jungle rot'.[12]

Even so, the Americans remained cocky and confident. They had been told, and they believed, that the battle to take Buna would be a 'push over'. The American official historian wrote that no one, either in Port Moresby or at the front, believed that there would be any difficulty in taking Buna. Reports of enemy weakness poured in, and with this the officers and men of the 32nd Division began to think in terms of a quick and easy victory. On 20 October, Harding recorded: 'A fair chance that we will have Buna by the first of November'. At the end of the October, he assessed the Japanese forces in the Buna–Gona area were relatively light and wrote to GHQ, suggesting 5 November as a suitable date for D-Day: 'Things look pretty favourable right now for a quick conquest of Buna'.[13]

By now, even Willoughby had revised down his assessments of Japanese numbers at the beachheads. With the Australian decisive victories at Oivi and Gorari, where the Japanese *South Seas Force* just days before had been badly mauled, he assessed there were now far fewer troops available to the Japanese to defend their positions, believing they had just: 'One depleted regiment and auxiliary units' available for service and that these were capable of fighting a delaying action only. Willoughby suggested that there would be close perimeter defence of the airfield and beachhead at Buna. He also assessed that further attempts to reinforce Buna were improbable, 'in view of the conditions in the Solomons, and the logistic difficulties and risks which are involved'.[14] Vasey and his Australian staff also badly underestimated Japanese strength, based on prisoner of war interrogations, and on 14 November, they concluded that all three beachheads in total numbered fewer than 2000 troops. At this point, before reinforcements from Rabaul arrived, there were around 8000 Japanese distributed between the three beachheads.[15]

Harding was increasingly optimistic and relying on information supplied by local Papuans; his intelligence officer estimated that the 'Buna area was garrisoned by not more than a battalion with purely defensive intentions'.[16] As recorded in the intelligence annex of Harding's first field order of the campaign: 'The original enemy force based at Buna is estimated as one combat team with two extra infantry battalions attached. This force has been withdrawing steadily along the Kokoda Trail for the past six weeks. Heavy losses and evacuation of the sick have reduced them to an estimated three battalions, two of which made a stand in the Kokoda–Wairopi area [Oivi and Gorari], with the third occupying Buna and guarding the line of communications. Casualties in the two battalions in the Wairopi area have reduced them to approximately 350 men, who, it is believed, are retiring northward along the Kumusi River Valley'.[17]

By the time the situation had leaked down to the troops on the ground, Chinese whispers had brought down the estimate of the

CHAPTER 3

Japanese defending Buna Village to a mere two squads. Told by their officers that the operation would be a walkover, and that only a small and pitiful group of survivors from the Owen Stanleys fighting remained to be dealt with, the American troops were sure that they could take Buna in a couple of days, and all that remained was to mop up isolated enemy pockets of resistance. This, however, was a spectacular miscalculation.

The Japanese were present in much greater strength than the Allied commanders had assessed. They had also spent four months preparing excellent defensive positions, which included strong bunker positions, interlocking machinegun fire, covering killing fields to any likely approach, as well as building an extensive criss-crossing crawl trench system, and critical reinforcements and supplies from Rabaul would soon arrive. The Japanese defenders were now waiting for the Australian and American advance.[18]

American squad leader Ernest Geber, with the II/128th Regiment, recalled just how ignorant they were of the Japanese and their defensive positions: 'We had been told this was going to be a pushover. It was generally believed that the Japanese there were sick, half dead, and not numerous. This was what we were told. Hell, we were whistling on the approach march. It wasn't until the end of the first week that we realised that we had a bear by the tail, and no one knew what was going on …. We didn't understand jungle warfare either. Worse yet, we didn't understand the Japanese'.[19]

4

'NATURALLY, THE STRIPS GAVE THE ENEMY FIELDS OF FIRE'

The Japanese defence was built around three main positions. To the west was Gona, in the centre Sanananda, and to the east Buna. Each was an independent position, but their inward flanks were well guarded, and lateral communications between them, except where the coastal track had flooded, were good. Gona, a sandy track junction covering the anchorage at Basabua, was well fortified, although its proximity to the sea made it impossible to defend in any depth. There were strong and well-designed defences along the Sanananda track and at the junction of the several branch tracks leading from it to Cape Killerton. East of the Girua River, equally formidable defences protected Buna Village, Buna Mission, and the airstrip positions.[1]

The Japanese line defending Buna was a strong one, representing a continuous front, difficult to flank. The defences began at the mouth of the Girua River, and continued south-east, cutting through a coconut plantation known as 'Coconut Grove', and then it turned southward to the track junction where the Soputa–Buna track forked to Buna Village on the left and to Buna Mission on the right. From here, the defences now swept north, the line enclosed the Triangle (as the fork was called), and then it turned eastward from that narrow salient to the grassy area known as the 'Government Gardens'. From there, the line led east through the main swamp to the kunai area at the lower or southern edge of Old Strip. It then looped around the strip and, continuing southward, around the bridge between it and

CHAPTER 4

New Strip. The key defensive line then swept at a right angle to New Strip, and then following the southern edge of the airfield to within a few hundred metres of the sea, it cut sharply north-east, emerging on the sea at a point about 750 metres south of Cape Endaiadere.[2]

The shallow one-metre water-table in the area ruled out the possibility of deep trenches and dugouts – the region was studded instead with hundreds of coconut log bunkers, most of them mutually supporting and organised in depth. In general, they were of two types: heavily reinforced bunkers located in open terrain, and smaller, less heavily reinforced bunkers built where the terrain was overgrown with trees and vegetation that offered the defenders a measure of protection against air bombardment or artillery fire. Where possible, depending on terrain, the Japanese had large, squat, earth-covered blockhouses, each capable of holding 20 to 30 men, while several concrete and steel pillboxes were located behind New Strip.[3]

Most Japanese bunkers in the area were constructed using heavy coconut logs, with the floors being a shallow trench were possible about a metre deep. The smaller bunkers were usually about three metres long and one metre wide, and the larger ones were up to ten metres long and three metres wide. Heavy coconut logs, about a third of a metre thick, were used for both vertical supports and crossbeams. The logs were cut to give the bunkers an interior height from about 1.5 metres to around two metres, depending on the foliage and terrain. The crossbeams forming the ceiling were laid laterally to the trench. They usually overlapped the supports and were covered by several courses of logs, and often by plates of sheet steel up to a quarter of an inch thick, taken from nearby stricken Japanese transports.

The walls were riveted with steel rails, I-beams, sheet iron, and log pilings. And 40-gallon oil and petrol drums, which had been used at the airstrips, now filled with earth. As soon as the framework had been built, the entire structure was covered with earth, rocks and short chunks of log. Coconuts, palm tree fonds and strips of grass matting were integrated into the earth fill to help cushion from high explosives, and the whole bunker was planted with fast-growing vegetation for camouflage and to help consolidate the earthen structure. The result could hardly be improved upon with the completed bunker merged perfectly within their surroundings, affording excellent camouflage.[4]

To further hide their presence, firing slits were usually so narrow as to be nearly invisible from the front. Those that were used solely as protection against mortar and artillery bombardment and from Allied aircraft had no slits at all. Entrance was from the rear, and sometimes there was more than one entrance, and they were placed so that they could be covered by machinegun fire from adjacent bunkers and support trenches. They were also usually angled to protect the occupants from hand grenades. The bunkers either opened directly onto fire trenches or were connected by shallow crawl tunnels, enabling the Japanese to move quickly from fire trench to bunker and back again without fear of observation or being targeted by Allied troops just a few metres away.[5]

These fortifications were cleverly located throughout the Buna position to provide interlocking fire support. Bunker and trench systems within the Triangle, in the Government Gardens, along Entrance Creek, and in Coconut Grove on the other side of the creek, protected the inland approaches to Buna Village, Buna Mission, and in turn, were honeycombed with mortar and gun emplacements. The main swamp also protected the southern edge of Old Strip, and bunkers, fire trenches, and barbed wire covered its northern edge. The bridge just south and between the two airstrips was also covered by several bunkers and gun emplacements, both at the front and rear, and the bridge area between the airfields could be swept with fire from both strips. There were bunkers, fire trenches, and breastworks behind New Strip and in the Duropa Plantation. Interlocking machinegun fire from the bridge, both strips, and the plantation defined the forward-killing zones. The airstrips provided clear fields of fire, enabling the

CHAPTER 4

Japanese to easily target any enemy troops seeking to cross or flank the strips, or attempting a front-on charge across the bridge.[6]

Old Strip was the original airstrip at Buna, which had been extended to 1300 metres long and 90 metres wide by the Japanese after invading the area in July 1942. At this point, it was not operational. They had also constructed New Strip, located south-east of the original strip. New Strip, however, was a dummy airfield, in an attempt to fool Allied intelligence.[7] The historian of the 2/10th Battalion described Coconut Grove, Old Strip, and the nearby Simemi Creek, which would figure prominently in the fighting to take the beachhead:

> The strip was covered to a height of four feet [1.3 metres] by kunai grass. It was honeycombed with strong posts and communication trenches. At the far end was a plantation of coconut trees, known to be held in strength by the enemy. This position was well dotted with solidly constructed pillboxes. The walls being of 44-gallon petrol drums filled with sand and wired together, whilst the roofs consisted of two layers of trunks of coconut palms. Beyond the plantation was the sea, and just above the beach the track that led from Buna Mission to Dobodura.
>
> The Buna strip was guarded on each side, for the full length, by deep swamp and jungle growth. Through the swamp on the right [east] ran the Sumemi [sic] creek, up to 12 feet [four metres] deep in places, and it meandered aimlessly through jungle-covered swamp about 200 yards [metres] wide. The swamp to the left of the strip was equally difficult; the mud, in places, being deeper than a man's height and heavily covered with thorny jungle plant life. At the bottom end of the strip, the creek made a sharp bend moving straight across the width of the strip. The banks, perhaps 15 feet high and practically perpendicular, were spanned by a flimsy wooden bridge. Beyond

the bridge to the west, the enemy looked down the full length of the strip from higher ground, for the terrain rose steadily and evenly from the bridge to the coconut grove seen in the distance'.[8]

Similarly, Lieutenant General Eichelberger's report on the fighting at Buna describes the significance of the terrain around the two airstrips and their interior lines of communications:

> Naturally, the strips gave the enemy fields of fire. Further, the impassable, jungled swamp between the Dobodura – strips track and the Soputa – Buna Village track precluded lateral communications between Allied forces attacking the Japanese flanks. For the Americans, it was a two-day march from their left flank near Buna Village to their right flank below Cape Endaiadere. But, at the same time, the terrain inside the Japanese perimeter was such that they could move reinforcements quickly to any threatened point by truck or marching.

> Thus, the enemy's brilliant terrain utilisation canalised all potential Allied attacks into four narrow fronts: (1) through the swamp in front of Buna Village; (2) against the fork, or so-called 'Triangle', of the Soputa-Buna track; (3) across the narrow bridge between the strips; and (4) through the coconut plantation below Cape Endaiadere.[9]

After the campaign, Eichelberger would write to Brigadier Floyd Parks, Chief of Staff, Army Ground Forces, based in Washington: 'The situation up there varied widely because the terrain in one place was usually entirely different from that two hundred yards away. Ordinary swamps, mangrove swamps, sago swamps, patches of kunai grass, abandoned native villages and deep saltwater streams, which divided our forces into many corridors, made the whole show a military nightmare'.[10]

CHAPTER 4

The Japanese line at Buna would force the Americans of the 32nd Division and the Australian commandos of the 2/6th Independent Company to attack the enemy where he was strongest – the Triangle, along the track leading to the bridge between the strips, and further east frontally in the Duropa Plantation. By forcing the Americans (and later the Australian battalions) into these narrow, well-defended killing fields, the Japanese, with short interior lines, could shift troops from front to front, not only on foot or by truck, but also by sea using landing craft. They were able to exploit their available strength to the maximum, no matter their numerical inferiority; the defences at Buna would be a hard nut to crack.[11]

* * *

With the drowning of Major General Tomitarô Horii, who had commanded the *South Seas Force* in mid-November 1942, the command west of the Girua River (Gona and Sanananda) had fallen to Colonel Yokoyama Yosuke, while those to the east (Buna) were commanded by Captain Yasuda Yoshitatsu, being the senior naval officer in this sector. By mid-November, the Japanese Buna garrisons were a collection of broken Army and Navy units suffering from battle casualties and riddled with disease. The defenders at Buna by late November and early December would be reinforced and resupplied from Rabaul, while the seriously wounded and sick would be evacuated, meaning there was probably around 4000 effectives at the height of their defence.[12]

The Japanese defences at Buna were defined by two sectors, which not surprisingly corresponded with the likely Allies' plan of attack. Men of the *Imperial Japanese Army* would confront the Allies of Warren Force, while those of the *Imperial Japanese Navy* would mostly confront those of Urbana Force.[13]

The Army units included the remnants of the *144th Infantry*, men of the *15th Independent Engineers*, the troops of the *III/41st Infantry*, the divisional cavalry detachment represented by *No. 3 Company, 55th*

Cavalry Regiment, and the troops of the *47th Field Antiaircraft Artillery Battalion*. The engineers, the anti-aircraft troops, and the service troops were all assigned to the defence of the coconut plantation, New Strip, and the bridge between the strips. In addition, a few artillery batteries were available, along with several rear echelon units, although most of the later had not seen combat.[14]

The Naval personnel at the start of the battle numbered around 500 marines from the *Yokosuka 5th* and *Sasebo 5th Special Naval Landing Party* (SNLP), and perhaps twice that number of naval laborers from the *14th* and *15th Naval Pioneer Units*. Yasuda also had several 75-mm naval guns, 13-mm guns and 37-mm pompoms, and half a dozen 3-inch anti-aircraft guns. The *Yokosuka 5th* and *Sasebo 5th SNLP* marines, as well as the naval laborers, were deployed in Buna Village, Buna Mission, the Coconut Grove, and the Triangle.[15]

* * *

Japanese *Imperial Headquarters* in Tokyo had realised for some time that, despite the emphasis on retaking Guadalcanal, troops would also have to be sent to the three Papua beachheads if they were to be held. The troops immediately available were several hundred replacements for the *144th Regiment* who had just reached Rabaul from Japan and men from the *III/229th Regiment, 38th Division* whose two sister battalions were on Guadalcanal. The men of the *229th Regiment* were combat-experienced, having fought in China, Hong Kong and Java, and the battalion was rated an excellent combat unit.[16]

Even so, the Japanese troops, especially those who had been involved in the ongoing fighting with the Australians over the last four months, were in a bad way. In the long retreat from Ioribaiwa Ridge through the Owen Stanleys, with the fighting at Templeton's Crossing and Eora Creek, along with the northern coast battles at Oivi and Gorari, closely followed by the crossing of the Kumusi River, the Japanese had lost against the Australian's irreplaceable men, weapons and supplies. In terms of equipment and supplies, their most critical

CHAPTER 4

shortages were in small arms, food, and medical supplies – items that Lieutenant Colonel Tomita, the detachment supply officer, had already been forced to hand out with a careful eye.[17]

All the weapons that could be scraped together were either in the frontlines or stacked where they could readily be supplied when the frontline troops required them. Except for troops immediately in reserve, most of the men to the rear had no weapons. Indeed, worried by the situation, Colonel Yokoyama, at Sanananda, issued orders for all troops without arms to tie bayonets to bamboo poles. If they had no bayonets, they were to carry bamboo spears, and these were to be carried at all times; even the patients in the hospital were to have them by their beds.[18]

The troops had been on short rations for some time now, and rations were progressively reduced further. To help stretch out food supplies, the few packhorses that were left were butchered. Most of the men were sick, and nearly all those admitted to the hospital for wounds and disease were also suffering from exhaustion, with almost all suffering from malaria, and a large proportion of the men were down with dysentery.[19]

Despite these difficulties, the position of the Japanese was not hopeless. They had good stocks of ammunition, a strong defensive position, and enough men and weapons to hold their positions for some time. They had also been told that their commanders in Rabaul would soon be sending reinforcements and supplies. Their orders were to hold, and, with a little help from Rabaul, they were prepared to do so indefinitely.[20]

5
'... DEPRIVE THE ALLIES OF ANY ROOM FOR A COUNTER-OFFENSIVE'

The Americans east of the Girua River advanced towards the positions they were to occupy before launching their attack upon the Japanese. On the right, Brigadier Hanford MacNider and his men of the 128th Regiment (Warren Force) had by nightfall made sporadic contact with advanced Japanese elements. Along the coastline, his troops of the I/128th Regiment (less 'A' Company, which was still at Pongani), under Lieutenant Colonel Robert McCoy, had moved out, advancing up the coast from Embogo, crossing the Samboga River, taking up a position at Boreo. This was located at a creek mouth just north of Hariko where MacNider had established his Regimental Headquarters. McCoy reported finding enemy outposts about 400 metres north of their position.[1]

Meanwhile, Lieutenant Colonel Kelsie Miller and his men of the III/128th Regiment were advancing from Warisota Plantation, five kilometres west of Embogo, and Embi. They encountered and scattered a small Japanese patrol at Dobodura that afternoon (killing three), and started for Simemi, their jump-off point for the attack on the bridge between the two airstrips. Behind them was Lieutenant Colonel Smith and his infantrymen of the II/128th Regiment. They were moving up behind Miller's battalion in reserve. These men had arrived at Dobodura with a company of engineers, and all set to work clearing a landing strip.[2]

At this point Allied troops still at Pongani – consisting of 'A'

CHAPTER 5

Company, I/128th Regiment; 'A' Company, 114th Engineer Battalion; Lieutenant Colonel Edmund Carrier and his men of the I/126th Regiment, and Major Harry Harcourt and his Australian commandos of the 2/6th Independent Company – were to leave for the front the next day, by luggers.[3]

Brigadier Albert Waldron, the 32nd Division artillery officer, using a Japanese barge captured at Milne Bay, had arrived at Hariko the night before with the two 3.7-inch mountain howitzers, from the Australian 1st Mountain Battery, their crews, and 200 rounds of ammunition. Waldron left before daybreak for Oro Bay to now pick up two Australian 25-pounders. His executive officer, Lieutenant Colonel Melvin McCreary, was put ashore at Hariko with the two mountain guns, which were ready to fire from their advanced position at Boreo that evening.[4]

It was clear as the advance got under way that the division's weakest link was its supply line. Until an airfield was established at Dobodura, American supplies, except for emergency drops by aircraft, would be entirely dependent upon the six remaining luggers or trawlers that Lieutenant Colonel McKenny was using to carry supplies up the coast from Porlock Harbour to Oro Bay, along with the captured Japanese barge then bringing forward the two 25-pounders.[5]

It was now that the tenuous American line of supply was targeted by Japanese airmen. At Buna, a message had been sent to Rabaul at 8 am, stating: 'Enemy transport ships are visible in the waters off Cape Endaiadere'.[6] It was reported at 10 am that six Allied small landing vessels were operating in Oro Bay, 13 kilometres south-east of Buna, and that a landing was being made on the left bank of the Samboga River by a force of around 1000 enemy troops. With this news, the Japanese launched from Rabaul a sortie of a dozen Val dive bombers, each armed with a pair of 60-kilogram bombs, escorted by six Zero fighters.[7]

Late in the afternoon, the barge, carrying the two 25-pounders commanded by Captain Charles Mueller, a 26-year-old accountant from Sydney, and his troops of the 2/5th Field Regiment (the troop had come round from Milne Bay to support the Americans), had left Oro Bay for Hariko, just north of Cape Sudest, in company with three luggers: *Alacrity*, *Bonwin*, and *Minnemura*. The *Alacrity* was carrying ammunition and the equipment and personnel of the 22nd Portable Hospital. The *Bonwin* was loaded with rations and ammunition, and the *Minnemura*, largest of the three, held ammunition, rations, radio supplies, 81-mm mortars, 50-caliber machine guns, and other heavy equipment not easily carried by the troops. Major General Harding was also on the *Minnemura*.[8]

The luggers and barge, protected only by machine guns mounted on their decks, were rounding Cape Sudest, while a small lighter from shore was soon off-loading ammunition from the *Alacrity*. It was now that the small flotilla was attacked by the Japanese airmen who appeared without warning from the north-west, strafing the craft. The troops aboard replied with ineffective machinegun and rifle fire. Within minutes, the barge and all three luggers were ablaze. Ammunition was exploding, and all crew members took to the water. The luggers, the Japanese barge, and virtually all their cargo were a total loss – including the two 25-pounder field guns.[9]

Casualties were heavy. Lieutenant Colonel McKenny and 23 others were killed (among them five Australians), and there were many wounded. The loss of life would have been even greater but for several daring rescues. The lighter that had been loading ammunition from the *Alacrity* reached shore under fire, and at great personal risk, the ordnance officer with the 32nd Division, Lieutenant John Harbert, went aboard and took off the ammunition. Rescue parties braving enemy fire, exploding ammunition, and the flaming debris, led by Colonel John Carew, commanding officer of the 114th Engineer Battalion, and Lieutenant Herbert Peabody, of the Division Headquarters Company, saved the lives of many who might otherwise have drowned or burnt to death. Harding and Waldron were forced to swim for shore.[10]

CHAPTER 5

The commanding officer of the 2/5th Field Regiment, Lieutenant Colonel John O'Brien, a 34-year-old engineer from Melbourne, went on to write the regimental history and recorded the attack:

> Three times a Zero made its swooping dives. Tracer bullets, leaving searing ribbons of flame in their paths, ripped into the hull of the barge and into the crouching bodies tightly packed aboard it. There was little that could be done in defence other than to keep cool and get behind anything offering a scrap of protection. These things the men did. A single light machine gun had been set up on the stern. As the bright coloured rain of death poured down in graceful curves, Gnr A. G. King[vi] stood to face the Zero. He fought the plane defiantly with this pitifully inadequate weapon …. Soon the barge was ablaze. Clouds of dense black smoke billowed upwards. Beneath this canopy the vessel was sinking fast.[11]

The Japanese airmen reported that three landing craft were sunk and that a further two were on fire and sinking after the Allied force was attacked at around 5 pm. A lone Japanese reconnaissance aircraft was despatched forty minutes after the sortie, to observe the results of the attack, later reporting that two landing craft had survived, and that wrecks of the destroyed vessels were visible in the area.[12]

*　*　*

That morning, Lieutenant General Hitoshi Imamura, who commanded the newly designated *8th Area Army*, had two armies under his command – the *17th Army*, under Lieutenant General Hyakutake Haruyoshi, who was responsible for the fighting in the Solomons, including at Guadalcanal, and the *18th Army*, under Lieutenant General Hatazo Adachi, who was responsible for operations in New Guinea. Adachi's main task was to hold the beachheads at Buna, Sanananda, and Gona,

---

vi   Gunner Alan King, a 24-year-old cost clerk from Sydney.

until the Americans had been driven off Guadalcanal, and to prepare for the next operations against Port Morsby.[13]

Adachi would arrive in Rabaul on 25 November and take command immediately of the *18th Army*. Historians Saburo Hayashi and Alvin Coox recorded in their study of the Japanese Army in the Pacific: 'In view of the new concept, Japanese troops were to pull back from the forward positions which they had been striving so mightily to maintain: the Port Moresby–Guadalcanal line. No changes whatsoever were affected in the former plan, which had called for the retention of strategic sites in the Solomons (centring upon Rabaul) and in eastern New Guinea (around Lae, Salamaua and Madang)'.[14]

Adachi's first task was to retrieve the reversals that had taken place since late September, with the withdrawal of the *South Seas Force* from Ioribaiwa Ridge just north of Port Moresby and the advance of the Australian 7th Division through the mountains. These Australians were about to assault the Japanese beachheads at Gona and Sanananda, while American forces were preparing to attack Buna. Sometime that day, Colonel Yamamoto Hiroshi, who had arrived in Rabaul to replace Colonel Kusunose Masao as commander of the *144th Infantry Regiment*, (who had been shipped back to Rabaul due to illness), was tasked with securing the Sanananda beachhead as well as the inland Soputa areas at all costs. He was also to protect the landing of reinforcements at these beachheads. Yamamoto was to lead a force that included the *III/229th Infantry Regiment*, commanded by Major Kenmotsu Hewishichi. This force, consisting of a four-rifle company structure, totalled 815 men, with 69 machine guns, and two small howitzers. Also included was *No. 2 Battery, 38th Mountain Artillery Regiment* (Lieutenant Shiiki Kazuo) and around 700 replacements for the much depleted *144th Regiment*.[15]

Meanwhile, having failed in their latest attempts to reinforce their stranded garrison at Guadalcanal, the Japanese chief of staff of the Combined Fleet noted with the Allied advance to the beachheads at Papua: 'Buna is becoming a bigger issue in this region than the

CHAPTER 5

problematic Solomon Islands, in terms of national defence. It is essential to nip this in the bud now and deprive the Allies of any room for a counter-offensive'.[16]

That morning, at 8 am, Yamamoto and the bulk of his 1500 men force left Rabaul on a five-destroyer convoy consisting of the *Kazagumo*, *Makigumo*, *Yūgumo*, *Oyashio* and the *Kagiroi*, for Buna, but they would mistakenly arrive just off close to midnight. Disembarkation was conducted under cover of darkness and was completed by 2.30 am.[17]

6

'IT IS IMPERATIVE THAT OUR FORCES PUSH FORWARD AT THE GREATEST SPEED ...'

The following morning, 17 November 1942, the Americans of the I/128th Regiment edged slightly forward along the beach while those of the III/128th Regiment on the left entered Simemi. Major General Harding now scheduled the main attack against Buna for 19 November. A simultaneous attack would commence along the water's edge and from the Simemi Track. Both would be supported by the two Australian 3.7-inch mountain howitzers, commanded by Captain Martin O'Hare, a 25-year-old regular soldier from Cunderdin in Western Australia, who had seen service in the Middle East. These were the only artillery available to Harding at the time. The 3.7-inch howitzers were very accurate and fast-firing weapons, each capable of getting off 12 rounds per minute without undue strain on the crews. Their shells were most effective, but the guns were worn, their connections so loose that closing a breech could throw a gun offline by as much as a degree. In temperate climates, they could have been moved successfully by packhorses, but these animals became exhausted after carrying the guns over about 15 minutes of level-going ground in the Papuan heat. Nor could Papuan bearers solve the problem, for about 90 were needed to carry each disassembled gun without its ammunition.[1]

Further west, there had been some uncertainty on the inland route. There, Colonel Tomlinson's 126th Regiment (less that part

CHAPTER 6

of I/126th Regiment at Pongani) had been pushing on from the Natunga–Bofu area to reach Dobodura by way of Inonda and Horanda. From there, they were to cover the left of the advance on Buna by following an alternative route west of Simemi through Ango and the village of Gerua. Although an Australian wireless detachment had been attached to Harding for the purpose of keeping him informed of the progress of the Australians west of the Girua River, he could not establish radio contact with Major General Vasey commanding this sector. During the early days of his advance, Harding was almost as ignorant of the whereabouts of the Australians on his left as he was about the Japanese.[2]

* * *

Meanwhile, the Japanese aerial attack, which had taken place the previous day against the small flotilla, was repeated when four Zero fighters targeted two of the remaining three luggers, one at Embogo and the other at Mendaropu. The first lugger, the *Two Freddies*, was badly damaged and had to limp back to Milne Bay for repairs; while the second, the *Willyama*, suffered even greater damage and had to be beached – a total loss. Only one small lugger, the *Kelton*, was left to supply the troops east of the river.[3]

The loss of these craft was a disaster. There were no replacement vessels and artillery, mortars, machine guns, and other essential matériel, which could not be replaced for days, had been lost on the very eve of the campaign against Buna. The whole supply plan for the operation had been disrupted. Since the stores of rations and ammunition at the front were in dangerously short supply, and the lone lugger could not possibly handle more than a small fraction of the American's immediate needs, Major Ralph Birkness – who had just replaced American quartermaster Lieutenant Colonel McKenny, following his death during the previous day's raid – arranged with the air force to have the most critically needed items dropped by air.[4]

This forced Harding to make some last-minute changes in plan. Brigadier Hanford MacNider, commanding the 128th Regiment, was ordered to halt his advance until the *Kelton* could come in and make up at least part of his supply deficiencies. Also the troops at Pongani, who were to have been moved to Embogo by boat, were ordered instead to advance on foot to Buna. Except for the engineer company, which was sent to Dobodura, the troops were ordered to Boreo, where they were to join with Lieutenant Colonel Robert McCoy and his men of the I/128th Regiment in the attack towards Cape Endaiadere.[5] With these troops were the Australians of the 2/6th Independent Company, who were finally on the move, as recorded in the 2/6th Independent Company war diary: '1530 [hours]: Coy moved off – strength ten off. 109 O/Rs – Rear HQ and sick remained behind. Detachment 1/126 and 3/128 moved with Coy 1730: Halted short of MISSION (MENDAROPU) so that men could cook and camp before "black out" came into force. Very wet night – heavy rain. CO went fwd. to get fuller details and to ask for a few carriers'.[6]

* * *

That day, General Blamey wrote to Lieutenant General Herring at NGF in Port Moresby: 'There are indications that [the enemy] is gathering transports and protective destroyers to land reinforcements at Buna. It is imperative that our forces push forward at the greatest speed to seize the sea front in the Buna Area and destroy any enemy remaining in the region of operations as early as possible'.[7]

Indeed, at Rabaul, a three-destroyer convoy consisting of the *Asashio*, *Umikaze*, and the *Kawakaze* up-anchored from Simpson Harbour just before midnight, with the remainder of Colonel Yamamoto Hiroshi's force. These men would arrive at Buna just on dusk, at 5 pm, the next day.[8]

7

'... FIRST DEFEAT AND CLEAN UP THE AUSTRALIAN FORCE'

Early on 18 November, Major General Harding had changed his plans, ordering Colonel Clarence Tomlinson, commanding the 126th Regiment, then at Inonda, to move some of his men across the Girua River boundary towards Popondetta and Soputa to ensure the American left flank was protected, as he was still out of contact with the Australians who were supposed to be west of the river. Harding's chief of staff, Colonel John Mott, sent Tomlinson the following order: 'Have strong patrol move from Inonda to contact with view of moving thence to Soputa as previously planned if Aussies now there'.[1] Tomlinson would send out early the following morning a detachment of the III/126th Regiment to hopefully contact the Australians, who by now should have been approaching Sanananda just west of the river.[2]

Meanwhile, the men of the I/128th and III/128th regiments were positioned at Boreo and Simemi respectively, with their attack set for 7 am the next morning. Supply, however, was still an ongoing problem, as demonstrated by a message from Lieutenant Colonel Kelsie Miller, leading the III/128th Regiment, to his CO, Brigadier Hanford MacNider: 'What has happened to the ammunition needed?'[3]

Three companies of the II/128th Regiment, representing the division reserve, were now ordered from Dobodura to Ango, to cover the junction of the Soputa–Buna and Ango–Dobodura tracks until the men of the 126th Regiment arrived to take over the left-flank attack against Buna Village and Buna Mission. The remaining company, joined by the engineer company when it arrived from Pongani (likely now moving towards the front with the Australian commandos), was to remain at Dobodura to help prepare the airfield there.[4]

* * *

Further east at Mendaropu, the men of the Australian 2/6th Independent Company left for the Buna front with remaining elements of the 32nd Division. The Australian adjutant recorded in the unit war dairy later that night: '0800 [hours]: Moved off – passed EMO MISSION 0900, picked up 11 carriers and 2 police boys for W/T [wireless transmitter] sets and Bren guns. 1200: Halted for lunch – very hard climb in stifling heat through tall Kunai grass areas over steep hillsides – no cover from sun. Several men had to return due to fever. After lunch moved into wooded and jungle country. 1745: Camped on high ground between creeks. Exceptionally wet night but most men built native type shelters'.[5]

* * *

At Buna that day, unnamed Japanese soldier [B] recorded in his diary, which was later captured and translated after the fighting: 'This morning, we mistook our men for enemy and fired upon them for a while. After that, as before, there were several air raids'.[6] He would write his last entry just days later.

At Rabaul, the commander of the Japanese *8th Area Army*, Lieutenant General Hitoshi Imamura, received an order from the *Imperial General Headquarters in Tokyo*: 'Cooperate with the Navy to first invade the Solomon Islands while securing key areas in New Guinea and preparing for future operations in that area … secure key areas around Lae, Salamaua and Buna in cooperation with the Navy'.[7] Securing Guadalcanal was the current priority, with the operational doctrine to: 'Continue to secure the Buna area with reinforcements consisting of the 21st [Independent] Mixed Brigade, first defeat and

CHAPTER 7

clean up the Australian force attacking from the Owen Stanley Range, then destroy the American force advancing on the Buna front from the coast'.[8]

The *Imperial Japanese Navy*, however, assessed that the campaign in Papua was going from bad to worse. They judged that if the Allied airfield under construction to the south of Buna was not quickly captured, not only would future operations to reinforce and supply the Japanese beachheads become problematic, it would also threaten the Japanese position at Rabaul itself. Consequently, the Navy wanted the airfield to be captured and occupied as soon as possible.

The Army opposed this by countering that even if military strength in the area was reinforced to seize the airfield, including the troops of the *65th Brigade* and elements of the *51st Division* being transported by the Navy, the current difficulty in supplying Guadalcanal would be intensified by any attempt to increase supply to a large force in Papua. The Navy countered, stating that with the capture of the Allied airfield south of Buna, and with the key areas secured, there would be no requirement to reinforce the area to any great degree, and greater aerial support could be provided for the final operation against the renewed attack against Port Moresby.[9] Indeed, the *Imperial General Headquarters* established a policy to 'prepare to rapidly capture the enemy's airfield under construction about ten km to the south of Buna'.[10]

Meanwhile, the remainder of Colonel Yamamoto Hiroshi's force, including elements of the *144th* and *III/229th regiments*, arrived just off Sanananda on dusk. As the last of these men were disembarking at 7.40 pm, a lone Allied bomber attacked the convoy, using the light of the moon. The *Umikaze* sustained some damage while the *Kawakaze* only suffered slight damage. The Japanese at Buna now had an additional 2500 troops to man the defences – almost half of them were newly equipped and fresh from Rabaul.[11]

Among these men was unnamed Japanese soldier [C], whose diary was recovered during the fighting by American troops on

27 December 1942: 'Landed at BASA 2.20. NIG Company went to GIRUWA by motor launch and landed there at 4.00. From there they went towards SOPUTA 4 KM away [associated with the defence of the Sanananda beachhead] and rested there taking up positions of readiness. At 1800 [hours] left there and headed towards BUNA'.[12]

Japanese Lieutenant Suganuma and his platoon were also part of Yamamoto's force. The Japanese officer recorded in his diary: 'Transferred to small boat. Saw a transport apparently run aground front of landing point. Signalling with Heliograph. Several motor launches come out to take us in. Landing point is a sandy beach and various units have already landed. I saw the MATSUO unit and the HITABE unit. Since the enemy bombings are fierce, we dispersed into the jungle. After a while we were given rations and the 1st Platoon was to leave. Even though it is low tide there were several times when the water was knee and waist deep when we crossed small streams. At dawn I found that we were on a small trail in the jungle'.[13]

8
'... ALL COLUMNS WILL BE DRIVEN THROUGH TO OBJECTIVES REGARDLESS OF LOSSES'

Torrential rains that would last all day began early on 19 November. As ordered the previous day, Colonel Clarence Tomlinson, commanding the 126th Regiment, sent a strong detachment of the III/126th Regiment across the Girua River during the morning. Tomlinson had ordered Major George Bond, commanding the III/126th Regiment, to conduct an advance towards Popondetta. With this, Bond and his men of 'I' and 'K' companies crossed the river to determine if the Australians had occupied the village. By 11.30 am, Bond and his men made contact with elements of the Australian 16th Brigade close to Popondetta, and they were informed that most of the brigade had already passed through the village heading for Soputa. As ordered, Bond and his men now made their way back towards Inonda, and with the rest of the regiment, they were soon marching out towards Buna via Horanda, with the II/126th Regiment leading the advance. Scarcely had Tomlinson reached Horanda when he received news that he had been placed under the temporary command of Major General Vasey, who was commanding the Australian 7th Division.[1]

Lieutenant General Herring, commanding NGF, had earlier decided to attack Japanese concentrations west of the Girua, with the maximum force available. To affect this, Vasey was given the alternative of taking direct command of the 126th Regiment or shifting the American boundary westward. He chose the former. Major General Harding was then informed that his role was to seize and hold a line from the Girua to the coast (including a crossing near Soputa), to prevent enemy penetration into his area, and to secure bridgeheads. Harding protested to Herring, but it fell on deaf ears.[2]

A scribbled message from Vasey to Harding records: 'I will assume command that portion 126th Regt in Inonda. Request you order it to concentrate at Soputa on 20 Nov, moving via Popondetta. Have already ordered det. [Australian] 3d Bn now at Popondetta to move Soputa 0730 hrs, 20 Nov. Am directing 25th Bde on Gona and 16th Bde on … Sanananda. My HQ arrives at Soputa 1200 hrs, 20 Nov'.[3]

The last-minute diversion of elements of the 126th Regiment to the 16th Brigade obviously upset Harding's plans. Robbed of the bulk of his left-flanking force, Harding had to commit his reserve, the II/128th Regiment, there instead. In ordering Lieutenant Colonel Smith and the II/128th Regiment to now attack Buna from the left, Harding was sending a single battalion to accomplish a task previously allocated to the three battalions of the 126th Regiment. He had no other force available and sent Smith forward, hoping that he might, with luck, do the job of a full regiment.[4]

Even so, this would not prevent Harding from going ahead with his planned attack that day by Warren Force. The men of the I/128th Regiment would attack from the beach, while those of the III/128th Regiment would launch their assault inland from Simemi Village.[5]

* * *

The American troops were drenched to the skin, and all aircraft were grounded. At 7 am, after the two Australian mountain howitzers fired a few unobserved rounds, the men of the I/128th Regiment, led by Lieutenant Colonel Robert McCoy, moved forward from Boreo, while to their left, the III/128th Regiment, under Lieutenant Colonel Kelsie Miller, marched out from Simemi towards the bridge

CHAPTER 8

south of the two airfields. Because of the supply situation, each man only had one day's supply of food and ammunition.[6]

The frontline supply situation was clearly still in a state of chaos, as indicated by the messages sent to Harding that day from the I/128th Regiment: '1st Bn 128 needs ammo out of ration', and 'McCoy out of rations. Request dropping at Hariko'. Harding also received similar messages from the III/128th Regiment, and so Harding sent an urgent request to NGF in Port Moresby: 'Miller Bn held for want of .30 cal [machine gun] ammo. Urgent drop by chute'.[7]

* * *

Meanwhile, Colonel Yamamoto Hiroshi, who had arrived to replace Colonel Kusunose Masao as commander of the *144th Infantry Regiment*, was ready. He had two full days to get the bulk of his fresh, well-armed troops from his own regiment, along with those from the *III/229th Regiment* into position. His main line of resistance, between 750 and 800 metres south of Cape Endaiadere, ran from the sea through the Duropa Plantation to the eastern end of New Strip and past it to the bridge between the two airstrips. At the immediate approaches to this well-built and strongly held defence system, he had an outpost line of emplacements. Although not continuous like the main line, it was strong with cleared fields of fire. It was covered by troops who manned concealed machinegun nests along the track at the lower (southern) end of the Duropa Plantation, and in the plantation itself. The Japanese Navy units of *5th Yokosuka, 5th Sasebo (SNLP)*, and supporting naval pioneer troops commanded by Captain Yasuda Yoshitatsu were deployed further west to protect Buna Village and the area around the Buna Mission, as well as the area just south known as the Triangle.[8]

* * *

At 8 am on the fringes of Duropa Plantation, about 1.5 kilometres south of the cape, McCoy and his men of the I/128th Regiment waited as the two Australian 3.7-inch mountain howitzers, commanded by Captain Martin O'Hare, provided a ten-minute bombardment against the Japanese forward positions. A scribbled note by the adjutant of the III/128th Regiment records: '0810 [hours] McCoy to Miller. Heavy ten min barrage. Commencing 0800. Our jump-off 0810'.[9]

After the bombardment, McCoy and his men advanced but were quickly targeted with concentrated machinegun and rifle fire, throwing them into confusion. He and his men also encountered heavy overhead jungle growth, which made it difficult for them to use their mortars and their grenades, as they could not observe the Japanese positions or where their fire was coming from. The Japanese weapons gave off no flash, and the reverberation of their fire in the jungle made it impossible to determine their whereabouts by sound.[10]

To make matters worse, the map then in use, *Buna Target Plan No. 24*, was later discovered to be inaccurate, which led to errors in the daily situation reports. This is clearly demonstrated by early messages of success by McCoy. This led to the following inaccurate messages just before 9.30 am: '0920 [hours] McCoy to Miller: Have advanced to within short distance of Cape Endaiadere. Still moving'. Soon after, Brigadier Hanford MacNider related to Miller: 'McCoy 100 yds [metres] from Cape Endaiadere and left advancing through Coconut Plantation'.[11] This was clearly not the case, as they were still at least a kilometre south of the cape.

Major David Parker, an engineer assigned to the I/128th Regiment, recalled at the time:

> The first opposition from the enemy here was a surprise and shock to our green troops. The enemy positions were amazingly well camouflaged and seemed to have excellent fields of fire even in the close quarters of the jungle .... Snipers were everywhere ... and they were so well camouflaged that it was nearly impossible to discern them. The enemy habitually

CHAPTER 8

> allowed our troops to advance to very close range – sometimes four or five feet from a machinegun post – before opening fire; often they allowed troops to by-pass them completely, opening fire then on our rear elements, and on our front elements from the rear ... the deadly accuracy and strength of the enemy machinegun and rifle fire from their camouflaged positions ... pinned down [our men] everywhere .... It was dangerous to show even a finger from behind one's cover, as it would immediately draw a burst of fire. It was impossible to see where the enemy fire was coming from; consequently, our own rifle and machinegun [fire] was ineffective during the early stages .... Grenades and mortars ... were difficult to use because, first, it was difficult to pick out a nest position to advance upon with grenades, second, the thick jungle growth, and high grass, made throwing and firing difficult, and third, because it was nearly impossible to observe our fire.[12]

Parker also recorded during this attack that the Fifth-Grade technician, Edwin De Rosier, a medical aid man with the 107th Medical Detachment, had moved out into the open repeatedly to treat the wounded while under intense fire, saving the lives of many. Edwin De Rosier would be killed-in-action two weeks later. He was awarded the Distinguished Service Cross (DSC) posthumously.[13]

Falling back a dozen or so metres at a time when strongly pressed, the Japanese covering the troops gradually fell back towards their main lines. Out of rations, and with the greater part of their ammunition used up, the men of the I/128th Regiment ended the day a badly shaken outfit. The official American historian of the campaign recorded: 'The troops had entered the battle joking and laughing, and sure of an easy victory. Now they were dazed and taken aback by the mauling they had received at the hands of the Japanese. Nor did it escape them that the bodies of the few Japanese left on the field were those of fresh, well-fed, well-armed troops – not, as they had been led to expect, the tired, emaciated, and disease-ridden survivors of the fighting in the Owen Stanleys'.[14] It was to be some time before these men recovered from the shock of finding that the battle was to be no pushover and that, 'instead of a short and easy mop-up, a long cruel fight lay ahead of them'.[15]

* * *

Even more abrupt was the baptism of fire for the men of the III/128Regiment. As Miller and his men trampled forward from Simemi Village, with his men of 'K' Company leading the way, the track became a narrow strip of corduroy 'road' enveloped by swamp land. As it approached the airstrips, this track entered completely cleared kunai grass country, little higher than the main swamp level. On the right, New Strip was bathed in sunlight; the bridge between the strips lay ahead with Old Strip to the left, and, on the immediate left, a 'scarecrow growth marked the line of Simemi Creek with grey arms of dead wood'.[16] As they entered this barren country, intense Japanese fire swept the Americans away. According to Miller, he and his men were 'stopped cold'.[17] The adjutant of the III/128th Regiment recorded within ten minutes of conducting their attack: '0820 [hours] Miller to McCoy. Still held up. Keep us advised'.[18]

Attempts to get his men through the open field about 300 metres south of the junction were met with concentrated fire from the western end of New Strip, from behind the bridge, and from machine guns forward of the junction, making further advance impossible. Nor could Miller do much to blast out the enemy with fire. He had no 81-mm mortars; a large percentage of his grenades were observed to be duds; and he had still not received a resupply of ammunition for their .30-caliber machine guns.[19]

One of the regimental staff members recalled the situation: 'Miller had to attack through swamps which were sometimes waist- and chest-deep, and through which it was impossible to carry any but light weapons. Here too, grenades (Mills bombs obtained from the

CHAPTER 8

Australians) became ineffective when wet. One of Miller's patrols threw seven grenades into a group of ten or twelve Japs whom they stalked, only to have all the grenades fail to explode and to suffer casualties from return grenade fire'.[20] By the end of the day, the men of the III/128th Regiment were still at the edge of the clearing south of the bridge. The battalion had suffered several casualties and made no further gain.[21]

Pinned down on a narrow front, out of rations, and with nearly all the ammunition expended, Miller concluded that they were fortunate that Colonel Yamamoto did not press his advantage by launching a counterattack.[22] It was recorded by the III/128th Regiment adjutant that night: 'Miller to MacNider: Rations for 800. 7 wounded and 12 MIA. Rain all night, with 1/3 ration for day'.[23]

* * *

An unknown Japanese soldier at New Strip recorded later that day: 'Near the plantation, and after firing two shots we captured two prisoners. The prisoners were executed by medical Captain Kato of *14th Pioneer Unit*. Army units with battalion guns, mountain artillery, machine guns, infantry, engineers, etc., passed by throughout the day'.[24]

Having landed the previous day at Sanananda, Colonel Yamamoto Hiroshi and the bulk of his force, including elements of the *144th* and *III/229th regiments*, had made their way to Buna. Among these men was unnamed Japanese soldier [C], who recorded in his diary: 'Reached BUNA. Due to activities of enemy planes withdrew temporarily to the mountaingun positions. Just as we reached the mountaingun positions, we received reports of enemy attack and immediately went forward. Engaged enemy near positions of the Navy NCO outpost and repulsed them. Received orders to return to Battalion. On shore watch tonight. Platoon leader Toyoda probational officer killed in action. 3rd platoon leader is Sgt Nishiyama'.[25]

BLOODY BUNA

Close by would have been Lance Corporal Uchiyama Seiichi, with Captain Matsuo, who led *No. 9 Company, III/229th Regiment*. His company went into action that day; Uchiyama recorded in his diary: 'Fierce hand grenade battle with enemy 20 metres away in the jungle. Horiguchi was wounded. I dragged him to the rear and became a machine gunner. Retreated while firing, established position in the area. While halting to return fire, Ikeda and Kanda were killed. Ordered to retreat in the morning because of enemy mortar fire. Lost a few men and abandoned several LMGs [light machine guns] and grenade discharges'.[26]

Japanese Lieutenant Suganuma, who was also with Yamamoto's force, had yet to reach Buna. He recorded in his diary the journey from Sanananda:

> We are following this trail. At about 1000 we reach GIRUWA. Here and there troops are present. There are some who say that they just arrived from the front. All are dispersed in the jungle to avoid being bombed. We too disperse according to squads and rest. When we will set out is not known. I hear stories of conditions in the new battlefields.
>
> We were told that we could not eat till after 1700 and it was not ten minutes after I started to prepare my mess that we would leave in ten minutes. I hurried as much as possible and somehow made it. We departed. Due to the full tide the swamps are full of water and there are places where the road is under water. What a place, I thought. It was a difficult march to the seashore. We rested at the seashore. Enemy planes flew over and dropped flares after which they strafed a motor launch that had been washed ashore. Here and there I saw shore patrol soldiers. They seemed very alert. On the small trail along the shore there were suspension bridges and broken-down bridges at places. This takes quite a while. They gave us a rubber boat. When we meet with soldiers and sailors, we ask how many kilometres it is to the

CHAPTER 8

airfield. The guides are very kind. Near entrance of airfield [we] made connection with the 3rd Platoon, which we met before, and was surprised. When we crossed the airport, it was getting a little lighter. We headed for Coconut Grove.[27]

* * *

Back in Port Moresby, General MacArthur was restlessly demanding a successful conclusion to the operations now just commencing not only at Buna but on the whole Buna–Sanananda–Gona front. He told General Blarney that his land forces must attack the Buna–Gona area vigorously the next day, and that 'all columns will be driven through to objectives regardless of losses'.[28] This was passed onto Harding with information that heavy air support would be provided at 8 am, the next morning. Allied infantry were to storm the Japanese positions as soon as the air sorties had concluded, even if weather prevented the aircraft from assisting the attack, and in that case, they would advance at 8.10 am.[29]

This rush to take the beachhead positions would characterise the fighting throughout November 1942 to January 1943. A lack of reconnaissance and careful planning replaced with demands by Army, divisional, brigade, regimental, and even by some battalion commanders to conduct ad-hoc rushed localised attacks, would result in literally hundreds, if not thousands, of casualties that could have been avoided. Many junior officers and men would forever feel justifiably bitter about the apparent lack of concern for their welfare by their senior commanders during the battles for Gona, Sanananda and Buna.

9

'... CHARGING AN ENEMY MACHINEGUN POST, SUBMACHINE GUN IN HAND'

Next morning – 20 November – Lieutenant Colonel Robert McCoy and his men of the I/128th Regiment resumed their attack. With assistance from the two Australian mountain howitzers and several strikes by a few B-25 and A-20 two engine bombers against Cape Endaiadere, the battalion attacked from a point about two-kilometres south. The Allies where not the only ones to commit aircraft to the battle for Buna that day as seven Japanese carrier-based fighters strafed American positions around Buna.

Lieutenant John Crow led his men of 'C' Company on the right, along the coast, while 'B' Company was to their left, a short distance inland. The Japanese were still well hidden and waiting, but the Americans had a better idea of what now lay ahead. Crow and his men succeeded in infiltrating and knocking out several enemy machine gun nests. The line moved forward a few hundred metres – where they were forced to dig-in for the night. In this advance, Lieutenant Crow was killed, along with one of his platoon commanders, Sergeant Paul Sherney; both had led their men from the front and paid the price.[1] Lieutenant Colonel Alexander MacNab, executive officer of the 128th Regiment, reported that Lieutenant John Crow was last seen 'charging an enemy machinegun post, submachine gun in hand'.[2] He was awarded the DSC posthumously.

Just south of the two airstrips, Lieutenant Colonel Kelsie Miller

CHAPTER 9

and his men of the III/128th Regiment remained dug-in as ordered and were preparing for the next day's attack against the entrenched Japanese positions near the airstrips.³

* * *

Earlier that morning, Japanese Lieutenant Suganuma, who was with Colonel Yamamoto Hiroshi's force, had reached the Coconut Grove since landing at Sananda days before recording in his diary: 'It started to rain again. 30 minutes after eating breakfast there was an alarm. At first, I thought that they told us to put up camouflage because of enemy planes. We hurriedly took off our extra weight and with light arms went towards the grass plain (dummy airfield) and went as far as the front edge of the coconut grove. Much firing heard. It was said that our scouts were firing at their scouts. The MATSUO unit steadily pushing on the left. After lunch we went out to the right edge of the coconut grove'.⁴

* * *

That afternoon, Lieutenant Colonel Edmund Carrier, and his detachment of 218 men from the I/126th Regiment, and Major Harry Harcourt and his 118 Australian commandos from the 2/6th Independent Company, who days before begun their marched forward from Pongani, arrived at Brigadier Hanford MacNider's headquarters. This post was located just behind the men of the I/128th Regiment and these men went into bivouac immediately behind McCoy's men. These reinforcements had arrived after an exhausting 40-kilometre march with full pack and were to join McCoy's battalion in their further attack against Cape Endaiadere the next morning.⁵

* * *

At Rabaul, the following agreement was made between the *Imperial Japanese Army* and the *Imperial Japanese Navy*: '1) The main strength of the 21st Independent Mixed Brigade will be transported to Buna and landed during the night of 23 November; and 2) As there are no prospects for the future operations of the Buna airstrip owing to its poor quality, make preparations to quickly seize the airfield under construction by the Allies approximately ten kilometres to the south of Buna'.[6] Nothing would come of this order.

The *21st Independent Mixed Brigade* commanded by Major General Yamagata Tsuyuo had just arrived at Rabaul, from Indochina [present-day Vietnam and Cambodia]. The nucleus of this force was the *170th Infantry Regiment*. Around 750 men from this force, mostly from the *I/170th Regiment*, however, would not set sail from Rabaul until the night of the 28 and early morning hours of 29 November to reinforce the Japanese beachheads.[7]

10
'THE PARADE OF INJURED GIs WAS HEARTBREAKING TO WATCH ...'

On the morning of 21 November, an order to General Harding arrived: 'TAKE BUNA TODAY AT ALL COSTS. MACARTHUR'.[1]

The attack that day was to be in greater strength, better supported and supplied than those of the previous two days. The plan called for Lieutenant Colonel Robert McCoy and his recently arrived men of the I/128th Regiment on the right, and Lieutenant Colonel Edmund Carrier and his troops of the I/126th Regiment (minus three platoons of 'C' Company and all of 'D' Company, who were then fighting at Sanananda) on the left, to move north on Cape Endaiadere on a 300-metre front. While this attack was progressing along the coast, Major Harry Harcourt and his 118 Australian commandos of the 2/6th Independent Company would infiltrate the eastern end of New Strip, while Lieutenant Colonel Kelsie Miller and his men of the III/128th Regiment, from their position astride the Dobodura–Simemi track, would seize the bridge between the airstrips. The attacks would be preceded by a heavy air bombardment. The time of the attack would be communicated to the battalion commanders once the air force could confirm the timing of the air soties.[2]

By the time Harcourt reported to McCoy at 7 am, Harcourt had been told that the men of the I/128th Regiment were holding a line some 600 metres south of Cape Endaiadere, south-west to the eastern end of New Strip near the beach – a position which meant the American left was well north of the strip. Harcourt's own reconnaissance, however, indicated this was incorrect, as the American left was not nearly so advanced and only slightly (if at all) above a line drawn due east from the strip. Two further patrols by Australian commandos confirmed Harcourt's assessment. Even so, the plan remained for McCoy on the extreme right and Carrier to his left to advance against Cape Endaiadere on a 300-metre front.

Harcourt was to protect the left flank of the coastal drive and oust the Japanese from their positions at the eastern end of New Strip, while Miller and his men of the III/128th Regiment would advance across the bridge, on the far left. Meanwhile, Lieutenant Colonel Smith and his men of the II/128th Regiment further west would push on from Ango Village, along the eastern bank of the Girua River, over six kilometres to Gerua, and from there they were to take Buna Village.[3]

The air attack by A-20 and B-25 bombers took place at 8 am, and while a few enemy machinegun nests were knocked out from the air, no ground attack followed the bombardment. Because of faulty co-ordination, neither McCoy nor Miller received prior notice of the bombardment orders telling them when to attack. Worse still, one of the planes, instead of dropping its bombs on Japanese positions, targeted some of Miller's forward troops, killing four and wounding two. Orders from regiment calling for an attack at 8 am were finally received by Miller at 8.40 am, and by McCoy at 8.50 am – late by 40 and 50 minutes, respectively, after the air bombardment had ceased.[4]

Major General Harding soon after arranged to have the airmen attack again at 12.45 pm. This aerial attack would be followed by an artillery and mortar barrage, and the troops would jump off at 1 pm. This time, however, no planes arrived, as the Air Force feared they would not be able to complete the attack within the specified time, so they held their planes back rather than run the risk of hitting friendly troops. Another aerial attack was slated, with the airmen arriving over

CHAPTER 10

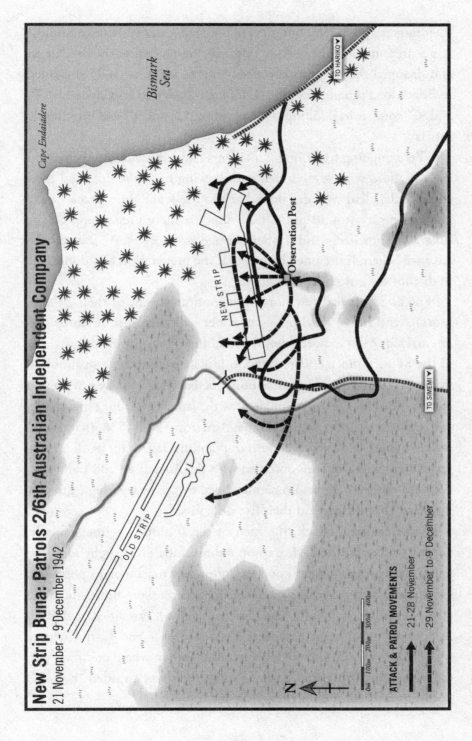

their targets at 3.57 pm, but most of the planes were unable to find the target area, and a flight of A-20 bombers even overshot the beachhead and dropped their bombs harmlessly out to sea. One B-25 unloaded its bomb load squarely in the midst of McCoy's two lead elements ('B' and 'C' companies), killing six, wounding 12, and almost burying 70 others.[5]

These ongoing friendly fire incidents had a disheartening effect on the battalion, with several men withdrawing from the line, and their commanders had to order them back to the front. The attack finally got under way at 4.30 pm, after a short artillery preparation by the Australian howitzers and a brief barrage by mortars. As soon as the advance began, it became obvious that the preparation had done little to disrupt the entrenched Japanese.[6]

The attackers had few heavy weapons, and most of their 81-mm mortars and heavy machine guns either had been lost at sea or had not arrived. All the mortar-bombs reaching the front, including those of the 81-mm mortar, were fused to impact on contact and thus had little effect against the Japanese bunkers. Forward observers were also handicapped by the heavy jungle growth, Japanese skilful camouflage, and communication failures. The American SCR 536 (hand-held walkie-talkie) used by the mortar platoons failed to work in the jungle; this had also been observed with the Australian 108-radio sets. Forward observers were also handicapped by the heavy jungle growth, Japanese camouflage, and their fire discipline.[7]

In their coastal attack, the men of the I/128th Regiment fought desperately with rifles, Thompson submachine guns, light machine guns, and hand grenades, knocking out a few machinegun positions, but little if any progress was made. Casualties were heavy. In three days of combat, 'C' Company alone suffered 63 casualties, including all four of its officers. Sergeants Reuben Steger and Carl Cherney were killed within a few hours of each other when commanding the company during that day's fighting; each was awarded the DSC posthumously for their actions that day.[8]

CHAPTER 10

The war diary of the 126th Regiment briefly records the day's events on the left: 'The battalion attacks with the north beach as their objective but are hampered by enemy machinegun fire, snipers, and jungle terrain. An attempt is made to neutralise the machinegun fire with our mortars, allowing company "A" to advance to the fork of the new airstrip. Our casualties are numerous'.[9]

* * *

Meanwhile, three patrols from the 2/6th Independent Company had been sent out to gain further intelligence of the Japanese positions before the main attack by the rest of the company. This attack would be led by Captain Rossall Belmer, a 27-year-old regular soldier from Sydney, totalling just 51 officers and men, and was scheduled for noon.[10]

The first two patrols were led by Lieutenant Robert Scott, a 26-year-old clerk from Margaret River in Western Australia, with three men of 'A' Platoon; and Lieutenant Richard Egan, a 39-year-old accountant from Haywood in Victoria, with three men of 'B' Platoon. Both patrols were tasked with locating the eastern part of New Strip and the Japanese defences north of this position. The third patrol, led by 29-year-old Lieutenant Arthur Tregarthen from Brisbane, with three men of 'C' Platoon were to locate the south-west part of New Strip and reconnoitre the Japanese positions there. Meanwhile, Belmer and the rest of the company moved to their forward positions, awaiting the return of the three patrols.[11]

The men of 'A' and 'B' patrols returned by 11.30 am. Scott leading 'A' Platoon reported reaching the eastern parts of the strip and the position of observed Japanese machinegun positions. Egan, leading 'B' Platoon, was unable to locate the strip but did encounter a Japanese patrol south of the strip, killing one, while suffering one man wounded. Both patrols observed: 'Only Americans seen and who appeared to be F.D.L. [Forward Defence Line] tps [troops]. were well S and E of position of E end of STRIP'.[12]

With this information, Belmer now planned to take out the identified Japanese machinegun positions. As recorded in the company war diary: 'Coy's Det. to advance in patrol formation and on striking of opposition to attempt encirclement or infiltration tactics. US plan was to advance from present F.D.Ls to coastline W of CAPE ENDAIADERE – we were to move up on LEFT flank and protect this'.[13] Soon, word came through that the attack was postponed to 12.45 pm, to enable further aerial bombing of enemy positions; however, even so, the attacking party was moving out by 12.20 pm.[14]

Belmer's attacking force was divided into two parties. The first contained Lieutenant Scott and Lieutenant Owen Folland, a 21-year-old shop assistant from the township called 'Hundred of Goode' in South Australia, and 24 commandos from 'A' Platoon; while the second party consisted of Lieutenant Egan and Lieutenant Geoffrey Fielding, a 30-year-old clerk from Fremantle in Western Australia, with 22 commandos from 'B' Platoon. At this point, the third patrol of Lieutenant Arthur Tregarthen from 'C' Platoon had not returned. The men were now waiting for the aerial bombard before launching their attack against the strip.[15]

Due to the failure of the aircover to appear, Belmer's attack was rescheduled for later that day. The war diary records the attack that afternoon: 'Two heavy bombs fell in line of left Support Coy of 1/128 and caused a great deal of disorganisation. In the end, however, the casualties caused were light, but this incident destroyed the confidence of the US Inf. in air bombing and settled decisively the position of their F.D.L. some 200 yds. S. of SOUTH-EASTERN horn at E. end of NEW STRIP. Our detachment moved fwd. at end of air bombing and came under heavy MG [machinegun] and sniper fire. Several MG posts were cleared, and some snipers shot down from trees, but the enemy moved his MGs to alternative positions as soon as they were attacked. The thick nature of the undergrowth made it extremely difficult to see the enemy until our men were on top of him or until he opened fire'.[16]

CHAPTER 10

Having lost two officers and three men to enemy fire, and with the failure of the attack by the coastal force, Belmer and his men were forced to fall back a further 100 metres south of the Japanese perimeter at New Strip, taking up a position to the furthest forward American position, about 150 metres from the Japanese frontlines. The company adjutant continued his diary entry that they were in danger of being fired on by the Americans to their left: 'The 1/128 were not advancing and had not moved from their previous positions, which made it possible for our men to be caught by both US and Jap fire'.[17]

With the Australian commandos was Private Stanley Martin, a 20-year-old stockman from Victoria River Downs in the Northern Territory, who fought on after he had been shot in the arm, wounded again in the leg, and shot a third time, in the torso – he only left the fight on direct orders. Private Stanley Martin received a mention in despatches for his actions that day.[18] In this action was 20-year-old Private Allen Osborne, from Sydney, with No. 4 Section, who recalled Martin's actions: 'On this particular day during the bit of an action, one of the Martin twins was wounded, not badly, I think. He was wounded in the arm, but he kept moving forward and his brother [James][vii] said: "How's your arm?" He said: "Not too bad, but my leg's a bit crook." He'd been wounded in the leg. He kept going and they said: "How's your arm and your leg?" He said: 'They're not too bad, but this one on my side's crook", and at that point [I] had to order him to leave the battle. He had been wounded three times'.[19]

Meanwhile, Lieutenant Arthur Tregarthen and his 'C' Platoon patrol, who had gone out further north-west earlier that morning, returned having not encountered any enemy patrols but had located a Japanese mortar position, which was bombing the command post of the I/128th Regiment and support lines. Soon after, Tregarthen was sent out with 11 men to destroy the mortar position and make a

---

vii Both brothers signed up together, as James' serial number is SX17641 with Stanley's being SX17642.

thorough reconnaissance of the kunai grass area between the coconut plantation and the Dobodura–Buna Track. Tregarthen later reported back that the Japanese mortar-bombs had set fire to the large kunai patch, and that Japanese snipers targeted them as they tried to advance into the general area.[20] With this patrol was Private Jim Kent, a 20-year-old clerk from Cottesloe in Western Australia, who recalled:

> Shrapnel whirled through the trees just above our heads, and I heard low-pitched chirping noises that had no connection with the exploding mortar-bombs. I raised my head and saw on one of the thin branches a nest with two babies in it, their small bald heads just peeping over the top of it. Mumma bird fluttered up and down just over their heads chirping in an agitated manner. Then three more bombs exploded, and the shrapnel flew dangerously close. Mumma bird became very agitated, fluttering up and down, hovering just above the nest, chirping away as she tried to pacify her two wee babies. She must have been absolutely terrified (I wasn't feeling too good myself) but she could not desert the nest containing her babies.
>
> There was a break in the firing, and she became less and less agitated, her chirping changed to what could be called re-assurance, and finally she perched on the side of the nest and nudged her young with her head. The little ones became calm, and she began to look around, eyeing us with curiosity, but completely unafraid. It was almost as if she knew we would not harm her or her babies. We stayed put for ten minutes or so and no more bombs fell, so we moved off deeper into the belt of timber. The devotion to her babies displayed by the tiny, feathered mother was most impressive.[21]

Tregarthen planned to take out the mortar position next morning.[22]

* * *

CHAPTER 10

To the left of the Australians, on the Simemi Track, Miller and his men of the III/128th Regiment failed to reach the bridge between the airstrips. A 20-round barrage by the 60-mm mortars was fired, and the troops moved out at 4.28 pm. At first, they made good progress, moving through the clearing where they had been held up the previous two days, sweeping past the junction, and several of the lead platoons advanced to within a short distance of the bridge. It was then that a withering crossfire completely pinned them down. The battalion suffered 42 casualties during the attack. At 5.50 pm, Miller ordered the troops to pull back to a less-exposed position south of the track junction, in bush below the western end of New Strip.[23]

* * *

Meanwhile, at Urbana Front, advancing further south from Ango Village on the extreme left flank, Lieutenant Colonel Smith and his men of the II/128th Regiment had reached Gerua village. Here, the main track forked – the right branch led to the Buna Government Station, while the left led to Buna Village. About 250 metres beyond each track where they diverged, two additional branches also parted to form an acute angle of only 20 to 30 degrees before they suddenly flung wide – defining the Triangle. From here the 'Coconut Grove' lay just beyond on the western track with the Government Garden to the right of the eastern track.[24]

As Smith's men approached the Triangle, his leading company narrowly escaped an ambush. It is likely that squad leader Ernest Gerber was with this advance. He recalled: 'My company walked down a trial towards the Triangle. We were feeling easy about the whole thing. We had run into one or two Japs along the way and had killed them. We thought this was going to be a snap, you know. When we hit the Triangle, where the Japanese were solidly entrenched, we immediately had two or three soldiers killed. We were going up the trail when this happened. We weren't thinking about going into the swamp. We were just going to walk up the trail and take things over. We backtracked, thinking maybe it would be a little tougher'.[25]

Smith immediately attempted to flank the Japanese position, facing the defences with one company on the track, holding a second in reserve, and sending one to either side. But his flanking companies plunged deep into swampland, and with this darkness, the Americans were forced to dig-in.[26] An unnamed American engineer witnessed the fighting here:

> The first opposition from the enemy was a surprise and a shock to our green troops. The enemy positions were amazingly well camouflaged and seemed to have excellent fields of fire even in the close quarters of the jungle .... Snipers were everywhere .... The enemy habitually allowed our troops to advance to very close range – sometimes four or five feet from a machinegun post – before opening fire; often they allowed troops to bypass them completely, opening fire then on our rear elements, and on our front elements from the rear.
>
> Our troops were pinned down everywhere .... It was impossible to see where the enemy fire was coming from; consequently, our own rifle and machine gun [fire] was ineffective .... Grenades and mortars ... were difficult to use because, first it was difficult to pick out a nest position to advance upon with grenades, second, the thick jungle growth, and high grass, made throwing and firing difficult, and third, because it was nearly impossible to observe our fire.[27]

Another unnamed soldier recalled: 'The parade of injured GIs was heartbreaking to watch .... The walking wounded struggled past us .... A few were being carried on litters, and some were left where they died, until the next day when they could be taken care of by special burial squads'.[28]

The experience of his men in 'G' Company, who were trying to flank the Japanese east in the swamp, was particularly difficult. These

CHAPTER 10

men had moved out into the swamp in the late afternoon, and as they made their way eastward, darkness fell. The acting company commander, Lieutenant Theodore Florey, decided to go on, but the swamp kept getting deeper. Since there was little chance of reaching dry ground before morning, Florey finally called a halt at 9 pm. The company spent a miserable night, with only a few men able to perch on the roots of trees, while the rest were stranded in the mire until first light. Wet to the skin and in need of sleep, all anxiously waited for first light.[29]

When Harding received news from Smith, he was not surprised. He assessed that Smith could not possibly hope to complete his objective with just one battalion – he had originally planned for the whole of the 126th Regiment to conduct this operation. He now asked Lieutenant General Herring, commanding Advance NGF, to return his men of the 126th Regiment attached to the 16th Brigade. Herring's reply to Harding's request states: 'Personal to Gen Harding. Re your previous message [20 November], and 7th Aust Div [19 November]. Vasey's assumption comd 126th Regt purely temporary and operational to ensure complete co-ordination Soputa area [Sanananda Beachhead area]. This decision must stand. Rely on your loyal cooperation avoidance misunderstanding and wholehearted determination to destroy the enemy. Consider Vasey action essential and minimum necessary to permit his force to bypass Soputa and take main enemy with all speed'.[30]

Even so, Herring left the decision to Major General Vasey, commanding the Australian 7th Division. Vasey agreed that Colonel Clarence Tomlinson, commanding the 126th Regiment (then at Soputa with the Australian 16th Brigade), should send Major Smith and his men of the II/126th Regiment off next morning to join Lieutenant Colonel Smith and his men of the II/128th Regiment located at Gerua Village.[31]

* * *

By 8 pm, Harding was readjusting his battalions. If Miller clung to his positions short of the bridge, on the approach to the two strips, he was likely to remain bogged down and unable to advance. Harding therefore instructed him to leave one company to hold their existing position while he brought the rest of his battalion to Simemi, to join McCoy and the others. They would all collectively attack on the right flank against Cape Endaiadere. Miller left Lieutenant Carl Fryday and 'I' Company behind to hold the ground just south of the bridge, while the rest of the battalion arrived just behind McCoy's position sometime later that night. The main thrust against the beachhead was now along two axes: the coastal strip at the Warren front, and the western approach at Urbana Front; the central thrust between the two strips was now on hold.[32]

Harding now also readjusted his command structure by advancing Lieutenant Colonel Alexander MacNab, executive officer of the 128th Regiment, to operational command of the coastal drive over the head of MacNab's own commander, Colonel Tracy Hale. Harding was dissatisfied with the co-ordination between the various units of Warren Force. He now ordered MacNab, an experienced and aggressive officer, to report directly to Brigadier Hanford MacNider, under whom he was to co-ordinate the coastal drive. He would arrive at the front the next day and immediately develop plans to take Buna and its airstrips.[33]

By now the supply situation had improved when the airstrip at Dobodura opened for limited service. The strip had been completed to a length of 1000 metres and a width of 32 metres – a notable speedy achievement by the engineers. Additionally, five luggers arrived on the scene from Milne Bay, but one broke up on a reef immediately upon arrival. Even so, the remaining four brought in their cargo safely. With the *Kelton*, Major Ralph Birkness now had five luggers for coastal operations. There was still a chance that the 32nd Division's supply, disrupted though it was, could be put on an even keel.[34]

With the sinking of the barge and the two 25-pounder guns on

CHAPTER 10

16 November, most of the surviving Australian gunners of 'F' Troop had walked back along the coast to Oro Bay and retraced their steps to join the battery commander, Major William Hall, a 36-year-old accountant from Essendon in Victoria, who had just arrived with 'E' Troop and four 25-pounder guns. At Wanigela, Hall had rafted his guns and stores ashore on 14 November. Two days later, he had positioned them for beach and airstrip defence. He now advanced to Hariko to learn more about the American plans, leaving his men under the command of Captain Lionel Nix, a 28-year-old solicitor from Sydney.[35]

At Hariko, Captain Mueller joined Hall, having left Lieutenant William Marr, a 23-year-old reporter from Dubbo in New South Wales, and a few helpers at Oro Bay to get his two remaining 25-pounder guns forward. Marr, on board the *Kelton* with his dismantled guns, was preparing to land, when he received word from the Americans that no landing could be made through the surf at Oro Bay. Nonetheless, Marr ignored the warning, and through pitch darkness and broken sea, he used a longboat and a canvas-assault boat to land his guns and ammunition on the night of 21 and early morning hours of 22 November. Once ashore, the guns were concealed beneath thick tropical vegetation and were soon moved just north of Hariko. Japanese Zeros, however, came over and strafed the gun positions, damaging the sights off one of the guns, putting it out of action for several days.[36]

By now more guns were on their way to the front. In Port Moresby, Lieutenant Colonel Keith O'Connell, a 34-year-old insurance assessor from Sydney, now commanding the 2/1st Field Regiment, who was a veteran of the African desert and Greek campaigns, had been alerted. His 2nd Battery was standing by for final orders to move to Buna by sea, while the 1st Battery waited in hopeful expectancy, and the 51st Battery was preparing to begin a flight to the coast on 23 November. One troop of the 2/1st Field Regiment constituting Blackforce under Major Arthur Hanson, a 31-year-old clerk from Killara in New South

Wales, was to land at Popondetta and support Major General Vasey, commanding the Australian 7th Division to the west; the second troop, constituting Bullforce under Captain Herbert Manning, a 29-year-old grazier from Mendooran in New South Wales, was to land at Dobodura and support the American at Buna.[37]

Even so, other problems now loomed large for the 32nd Division. They needed to adjust their own approach to the objectives; and they needed further support of greater weight than infantry alone could muster. It was true that considerable air support had been provided, but the nature of the vegetation made it impossible to see the recognition signals on the ground. Added to this was the inexperience of the soldiers combined with the lack of practice and skill of some of the pilots in close-support operations. Complicating things further was the skilful construction of the Japanese defences, which made them invisible from the air and almost impervious to bombing (except by a direct hit), rendering air attack largely ineffective against prepared positions.[38]

Although the Australian commanders had generally shared the Americans' expectations that resistance in the Buna area would be light, some provision had been made earlier for tank support. It was now clear that these would be the only answer to the solidly prepared and tenaciously held, extensive Japanese bunker system.

On 13 November, Major General Cyril Clowes, a 50-year-old professional soldier and Duntroon graduate from Warwick in Queensland[viii], had been ordered to send from Milne Bay to Pongani or Oro Bay (to be determined by Harding) one troop of M3 Stuart tanks from a squadron of the Australian 2/6th Armoured Regiment. Lack of shipping, however, defeated this plan, as when the first tank was loaded on the only available craft thought to be suitable (a captured Japanese landing barge), both barge and tank sank to the bottom.

---

viii Clowes had commanded Milne Force, which inflicted the first significant victory against Japanese land force in the Pacific War when his men of the Australian 7th and 18th brigades repelled the Japanese invasion of Milne Bay in late-August 1942.

CHAPTER 10

Although both were subsequently salvaged, it was clear that there was no immediate hope of moving the tanks from Milne Bay to Oro Bay. Instead, as a temporary measure, Clowes was told on 21 November to send a platoon of Bren gun carriers, which would turn out to be a tragic disaster for all concerned.[39]

* * *

At Buna that day, unnamed Japanese soldier [B], who days before wrote of mistakenly firing at his own men, recorded in his diary: 'Today the enemy suddenly took the offensive. The mortar bursting on our front is fierce and the enemy definitely has superiority in the air. Enemy bombers and fighters raided rear positions and afterwards strafed. Because of that, our forces could not move'.[40]

11
'STIRRING UP THE JAPS'

During the morning of 22 November, Colonel Clarence Tomlinson, commanding the 126th Regiment, had entered the battle to take Sanananda to the west of Buna, in support of the Australian 16th Brigade. However, Major Smith and his exhausted troops of the II/126th Regiment, who were to be his reserve, had the previous day been ordered back across the Girua River to strengthen the main American attack that had stalled around Buna. Tomlinson, for now, was to remain in the Sanananda sector and was left with just his Headquarters Company; Major George Bond and his men of the III/126th Regiment; Major Richard Boerem and his detachment of men from 'C' and 'D' companies, I/126th Regiment; the regimental Cannon Company; Antitank Company; and a detachment of the Service Company, totalling 1400 men – this was less than half of his regimental command.[1]

* * *

Meanwhile, Lieutenant Colonel Alexander MacNab arrived at the Warren front. He was tasked with co-ordinating the coastal drive and was answerable directly to Brigadier Hanford MacNider. He immediately placed all the available mortars at the front in a battery, connecting them by field telephone with a central observation post in a tall coconut tree overlooking the Japanese positions.[2]

Most of Warren Force had dug-in and were preparing for their attack against the Japanese, which was scheduled for 24 November. Harding sent a message to Brigadier Ennis Whitehead with the US Fifth Air Force, concerned about potential casualties from close-order

CHAPTER 11

air support: 'Japs holding Giropa Pt, Buna Mission and old airdrome. Do not, repeat not, attack Cape Endaiadere or New Strip. Our troops too close. Notify us without fail, time and place of any contemplated air action'.[3]

The only significant activity that day was by Captain Rossall Belmer and his Australian commandos who were tracking down Japanese posts at the eastern end of New Strip. Belmer's attacking force of 50 men were still just 150 metres south of the airstrip between the Americans. His CO, Major Harry Harcourt, had planned a local attack in support of the Americans on 24 November.[4]

Harcourt was informed the I/126th and I/28th regiments to his right would 'attempt to get fwd. by infiltration', but nothing would come of this.[5] He ordered Belmer to assist the American troops by conducting strong reconnaissance of the Japanese positions around New Strip, with a view of conducting an attack that afternoon. By 2 pm, Lieutenant Arthur Tregarthen leading 'C' Platoon's patrol, who had gone out to the north-west to silence the Japanese mortar position, reported back. As they advanced earlier that morning, they soon encountered large areas of deep swamp, at least chest-deep, and were forced to return to the company HQ position. They were told to get some food, a quick rest and be prepared to reinforce Belmer's group, which would likely be tasked with attacking New Strip later that afternoon.[6]

By 4 pm, Belmer's patrols, were attacking the Japanese positions in strength close to New Strip, but intense enemy automatic fire meant the commandos could not infiltrate the Japanese positions although, as recorded in the unit diary: 'In using grenades and stalking tactics, some success gained but could not overcome opposition'. By 5.30 pm, elements of Belmer's men had made their way to the eastern end of New Strip, and the position of the Americans in this area was now better known. The unit war diary reports that Belmer and his men were south of the eastern end of New Strip. The American flank, as defined by the headquarters staff of the I/128th Regiment, admitted they were just left of the eastern end of New Strip, while the III/128th Regiment (less one company) had moved east to the coast from their former position south of the bridge area between the two strips. One company of this regiment remained in a holding action south of the bridge. Belmer's small force lost another six men that day while conducting theses patrols.[7]

Meanwhile, Harcourt was informed the next day that the men of the 128th Regiment would advance their line, using infiltration tactics and all three battalions. Belmer's force was to support the American advance by attacking the eastern end of New Strip. Just on dusk, another eight commandos, who had just arrived, were sent forward to reinforce Belmer. The company war diary records the situation at 6 pm: 'Lieut. TREGARTHEN with section "C" Pl. moved out to thoroughly recce swamp area – ways through and round it – and if found, route out enemy patrols or detachments and endeavour to silence mortar. Enemy very active on front with small arms fire and HMG [heavy machine gun] but little shelling. On occasions he appeared to be using an A/A gun firing horizontally. The shells burst about 40/50 feet [15 metres] in the air and did little damage – they were, however, noisy and disconcerting until one became used to them. Some enemy MG fire on US positions'.[8] The unit diary also records that the strength of the 2/6th Independent Company at this point was nine officers and 107 other ranks.[9]

It was now that reports reached Harcourt from American officers concerned about his fighting patrols that were seeking out the Japanese and attacking identified positions and targeting their snipers in the trees. They complained that the company's habit of hunting down Japanese snipers was merely: 'Stirring up the Japs'.[10] A request was issued requesting that they cease this practice – needless-to-say, this request was duly ignored.[11]

That night, Harding's staff at the 32nd Division Headquarters in Embogo, generated Sitrep No. 58 recording the situation at the Warren front. The men of I/128 Regiment and combat teams from the

CHAPTER 11

I/126th Regiment, along with the Australian commandos started their advance at 11 am by infiltration of small patrols against well-prepared Japanese machinegun and mortar positions and snipers in trees. The adjutant recorded incorrectly regarding the American advance: '1st Bn 126 C.T. and 1st Bn, 128 have reached Cape Endaiadere, an advance of about 350 yards. 6 Ind. Co. advancing along new strip with similar opposition. 2nd Bn astride Popondetta track 1500 yards south of Buna held up by heavy machinegun and mortar fire. One Coy moving around right flank. One Co 3rd Bn still in position astride Dobodura – Buna track at SW corner new Strip …. All streams in flood'.[12] The stated advance to Cape Endaiadere by the men of the I/126th and I/128th regiments was grossly inaccurate. This position would not be taken until 18 December by the Australians of 17 Platoon, 'D' Company, 2/9th Battalion.[13]

The adjutant of the 126th Regiment recorded in the unit war diary that day that the attack continued. The men of 'B' and 'C' companies withdraw and were replaced by 'A' Company. Soon after, 'B' Company was tasked with relieving pressure on the 128th Infantry. A patrol from 'A' Company successfully advanced on the right to determine the Japanese strength.[14]

* * *

Meanwhile, unnamed Japanese soldier [B], who had recorded the heavy fighting that had broken out the day before along Warren front, wrote in his diary: 'Enemy mortar fired from morning, bursting fiercely around us. Enemy scouts appear everywhere and attack, shooting automatic rifles. Today, enemy planes again flew over and because of this we could not step outside'.[15]

* * *

Along the Urbana front, Lieutenant Colonel Herbert A. Smith and his men of the II/128th Regiment were in front of the Triangle. Smith was determined to flank the Japanese entrenched here. His men of 'G'

Company had already advanced on the right, and now he planned for his men of 'F' Company to do likewise on the left. His men of 'H' Company were given orders to engage the enemy frontally, while 'E' Company was held back in reserve.[16]

The men of 'G' Company, who had spent the night in the swamp, moved out at first light. After a slow and difficult march, they hit dry land at about noon. Taking their bearings, the troops discovered that they were on one of two kunai flats running south-east of the Triangle, and that only about 200 metres of sago swamp lay between them and the flat adjacent to their objective. They were in a jumping-off position to attack, if only they could be resupplied.

Even though Smith now had 'G' Company in position to strike, he had doubts whether an attack there could succeed, as reports from the accompanying Ammunition and Pioneer Platoon, who were carrying rations forward to 'G' Company, as well as from a wire-laying party, convinced him it was virtually impossible to supply these men at their current position. Since the reports from 'F' Company, on the left, were more favourable, indicating that the morass in this area was no more than waist-deep, Smith decided to pull back 'G' Company and concentrate his entire force on the left, where the going, though far from good, was better.[17]

Indeed, the men of 'F' Company had continued their advance left of the Triangle along the Dobodura–Buna track, knowing nothing of the Japanese defences. At 1.30 pm, Sergeant Irving Hall, leading at point, caught a swift glimpse of a Japanese machine gun position about 50 metres away. Coolly turning his back on the gun, to give the impression that he had not seen it, Hall motioned his men off the track. Before the Japanese knew what he was up to, Hall turned around and fired a burst from his submachine gun into the enemy position. In the heavy fire fight that ensued, the point team suffered one casualty.[18]

* * *

CHAPTER 11

Facing Smith was Captain Yasuda Yoshitatsu and his force of the *5th Yokosuka, 5th Sasebo* (*SNLP*), plus the supporting naval pioneer troops dug-in at the Triangle. The Japanese here outnumbered the Americans by at least 2:1 and were alert and waiting for the Americans to attack. Yasuda had a series of concealed machinegun positions south of the Triangle covering the track, and an elaborate system of bunkers in the Triangle itself. There was heavy swamp on either side of the Triangle, and the bunkers had the effect of turning it into a position of almost impregnable strength. Strong bunker positions in the Coconut Grove, north of the Triangle, and in the Government Gardens north-east of it, lay astride the tracks leading to the village and the mission; both positions were honeycombed with bunkers. The defensive position here was excellent. Yasuda had the benefit of interior lines, which enabled him to concentrate almost his full strength at any given point and any given time.[19]

12

'I AM BEGINNING TO WONDER WHO WILL REACH ZERO FIRST'

On 23 November, Lieutenant Colonel Alexander MacNab ordered the coastal drive to begin afresh. With this, lieutenant colonels McCoy and Carrier attempted an advance beneath the cover of artillery fire, supported by concentrated fire from the heavy mortar battery. This fire, however, achieved very little, as the shells and bombs were ineffective because they remained on instantaneous fuses. This meant that when they hit a Japanese bunker or entrenched position, they exploded on impact. Delayed fuses, to postpone the explosion until the projectile had buried itself deep in the target, would have been much more effective, but none were available. Therefore, the attacks on the right and left made very limited progress. Quiet settled over the coastal strip, except for Captain Rossall Belmer and his Australian commandos who were still trying to track down Japanese posts at the eastern end of New Strip.[1]

Belmer and his advance party of the 2/6th Independent Company were that morning reinforced with 23-year-old Lieutenant Cyril Ireland, from Sydney, and 12 other ranks. Belmer was tasked with advancing and covering the American left flank as it advanced to infiltrate the Japanese perimeter east of New Strip. But the American advance was restricted to about 100 metres on the coastal flank, while there was little if any movement on the left. As recorded in the war diary of the 2/6th Independent Company: '0930 [hours]: There was still some differences of opinion between Americans and us as to the

CHAPTER 12

location of their line on left flank. They claimed still that it was 200 or 300 yds NORTH of EASTERN end of NEW STRIP. BELMER told to complete recce of "Y" end of NEW STRIP with view to attacking on following day, be aggressive and shoot any enemy or snipers seen. Asked 128 Regt HQ to ask supply line to hasten forward extra rifle dischargers, 68 and 69 grenades, and SAA [small arms ammunition] for which signal had been sent'.[2]

At 4 pm, Major Harry Harcourt had made his way forward to discuss the next day's attack. The Company CO stated to Belmer: 'To approach with parties (sections under comd. of an officer) on a front and when held up to infiltrate and make encirclement movements. Sections not to be crowded together'.[3] The Australians would receive no artillery or mortar support; they were to dominate the enemy, using their rifles and grenades alone. Non-Commissioned Officer (NCO), John 'Bill' Anderson, a 28-year-old from Windsor in Victoria, with No. 4 Section, recalled the situation at this point: 'The Company was given the job of probing the Jap defences, and we were constantly in contact with Jap patrols, and the whole area in front of the bunkers was alive with snipers up trees with camouflage nets underneath them'.[4] By 5 pm, Belmer had re-established his command post in a tree at the edge of the Coconut Grove where good observation was provided of New Strip all the way to its western end. It was observed that the Japanese were moving about and working on earthworks during the day.

At this point, Harcourt provided the following sitrep from Belmer to Brigadier Hanford MacNider:

> Commander of patrol at E [east] end of new strip says he has not been able to locate definitely positions of any mortars near the E end but says that there are one or two near 'D'. Some machine guns are near E end of strip, and these he is trying to silence. He says he has had a small patrol into 'X' – between the houses of the new strip. The new *strip* is not cleared and is

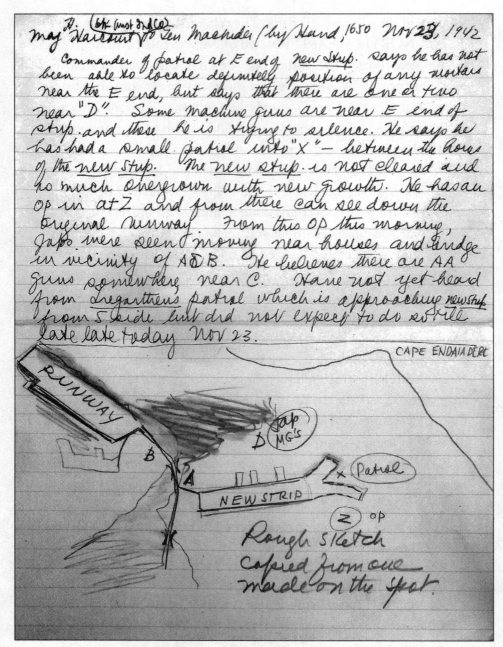

Patrol report from Major Harry Harcourt commanding Australian 2/6th Independent Company to Brigadier Hanford MacNider commanding the US 128th Regiment, 32nd Division

CHAPTER 12

much overgrown with new growth. He has an OP in at Z and from there can see down the original runway. From this OP this morning, Japs were seen moving near houses and bridge in vicinity of A & B. He believes there are AA guns somewhere, near C. Have not yet heard from Tregarthen's patrol, which is approaching new strip from S side, but did not expect to do so until late today.[5]

An hour later, word came in from Lieutenant Arthur Tregarthen, reporting he and his patrol had moved up through the swamp to the north-west, and while they had not been able to silence the troublesome Japanese mortar, they had forced the mortar team to fall back and were waiting in an ambush position should the Japanese try to reoccupy the position.[6] Twenty-year-old Private Gordon Green, from Roma in Queensland, with this patrol, recorded the situation: 'Eight section, the only C Platoon there under Lieutenant Tregarthen and much patrol work, out all night in the swamps, listening and crawling about'.[7]

Private Allen Osbourne with No. 4 Section later recalled the conditions they faced on a daily basis:

> It was a very miserable place. We were almost, nearly all the time under some sort of fire. The Japs had some three and 75 mill dual-purpose ack-ack anti-tank guns and they'd bring them down and they used [them] to fire these huge shells which would explode over us all the time. Bloody disconcerting, you know, to say the least. All the bang, bang, bang, and all the time, day and night, there was gunfire of one sort or another, either mortar fire or machinegun fire. And, you know, if you lay in the ground you lay in bloody water. You couldn't dig a hole, you couldn't dig any cover for yourself, you'd drown if you got in it. And it was a very unpleasant place. We attacked it a number of times. We did a reconnaissance through it, we sneaked through

it a couple of times and got away with it. We made some maps; there were no maps. And opposite where we were, the Japs had cut the coconut trees down to make another airstrip. And the Japs cut the trees off … fallen over trees and fronds, and it was a great tangle of fallen coconut trees. And they were on the other side of it, as we found out, we didn't realise it. And they had used, once again as we found out, these coconut logs to make little forts, pillboxes. And they'd thrown over logs, and basically the first time we saw them, we just thought they were tangles of coconut logs but they weren't, under them [were] little slots … and small arms fire would make no effect on them ….

There must have been tens of thousands of coconut trees and by the time we left, I don't think one had a top still in it. The first attack we made on the place we had done some reconnaissance and we'd made some maps, which we'd given to the Yanks. OK start-line, bang, away we go. Well as soon as we got across the start-line into the scrub, we all lost contact with each other. You couldn't see. I was with my section, I used to travel number three. One bloke [was] in front and then me, and I used to link up with the section. As soon as we got going, we lost sight of everyone. We could hear them, but we couldn't see them. And we got well across, we got into the cut coconuts and that's when the trouble started because you couldn't keep going ahead. You couldn't climb over them, you had to go this way, [then] that way …. In fact, it was difficult in the end to know what direction you were going, because you were changing direction so many times.[8]

* * *

Brigadier MacNider, the commander of Warren Force, came up during the afternoon from his headquarters at Hariko to observe the fighting along the line. He was wounded at around 6.30 pm

CHAPTER 12

by an enemy rifle grenade while inspecting the frontlines and was immediately evacuated. On Major General Harding's instructions, Colonel Tracy Hale succeeded him as overall commander of Warren Force.[9]

* * *

To the west on the Ango Track, Major Herbert M. Smith with his men of the II/126th Regiment were approaching Lieutenant Colonel Herbert A. Smith and his men of the II/128th Regiment south of the Triangle. To help avoid confusion, it was agreed that day that Major Smith would be called 'Red Smith', while Lieutenant Colonel Smith would be referred to as 'White Smith'.[10] The two battalions, assigned to Urbana Force, were widely separated by swamps, with Lieutenant Colonel Smith in overall command. But now, Smith was in difficulties with his own two flanking companies still dispersed in the swamps, with 'G' Company, II/128th Regiment, who were still on the right flank, in particular trouble.[11]

Lieutenant Colonel Smith gave the major a quick tour of the area. Major Smith would have little time to familiarise himself to the terrain, vegetation, and Japanese and American positions before he and his men were committed to help take the Triangle. He recalled: 'Buna was a nightmare …. Of jungle … kunai grass higher than a man's head … and swamps … that rose and fell with the tides …. The Japs had built bunkers [with] excellent fields of fire covering approaches from inland routes …. These bunkers [were] practically invisible'.[12]

Lieutenant Colonel Smith sent a message to Harding, informing him of his plans to extricate 'G' Company, explaining that the supply route was 'neck-deep in mud and water', and he asked permission for the company's withdrawal. After waiting until about 2 pm with no reply, Smith ordered the company to pull out of the swamp and report back to battalion for further orders. The company severed its wire connection with Battalion Headquarters and started for the rear. Harding, however, did not received Smith's message until around 2 pm. Because of an error on the part of the decoding clerk, Harding incorrectly understood it to say that the supply route to 'G' Company was 'knee-deep in mud and water'.[13] Harding replied at 2.25 pm: '32d Div to White Smith. "You will not withdraw. Continue efforts to go around"'.[14]

On receiving this message, Smith sent a runner to intercept 'G' Company, stating they were to return to their former position. Having only limited knowledge of the Japanese positions, Lieutenant Colonel Smith was supposed to attack the Triangle. Smith recalled: 'I then asked Division for a delay of a day or two in order that our patrols might learn a little more of the terrain and the Japanese positions and find, if possible, a better route of supply. In reply, I was informed that there would be an air strike at 0800 on 24 November, and that we would follow this with an immediate attack'.[15]

At 11.30 pm, Major Smith had made his way to Lieutenant Colonel Smith's command post (CP), which was about 1200 metres south of the nearest Japanese positions. There they worked out a plan that included simultaneous thrusts against the Triangle from left, front, and right. It was agreed that on the right, the men of 'G' Company, 128th Regiment, reinforced with 'E' Company, II/128th Regiment would attack, while a frontal attack would be launched by the men of 'F' Company, II/126th Regiment. On the left, the men of 'E' Company, II/126th Regiment would launch their assault. These men would also relieve the exhausted men of 'F' Company, II/128th Regiment left of the Triangle along Entrance Creek.[16]

The Australian four 25-pounder battery, which had just reached Dobodura that day, would fire from Ango in support of the attack as soon as they got the range. Indeed, earlier that morning, the Bullforce guns and gunners had begun arriving at Dobodura, and Captain Manning, unable to report directly to Harding at Embogo, reported to Lieutenant Colonel Smith instead. Manning recalled: 'As he [Smith] refused to adopt us [I] had to wait to contact General Waldron by wireless'. Waldron informed Manning that he was to

CHAPTER 12

support the attack on the Urbana front the following day. Manning had his 25-pounder guns ready for action by nightfall.[17]

The terrain facing Smith's men, especially on the right, was according to him truly appalling. The main track was deep in mud, and 'G' Company, still attempting to advance on the right, had hit stretches of swamp in which the troops often found themselves up to their necks in water. Meanwhile, the men of 'F' Company, II/128th Regiment had met better terrain on the left but discovered that Entrance Creek, which paralleled the left-hand fork of the Triangle, not only was tidal and unfordable but was covered by enemy machine guns at every likely crossing.[18]

* * *

Still at the Warren front was unnamed Japanese soldier [B], who had been recording the heavy mortar and aerial activity of the enemy. He wrote in his diary: 'In the afternoon, enemy mortar opened fire ferociously. The shells are passing our hut and landing in the shore area. I feel that our lives are finally being shortened'.[19]

* * *

Sometime that day, Major General George Vasey, commanding the fighting at Gona and Sanananda, wrote to Lieutenant General Herring: 'The Jap is being much more stubborn and tiresome than I thought, and I fear a war of attrition is taking place on this front. The Jap won't go till he is killed, and in the process, he is inflicting many casualties on us. I am beginning to wonder who will reach zero first'.[20] The same applied to Buna.

13
'AT THIS RATE, WE CAN'T HOLD OUT'

At 8 am on 24 November, attacking P-40 fighters swept over the Urbana positions, covering the left flank of the American advance. However, only 12 aircraft arrived, and they all missed their target area; the infantrymen wondered what had happened to the bombers. Lieutenant Colonel Smith now delayed his attack and asked for a second attempt.[ix] It was arranged that this would be made again by another 12 fighters, as no bombers were available, but only four fighters made up the second sortie. While these fighters left the Japanese positions untouched, they strafed Smith's headquarters. Smith recalled: 'I waited a little longer to see if more planes would follow, but when no more arrived, I decided that this was our "air strike" and ordered our attack to begin without the air attack'.[1]

Following a short mortar preparation from the 60-mm mortars (the two battalions then had only two 81-mm mortars apiece, with little ammunition), the troops jumped off at 2.28 pm. Ten minutes later, the Australian 25-pounders at Ango found the range and supported the attack.[2]

On the left, as planned, 'E' Company, II/126th Regiment (having relieved 'F' Company, 128th Regiment) swung wide around Entrance Creek, and then moving north about 400 metres, these men turned north-east. Just as they had finished covering another 400 metres

---

[ix] The then Colonel Smith in 1950, responding to a request from the American Official Historian of the campaign wrote that NO aircraft arrived at 8 am, and the same is said to have happened for a reschedule sortie at 1 pm., and only three P40s arrived later that afternoon at around 3 pm, strafing his own CP.

CHAPTER 13

and were approaching a small bridge over the creek north-west of the Triangle, a strong Japanese force targeted them with accurate machinegun fire. The troops dug-in at once; their foxholes immediately filled with water. They went no further that day.[3]

With 'E' Company was Sergeant Paul Lutjens. He had scribbled in his diary the night before on being briefed of their mission: 'God only knows what we are about to face. If I said I am not afraid I would be a liar. Reread an old letter trying to place myself back in the states. To find something to fight for …. I'm afraid of dying as much as anybody else. Maybe life wasn't so pleasant for me, but God it seems good now. If I don't come through this, it will be God's will'.[4] Lutjens also recalled the fighting here:

> Everybody flopped down and sank hid face into the mud. I don't know exactly how the rest of the guy's felt, but it scared the hell out of me. Somebody whispered, 'That's a Jap' …. The Japs had automatic fire emplaced in coconut trees, and as soon as they saw the matches flare up, they let us have it – not from just in front, but from all sides. We'd walked right into the middle of them. We stared to dig-in, and I think quick. Three of us dug a hole in five minutes flat, with our hands. We thought it was all over with. We couldn't see a thing. The Japs were shooting all around us. They stopped for a while, and by the next morning we were all dug-in. They couldn't spot us too well through the jungle, but every time a man moved, they'd open up. One guy had the tip of his bayonet shot off. He didn't move a muscle. Nobody fired. I sometimes think it took more guts not to than it would have to shoot back. Then it began to rain. It was a cold, cold rain. We had left our packs behind when we started, and all we had with us was a few rations in our pockets. Then the tide began to come up through our foxholes.[5]

Meanwhile, 'F' Company, II/126th Regiment – supported by 'H' Company, II/128th Regiment, which was part of Lieutenant Colonel Smith's heavy-weapons company – were only able to advance about 300 metres in their frontal attack against the Triangle. These men encountered heavy barbed wire entanglements strung across the track, with Japanese troops covering the wire with concentrated fire. Having neither wire cutters or any means of removing the obstacle, the Americans dug-in and requested engineers with explosives to clear the way.[6]

On the right, the men of 'E' and 'G' companies, II/128th Regiment were faring no better. Captain Bakken and his men of 'E' Company were advancing to join Lieutenant Theodore Florey and his men of 'G' Company at their position. Using newly found short cuts through the deep swamp, 'E' Company managed to reach the kunai flat in much less time than 'G' Company had taken to reach it on 21 November. The men of 'E' Company joined 'G' Company in plenty of time for the attack.[7]

Leaving Lieutenant Ferguson and his weapons platoon, 'G' Company, on the flat with 'E' Company, Lieutenant Florey and 'G' Company, started moving north-west through the sago swamp to flank the Triangle from the east. A little less than 200 metres out, the leading platoon, led by Lieutenant Bell, arrived at a small grassy area, just outside the Triangle, where it surprised a group of Japanese working on what appeared to be an anti-aircraft position. The Americans opened fire, but there were more Japanese than originally thought, and the company, after suffering several casualties, was forced back into the swamp. Lieutenant Colonel Smith recalled: 'The enemy almost immediately opened fire against Company G with light machine guns, followed shortly by heavy machinegun fire. The grassy strip offered no cover except along the edge where the ground sloped into the swamp, and after suffering several casualties, the men pulled back to the edge. The [lead] platoon then started working along the edge of the grass to the West'.[8]

CHAPTER 13

While the main body of 'G' Company was held up just outside the right-hand fork of the Triangle, the Japanese from the Government Gardens moved forward to within firing distance of the kunai flat held by Captain Bakken and his men of 'E' Company, and the weapons platoon of 'G' Company. The enemy attacked just as it was turning dark. The weapons platoon had spent two days getting their weapons in order after its march through the swamp, while those of 'E' Company had been on the kunai flat for about six hours, long enough for them to do likewise. Even so, they lacked oil, and parts of the equipment were wet. Then for whatever reason, they were caught in the open, with the sounds of Japanese yells coming from a short distance away, so the men tried to hit back at the unseen enemy as best they could, only to find that their weapons would not function properly.[9]

Lieutenant Colonel Smith recalled: 'Mortars fell short because increments [the propelling charges in the mortar ammunition] were wet. Machine guns jammed because web belts were wet and dirty and had shrunk. Tommy guns and BARs were full of muck and dirt, and even the M-1s fired well only for the first clip, and then jammed because clips taken from the belts were wet and full of muck from the swamp'.[10] Low on ammunition, completely out of food, and fearing that they were being surrounded, the troops pulled back hastily into the swamp, leaving some of their weapons behind. In this counterattack, the Americans suffered one man killed and five wounded.[11]

Meanwhile, Lieutenant Colonel Smith had been in communication with 'E' Company by telephone. Smith recalled: 'At this time it was getting dark, and the reports coming in were both garbled and alarming. To add to our confusion, the telephone line began to go out. Fearing that I might soon be out of communication altogether, I told the S-2 [Intelligence Officer] to have both companies remain where they were, and that I would join them as soon as possible after daylight in the morning. I told him that, it if was necessary, they could pull into the edge of the swamp, but that they were to remain there until I arrived. At this point the phone went completely dead, and we had no further contact'.[12]

At this time, Captain Bakken and his men of 'E' Company were strung out in a single file all the way back from the kunai flat, with the weapons platoon of 'G' Company somewhere in the middle of the line. Near the end of the line, nearest to battalion, was the executive officer of 'E' Company, Lieutenant Orin Rogers, and at the head of it, near the kunai strip at the dead telephone, was Bakken.[13]

Shortly after darkness, an order was passed down the line to Rogers to move back to the battalion CP. The young lieutenant assumed that the phone to Bakken was working again and that there had been a change in orders. Rogers, however, made it a point to ask if the order had come from the captain. The answer came back a few minutes later that it had. Rogers, therefore, started to lead the troops back to the CP. At the other end of the line, Captain Bakken had also received an order to move to the rear. Knowing that the phone was out, he assumed that a messenger from Battalion Headquarters had delivered a similar message to Rogers, and just to make sure, he asked whether the message had come from Battalion Headquarters. The answer came back (again via the chain method) that it had, and the entire column started moving to the rear, with the weapons platoon of 'G' Company included.[14]

The rest of 'G' Company, under Lieutenant Theodore Florey, were still pinned down just beyond the grassy strip leading to the Triangle. Florey had sent a runner back with orders to the weapons platoon to bring up more mortars. The runner returned with the report that 'E' Company and the weapons platoon were gone. So, an officer was sent back to the kunai flat to check. When this officer returned confirming the information, 'G' Company, after waiting for further orders and receiving none, also began to withdraw.[15] Smith recalled: 'Realising that they were alone and having a number of wounded men on their hands, Bell and Florey, after a conference, decided that if they received

CHAPTER 13

no further orders, or if no help appeared, they would pull out after dark and return to the battalion. According to Lieutenant Florey's statement, it was not until he rejoined the balance of the unit that he discovered that the weapons of the weapons platoon had been left behind when Lt Ferguson took the platoon to the rear'.[16]

The men of 'E' Company and the weapons platoon of 'G' Company reached Lieutenant Colonel Smith's CP post in the early hours of 25 November, and 'G' Company, except for a few stragglers, arrived there by 10 am.[17]

* * *

Meanwhile, at Warren front, which was now commanded by Colonel Tracy Hale, the Australian 25-pounder guns began to register the enemy positions along the coastal track and in the New Strip area. The fire was effective, and Lieutenant Colonel Robert McCoy and his men of the I/128th Regiment, and Lieutenant Colonel Edmund Carrier and his troops of the I/126th Regiment attacked the Japanese outer defences. The lead companies were able to push the enemy back against their main line of resistance. To their left, the Australians of the 2/6th Independent Company, operating off the eastern end of the strip, made some progress. Ordered to hold tight, Lieutenant Carl Fryday and his men of 'I' Company, III/128th Regiment – who were still in position off the south-west end of New Strip, south of the bridge between the strips – remained dug-in.[18]

At 7 am, Captain Rossall Belmer and his commandos attacked the Japanese positions at the 'Y-shaped' dispersal bay area at the eastern end of New Strip. Belmer had divided his force into four sections. No. 1 Section consisted of riflemen; No. 4 Section contained men with machine guns who would attack the dispersal bays; No. 6 Section was to attack with machine guns along the southern arm of the 'Y' Shape dispersal bay; while No. 5 Section would be held in reserve and committed as needed. When the commandos moved out, they were immediately targeted with concentrated Japanese rifle and machinegun fire. While they inflicted many casualties against the enemy, by 9.30 am, the attack had ground to a halt, taking up a position just south of the dispersal bays. In this advance, Belmer suffered two killed and four wounded.[19]

In this attack was NCO John Anderson, who recalled: 'Tragically lost two of my best men. Larry Hartt[x], a marvellous bushman, was forward scout and was killed by a sniper, and the whole patrol came under intense Jap machinegun fire, [but] we held our ground until ordered to withdraw, and, unfortunately Toby Atkins[xi] was shot and killed by a sniper. He was only 21 and a splendid fellow'.[20] Also in the fighting here was Private Allen Osborne with No. 4 Section, who recalled:

> As we started to move across the strip, we caught glimpses of Japs running through the trees on the other side. We would snap off a few shots and they would drop down and disappear. The rifle fire from their side was becoming more intense but fortunately they weren't very good shots. The tangle of fallen coconut trees prevented us from seeing anyone from the sections on either side of us, although we could hear them. At about this time, the Japanese opened up with a light machinegun, and it was obvious they could see us. We could see blue smoke coming from a big tangle of logs at the edge of the strip, and it was obvious that the LMG was there.

> We brought the Bren half-way across the strip and fired a couple of magazines into the position. It quietened them down for the time being. They then opened up with another light machine gun further along the strip and started to hammer into the section on our left. I'm not sure if it was 5 or 6 section.

---

[x] Thirty-two-year-old Private Lawrence Hartt from Brisbane is listed as killed-in-action on 24 December 1942

[xi] Twenty-year-old, Lance Corporal Victor Atkins, from Sydney is listed as killed-in-action on 24 December 1942

CHAPTER 13

What I have just described was just 4 Section, or part of 4 Section's part of the attack. There was plenty going on, to the right and left of us but we couldn't see it.[21]

False claims came into Major Harry Harcourt's CP that the Japanese appeared to be using explosive bullets: 'Reports that Japs are using explosive bullets is thought to be unfounded. Many bullets have been examined but no explosive type found. Impression believed to come from fact that bullets strike trees, which mostly being of soft nature (coconut and mangrove) cause the strike to sound sharp and like a rifle shot fired from close range. This feature is inclined to be disconcerting because the impression is given that snipers are up in trees in the vicinity'.[22]

***

Harding was angered by the failure of the attack along the whole line, especially perturbed by the failure on the right flank by Warren Force. Even so, he was not prepared to listen to Smith's explanations for failure along the Urbana front. Smith informed Harding that he had ordered his companies to remain on the edge of the swamp until morning – and then Harding was informed that these men had straggled back to the rear. Smith, however, defended his men, stating they were hungry and exhausted and incapable of further effort for the moment. Smith was also still of the opinion that any attack from the right of the Triangle could not succeed.[23]

Harding also sent a message to Brigadier Ennis Whitehead with the US Fifth Air Force, concerning the lack of air support, stressing that if the full weight of aerial bombing and strafing could not be supplied, he requested that none be provided, stating: 'Under the existing conditions, a few planes do no good. For instance, the bombing and staffing you did for us on our left flank [today] …. was too little to have any appreciable effect. In brief, if you can't shoot the works, say so and we'll re-adjust out time and wait until you can. Before you receive this, you will have had a request for a heavy bombardment and strafing of the west end of the Strip at a given hour tomorrow. Purpose of this, is to blast out what appears to be a strong defensive set up from which machinegun crossfire holds up our advance. The bombardment will have to be heavy to do any good. I think it should include some 500 lb bombs'.[24] This attack would be delayed for 24 hours, taking place on 26 November.

* * *

Meanwhile, a new artillery aid was now beginning to lessen the disadvantages of lack of observation from the ground. That day, NGF in Port Moresby had arranged for No. 4 Army Cooperation Squadron R.A.A.F. (Royal Australian Air Force), who were equipped with the 'slow almost weapon-less Wirraways and manned by skilful pilots and observers', to be made available for air spotting.[25]

* * *

Still at the Warren front was unnamed Japanese soldier [B]. The previous day, he had written that his life was 'shortening' and recorded his second-last diary entry: 'At this rate, we can't hold out. Taking the advantage, the enemy is gradually pressing on. As time passes on, enemy bombing becomes more fierce. Today's were the fiercest yet. In the afternoon, the enemy suddenly took the offensive. Mortar shells are really bursting close by. At night we had our first encounter. The enemy sent a three-man scouting party to reconnoitrer our positions. Went out to check this party. It was fairly dark when suddenly alarming sounds of fire, rifle and automatic, were heard. Here they come. We replied with mortar fire and the enemy finally withdrew, but we had one man killed in action'.[26]

14

'OUR UNIT DAILY BECOMES WEAKER'

It was a quiet day on the Warren front during 25 November 1942. That day, a message was penned to the ordinance officer located at the 32nd Division Headquarters: 'Weapons have many stoppages due to sand. Men losing confidence in BARs and Tommy guns. Need toothbrushes, oil, and M-1 clips'.[1] Problems of logistical support was an ongoing problem for the frontline troops.

Lieutenant Colonel Kelsie Miller and his men of the III/128th Regiment relieved Lieutenant Colonel Robert McCoy and his troops of the I/128th Regiment in the frontline, but no advance was attempted that day. The lull was being used to prepare for a co-ordinated attack on Cape Endaiadere and both ends of New Strip, which was planned for the next day – 26 November – American Thanksgiving Day.[2]

Meanwhile, Captain Rossall Belmer and his Australian commandos located close to the bays at the eastern end of New Strip conducted fighting patrols to locate and, where possible, take out the Japanese positions in their immediate area. The company war diary records: 'Our patrols carried on active patrolling and shot several Japs with no loss to ourselves'.[3] At this time, his CO, Major Harry Harcourt, was provided details of the planned advance scheduled for the next day. He was informed that I/126th Regiment would be on their right and would advance to take Cape Endaiadere and New Strip, as well as the large kunai area after the air force and artillery had completed their sorties and bombardments, which would begin at 7.30 am and end two hours later. The Australians were to cover their left flank.[4]

BLOODY BUNA

American GI Dick Randle was with the 32nd Division and fighting on Warren front, located just south of Duropa Plantation. He recalled:

On the coast, there was nothing you could really call a front. There were people in little slit trenches. When you walked up there, they told you to get down. The snipers were shooting at you. This was on the coast. Just south of the Duropa plantation. The ground was level, a swamp to the left .... The snipers were up in the coconut trees. You can't see the snipers. You shoot at the trees, but you've only got so much ammunition, so you can't just blindly shoot. We didn't have the slightest idea of what was in front of us: not the slightest idea. Our unit was acting in the dark. We were hung up for days and days. You'd get up in the morning, do a patrol, and look around. Once in a while you'd get a shot at someone going to the chow line in the Japanese communication trenches .... The front did not move. It was stagnant within 50 to a 100 feet [15 to 30 metres] for weeks. There was no way to move .... You couldn't see the Japanese positions, but they had their fire lanes cleared. They knew what we were doing all the time. Funny thing, though, I saw live Japanese often. Some guy walking along the trenches. Going from bunker to bunker. If the Japs got down on all fours, we couldn't see them, but they'd be in the water. It was that close to sea level. They'd get lazy and walk around. As soon as you'd see one, you'd blast away. They'd fall right away, but you never knew if you'd hit him or not. All this time we were taking causalities.[5]

* * *

Japanese medic Yokoyama Yoriichi was with the original elements of the *South Sea Force*, having fought along the Kokoda Track. As such, he was likely either with the *144th Regiment* or the *41st Regiment*. He was now based at Buna, and not being a marine, he was almost

CHAPTER 14

certainly at Warren front. He would not only survive Buna, but the war. Yokoyama recalled many years later his experience of the fighting at Buna and being targeted by an Australian patrol:

> One day we were told to search for some enemy who were approaching the Buna position. I went with a section from my platoon, and we took a light machine gun. There were three of them at the front and I was next to the sergeant and the rest followed behind us. Then I heard a shot from the jungle, and the soldier at the front was shot. Soon after, the next two men, the light machine gunners, got shot too. They were all shot in the head. What I remember next is that the sergeant shouted, 'I'm going forward!' But soon after, he got shot in the arm, then he ran back to me. I gave first aid to him. I told him not to move but he didn't listen. I guess it's normal to be really afraid of bullets once you have been hit, no matter how strong and brave you are. While trying to get back to our lines he was hit again, this time killed outright. Fortunately, I did not get hit, but by then everyone else had been. Then a voice from the rear called out, 'Yokoyama, tell me what the hell is going on up there!'
>
> I was in shock at the start of it all and screamed out, 'The squad leader got killed,' but whenever I raised my voice, bullets came my way. So, I stayed there quietly. Then someone from the rear said. 'I think Yokoyama is dead now too. I can't hear his voice anymore. Let's get out of here. It's getting dark. We'll come back and collect the bodies tomorrow'. I couldn't make a noise to let them know that I was still alive, nor move from there. Moments later, several Australian soldiers appeared and started to dig a hole. I thought the hole was for the dead bodies, but it turned out that it was in fact for their position. Luckily, they didn't come over to check the dead, despite the number of us they had killed.

I felt like hiding in the grass forever. I was desperately waiting for an opportunity to escape. When it became dark, I thought I would be left alone in the middle of the enemy if I didn't get out now. I grabbed the machine gun and a rifle, then ran like a rabbit.

When I met my friends again, my good mate said, 'Hey! You're still alive. We were sure you didn't make it, so we went without you.' He said it in a sarcastic way, but I knew he meant well. I was really happy that there was someone like him in my platoon. He also died at Buna, like everyone else.[6]

* * *

To the west, the men of Urbana Force were recovering from the previous day's attack against the Triangle. By 10 am, the men of 'E' and 'G' companies, 128th Regiment arrived back at the battalion CP. Despite a thorough investigation, Smith was unable to discover who sent the message to fall back. He later wrote to the American official historian: 'A number of men told of passing the messages back and forth, but no one could say definitely where they originated, and many of the men did not even know who stood next to them, especially where Company E and the Weapons Platoon of Company G were badly intermingled'.[7] Lieutenant Colonel Smith decided that 'faulty communication' was the reason for their return to the rear, in contravention to his orders.[8] Smith recalled his dilemma:

> As the troops arrived at the CP, it became evident that most of them were utterly exhausted and that it would be necessary to give them food and rest before any other action could be taken. Next, I was confronted with the necessity of making the decision as to whether I should take these two companies, return to the kunai strips and take up the fight where it had been broken off, or whether I should abandon efforts in this

CHAPTER 14

direction and concentrate on the left. I realised that I stood less chance of being personally criticised if I selected the first of these two choices. However, I had never been convinced of the practicability of this plan, and I now felt, more than ever, that its only hope of success lay in our ability to quickly seize the Triangle (and there appeared very little chance of this), and thus open the Buna–Soputa Trail for a supply route. I was certain that we could not hope to support any extensive action over the route then open to us. My decision was to abandon, for the time being, any action on the right and concentrate on the left, but to continue patrolling on the right in the hope of finding a suitable route forward. This was approximately the situation when Colonel Mott arrived and assumed command of the Urbana Force.[9]

Harding now shared Smith's views about the impracticality of an attack against the right of the Triangle, and it was agreed that the main effort would be on the left. Harding concluded from studying a map of the track, which branched off to the left of the Triangle, leading directly to Buna Village and Buna Mission Station, that it would be possible to bypass the Triangle. In doing so, they could take both the village and the mission, if his men could capture the large kunai area north-west of the Triangle. Hardy now ordered Smith to contain the Triangle with a portion of his men and deploy the bulk of his force in the swamp south of the grassy area to the west, in preparation to seize the large kunai patch, which would place them in a better position to move against the village and mission.[10]

* * *

Unknown Japanese soldier [D] at Buna made an entry in his diary: 'I wonder what our replacements from Rabaul are doing, also, what our planes are doing. Passing the day like this means only waiting for death. Dried bread is issued now and then; however, this is only temporary relief. Every day, from morning till night, there are enemy air raids. Our unit daily becomes weaker. There is food, but we cannot cook it. There is water, but we cannot drink it. I pray fervently that the following on units will land. From 1400 there was very heavy rifle and machinegun fire …. I thought there was going to be a charge. During the night, we made a cover for the trench'.[11]

Another unidentified diarist wrote: 'The enemy has surrounded us and are attacking from the front. Our morale is to fight until we are killed. Heard from the Commander of the Combined Fleet [in Tokyo] – Buna garrison is fighting desperately, and the entire Navy is co-operating, so he expects a change soon. Those were welcome words'.[12] That is what they were, however, merely words and empty promises.

15

'... THE JAPS HAD HURRIEDLY WITHDRAWN'

On 26 November, Lieutenant Colonel Smith began deploying his troops for his renewed attack against Buna Village and Buna Mission Station. Early that morning, he received a communique from Lieutenant General Herring at Advance NGF Headquarters:

My dear Harding,

> Glade to be in touch with you after your many and varied adventures. Am sorry you have so [much] mud on your side and swamp, [with] so little room to manoeuvre. Hope you are able to make progress today after bombing, which should shake the enemy. If no progress, suggest you try movement forward at night.
>
> Am looking forward to seeing you [at] DOBUDURA very soon. Vasey is still hopeful he will clear his side, but his Australian forces are very short in numbers, and though he has more room than you, he hasn't the men available. He has met like you a good deal of swamp, but Jap resistance Nth of SOPUTA is really South of the bad swampy country.
>
> All [my] best wishes, let's know what you need, [and] we will lay it on if it is humanly possible.
>
> Regards to Mott.[1]

* * *

Colonel Tracy Hale, commanding Warren Force, and Lieutenant Colonel Alexander MacNab, the executive officer of Warren Force, had worked out their detail plan for the day's attack. Lieutenant Colonel Kelsie Miller and his men of the III/128th Regiment (less 'I' Company) had already relieved Lieutenant Colonel Robert McCoy and his troops of the I/128th Regiment in the most advanced positions along the beach. Forward of Miller, at 7.30 am, the Allied fighters opened what was to be the largest air attack yet undertaken against the Japanese coastal positions, likely in response to Major General Harding's criticism of 24 November. Bombers came in behind the fighters at 8 am, and the attacks continued until 9 am – 50 aircraft participated. The Japanese anti-aircraft defence unit at Buna reported shooting down four of these aircraft.[2]

After the air sorties were complete, the artillery and mortars bombarded the Japanese positions. Captain Martin O'Hare's howitzers, concentrating against Cape Endaiadere, and Captain Manning with his four 25-pounders of Bullforce were still in action around Ango; while Captain Charles Mueller and his two 25-pounder near Hariko brought their fire down along the western edge of New Strip and on the bridge between the strips, with twelve 81-mm mortars and four heavy machineguns adding to the barrage.[3]

The infantry waited for the order to advance. The men of the III/128th Regiment were to thrust directly north along the coastal track against Cape Endaiadere, while Lieutenant Colonel Edmund Carrier and his men of the I/126th Regiment would move out on Miller's left. McCoy's troops were to follow Carrier's men at an interval of 1000 metres and be prepared to push through them if necessary. The Australians of the 2/6th Independent Company were to continue attacking the eastern end of New Strip, while covering the left of the Carrier's battalion. The men of 'I' Company, III/128th Regiment, from their position south of the track junction near the bridge south of the two airstrips, would represent the left flank of

CHAPTER 15

the attack. These men were to establish themselves on the western end of New Strip, if possible.[4]

High hopes were held for the success of the operation, and Major General Harding had left his headquarters at Embogo the night before to observe it directly. Having no motorboat for command use, he caught a ride on the lugger *Helen Dawn*, which was carrying ammunition to the forward dump at Hariko. About ten kilometres out, the lugger ran onto a sand bar, and the general had to complete the remaining five kilometres in the lugger's rowboat. Harding arrived at Colonel Tracy Hale's CP at Hariko at 4.45 am. After visiting McCoy and Carrier, he moved on to Miller's CP.[5]

* * *

At 9.30 am, Miller's battalion went in on the right to drive directly northward along the track to Cape Endaiadere. To no one's surprise, the Japanese were waiting and rose practically unscathed from their bunkers and strongpoints and stopped the Americans almost dead on the track and its bordering swamps. Miller's men came up against the strongest part of the Japanese line and suffered 50 casualties by noon and could not move forward. His men of 'K' Company, which had sustained the bulk of the casualties, were pinned down, and 'L' Company, out of contact with Carrier's battalion, was immobilised. To make matters worse, Japanese zeros from Lae arrived and strafed the Americans as they attacked.[6]

On his left, Carrier and his men of the I/126th Regiment moved out 15 minutes after Miller's men, tasked with advancing north-west to capture Strip Point. This battalion, however, added to the day's confusion when Carrier unknowingly went east instead of north-west. Moving through waist-deep swamp, Carrier's lead troop first turned apparently too sharply to the west, and then cutting too soon to the east. They managed to get themselves completely turned around, and by 2 pm, Carrier reported that his troops were nearing the sea. Then at 3 pm, he found – to his embarrassment – that they were coming out on the coast just behind Miller's men. Realising his error, Carrier resumed the attack, this time striking towards the Duropa Plantation. He made some minor gains against strong enemy opposition, and by next morning, the two battalions presented a continuous front to the enemy, with Carrier's men again left of Miller's battalion.[7]

The adjutant of the 126th Regiment briefly recorded for 26 November: 'Following air and artillery barrage, our attack is started. The troops attacking are subjected to enemy strafing from the air. One company advances to within 75 yards of the coconut grove on Cape Endaiadere. Troops are shelled by enemy mortars. The Australian 25-pounders return fire'.[8]

In the fighting here, Private Howard Eastwood, with the lone platoon of 'C' Company, I/126th Regiment, was reported as single-handily attacking a position held by ten Japanese to the front of the company's scouting party. Standing upright in the kunai grass, he 'engaged the Japanese with fire from his submachine gun, killing several and dispersing the others. He was soon after killed by a sniper in the area'.[9] Private Howard Eastwood was awarded the DSC posthumously for his actions.

The unit war diary of the 2/6th Australian Independent Company comments on the aerial attack and artillery barrage, which preceded the attack. With the ending of the bombardment, Major Rossal Belmer's attacking force numbering around 60 men advanced from their position close to the bays at the eastern end of New Strip, but as they advanced, it was noted in the diary: '0950 [hours] No sign of US Inf. movmt .... Belmer's party found themselves well in front of US inf'.[10] Carrier's confusion had left the Australian right flank exposed.

While the commando patrols skimmed the southern edge of New Strip, it was impossible for them to assault the strip itself due to the commanding Japanese fire, and any other approach was impossible because of the surrounding swamp. Also, like all others that day, these men had to endure either rain or blazing sun. To their left, Lieutenant Carl Fryday and his men of 'I' Company, III/128th Regiment were

CHAPTER 15

still in position on the approach south of the bridge; they had been unable to secure the western end of the airstrip, as planned due to concentrated Japanese fire.[11]

Later that afternoon, Corporal John McKitterick, a 38-year-old mechanic from Claremont in Western Australia, with two of his men noted a five-man Japanese patrol moving from a small island of bush directly towards their position. Given they had orders to not engage the Japanese, but to reconnoitre and gain information on the Japanese positions, they quietly fell back and let the enemy troops pass by.[12]

Meanwhile, Lieutenant Arthur Tregarthen and his patrol to the north-west in the swampland, who for days had been trying to find a path through the morass towards the Japanese positions, reported: 'They thought they had "put up" a Jap patrol ... and that the Japs had hurriedly withdrawn'.[13] He also reported that they could still find no way through the swamp to the enemy perimeter. The reply from Major Harcourt, was: 'Patrol told to keep on move and make sure Japs did not patrol the area at all after this date. Patrol contacted Coy of 3/128'.[14] The adjutant concluded in the unit war diary that night:

> Observers from our OP tree could see most of the strip and would be able to direct arty fire onto targets. Three dummy planes were seen on the strip – these were crudely made. The strip appeared unfinished. During the night ... the sound of a motor truck or trucks had been heard – the sound appeared to come from the W. end of NEW STRIP or just N. of that. Strength – 9 Off. 114 O/Rs. Conditions in swamp area where most of Coy now located are very bad – water underfoot everywhere – and no shelter from sun or rain. Expect fever to affect personnel – Resting a few each day when possible. About 30 sick at Coy HQ. Decided to occupy bush islands as soon as possible and endeavour put OPs in them.[15]

* * *

Meanwhile, at Urbana front, the men of 'F' Company, II/128th Regiment, and 'G' Company, 126th Regiment moved into the area west of the bridge over Entrance Creek, which had been occupied and patrolled by 'E' Company, II/126th Regiment since 24 November. These men had scarcely begun moving when Harding, who had already determined that the attack on the Urbana front was not being pressed with sufficient vigour, ordered his chief of staff, Colonel John Mott, to Smith's position. Mott was instructed by Harding that he was to take strong action when he got there and, if he thought the situation required it, he was to take direct command of operations there.[16]

* * *

Harding that night recorded the day's events in his diary:

> I called Colonel Hale about nine o'clock to find out what had happened on his front after I left. The report was to the effect that Carrier had moved forward some distance in the coconut grove in front, meeting much opposition, but that the other units had been held up without any appreciable advance. He was not entirely sure of the exact location of the troops, and his description of the line that he believed to exist had Carrier in an exceedingly vulnerable position in case the Japanese made any countermove. I asked Hale what he proposed to do, and he replied that he was going on with the original plan, which was to have Carrier push on into the coconut grove. Since the other elements of Hale's force hadn't made the necessary progress for a continuation of the original plan, I directed him to alter his dispositions to provide for a continuous front with adequate protection for Carrier's left flank, which as he described it was 'in the air'. The new disposition left his line with a slight bulge into enemy ground. I also talked to Mott, who had arrived at Dobodura during the day and was leaving the following morning

CHAPTER 15

for the front before Buna, where the 2d Battalion of the 126th and the 2d Battalion of the 128th, under the command of Lt Col Smith, were having difficulties.[17]

* * *

The Allies were not to have the skies to themselves that day, as the Japanese deployed 12 carrier-based fighters and four carrier-based bombers to raid the Dobodura airstrip. An additional seven fighters and four bombers were sent to attack land troop concentrations and transport ships in Oro Bay. A night raid was also conducted by three Japanese land-based attack aircraft against the airstrip at Embogo, just south-east of Buna, as well as against Port Moresby.[18]

Having landed eight days before at the Sanananda beachhead with Colonel Yamamoto Hiroshi's force, was unnamed Japanese soldier [C]. He had since dug-in around the New Strip and plantation area at Buna. That day, he briefly recorded in his diary: 'There were many duds in enemy mortar shells. One out of five shells exploded'.[19]

* * *

In Rabaul, the Japanese commander of the *8th Area Army*, Lieutenant General Hitoshi Imamura, and his staff were debating whether to reinforce or abandon the Papuan beachheads. Indeed, Colonel Suigita Ichiji argued for the abandonment of both Guadalcanal and the beachhead positions, as he believed holding them was untenable. That day, however, an operational order was issued, placing the main strength of the *21st Independent Mixed Brigade* and one infantry battalion from the *38th Division* under the command of the *18th Army* to, 'first secure the key areas around Buna village'.[20] At this point, the Japanese troops defending the Buna sector were as follows:

1. Reinforcement units led by Colonel Yamamoto Hiroshi, replacement commander of the *144th Infantry Regiment* (around 700 men).

2. Captain Yasuda Yoshitatsu, and his men of the *5th Yokosuka, 5th Sasebo* (*SNLP*), and supporting naval pioneer troops (around 800 men).
3. Men of the *III/229th Infantry Regiment*, led by Major Kenmotsu Heishichi.
4. *No. 2 Company, 38th Mountain Artillery Regiment*, commanded by Lieutenant Shiiki Kazuo.
5. One company of the *47th Field Anti-aircraft Artillery Battalion*.[21]

16

'THIS IS THE MDS, OR WHAT'S F...G LEFT OF IT!'

The next day, 27 November, Major General Harding sent the following abrupt message to Major General Cyril Clowes: 'Re transport tanks. Three tanks at Fall River assigned to me are urgently needed. Reply to my request that they be sent fwd. Stated that available barges would not carry them. Do what you can to have Jap landing barges now used at Goodenough Island made available to fwd tanks'.[1] Such a request should have gone through NGF Headquarters, for Harding was not in a position to be making demands directly to Clowes. That said, Clowes was doing all in his power to get the tanks to Buna.

Another friendly fire incident occurred that morning when Allied aircraft attempting to bomb Japanese positions along New Strip, mistakenly targeted – with a string of demolition bombs – Lieutenant Carl Fryday's men of 'I' Company, III/128th Regiment. These men were still located south-west of the strip. Three men were seriously wounded, and Fryday temporarily pulled his company back into the jungle, south of the position from where the first attack of his battalion had been launched on 19 November.[2]

At this time, the Australian commandos of the 2/6th Independent Company had a quiet day, remaining in the swamp. Major Rossall Belmer was still located further north near the eastern end of New Strip, with his advanced party of around 50 men. While patrols were sent out, they could not make much headway, due to the Japanese snipers located in the trees close to the strip, as recorded by the company adjutant: 'Shot at few Jap positions N. of NEW STRIP. Results not known but enemy fire ceased. Enemy fires with many MGs at all our A/C which fly over – at these times difficult to plot accurate positions unless near to conspicuous points, which are also marked on maps, of which there are few. Compass bearings taken whenever possible'.[3] It also recorded that 24-year-old Captain Gordon King and 25-year-old Lieutenant Gordon Blainey, both from Sydney, along with six men arrived as reinforcements, with the company strength now at 11 officers, 120 other ranks. Of these, 40 were sick at the company headquarters. The adjutant concluded that day: 'Many men are getting fever and tinea on their feet. Not possible to relieve other than the worst. Enemy MG and our arty fire during the night'.[4]

* * *

Meanwhile, and as instructed by Harding the previous day, Colonel Mott arrived at Urbana front that afternoon. Surveying the situation, he assumed command, with Lieutenant Colonel Smith reverting to command the II/128th Regiment. At once, Mott relieved the commanders of the two companies that had failed on the right: Captain Bakken of 'E' Company, and Captain Spraetz of 'G' Company. However, Bakken was reinstated soon after, and Spraetz was evacuated sick with Malaria. Smith also recalled that Captain Haggestad leading 'H' Company was also relieved, merely because he was unshaven; he too was soon after reinstated. Mott now ordered patrols into the area forward of the kunai flat to the right of the Triangle, from which the Japanese had driven 'E' Company and the weapons platoon of 'G' Company two days before. He also ordered 'E' and 'G' companies to retrieve their abandoned weapons on the kunai flat. They did so by sundown, but 'E' Company returned without one of its mortars, and these men were sent back a second time to retrieve it.[5]

Years later, Lieutenant Colonel Smith replied to a request for information by Samuel Milner, who was then completing the American official history. Smith wrote that Mott that day had sent

CHAPTER 16

him out to lead a patrol: 'I was ordered to take a ten-man combat patrol and ambush some Japs who were reportedly using a trail along a stream (later proved to be the Girua River) to the west'.[6] Allocating a battalion commander to such a task was strange, to say the least, and indicated that his next claim had some validity – Smith continued: 'Upon my return about 36 hours later, I was directed to take Company G and protect the right flank of the Urbana Force. In order to deceive the Japs as to our strength and intentions, I was directed to patrol aggressively, and then very dramatically was told that, if necessary, we would die in our tracks, but we must not retreat one step. I am positive that the order for me to remain with Company G was prompted, not by the need for my presence at that point, but by the desire of Colonel Mott to keep me away from my CP'.[7]

Mott now continued Smith's plan of concentrating his attack to the left of the Triangle by assaulting the grassy strip leading to the village. The men would launch their attack from the two smaller grass strips just south of the larger kunai patch. Major Smith and his men of the II/126th Regiment were ordered to assemble near the Girua River, directly south of the two strips that were to be the jump-off point for the attack. The men of 'F' Company, II/128th Regiment occupied the area west of the bridge over Entrance Creek. The troops of 'G' and 'H' companies, II/128th Regiment, under Lieutenant Colonel Smith, were ordered to take over the positions south of the Triangle, to contain the enemy there, while 'E' Company, in reserve, was deployed around Urbana Force headquarters.[8]

Mott reported to Harding at around dusk, as recorded in Harding's diary: 'At about six o'clock, Mott reported in. He had found the troops on the left flank badly disposed and had taken over command and rearranged the companies so that the battalions could operate under their proper commanders. The dispositions and the positions at which the companies were reported impressed me as being highly favourable for an attack in the direction of Buna the following day. I discussed this matter with Mott, who urged a delay of one day, to complete the preparations necessary to give the attack its greatest chance of success. I agreed to the delay, and the attack was set for the morning of the 29th'.[9]

* * *

Early that day, the Soputa airstrip was targeted by Japanese aircraft. This airfield was relieving the pressure on the Australian 2/4th Field Ambulance by evacuating casualties; however, the Japanese also struck a heavy blow against the nearby Main Dressing Station (MDS). Three days before, a Japanese low reconnaissance aircraft had flown over Soputa where the MDS and the American Clearing Hospital were sited. This resulted in six Val dive-bombers (each with a heavy load of five 60-kiogram bombs) and 13 Zero fighters bombing and strafing the medical stations. At the Australian MDS, located in a clearing by the roadside and almost void of cover, 22 Australians were killed, with around 50 wounded, including patients, members of the field ambulance, visitors to the hospital, and Papuan carriers and patients. Among the killed were two respected and admired Australian medical officers: Major Ian Vickery, a 28-year-old physician from Sydney, and Major Hew McDonald, a 30-year-old physician from Queenscliff in Victoria; both had done outstanding work during the campaign across the mountains. At the American Clearing Hospital, six Americans were also killed.[10]

Sergeant Bill Sweeting, with the 2/4th Field Ambulance, recalled this attack:

> Japanese aircraft attacked the still crowded MDS. I was at the entrance to the admission centre as the first bomb fell and dived into a nearby drain. 'Charlie the Crane', the nursing orderly on duty, was just ahead of me. His backside was protruding above the shallow drain, and he was trying to protect it with a folded

CHAPTER 16

parachute. The protective value of the parachute was never tested, perhaps fortunately for Charlie. The aircraft dropped five bombs on the MDS, in an area about 75 yards by 40. Then they returned to strafe the area.

The raid had hardly ended when the sound came of a revving motor from the direction of Popondetta. 'It's on again', yelled a voice, and the men, just beginning to recover their composure, scattered for cover again. Then a jeep drove through the MDS without stopping, a bemused driver at the wheel – he must have thought the removalist had been in. Someone shouted – it might have been me – 'It's only a jeep', and the cry was taken up, 'It's ok. It's only a jeep. It's only a jeep; it's ok', and we returned sheepishly to the clearing. The phone rang at the admission centre and Skinny Hurkett answered it. It was Divisional Headquarters. 'Is that the MDS?' a voice inquired. 'Yeah,' responded Skinny, never one to mince words, or given to exaggeration. 'This is the MDS. Or what's f … g left of it.'[11]

The Australian journalist, Geoffrey Reading, who had just arrived from Moresby, later wrote: 'I walked down the road to the Australian hospital and was appalled and sickened at the desolation. More than three bombs had fallen directly amongst the wards, transforming this place of healing into an open grave. Sixteen patients and two doctors were killed instantly. The wounded were brave, and few cried out, but never before had I seen so much pain in so small a place. Major Vickory, my friend of Myola days, had been blown to pieces'.[12]

* * *

At Rabaul that night, Major General Tsuyuo Yamagata, commanding the Japanese *21st Independent Mixed Brigade*, along with the bulk of his 750 men of the *I/170th Infantry Regiment* boarded four destroyers – they were scheduled to land at Gona the next night under cover of darkness.[13]

17

'THE EMPEROR ... HAS ASKED THAT BUNA BE DEFENDED TO THE LAST MAN!'

On 28 November, Lieutenant General Herring, commanding Advance NGF, had opened his advanced headquarters at Popondetta and again suggested to Major General Harding that he might consider launching night attacks against known Japanese positions. Herring was concerned that he remained largely ignorant of the details on the ground at Buna and had asked Harding for a sitrep of the situation. Harding replied with a lengthy report, full of excuses for the current stalemate, including problems with supply, the poor physical condition of the men, lack of artillery and aerial support, low morale among officers and men, and provided very little details of the Allied or Japanese troop dispositions within the Buna sector.[1]

Harding also expressed dissatisfaction with the temporary allocation of the III/126th Regiment to Major General Vasey, while also requesting that the 127th Regiment, then based at Port Moresby, be sent to him: 'I have requested that the 127th Infantry be flown to Dobodura at the earliest practicable date. Depending on the situation when the regiment becomes available, I propose to use the 127th either to relieve the frontline units or in an attack .... I am finding this flank of the Buna–Gona area a lot tougher nut to crack than I thought it would be. The Japs are evidently set to make it a little Tobruk or Bataan affair'.[2]

CHAPTER 17

Herring drafted his response to Harding, dated 28 November:

Dear Harding,

I have now moved forward with a small staff to the POPONDETTA area, and I am hopeful that I may now be able [to] make personal contact with you. As still not clear if and when you move to DOBODURA.

Vasey attacks GONA tomorrow with 21 Bde, which has just come up unfortunately only about 1000 men strong, with 25 Bde joining in with fire and five AP bombing strafing during first phase. He is also getting Tomlinson to take the offensive on the SOPUTA–SANANANDA RD, so as to give the appearance of the arrival of fresh troops at both places. Have consequently sent you a signal today at 1430 hrs, asking you for some aggressive action during the 29th.

The other matters referred to in the Signal relate first to information from secret sources that BUNA is to be further reinforced in the very near future. So far, the reinforcing attempted has a business costly to the enemy in ships and men, but there is always a chance they may be successful one night and ship a Bn or more ashore. The sooner therefore the position is cleared, both on your side and on Vasey's, the better for all. Your left flank seems to offer opportunities of turning his defences on the main strip inside out. In any event, aggressive action is needed, and I am sure that while a quick success may entail heavy casualties, there will be a nett saving in the long run if we take them early and clean the positions quickly.

Arranged before I left for dispatch of Signal personnel as soon as plane available, as sought by your Signal … cannot agree to despatch one Bn [of] 127 at the present, because I cannot see what it is needed for, as you seem to have ample reserves. Supply problem also makes it undesirable to increase your numbers unless they can be fed from the sea. Would you let me know your reasons for requiring it at the moment; with all the planes loads involved, which being devoted to troop carrying, are taken from what is just now our very vital, most pressing need, the supply of food and ammunition.

Would you let the bearer of this letter have all the news of your doings' proposals for the final capture of BUNA and the destruction of the Japanese garrison. I hope to hear of further advances in today's sitrep. My kind regards to Mott and Waldron, was very sorry to hear of MacNider's misfortune.[3]

***

To the east, Warren Force was still dug-in, facing the Japanese, having made little progress. Still forward near the eastern end of New Strip was Captain Rossal Belmer and his Australian commandos, who were reinforced that day by Lieutenant Blainey, a 25-year-old assistant manager from Sydney, with ten men. This officer had just arrived in the Buna sector the previous day. By 11 am, and further back, the rest of the company finally managed to occupy the small islands of bush, forward of 'I' Company, III/128th Regiment, who were still entrenched to their left. More Australians fell out that day due to fever.[4]

Harding now ordered an attack that night; however, he later agreed to postpone it until the morning of 30 November, as this attack would partly correspond with Mott's planned night attack on Urbana front on 29 November – the effect would be an almost simultaneous attack on both flanks.[5]

These attacks were to be supported by more closely integrated artillery fire than any previously attempted and directed by Brigadier Albert Waldron. The guns were still all Australian – Major William Hall's two 25-pounders forward of Hariko; Captain Martin O'Hare's two howitzers in the same general area; and Captain Herbert Manning's

CHAPTER 17

four guns near Ango. One American 105-mm howitzer of 'A' Battery, 129th US Field Artillery Battalion would land at Dobodura on 29 November, but it would not be ready to support the attack scheduled for 29/30 November.

The Australian gunners were gradually reducing the problems associated with the flat coastal country. Manning reported that at first, he had no accurate maps of the area but was able to construct a satisfactory one from aerial photographs recently supplied. His main difficulty was observation: 'No command at all, practically impenetrable jungle with open strips and all perfectly flat'.[6] Manning had originally relied on information from the infantry and reports of sound bearings from listening observation posts. Skilful calculations, however, enabled him to fire with sufficient accuracy to guarantee his shells falling within 200 metres of a given target. Even if that estimate were correct, however, it was still not sufficiently accurate to provide well-trained infantry the close artillery support they needed; such men would advance as near as 30 metres to the fall of the exploding shell.[7]

Harding was still painfully aware that his men needed the kind of support that only tanks could provide, if they were to overcome the solidly entrenched Japanese; he had again requested the tanks from Milne Bay be brought forward. Still lacking sea craft capable of carrying tanks prevented their dispatch. Clowes had been swift to get Bren gun carriers on the water, to help alleviate the situation. However, he was fully aware that these open-tracked and lightly armed vehicles were no real substitute for tanks. The first of the carriers and their crews had arrived at Porlock the previous day, and Harding was informed that at least four would reach him within the next two days and, in consequence, he hoped to employee these new weapons in supporting the attack at Warren front on 30 November. But once again, the lack of shipping would stifle his plans. Now, he was informed that he would not be receiving the air support he expected, as a Japanese convoy had been spotted heading for

Buna, which was to be the prime target for the airmen.[8] The official American historian recorded:

> The men on both the Urbana and Warren fronts were tired and listless. They had not been sufficiently hardened for jungle operations and, with few exceptions, had not been fresh when they reached the combat zone. Thrown into battle in an exhausted state, most of them had had no chance to rest .... The troops were half-starved. Most of them had been living on short rations for weeks and their food intake since the fighting began had averaged about a third of a C ration per day – just enough to sustain life. They were shaggy and bearded and their clothes were ragged. Their feet were swollen and in bad shape. Their shoes, which had shrunk in the wet, often had to be cut away so that the troops could even get their feet into them .... Morale was low. Instead of being met, as they had been led to expect, by a few hundred sick and starving Japanese, they found themselves facing apparently large numbers of fresh, well-fed, well-armed troops in seemingly impregnable positions, against whom in almost two weeks of fighting they had failed to score even one noteworthy success.[9]

Both Urbana Force and Warren Force were now scheduled to attack on 30 November, Urbana Force a few hours before Warren Force. Nevertheless, each was still suffering from the most acute deficiencies of supply – all but one of the newly arrived luggers that had come in on 21 November having by now either gone aground or been destroyed by the enemy aircraft.[10] Harding wrote to Herring that night: 'That finishes the Red Arrow freighters. There is nothing left except one small craft with a kicker that will make two knots ....'.[11]

* * *

CHAPTER 17

As requested, No. 4 Army Cooperation Squadron RAAF and one of their slow, almost weapon-less Wirraways was allotted to the 32nd Division, while another would support the 7th Australian Division. Soon their numbers would increase, given their success in aiding the artillery. From now on, these aircraft would play an increasing part in the coastal battle, at first landing at Dobodura for briefing before every mission, and later remaining at Dobodura and Popondetta for several days at a time, subject to the demands of the artillery. Although the threat of Japanese Zero fighters restricted their use to some extent, they were handled so boldly that the soldiers soon became used to seeing them circling slowly, seeming almost to hover, over the Japanese lines and passing detailed directions to the guns.[12] The official Australian history records: 'They spotted shell bursts, lured enemy AA into disclosing their positions, reported Japs trying to escape; they were forced down and occasionally crashed in flames; and one daring Wirraway actually shot down a Zero. Their work, according to the official artillery report, was "superb"'.[13]

As recorded by aviation historians Michael Claringbould and Peter Ingman: 'One of the more famous and unlikely aerial victories in the South Pacific occurred at 1135 [hours]. A No. 4 Squadron Wirraway[xii] on an artillery-spotting mission flying at 1000 feet [330 metres] saw a "Zeke" flying below in the vicinity of the Gona wreck. Being in a favourable position, Pilot Officer John Archer made a front-quarter attack firing 50 rounds from each of his forward-firing 0.303-inch calibre machine guns. Archer's observer, Sergeant James Coulston, saw the aircraft crash into the ocean in flames'.[14] The Japanese pilot was later identified as Fuji'i Hiroichi flying a Nakajima Model I Ki-43 Hayabusa and assigned to the *Headquarters chutai, 11th Sentai*.[15]

During the later stages of the coastal battle, as these aircraft increased the effectiveness of artillery fire and more guns arrived in the forward areas, the supply of ammunition became a great problem. At

---

xii The forward fuselage of Archer's A20-103 is preserved at the Australian War Memorial in Canberra.

this stage, however, the problem was not so acute: shells were brought by air to Dobodura and then taken out along the track on four jeeps for Manning's guns at Ango.[16] Major Hall's dump of the 2/5th Field Regiment was well to the rear of his gun positions, to which the shells had to be manhandled, as recalled by the regimental historian:

> At night, ammunition was loaded into canvas assault-boats which were then pushed and pulled along the surf. While so engaged, the men watched anxiously for aerial flares from Cape Endaiadere, for they would then be clearly visible to the enemy, who were strongly entrenched in that area. To pull an assault-boat along, one man had to walk in the water, chest-deep most of the way, well outside the line of breakers. There was about two miles [three kilometres] to travel, and after a few hundred yards even the strongest was exhausted. Sometimes the boats would be swamped, and then it was a case of diving for the boxes which, when full of water, became harder than ever to handle. Once the ammunition was ashore, it would be carried to the guns through the dark jungle. The usual routine was for each man to hold the belt of the man ahead, the leader trying to follow the telephone line. If he lost the wire, the file would soon be off the track. Everyone would then crawl on hands and knees until the line was found again. Although this trip through the jungle was only about a mile, it took up to two and a half hours in the dark.[17]

* * *

That day, six Japanese carrier-based bombers and 12 carrier-based fighters attacked a transport convoy near Oro Bay, with the airmen on their return reporting they left a 500-ton transport on fire. Three other carrier-based bombers raided an American staging point at Sumpit Village, near Buna.[18]

CHAPTER 17

Meanwhile, Major General Tsuyuo Yamagata, commanding the Japanese *21st Independent Mixed Brigade*, along with the bulk of his 750 men of the *I/170th Infantry Regiment*, were onboarded four destroyers. These ships were discovered later that day by Allied airmen flying B-17s from the 63rd, 65th and 403rd bombardment squadrons based at Seven-Mile drone, Port Moresby. Major Thomas Charles, with the 403rd United States Army Air Force Bombardment Squadron flying a B17, was sent out to shadow the destroyers. By 5.30 pm, the crew radioed that they had contacted the convoy in the Vitiaz Strait, but the 11-man crew were never heard from again, and no trace of their aircraft has ever been located. It was likely shot down by anti-aircraft fire or fell prey to bad weather.[19]

* * *

Sometime that day, unknown Japanese soldier [D] recorded in his diary: 'From morning, we are heavily bombed. It is more terrifying than that of the 25th. The daily enemy air and assaults kill off my comrades. Hunger assails me and there is nothing I can do but await death'.[20] He recorded next day: 'This morning, the enemy persistently worries us with mortar fire'.[21]

Also at Buna was unnamed Japanese soldier [B], who had previously recognised that his life, along with those of his comrades, was slipping away. He wrote his last entry in his diary: 'At last our lives are … shorter. Look at the fierceness of the enemy mortar fire, which burst near us. Today, the word that the Buna Crisis is imminent has reached the ears of the Emperor and he has asked that Buna be defended to the last man'.[22]

18

'TO A GIRL I LOVE'

Preparations for the night attack on the Urbana front were complete by the late afternoon of 29 November 1942, with the attack to now be launched around midnight. In a tall coconut tree that overlooked the front, Colonel John Mott had an observation post connected by telephone with the artillery at Ango and the mortar teams. Both artillery and mortars were registered on the objective – the large grassy kunai area just north of the two clearings south of the area Urbana Force, where the troops would form up for the attack. Mott's CP was a hundred metres behind the most forward element of 'E' Company, II/126th Regiment. His aid station and part of a collecting company were in place near the Girua River.[1]

The final details of the attack had been worked out, with Major Smith commanding the II/126th Regiment. The troops would move off towards the large kunai patch just after midnight. A 30-minute mortar and artillery preliminary bombardment would be laid down on the kunai strip. Immediately after this ceased, the men would proceed to their objective in darkness. Lacking white material for armbands to assist with identification, even underwear, the men would have to keep in close contact with one another.[2]

The men of 'E' and 'F' companies, II/126th Regiment would attack in a north-easterly direction and occupy the main kunai patch, making sure that they first secured the area nearest to the Coconut Grove, a small coconut plantation immediately north of the bridge over Entrance Creek. Meanwhile, the men of 'G' Company, II/126th Regiment would attack along the track and take Buna Village, while the men of 'F' Company, II/128th Regiment, after being relieved from

CHAPTER 18

their present positions by 'E' Company, II/128th Regiment, would proceed to Siwori Creek, covering the extreme left of the attack. They were to seize the crossing near its mouth and occupy the area between the creek and the Girua River. Captain Arnold Haggestad (who would be killed that day) and his men of 'H' Company, II/128th Regiment would be immediately behind 'E' and 'F' companies, II/126th Regiment, in support, while 'E' Company, II/128th Regiment, who was operating immediately to the right of 'E' Company, II/126th Regiment, would clear the Japanese out of the Coconut Grove. Finally, those of 'G' Company, II/128th Regiment would operate south of the Triangle and cover the track, supported with fire from the Australian artillery at Ango.[3]

Still with 'E' Company, II/126th Regiment was Sergeant Paul Lutjens, who after being briefed of the next day's attack, wasn't feeling particularly positive about his future. It finally gave him the courage, however, to write to the girl of his dreams back home, Francis 'Lorraine' Phillips. He had known her since school and had fallen for her at first glance, but he had never had the guts to admit it to her. That night, he penned her a letter that was only meant to be sent if he was killed, after being recovered from his body.[4]

To a girl I Love.

Dearest,

You will never know what you have meant to me since I have known you. I guess I've loved you since the first day I saw you ten years ago. Many times, I have tried to drive you out of my thoughts, knowing how hopeless it was. Just to know that one day you smiled on me gives me courage to face most anything .... You probably don't even know I'm alive. Many a night, lying in the mud and hell of this country, you have been my consolation and friend, my courage and my life. The only time I would ever think of saying this is now when my life means nothing. Forgive me for taking this unforgivable privilege and please don't laugh …. If I do come through this, everything will go back as it was. Never would I dare to mention this. Only God will know.[5]

* * *

At the Warren front, it was a relatively quiet day. The Australian commandos of the 2/6th Independent Company sent out several patrols, as recorded in the unit war diary: '0830 to 1200 [hours]: Our patrols went across NEW STRIP in several places from these and [from] the OP much good information was obtained and sent to HQ 128 US Regt. Japs were frequently seen moving about on the BUNA Runway and near the bridge SE of it. Gave instructions that no sniping was to take place from OP "[bush] island". Suggested to 128 US Regt HQ that indirect MG fire should be used on selected points near which Japs are seen'.[6] Major Harry Harcourt was also informed that the following day, the Americans of the 128th Regiment would advance along the coast towards Cape Endaiadere and north-west to New Strip. His commandos were tasked to support this attack against the eastern end of the strip and protect the American left flank, as well as to 'neutralise fire from area near and EAST of bridge'.[7]

* * *

On the other side of the wire at the Warren front was unnamed Japanese soldier [C], who was part of Colonel Yamamoto Hiroshi's force dug-in around the New Strip and plantation area at Buna. He recorded in his diary: 'The Emperor has heard of our situation and given words of praise to the Army and Navy in the BUNA Area. Morale very good'.[8]

* * *

CHAPTER 18

Back in Australia, Lieutenant General Eichelberger was training the American 41st Infantry Division in jungle warfare near Rockhampton in Queensland. That day, he received two messages. The first was a warning from Brisbane telling him to stand by, advising him that he and a small staff might be ordered to Port Moresby at short notice. Later that night, the second message arrived confirming the earlier order. By that time Eichelberger, Brigadier Clovis Byers, his chief of staff, six staff officers, his aide, and nine enlisted men, mostly clerks, were packed and ready. They would board two C-47 transport aircraft for Port Moresby early the next morning.[9]

* * *

Major General Tsuyuo Yamagata, commanding the Japanese *21st Independent Mixed Brigade*, along with the bulk of the *I/170th Infantry Regiment* were still on board the four destroyers that had been spotted the previous day by Major Thomas Charles. During the afternoon of 29 November, these ships were targeted by American airmen and the destroyer *Shiratsuyu* suffered substantial damage, while the *Makigumo* suffered a near miss, but a fire broke out in her boiler room. These two ships, by 5 pm, were heading back to Rabaul, and while the destroyers *Kazagumo* and *Yūgumo* proceeded to Gona, they were again targeted by Allied aircraft and forced to sail back to Rabaul, having not landed any of the reinforcements or desperately needed supplies.[10]

19

'BUNA IS GRADUALLY FALLING INTO A STATE OF DANGER'

The following morning, 30 November 1942, was the date set for the two attacks by the men of Warren and Urbana forces tasked with breaking through the main Japanese defences. Major General Harding, commanding the 32nd Division, was now convinced from the previous week of fighting that it would take tanks to clean out the enemy bunker defences in the Duropa Plantation. He radioed Brigadier Dwight Johns of COSC on 27 November, asking him to do his best to get the Australian tanks at Milne Bay sent to him. He suggested that Johns try to get some of the Japanese landing barges captured on Goodenough Island in the hope that they might prove large enough to ferry the armour to his position. New Guinea Force, however, replied for Johns that there were no barges anywhere in the area big enough to carry the tanks. He would have to conduct operations without tank support until these vehicles could be ferried to his position. Even so, the four Australian Bren gun carriers were scheduled to support the attack by the troops of Warren Force, but within hours, Harding was informed that because of an acute shortage of shipping at Porlock Harbour, the Australian Bren gun carriers would not arrive as scheduled, and the attack would have to be launched without them.[1]

* * *

During the early morning hours, the men of Urbana Force had been involved in an intense struggle around the Triangle and beyond the

CHAPTER 19

swamps, which spread west of the strips. Colonel Robert Mott was assigned the most difficult task, even before the fighting began: an advance by ill-trained and apprehensive troops through darkness and swamps. It was true that the distance was short from the two grassy strips which he had selected as his forming-up areas, but even this short distance under such circumstances would prove too much. The plan, though bold, was far too intricate and ambitious – especially for their raw troops. Mott's timetable was disrupted, even before his initial moves began. He planned to advance on to his objective just after midnight behind the barrage from Captain Manning and his 25-pounders, along with his own mortar teams, both of which had ranged in on the large kunai patch, but the infantry would not attack until just after 4 am that morning.[2]

At this point, Manning had conferred with Mott, later reporting that liaison between his guns and the American commanders was difficult due to faulty radio and telephone communications, often requiring a 15-kilometre slog through mud by liaison officers and runners. He later reported: 'Use of air co-operation most affective shooting. Infantry apparently well pleased with use of guns – main difficulty to be allowed to use them. The US Infantry commanders have no appreciation of Arty as a support weapon – their troops do not make best use of neutralising fire. Effect on morale of troops appears to be extremely good'.[3]

The delay in the attack was attributed to several factors, including: enemy fire from the strip; flares from enemy aircraft that flew over the area during the night; the rising tide in the swamp; and the confusion with moving so many men through the swampland in the dark. Lieutenant Robert Odell, with 'F' Company, II/126th Regiment recalled: 'As soon as it was dark, preparations began. When these were completed, we each grasped the shoulder of the man in front, and slowly shuffled forward in the pitch black of the night. Our only guide was the telephone wire leading to the jump-off point, and the troops in the foxholes along the way who had been holding the ground recently captured. There was no trail, and consequently, several hours were required to travel many hundreds of yards. We all had bayonets. Rifle fire was forbidden until after the attack was well under way. Japs encountered along the way were to be dealt with silently'.[4]

Just after 4 am, the men of 'E', 'F', and 'G' companies, II/126th Infantry finally attacked. It was still dark, and about one hundred metres out, they made their first direct encounter with the Japanese – a line of machine gun posts dead ahead. At that moment, Odell recalled: 'All hell broke loose. There was more lead flying through the air … than it's possible to estimate. Machinegun tracers lit the entire area, and our own rifle fire made a solid sheet of flame. Everywhere men cursed, shouted, or screamed. Order followed on order …. Brave men led, and others followed. Cowards crouched in the grass literally frightened out of their skins'.[5]

The men of 'E' and 'F' companies, II/126th Infantry overran the enemy outposts and gained their objective – the eastern end of the large kunai patch. There they found and dispatched several Japanese and began to consolidate their position. Sergeant Boyd Lincoln, a squad leader with 'E' Company, was killed during the fighting here after leading his men with great distinction all day against the Japanese outpost on the outskirts of Buna Village and was awarded the DSC posthumously.[6]

Sergeant Paul Lutjens, with 'E' Company, recalled seeing his men being blown apart, and the track was, 'so slimy with blood of the wounded … that you could hardly keep your balance …. Men coming back with their faces shot away and their hands where their chins had been, trying to stop the flow of blood. [Men] with their guts sagging out … yelling in pain'.[7] Somehow, to his surprise, he came out of it unscathed.

The men of 'G' Company, II/126th Regiment, who were to take the track to Buna Village as soon as they gained the western end of the large kunai patch, accomplished only part of their mission. Led by Lieutenant Cladie Bailey, these men overran strong enemy opposition

CHAPTER 19

on their part of the patch, but they lost their way when they tried moving towards the village. By daylight, the company found itself in the swamp along the northern edge of the Kunai strip. Finding 'G' Company out of reach, Colonel Mott immediately assigned 'E' Company, II/126th Regiment the task of taking the village. Moving directly on Buna Village by the main track, the company attacked at 6 am. About 300 metres out from the village, it ran into a well-manned enemy bunker line, unable to advance because of intense enemy crossfire.[8]

Meanwhile, on Major Smith's orders, Captain Harold Hantlemann, leading 'H' Company, II/126th Regiment came up with Lieutenant Erwin Nummer, commanding 'F' Company, and some troops from the Headquarters Company. Putting Hantlemann in charge of the mortars, and Nummer in command of the rest, Smith made a determined effort to take Buna Village. Preceded by a heavy concentration of mortar fire, the second attack met even fiercer resistance. Again, the troops could make only slight headway. When the attack was finally called off that afternoon, they had taken considerable casualties but had gained very little. During the fighting, Nummer was wounded, but he continued to lead his men. He was later awarded the DSC for his actions.[9]

To their left, 'F' Company, II/128th Regiment, after skirting the defences, had flung themselves widely to the west as far west as Siwori village. They were to secure the left flank of Urbana Force from enemy attack and cut the Japanese land communications between Buna and Sanananda. They secured the crossing over Siwori Creek and occupied the track between the creek and the bridge over the Girua River. The troops east of Siwori Village had already killed several Japanese from Buna, who had tried to cross the bridge, presumably to get to Sanananda.[10]

The other companies of the II/128th Regiment were less successful in gaining their objectives. The men of 'E' Company, attacking from the south-east end of the large kunai patch, failed to take the Coconut Grove, and 'G' Company had very little success in its attacks into the

BLOODY BUNA

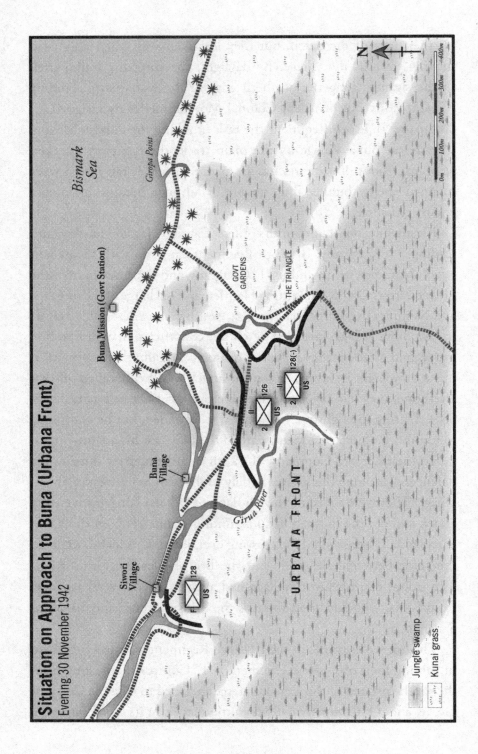

CHAPTER 19

southern tip of the Triangle. Both were subsequently ordered by Mott to consolidate; they were to make no further attacks until ordered.[11]

By the end of the day, at the large kunai patch, Americans were conducting mopping-up operations, having overran a Japanese headquarters area from which many Japanese troops had just fled. The location consisted of a headquarters building, an infirmary, and several huts containing weapons, ammunition, food, and medicine. The two main buildings had bunkers to the rear connected by tunnels. The buildings were of canvas and frame construction with wooden floors covered with mats. The headquarters building was found to be strewn with military documents, codes, and diaries, and contained a large radio set, which took eight men to carry. After removing the papers, the radio, the food, and the medical supplies, the buildings were burned to the ground and the connecting bunkers destroyed. With darkness now descending, Mott assessed his men had lodged more firmly on and around this key position.[12]

* * *

At Buna, 1st Class Mechanic, Kuba Satonao, with the *Imperial Japanese Navy*, had been assigned to *Tsukioka Transport Unit*, which had been under the command of Lieutenant Colonel Tsukamoto Hatsuo, commander of the *I/144th Regiment*, who with his men had fought the Australians along the Kokoda Track at Oivi and Gorari. Kuba recorded in his diary that day: 'Since the beginning of the battle … the enemy flies over in planes. All we do is get severely bombed. Buna is gradually falling into a state of danger'.[13] Kuba's diary was recovered by American troops on the Urbana front at Buna on 23 December.

* * *

Meanwhile, the men of Warren Force commenced their attack later that morning. The battalion commanders had only hours before been informed that they would be attacking without the Bren gun carriers.[14]

The attack called for Lieutenant Colonel Robert McCoy and his men of the I/128th Regiment, which had been reorganised into two rifle companies and one heavy weapons company (due to casualties), to advance straight up the track in a column of companies, with 'A' Company leading, before shaking out into a 350-metre front. They were tasked with taking Cape Endaiadere. To their left would be Lieutenant Colonel Edmund Carrier and the I/126th Regiment, with the Australian commandos covering the left. This force was to strike westward in the area immediately south of New Strip. The four 81-mm mortars from 'M' Company, III/128th Regiment would support Carrier's attack. Lieutenant Colonel Kelsie Miller and the III/128th Regiment, less 'I' Company, would be in reserve, ready to assist either McCoy or Carrier, as required. The men of 'I' Company would remain in their current blocking position astride the Dobodura–Simemi track, a few hundred metres south of the bridge between the airstrips.[15]

The infantry was to commence at 6.30 am. The Australian artillery would open the offensive at 6.15 am with a series of barrages. The 25-pounders would lay down fire on the south-west end of New Strip and would then switch their fire against the woods north-east of the strip, to knock out known Japanese mortar and artillery concentrations. Meanwhile, the Australian 3.7-inch mountain howitzers would first fire against the positions around Cape Endaiadere and then switch to local support of McCoy's advance. The air force, having repulsed the enemy convoy that had been bound for Buna, were still planning further attacks against the Japanese shipping, but they were able to provide aircraft to bomb and strafe the Japanese positions. A flight of Australian Wirraways, had also just arrived from Port Moresby to further aid the artillery in its spotting of enemy targets.[16]

As planned at 6.15 am, artillery and mortars opened a 15-minute barrage against the Japanese positions in front of Warren Force. Fifteen minutes later, the American GIs crossed their start-lines, with McCoy

CHAPTER 19

and his men of the I/128th Regiment leading the advance straight up the track. Within a hundred metres, however, the vanguard, defined by the men of 'A' Company, faced a log barrier, from which the Japanese poured fire into the approaching Americans, supported with intense enfilade from both flanks. The gunners at Boreo were unable to reduce the barricade and sustained fire from 81-mm mortars and from a 37-mm gun brought up specifically for the purpose made little if any impression on it. By noon, the advance by 'A' Company had come to a halt with the men digging-in.

Later that night, when 'A' Company was relieved by the men of 'B' Company, it was reported they were positioned about 900 metres south of the Cape. Its right flank was still in front of the barricade, and its left, which had not kept up, was curved almost all the way back to the line of departure.[17]

Meanwhile, on McCoy's left, Carrier, leading the I/126th Regiment, had been trying to breech the Japanese perimeter at the eastern end of New Strip. With a view of striking along its northern edge, 'B' Company tried to fight north into the fork but was stopped by Japanese fire from a strongpoint dominating the spur and the strip. To their left, the men of 'C' Company got no farther than half-way along the airstrip's southern edge before they too were forced to dig-in to survive the storm of ordinance sweeping across and along the open space, which had obviously been ranged as a killing field by the Japanese.[18]

Earlier, Allied bombers, after successfully chasing the enemy convoy back to Rabaul, joined in the battle at 9 am. Forty-five minutes later, another artillery barrage targeted the Japanese positions, while at 1.45 pm and 2.48 pm, Allied airmen conducted additional sorties, strafing and bombing the enemy. Pressed tightly against the Japanese defensive positions and without enough heavy artillery using projectiles with delayed fuse to demolish the Japanese bunkers and fortifications, the Americans could make little headway. The troops had fought desperately, but they could not get through the Japanese protective fire, which was defined by killing grounds of interlocking fire.[19]

* * *

On the extreme left, the small force of Australian commandos of the 2/6th Independent Company were handicapped, as the American advance had ceased almost before it began. Even so, the Australian patrols on the right located Japanese machinegun positions to the north of the airstrip's eastern end with elements of this small force linking up with Fryday to the west, south of the bridge.[20] The commandos reported on the Japanese defences, as recorded in the unit war diary:

> All emplacements appeared to be made of coconut logs laid lengthwise with others placed on bearers forming the roof. The whole was then camouflaged according to the country in which they were situated. In the case of those to the WEST of the STRIP, kunai grass was festooned all over them with small bundles standing upright in front, while at the EASTERN end near the 'Y' were covered with coconut leaves – bits of scrub and heaps of fallen coconuts or husks. In most cases the loopholes were hidden to view by the screen of bush or camouflage, although vision from inside out was still possible, and in nearly every case the pillbox or emplacement was not discovered until you were right on to it. The openings were difficult to see from the front and only in two cases – those near the bridge – were they located, nor could the width or size of the loopholes be ascertained. Able to get arty fire on them directed from OP: No indirect MG fire yet arranged.[21]

Meanwhile, Lieutenant Arthur Tregarthen and his 11-man patrol, who were still out to the north-west in the swampland, reported that they had now occupied a small 'island' within the swamp. The company adjutant concluded for the end of November that the company

CHAPTER 19

strength was now 11 offices and 90 other ranks, with two officers and 25 men sick. Most of the sick would be evacuated back to Moresby – they would not be the last. It records: 'A form of swamp fever seems to be main ailment – Unit is holding position in waterlogged area …. No relief can be obtained. Hot meals still being sent fwd. to troops in F.D.Ls. Warm day – quiet clear night'.[22]

Major Harry Harcourt was not happy with the role his commandos were playing in the current campaign. Attached to the 128th Regiment, he took his orders from McCoy, and Harcourt wrote in his report for operations in late November: 'When issue was joined near Cape Endaiadere, the Coy was used more or less as infantry. There was little chance of employing any other tactics in the role we were given. The only part in which we may have operated in an independent manner was on the coast towards Cape Endaiadere where the Jap pillboxes or machinegun emplacements may have been broken down by [our] cutting-out tactics. Permission to attempt this towards the Cape or towards the Bridge west of New Strip was refused because US Inf. had been allotted these fronts.'[23]

* * *

By the end of the day, the situation for Warren Force was precarious. Despite repeated attacks, the Japanese line was intact. In the two weeks since the 32nd Division had marched out so confidently on the Japanese positions at Buna, it had sustained close to 500 battle casualties, but they had yet to penetrate any part of the Japanese perimeter. It was obvious that something would have to be done to intensify the attack. Harding again was in desperate need of the Australian tanks of the 2/6th Armoured Regiment at Milne Bay.[24]

That night, Harding recorded in his diary: 'Reports from Hale and Mott on the day's operations chalked up some progress on the right flank and a substantial gain on the left. Mott's attack had gone clear through to the outskirts of Buna and had overcome a considerable area in which the Japanese defenders of the place had been living.

BLOODY BUNA

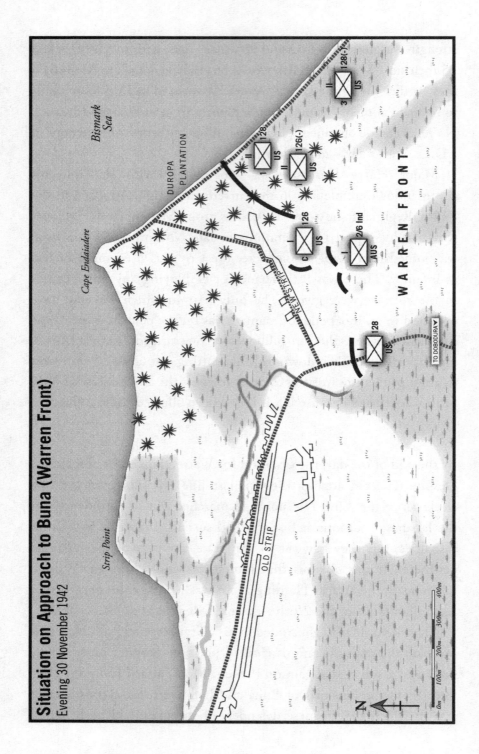

CHAPTER 19

He reported many Japs killed and fairly heavy casualties on our side. I asked Mott what he posed to do for the next day, and he told me he intended to devote it to reorganising his units and getting set for another push on the day after. I okayed this proposal'.[25]

* * *

In response to the Emperor's demand on 28 November that Buna be defended to the last man, Corporal Tanaka, with Colonel Yamamoto Hiroshi's force, wrote what he believed would be his final letter to his comrades that morning: 'Thank you very much for your personal and public co-operation. Enemy attacks have been heavy from 19 November. Today, Battalion Commander Yamamoto and subordinates organised a suicide squad. Guard Leader Hujita and four men are included. Death is the ultimate honour. After my comrades and I are dead, please bury us in your leisure time. I ask this because it is dishonourable to remain unburied. Please take care of your health and serve your country. I regret to say that Section Leader Nakayama is missing, and we have no information regarding his whereabouts. Enemy trench mortar fire is increasing in intensity, so I shall close. My best regards to you. Time 07.00. 30 November'.[26]

Likely close by was unnamed Japanese soldier [C], who was now part of Colonel Yamamoto Hiroshi's force dug-in around the New Strip and plantation area. He recorded in his diary: 'Monday. Fair. From early morning the enemy bombed us. All along the front enemy scouts approaching. Seems like the enemy has received light MG's, and it seems that cannons have arrived too, for there are bursts, but there is no firing heard. It is also lively at night'.[27]

* * *

At Rabaul, in late November, the Japanese *18th Army Headquarters* estimated there were around 10,000 troops deployed in the Buna, Sanananda and Gona beachheads. A plan of supply was issued, with expectations of a renewed advance to capture Port Moresby.[28]

Japanese victory fever was clearly still prevalent within the high command.

Outline of resupply plan for the Buna area:

1. Policy

    Quickly strengthen supply to the *South Seas Force*, restore the fighting strength of the troops, and make preparations to reactivate the invasion of Port Moresby.

2. Outline

    1. First, carry out land operations in the Buna sector. While applying reinforcement units, carry out transport of supplies of food for the *South Seas Force* and strengthen Buna as a supply base. It is assumed that the Buna sector requires supplies for approximately 10,000 men. Supplies will be loaded on vessels used for landing operations sufficient to supply these troops for one month. If these operations are successful, sufficient supplies for three months will be successively advanced to the area.

    2. The Buna base will be strengthened in preparation for a future assault against Port Moresby. In addition, new bases will be established near the mouth of the Mambare River, Zaka, and Morobe. A new line of communication will be established from Zaka sector to Port Moresby.[29]

20
'WANT YOU TO TAKE BUNA, OR NOT COME BACK ALIVE'

Earlier that day, 30 November 1942, General Douglas MacArthur had sent his chief of staff, Major General Richard Sutherland, to meet with Lieutenant General Herring commanding Advanced NGF at Popondetta; he was also to meet with Major General Harding to directly observe the situation at the Buna.[1]

Herring had established that even with his advanced headquarters at the front the previous day and with Harding's communique of 28 November, he still remained largely ignorant of the troop disposition in the Buna sector. Herring sent his senior liaison officer, Lieutenant Colonel William Robertson, a 25-year-old university student from Melbourne, to visit Harding. Herring himself would soon make his own way to Harding's headquarters on hearing of Sutherland's imminent arrival there.[2]

Robertson flew to Dobodura and saw few signs of life as he looked about the airstrip. Then a wisp of smoke curling among the trees on the edge of the field attracted him. As he approached, he could see an American GI bending over a fire and stirring a pot. Robertson soon came across a colonel who informed him that Harding was just down the track and would be along soon. But he had a long wait before Harding appeared, and when he did arrive, the general could provide little details of his infantry positions. He explained that he was quite out of touch with his forward troops. Nor could his signals officer give him much hope that communications would be restored any time soon, saying that the signallers had found the going too hard to carry the divisional headquarters wireless set and had thrown it into the bush some kilometres back.

Robertson was astonished and dismayed and soon reported his impressions to Herring on his arrival at the Buna sector. Indeed, as he was making his report, Sutherland arrived and both Herring and MacArthur's chief of staff listened gravely to the Australian officer. Robertson's report would soon confirm Sutherland's own views and likely accounted in some measure for the grave report he would provide MacArthur on his return to Port Moresby that afternoon.[3]

Harding had already expressed his dissatisfaction to Herring about the temporary allocation of his 126th Regiment to Major General Vasey, who was commanding the Australian 7th Division. He had also requested that at least one battalion of the 127th Regiment be sent to him. Harding recorded in his diary:

> The chief topic we discussed was the bringing in of part or all of the 127th Infantry. In one of his letters to me, General Herring had stated that he disapproved of previous requests that part or all of the regiment be thrown in, on the ground that we had plenty of reserves. I explained, somewhat heatedly, that we had no reserves, and I argued to the best of my ability for additional troops, not to relieve those in the line, but to strike in another quarter. General Herring remained unconvinced of the need or desirability of the proposed move despite all my protestations ….
>
> I tried to give Herring the picture by letter, radio, and finally face to face, but he never seemed to get it. He was a gentleman … a scholar, and a pretty good guy withal, but his heart, I am sure, was with the Australians. He seemed to take an almost detached view of the trials and tribulations of my all-American contingent. I felt all along that he had very little scope for independent decision.[4]

CHAPTER 20

The three senior officers were now gathered at Harding's headquarters discussing the situation. Sutherland agreed with Herring that the 127th Regiment was to remain in Port Moresby for the time being. He too argued that issues of supply made their movement to Buna impracticable, stressing that the troops already in the area were taxing the air force to the utmost. Harding himself had expressed such concerns in his letter to Herring of the previous day. Sutherland stated that it would be unwise to bring in more troops until a stockpile had been built up at Dobodura. Even so, Harding requested that at least one battalion of regiment be brought forward to strike in a new sector, but Sutherland was adamant. The supply situation would have to be resolved before such a move could be considered.[5]

Harding also recorded in his diary: 'Another matter which came up for discussion was the 126th Infantry force operation with the Australians west of the Girua River [Sanananda sector]. Sutherland said something to the effect that Tomlinson wasn't acting aggressively. I remarked that if they would return him to my command, I felt sure that I could get plenty of aggressive action out of him .... General Herring and General Sutherland both gave me the brush-off on this proposal'.[6]

At the close of the discussion, Herring flew back to Popondetta, while Sutherland stayed for lunch. Harding now again pressed Sutherland about the 127th Regiment, recording in his diary: 'I asked if the Australians were going to use it on the other side of the river. His reply was startling. He said that that had been discussed, and that Blamey had spoken disparagingly of the fighting qualities of the American troops and told MacArthur that he preferred to use his militia brigade in that quarter. He had also dropped one or two remarks to the effect that the Americans weren't showing the fight they should. I told him that anyone who thought that didn't know the facts – that while we hadn't made much progress, it wasn't because we weren't in there fighting, and I reminded him that our casualties would testify to the hard fighting that had been going on'.[7]

BLOODY BUNA

While General Blamey had indeed spoken disparagingly to MacArthur of the performance of the 32d Division, MacArthur and his staff had for months now been telling all who would listen, especially those in Washington, that the Australians were performing dismally against the Japanese since their invasion of Gona and Buna in July 1942. He sent communique after communique to Washington about the poor quality of the Australian troops, who were fighting and dying along the Kokoda Track, while MacArthur and his staff were comfortably ensconced in Brisbane, seemingly ignorant of events playing themselves out along the track. Indeed, MacArthur only seemed to become actively involved in the fighting in Papua soon after the Australians launched their northward thrust from Ioribaiwa Ridge just north of Port Moresby in late September, which would see them reach the Japanese beachheads by mid November.[8]

The conversation between MacArthur and Blamey had taken place just days before at Government House, which was General MacArthur's headquarters at Port Moresby. Major General George Kenney, who was then commanding the Allied Air Force and who had been present (and had made a note of Blamey's remarks), felt that it had been 'a bitter pill for General MacArthur to swallow'.[9] It must have been, for it was about this time, as General Kenney recalled, that General MacArthur 'began to be worried about the calibre of his infantry'.[10]

The American official history, states that American troops were refusing to fight, even recording that some men had thrown away their weapons and fled in panic from the Japanese. Such reports had by now already reached MacArthur's headquarters. Other American reports noted that the troops and their officers lacked aggressiveness, that many of the junior leaders did not seem to know their business, and that 'too many' commanders were trying to conduct operations from a CP far behind the frontlines. The American official historian also recorded that at least one report stated: 'The 32nd Division would not fight'.[11] MacArthur's ongoing derogatory remarks about the lack

CHAPTER 20

of fighting ability of the Australian troops was now coming back to haunt him. Matters also came to a head when Colonel David Larr, deputy to Brigadier Stephen Chamberlin, who was part of MacArthur's staff, visited the front on 27 and 28 November and returned to Port Moresby with an extremely unfavourable report on the situation at Buna.[12]

Sutherland mentioned Larr's report to Harding during their lunch, telling him that MacArthur had sent for Lieutenant General Eichelberger and would probably order him to the front. Sutherland asked Harding whether he intended to make any changes in his top command, perhaps trying to give Harding a lifeline. His two field commanders, colonels John Mott and Tracy Hale, were not highly regarded by the senior officers of I Corps and GHQ. Harding confessed that Mott had a talent for 'antagonising superiors, subordinates, and contemporaries,' and that Hale lacked abilities as a regimental commander. Even so, he replied he had no plans to remove either of them from their commands, and he defended his commanders, stating that Mott was doing an excellent job on Urbana front and, while he 'questioned whether Hale had the qualifications to lead a regiment in battle,' he considered he was 'doing fairly well in the only chance he had had to show his stuff'.[13]

Harding recorded in his diary at the time that Hale – being his last regimental commander from the National Guard, in a division where the bulk of the officers were from the Guard – should be given a chance and more time to demonstrate his abilities, especially since Lieutenant Colonel Alexander MacNab, who was on the ground, could be trusted to 'keep him out of trouble'.[14]

Harding's refusal to reshuffle his command structure was likely enough for Sutherland, who on returning to Port Moresby that afternoon recommended to MacArthur that Harding be relieved of his command. It is also possible that Blamey had shared a letter with MacArthur that Herring had penned to him, which stated in part: 'I think it is fair to say that 32 US Div. has still not realised that the enemy will only be beaten by hard fighting, and that while bombing, strafing, mortars and artillery may soften his resistance to some extent, the men who are left will fight it out and will have to be taken out and killed in hard fighting. This I was at pains to explain to Harding this morning. He is anxious to have more men but still hasn't really made anything like full use of the men he has …. On the east side [Girua River] there does not seem to have been any really organised plan but just a lot of what Gen Vasey calls milling around. The organisation of HQ is worse than primitive'.[15]

Indeed, in Port Moresby, MacArthur was frustrated by the ongoing failures; nowhere had his forces been able to achieve any breakthroughs. In the two weeks since they had started forward, the 32nd Division had lost 492 men in battle with nothing to show for the sacrifice: 82 killed, 325 wounded, 85 missing – most of those listed as missing would be recorded as killed in action. The main Japanese line was still unbreeched. At Sanananda and Gona, the strength of the Australians was waning fast.[16]

The Australians had already been fighting the Japanese for months now, involved in significant battles along and the Kokoda Track, and the northern slopes around Oivi. They were in desperate need of rest, reinforcements, along with reorganisation and resupply. Any other troops would have been pulled out of the line before the battles for the beachheads, but NGF had no choice – these were the only Australian troops immediately available. It would not be long, however, before the veterans of the Australian 18th Brigade would be brought forward from Milne Bay to conduct the spearhead attacks to finally take Buna, and soon after Sanananda.[17]

* * *

Earlier that morning, Lieutenant General Eichelberger and his staff had boarded two C-47 transport aircraft for Port Moresby that morning, and, after an uneventful flight over the Coral Sea, landed at Seven Mile Airdrome in the afternoon. They were met at the airstrip

CHAPTER 20

by Colonel Larr, who told Eichelberger that he would be given four or five days to be briefed on the situation at Buna before he and his staff would be sent over the mountains.[18]

Eichelberger and Byers were given quarters at Government House, MacArthur's headquarters. It was a comfortable sprawling place, which in pre-war days had been the official residence of the lieutenant governor of Papua. They had scarcely arrived when they were ordered to report to immediately to MacArthur. The two senior officers found MacArthur with Kenney and Sutherland on the long breezy veranda at the front of the house.[19] Eichelberger later wrote of his meeting with MacArthur in his memoirs, *Our Jungle Road to Tokyo*:

> Byers and I were conducted to a sweeping veranda where General Sutherland sat at a desk, grave-faced. He had just flown back over the Owen Stanley Mountains from Dobodura, and it was plain that his report on conditions at Buna was responsible for my abrupt summons. General MacArthur was striding up and down the long veranda. General Kenney, whose planes were to do so much to make the ultimate victory possible, was the only man who greeted me with a smile. There were no preliminaries.
>
> 'Bob,' said General MacArthur in a grim voice, 'I'm putting you in command at Buna. Relieve Harding. I am sending you in, Bob, and I want you to remove all officers who won't fight. Relieve regimental and battalion commanders; if necessary, put sergeants in charge of battalions and corporals in charge of companies – anyone who will fight. Time is of the essence; the Japs may land reinforcements any night.'
>
> General MacArthur strode down the breezy veranda again. He said he had reports that American soldiers were throwing away their weapons and running from the enemy. Then

he stopped short and spoke with emphasis. He wanted no misunderstandings about my assignment. 'Bob,' he said, 'I want you to take Buna, or not come back alive.' He paused a moment, and then, without looking at Byers, pointed a finger. 'And that goes for your chief of staff too. Do you understand?'

'Yes, sir,' I said.[20]

MacArthur went on to inform Eichelberger that given the urgency of the situation, he and his staff were to fly to the front the very next morning. At some point, MacArthur informed Eichelberger that he would find his force: 'Strong in the rear areas and weak in the forward areas'.[21] Subsequent briefings and conferences lasted long into the night. In the morning, immediately after breakfast, Eichelberger and his staff would depart for Buna.[22]

PART 2
STALEMATE

21

'AT THE BREAK OF DAWN, THE ENEMY CHARGED'

During the morning of 1 December, Lieutenant General Eichelberger and his staff prepared to board their transport aircraft for Buna. He recalled meeting General MacArthur earlier that morning: 'After breakfast he put an arm around my shoulders and led me into his office. "If you capture Buna", the Allied commander said, "I'll give you a Distinguished Service Cross and recommend you for a high British decoration. Also, he continued, referring to the complete anonymity under which all American commanders in that theatre functioned, "I'll release your name for newspaper publication"'.[1]

Eichelberger landed at Dobodura at 9.58 am, and by 1 pm, he had assumed command of all American troops in the Buna Area. Major General Harding, who had been writing a letter to Major General Sutherland when Eichelberger arrived, noted in his diary that night: 'Eichelberger had come fresh from the presence of MacArthur who had given him an earful of instructions concerning what he, Eichelberger, was expected to do. First of all, he was to take command of American troops in the sector. I wasn't sure just where that left me, but I gathered MacArthur was much dissatisfied with [the] way things were going. Among other things, he had told Eichelberger that he was to take Buna or die before it. Eichelberger expressed his intention of finding out for himself how things were going. I told him that I was glad to hear him say that, for I felt that he would find that the men were doing a good job under exceedingly difficult conditions'.[2]

After explaining how MacArthur felt about the situation, Eichelberger asked Harding what changes he proposed making in his command to get things moving. When Harding confirmed he intended on relieving no one and that most of his commanders deserved to be decorated not relieved, Eichelberger pushed the matter no further and left for Dobodura, to find out what he could there, and inspect the front the following day. Two of his staff officers – Colonel Clarence Martin, his Operations Officer, and Colonel Gordon Rogers, his Intelligence Officer – would, the following morning, make their way to Warren front to observe the fighting there, while Eichelberger, Harding and a few others would make their way to Urbana front to observe the fighting in that sector.[3]

That night, Eichelberger wrote to Sutherland that judging from what he heard during the day, things were not as bad as he had been led to believe – however, he would not hold this view for long. Colonel John Mott was reporting progress and said his men were within a hundred metres of Buna Village. Eichelberger referred to a conversation he had that day with Brigadier Ronald Hopkins, a 45-year-old regular soldier from Stawell in Victoria, who was chief of staff to Lieutenant General Herring. Hopkins, he said, had stated that Herring wanted Buna Mission taken and was not particularly interested in the capture of Buna Village.

Eichelberger recalled: 'I told him that I had directed, prior to seeing him, that Buna Village be captured tonight, and while I was anxious to get in Buna Mission, I did not want to leave the force in Buna Village on our front and rear. I shall go forward in the morning to gain first-hand knowledge of the situation'. While he was not willing to admit anything, Eichelberger said, until he had 'personally surveyed the situation well forward', he felt that he could already recommend the dispatch to the beachhead of 'at least one battalion

CHAPTER 21

less two companies of the 127th Infantry, because we may need a fresh impetus to carry into Buna Village'.[4]

* * *

On Warren front, Lieutenant Colonel Robert McCoy and his men of the I/128th Regiment were stuck near the water's edge. It was decided the next day that an attack by Lieutenant Colonel Edmund Carrier and his men of the I/126th Regiment towards New Strip would coincide with an attempt to push forward across the bridge between the two air strips by Lieutenant Carl Fryday and his men of 'I' Company, III/128th Regiment, supported by Major Harry Harcourt and the survivors of his commandos of the 2/6th Independent Company.[5]

Harding had already concluded that to attack Cape Endaiadere and New Strip simultaneously was unwise, as the attacks from the eastern end of New Strip were on divergent lines. He now shifted the main attack to New Strip. At 10.45 am that morning, he ordered Colonel Tracy Hale and his men of the 128th Regiment to stop pressing the attack on Cape Endaiadere, next day they were to support Carrier in an attack against New Strip. The men of 'B' Company, I/128th Regiment were to remain in position about 900 metres south of Cape Endaiadere and from there they were to launch several feints to deceive the Japanese. Meanwhile, McCoy and the remainder of his troops of the I/128th Regiment would attack New Strip in support of Carrier and his men. Their object was essentially exploratory, to discover a weak point in the Japanese line and to 'go all out' if it found a hole.[6]

Meanwhile, the men of 'A' Company, I/128th Regiment, with 'B' Company, I/126th Regiment, and what was left of 'C' Company, I/128th Regiment would launch an east-west attack from the coastal flank towards the aircraft dispersal bays off the eastern end of the airstrip. At the other end of the strip, 'A' Company, I/126th Regiment would join Lieutenant Fryday and his men of 'I' Company, III/128th Regiment in an attack on the bridge between the strips. Finally, Captain Rossall Belmer and his advance party of Australian commandos, 2/6th Independent Company, would patrol the area facing the strip, tasked with maintaining contact with the forces attacking either other end. The drive from east to west would be under command of McCoy; that from south to north, under Carrier.[7]

The 2/6th Independent Company received verbal instructions from the headquarters of the 128th Regiment regarding the next day's scheduled attack against the bridge between the two strips and defences at the western end of New Strip. Allied airmen would bomb and strafe the area north and north-west of the bridge, followed by an artillery barrage and mortar bombardment of bridge and Japanese defences adjacent to it and the timber east and west. Smoke bombs would be dropped by guns and mortars to help cover the advance of the infantry. The men of 'I' Company, III/128 Regiment would also be reinforced with 'A' Company, I/128th Regiment. The American troops were to form up before the barrage and behind the smoke screen as the bombarded ceased at 8.45 am.[8]

The 2/6th Independent Company war diary concludes with the tasks of the commandos: 'To have one patrol on LEFT of Inf. protecting them from attack from timber in SW corner ... (BLAINEY detailed for this task) and the remainder on RIGHT to advance in and neutralise enemy action from edge of timber behind pillboxes to E. of bridge (FIELDING & SCOTT detailed for this)'.[9]

Indeed, smoke bombs were used by the artillery to also range in on Japanese targets, as high explosive shells were difficult to observe. Forward artillery observers would go out to the front and from the flank's range in the guns and quickly walk the shells onto the Japanese targets, before a full barrage was put down.[10]

That day, Harcourt recalled how an American officer approached him and asked him about his laundry unit because he wanted his uniform cleaned as he had heard that Lieutenant General Eichelberger was due to arrive soon. Harcourt pointed him down a track to where

CHAPTER 21

the officer would find his commandos 50 metres away washing themselves in a creek, informing the American he was free to join them.[11]

*　*　*

That day, Japanese Lieutenant Suganuma, who was with Colonel Yamamoto Hiroshi's force, was now in the Coconut Grove, near New Strip; he recorded in his diary: 'The enemy scouts which have been bothering us all night quit their activities about two hours before dawn. The day is slowly dawning. The night of strain has passed. Thought of clearing the field of fire in front of position which I have been planning for several days and put the whole squad out under sufficient protection, but after a few minutes of work, three enemy scouts opened fire. SHIMIZU MASAYUKI hit in chest. About 1600 in front of 3rd MG squad, enemy troops infiltrated. They were fired upon; NAMIDA wounded'.[12]

Corporal Tanaka, at Warren front, who had just days before written what he thought would be his last letter, was still alive, and he penned another to a friend at 8 am that morning – this would be his last letter: 'I was able to stand up against the enemy trench mortar fire. At about 05.00, there was heavy mortar and artillery fire. At the break of dawn, the enemy charged. We repulsed them once. Later, the attack was intensified, and it is now merely a case of waiting for death. Most of the officers have been killed, so there isn't much we can do …. We have not eaten for over a week and have no energy. As soldiers, we are ready to die gallantly. Take care of yourself and do your best. Excuse my hasty writing'.[13]

Close by would have been unnamed Japanese soldier [C], who was also part of Yamamoto's force dug-in around New Strip and the plantation area. He recorded in his diary: 'Tuesday. Fair. Enemy appeared about 50 metres in front in line of sweeping fire and fired from left to right. I chose a large silhouette of the enemy and fired and saw one fall. At night, the enemy still remained. Placed in emergency alert positions. They throw three hand grenades. There was no damage'.[14]

* * *

The night before and early morning hours of 1 December had been an uneasy one for the men of Urbana Force. The Australian 25-pounders and the mortars had laid down fire on Buna Village. However, only a few unarmed Japanese were observed to have been killed, trying to get back to their headquarters, which was already occupied by the Americans. These enemy troops were likely trying to recover some of the food and weapons left there. There was little action during the night, but the exhausted troops from both sides were expecting counterattacks, so few likely got any real rest.[15]

That morning, the men of Urbana Force made another attempt to take Buna Village. Detachments from both headquarters' companies of the 126th and 128th regiments, and a section of machine guns from 'H' Company, II/126th Regiment were sent forward to reinforce 'E' Company, II/126th Infantry. They were to move on Buna Village through the relatively open area just south of the bridge over Girua River, instead of directly up the main track. The attempt was preceded by a barrage from the Australian 25-pounders at Ango and from all the available 60-mm and 81-mm mortars now in battery – the latter under Captain Harold Hantlemann, 'H' Company, II/126th Regiment. Initially, the fighting went well, with several bunkers knocked out. Then, just as the troops were at the point of breaking through 'E' Company, instead of pressing the attack, withdrew. Whether they did so because there was a mix-up in signals or because the men were 'jumpy', Colonel John Mott was unable to say.[16]

* * *

Manning the Urbana front, Japanese 1st Class Mechanic, Kuba Satonao, with the *Japanese Imperial Navy Tsukioka Transport Unit*,

CHAPTER 21

recorded in his diary: 'Our troops are expected to come in today, but I have doubts. Two thousand at BASABURA; there seems to have been an aerial fight. Four destroyers may have entered Buna. A few enemy appeared in front of us; we took up positions'.[17]

22

'HAVE YOU TAKEN OUT THE TRIANGLE YET?'

During the morning of 2 December, colonels Clarence Martin and Gordon Rogers, as planned, made their way towards Warren Force while Lieutenant General Eichelberger, Major General Harding and Brigadier Albert Waldron made their way to Urbana front to observe the fighting with Colonel John Mott.[1]

* * *

Warren Force's right flank was anchored near the water's edge and its left near New Strip. Lieutenant Colonel Robert McCoy, commanding the I/128th Regiment, left 'B' Company immediately south of the Cape Endaiadere position to conduct several feints along the track to keep the Japanese occupied. The rest of his men would probe towards the eastern end of New Strip, with Lieutenant Colonel Edmund Carrier supplying him 'A' Company, I/126th Regiment in support. At the same time, the companies just south of the bridge between the airstrips would attack north and north-west. McCoy would command the east-west advance, while Carrier would command the advance from the south. Major Harry Harcourt and his Australian commandos would again link the two attacking groups. One of their patrols, under Lieutenant Gordon Blainey, would operate on Carrier's extreme left, south-west of the bridge. These attacks were to be supported by artillery, mortar and aerial bombardment.[2]

As planned, the air strafing and bombing of Buna Village, New Strip, and the bridge between the strips commenced at 8 am, lasting for around 15 minutes. Most of the bombs hit the target area, but

CHAPTER 22

the last flight, however, forgot to drop flares (the prearranged signal that the bombing was complete), and the artillery and mortars waited some time before realising the strike had finished. As such, their bombardment commenced sometime after the aircraft had departed. The troops, who had pulled back temporarily to avoid being hit by friendly fire, did not jump off until after 9 am, but by then, the Japanese were ready and waiting. The Allied troops made little progress, as Colonel Yamamoto Hiroshi and his men had not been taken in by the feint of 'B' Company towards Cape Endaiadere. When the bombing began, they had taken shelter in their earthen bunkers, and when it was over, they emerged and laid down concentrated fire, forcing the Americans and Australians to ground.[3]

During the day's fighting, Sergeant Delmar Daniels, with I/128th Regiment, led three volunteers against a Japanese strongpoint near the dispersal bays at the eastern end of New Strip, which had held up the advance for some time. He was killed, as he unsuccessfully attempted to finally clear out the Japanese position. Sergeant Daniels was awarded the DSC posthumously for his actions that day.[4]

The results of the day's fighting were not encouraging. The heat was intense, and there were as many casualties from heat exhaustion as from Japanese fire. The troops on McCoy's front knocked out only a few bunkers before they were forced to ground. On Carrier's front, the troops initially made small gains but were also stopped in their turn by machinegun enfilade from positions in the western part of the strongpoint between the strips. The regimental adjutant recorded: 'The attack is continued – "A" Company meets heavy machinegun fire and "B" Company meets mortar fire. There is heavy allied air bombardment of enemy positions'.[5]

In the centre, linking the two American flank attacks, was Harcourt and his commandos. He had sent forward his advanced party under Captain Rossall Belmer. Earlier that morning, Belmer was reinforced with Lieutenant Arthur Tregarthen and his section, who had returned from the south-west patrol earlier that morning. Lieutenant Gordon Blainey and his section was on the left, while Tregarthen and his men were in the centre, with Belmer, Lieutenant Geoffrey Fielding and Lieutenant Robert Scott on the left. Scott and his section were just behind the exploding smoke screen, with Fielding and his men behind, in support.[6]

The commando unit war diary records that at 9 am the American infantry moved forward to their staging point, waiting for the smoke barrage to cease. Blainey's patrol was in the timber on the left and moved forward as the Americans advanced until they were about 150 metres off the Japanese forward defences. Then several enemy machineguns opened fire, tearing into their ranks, and here the advance stalled. The company adjutant recorded the situation at this point: 'BLAINEY on the LEFT moved through bush to a position within 30 yds., in rear of S. end of defences S. of BRIDGE. Here patrol came under accurate MG fire from an emplacement facing to the rear – roughly S. to W. and patrol was held up. Attempts to throw hand grenades into emplacement drew heavy fire'.[7]

Nearby, Captain Rossall Belmer was trying to find a way forward for his men, and it was now that this gallant officer was killed by a Japanese sniper in a tree overlooking the line of advance. Lieutenant Geoffrey Fielding took over. On the right, Scott and his men engaged the pillboxes with rifle and light machinegun fire but could not break through the enemy defences. At around 9.50 am, the commandos observed the American infantry withdrawing. An hour later, Blainey was unable to see any Americans to his left and sent out a runner to contact them, but the runner was killed. It was not long before the artillery was firing close to their position, and Fielding was forced to withdraw.[8]

* * *

Meanwhile, Martin and Rogers had reached Colonel Tracy Hale's headquarters at Hariko at around noon, after catching a lift part of

CHAPTER 22

the way to Simemi in a jeep. They left Hariko at 2.10 pm and at 3.30 pm reached McCoy's CP. After a short discussion, they went forward with Lieutenant Colonel Alexander MacNab, the executive officer of Warren Force, to the area off the eastern end of New Strip. By the time the senior officers arrived, the action had died down to virtually nothing. They would soon after report that there was no firing, with Martin recalling there were times when the front was 'as quiet as the inside of an empty church'.[9]

Having beaten off a succession of American attacks, the Japanese were resting. They were seen to not even fire at targets in full view – it was also noticed that this also applied to the American troops just opposite the Japanese. These men were now focused on bring up supplies and preparing for the next day's attack. Although Martin admitted 'in the light of subsequent knowledge' that the attacks could not succeed, even had they been 'continued throughout the day with the utmost vigour and daring', the total absence of fighting when the inspection team reached the front led them to incorrectly question whether there had been any fighting at all that day.[10]

These officers were especially struck by the poor physical condition of the men. Rogers was critical of Hale for remaining too far behind the lines, while Martin was critical that unsanitary conditions had been allowed to develop at the front. He recalled seeing a great deal of unnecessary litter, quantities of un-salvaged equipment, and piles of empty ration tins swarming about with flies.[11]

By 5 pm, Martin and Rogers arrived back at McCoy's CP and left on foot for the rear at 6.20 pm, not reaching Dobodura and Eichelberger's headquarters until 10 pm. On arriving they would learn of a major shakeup in the command structure of the 32nd Division which had been implemented on Eichelberger's return from Urbana front.[12]

* * *

That day, unknown Japanese soldier [E] – who had landed at Buna with Colonel Yamamoto Hiroshi and his force, consisting of reinforcements of the *144th Regiment*, along with the men of the *III/229th Regiment*, who were then positioned in the plantation and at the north-east end of New Strip – recorded in his diary: 'Bombings in the morning. Severe mortar fire morning and afternoon. Concentrated fire around shelters. YOSHIKAWA wounded by shell fragment. AIZU also wounded by shell fragment. KUCHIKI wounded by bullet. YOSHIKAWA severely wounded, the rest have only slight wounds. YOSHIKAWA sent to the rear'.[13]

Nearby would have been Japanese Lieutenant Suganuma and his platoon also with Yamamoto's force, dug-in around the Coconut Grove near New Strip: 'From early morning, enemy planes flew over. In formations of three, three combinations and four groups flew over. They bombed and strafed us as usual, and with this there were a few mortar and infantry guns firing. In co-ordination with this, the enemy ground troops opened fire heavily. They could not be seen, only rifle firing heard. Four or five seen on edge of field of fire clearing. Withdrew after heavy MG and mortar. Following this there was concentrated mortar and mountaingun fire. They fired several hundred rounds continuously until I thought they would run out of shells. One enemy mountaingun shell exploded between the 2nd and 3rd squad near the Coconut Grove. 3rd squad is resisting enemy ground forces'.[14]

*　*　*

Eichelberger, accompanied by his aide, Captain Daniel Edwards, along with Harding, Waldron and several others, had left Dobodura for Urbana front at 9.30 am. They only got a short distance by jeep; the rest of the way they had to slog along the main track to Mott's headquarters. Harding recorded in his diary: 'Leaving the jeep, we proceeded on foot by a tortuous and poorly marked footpath through the jungle towards Mott's CP. Just about the time we started

CHAPTER 22

walking, the artillery opened up behind us, firing at Buna. Our walk was made to the accompaniment of guns firing behind us, shells passing overhead exploding somewhere to our front'.[15]

Eichelberger stopped at the aid station where he found several unwounded men who had been sent to the rear for a few days to recover from dengue fever or exhaustion. Some had 'cracked up in combat'.[16] Eichelberger questioned these men closely as to why they were not at the front, with the most common answer being: 'They had been sent to the rear for a rest, and the same answer was given by two or three other unwounded individuals closer to the front, who either were dozing at the roots of trees or were on their way to the aid station'.[17]

Meanwhile, Mott had telephoned Lieutenant Colonel Smith, who was commanding the II/128th Regiment. Smith recalled vividly this conversation to the American official historian Samuel Milner in 1950. Clearly, the growing animosity between these two officers was palpable:

Mott: 'Have you taken out the Triangle yet?'

Smith: 'No, Sir! We have been following your orders, which were to keep patrolling aggressively to deceive the Japs as to our strength and intentions.'

Mott: 'Now long will it take you to take out the Triangle?'

Smith: 'That I cannot say. If you order us to attack, we will do the best we can, but I cannot say how long it will take.'

Mott: 'I want you to tell me how long it will take you to take out the Triangle.'

Smith: 'Obviously, I cannot answer that.'

Mott: 'Then I'll tell you! Either you take out the Triangle by two o'clock this afternoon or be prepared to go to the rear.'[18]

Smith went on to conclude: 'Since I was unable to take out the Triangle with the 25 men then available, I would very probably have been relieved that day except for the fact that General Eichelberger chose this time to make his first visit to the Urbana front CP. There he found that the reports Mott had been sending in were grossly exaggerated, if not deliberately falsified…'.[19]

Eichelberger, Harding and Waldron reached Mott's CP at around 11.40 am. At this point, the Australian artillery ceased firing, and it was hoped that the bunkers holding up the advance had finally been destroyed. Harding recorded in his diary: 'Shortly after our arrival at the CP, the artillery stopped, and we heard the yells of the men as they followed it with a charge. Then we waited, hoping a report would come back in a short time that the town [village] had been taken …. When word did come in, an hour or so later, we learned that the Japs had emerged from their dugouts in time to lay bands of machinegun fire across the front to stop the attack. The artillery preparations, splendid though it was, had not blasted out the bunker that was the key to the Japanese defences of the line we were attacking'.[20]

Mott had available for the attack the men of 'E' and 'H' companies, and as promised the Cannon Company, 126th Regiment, along with a platoon of 'F' Company, II/128th Regiment, which he had ordered up from the other side of the Girua River. He also had eight additional mortars that Harding had rushed up to him. The artillery provided a concentrated bombardment on the identified Japanese bunker positions, which had been holding up the advance followed by the mortar teams blasting the same positions. The artillery fire was accurate, and the mortar barrage intense and well placed. As soon as the Americans attempted to advance, however, they were stopped by heavy streams of enfilade across their approach. During the fighting here, Captain Harold Hantlemann and Lieutenant James Hunt, with the Headquarters Company, were recognised for their gallantry. Hunt, at his own request, led a platoon against the village; both officers were awarded the DSC.[21]

CHAPTER 22

Now weakened by fever and suffering from hunger and exhaustion, the men were in a bad way. Mott observed that the men were suffering from the ongoing fighting, lack of food, and lack of sleep, as well as from 'the long marches and short rations on which they had been subsisting even before the fighting started'.[22] An entry that day in the journal of the II/126th Regiment made just after the Japanese had repulsed 'E' Company's fifth attack on Buna, reads: 'The troops that we have left are weak and tired and need rest and reinforcement'.[23] It was clear that until these men were reinforced and provided with much-needed rest and reorganisation, it would be impossible for them to close the last few hundred metres between them and Buna Village.[24]

With the news of another failure, Eichelberger announced that he was going forward to see for himself how things were. He ordered Waldron to remain at the CP while he went up the line. Harding, who refused to remain behind, went with him. The Japanese, after repulsing several attacks, were not firing, and the two generals were able to inspect the frontline without drawing any fire.[25]

As they approached the frontline, Harding recalled that Eichelberger became increasingly critical – he found a great deal to be angry about. He had been told, and had reported in good faith to NGF, that there had been a strong Japanese counterattack. On questioning Major Smith, commanding the II/126th Regiment, however, Eichelberger discovered that there had been no counterattack, only a feeble attempt by a few Japanese to get back into the main kunai strip south-east of the village. Eichelberger noticed both light and heavy machine guns were positioned in the open, and not dug-in or concealed. He was angry on discovering that the frontline troops, though hungry, had not been permitted to cook captured rice, as it might have drawn enemy fire from the smoke arising from the wet timber. He assessed that lack of aggressiveness kept the troops from firing, and he was further angered when he asked for volunteers to see what lay immediately ahead; the men he spoke to did not respond.[26]

Indeed, while the general was questioning these men, he also interviewed three machine gunners who informed him that they knew that there was an enemy machine gun close by, which had fired on the troops who tried to advance. Eichelberger asked if any of them had gone down the track since then to see if the Japanese were still there. The men replied, 'No'.[27] Eichelberger then offered to decorate any man who would go forward 50 metres to find out the situation there. Again, no one volunteered. Instead, Eichelberger's aid, Captain Daniel Edwards, crawled out making his way to the outskirts of Buna Village. He soon returned without being fired on, an exploit that only deepened Eichelberger's irritation with the troops over their failure to show any inclination to fight.[28]

Although his frontline was now less than 300 metres from Buna Village, Mott decided to make no further attacks that day. His plan was to attack again in the morning, with the aid of the Cannon Company, 128th Regiment, which had been promised to him by Harding. The upshot of this decision was voiced by Eichelberger on his return to the CP. The CO had some 'caustic comments' to make on what he had seen at the front.[29] The corps commander delivered damning remarks on the unwounded men at the aid station, the exposed machine guns, the hesitancy to stir up enemy fire, and the failure of frontline troops to volunteer 'even for a decoration'.[30] He went on to accuse the men as having failed to even advance. Mott flared up at this and spoke of the hardships his men had been through and argued vigorously in their defence – a point Harding made clear he agreed with by 'demonstratively dashing his cigarette to the ground when Mott finished speaking'.[31]

Mott recalled that Eichelberger's voice: 'Rose and he said, "You're licked", and indicated in various ways that the troops had done a very poor job and included a great many cowards. After having observed General Eichelberger's manner, I refrained from further attempts to state my side of the case and that of the soldiers under me, and shortly thereafter, General Eichelberger ... left my command post'.[32]

CHAPTER 22

At the time, Harding recorded the incident in his diary, writing that Eichelberger: 'In his remarks, he showed no appreciation of what the men had been through, or the spirit shown by most of them in carrying on despite heavy casualties, the roughest kind of opposition, and the most trying conditions. Most everything he said was critical'.[33]

* * *

Eichelberger later recalled the situation on 2 December, as it related to both Warren and Urbana fronts:

> When I went to the front on 2 December, I couldn't find a front. I had been told the day before that our men were within 75 yards of Buna Village and attacking. I knew that 400 artillery rounds had been laid into the troubled sector. When I came back that evening to my headquarters' tent on a creek bank ... I wrote to General Sutherland in Port Moresby.

> 'The rear areas are strong, and the frontline is weak. Inspired leadership is lacking. In a circuit of Buna Village, I found men hungry and generally without cigarettes and vitamins. Yesterday afternoon, the men immediately in contact with the Japanese had had no food since the day before. About four o'clock, the rations arrived, two tins of C ration!'

> Here is what Colonel Rogers, then I Corps Intelligence officer, wrote me about his inspection trip: 'The troops were deplorable. They wore long, dirty beards. Their clothing was in rags. Their shoes were uncared for or worn out. They were receiving far less than adequate rations and there was little discipline or military courtesy .... Troops were scattered along a trail towards the frontline in small groups, engaged in eating, sleeping, during the time they were supposed to be in an attack. At the front there were portions of two companies, aggregating 150 men.

> Outside of the 150 men in the foxholes in the frontlines, the remainder of the 2000 men in the combat area could not have been even considered a reserve – since three or four hours would have been required to organise and move them on any tactical mission …'
>
> Our patrols were dazed by the hazards of swamp and jungle; they were unwilling to undertake the patrolling, which alone could safeguard their own interests …. One result of [the] … lack of communication and the density of the jungle was that companies and platoons were as scrambled as pied type on the floor of a printing office …. I stopped all fighting, and it took two days to affect the unscrambling of the units and [implement] an orderly chain of command.[34]

After the war, Lieutenant Colonel Smith was concerned on reading a draft of the American Official History of the campaign, stressing that many senior American officers located well behind the frontlines were all too easy to criticise the performance of the American troops at Buna. He provided to the official historian a detailed informative response to questions asked of him, as well as providing his own insights. As a frontline commander, his assessment should be given some weight. He wrote in part:

> In consideration [of] the very early fighting at Buna, I think we must keep in mind several factors …. The troops not only were green and untried, but they were confronted with a situation entirely foreign to anything they had ever encountered before. They received fire from the Japs, but they could not determine where it came from, and so could not fight back. In order to get to where they thought the Japs were, they had to wade through deep swamps, the like of which they had never seen before, and which for all they knew might be filled with crocodiles [they were], even more dangerous than the Japs. Or they might step

CHAPTER 22

into soft gooey mud and sink from sight. Also, we were fighting an enemy, who in my opinion, had been greatly 'over sold'. The high command had indoctrinated us with tales of the Jap's prowess as a jungle fighter until we had come to look upon him as a sort of a 'super-man' of the jungle. Instead of just a healthy respect for him as a fighter, there was born in the minds of many, an actual fear that he was too good for them to cope with, and every bullet that cracked overhead made them think there were snipers in the trees, or that the Japs were working around to cut them off from supplies and reinforcements.[35]

* * *

Eichelberger understood that MacArthur had spoken in anger on his arrival at Port Moresby, when he ordered him to relieve Harding. As corps commander, however, he was under no obligation to take that step if he thought the relief was unnecessary and detrimental to ongoing operations. That evening, shortly after his return from the front, he called in Brigadier Clovis Byers, his chief of staff, and several other corps staff and informed them of the situation on Urbana front. He described the scene in Mott's headquarters, informing them that Harding was sympathetic with Mott throughout, and asked them what they would do if they were in his place. The officers unanimously told him that he had only one choice: to comply with MacArthur's instructions and immediately relieve Harding.[36]

Soon after, Harding approached Eichelberger in his tent to discuss a new plan to take Buna. He described the plan, which included an air sortie of bombers and fighters and an artillery bombardment, with the infantry assaulting to finally take Buna. Waldron was also present. Harding recorded in his diary that night, on entering the tent: 'Eichelberger listened but did not seem to be impressed. He had other matters on his mind, and I soon found out what they were. He started talking about what he had found out that day that was allegedly wrong. I took issue on one or two points, and finally said, "You were probably sent here to get heads, maybe mine is one of them. If so, it is on the block." He said, "You are right, it was, and I am putting this man" pointing to Waldron "in command of the division". I said, "I take it I am to return to Moresby." He said, "Yes." I stood up and stepped outside the tent'.[37]

As soon as Harding left, Eichelberger suggested replacing Hale with Martin, an offer that Waldron promptly accepted. Sometime later, while Waldron was still in Eichelberger's tent, Martin and Rogers reported to Eichelberger from Warren front. Martin recalled that scarcely had he started to give the report of what he had seen, when: 'General Eichelberger, turning to General Waldron, stated rather than asked, "Shall we tell him now." Whereupon he turned again to me and said, "Clarence, my boy, you have always said you would like to command a regiment. I am going to give you one. You will take command of the 128th Infantry and the Warren front …." I immediately replied, "Yes, sir, that is true, but I never imagined it would be under circumstances such as these." Then, I added, "Since I am to take command of the 128th Infantry, I would prefer [that] Colonel Rogers made the report." Rogers then continued and made the report orally. We had just returned, it was dark, and there had been no time to write a report'.[38]

Harding was officially relieved of his command early the next morning, as were Hale and Mott. Martin replaced Hale as commander of Warren Force, and Lieutenant Colonel Melvin McCreary took over from Mott as commander of Urbana Force. McCreary, however, was replaced on 4 December by Colonel John Grose, Eichelberger's inspector general, who Waldron accepted for the post after deciding that he needed McCreary to command the critical role of the artillery. The task of straightening out the chaotic supply position was given to Colonel George De Graaf, his own corps supply officer. Thus, with three of his own officers in the key positions under the already tried Waldron, Martin was now ready to confront the entrenched Japanese.

CHAPTER 22

The I Corps had taken over completely, and the responsibility for taking Buna was now firmly in the hands of Eichelberger.[39]

The historian of the 32nd Division recorded Mott's bitterness. The previous day; he had been informed by Eichelberger that he was to be decorated with the Silver Star and the Purple Heart. Mott, however, had not been wounded and so did not receive the latter. Mott stated soon after: 'I really should have got that too since I got my throat cut'.[40]

* * *

Meanwhile, holding the line along Urbana front, Japanese 1st Class Mechanic, Kuba Satonao, with the *Imperial Japanese Navy Tsukioka Transport Unit* recorded in his diary sometime that night: 'Until now the enemy did not bomb us at night but now, they are coming over at night. We lived till today, but it is something unusual. There are tears in my eyes as I realise the meaning of the fact that I am alive. To the Truck Company Commander, thank you for all you have done for me. Since landing at Buna, I haven't been able to do anything, and I have nothing I can say in apology. I am grateful that you readily released me so that I could volunteer. Please hold BUNA. The BUNA BASE that COMMANDER TSUKIOKA captured. Hurrah for the Emperor, Hurrah for Japan. Regards to the people in Rabaul. Here's to the health of one and all'.[41]

23

'... WATCHED PARACHUTE TROOPS MAKING A SAFE LANDING'

On 3 December, Lieutenant General Eichelberger made a request to Lieutenant General Herring, commanding NGF, that Colonel Clarence Tomlinson, who was commanding the 126th Regiment, and his headquarters be transferred from the Sanananda to Buna. Given that the fighting at Sanananda had seemingly become a stalemate, Eichelberger was keen to have his regimental commander and his headquarters, rejoin the bulk of their men of the 126th Regiment now fighting at Buna. Tomlinson would move out the next day with most of his headquarters, leaving Major Bernd Baetcke in overall charge of the remaining Americans at Sanananda, consisting of the III/126th Regiment, with most of the men from 'C' and 'D' companies, I/126th Regiment.[1]

Lieutenant General Herring wrote to General Blamey, regarding Eichelberger's visit to the front during the previous day: 'There is no doubt that Eichelberger's visit to see for himself exactly what the forward troops are doing has had a great effect. He practically walked into Buna Village. No one could deter him, tho' I gather a number of windy gentlemen tried to'.[2] Meanwhile, in preparation for a major attack to be launched on 4 December, Eichelberger and his new commanders of Warren and Urbana forces gathered up their scattered command and reorganised them once more into a homogeneous force.[3]

* * *

CHAPTER 23

When Colonel Clarence Martin went forward to Warren front that morning to take command, he discovered the troops 'had little in the nature of weapons and equipment of what was normally considered necessary to dislodge an enemy from a dug-in, concealed position'.[4] At his forward headquarters, he found a mere 'single shelter half-suspended horizontally about five feet from the ground, under which the CP telephone rested against a log on the ground'.[5] Martin recalled his regimental operations officer, Major Milton Ziebell, had with him a printed map 'inaccurate for artillery fire [and] half of a small writing tablet, the kind selling in ten-cent stores for a dime, and a pencil'.[6] When Martin asked the adjutant for his files, the soldier 'patted the pocket of his denim jacket, which was a shade of black from the swamp mud, and said that he was keeping what he could there'.[7]

Martin set about improving conditions. One of his first actions was to call an officers' meeting, at which he told them that the men, 'would be required to do all they could to better their conditions, their personal appearance, and their equipment'.[8] Sanitation needed to be a priority, and more attention was to be given to the care of equipment. Officers were to cease commiserating with the men – an attitude he noticed seemed to dominate their thinking. He also told them there would be no relief until 'Buna was taken'.[9] The CO knew that this news would come as a shock, 'but I was certain that after the shock was over, the troops, knowing their task, would fight better than those just hanging on and continually looking over their shoulders for relief to come'.[10]

On reorganising Warren front, Lieutenant Carl Fryday and his men of 'I' Company, III/128th Regiment – who had been operating under Lieutenant Colonel Edmund Carrier, commanding the I/126th Regiment at the south-west end of the strip – were returned to their regiment. The men of 'A' Company, I/126th Regiment – who had been under Lieutenant Colonel Robert McCoy, commanding the I/128th Regiment, located off the south-east end of the strip – now also returned to their parent unit.[11]

Miller and his men of the III/128th Regiment were now positioned to the right of New Strip on an arc extending from the sea to a point just south of the aircraft dispersal bays at the eastern end of the strip. McCoy and his troops of the I/128th Infantry moved in on Miller's left, just south of the strip, while Major Harry Harcourt and his surviving commandos covered the gap between Carrier and McCoy. Carrier and his men of the I/126th Regiment moved from the coastal position to the Dobodura–Buna Track south of the bridge between the airstrips. Warren Force had no reserve, but each battalion held small reserve elements out of the line.[12]

* * *

By now, Harcourt and his men of the 2/6th Company were in desperate need of rest and reorganisation. His frontline force was down to just nine officers and 61 other ranks, even with ongoing reinforcements. The company diarist recorded the situation: 'Our OP still observing but little to report this day – Our A/C [aircraft] overhead – only little Jap A/A gun and no LMG ... opposition – slight arty. Activity. Patrols outposts taken over by US Inf. and our men had support position. TREGARTHEN's patrol withdrawn for rest. Sickness still a problem – mostly fever and tinea due to waterlogged area'.[13] Of this force, four officers and 37 men remained in the forward area, while the remaining five officers and 24 men (most sick with fever) remained at the headquarters' position.[14]

Private Allen Osborne, with No. 4 Section, recalled the atrocious conditions that he and his mates were forced to endure for weeks; indeed, he recalled the men were seriously unwell even before they were involved in the initial fighting around Buna: 'The conditions in the coconut plantation were appalling. The plantation was at sea-level, and normally it had been drained by a series of drains that were criss-crossing it. However, since it had been abandoned, these had chocked up with weeds and coconut fronds and bits and pieces, and the water table was right up at the surface .... We were starting

CHAPTER 23

to get sick – plenty of malaria, dysentery, blokes had hookworm, ringworm, a little bit of scrub-typhus [usually fatal] – you name it. Before we had been in any substantial action, we were pretty-well knocked out of action'.[15]

The American GIs were also suffering from sickness, as recorded by Australian journalist George Johnston, who was writing for the *Sydney Morning Herald*, the Melbourne *Age*, the *Daily Telegraph* in London, and Australian United Press. During the war, he published his book, *New Guina Diary*, writing: 'When you see these young Americans moving up towards the shattering noise of the frontline, or coming back wounded, or sick with the strange jungle fever that is not malaria, nor scrub typhus, nor dengue, you are immediately amazed at how young they look. Many of them look like kids out of high school. I suppose our own troops looked as young when they went abroad [to the Middle East, North Africa, and Greece] three years ago. The Americans are finding now that war is grim, bloody, callous, dangerous, hard work …. And yet whenever you speak to any of them, they have the same boyish grins, the same disarming candour, the same naivety, and the universal wish: "I sure want to get me a Jap"'.[16]

* * *

That day was the first of two missions by Japanese airmen to supply the garrison at Buna by air. Just before 3 pm, nine Japanese bombers, escorted by 14 Zeros, dropped about 30 large crates of supplies on Old Strip. Private Noburo Wada with *Yokosuka, 5 SNLP*, who was further inland at Urbana front, recorded mistakenly: 'Our Army is pressing the enemy by dropping parachute units. Our courage increased a hundred-fold as we watched parachute troops making a safe landing'.[17]

That day, unnamed Japanese soldier [C] who was part of Colonel Yamamoto Hiroshi's force dug-in around the New Strip and the plantation area at Buna, recorded in his diary: 'Thursday. Rain later fair. They dropped bombs uncomfortably close during the morning.

All were parachute bombs, but there was no damage done. Extremely quiet in the afternoon. About 0200 repaired shelters of the Mizaki squad. From today rations out, but there is an abundance of provisions and morale is high and there are reports that our troops are landing continuously'.[18]

Close by would have been Japanese soldier [E]. He had also landed at Buna with Yamamoto and was now dug-in around the plantation and at the north-east end of New Strip. He recorded in his diary: '2 GO 5 SHAKU (… about a handful) rations now. Bombing and mortar fire during morning. Fired Battalion gun at 3:30 AM. Our planes flew over today. 6 heavy bombers and 3 fighters'.[19]

Also in this area was Lieutenant Suganuma and his platoon; he recorded in his diary: 'Utilising early dawn strengthened shelter of MIZAKI MG Squad. This morning, enemy planes are late, [at] about 0800 [hours] enemy fighters flew over. Bombed and strafed. Wonder if the enemy has withdrawn. There have been no enemy patrols today for a change. At sundown, command section news, 23 enemy planes downed, seven burned to ground that was why enemy planes didn't come over today. For once the soldiers are not busy. Within the shelters listened to stories by first year soldiers …. There were many interesting stories of men who have been in their third battle and have spent two … years in the field. New Years in "KOMON" and Hong Kong. What about this new year? Will I greet new years in this trench? No, no if the main force comes, we will go forward …. I wondered what would happen to us …. Battalion commander instructions. Carried out reinforcements of shelters'.[20]

* * *

At Urbana front, Colonel John Grose had little opportunity to inspect his forces now in his command. He had just flown in from Australia that morning and made a hurried inspection of the frontline that afternoon. The following day, when he took official command, he

CHAPTER 23

found Lieutenant Colonel McCreary supervising a reorganisation of the positions, and he asked Eichelberger to postpone the attack for a day, which was approved, and the attack on the Warren front was also now rescheduled for 5 December.[21]

It was now that the scattered units of the II/126th Regiment, commanded by Major Smith, who had been at Entrance Creek north of the Coconut Grove, rejoined their battalion and the Cannon Company, 128th Regiment in front of Buna Village. The II/128th Regiment, commanded by Lieutenant Colonel Smith, now took over the sector following the west bank of Entrance Creek. The men of 'F' Company, II/128th Regiment continued to hold the blocking positions between the Girua River and Siwori Creek.[22] Lieutenant Colonel Smith recalled to Samuel Milner in 1950: 'Lt Col McCreary was placed temporarily in command of the Urbana Force, and he phoned me and told me to return to the Battalion CP and resume active command of the entire battalion'.[23]

* * *

The planned attack for 5 December would again follow the pattern that, up until now, had been unsuccessful – a frontal assault with air, artillery and mortar support. Lieutenant Colonel Keith O'Connell, a 34-year-old loss assessor from Sydney, now commanding the 2/1st Field Regiment, had just flown in from Port Moresby and was placed in charge of the guns. The two guns near the Hariko ammunition supply had been an acute problem, which would only be relieved just before the attack with the arrival of the small craft ferrying in 1000 shells, and their delivery enhanced by the construction of a rough track from Hariko to Simemi. Even so, movement to the dump and gun positions was still slow and awkward. As the gunners manhandled the shells from the vessels at the water's edge, they stumbled over roots and collided with one another in the darkness. The track from Simemi provided only a trickle of ammunition.[24] Over this track, the gunners' only jeep, 'brakeless, running on kerosene, and with stuttering regularity, went bucketing to Dobodura to carry a mere 40 rounds a trip'.[25]

There would, however, be one new development in the attack, brought on by delaying the attack until 5 December. Two weeks before at Milne Bay General Cyril Clowes had ordered Brigadier Murray Moten, a 43-year-old bank official from Woodville in South Australia, commanding the Australian 17th Brigade, to provide men to crew 13 Bren gun carriers supplied by the 18th Brigade. This improvised platoon of Bren carriers would be sent to Buna to help break the stalemate there. Each carrier was armed with two light machine guns, with each section also having an anti-tank rifle. Moten placed Lieutenant Terence Fergusson, a 22-year-old Jackeroo from Corowa in New South Wales, as the commander of this force. All were banking success on the sound training that this young officer had received in carriers as a trooper in his father's 6th Divisional Cavalry Regiment, before being commissioned and posted to the 2/7th Battalion.[26]

On 29 November, Fergusson had brought five of his Bren gun carriers into Oro Bay, although the shipping and unloading difficulties forced him to return the other eight carriers to Porlock Harbour. He then had troubles finding an overland route by which to get farther forward, but his 2i/C, Lieutenant Ian Walker, a 23-year-old jackeroo and bookkeeper from Essendon in Victoria, had managed to get the five carriers on another barge. By the early hours of 4 December, Walker would have his five-section carrier force ashore and, in the afternoon, they would move forward to an assembly area in preparation for the attack planned for 5 December.[27]

* * *

During the previous week, the average daily ration for the troops on both Warren and Urbana fronts had consisted of just a single can of meat and an emergency bar of concentrated chocolate, just enough to subsist on. Even though rations were still in short supply, the men ate their first full meal in some time that day.[28]

24
'... THESE ARE NOT TANKS'

By 4 December, the 32d Division's supply situation, which had been hopelessly inadequate during November, was now beginning to improve. There were several reasons for this, including increased airdrops, emergency movements by sea, which had staved off disaster, and the arrival of supplies, which Major General Harding had requisitioned some time before. In addition, the opening of additional airfields at Dobodura and Popondetta, as well as the completion of the Dobodura–Simemi jeep track (and associated tracks), the arrival of a new flotilla of luggers to replace those destroyed in November, and the establishment of a separate service organisation at Dobodura, known as ALMA Force. Indeed, Lieutenant General Eichelberger's efforts, and those of his quartermaster, Colonel George DeGraaf, and the continuing efforts of the division's supply officers all went to significantly improve the supply situation.[1]

That morning also witnessed the reorganisation and regrouping of Warren and Urbana units being finalised. Fortified by a much-needed two-day's rest, the men received rations and ammunition and prepared to resume operations under their new commanders; all were now preparing for the next day's attack. The plan for the American–Australian assault was embodied in a field order drawn up the day before by Brigadier Albert Waldron. Warren Force and the five Bren gun carrier section, supported by elements of the US Fifth Air Force and Australian artillery, were to target the Japanese positions in the Duropa Plantation–Buna Strips area at 8.30 am. Their objective was to capture the entire area east of a line drawn along the coast south-west from Strip Point and extending inland to Old Strip. Meanwhile, to the west, Urbana Force, also supported by artillery and an aerial bombardment, was to jump off at 10 am with the task of taking Buna Village. Both attacking forces were to make an all-out effort.[2]

* * *

That morning, the five Australian Bren carriers were approaching Buna and, in the afternoon, they reached the American positions. They were allocated to Colonel Clarence Martin's attack against the Japanese positions in the Duropa Plantation. In the attack scheduled for the next day, four carriers would be manned by crews from the Australian 2/7th Battalion, while the remaining carrier would be crewed by men with the 2/5th Battalion under Corporal Norman Lucas, a 25-year-old cabinet maker from South Perth. One of the crews from the 2/7th Battalion was led by Sergeant Douglas 'Jock' Taylor, a 35-year-old labourer from Melbourne, who was described in the Australian official history as having 'shown himself in the African desert and Greece to be one of the outstanding fighting men of the AIF'.[3]

On arriving, Martin and Lieutenant Colonel Alexander MacNab, the executive officer of Warren Force, gave Lieutenant Terence Fergusson, commanding the carrier force, a briefing on the terrain. MacNab recalled after the war: 'Col Martin and I both briefed Lt Ferguson [sic], cautioning him about the condition of the ground throughout the plantation and pointing out the likelihood of his carriers being "bellied" by the stumps and other inequalities of the surface'.[4] MacNab sent Fergusson and Lieutenant David Anderson, commanding officer of the regimental Reconnaissance Platoon, to observe the ground. Though under no illusions about the risk of the attack, Fergusson reported he judged his carriers could negotiate the terrain; however, he requested additional automatic weapons for his men, which were provided.[5]

CHAPTER 24

Although Fergusson and his men were keen for action, some misgivings must have occurred as they assessed the nature of the country, and the task assigned them. The open-top and lightly armoured Bren gun carriers were designed principally as reconnaissance vehicles. It was due to their light armour that they were able to move rapidly and transport troops and weapons across bullet-swept ground. Their armour could stop small-arms fire, but in some cases, even some of that was likely to penetrate at close range. Brigadier Ronald Hopkins, chief of staff to Lieutenant General Herring, had gone to Buna earlier to argue against the use of carriers. He later wrote in his history of the Australian Armoured Corps: 'The carriers were too lightly armoured and the crews too exposed, for them to be used as tanks. Any attempt by the carriers to close with enemy bunkers would be fatal, especially since it was known the Japanese had several quick firing anti-aircraft and anti-tank guns. Definite instructions were given that each carrier was to have an infantry escort to protect its crew from snipers in the trees and enemy grenade attacks'.[6]

A basic doctrine of infantry training had always been that carriers were not tanks and should not, and could not, be used as such. Even so, they were now essentially being asked to perform in that capacity, to assault deeply entrenched positions manned by determined Japanese defenders. As recorded in the American official history: 'Sending the thin-skinned vehicles, open at the top and unarmoured below, against the formidable enemy positions in the plantation area was a desperate venture at best. The least the Americans could do was to give the Australian crews, who were to spearhead the attack, all the weapons they could use'.[7]

Meanwhile, the Australian commandos under Major Harry Harcourt were close to being a spent force. Harcourt, that morning, ordered that the advance party, which was commanded by Lieutenant Geoffrey Fielding, to return to the headquarters' position for a few hours rest out of the line. Even so, 28-year-old NCO Frederick

McKittrick, from Sydney, and Private Albert Stuart, a 28-year-old milk vendor from Wayville in South Australia, remained at the OP.[8] These men reported to Harcourt that day: 'Some A/A fire from RUNWAY AREA. The Japs seem to move their guns a good deal or have several because fire seems to come from different sources. Our arty fire on several targets. Arrival of recce party to place 37 [mm] gun in position vicinity of OP – told NOT to put gun too close'.[9]

Private Les Gosden, a 21-year-old turner from Melbourne, at the company headquarters recalled the splendid work of these two men: 'The 25-pounder guns, which were shelling the Jap positions at Buna, would have been virtually useless had it not been for Fred McKittrick and *Dagwood* Stuart who were positioned high up in a tree bordering the Buna strip'.[10]

While attending a conference at the headquarters of the 128th Regiment, Harcourt was informed that Australian Bren gun carriers were to be used in the next day's attack. He also raised concerns, as recorded in the company war diary: 'Bren carriers from 2/7 Bn. A.I.F. to be used to support infantry – these [carriers] have a tank task to do for which they are unsuited. Pointed this out to US comdrs. and emphasised that Inf. must move on heels of carriers all the time as these are NOT tanks. Must be used in packs of at least three and NOT singly'.[11]

Even so, Harcourt set about improving the approach of the carriers by getting the company engineers to build a sand crossing over the estuary; fortunately, that morning, the tide washed sand into the mouth of the estuary and effectively closed it, proving a path for the carriers. Just days before, these men had also built a bridge south of the estuary, enabling the troops to cross unobserved by the Japanese, and it was found that the structure was strong enough for the carriers to use, even though all witnessed it stained under the weight of the four-ton vehicles.[12]

Orders were issued that day to Lieutenant Fielding and other

CHAPTER 24

officers regarding their next day's objectives: 'To provide contact patrols between I/128 and I/126 and to take any chance of inflicting casualties on enemy or opening avenues through which Inf. advance could move. To be in position by 0700 hrs. 5 Dec. Strength 9 off. 63 O/Rs – more sick evacuated to hospital'.[13]

* * *

That day, Japanese Colonel Yamamoto Hiroshi and his troops were dug-in and ready for the expected attack. Yamamoto had the bulk of his relatively fresh troops of the *144th* and *III/229th regiments* in the plantation and at the north-east end of New Strip. The rest of his troops were holding the bridge between the strips, together with the troops of the *15th Independent Engineer Regiment*, led by Colonel Yokoyama Yosuke and Lieutenant Colonel Fuchiyama Sadahide and his men of the *47th Field Antiaircraft Battalion* who were originally assigned there.[14]

Unnamed Japanese soldier [C], who was part of Colonel Yamamoto Hiroshi's force dug-in around New Strip and the plantation area at Buna, recorded in his diary: 'Friday. Our troops and enemy troops are quiet today. Only once in a while a plane flies over. Cleared out the zone of fire taking advantage of the dusk. While clearing up, 1st Class Private Suzuki found an automatic rifle, and 1st Class Private Furuta found a rifle and 112 rounds [of] ammunition'.[15]

Close by would have been Japanese Lieutenant Suganuma, who was also with Yamamoto's force now in the Coconut Grove area near New Strip. The young officer recorded the day's events in his diary:

Planes circling around and no rifle fire, only a few sniper shots in front of 3rd Platoon. Came the dawn. Carried one coconut tree and filled in all of the shelter. Now we are safe from mortar fire .... There has been no appearance of enemy. The usual strain of the night. With bloodshot eyes and all nerves strained listening all night, we sleep when dawn comes, leaving a relief solder and sentries. We start up when we hear rifle fire. That is how we maintain our alertness and go to sleep. Surprisingly, there are no enemy planes, but an airplane sometimes like an observation [RAAF], which may be ours or the enemies, has been reconnoitring must be reconnoitring enemy landings. Flyers that were not here before have gradually begun to increase. They must have increased because of the dead enemy bodies in front of protection. About 1630 [hours] carried out clearing of field of fire. At this time ... Lance Corporal MIYOSHI wounded in stomach.[16]

* * *

To the west, at Urbana front, Colonel Clarence Tomlinson, commanding the 126th Regiment, arrived with his headquarters from the Sanananda Front. His regiment had been split to support the Australians at Sanananda and Americans at Buna. Also arriving were advanced parties of the newly arrived 127th Regiment, which was now also committed to the Urbana front. By now, the troops in the line, the II/126th Regiment, the II/128th Regiment, and the Cannon Company, 128th Regiment had had a little rest. They would now have another chance to finish the job that they had not been quite able to complete on 2 December.[17]

Still near the Triangle was squad leader Ernest Gerber, with the II/128th Regiment, who recalled the effectiveness of the Japanese weapons: 'Japanese weapons, and especially their rifles, were generally smokeless. We couldn't see where the gun was firing from. Noise is very deceptive. You hear something. One guy yells, "It's over there!" Another guy yells the same thing but points in the opposite direction. This is where you need fire discipline. Its [sic] so easy to just start blasting away at anything. That gives away your position and, if you're firing blind, the chances of you hitting one of your own men is pretty high. So, you had to look, watch, be patient. In retrospect,

CHAPTER 24

the situation was very interesting. At the time it was hopeless from the military point of view'.[18]

* * *

Meanwhile, on the other side of the wire, Captain Yasuda Yoshitatsu and his marines of the *5th Yokosuka*, *5th Sasebo* (*SNLP*), as well as supporting naval pioneer troops were defending Buna Village, the Triangle, and the Buna Mission. The Japanese had thrown back every attack thus far, and they were confident of doing the same again.[19]

* * *

That day, General Blamey wrote to the Australian Prime Minister, John Curtin, with his assessment of the status of the campaign to take the Japanese beachheads – designated: 'Most Secret and Personal'.[20] As per usual, Blamey took credit for the strategic success and used others as scapegoats for the tactical failings; the letter also demonstrates General MacArthur's knee-jerk reaction to any reversal, and his similar tendency to blame others:

> I had hoped that our strategic plans would have been crowned with complete and rapid success in the tactical field. It was completely successful strategically in as much as we brought an American Division on to Buna and an Australian Division on to Gona simultaneously. But in the tactical fields after the magnificent advance through the most difficult area, the Owen Stanley Range, it is a very sorry story.
>
> It has revealed that the American troops cannot be classified as attack troops. They are definitely not equal to the Australian militia, and from the moment they met opposition, [they] sat down and have hardly gone forward a yard. The action, too, has revealed a very alarming state of weakness in their staff system and in their war psychology. General MacArthur has relieved the Divisional Commander and has called up General Robert

Eichelberger, the Corps Commander, and sent him over to take charge. He informs me that he proposes to relieve both the regimental commanders, the equivalent of our brigade commanders, and five out of six of the battalion commanders; and this in the face of the enemy. I am afraid now that the bulk of the fighting will fall on our own troops, in spite of the greatly larger numbers of the 32nd US Division.

The brigades that went over the mountain track [Australian 16th and 25th brigades] are now so depleted that they are being withdrawn, and I am utilising the only remaining AIF brigade in Port Moresby [21st Brigade] and a brigade of Militia [30th Brigade] that has been intensely trained here, and I think we will pull it off all right.[21]

25

'WE HAVE HIT THEM AND BOUNCED OFF'

As scheduled, from 8.20 to 8.35 am, on 5 December, six twin-engine medium bombers gunned and bombed the Japanese positions between Cape Endaiadere and Old Strip. Without waiting for the aircraft to finish, the artillery commenced firing at 8.30 am. Twelve minutes later, the infantry and Bren gun carriers went forward, leaving their start-lines. There, Lieutenant Terence Fergusson and his carrier section formed the spearhead for Lieutenant Colonel Kelsie Miller and the III/128th Regiment's attack against the Duropa Plantation.[1]

On the left, Lieutenant Colonel Robert McCoy and his men of the I/128th Regiment were attempting to break through the eastern end of New Strip. From his positions south of the bridge, Lieutenant Colonel Edmund Carrier and his troops of the I/126th Regiment were thrusting against the resolute Japanese defenders who would give no ground. Between McCoy and Carrier was Lieutenant Geoffrey Fielding, commanding the most forward Australian commandos. They were tasked with maintaining contact between the I/128th and I/126th regiments and assisting the Americans in any way of breaking into the Japanese defences.[2]

* * *

Miller and his men of the III/128th Regiment on the right were to take Duropa Plantation. Captain Samuel Horton was leading 'L' Company and his men, using small-arms and machinegun fire, sweeping the treetops to kill Japanese snipers. Supported by mortar and machinegun fire from 'M' Company, the Bren gun carriers and 'L' Company left the line of departure at 8.42 am. The carriers broke cover, each with a crew of four, their speed held down to three kilometres an hour to enable the infantry to keep pace. The ground was also spongy under their narrow tracks and littered with fallen logs, further reducing their speed.

On the right were the two carriers driven by Corporal Norman Lucas and Sergeant Douglas Taylor. In the centre was Lieutenant Fergusson in his carrier. Covering the left were the two carriers commanded by Corporal James Orpwood, a 24-year-old factory worker from Nagambie in Victoria, and Corporal Cecil Wilton, a 23-year-old grocer's assistant from Orbost in Victoria. The carriers were to attack straight up the coast on a 200-metre front. The Americans of 'I' Company were to follow in a column to the left rear of 'L' Company, and machinegun crews of 'M' Company were to advance along the line of departure and immediately to the rear, to clean out any remaining snipers in trees and to provide direct support to the advance.[3]

A great volume of fire hit the attackers as they advanced into the cleared space, and as feared, the Bren carriers bellied up badly on the uneven stump-filled ground and their progress was slow. As their fronts rose while clearing stumps and other obstacles, the carriers were easy targets for the Japanese machine gunners and the Japanese snipers in the trees, as well as those in the trenches who lopped hand grenades over the sides and attempted to attach 'sticky' bombs against their superstructures. They were also targeted by at least one anti-tank gun.[4]

On the extreme right, Lucas' carrier bellied on a log hidden in the kunai grass after it had advanced just 40 metres. The crew fought on from its shelter to cover Sergeant Taylor's advance on their left, who was engaging a Japanese machinegun bunker position about 50 metres to the carriers left. Taylor had crossed about 75 metres of cleared space when a torrent of fire from this position stopped him momentarily. He and his men pounded the bunker with grenades and poured machinegun fire against it. They then circled to take it from the rear,

CHAPTER 25

but not before a mortar-bomb had exploded in the back of the carrier, killing one of the crew. Just before they silenced this post, an enemy soldier attempted to lop a grenade into the open carrier. Taylor leaped from the vehicle and killed the enemy soldier in the open.[5]

Swinging his carrier to the right, Taylor now silenced another Japanese position. As the sergeant was engaging a third post, a burst of machinegun fire shattered his left arm. With blood pouring from his wound, he left the carrier to go to the assistance of Lieutenant Fergusson, who was experiencing difficulties farther to his left, while his crew member, Private Leslie Locke, a 25-year-old carpenter from Grafton in New South Wales, provided covering fire. As the carrier moved into the Japanese position, its damaged motor gave out and the carrier came to a halt. Desperately, the driver, Private Angus Cameron, a 32-year-old truck driver from Beaumaris in Victoria, emptied his rifle into the Japanese until it jammed. Cameron now also struggled to fix a stoppage in the Bren gun. As he was doing so, he was hit in the head. Locke got him out of the carrier and then, badly wounded himself, fell among the torn scrub.[6]

Meanwhile, in the centre of the section's advance, Lieutenant Fergusson, had been heavily engaged not just by the Japanese to his front, but snipers commanding his open vehicle from the treetops. When his driver was hit, Fergusson took over the driver's seat. He turned to look for the Americans who should have been supporting him, and it was now that his carrier became jammed among fallen trees. As Fergusson stood up to call to Taylor, near him on the right, a Japanese marksman shot him through the head. At once, from Taylor's carrier, Locke shot this sniper out of the tree, but within seconds, Corporal Frank Davies, a 25-year-old carpenter from Richmond in Victoria, was also shot dead when he struggled to move Fergusson's body from the driver's seat.[7]

By now, Corporal Orpwood in the fourth carrier to the left of Fergusson, had been wounded, mortally. After he had advanced about 100 metres on Fergusson's left, a grenade burst over his carrier's open top. Turning to crush the thrower, Orpwood became the target for a sniper perched above him in a tree. He fell across the driver, who temporarily lost control of his vehicle and then reversed into the cover provided by some bush and, under the protection of the forward infantry, removed his dying friend. Soon after his carrier became stuck as it tried to cross a fallen log. While Orpwood had been reversing, he had passed Corporal Wilton's carrier, which was helpless astride a log that had lain across the path; Wilton had been covering Orpwood's left rear. In a free-for-all, the Japanese riflemen engaged them from trees, and Wilton's two gunners were wounded. The crew then fought on for some time with the forward infantry. About midday, Wilton sent the two wounded men back, while he attached himself and his remaining crew to the Americans of 'L' Company; they would remain with these troops until the next evening.[8]

Lieutenant Colonel Alexander MacNab at his CP recalled the situation after Lieutenant Fergusson had been killed: 'Shortly after the action started, a runner from the Australians came to the CP with a request for the 2nd in command of the Bren Carrier Platoon to move up as Lt Fergusson had been hit'.[9] With this, Lieutenant Ian Walker, Fergusson's 2iC, hurried forward from the carriers' rear headquarters. Covered by fire from 'L' Company, III/128th Regiment, Walker and another soldier methodically removed the guns and ammunition from the three closest carriers. Walker then ordered the enlisted man back. The young lieutenant with a submachine gun went forward alone towards the two remaining carriers, determined to recover their guns. Before he could reach the nearer of the two, he fell, mortally wounded. The Japanese succeeded in stripping the gutted hulks of the two carriers that night before a patrol of Warren Force sent out to recover the guns could get to them.[10]

Within 30 minutes, the five carriers lay abandoned, proof of the truism that carriers were not tanks. And, just in rear of them, Captain Horton leading 'L' Company in support of the Bren gun carriers in their disastrous attack, had suffered appalling casualties. The

CHAPTER 25

centre platoon suffered so many dead and wounded during the first 30-minutes of the fighting that it required help from the left platoon just to hold their position; even though this platoon was itself under heavy fire. A platoon of 'I' Company had to plug the resulting gap on the left before the attack could continue.[11]

Even though the men tried to advance, they were forced back. They were blocked, not only by the intense fire from the log barricade a few metres in from the coast, but also by the hidden and carefully sited bunkers in the plantation. To make matters worse, the intense heat of the morning sapped the men's strength, with men falling out from heat exhaustion. By 10.10 am, the battalion had gained less than 40 metres, and it would make no further advance that day. Miller's infantry assault was halted almost before it began.[12]

Years later, MacNab recalled to the American official historian of the campaign, Samuel Milner: 'This action cost us heavy casualties and the Bren platoon [*sic* section] lost its two officers and about 15 men killed and wounded. The gallantry displayed by the Bren platoon was outstanding, realising as they did the basic inadequacy of their effort. Jap sticky bombs, grenades and the "bellying" of their vehicles were insurmountable obstacles'.[13]

As recorded in the 2/5th Field Regiment War Diary: 'Five Bren carriers arrived this morning and moved forward to lead the attack, resulting in all telephone communications being disrupted for an hour, despite the fact that all lines were overhead. Once again it was proved that Bren carriers are not tanks, as all five carriers were out of action in half an hour. And several men were killed, including Lieut. Fergusson. The other subaltern died of wounds (Lieut. Walker) received while attempting to salvage arms from carriers. Small gains were made by all three bns .... Maj. Hall spent the day from 0800 to 1700 at the Regt Inf fwd OP and gained the impression that American Inf are not fully aware of the advantages of "fire with movement"'.[14]

* * *

That day, unnamed Japanese soldier [C], who was part of Colonel Yamamoto Hiroshi's force dug-in around New Strip and the plantation area at Buna, recorded the day's fighting: 'The enemy attacked all day long. They drop bombs, fire artillery, mortar, automatic rifles, LMG and put all their fire power into it and attack. It's too bad that we can't see their forms. We know roughly where they are, but we cannot see their figures. They fire so much that we retaliate with a few grenades. Around evening heard from the unit commander that there were tanks [sic] in front of the 11th Company. The enemy attacked today with tanks. Out of the five tanks one returned. Four tanks had some trouble or other. In that condition they were bombed during the night. Heard two explosions and felt relieved. The platoon, hearing of these tanks made trenches and reinforced the shelter positions'.[15]

Sometime that day, unknown Japanese soldier [D] recorded his last diary entry: 'Receiving concentrated fire incessantly from early morning. We are more dead than alive. Reinforcements do not arrive. The gradual extermination of my fellow soldiers makes me feel lonely at heart'.[16]

Close by Japanese Lieutenant Suganuma, who was also with Yamamoto's force and had dug-in around the Coconut Grove near New Strip. The young officer recorded the day's events in his diary:

> MIYOSHI killed in action. Burial early morning. About 0600 many enemy planes flew over and dropped parachute bombs all around and strafed us. Following this mountain artillery and mortar fire and ground force fire all at once. They fire recklessly from the jungle when our field of fire is not effective. Probably fired most today. Fired about one hour and quit all of a sudden. After, only three or four enemy seen to move about. About 1100 again they started firing all at once for about ten minutes. Mortar and artillery fire followed. Fire so much I wondered whether their ammo. would last. Heavy firing in

CHAPTER 25

front of 1st squad. Seem like enemy infiltration. Sundown four men screamed. Must be hit. According to Sgt YAMADA 'the enemy has received almost no training, even though we fire a shot they present a large portion of their body and look around. Their movements are very slow. At that rate they can't make a night attack' – so he says. According to reports at evening five enemy tanks [sic] appeared in front of the HITABE unit and the enemy attacked but were repulsed. It is the same as at Hong Kong. If we shot the men on the tanks and stopped them, they withdrew. We pursued them and inflicted severe losses on them. It was very effective when hand grenades were thrown in them. So, it was at Hong Kong. The enemy who went so far as to bring a tank and was repulsed is, as Sgt YAMADA says, dependent upon fire power.[17]

The Japanese official history recorded the attack by the Australian carriers that day: 'The battle in the eastern sector started on 5 December. For 35 minutes from 6.20 am, six Allied fighters strafed the outer camp from the direction of New Strip. Supporting artillery fire began at the same time, while frontline infantry troops with armoured reconnaissance carriers began advancing at 6.42 am. The Japanese garrison at the eastern sector targeted the carriers with hand grenades, adhesion mines, and some anti-tank artillery. The five carriers were all destroyed within only 20 minutes'.[18]

* * *

It was a similar story for McCoy and his men of the I/128th Regiment as they attempted to break through the eastern end of New Strip. Here the men moved forward 13 minutes after Miller's assault was launched through the coarse kunai grass and in the unbearable heat and humidity. At 8.55 am, the 83 men of 'A' Company, led by Lieutenant Robert Scott, pushed off from the 'Y-shaped' dispersal area at the eastern end of New Strip. The men of 'B' Company, led by

Lieutenant Milan Bloecher, were on Scott's left rear, waiting to go in, while those of 'D' Company were positioned along the line of departure, supporting the advance with covering fire.

Scott's men moved slowly and cautiously through the tall kunai grass. Despite the heat and heavy casualties from enemy fire, they made good progress at first, and by 11 am, most of the men had crossed the lower arm of the 'Y' of the strip. There, however, they were halted by rifle grenade, mortar, and machinegun fire to their front, as well as enfilade from the right and left. Men who tried to advance were caught in this crossfire and were either killed or wounded. By noon, Japanese resistance and the heat and humidity had seriously reduced 'A' Company's strength, and 'B' Company, under Bloecher, was ordered in on its left to help relieve the pressure. By the late afternoon, the situation was considered hopeless, and Colonel Clarence Martin ordered 'A' Company to fall back as soon as it could. That evening, the survivors were relieved.[19]

Two hours later, Lieutenant Bloecher and his men of 'B' Company reached the south-eastern end of the strip at a point just west of the dispersal area occupied by 'A' Company. Setting up their light machine guns on the left to cover the strip, Bloecher tried to move his men across the exposed ground, but Japanese fire made this impossible. As the men crawled out of the sheltering kunai grass into the heat drenched strip, concentrated fire from bunkers and hidden firing positions in the area forced them back. Those who managed to get halfway across were trapped; they could not advance or retire. Since further advance was impossible, the company consolidated their position at the eastern end of the strip.[20]

* * *

At the western end of the airstrip, Lieutenant Colonel Carrier and his troops of the I/126th Regiment did little better. The men of 'A' Company on the right and the much depleted 'C' Company (most of the company was at Sanananda) on the left moved out against

CHAPTER 25

the bridge between the strips at 8.50 am, and at first, they reported good progress. Aided by the mortars and the 'M' Company's 37-mm gun, they succeeded in knocking out seven enemy pillboxes during the first two hours of fighting. With the Japanese fire from the pillboxes suppressed, the GIs began to close in on the bridge, only to be halted by heavy concentrated fire from front and enfilade from the left just 150 metres from their objective. Artillery fire was called in for support, but it proved ineffective. The Japanese fire only increased in intensity.[21]

Carrier's troops were suffering from the heat, like the other companies of Warren Force, but they still attempted to make repeated attempts to advance. The Japanese fire was, however, too heavy. This frontal attack was abandoned – with 'B' Company relieving 'A' Company – and an attempt was made to cross Simemi Creek in the hope of flanking the bridge. The attempt failed, as there was quicksand around the crossing area and the creek was too deep. By day's end, the Japanese still held the bridge between the strips, and Carrier's troops were dug-in about 200 metres south of it.[22] The regimental adjutant recorded the day's fighting by the men of the I/126th Regiment:

> After heavy artillery fire, the attack moves onward, meeting heavy resistance of machinegun fire from enemy pillboxes on Simemi Creek. These are neutralised by direct fire from 37-mm guns. Excellent results are had from crew [servicing] weapons, the firing of which is directed by Lt Kucera from an observation post constructed in a tree. 'B' Company patrols get in behind enemy machine [gun] bunkers at the junction of the Dobodura track and Simemi Creek. Both 'A' and 'C' companies advance. 'B' Company is sent up to relieve Company 'C' now located on the bridge that crosses the creek. Much rifle and grenade fire from the enemy. Their mortars and machine guns hold up our forces. The troops are withdrawn a short distance, and these areas of resistance are subjected to artillery fire following,

which our troops are able to move onto the new airstrip again. Company 'C' is sent up to relieve Company 'A'. The enemy delivers heavy fire with mortars and artillery.[23]

* * *

Between McCoy and Carrier, Lieutenant Geoffrey Fielding commanding the most forward Australian commandos was able to penetrate through the eastern end and across the centre of the strip, with most of the Japanese fire passing over their heads.[24] Three fighting patrols had been sent out at 6 am. On the right was Lieutenant Gordon Blainey and his section in contact with the I/128th Regiment; in the centre was Lieutenant Robert Scott and his men; and on the left was Lieutenant Arthur Tregarthen and his section in contact with the I/126th Regiment. With no infantry coming up in support, however, this small force of determined fighters was forced to withdrew later in the day.[25] The war diary of the unit records the situation at this point for the battle-weary Australian commandos:

> An excellent smoke screen was placed across front of enemy defences near the BRIDGE .... The 37-mm gun placed in vicinity of OP fired at emplacements near the ... BRIDGE.

> On RIGHT the Inf. were unable to advance more than a few yards and the carriers were put out of action .... Lieutenant BLAINEY's patrol moved fwd. and across E. end of NEW STRIP but could not move further forward alone. They patrolled to the LEFT across the STRIP and contacted the centre patrol and after patrolling fwd. towards timber ... moved back to far side of NEW STRIP. SCOTT's patrol in the centre moved fwd across the NEW STRIP and failing to wait for the Inf. advanced moved fwd. until they were nearly into the timber N. of the STRIP. Here they waited for the Inf. advance to come up to them.

CHAPTER 25

The enemy SA [small arms] fire did not seem to be directly aimed at these two patrols – they were able to pass through the fire screen unharmed as most of it passed over their heads. The Inf. on the LEFT moved to the advance a little too late to obtain full benefit from the smoke screen and the enemy opened heavy MG fire. The line went to earth and was not again able to move forward. Enemy mortars joined in the fire on the LEFT, but their shells appeared to be badly aimed or directed as all fell behind our lines in open patches of grass.

1335 [hours]: Our 25 pdrs. again, began shelling the enemy positions E of BRIDGE … and it was presumed that the advance had ceased for the day. SCOTT's patrol withdrew to line of NEW STRIP as 25 pdr. Shells were falling very near his patrol position.

1500: Lieut. TREGARTHEN with his patrol given instructions to endeavour to find line of approach through bush and swamp … with view to outflanking enemy positions on our LEFT. If passage through not possible to the NORTHWARD patrol were to try further SOUTH. The patrol was to contact 1/126 Bn. on its way out.

Weather – fine, slight breeze from EASTWARD. Quiet night – some rain – heavy towards morning of 6 Dec.[26]

* * *

Meanwhile, back at Milne Bay, the officers and men of the 17th Brigade would remain ignorant of the attack made by their Bren gun carrier crews for another week. The adjutant of the 2/7th Battalion recorded on 12 December on receiving a letter arrived from a member of the carrier section to the battalion CO, indicating that 'the carriers had been in action …. It also inferred that Lieuts Fergusson, and Walker had been killed and other personnel wounded'.[27] With this news,

BLOODY BUNA

Captain Septimus Cramp, a 28-year-old radio operator from Mildura in Victoria, commanding 'A' Company, immediately volunteered to go to Buna to get further details and take command of their men at Buna – he left later that day.[28]

* * *

The all-out attack of Warren Force to finally capture Buna had failed all along the line. Japanese Colonel Yamamoto Hiroshi, commanding the garrison here, had the situation well in hand. As Martin put it in a phone call to Brigadier Clovis Byers, Eichelberger's chief of staff, that night: 'We have hit them and bounced off'.[29]

26

'... MUCH TO BE PROUD OF DURING THE DAY'S OPERATIONS'

Meanwhile, to the west at the Urbana front, the plan was for the Cannon Company, 128th Regiment, and Major Smith and his men of the II/126th Regiment to attack at specified points on the Japanese perimeter defending Buna Village. Having suffered heavy losses during the attacks of 2 December, the men of 'F' Company II/126th Regiment would now be in reserve. The Cannon Company would remain on the left of the 126th Regiment and continue to support its operations. Lieutenant Colonel Smith and his men of the II/128th Regiment, on Major Smith's right, would complete the penetration from the left bank of Entrance Creek. Air sorties and an artillery bombardment would support the attacks. From positions behind the large kunai strip west of Entrance Creek, eight 81-mm mortars would fire on the village. The troops of 'F' Company, II/128th Regiment from their positions on the west side of the Girua River, would also provide supporting fire with two 81-mm mortars, a 37-mm gun, and several light and heavy machine guns.[1]

Colonel John Grose went to the front early in the morning, and after getting the men into line and making a final check of their positions, he returned to his CP about 10.15 am. There he found waiting for him Lieutenant General Eichelberger and members of his staff, including his aide, Captain Daniel Edwards – all keen to observe operation from Crose's headquarters' position.[2]

The attack opened at 10 am with a raid on Buna Mission by nine

B-25 bombers. After they departed, the artillery and the mortars began firing on the village. At 10.30 am, the fire ceased, and the infantry moved forward. On the left of the attack, the Cannon Company, 128th Infantry attacked along the east bank of the Girua River. To their right, Major Smith and his men of the II/126th Regiment also moved out against Buna Village after nine Australian Kittyhawk fighters attacked the Government Station at 10.30 am to disorganise any move to send reinforcements from that area. This was the only possible avenue of reinforcements to the Japanese village, and the guns and mortars also bombarded the area. Directly south of the village, the men of the regiment tried to advance with 'H' Company on the right, 'G' and 'E' companies in the centre, and the Cannon Company continuing their advance on the extreme left.[3]

* * *

The Japanese commander in the area, Captain Yasuda Yoshitatsu, and his marines of the *5th Yokosuka*, *5th Sasebo*, *SNLP*, with supporting naval pioneer troops totalled around 200 men in the village, enough for its immediate defence. With the help of the bunkers, barricades, and trenches, he could count on holding the village for some time, even though it was his least defensible position.[4]

* * *

In the centre, the advance of 'H' Company was soon bogged down, while on their left, two platoons of 'G' Company commanded by Captain Cladie Bailey went to ground under fire. His third platoon, led by Staff Sergeant Herman Bottcher, with 'H' Company, who had been attached to 'G' Company for the attack took quick advantage of an opening to overcome several enemy positions and halted only when they reached the sea at 1.30 pm. There, with 18 men and one machinegun, Bottcher dug-in on a narrow sand spit just east of Buna Village. He and his men now commanded the line between the Government Station just east and the village just west.[5]

CHAPTER 26

To the left, 'E' Company, commanded by Captain Melvin Schultz, also met tough opposition from the intrenched enemy. Largely because of the leadership of two young leaders – Lieutenant Thomas Knode, and Sergeant Paul Lutjens, both of whom were badly wounded – the company got within 50 metres of the village before they were stopped. Lutjens was out in front and hit by a grenade; however, he managed to slowly drag himself back to his lines through the thick mud, but in the process, he was wounded again. Historian James Campbell recalled: 'It was a miracle: Somehow, he snaked his way to a medic who was sitting in a foxhole with his hands in a man's gut. Scattered around him lay dead and wounded soldiers. The medic gave Lutjens a handful of sulphanilamide pills and went back to work on the soldier. Lutjens was full of shrapnel and lead, but the belly wounds came first'.[6]

Meanwhile, Sergeant Harold Graber had also helped to push the line forward. When the platoon was pinned down, Graber leaped to his feet, fired his light machine gun from the hip and cleaned out a Japanese strongpoint, which had been holding up their advance; Sergeant Harold Graber was killed while doing so. Lieutenant Thomas Knode, Sergeant Paul Lutjens[xiii], and Sergeant Harold Graber were each awarded the DSC for their actions that day.[7]

Disappointed that the attack had bogged down just outside the village, Eichelberger took direct control of operations. He called Grose forward to the observation post and sent Tomlinson back to the CP. He now ordered 'F' Company, then in reserve, to pass through 'E' Company and take the village. Grose immediately protested the order. Instead of committing 'F' Company, his last reserve, to the centre of the line, Grose had hoped to use it at a more favourable moment on the left. He informed Eichelberger that there was nothing to be gained by hurrying the attack, that it was the kind of attack that might take 'a day or two', but Eichelberger was determined to take Buna Village that day and overruled the protest.[8]

[xiii] Sergeant Paul Lutjens would survive the war and soon after marry his childhood sweetheart, Francis 'Lorraine' Phillips.

Summoned to the observation post, Lieutenant Robert Odell, who had taken command of 'F' Company a few days before, was, as he put it, 'surprised to see a couple of generals – one a three star – in addition to the usual array of majors and colonels'.[9] Odell recalled:

> The Lieutenant General explained what he wanted, and after a brief delay, I brought up the company and deployed accordingly. [Sergeant George] Pravda was to take half the company up one side of the trail, and I the other half on the other side. We were given ten minutes to make our reconnaissance and to gather information from the most forward troops which we were to pass. It was intended that we finish the job – actually take the village – and [it was thought] that we needed little more than our bayonets to do it. Well, off we went, and within a few minutes our rush forward had been definitely and completely halted. Of the 40 men who started with me, four had been (known) killed, and 18 were lying wounded. We were within a few yards of the village, but with ... no chance of going a step further ... [Pravda] was among the wounded, and casualties were about as heavy on his side.[10]

Scarcely had the attack in the centre been brought to a standstill when news was received from Captain Bailey that Sergeant Bottcher with his platoon had pushed north from their position on the far right. Here, Japanese counterattacks were launched from both the village and the mission, but Bottcher and his men, with the senior NCO himself at the machine gun, repulsed the attacks. The beach on either side of Bottcher's Corner (as the position would become known) was soon piled with Japanese dead. Sergeant Herman Bottcher would be awarded the DSC for his actions over the next few days, and be promoted in the field to the rank of captain.[11]

The Japanese official history records the breakthrough by Bottcher and his men: 'The Japanese naval units led by Captain Yasuda returned

CHAPTER 26

heavy fire and halted the American advance. Meanwhile, a platoon from the American 126th Regiment, in defiance of the Japanese attack, penetrated into the coastal sector between the Buna Mission and [Buna] Village. This unit encircled and attacked the Japanese position from both sides. The Japanese units were not destroyed, however, and fought all the stronger for being cornered in the village'.[12]

Meanwhile, on the extreme left, the Cannon Company, 128th Regiment faltered below an open space just south of the village. The company sent out patrols to flank the enemy, and the mortar men on the west side of the Girua River began firing on the village to relieve pressure. Later that afternoon, divisional staff officer, Major Chester Beaver, took command to get the company moving again. It had by then also been reinforced with Lieutenant Paul Schwartz and his platoon from 'F' Company, II/126th Regiment, which was Major Smith's reserve company.

Nonetheless, none of these measures could get the bulk of the men to advance as the Japanese continued to lay down concentrated fire. Beaver, with Schwartz, acting as his 2i/C, managed to clear out the enemy positions immediately to the front and then crawled through muck to bring his patrol to a position along the southern outskirts of Buna Village. Beaver and Schwartz were, however, forced to withdraw when night fell, but by the following morning, the Cannon Company and Schwartz's platoon of 'F' Company were back on the outskirts of the village, which was the position they had tried in vain to reach the day before.[13]

Meanwhile, Lieutenant Colonel Smith and his men of the II/128th Regiment on the right had advanced along the western bank of Entrance Creek to a point where he controlled the entire length on this side of the creek, except for the area of the Coconut Grove, which was still strongly held by the Japanese. With Smith's commanding position, Bottcher's breakthrough, and the position held by Major Smith's companies and the Cannon Company, Buna Village was effectively cut off; it was therefore only a matter of time before this stronghold would fall, provided the Japanese did not in the meantime succeed in recapturing Bottcher's Corner.[14]

Even so, the success of this day on the Urbana front was much less than it should have been. Two factors had swung the delicate balance in the Americans' favour. First was Bottcher's brilliant and brave opportunism; Eichelberger would write: 'On my recommendation the Allied commander commissioned Bottcher as a captain of infantry for bravery on the field of battle. He was one of the best Americans I have ever known. He had been born in Germany and still talked with a faint Germanic accent. A profound anti-Nazi, he came to [America] early in the 1930s, took out his first papers, spent a year at the University of California, and then went to Spain to fight against Franco. His combat experience was extremely useful in Buna, and his patriotism as a new American was vigorous and determined'.[15]

The second factor was the heroism of several individuals. These fell into two main groups: there were those who, like Bottcher, fought through to complete their objectives, and those senior and extra-regimental officers who took command from ineffective junior officers and NCOs to lead the men forward. Eichelberger again recorded:

> I watched the advance from the forward regimental CP, which was about a 125 yards from Buna Village. The troops moved forward a few yards, heard the typewriter clatter of Jap machine guns, ducked down, and stayed down. My little group and I left the observation post and moved through one company that was bogged down. I spoke to the troops as we walked along. 'Lads, come along with us.' And they did. In the same fashion we were able to lead several units against the bunkers at Buna Village .... When I arrived at Buna there was a rule against officers wearing insignia of rank at the front because this might draw enemy fire. I was glad on that particular day that there were three stars on my collar which glittered in the sun. How else would those sick

CHAPTER 26

and cast-down soldiers have known their commander was in there with them?[16]

* * *

Brigadier Albert Waldron, accompanied by his operations officer, Lieutenant Colonel Merle Howe, who had just arrived, had also been up front pushing the assault in the right centre of the line. During 'F' Company's attack, he received a shoulder wound and had to be evacuated. On Eichelberger's orders, Brigadier Clovis Byers, Eichelberger's chief of staff, succeeded Waldron as commander of the 32nd Division.[17]

Eichelberger and his party left for the rear at around 6 pm, less Captain Daniel Edwards, who had been wounded and evacuated earlier in the day, while Grose was left to reorganise and consolidate the ground captured. Grose had nothing but praise for the way the troops had performed, writing: 'The battalion's men have been courageous and willing, but they have been pushed almost beyond the limit of human endurance [they were] courageous, fine men [who gave] the utmost cooperation'.[18]

In a letter to Brigadier Floyd Parks, who was based in Washington DC, Eichelberger described the wounding of the then recently promoted Edwards: 'My aide Major Edwards had the hardest time because he was hit with one of those soft-core bullets which melt and spread. It is their new substitute for the dum-dum bullet and reports are being written about it. When I returned to the spot where he was shot some days later, I found that the little lad who had shot him from a distance of about ten feet [three metres] had a hole scooped out under the roots of a tree. He could hide in there or climb into the tree as he desired'.[19]

Although the troops had failed to take Buna Village, Eichelberger had revised the opinion he expressed on 2 December that they lacked a fighting spirit. He wrote to Major General Sutherland the next day, noting the troops had fought hard, that morale had been high, and that there had been 'much to be proud of during the day's operations'.[20] As far as he was concerned, Eichelberger went on, MacArthur could begin to stop worrying about his men's conduct in battle. Australian Lieutenant General Herring, commanding Advance NGF that day, also highly praised the bravery of the GIs of the 32nd Division.[21]

* * *

Manning the Japanese perimeter at Urbana front, Japanese 1st Class Mechanic, Kuba Satonao, with the *Imperial Japanese Navy Tsukioka Transport Unit*, recorded in his diary: 'In the battle following bombing, out of the 4th squad, four killed, four wounded by mortar. Our troops do not come. Even [when] they do come, they are driven away by enemy planes. Every day my comrades die one by one, and our provisions disappear day by day. There are no replenishments from our troops. It's just like waiting for death. However, there is no fighting at night, and it is that much less of a strain. When the sun sets in the West, we look at each other and wonder that we lived till now. How long will this battle last. We are waiting only for our troops'.[22]

27

'... THERE IS ALWAYS ENEMY MORTAR FIRE'

Dawn on 6 December at Warren front was relatively quiet, and it would remain so for a few days to come. During that time, several American patrols were sent out to identify the Japanese strong points. The Australian commandos of 2/6th Independent Company also continued to conduct fighting patrols against the Japanese perimeter around New Strip. Lieutenant Geoffrey Fielding, still commanding the three forward patrols, was instructed by Major Harry Harcourt to maintain a small outpost along the line of New Strip and to hunt down Japanese snipers who were active in the area. Several 'kills' were recorded that day.[1]

Lieutenant Arthur Tregarthen, leading his patrol, reported that afternoon that he and his men were moving westward through bush west of the Dobodura–Buna Track, reporting that the ground there was very swampy and that he was doubtful, 'if movement of large parties would be practicable. If not successful in this line will try further to SOUTH'.[2]

It was also reported that day that a Japanese mountain gun opened fire on an Australian gun position. The commandos observed that this enemy gun was firing from a point north-east of the main track and about a kilometre distant. The 2/6th Independent Company OP sent out the bearing of this gun. The Australian artillery, along with several mortars, bombarded the area, and the enemy shelling ceased. Whether the gun was hit or not remains unknown.[3]

The unit war diary records the situation as darkness fell at around 6 pm, as provided by the men at the OP: 'Considerable Jap movement was observed in and about BUNA RUNWAY …. Requests repeated to 128 Regt. For HMG harassing fire to be used. Offered to take over HMG and man them … rain had made conditions in swamp area very bad'.[4] After all these men had been through, they were still concerned that they might be withdrawn before Buna fell – even though their numbers were pitifully small. The unit war diary records: 'Heard during day that Adv. HQ HGF wanted to recall the Coy. Hope this not true as we want to be in at the finish'.[5] The adjutant recorded that the strength of the company was now down to nine officers and 50 other ranks, with just four officers and 27 other ranks in the forward defensive line, concluding that it was a quiet night with Allied airmen patrolling the coast and dropping flares during the night.[6]

***

That day, unnamed Japanese soldier [C], who was part of Colonel Yamamoto Hiroshi's force dug-in around New Strip and the plantation area, recorded the day's fighting: 'Sunday. Fair later rain. Very quiet during the morning. Mortar fire in the afternoon. Seems that the enemy are now using short, delayed action fuses. It is necessary to further reinforce our position. Took advantage of the dusk and assembled material. Towards evening saw a red light out at sea. Thought it might be enemy landing parties and we were put on emergency alert. The Iwata platoon is in readiness near location of the Battalion HQ. The Nishiyama platoon has put in a protective screen to the front. Received ten days provisions. 1 GO 6 Shaku a day per man'.[7]

Close by, Lieutenant Suganuma, also with Yamamoto's force, was dug-in around the Coconut Grove area near New Strip. He recorded in diary sometime that night: 'Perhaps it may be due to the fact that the enemy who, depending only on fire power attacked [yesterday] and was repulsed, but it is very quiet today. But their patrolling is as usual. Had terrific rainstorm last night and my equipment and clothes got wet. Very hard to dry out. At times they fire in front of HITABE unit. Automatic rifle fire sounds very near. Seems cloudy tonight. At

CHAPTER 27

about 2000 liaison soldiers arrived. Reports that enemy may land on beach so kept strict guard'.[8]

***

Meanwhile, to the west, on the Urbana front, bitter fighting continued almost without respite. The Japanese in Buna Village were surrounded. Fire was hitting them frontally and from across Buna Creek. Even so, the Japanese held their positions with tenacity, and it began to look as if it would be necessary to 'root them out of their bunkers individually, as had been the case at Gona'.[9]

Colonel Grose had been promised command of the 127th Regiment, which was then on its way to the front. He had left the reorganisation of the dispersed II/126th Regiment to Colonel Tomlinson and the battalion commander Major Smith. Grose attended to issues of supply and the readjustment of the positions held by Lieutenant Colonel Smith's II/128th Regiment, on the right. Believing the command of Urbana front should be given to Tomlinson, as there was no use in having two regimental commanders at the front, Grose asked Brigadier Clovis Byers, now commanding the 32nd Division, that afternoon if Tomlinson could be given the command. Byers agreed and Grose returned to the rear, while Tomlinson went on with preparations for an attack scheduled to be commence the next morning.[10]

The attack was to have better artillery support than that previously provided, with all the guns east of the river scheduled to go into action, with the mortars being used more effectively – now amassed based on artillery practice. Because the men could not control their mortar fire in the dense jungle and undergrowth, Lieutenant Colonel McCreary – now commanding the artillery and mortars consolidated the seventeen 81-mm mortars on his front into one unit, made a fire-direction chart from a vertical photograph, and by observation and mathematical calculations, he fixed the position of the mortars in relation to the Japanese positions. McCreary formed these mortars into three batteries, two of six mortars, and one consisting of the remaining five mortars. After adjusting the mortars and training the crews in artillery methods, he spent 'the next two days 60 feet [20 metres] up in a tree less than 200 yards from the Jap forward elements, throwing hammer blow after hammer blow (all firing at once fairly concentrated) on the strong localities, searching through Buna Village'.[11]

The 2/5th Field Regiment adjutant recorded receiving orders that day for the 3.7-inch howitzers, 1st Australian Mountain Battery, commanded by Captain Martin O'Hare, to be prepared to move from their current location, just north of Hariko, to a position about 1.5 kilometres south of the bridge between the airstrips. It was also recorded: 'A ship arrived under fighter escort today with stores and 576 rds of 25 Pdr amn. We were shelled today, about 20 rds in RHQ area. We did NOT ring the guns and ask them "what are they going to do about it". Received news tonight that nine fighters and six Jap bombers landed at Lae'.[12]

The renewed attack against Buna Village would be launched during the early afternoon of the next day by Major Smith and his men of the II/126th Regiment, less the gallant Sergeant Herman Bottcher and his men who were still holding out at Bottcher's Corner, located near the beach. The men of 'E' and 'G' companies would attack on right and left respectively, and the weapons crews of 'H' Company would support the attack with fire from a position to the right of 'G' Company. Sergeant Bottcher and his men were to maintain their position, and 'F' Company would be available as required for the reinforcement of the other companies. The Cannon Company, 128th Regiment, now in reserve, would take up a holding position in the area immediately south of Musita Island, and the II/128th Regiment would continue to cover the right flank of the 126th Regiment. The Japanese, however, would beat them to the punch.[13]

* * *

Still defending his position on Urbana front was the Japanese 1st Class Mechanic, Kuba Satonao, with the *Imperial Jaspanese Navy Tsukioka*

CHAPTER 27

Transport Unit. He recorded in his diary: 'About 1130 [am] our heavy bombers in formation of 15 fly over northward (Rabaul). Probably bombed Moresby. Two or three times a week enemy transport planes drop ammo and provisions. After they are dropped there is always enemy mortar fire'.[14]

* * *

The complete failure on 5 December at Warren front had convinced Eichelberger that the Japanese defences were too strong to be breached by frontal assault. In discussing this with Lieutenant General Herring, he was told he was about to finally be supplied with tanks, as well as fresh Australian troops for action on his side of the river. Eichelberger decided there would be no more all-out frontal assaults against Warren front until the Australian tanks and infantry reinforcements arrived. Meanwhile, he intended to do everything possible to weaken the enemy positions.[15]

Herring had suggested late on 5 December that Eichelberger should try pushing forward on Warren front by concentrating on the destruction of individual pillboxes and machinegun nests that lay in the way. The following day, Eichelberger assured Herring that this was the approach he would now adopt. Since the Japanese perimeter to his immediate front was known to be well defended, he added, he would make the main effort on the left while containing the Japanese on the right – instead of making frontal assaults, which had gotten Warren Force nowhere. The troops would now soften up the Japanese perimeter by attrition and infiltration, before making the final breakthrough with the tanks and Australian infantry reinforcements.[16]

Eichelberger sent out revised orders to Colonel Martin, informing him that his men of Warren Force were to begin vigorous patrolling to locate and pinpoint individual Japanese strong points. As soon as they were located, they were to be destroyed.[17]

* * *

That night, Major General Tsuyuo Yamagata, commanding the Japanese *21st Independent Mixed Brigade*, managed to land at the mouth of the Kumusi River, about 30 kilometres north-west of Gona, with supporting elements to join his men of *III/170th Regiment* who had landed in this area on 2 December. He landed with few men, just the remaining elements of the *III/170th Regiment* who had not landed with the first echelon five days before in the same area. Yamagata's men of the *Ist Battalion*, along with supporting elements, were still stranded in Rabaul[xiv] [18]

That morning, the commander of the *18th Army* had placed Yamagata in direct command of the defence of Gona and Sanananda (he was, on paper at least, commanding all Japanese forces at the three beachheads). He was to take direct command of the *41st Regiment*, elements of which were located at both beachheads, with its *1st Battalion* stranded west of the Gona River. The sole exception was the remaining men of the *144th Regiment*, who would stay under the overall command of Colonel Yamamoto Hiroshi. The complete failure of communications within and between the beachhead perimeters now made this a meaningless command, existing only on paper. Yamagata's force, trapped west of Gona, was designated with the confusing title: *Buna Detachment*, and his immediate priority was to stabilise the situation around Gona. He and his men were to advance east to reinforce the garrison there. This would lead to ongoing fighting around Haddy's Village, just west of Gona Creek, a week after Gona fell to the Australians on 9 December.[19]

Even though Yamagata was in overall command of the Japanese defences at Gona, Sanananda, and Buna, he would never be able to fight his way through the Australian troops around Gona. He would be trapped west of Gona Creek, and therefore, his command of these beachheads was essentially null and void.

---

xiv The *2nd Battalion* of the *170th Regiment* (*II/170th Regiment*) did not serve with the unit in Papua New Guinea, as it had taken up garrison duties on Wake Island.

28

'DURING THE DAY, CONSIDERABLE JAP MOVEMENT WAS OBSERVED ...'

On the morning of 7 December, the one-year anniversary of the attack against Pearl Harbour[xv], Colonel Tomlinson – who was now in command of Urbana front – was preparing to send Major Smith and his battalion once more against Buna Village later that day. The Japanese, however, moved first.[1]

At 6 am, a more determined attempt was made by the Japanese to recapture Bottcher's Corner. They attacked from both the village and the mission station. Sergeant Herman Bottcher and his men were a major thorn in their sides. Bottcher had just been reinforced with a fresh platoon from 'H' Company. Bottcher's men initially concentrated on the attack from the mission, and soon a fresh pile of Japanese dead and dying surrounded their perimeter.

Meanwhile, the attack from the village group, which had remained unseen, was closing in from the other side. Corporal Harold Mitchell, who had joined the garrison the previous day, was now positioned in a forward outpost. The corporal detected the enemy troops from the village while they crept forward under cover of the jungle. Just as these Japanese were about to launch their attack, Mitchell charged the Japanese, yelling with his fixed bayonet. He was quickly and single-handedly among the Japanese. There, he shouted in fury to warn his

---

xv Note, the Japanese attack against Peral Harbour occurred on 8 December, Australian and Japanese time.

pals of the Japanese attack. Mitchell's courage momentarily stunned the Japanese, giving Bottcher and the rest of his men enough time to bring their machine gun and rifles into action to repel the attack from the mission. Miraculously, Mitchell escaped without a scratch and was awarded the DSC for his outstanding courage.[2]

Urbana Force soon after telephoned to Eichelberger the following description of the action: 'Bottcher opened fire on the Buna Mission force first, stopping that attack. He then turned his gun on the Buna Village force and stopped that attack. During the attack, Bottcher was shot in the hand. He was given first aid treatment and is now [again] commanding his gun'.[3]

Meanwhile, 'E' and 'G' companies, II/126th Regiment had advanced at 1.35 pm after a 15-minute artillery and mortar barrage. In their advance, they met heavy opposition and made little progress against the stubborn Japanese defence. To encourage his troops, Major Herbert Smith moved to the most exposed forward positions but was severely wounded as a result. He was later awarded the DSC for his actions. Captain William Boice, the regimental intelligence officer, who had made the first reconnaissance of the track to Jaure over the Owen Stanleys, immediately replaced him as battalion commander, but the attack here stalled. At 2.30 pm, the men of 'F' Company were committed to support 'E' and 'G' companies, and the remaining platoon under Lieutenant Robert Odell was ordered to reinforce Bottcher's Corner.[4]

Lieutenant Odell was also tasked, while moving forward, to clear out two suspected enemy outposts: one north-west of Bottcher's Corner; the other closer to the village. The first outpost fell readily, as the defenders were either dead or dying. The second was a different matter. Odell and his platoon, numbering just a dozen men, began closing in on the objective when they found themselves facing about 50 Japanese in a hastily dug trench. As Odell and his men edged forward, one of the Japanese called out in English that he and his comrades would surrender if the Americans came over to them first. The ruse

CHAPTER 28

was ignored, and the Americans stormed the trench and mopped up the Japanese, but heavy fire from the village soon drove them out. Odell and his men now made their way to Bottcher's Corner.[5]

The Japanese were still not ready to admit defeat to Sergeant Bottcher and his men. In the gloom of the evening, Captain Yasuda Yoshitatsu, commanding the marines of the *5th Yokosuka, 5th Sasebo, SNLP*, with supporting naval pioneer troops, sent a small force on several boats from the Government Station to attack the stubborn American defenders from the sea. But Bottcher's men saw a barge being launched, and their machine gun set the boat on fire – this attack washed back with the tide. The barge, now a blazing hulk, was pulled back to the mission.[6]

* * *

At Warren front, as ordered, intense patrolling became the order of the day. The 37-mm gun and mortar crews fired on the bunkers as their positions became known, and the artillery, aided by Australian Wirraway aircraft now based at Dobodura, provided details of the Japanese positions. The shells of the 37-mm guns and the bombs of the mortars, however, were too light to have any real impact against the bunkers, and the Australian 3.7-inch howitzers and 25-pounders, using high explosive shells with immediate fuses, proved ineffectual against the strong points. Brigadier Albert Waldron had earlier stated the situation regarding the Japanese bunkers: 'The 25-pounders annoyed the Japanese, and that's about all'.[7] What was effective was the lone American 105-mm howitzer with its higher angle of fire and its shells with delay fuses. When its shells struck the bunkers, they buried themselves into the earthen structures before exploding. This howitzer was the only effective weapon on the front to deal with the Japanese bunkers.[8]

Unfortunately, the supply of ammunition for the 105-mm howitzer was ad-hoc. After having fired its original supply of around 200 shells, the howitzer had to remain silent for days. The day before, 6 December, the I Corps ordnance officer at Port Moresby wrote to the front: 'I've been burning the air waves since 2 December to have 800 rounds of 105-mm ammunition flown [to you]. The stuff has been at Brisbane airdrome since the night of 3 December .... The general asked for 100 rounds per day for ten days starting 5 December, and there isn't a single damned round here'.[9] Ammunition for the 105-mm howitzer would finally begin arriving at the front during the second week in December, but even so, it would only do so in small amounts. For most of the time, when it could have made an appreciable difference in the fighting, it stood useless while artillery pieces less suited to the task, the Australian 3.7-inch howitzers and 25-pounders, tried vainly to deal with the Japanese bunkers.[10]

During the fighting, the American and Australian troops recognised just how effective the Japanese employed their grenade launchers. Impressed by their effectiveness, the troops at Warren front now began to experiment with rifle grenades. Australian grenades were used, as no American grenades were available. Using Australian .303 Lee Enfield grenade rifle the men found the few grenades on hand extremely effective. The small supply, however, soon ran out, and they received no more during the campaign.[11]

Still at Warren front, the situation for Lieutenant Colonel Carrier and his men of the I/126th Regiment during this period was one of hardship, as recalled by Martin: 'The positions occupied by the 1st Battalion, 126th Infantry were almost unbearably hot in the daytime as the tropical sun broiled down, the grass shut off all air, and held in the steaming heat. Due to enemy observation any daylight movement among the forward positions had to be by crawling which added to the misery from the heat. There were cases of heat exhaustion daily, and some of the company commanders strongly urged the battalion commander to permit the troops to withdraw about 300 yards in daytime to positions where there was shade and reoccupy the forward positions at night'.[12]

Martin overruled these requests, believing that to allow daily

CHAPTER 28

withdrawals would contribute nothing to the harassing and softening up of the enemy and 'would be psychologically bad [and] would hurt the rebuilding of their offensive spirit'.[13] The renewed tactics of slow methodological destruction of Japanese strongpoints, made few gains anywhere along Warren front. Carrier and his men met repeated setbacks in their efforts to cross the bridge between the strips, and Miller and his men of III/128th Regiment, with McCoy and his men of the I/128th Regiment moved ahead only a few metres. The fighting there essentially settled into a stalemate.[14]

The Australians of the 2/6th Independent Company fared little better. The unit diary records how Allied airmen that day strafed Old Strip several time and that some dogfights were observed with planes falling into the sea – they were too far away to determine which side got the better of the combat. It was also recorded: 'During the day, considerable Jap movement was observed in and about the RUNWAY area. [American] MG harassing fire would stop a lot of this. The positions to and from which they move are all recorded'.[15]

At around 7 pm, a Japanese four-man patrol was observed moving towards the commandos' forward OP position, they were observed to lay in the grass for a short time, then fell back. These Japanese were not targeted, as they did not want to give away the position of the OP. A few hours later, it was reported that the Japanese were moving between the emplacements east of the bridge and a machine gun position west of it, while trucks could still be heard driving down one of the strips and was soon observed to be loaded with troops heading for the bridge located between the airstrips.[16]

* * *

Still in the Warren front area was unnamed Japanese soldier [C], who was part of Colonel Yamamoto Hiroshi's force. He briefly recorded in his diary that day: 'Cloudy. Quiet since yesterday. Considerable mortar fire. Aerial combat about 1300'.[17] Close by, Lieutenant Suganuma, also with Yamamoto's force, was dug-in around the Coconut Grove.

He also wrote in his diary: 'During the morning three to four groups of three plane formations flew over. Bombed blindly the A/A position area. Enemy patrols infiltrating in front of HITABE unit and firing automatic rifle and withdrawing. At times it seems that we fired our infantry gun. The planes seem to fly very high. We can hear them but can't see them. Concentrated mortar fire. Everyone in shelters. Heard reports of our troops being reinforced'.[18]

* * *

At this point, the Australians had fielded three of their veteran 2nd AIF brigades (the 16th, 21st and 25th brigades) and two of their most seasoned militia units (the 3rd and 39th battalions). All had fought the Japanese along the Kokoda Track through the Owen Stanley Range, with most also participating in the brutal fighting to take Oivi and Gorari just below its northern slopes just west of the Kumusi river. All were now involved in the ongoing battles to take Gona and Sanananda. Along the Sanananda Track, the Australian 30th Militia Brigade was on the eve of also being thrown into the bloody battles for the coastal beachheads.[19]

Based at Milne Bay, the 17th and 18th brigades of the 2nd AIF and the 7th Militia Brigade were a pool from which rested and battle-hardened units could be called on for quick service against the enemy defences at Buna, Sanananda and Gona. Even so, General Blamey could not commit these formations lightly as he had to balance: 1) the potential for the Japanese to launch fresh seaborne attacks against south-east New Guinea and the adjacent islands; 2) the need to take the Papuan Japanese beachheads; and 3) a need for fresh and experienced troops to carry the fight deeper into Japanese-held territory after the Papuan phase had ended. But events made the second of these needs so urgent that it demanded the immediate use of experienced men. Unknown to Blamey, the Australians would finally take Gona within days, and a week later, they would decimate the large Japanese reinforcements that had landed just west of Gona Creek.[20]

CHAPTER 28

Even so, Lieutenant General Herring, commanding Advance NGF, and his chief of staff, Brigadier Ronald Hopkins, visited Lieutenant General Eichelberger's headquarters at Henahamburi to make arrangements for the reception of the Australian troops and tanks. Blamey had decided that Brigadier George Wootten, a 51-year-old Duntroon graduate from Sydney, and his men of the 18th Infantry Brigade would reinforce Buna. Eichelberger at once offered to put Wootten in command of Warren Force with Colonel Martin as his 2i/C, an offer which Herring promptly accepted.[21]

Blamey had discussed the matter with General MacArthur, and the two commanders had agreed that the operation would require the immediate despatch of at least a battalion of troops from Milne Bay and a suitable number of tanks now at Port Moresby. Since Blamey did not have enough small ships to move the battalion, he asked MacArthur to prevail upon the Navy (who had been unwilling to send its ships into the waters around Buna) to provide corvettes or destroyers to get the troops forward. The next day, the Navy agreed to provide three corvettes, and NGF issued its first orders relating to the movement of the 2/9th Battalion (18th Brigade), one battalion of the 7th Brigade, along with two troops of tanks from the 2/6th Armoured Regiment to Buna.[22]

29

'... MAY START A GENERAL ATTACK IN REVENGE OF HAWAII'

The next day, 8 December, at Urbana front, the men of the II/126th Regiment, now commanded by Captain William Boice, made another attempt to finally take Buna Village. Artillery, mortars, and machine guns opened their barrages at 2 pm, and the troops started moving forward 15-minutes later. Lieutenant Colonel McCreary, commanding the artillery and mortars, organised for his three mortar batteries to lay down fire just 50 metres to the front of the battalion's advance, but the Japanese held firm, and the attack was repulsed once again.[1]

A courageous but futile attempt was made to use a flamethrower to burn out a Japanese bunker on the southern edge of the village, which had resisted capture for several days. The bunker was on the corner of a kunai flat, with dense jungle and swamp to the rear. Two primitive flamethrowers had arrived that day, and one of them was immediately pressed into action. Covered by the fire of 20 men, the operator managed to get within ten metres of the bunker without being detected. Then he stepped into the open, intent on sending out a ball of flame to engulf the entrenched Japanese. However, as he squeezed the trigger of the flamethrower, all that came out was a three-metre dribble of flame, which set the grass on fire. As the operator and his two-covering party courageously moved closer, they were shot down, as was his officer, who went forward to their assistance.[2]

* * *

CHAPTER 29

That evening, Captain Yasuda Yoshitatsu made his last diversion in favour of the beleaguered troops in the village. While the Japanese there counterattacked on the left with about 40 men, a second force of around 80 men moved from the mission by way of the Mitsu Island and hit the right flank of the II/126th Regiment. The force from the mission advanced to the attack, screaming and yelling, but the battalion mortars and machine guns beat back the enemy in short order. The battalion war journal records: 'Our heavy weapons quieted them down rather fast'.[3]

The Japanese official history also records: 'The Japanese Navy units again mounted a counter-offensive on 8 December. Approximately 40 men from Buna Village attacked the American's left flank, and 100 men from the mission sector sortied against the Americans' right flank. After a brief encounter, the sallying parties were forced back by heavy mortar and machinegun fire. However, the strong defences of the Japanese garrison withstood over 12 assaults by the American force'.[4]

Still defending his position here was Japanese 1st Class Mechanic, Kuba Satonao, with the *Imperial Japanese Navy Tsukioka Transport Unit*. He recorded in his diary that day: '8 December is the 1st anniversary of this war. The enemy doesn't offer much battle today, but the enemy may start a general attack in revenge of Hawaii. If reinforcements come by then, all will be well, but if not, BUNA BASE may be completely lost. I will fight to the last – while my eyes are open. Thought it unusually quiet for the 1st anniversary, but in the afternoon, there was fierce mortar barrage. Received a light wound. There were two shells that hit our position. Towards evening five scouts picked, myself among them. We rushed the enemy, but they had already left. We returned'.[5]

Corporal Okajima, at Buna, wrote on the one-year anniversary of the start of the Greater East Asian War: 'Never thought I would be spending this day in a bomb shelter in New Guinea'.[6]

* * *

At Warren front, Colonel Martin wanted to move up a few of the artillery pieces for direct fire against the bunkers, but there were too few guns on hand to risk any of them so far forward. The arrival by sea that morning of two more Australian 25-pounders of the 2/5th Field Regiment made it possible to relocate the guns. The newly arrived guns were emplaced just north of Hariko, while the O'Hare Troop of two 3.7-inch howitzers, 1st Australian Mountain Battery, began moving from Hariko to take up their new position 1.5 kilometres south of the bridge between the strips; they would be in position by 11 December.[7]

The adjutant of the 2/5th Field Regiment recorded sometime that night: 'Maj. Hall accompanied Col Martin to Bn HQ (left flank) 1 Bn 126 Regt. Recce of the New Strip area was carried out, and the "dummy plane, dummy AA guns" and the MG oil boxes in that area were viewed from 200 yds. As a result of this recce, it was decided to shoot both the 3.7 and 25 Prs on the pillbox area this evening, and to support an attack on them tomorrow morning at 0700 hrs. 2/1 Regt to shoot on two areas, 3.7 and 25 Prs each to engage two areas. Gen Byers inspected Capt. Mueller's OP and observed the shoot. He expressed complete satisfaction and was pleased with results'.[8]

Meanwhile, the two 25-pounders Hall had left with Captain Lionel Nix at Wanigela in the middle of November had the previous week been ordered forward. On 27 November, Nix loaded the two guns on S.S. *Kuri Marau* and set out for Oro Bay. They arrived there in darkness at the beginning of an odyssey, as recorded by the commanding officer of the 2/5th Field Regiment, Lieutenant Colonel John O'Brien:

> The skipper could get no response to his oft-repeated signals. Accompanied by Nix, he rowed ashore. After a search along the blacked-out beach, the pair stirred up the soundly sleeping members of an American defence post. They then located the much-harassed Harbour Master, who, learning the nature of their cargo, cried 'Hell, I want food, not guns and ammunition'

CHAPTER 29

.... There was no way to get the guns ashore. The ship turned back, its cargo still aboard, to be clear of the danger area by dawn. On arrival at Porlock Harbour the *Kuri Marau* received orders to proceed immediately to Milne Bay. The guns had to come off .... The Harbour Master at Porlock was, like all of his kind on the New Guinea coast, very short on ships and very long on conflicting orders from above. Nix and company pestered him until he was glad to uphold their claim to a large, flat-topped barge, which they commandeered, so long as he got rid of them ... when a ship could be got from somewhere to tow the barge.

Spirits were ebbing fast when the familiar *Kuri Marau* appeared on the scene again. At Milne Bay it was discovered that there had been a mistake, the vessel had been required at Porlock, of all places. Nix pressed his claims so vigorously that *Kuri Marau* soon started on its way to Hariko, the big, awkward barge blundering along in tow .... Just before dusk, three Jap planes came bombing and strafing .... The damage forced the ship to return to Porlock. Worse, it was ordered to Milne Bay again. The section seemed fated never to leave Porlock.

But new hope dawned the following day. Two small vessels were obtained to tow the barge in tandem. This time the journey was going to be done entirely in the dark. The barge arrived off Hariko on the night of 8 December without further mischance .... The waves were tossing the barge several feet up and down on the edge of the beach, and so landing the guns was a hazardous business.[9]

Major Hall now had four 25-pounders in action north of Hariko. Soon after, Captain O'Hare, who's strength recently increased by the arrival of an additional howitzer, moved to the new site on the Dobodura–Buna track, south of the bridge between the strips. Even though the howitzers would at once begin targeting Japanese positions behind both strips with greater effect than before, they were still unable to make any appreciable impression against the Japanese perimeter, so well was the enemy entrenched.[10]

A report in the 2/1st Field Regiment provides details of a meeting held that day between the airmen of No. 4 Army Cooperation Squadron RAAF and Lieutenant Colonel Keith O'Connell, commanding the regiment, to better co-ordinate targeting positions at the Buna front:

> I endeavoured on BUNA front to … assist pilots generally by providing them where possible with obliques on which the target was marked by me. This was particularly valuable in BUNA MISSION area in which there are a number of buildings and ensured that any pilot would engage actual target desired. These obliques were also valuable where speed was essential, for instance, information was desired on STRIP point where there were some suspected (from air photos) enemy works. The pilot had finished his mission but was prepared to do a quick sortie on his way home. A photo was given [to] him, guns laid on target from information got from map and other shooting and he plotted H.E. rounds of first salvo (since they fell near the target) and dropped the marked photo. Corrections could be applied later by a scale made on the photo from the map of the locality (the map had been made from verticals, so a comparative scale was made with reference to detail near the target. Actually, this salvo fell approx. 75 yards from target.[11]

Meanwhile, at the forward OP of the 2/6th Independent Company, a wounded American wandered into their outpost. He had been hit in the arm. The diary records: 'He was rather incoherent but stated he thought the other two members of his patrol were killed'.[12] Again, the OP reported that Japanese were using trucks along the airstrips during darkness, heading for the bridge area. This was reported to the

CHAPTER 29

Australian gunners who soon after opened fire. An observer noted that the first shell landed about 50 metres left of the trucks and that the Japanese scattered into the trees to the right of the bridge. Correction shots were soon bombarding these trees, tearing the timber into deadly timber shrapnel, and likely inflicting several casualties against the enemy who had sort shelter there.[13]

* * *

Lieutenant Suganuma and his men were still dug-in around the Coconut Grove near New Strip:

> According to instructions from battalion commander, at 0430 each squad within shelter bowed towards the Imperial Palace. Told the meaning of Great[er] East Asia War to the squad. Bombing during the morning. Morning and afternoon concentrated mortar fire. Several burst in front of 3rd squad. Until night there was firing in the jungle. It is not in front of the HITABE unit, and it isn't in front of our unit. Only firing heard. There were no bullets coming our way. We could not see them, yet they are shooting LMG and automatic rifles and rifles. Soldiers impressed by the firing.
>
> Enemy worn out by attackers. Furthermore, the enemy has been repulsed by our keen-eyed snipers and nowadays they seem very quiet. The enemy who depends solely on fire power must be afraid because of the severe losses they suffered. In the jungle it seems that they fire at any sound, due to illusions. They must be frightened by the little animals and shoot at them. From sundown till about 2000 [hours] they fired LMG and threw hand grenades recklessly. However, because of the feeling that the enemy is near, we have heavy guards. According to reports our troops are continuously landing. We just have to hold on only a little longer.

From tomorrow we will get 1 GO 7 SHAKU (about a handful) of rice, but today we have 2 GO. However, even though we get 2 GO I am still hungry. I said I would positively eat only twice, but about 0700 [hours] after breakfast, I eat [at] about 1300 [hours] after all and leave some for super. Ate three coconuts, but there are no more coconuts in the rear. We must go in front of the outposts to get them. There were lots of coconuts before, but due to the constructing of trenches and shelters they have been ... used up. It is said that a bullet cannot pierce a coconut [tree] and are used widely. At RABAUL we ate coconuts and drank coconut milk and didn't think much of it, but here at the front, coconuts are about all we can get to eat at hand. The coconut and milk are eaten, and the outside is used for tobacco. Coconuts meat is slightly sweet and is hard; the inner part is water. It doesn't fill the stomach very much, but it is good. Maybe it is because I haven't had much sugar to eat since landing, but the sweetness of the coconut tastes very good.[14]

Likely nearby was medic Yokoyama Yoriichi. He later recalled the food situation: 'No regular food supplies were provided. I heard that they put rice and dried fish in drums and submarines threw them into the ocean offshore for us, but we failed to find any. Usually, you measure rice with a cup .... In those days, we measured rice by counting grains .... We picked some bracken, like a fern, and mixed in the rice with water. It wasn't like eating rice, but more like eating fern porridge with a little rice floating in it. The soldiers positioned close to the seaside were able to obtain salt, but since I was stationed well inland, I couldn't leave my position just for salt. Having no salt at all, I was lucky to find a lemon tree, but, as I suspected, lemon cannot replace salt'.[15]

* * *

CHAPTER 29

General Blamey sent a peremptory summons for Brigadier Wootten, commanding the Australian 18th Brigade. At the time, Wootten was visiting his 2/12th Battalion on Goodenough Island. Presently, his 2/10th Battalion, the original nucleus of the force that had been flown into Wanigela, was divided between there and Porlock Harbour. Wootten now only had the 2/9th Battalion at Milne Bay. These men had narrowly missed being committed to the fighting at Buna, as Blamey had planned to land them on the beach immediately east of beachhead in co-ordination with an overland thrust by infantry and tanks from the south. But, to his intense chagrin, the Navy had refused to make available the two destroyers and two corvettes needed to ferry these men, and he could only collect enough small boats to carry about 400 men. He had been forced to abandon the plan. Even so, the men of the 2/9th Battalion were training for an opposed landing.[16]

Blamey now planned to move the Australian 18th Brigade to Wanigela as soon as the men of the remainder of the 17th Brigade arrived at Milne Bay. There was still considerable concern that the Japanese might launch another invasion to take Milne Bay and its airstrips. In late August, the men of the 18th Brigade decisively defeated a Japanese invasion of Milne Bay, which was supported with a naval bombardment followed by troops landing with artillery and tanks. This attack was to help isolate Port Moresby and capture the airfields at Milne Bay under construction. The battle for Milne Bay would go down in history as the first decisive defeat of Japanese land forces in the Second World War.[17]

Indeed, the future Field Marshal, Lord Slim, commanding the 15th Indian Corps in Burma (Myanmar), recalled after the war: 'We were helped too, by a very cheering piece of news that now reached us, and of which, as a morale raiser, I made great use. In August and September 1942, Australian troops had, at Milne Bay in New Guinea, inflicted on the Japanese their first undoubted defeat on land. If the Australians, in conditions very like ours, had done it, so could we. Some of us may forget that of all the Allies, it was Australian soldiers who first broke the spell of the invincibility of the Japanese Army; those of us who were in Burma have cause to remember'.[18]

30

'... WE HAVE BULLETS OF FLESH'

With the capture of the Gona beachhead on 9 December by Australian troops of the 39th and 2/14th battalions, it became clear that the remaining Japanese beachhead garrisons at Sanananda and Buna could no longer be supplied easily by sea. But the Japanese could still use the airfields at Lae in western Papua and Rabaul in New Britain to possibly drop supplies to their stranded troops. The next day, Japanese bombers, escorted by Zeros fighters, would fly nonstop from Rabaul and drop food and ammunition onto Old Strip. This flight was the second, and last, air supply mission ordered by the Japanese headquarters at Rabaul to supply the two beachheads.[1]

* * *

At Warren front, since the attack of 5 December, there had essentially been no gain, as the 'active patrolling' and attacks against localised Japanese strong points had failed, and the whole front had settled into stalemate. Even so, a limited attack was launched that day against New Strip by American troops of the I/128th Regiment and the Australian commandos.[xvi] Unknown to Major Harcourt and his men of the 2/6th Independent Company, 9 December would see their final battle against the Japanese at Buna. The war diary of the commando unit describes their final attempt to break through the Japanese lines.[2]

The adjutant of the commando unit recorded what happened

---

xvi It is interesting that neither the Australian nor the US official history mention this attack at all.

that morning. At about 7.25 am, the smoke from a smoke screen was clearing, and about 20 GIs advanced towards the Japanese positions east of the bridge, followed by another four men. At around 7.30 am, several Japanese apparently wounded, moved, or limped from their forward positions and moved back along New Strip. Japanese machinegun and mortar fire targeted the Americans, but no Japanese troop movement could be seen. Just after 9 am, ten GIs withdrew from the enemy position east of the bridge, back to their original position. About ten minutes later, Allied planes bombed the timber east of the strip, including the Coconut Grove, north-east of the eastern end of the runway. At 9.58 am, supporting mortar fire exploded in nearby enemy emplacements. Even so, the Americans and the remaining GIs in the emplacement withdrew – no reason was given, as it was observed Japanese small arms fire 'was only spasmodic and not heavy'.[3]

Soon after, Lieutenant Robert Scott passed through to take up a position behind the woods, noting the enemy position was empty. Scott considered that if his patrol had been larger, he could have occupied the emplacement, but he was not sure he could have held it unaided. Now the 'friendly' mortar-bombs were exploding close to Scott's position.[4]

Meanwhile, Lieutenant Geoffrey Fielding, who was commanding the three forward patrols, stated that although there was some enemy fire from west of the bridge, he too believed that if he had more men, or if the GIs had occupied the emplacement east of the bridge, this area could have been held and the fire coming from the west silenced.[5]

To the east, Lieutenant Gordon Blainey and his section had moved up with the men of the I/128th Regiment, near the eastern end of New Strip. If enemy opposition was not great, the GIs and Blainey intended to advance to the timber area behind the strip; however, they were quickly targeted with concentrated small arms and machinegun fire.[6]

By 12.15 pm, Japanese movement and a mountain gun were observed positioned along the north-east side of the strip. This enemy

CHAPTER 30

force appeared to be trying to locate the mortars now positioned behind the commando's OP, with some shells exploding close to the post, spraying deadly shrapnel throughout the area.[7]

Supporting this attack were the Australian gunners of the 2/5th Field Regiment. The regimental diarist recorded that the gunners opened fire against the Japanese positions at 7 am, and during the last ten minutes of the barrage, one round of smoke was fired every two minutes. It was observed from the exploding smoke shells, that the guns were on target and no corrections were required: 'The SMOKE was most effective but owing to lack of experience on the part of the Inf the attack was not entirely successful. The Arty Board is now in full operation at the Comd Post, and all targets registered by both the Arty from the coast and the 2/1 inland are on the same grid and are reported to each other. The CCRA, [Commander in Chief Royal Artillery] and Col [Horace] Harding, US Army, and now commanding all artillery in the attack on the BUNA area visited the coastal area and expressed themselves perfectly satisfied with gun posns in this area. During the night 8–9 Dec Capt. Nix arrived with two F Tp guns, and 1000 rds of amn., Lieut. [Arthur] Outridge and 23 ORs. These guns are in action in the old 3.7 Mtn Bty posn [mountain battery position], and will be shot in tomorrow, Capt. Nix has had to report sick, but is still on duty'.[8]

It was also recorded that a reconnaissance was to be carried out the next day for a new position for the 3.7-inch howitzers to be located on the Buna-Simemi Track, to place them in direct support of the left flank of Warren Force. Here, Lieutenant William Marr was in position as the Forward Observation Officer (FOO). During the late afternoon, Major William Hall was informed by Captain Mueller's OP that around 15 Japanese troops were moving about several machinegun position, and with this, the area was swept with artillery fire.[9]

Meanwhile, at 3 pm, commando Lieutenant Arthur Tregarthen, who was leading his patrol, returned to the OP, reporting he had located a narrow passage through the swamp south-west of the airstrip, but it was impracticable for passage of troops in any number, as they would be observed by nearby Japanese emplacements. The swamp water at this point was described in the unit war diary as being between 'four to six feet deep [one to two metres] in places and bush very thick. Patrol pushed through to kunai grass clearing … but a body of troops could not have reached there undetected'.[10]

An hour later, Major Harry Harcourt received orders from the 128th Regiment that the 2/6th Independent Company would 'cease to be under their comd. as from 1200 hrs. 10 Dec. and were to procced to HQ 7 Div. at SOPUTA. Contacted fwd tps and told them to hand over OP to 128 Regt and report to Coy HQ'.[11]

* * *

Still in the Warren front area was unnamed Japanese soldier [C], who was part of Colonel Yamamoto Hiroshi's force. He recorded:

> Wednesday. Rain later fair. From early morning today there was mortar fire around us. From the left there is a considerable large artillery fire (cannon) which lands to the left rear of us. There is a constant flight of enemy planes overhead. We are now in a delaying and holding action. The amount of provisions is small and there is no chance of replenishing ammunition. But we have bullets of flesh. No matter what comes we are not afraid. If they come, let them come, even though there are thousands of the enemy, we will not be surprised. We have the aid of Heaven. We are warriors of YAMOTO. The enemy fired 990 mortar shells this morning. Didn't think they could do it. One shell hit our shelter but there was no damage done. In one squad a soldier was slightly wounded. From the Army commanding officer to the Kimmochi unit there were words of praise. Tomorrow, they expect provisions by air.[12]

CHAPTER 30

Close by in the Coconut Grove was Lieutenant Suganuma and his men. The young officer recorded sometime that day:

> Sunrise at 0400 [hours]. From today one man gets 1 GO a day. Other auxiliary food is the same as before, MISO SHOYU 5 grams. Most of us finish breakfast around 0500. I think that just one more mouthful, just a little more won't lessen the amount, but before I know it, I have eaten more than I have planned. Nothing like one-third of the food, I eat most of it. About 0600 there is mountain artillery fire. The shells seem to be dropping way in the rear. Following this there is concentrated mortar fire. There is reckless firing before and after this the same as yesterday. However, today perhaps due to the increased number of our planes, they do not fly low but high making a lot of noise. I cannot tell whether they are patrolling or reconnoitring or whether they are our planes or the enemies!
>
> But the mortars are pouring heavy fire on us. Really 'pot fish shooting'. Concentrated fire with three mortars. The one on the very left is aimed at the HITABE unit, the centre one is aimed at the 2.3 squad [2nd and 3rd]. The one on the right seems to fire way to the right. They fire 30 or 50 rounds of concentrated fire. The firing stops all of a sudden and everything is quiet. After a while rifle shots are heard in the jungle. Then there is concentrated fire with the 10 cm guns. No time for rest. Feeling that enemy scouting patrol infiltrating but since the target isn't definite, restrained from firing. We are waiting for one good shot. The enemy comes in feeling safe because we do not shoot. It seems as if these scouts are observing where the shells are landing. Shells fall continuously around the 2nd and 3rd squads.
>
> Even though it is but a mouthful I eat my meagre noon meal. Mortar fire has died down. The squad leader's trench is full

of mud. There are marks on his rifle. There is a hole left by a fragment in SHIMIZU's mess kit. Corp WATANABE has a wound on his nose due to a shell exploding near the entrance of the trench. From noon there is continuous concentrated firing [and at] about 1530 [hours], the mortar fire ceased. There is no firing in the jungle. About 1630 it became cloudy, and it felt as if it were evening. TAKASE was feverishly reinforcing his trench. Suddenly there was automatic rifle firing. I told them to hurry and jump into the trench. I wondered how TAKASE was but he had been shot through the head. Almost unconscious. He had reinforced his own trench and piled dirt up so that it would shelter him from mortar fire, and while he was just putting on camouflage, rear part at that, he was wounded, without entering the trench that he himself had dug out. He lost consciousness. He was a man who strived till the last. He died around evening. In this battle his helmet was hit, and again he was scraped on his leg by a piece of mortar shell. Surprisingly enough, both wounds were light but on the third time due to a wound in the head he died. By the same fire, KATO of the 3rd squad was wounded in the hand.[13]

* * *

At Urbana front, Lieutenant Colonel McCreary, commanding the artillery and mortars, continued his hammer blows against the Buna Village, but the Japanese still held their positions. The Japanese official history records that this bombardment inflicted many casualties: 'A concentrated barrage of over 2000 artillery shells in the half hour from 5.30 am on 9 December destroyed the second-line other-ranks sentry position, which consisted of 130 men. Many of these men were buried alive'.[14]

During the afternoon, Lieutenant James Downer, now commanding 'E' Company, II/126th Regiment, led a patrol against

CHAPTER 30

the same bunker position that the flamethrower failed to reduce the previous day. Covered by fire from the rest of the patrol, Downer moved out against the enemy positions alone. However, as he made his way forward, he was spotted and killed by a hidden sniper just before reaching the bunker. Downer's body was recovered, and the fight for the bunker continued. Enemy fire slackened by evening, and the bunker was finally taken after costing the attackers heavy casualties and several days of fighting. Lieutenant James Downer was posthumously awarded the DSC for his actions that day.[15]

Captain Herbert Manning, commanding the Australian guns of Bullforce, reported the day's events, which appeared to have been one of overall confusion:

> Buna Mission consisting of a number of fortified huts, MG and A/A posts engaged with 25 rounds .... [Japanese] OP partially demolished. Task on enemy OP area fired to support 2 Bn 126 Regt attack on Buna Village. Was effective in neutralising enemy fire – but as [the] infantry [was] delayed five hours with one Coy, this was of little use. Could not repeat as other Coy had gone forward .... Present operations include attack on Buna Village area which we are supporting when possible. Lieut. HAYWOOD endeavouring to find fresh Ops. Lieut. ARNOLD going to US troops on coast to act as LO and observe if possible. Using wireless .... A pillbox on BUNA VILLAGE was engaged by Lieut. HAYWOOD from Buna Creek. The infantry wished this destroyed – despite advice that it was not practical. A verified 25 yd bracket was obtained, and 120 rounds fired raising and lowering angle of sight. No direct hits were observed. Shoot was discontinued.[16]

By now, Major Smith's II/126th Regiment had launched 12 futile attacks on the village. In doing so, the battalion strength was fewer than 250 men. Indeed, 'E' and 'F' companies each had less than

50 effectives left. But fresh troops were now available, as the 127th Infantry Regiment was moving forward. Colonel Grose, as promised earlier, took over command of the 127th Regiment, and Lieutenant Colonel Edwin Schmidt, the regimental commander, became his executive officer.[17]

* * *

Meanwhile, Japanese 1st Class Mechanic, Kuba Satonao, with the *Imperial Japanese Navy Tsukioka Transport Unit*, was still holding his position along Urbana front. He recorded in his diary that day: '0500 [hours] heavy mortar barrage. TODA, UYEMURA and myself [*sic*] had been sent to the YASUDA Unit since last night. There are only five in our position. We have only rifles. This may be the place where I will meet my death. I will fight to the last. 1800 ordered back to HQ to find that the mortar barrage during the morning had hit our position and three had been killed out of the 2nd squad and one killed from my squad (3rd). Our platoon leader was wounded, and our company commander (1st Lt. NIORII) was killed. If we had not been sent out we may have been killed too. It is only fate that I am alive today'.[18]

31

'FOUR TANKS HAD JUST ARRIVED AT HARIKO'

On 10 December, Eichelberger informed Major General Sutherland in Port Moresby: 'I am changing some of my leaders on the right flank. Young Clarkson who only left the military academy in 1938 is going to take one of the battalions on the right flank and Carrier is being relieved by Major Beaver. I know Clarkson well, for I raised him from a pup …. He is full of fight and will do what I tell him'.[1]

The three American battalion commanders who had endured weeks of combat were now not surprisingly beginning to show signs of stress and exhaustion. Lieutenant Colonel Carrier, suffering from angina pectoris, would be evacuated on 13 December. Major Chester Beaver, who had fought with such determination on Urbana front, now replaced him as the commander of the I/126th Regiment. Lieutenant Colonel McCoy, commanding the I/128th Infantry, was replaced with Major Gordon Clarkson with the staff of I Corps. McCoy returned to division headquarters. Lieutenant Colonel Miller, commanding the III/128th Regiment, was replaced with Lieutenant Colonel MacNab, who had been executive officer of Warren Force, with Miller becoming executive officer to Colonel Martin.[2]

The war of attrition ordered for Warren front had still not resulted in any advance, but the relentless pounding by the mortars and artillery, and the sharp probing forays of the infantry were assessed (rightly or wrongly) to be having the effect intended by Eichelberger, wearing down the enemy physically and mentally and softening up their defences for the final battle to take the beachhead.[3]

The 2/5th Field Regiment war diary records how Captain Lionel Nix and his two guns were finally in place to assist the fighting at Buna. He spent some time with Major Hall and Captain Charles Mueller, examining maps and aerial maps of the area prior to occupying his OP. The four remaining Bren gun carriers and their personnel were placed under Hall's command temporarily, as the most 'senior man left is a Sgt'.[4]

Just as 32-year-old Lieutenant Arthur Outridge, from Sandgate in Queensland, and his gunners with 'F' Troop opened fire against the Old Strip position, several Japanese medium Betty bombers, escorted by Zeros, arrived from Rabaul and began to drop food and ammunition supplies onto the strip.[5] The war diary of the 2/5th Field Regiment records their arrival: 'This [first] shot had just been completed when 16 enemy bombers and eight Zeros flew over the Old Strip and released 200 to 300 parachutes of food and/or amn. Guns were immediately laid on the area awaiting the attempted recovery of the bundles by Japs. Within 30 minutes of the droppings a force of Beaufighters and A20s strafed and bombed the area from low level, where the droppings had taken place. The strafing started a little too far south and one of our FOOs had branches shot off his tree (Mr Outridge and Capt. Mueller had shots unpleasantly close)'.[6] Also supporting the barrage here were the guns of 'E' Troop.[7]

*　*　*

That day, Japanese soldier [E] who had landed at Buna with Colonel Yamamoto Hiroshi and was now dug-in around New Strip recorded in his diary the aerial resupply: 'Our planes flew over and dropped a lot of provisions for the rear Navy Mess'.[8] Close by would have been unnamed Japanese soldier [C], who was also part of Colonel Yamamoto Hiroshi's force. He briefly recorded in his diary the appearance of their airmen: 'Thursday. Fair. Continued from yesterday there is mortar fire. Thirty of our planes flew overhead'.[9]

CHAPTER 31

Still at the Coconut Grove was Lieutenant Suganuma and his men; this officer recorded in his diary:

TAKASE's body was buried last night, and we pass a night of strain. About 0800 [hours] there was rain as usual. We are soaked through and through. These last three or four days it rains every day. Even though we are directly under the equator it is cold at night. We take advantage of the dawn and putup camouflage. Before sunrise there is concentrated mortar fire. Today we expect enemy ground troops. Everyone alert.

Today they say that provisions and ammo will be dropped from planes for us. We just have to bear and have patience for three or four days more, so the unit commander's instructions say. The main force of the Army will make an enforced landing against the enemy, so they say. The advance unit is already at GIRUWA. I instruct everyone for the next three or four days we must hold this present position to the last man. There has been a telegram from the Army commander to the effect. 'The KIMMOCHI unit has securely held the airport against a superior enemy and under difficult conditions, we are grateful'. Morale was greatly boosted.

Noise of planes heard but can't tell whether they are enemy planes or ours. They may be our planes dropping provisions. Yesterday's mortar and artillery rounds fired until 1200. They certainly fired a lot. A fighter plane flew very low. Thought it was one of ours, but it was an enemy plane. After that it seems they are flying high. As usual, I wonder how the dropping of provisions has turned out. Due to lack of food [at] around 0900 SAIMIZU asks whether it is time to eat and when I tell him there are still two hours left, he answers 'my, my'. We burry Superior Private NAKAYAMA from 1st squad.

The enemy approaches close by, the sound of the cracking of coconuts attracts them, so for the time being, we are prohibited to eat them. Relief of sentries etc., during the daytime, will be absolutely carried out by crawling on all fours. The next three or four days will be tough so until then no matter what happens, hold out. During the daytime those who do not have any business must not go outside of the trenches etc. – so I tell my men. Two or three enemy infiltrate and start sniping. During the morning there was mortar fire, but after that although some fell in front of the HITABE unit none fell around here. It is too early to feel safe. It is 1200 now. Although there are enemy planes there is no bombing. It is surprising. Maybe after observation they may come and bomb ….

Today from noon there isn't a cloud in the sky. About 1230 there were explosions. Didn't jump into trenches, and when I looked closer, [I] found it was a large formation of our bombers. Nine Navy bombers in two formations with a few fighter planes flying over and [then] flew away. Probably bombed enemy airfields and were on their way back. About 30 minutes later, I heard the roar of motors and I thought that our planes had come again, but they came in turn and bombed and strafed the AA position vicinity, and CP vicinity. About six or seven planes flew over. After that only the roar of the motor was heard. [Earlier] the enemy came into our position to the front edge of the field of fire clearing at 0890 and started sniping. About three o'clock they went towards the 1st squad but the situation there is the same. Two rounds of infantry gun fired into them, but it didn't do so well. As soon as the infantry guns quit firing there was concentrated enemy mortar fire. Fired about 340 rounds.[10]

* * *

It was also now that Major Harry Harcourt and his commandos of the 2/6th Independent Company finally returned to the Australian 7th Division west of Girua River. The unit war diary simply records:

CHAPTER 31

'1000 [hours]: Preparations made to move. FIELDING's party withdrawn from fed. Area – four offs. 38 O/Rs. Decided that as they had been in line without rest for 19 days to let them wait at HARIKO until 11th or 12th. Men tired and feet very bad owing to constant wet. 1300: HQ part (5 Offs. 26 O/Rs) moved out to SOPUTA via HARIKO and SEMEMI.[11]

After the fall of Buna, a month later on 9 January, General MacArthur would issue his Order of the Day. It was the only one he ever issued during the war and was his most important statement until the announcement of the Japanese surrender in 1945. The order received wide international publicity: 'While all ground troops have performed admirably, elements of the 6th and 7th Australian divisions and the 32nd and 41st US divisions, the 6th Independent Commando Unit [sic], Mountain Artillery Batteries of the First Australian Corps, elements of the [Australian] Armoured Division and the native Papuan carriers have been especially prominent'.[12]

As the historian of the company, Syd Trigellis (a 2nd AIF veteran with the 2/2 Field Regiment) recorded: 'The 2/6 Australian Independent Company was the only unit specifically mentioned by General MacArthur – even if he did get it wrong! Perhaps that should be the company's accolade for the achievements in the campaign and the last world on its first major battle'.[13]

* * *

Eichelberger was now almost ready for what he planned would be the final attacks to take Buna. The bewilderment, and the reluctance of some of his troops, was now being replaced by a higher resolve and a feeling of greater confidence. His total casualties to date were calculated at 113 killed, 490 wounded, 64 missing, and 1260 evacuated sick. This left him with an effective strength of 55 officers and 1062 men in Urbana Force, and 114 officers and 1955 men in Warren Force. The arrival of the 127th Regiment was heartening, with more vigorous officers encouraging the men. Also, under Colonel De Graaf's capable direction, more supplies were arriving, including mail, which always boosted the men's morale. It was also now becoming known that Australian tanks and infantry would soon be joining them.[14]

The day before, the four tanks from 'C' Squadron, 2/6th Australian Armoured Regiment had arrived at Oro Bay. The unit war diary records for 10 December: 'Spent day under cover of mangrove swamp at Harvey Bay. Party arrived at Hariko at night. Two barges stuck on reef, were hauled off the following morning and returned to Harvey Bay, [would] rejoin unit on night 12/13 Dec'.[15] Lieutenant Colonel Charles Hodgson, a 39-year-old engineer from Sydney, commanding the 2/6th Armoured Regiment, later recalled: 'Four tanks had just arrived at Hariko, and the others were due that night or the next. Hariko was the name of a small collection of huts near the coast. There was no harbour or jetty and as the Japanese had control of the sea and the air, the tanks were towed up – two on a flat open barge – and when the barge grounded, the tanks drove off into two or three feet [one metre] of water'.[16]

* * *

Japanese 1st Class Mechanic Kuba Satonao was still holding his position along the Urbana front. He recorded in his diary: '1400 [hours] bombed and strafed by enemy Martin planes [likely twin-engine B26 Marauders] but no changes. About 1330 eleven of our planes were over but went back without bombing or strafing. They dropped supplies (provisions and ammo). Today again our troops did not come in. The enemy has superiority of the air, and our transports can't sail as they would like'.[17]

* * *

Meanwhile, Brigadier George Wootten, who was commanding the Australian 18th Brigade, flew into Port Moresby to report to General Blamey. The Australian Supreme Commander informed Wootten that he and his men of the 2/9th Battalion at Milne Bay, along with

CHAPTER 31

a battalion of the Australian 7th Brigade, were to be sent to Buna. Wootten was told that four M3 Stuart tanks from 'C' Squadron, 2/6th Australian Armoured Regiment had already arrived at Oro Bay the day before to support the fighting at Buna, with another four tanks from 'B' Squadron scheduled to arrive there soon. His task was to clear the Japanese from the area enclosed by Cape Endaiadere, New Strip, Old Strip, and Buna Government Station. Wootten naturally preferred to work with his own men and requested that the 2/10th Battalion be substituted for the 7th Brigade Battalion; Blamey agreed.[18]

The remaining tanks were to go forward in the Dutch ship *Karsik*, a 3300-ton, four-hatch freighter of the KPM Line; the Australian corvettes *Colac*, *Ballarat*, and *Broome* were to carry the troops. The *Karsik* was to pick up supplies and ammunition at Milne Bay before moving on to Oro Bay, where it was to be unloaded on the night of 11–12 December. The three corvettes would reach Milne Bay on 12 December. After taking on Brigade Headquarters and the 2/9 Battalion, they would make a speedy run northward and rendezvous the same night off Soena Plantation just south of Cape Sudest, with landing craft from Porlock Harbour to ferry the troops and their equipment ashore.[19]

The following day, Wootten was to go to Popondetta to discuss the situation with Lieutenant General Herring, commanding Advance NGF, before going on to Dobodura to confer with Eichelberger. There he would spend the afternoon reconnoitring the situation in the New Strip area.[20]

* * *

Meanwhile, at Rabaul, the commander of the Japanese *18th Army*, Lieutenant General Adachi Hatazo, had been discussing the urgent issue of supplying his troops with the *8th Area Army* commander, Lieutenant General Hitoshi Imamura, along with several senior officers of the *Imperial Japanese Navy*. In response to the aerial drop, which included pickled plums, powdered miso, and soy sauce, troops at Buna demanded only rice, powered miso, and rifles and ammunition be supplied. All other supplies were considered a luxury and only reinforced to many just how out of touch the Army High Command was regarding their desperate situation. A week later, resupply by submarine was also undertaken three or four times; however, disembarkation took place at the mouth of the Mambare River, around 75 kilometres of Gona.[21]

32
'THEY FIRE RIFLES A LOT'

By 11 December 1942, a distinct improvement in morale had become evident among the troops. The reasons for the improvement were due to several factors. The men had gained valuable experience in combat – reflecting this was the steady gains made at Urbana front. Also, due to news that the Australians had finally taken the Gona beachhead just days before, and the fact there were Australian reinforcements, including tanks, along with news of the imminent arrival of the 127th Regiment, the men's morale had improved significantly.[1]

There was also increased recognition by officers and men alike of the improved supply situation. More luggers were available, and Brigadier Dwight Johns, Deputy Commander of COSC, had sent large freighters into Oro Bay. The airlifts were also now transporting vast amounts of supplies, with the establishment of new and improved airstrips in the area. On 14 December, the air force conducted 74 individual flights between Port Moresby and the airfields at Dobodura and Popondetta, bringing in 178 tons of high-priority supplies and ammunition.[2]

Other positive factors were now also coming into play. Improved communications were provided by the sound-power telephone; these were now being used for artillery fire control, which was proving highly efficient within a three-kilometre range. The introduction of the new 4-inch to 1-mile (100-cm to 1.5-kilometre) Buna Map was now being circulated to replace the poorly improvised Buna Target Plan No. 24. With a more accurate base map, improved communications with the forward observers, and observation provided by No. 4 Army

Cooperation Squadron RAAF, the impact of the artillery against the Japanese positions was improving. The artillery was executing fire missions on bunkers adjacent to the bridge between the strips, as well as on those flanking the dispersal bays off the north-eastern end of New Strip. The Australian gunners were now laying down harassing fire on the enemy front and rear. Direct hits were slowly but surely chipping away at the Japanese defences; however, except in the case of the lone American 105-mm howitzer, the Australian shells without delayed fuses had little effect on the enemy bunkers themselves.[3]

The 2/5th Field Regiment war diary records a disturbing plan by Martin to use the surviving Bren gun carriers and their personnel as a replacement force for the commandos of the 2/6th Independent Company. Major Hall, who was commanding the survivors of this unit after the disaster of 5 December, was able to argue against this plan. His adjutant recorded: 'Col Martin is desirous of using Bren carrier personnel in the role formerly carried out by the 2/6 Ind Coy, which has been detached from this force. This was considered undesirable, and Maj. Hall suggested an alternative role of Bren gun beach defence, which has been adopted'.[4] The regimental diarist also recorded: 'It was decided to carry out a destructive shoot on the morning of 12 Dec on an earthen emplacement in the Bridge area. Brig. Wooten and Brig. Hopkins and Col Brady (US Army) visited this area today and did a thorough recce of the approaches to the New Strip area …. New defensive fire tasks were decided on in conjunction with mortars. A light field piece, which has not yet been located, fired 12 rds in an area 400 yards west of E Tp. During the day, mortar fire was brought to bear on our Regt OP area'.[5]

* * *

The Japanese 1st Class Mechanic, Kuba Satonao, was still holding his position along Urbana front, recording in his diary: '0600 [hours] about 200 metres front of the Independent Platoon the rapid-fire gun, which fired two days ago, fired ten rounds. Platoon leader of the

CHAPTER 32

Independent Platoon was wounded but it was very light and would not hinder him'.[6]

* * *

On the more strongly defended Warren front, what was needed above all was special equipment for the reduction of bunkers. This required the use of tanks. While they would later become a key factor of the fighting throughout the Pacific War, at this point, tanks were simply not to be had at Buna. It was expected that the arrival of the Australian tankers and their American M3 Stuart tanks would finally make up for these deficiencies.[7]

Meanwhile, at Urbana front, the men of 'I' and 'K' companies, III/127th Regiment relieved 'E' and 'G' companies, II/126th Regiment. The men of 'I' Company took up a position at Bottcher's Corner between the village and the mission, and the battle-weary and exhausted men of the II/126th Regiment moved into a reserve area along the supply track. Indeed, the day before, Private Walter Bajdek, with the Headquarters Company, made a dash under heavy Japanese fire to re-establish communications with an advanced observation post overlooking the Japanese positions and was awarded the DSC for his actions.[8]

* * *

At Warren front, unnamed Japanese soldier [C], who was part of Colonel Yamamoto Hiroshi's force, recorded in his diary: 'Friday. Cloudy, rain. As usual there is mortar fire. They fire rifles a lot. We are quiet. Our chance is not yet ripe. Enemy approached to about 50 metres. Difficult to distinguish their forms in the jungle. How can we hit them when we must make every bullet count. If one goes according to the theory of hitting an enemy every time one shoots, then one simply cannot shoot'.[9]

* * *

Brigadier Wootten flew to Popondetta at dawn that morning. After conferring with Lieutenant General Herring and Brigadier Hopkins, he and Hopkins flew to Dobodura where they met Eichelberger. Wootten spent the afternoon reconnoitring Warren front, and that night, while he slept at Eichelberger's headquarters, the *Karsik* arrived at Oro Bay.[10]

The *Karsik* had in its hold the remaining four Stuart tanks of the 2/6th Australian Armoured Regiment. It also unloaded seven days' worth of supplies for the men of the Australian 2/9th Battalion, 18th Brigade. Major Carroll Moffatt, an American officer serving with COSC, supervised the unloading. Moffatt had just reached the area from Milne Bay with six Higgins boats and two Australian barges, the first Allied landing craft to reach the combat zone. The unloading of the tanks and supplies was done by American troops of the 287th Port Battalion who had also come in on the *Karsik*. They quickly and efficiently unloaded the ship, and the *Karsik* got away safely before daylight. The tanks were now loaded onto specially constructed barges, which had arrived just days before, and they were towed to shore, were they were unloaded and hidden in the jungle. They would, the following night, be reloaded on the barges and towed by luggers to Boreo. There they would be landed, run into the jungle, and hidden at a tank lying-up point a few hundred metres north of the village.[11]

PART 3
TAKING NEW AND OLD STRIPS AND BUNA VILLAGE

33

'BUNA WILL NOT BE REINFORCED BUT SHOULD EVENTUALLY BE EVACUATED'

On 12 December 1942, the planning was underway for the new assault against Buna. At Warren front, the men of the Australian 18th Brigade and the supporting tanks of the 2/6th Australian Armoured Regiment were tasked with taking Cape Endaiadere, Strip Point, Old and New strips, and the Buna Government Station, where possible with American infantry support.[1]

Present at the day's conference were Brigadier Wootten, Lieutenant General Herring, Lieutenant General Eichelberger, Brigadier Byers, and Brigadier Hopkins. With the arrival of his Australian troops, Wootten would take over Warren Force, including all American troops within the sector. As recorded in the 18th Brigade war diary: 'At this conference it was decided ... after the arrival of tps of 18 Aust Inf Bde, Brig. WOOTTEN should assume comd of the NEW STRIP sector with ... 128 US Regt (Comd, Col MARTIN) comprising 1/126, 1/128 and 3/128 US Bns and attached units'.[2] By now, Wootten had established his brigade staff around him, including Lieutenant Colonel Charles Hodgson, commanding the 2/6th Armoured Regiment. Also attached were the Australian engineers and sappers of the 2/4th Field Company.[3]

To the west, at the Urbana front, it was a relatively quiet day with the newly arrived men of 'I' and 'K' companies, III/127th Regiment probing the Japanese lines, making small gains, and consolidating their positions. The 126th Regimental war diary records: 'While in reserve the battalion was reorganised and got much-needed rest. It was then called on to act as reserve for the 127th Infantry .... Our forward patrols active'.[4]

Wootten planned a three-phase operation to finally take the Buna beachhead.

Phase one would see the 2/9th Battalion, supported with the eight Stuart tanks, clear the area around Cape Endaiadere, Strip Point and Simemi Creek. In addition to the battalion's own mortars and medium machine guns providing support, a battery of the 2/5th Field Regiment and the mortars of II/126th Regiment would also be made available to directly support this phase of the operation.

Phase two would consist of the men of the 2/10th Battalion clearing the area around Old Strip to the mouth of Simemi Creek.

Phase three would see the Australians of the 2/12th Battalion, which were then still on Goodenough Island (near Milne Bay), supported where possible with US troops, clear the mouth of Simemi Creek to Giropa Creek, which enters the sea at Giropa Point.

The day to launch phase one was originally set for 17 December, but it was soon after moved back to 18 December, as Lieutenant Colonel Clement Cummings, a 34-year-old accountant from Atherton in Queensland, who was commanding the 2/9th Battalion, argued that his men would need a day's rest after their hard slog from Oro Bay.[5]

Lieutenant Colonel Charles Hodgson and his then 2i/C, Captain Norman Whitehead, went out to reconnoitrer the lay of the ground in which their Stuart tanks would be operating. Many years later, the CO recalled arriving at the headquarters of the 128th Regiment: 'The regimental CO [who] was a way back – sent us with a guide to the company commander – who sent us with a guide to the platoon commander – who sent a sergeant out to show us the Jap position. He was first class and took us so near we had to

CHAPTER 33

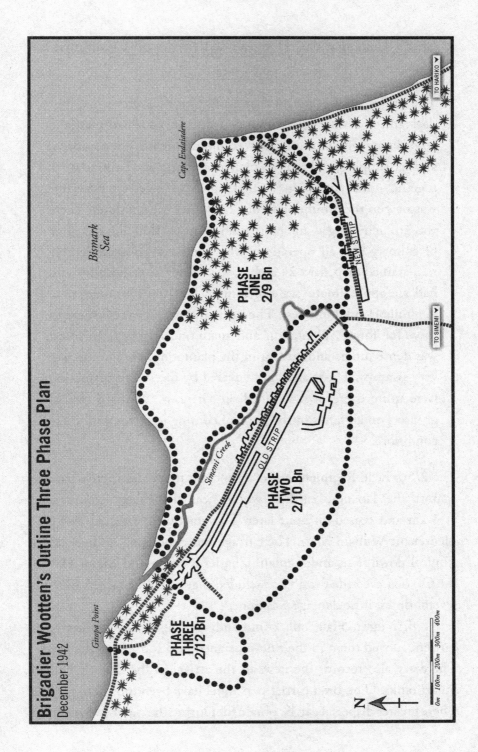

whisper'.[6] Later that day, Hodgson conferred with Cummings. He recalled:

> The arrival timings meant that I and four tank crews had four days and the other four crews two days in which to plan and co-ordinate with Cummings, reconnoitre the lines of approach, arrange supplies, and evolve a plan for infantry and tanks to work together under conditions neither had experienced.... Everyone was new to the ground, and one could not see anything. There was no such thing as an observation point overlooking any piece of country and all operations were on a very close scale. My rain-stained map, 36 x 24 inches, was called 'Buna Locality' and had an 'approximate' scale of four inches [ten centimetres] to one mile [1.5 kilometres]. The printed symbols were limited to those for 'forest', 'plantation' and 'main track'. In fact, the forest was dense jungle and, except in the plantation, the ground was very swampy. Those areas not covered by forest and plantation were quite overgrown with tall kunai grass. We used [track] grousers on all tanks in the hope of coming to terms with these conditions.[7]

The 2/5th Field Regiment war diary records that a destructive barrage against the Japanese earthen works near the bridge commenced at 3 am and ceased an hour later. The guns were directed by FOO Lieutenant William Marr. The barrage was conducted under a heavy tropical downpour, and Captain Charles Mueller and Major Hall at the OP observed the fire and concluded that while the targets were hit several times, little damage was done.[8]

At first light, Hall, still commanding the remaining Bren gun carriers, moved them to their new assigned positions along the beach. The diary also records the news of the arrival of the first of the M3 Stuart tanks: 'The Bren carrier personnel have been moved to an area where greater dispersal can be obtained. During the night two medium

CHAPTER 33

tanks were off-loaded at Hariko. Lieut. [Grant] Curtiss (Aust Offr in charge) has been shown the "new" and "old" strip areas from tree OP. Following on a recce it has been decided to endeavour to recover two of the lost Bren carriers'.[9]

Meanwhile, the Brigade Headquarters, the men of the 2/9th Battalion, and the commanding officer of the 2/10th Battalion, Lieutenant Colonel James Dobbs, a 43-year-old accountant from Mitcham in South Australia, moved out from Wanigela on the Australian corvettes *Colac*, *Broome*, and *Ballarat* early that morning. Travelling at high speed, they reached the rendezvous point off Cape Sudest and found Major Moffatt and the eight-landing craft waiting for them. Unloading began immediately, but scarcely had the first 75 men, including the two battalion commanders, stepped into the two leading Higgins boats when the captain of the *Ballarat*, the senior officer in charge of the small task force, was informed that a large Japanese naval force was moving on Buna from Rabaul. The commander immediately pulled the corvettes back to Porlock Harbour, with the rest of the troops still aboard. During the early morning hours, they would be informed that this was a false report and would set off again for Oro Bay, arriving during the early morning hours of 14 December, under the cover of darkness.[10]

* * *

That day, Japanese soldier [E] who had landed at Buna with Colonel Yamamoto Hiroshi, and was now dug-in around the plantation and at the north-east end of New Strip, recorded in his diary an Allied gun targeting their positions: 'Firing of rapid-fire gun in front of Navy positions'.[11]

* * *

At Rabaul, Lieutenant Colonel Kita, a staff officer with the *18th Army* – who had accompanied Major General Yamagata Tsuyuo, commanding the *21st Independent Mixed Brigade*, to the beachheads – had returned to Rabaul with his report entitled, *Conditions in the Buna Area*. This report was discussed during a briefing with Lieutenant Colonel Imoto, who later recorded: 'According to reports from staff officer Kita of the 18th Army, the actual situation in Buna area is as expected and does not seem to be acute. With the exception of continuing supplies of food, there seems to be absolutely no difficulty in securing the area at this time'.[12] However, Imoto also recorded: 'Although the words of the report were delivered with no particular emphasis or importance, the circumstances they described were especially tragic. I was later asked by Kita: "Is it possible to withdraw (towards Salamaua)?" I replied that, "Such an action would be a debacle"'.[13]

On the same day, the commander of the *18th Army*, Lieutenant General Adachi Hatazo, received 'Staff telegraph order no. 119' from the *Imperial Headquarters* in Tokyo, stating: 'Great importance must be placed on securing the north-eastern end of New Guinea', but it was immediately followed by the apparent contradiction: 'Buna will not be reinforced but should eventually be evacuated'.[14]

34

'A GUARDIAN ANGEL WAS WATCHING OVER ME'

On 13 December 1942, Buna Village at Urbana front was subjected to heavy fire from the Australian 25-pounders at Ango, and a heavy mortar concentration was laid down in preparation for a final assault the next day. The Japanese in the village were now down to fewer than 100 men, who were ordered to vacate their position after dark. Before the Japanese withdrew, Sergeant Samuel Winzenreid, 'I' Company, III/127th Regiment, on his own initiative, single-handedly reduced a strongly held enemy bunker with hand grenades and was awarded the DSC for his actions. After dark, the Japanese survivors of the battle for the village area made their way to the Sanananda beachhead at Giruwa to the west.[1]

* * *

The four Australian officers who would take the first tanks of the Australian Armoured Division into action were: Lieutenant Colonel Charles Hodgson, commanding the 2/6th Armoured Regiment, described by the Australian official historian as a, 'tall, spare, aloof, a cool and confident leader and hard taskmaster, greatly respected by his men'; Captain Norman Whitehead, a 33-year-old grazier from Urana in New South Wales, described as a 'massive fourteen-and-a half stone [92 kilograms] product of the land, broad shouldered and confident; Lieutenant Grant Curtiss, a 29-year-old clerk from Sydney, said to be a troop commander, 'short and plump, determined not to fail those who looked to him'; and Lieutenant Victor McCrohon, a 26-year-old engine driver from Armidale in New South Wales, described as a 'tall and straight, a veteran of the Western Desert where he had served in the 6th Divisional Cavalry'.[2]

Now just behind 18th Brigade Headquarters were the first four of the M3 Stuart tanks three from 10 Troop and one from 12 Troop, 'C' Squadron, 2/6th Armoured Regiment, commanded by Whitehead. By 16 December, they would be joined by the other four tanks three from 5 Troop, 'B' Squadron, command of McCrohon, along with another from 'B' Squadron Headquarters Troop. These eight tanks from 'C' and 'B' squadrons would collectively constitute an improvised half-squadron designed as 'X' Squadron under the command of Hodgson.[3]

Dudley McCarthy, the Australian official historian of the campaign, succinctly recorded the great efforts involved in just getting these vehicles to the front:

> The courage and ingenuity of such officers, and the men they led, were to be severely tried even before they entered action, merely in getting their clumsy 14-ton vehicles forward at all. It will be recalled that the mid-November attempt to do this had resulted in the only available craft sinking at its moorings at Milne Bay, taking with it the first tank that was loaded. Though the availability of ships like the *Karsik* partly overcame this problem it did not solve it completely. Whitehead's and McCrohon's tanks (and those which followed later) were off-loaded at Oro Bay on to clumsy barges which they rode precariously, the water lapping a mere two-inch [five centimetres] freeboard. Motor launches then towed these through the reefs until they were off Hariko. There the launches, swinging as close inshore as possible, cast the barges off, of necessity [was] leaving the tanks to get ashore as best they might. The crews then drove the tanks over the side with a lurch and a splash. Once ashore they followed the beach along to their assembly area with one

CHAPTER 34

set of tracks in the sea and the other just above the low water line so that the incoming tide would wash away the marks of their approach. 'The transportation and landing of these tanks in and around Hariko, [a] few miles from the battlefield, was an amazing achievement in view of the equipment available to the men charged with the task', General Herring was to write later.[4]

The American M3 Light 'General Stuart' tank was around five metres long, three metres high and about two-and-a-half metres wide. It was propelled by a 250-horsepower radial engine, capable of a maximum speed of about 65 kilometres an hour, armoured to an average thickness on the hull of around 25 centimetres and 40 centimetres on the front of the turret. Each turret was mounted with a 37-mm gun and a co-axial .37 calibre machinegun, along with a .30 calibre machine gun in the front of the hull, with a spare inside. Each was fitted with a No. 19 wireless set under normal conditions, providing internal communication from the tank commander to his four men, as well as voice transmission up to about 15 kilometres, and communication with the standard infantry pack set (although as demonstrated during the ongoing fighting in Papua, all wireless communications were at the best intermittent). Cross-country performance was good on suitable ground but was significantly reduced when encountering heavy timber, water, swamp, extremely broken up and rocky ground, and wide trenches. The crews would not normally use their vehicles at night, although they had powerful headlights. The smallest tactical unit was a troop of three tanks.[5]

The tank crew were highly trained men who had been carefully chosen when the Australian armoured division begun forming in 1941. All believed they would be fighting the Germans in the Libyan desert. It was straight from intense training in New South Wales that the 2/6th Armoured Regiment (claiming descent from the Great War veterans of the 6th Australian Light Horse) had been sent to Papua. This was a battlefield, with its mud, swamp and jungle, which was the complete opposite to what they had encountered during their training. The officers and men were not to know that their detachment heralded the gradual break-up of the armoured division as its regiments and squadrons were destined to fight piecemeal throughout the Pacific.[6]

* * *

Still in the Warren front area was unnamed Japanese soldier [C], who was part of Colonel Yamamoto Hiroshi's force. He briefly recorded in his diary: 'Sunday. Fair. It is a clear day. Enemy planes around all over. Enemy fire has become considerably accurate. The coconut trees around here have been badly hit by shells. The leaves are gone or rotting. It is a barren sight. During the night [I] heard motors which may have been enemy landing party. Placed on emergency alert'.[7]

Helping to cover the Japanese right flank at Buna was Japanese 1st Class Mechanic Kuba Satonao with the *Imperial Japanese Navy Tsukioka Transport Unit* still holding their position along the Urbana front. He recorded his second last entry in his diary some time that day: 'While on night sentry duty, myself and 1st Mechanic TOZAWA fired on by mortar. About five metres away one dropped. I was only covered with dirt and rocks. A guardian angel was watching over me. Expect our troops to land today. Hope they land safely'.[8] The expected landing at Buna of reinforcements was obviously a false report, and he would have been gravely disappointed on hearing that they were still stranded and seemingly forgotten by the Japanese high command in Rabaul.

35

'CAPTAIN HONDA GRACIOUSLY DIED IN ACTION'

During the early hours of 14 December 1942, the convoy ferrying the men of the Australian 2/9th Battalion finally arrived at Oro Bay. These men immediately set off on a forced march to the Buna front, arriving at Hariko, where they spent the night. By first light the following morning (15 December), they would arrive at the Brigade Headquarters' bivouac area. As recorded in the 18th Brigade war diary: 'This march was one of a most exhausting nature, involving as it [marched] in battle order along almost continual soft sand and the crossing of the SAMBOGA RIVER which was chest-high and in a hot muggy atmosphere'.[1]

Corporal Maurice 'Mervyn' Cotteral, a 25-year-old station hand from Toowoomba in Queensland, with 'B' Company recalled the exhausting march:

> We came to one of the many narrow, deep, fast-flowing creeks with a tree across it which had to be walked over to get across. The tree was smothered with mud from a couple of hundred pairs of boots ahead of us on the march. It was like the greasy pole. I was nearly across when I knew I was going in. Why I stared laughing I will never know. I came up with water around my neck. 'How deep is it, Toad?' asked Bernie. In he goes, in full marching order, plus Bren gun tripod on his shoulders and completely out of sight. All we can see is a stream of bubbles moving downstream. I eventually got him up like a drowned

rat. He received no sympathy from anyone, certainly not from me. I pushed him up the bank and said, 'Up there, you little bastard. You've been told not to play in deep water!'[2]

Many veterans of the desert fighting in North Africa judged this march to be worse than the forced march from Tobruk Harbour to the frontline perimeter, which covered 25 kilometres in full marching order – weapons and ammunition.[3]

That morning, at a conference held in the headquarters of the 128th Regiment, Major Hall was informed that his artillery was only to be fired when definite targets of opportunity presented themselves, as there was a recognition that ammunition had to be conserved for the next all-out assault. Also present were the two Australian commanders of the 2/9th and 2/10th infantry battalions.[4] The details of the next attack were outlined, as recorded in the 2/5th Field Regiment war diary: 'A detailed plan of an attack by the 2/9 was discussed. 55 Bty is to support the attack along the beach on the right, 2/1 Regt on the left, and 3.7 Mtn Bty in the centre, fire to be controlled by representatives of each Bty, who are to be with the Bn Comdrs. It was decided that Capt. Mueller should do the job for 55 Bty with Capt. Nix fully in the picture as emergency'.[5]

Later that night, 18th Brigade Headquarters received a communique from Colonel Martin, commanding the 128th Regiment, that he would not be receiving any significant American reinforcements soon: 'I just talked to Gen. Eichelberger about the extra battalion for our operations. Gen. Eichelberger stated that there would be no extra battalion; that I would use one of my present battalions'.[6]

* * *

Still at Warren front area in the Coconut Grove area was unnamed Japanese soldier [C], who was part of Colonel Yamamoto Hiroshi's force. He recorded: 'Monday. Rain, later fair. The enemy approached

CHAPTER 35

close as usual and fired tommy guns and rifles on our positions. But only once in a while they fire mortars. It seems that since yesterday their mortar fire has decreased somewhat. Maybe they are short on shells. Still, they scatter a large amount of bursts. We are quiet as usual'.[7]

* * *

At Urbana front, an intense barrage by the 25-pounders and mortars was put down on Buna Village at first light. Leaving a small holding force at the corner, the men of 'K' Company, III/127th Regiment moved forward at 7 am against the village. In support was 'I' Company on their left, with one of its platoons also protecting 'K' Company's left rear. The advance continued steadily and cautiously. There was no opposition. By 10 am, the entire area was occupied. Moving slowly and cautiously, as they feared a trap, the GIs discovered that the Japanese had evacuated the village. After all the bitter fighting on the village outskirts, it had fallen without a shot being fired.[8]

The village ceased to exist, now represented by its few huts having been blown to pieces and the surrounding coconut palms splintered and broken by shellfire, with shell craters dominating the ground. The bunkers still stood, most were not affected by the bombardments, even when they had clearly scored a direct hit. The Japanese had left little equipment or food behind. The only items recovered were just a few rifles, some discarded clothing, a supply of canned goods, and a store of medical supplies. The official American historian recorded: 'Thus anticlimactically had Urbana Force taken its first objective. The Coconut Grove remained as the only position on the left bank of Entrance Creek still in Japanese hands. This labyrinth of trenches and bunkers was next'.[9]

Lieutenant Colonel Smith, commanding II/128th Regiment, had been told by Brigadier Byers a few days before that he would be called upon to take the Coconut Grove when Buna Village fell. Smith and his executive officer, Major Roy Zinser, now set about preparing their plans, which called for one company of the battalion to attack on the right under Smith and a second company to attack on the left under Zinser.[10]

* * *

Earlier at 4 am, the Japanese of the *I/170th Regiment* were able to reach Papua, landing at the mouth of the Mambare River (about 75 kilometres west of Buna). The force in all numbered around 800 men. With them was Major General Kensaku Oda who took over command of Major General Tomitarô Horii's *South Seas Force* following his drowning in mid-November. It had been decided to open a new beachhead at the mouth of the Mambare River. There, a well-concealed base was to be established, and small craft could bring in supplies and reinforcements for the main battlefront. Here, the sick and wounded from the beachhead positions could be ferried to by several barges. Luckily for the Japanese, bad weather covered the convoy from Allied aerial observation, and Oda and the *I/170th Regiment* reached the Mambare River mouth without loss. They rapidly unloaded troops and stores during the night and early morning hours. By the time the Allied aircraft located the convoy, after daybreak, all the men were ashore with most of their supplies and the small watercraft they had brought with them; the destroyers got clean away. The Allied airmen sank a few of the small vessels, and some of the supplies wrapped in waterproof coverings lashed to buoys so they could be collected.[11]

Sergeant Hiroshi Kasahar, with these reinforcements who was attached to *No. 3 Company, I/41st Regiment*, landed with ten days rations, ready to engage the enemy. Near him, Major Nojiri with the headquarters of the *170th Regiment* also landed; however, he recorded that the bombing had resulted in significant casualties. He recorded soon after landing: 'Bombed – heavy casualties; impossible for commanders to control according to plans. After dark, will move to Buna. Went to the landing point of the *Omura Unit* – nothing but

CHAPTER 35

dead bodies of the unit there. Our own landing point heavily bombed. Captain Honda graciously died in action'.[12]

Among the allied airmen tasked with bombing this convoy was American Lieutenant Garrett Middlebrook in a B25 bomber with the 38th Bomb Group; he recalled: 'We went back next morning early … the convoy was gone but we found that they had put troops ashore near the Mambare River mouth … we strafed the area until we ran out of ammo. Then we discovered hundreds of buoys floating a mile or so off the coast, each with a little Japanese flag attached to the top of the buoy stem. Upon closer examination, we could see that each buoy had containers attached with supplies inside'.[13]

It would be another four days before Oda and his force could be ferried on barges to the mouth of the Amboga River to support Major General Tsuyuo Yamagata, commanding *Buna Detachment*. Even so, there was only enough room in the available vessels for a portion of the *I/170th Regiment*. Hugging the coastline, and moving only at night, Oda and the battalion's advance echelon reached the river on 18 December – far too late to have any significant impact on the fighting west of Gona, as this beachhead, including the area just west of the river around Haddy's Village, had already been taken by the Australians.[14]

Meanwhile, Japanese 1st Class Mechanic, Kuba Satonao, with the *Imperial Japanese Navy Tsukioka Transport Unit* in the Urbana sector, wrote his last diary entry: 'Quiet during morning. About two in the afternoon there was sudden rapid fire from the enemy. They hit our positions, but no one was hurt. Only covered with dirt'.[15] 1st Class Mechanic Kuba Satonao, obviously was not so lucky during the next round of fire/fighting as he was likely killed soon after making this diary entry. His diary was recovered by American troops on 23 December 1942.

36
'BORROWED CLIPPERS AT NIGHT AND ALL HAD HAIRCUTS'

The next day, 15 December, would witness further fighting along Urbana front to clear the Coconut Grove area. At 1 pm, General Byers arrived at the CP of Lieutenant Colonel Smith, west of the grove. Byers ordered him to launch his planned attack at once. The men of the II/128th Regiment now numbered about 350 men. However, these men were scattered along a front measuring about 1750 metres, all the way from the apex of the Triangle, along the left bank of Entrance Creek, to a point just south of Musita Island.

Not counting a platoon of heavy machine guns from 'H' Company, which was to play a supporting role, Smith had less than 100 men immediately available for the attack. He had about 40 men from 'E' Company, about 20 from a platoon of 'F' Company, 20 men from the Battalion Headquarters Company, with about 15 men from the Regimental Cannon Company. Smith, therefore, requested more troops, and specifically asked for the rest of 'F' Company, which was then in the Siwori Village area protecting the left flank. Byers, however, found it impossible to give Smith the men he needed, even so, the attack was ordered to begin at 3 pm with those he had.[1]

Smith divided his strength in half, giving Major Roy Zinser the platoon from 'F' Company, most of the troops from the Battalion Headquarters Company, and a few men from the Cannon Company detachment. Smith himself took 'E' Company and a few men from

CHAPTER 36

each of the other units. The two forces then moved out quickly to their respective points of departure. At 3.10 pm, with the troops in position and ready to go, Lieutenant Colonel McCreary gave the orders for the mortars to bomb the Coconut Grove.[2]

Still at the Triangle was squad leader Ernest Gerber with the II/128th Regiment; he recalled: 'The terrain varied according to the tide. The water could be up to your ankles, or up to your neck. In the area where we were, the famous "Triangle", our only dry ground was the trail which was built up, maybe two or three feet [one metre] higher than the surrounding terrain. That was the only dry land we were on for a period of three or four weeks. Anything to the right, left, front, or rear was swamp. There were trees that seemed two or three hundred feet high [100 metres]. You couldn't see the sun during the day or the stars at night. The underbrush was such that you could maybe see two or three feet ahead of you. If you were lucky, you might see occasionally twenty feet [seven metres]'.[3]

The mortar preparation consisting of about 100 rounds hit the target area but had little effect. One soldier recalled that it merely 'blew a little dirt from the Japanese emplacements'.[4]

At 3.20 pm, the bombing ceased, and the troops moved out with the help of fire from the platoon of 'H' Company. The Japanese, however, had the approaches covered and laid down concentrated fire on the attackers. Progress was slow, but Smith's men had pressed up tight against their objective by nightfall. Heavy rain fell during the night, drenching the troops and filling their foxholes with water.[5]

* * *

Meanwhile, further east at Warren front, the Australians of the 18th Brigade had moved up to their bivouac area about two kilometres north of Boreo and one kilometre inland. That day, Lieutenant Colonel James Dobbs, commanding the 2/10th Battalion, accompanied Major William Hall on a reconnaissance to the forward positions that he and his men were to occupy. Hall outlined the areas his guns would target during their attack. Later that afternoon, Hall repeated this recce with Lieutenant Colonel Cummings, commanding the 2/9th Battalion, providing him with the relevant information regarding the forward sector that he and his men were to occupy.[6]

That night, the Australian gunners of 'F' Troop engaged a Japanese artillery piece that was firing from the south-east end of New Strip. Soon after, the regimental diarist recorded receiving a note originating from an American officer: 'A message was received from Bde that Japs were digging in on the beach near a small white flag. It was investigated by Maj. Hall, who found that the small "white flag" was a jam tin and a stick planted by him the previous day as a range marker and the "digging Japs" the branches of a tree lying on the beach'.[7]

Meanwhile, that night and during the next early morning hours, the *Karsik* unloaded 100 tons of cargo, along with the four M3 Stuart tanks from 'B' Squadron, 2/6th Armoured Regiment at Oro Bay. These tanks were placed on barges, towed to Boreo, unloaded by next day, and had moved up the beach to the tank park positioned to the rear of 18th Brigade Headquarters. With the four tanks from 'C' Squadron, they were organised into the newly designated 'X' Squadron.[8]

* * *

Still in the Warren front area was Lance Corporal Uchiyama Seiichi, with Captain Matsuo who led *No. 9 Company, III/229th Regiment*. He recorded in his diary that he had lost his light machine gun in the fighting and his unit was now below half-strength: 'We now only wait for the final moments to come …. I am disgusted with myself, thinking only when my end will come. As a lance corporal, I must encourage the soldiers, saying to my subordinates that the fighting has just started – fight to the end!'[9]

Major General Edwin Harding, commanding the US Army 32nd Division was originally tasked with taking Buna.

Australian Lieutenant General Edmund Herring commanding New Guinea Force and US Lieutenant General Robert Eichelberger, commanding the American I Corps.

Advanced party of Australian commandos of the 2/6th Independent Company leading the way towards Buna somewhere between Wanigela and Pongani.

Brigadier Hanford MacNider, commanding the US 128th Regiment (centre, seated with helmet) discusses plans with his officers to take Buna – Warren Front.

Lieutenant Colonel Alexander MacNab (right), Executive Officer, US 128th Infantry Regiment takes time out for a cigarette.

Colonel John Grose at the US 127th Infantry Regimental Headquarters at Urbana Front.

Sergeant Herman Bottcher, US II/126th Regiment was promoted to Captain in the field and warded the Distinguish Service Cross for his courage during the fighting along Urbana Front.

Lieutenant Colonel Herbert Smith, up front commanding the US 2nd Battalion, 128th Regiment (II/128th Regiment) at Urbana Front.

Lieutenant General Robert Eichelberger at the 'Triangle' – Urbana Front – after its capture by troops of the US 126th Regiment.

Typical Japanese coconut log constructed bunker at Buna with shallow and narrow crawl Trench.

Major Harry Harcourt (seat second left with beret), commanding the Australian 2/6th Independent Company, provided critical support to the Americans during the first month of fighting to take Buna along New and Old Strips, Warren Front.

An American 30-calibre machine gun, I/128th Regiment in action along Warren Front.

Australian Brigadier George Wootten would soon take command of the fighting at Warren Front as the men of the 2nd AIF 18th Brigade took over this sector from the Americas.

Captain Norman Whitehead, commanding the composite 'X' Squadron of M3 tanks, the Australian 2/6th Armoured Regiment, was wounded during the fighting along Warren Front, 18 December.

Lieutenant Colonel Arthur Arnold commanding the 2/12th Battalion, 18th Brigade.

Lieutenant Colonel Clement Cummings commanding the Australian 2/9th Battalion, 18th Brigade.

Lieutenant Colonel James Dobbs commanding the 2/10th Battalion, 18th Brigade.

American anti-tank gun pouts fire into Buna mission, Urbana Front around 2 December 1942.

Burnt out Bren gun carriers of the Australian 18th Brigade, resulting from the attack on 5 December along Warren Front – the Australians paid a high price for this gallant but futile attack.

Interior of Japanese bunker after capture.

Tankers of 'C' Squadron, part of the composite 'X' Squadron the night before the attack to take Endaiadere Point and Duropa Point, Warren Front, on 18 December.

Lieutenant William McIntosh and Private Syd Bourne, 2/9th Battalion, during advance through Duropa Plantation, Warren Front, 18 December.

Australian infantrymen using a Bren gun fires at Japanese snipers in the trees, near New Strip, Warren Front.

Men of the 2/9th Battalion being supplied grenades by the tankers during the fighting to take Duropa Plantation and Endaiadere Point, Warren Front, 18 December.

Sergeant Jack Lattimore's M3 was one of four Australian tanks targeted and hit by Japanese anti-aircraft guns, while supporting the 2/10th Battalion's attacks to take Old Strip, Warren Front, 24 December, picture taken a few days later.

Bridge over Simemi Creek with New Strip in the background, Warren Front.

Australian troops, 2/9th Battalion, with Australian M3 tank support fight their way to Endaiadere Point, Warren Front, 18 December.

Christmas Day 1942, the wounded Private George Whittington, 2/10th Battalion, being helped along a track to Dobodura field hospital.

The famous, 'Carson's gun', manned by Sergeant Roderick Carson and his gunners, 'F' Troop, 55th Battery, 2/5th Field Regiment was an Australian 25-pounder gun which was used to 'snipe' several Japanese anti-aircraft guns along Old Strip, Warren Front.

Major William Hall, 55th Battery commander, in his high observation post identifying potential targets for the Australian gunners, Warren Front.

Footbridge over Entrance Creek to Musita Island, Urbana Front.

Destroyed Japanese 13 mm duel anti-aircraft gun located around Old Strip, Warran Front.

Japanese Model 96 Type 2 25 mm Anti-aircraft gun around Old Strip, one of several taken out by 'Garson's gun', Warren Front.

Knocked out Japanese dual-purpose 3-inch gun at the western end of Old Strip, Warren Front.

Japanese zero found on Old Strip – Lieutenant Victor McCrohon, tank commander with the Australian 2/6th Armoured Regiment second from left standing on wing.

Australian photojournalist George Silk, who was a great friend of fellow photojournalist, Damien Parer, was responsible for taking many of the most iconic images of the fighting around the Japanese Beachheads.

New Year's Day, 1943, Corporal Roy Rodgers, 17 Platoon, 'D' Company, 2/12th Battalion, points out an enemy bunker to the tankers during the final days of the fighting around Buna, Warren Front.

Australians of the 2/12th Battalion, during the final days of fighting firing on fleeing Japanese from a wrecked bunker, Warren Front.

Giropa Point with supporting M3 tanks, 7 Troop, 'B' Squadron, 2/6th Armoured Regiment with a 2-incch mortar firing on a Japanese position.

Detail of George Silk's censored photograph of Australian machine gunners, at Buna 1 Jan 1943 - showing a dead Australian, for this reason it was censored.

Lieutenant Duncan Clarke, 2/12th Battalion beside a dead Japanese soldier and his smashed bunker.

Colonel Yazawa Kiyoshi, commander of the Japanese 41st Infantry Regiment, was towards the end of the fighting to Buna, sent on a near suicidal mission to relieve Buna.

Sappers of the Japanese 15th Independent Combat Engineers were responsible for constructing the Japanese beachhead defensive positions from the day of the Japanese invasion on 21 July 1942.

Surviving elements of the Japanese 144th Infantry Regiment, who had led the advance south along the Kokoda Track, were months later called on to help defend the beachheads at Buna, Sanananda and Gona.

CHAPTER 36

Close by would have been unnamed Japanese soldier [C], who was part of Colonel Yamamoto Hiroshi's force. He recorded briefly in his diary: 'Tuesday. Fair. Enemy planes overhead all day. Our anti-aircraft machine gun fired at them at times. Enemy condition same as yesterday. Borrowed clippers at night and all had haircuts'.[10]

37

'THE SERGEANT COMMANDING THE CARRIER PLATOON AND I CONCOCTED A PLAN ...'

On 16 December, at Urbana front, the fighting to take the Coconut Grove continued. Lieutenant Colonel Smith and Major Roy Zinser both pressed the attack forward. Zinser and his force – which consisted of a platoon from 'F' Company, II/128th Regiment, with most of the men from Battalion Headquarters Company, and a few men from the Cannon Company detachment – took the initiative. Running into a troublesome bunker, Zinser brought forward a flamethrower of the same type that had failed so miserably the week before in front of Buna Village. The result was the same, as recalled by the officer to Brigadier Byers: the flamethrower 'fizzed out and Japanese shot it up'.[1]

The fighting continued, with the GIs targeting the position with grenades and small arms fire. On the left, they discovered a large bunker that commanded their approach to the grove. The bunker was accessible by both Smith and Zinser's men and they began converging on it, clearing out intermediate obstacles as they advanced. In this fighting, Zinser demonstrated conspicuous leadership, but it fell to two men of 'E' Company on the right – Corporal Daniel Rini and Private Bernardino Estrada – to clear out the bunker position. Rini and Estrada, members of the same squad, had been in the forefront

CHAPTER 37

of the company's advance, and Rini, covered by Estrada who was equipped with a Browning Automatic Rifle (BAR), got close enough to the main bunker to kill the Japanese occupants by using hand grenades.[2]

Smith had been watching Rini and Estrada about 40 metres behind them, occasionally helping them with fire. Just as Rini reached the bunker, Smith was called to the phone tied to a tree to talk to Colonel Tomlinson, commanding the regiment. He had scarcely lifted the receiver when he heard shouting from the direction of the main bunker: 'I sensed that this was probably the break we were looking for, so I told Colonel Tomlinson that I must get forward and see what was happening. I arrived just in time to see Corporal Rini on top of the big bunker and the rest of the squad closing in on it. Later I learned that Rini, after working up as close as he could, had suddenly made a dash, jumped on top of the bunker, and leaning over had pushed hand grenades through the firing slits'.[3]

Smith, realising he needed to move fast to take advantage of this breakthrough, ordered an all-out attack on the remaining enemy positions. Charging at the head of a squad, Smith cleared out a bunker in the centre, while Captain Joseph Stehling, leading 'E' Company, did the same on his right. The bunkers fell in quick succession. Tragically, during the mop-up operations resulting, both Corporal Rini and Private Estrada, were killed. Rini was shot by a wounded Japanese soldier as he tried to render him first aid, while Estrada fell not long after while helping to clear the last enemy position in the Coconut Grove. Both Corporal Daniel Rini and Private Bernardino Estrada were awarded the DSC for their actions.[4]

The Coconut Grove was in American hands by the early afternoon, and the next day these troops buried 37 Japanese; more were found and buried subsequently. The cost to the II/128th Regiment to take the grove was four killed and 13 wounded. Material recovered included 900 kilograms of rice and oatmeal, several kegs of malt and barley, a quantity of small arms, several light machine guns, and a hut full of ammunition. One badly wounded Japanese sergeant was taken prisoner.[5]

As soon as the grove was captured, Smith sent patrols over a footbridge built by the Japanese across Entrance Creek and the Ango–Buna track bridge. Although the Ango–Buna track bridge lacked flooring, its piling and stringers were still intact. The patrols met no opposition, and two heavy machine guns were immediately set up to cover the approaches to the bridges. Late in the afternoon, while the engineers were making some repairs on the track bridge, a Japanese officer was observed to be attempting to mass troops in the Government Gardens, presumably for an attack on the newly won beachhead east of Entrance Creek. This counterattack, however, was repulsed before it began, with fire from the heavy machine guns both east and west of the creek.[6]

Brigadier Byers had been wounded in the frontline during the attack on the Coconut Grove, and Lieutenant General Eichelberger, as the only American general officer present, took command of the American forces here.[7]

* * *

Meanwhile, Brigadier Wootten's initial allocation of his troops for the forthcoming battle to finally take the Buna beachhead was complete. He had available the men of the 2/9th Battalion, consisting of 26 officers and 638 men, including 127 reinforcements who had just arrived; the squadron of the 2/6th Armoured Regiment; five Bren gun carriers from the 18th Brigade carrier group, crewed by men of the 17th Brigade; and detachments of the 2/4th Field Company and the 2/5th Field Ambulance. At Porlock, there were now the 34 officers and 648 men of the 2/10th Battalion preparing to embark on the corvettes next day. The battalion war diary records for 16 December: 'Bn busy both days preparing for onward move by boat to Buna area. Bn on move to Buna known as Sledge Hammer

CHAPTER 37

Force'.[8] The main artillery support would remain as the field gunners under Major Hall and Captain Herbert Manning. Hall's four guns of the 2/5th Field Regiment were still just forward of Hariko, while Manning's four guns of the 2/1st Field Regiment were deployed off the track near Ango. Also, the three 3.7-inch howitzers under Captain Martin O'Hare had just days before been moved to a position on the Buna–Simemi Track about 1.5 kilometres south of the bridge between the two strips.[9]

Reports continued to come into 18th Brigade Headquarters regarding the Japanese defences around New Strip, with one recording:

> Enemy pillbox posns were both numerous and strong and had proved practically impervious to gunfire with instantaneous fuse. These pillboxes were so sited as to be mutually supporting while they were themselves inter-connected by a series of fire and crawl trenches. As a result of this appreciation, Bde Cond decided to attack on a one Bn front past the East end of NEW STRIP up the coast to CAPE ENDAIADERE and hence west to the line of SIMEMI CREEK with the object not only of clearing this area of enemy and facilitating supply by sea but of turning the enemy's flank by securing a bridgehead over the SIMEMI CREEK in the vicinity of its mouth. At the same time US bns were to maintain pressure and gain all possible ground to their respective fronts.[10]

Wootten was still ignorant of the amount of 25-pounder artillery ammunition he had available for the forthcoming battle. The CCRA had promised to update him on the situation, but so far, all he had was an estimate of about 250 shells per gun being available to support the attack. The ranging gun was focused on a position about 100 metres beyond the proposed line of concentration along the beach. During the last few days, it was observed that several duds had been fired. Since then, the shells were being carefully graded, with suspected duds removed. That night, the gunners of 'F' Troop again targeted the area of a suspected artillery piece at the eastern end of New Strip. Soon after, it was arranged for American mortars with the I/128th Regiment to target this gun, while the men of the III/128th Regiment attempted to unsuccessfully infiltrate parts of the Japanese perimeter.[11]

The Americans of Warren Force still included the men of the III/128th Regiment, now under Lieutenant Colonel Alexander MacNab, holding the line from the coast to the eastern end of New Strip. To their left were the Americans of the I/128th Regiment who extended westward to the southern edge of New Strip. This battalion was commanded by Major Gordon Clarkson, formerly of Eichelberger's staff. The incomplete I/126th Regiment – now led by Major Chester Beaver, who was of the divisional staff and had proved himself a brave and resourceful leader – was still south of the bridge separating New and Old strips.[12]

Years later, MacNab recalled the planned use of carriers in this attack; he had been concerned about the results of the attack of two weeks prior: 'The sergeant [now] commanding the carrier platoon and I concocted a plan whereby he and I and a dozen volunteers were to snake out two of the carriers just before dawn on 15 December, but this plan was abandoned when definite assurance came up that we were to have tank and troop support shortly. In fact, the 18th Brigade started to pull in on the 16th. The original plans called for the show to start on 17 Dec, but we had to postpone it until the 18th in order to get the tanks properly into position'.[13]

* * *

Captain Yasuda Yoshitatsu – commanding the marines of the *5th Yokosuka, 5th Sasebo, SNLP* and supporting naval pioneer troops – faced Urbana Force, while Colonel Yamamoto Hiroshi – commanding the bulk of his relatively fresh troops of the *144th* and *III/229th regiments*, along with the *15th Independent Engineer Regiment* and

CHAPTER 37

the *47th Field Antiaircraft Battalion* – confronted the men of Warren Force. Both were about to be caught in pincer movements from which there was planned to be no escape or mercy shown.[14]

That day, unnamed Japanese soldier [C], who was part of Colonel Yamamoto Hiroshi's force that was likely positioned within the coconut plantation area near New Strip, recorded briefly in his second-last diary entry: 'Wednesday. Rain, later fair. Corp Munari interchanged with officer candidate Watananbe. The enemy approached within 20 metres and threw grenades at the 2d platoon. We fired ten rounds with a captured rifle. In the afternoon we took advantage of enemy mortar fire and cracked some coconuts. Made loopholes and posts for sentries at night. At night there is artillery shelling. About 1700 [hours] the 6th Squad opened fire. The enemy shouted. Can't see their figures but it seems that the firing was effective'.[15]

Close by was unknown Japanese soldier [E], also with Yamamoto's force: 'During the morning there was a little mortar fire. No change in enemy situation. The rapid-fire gun which seemed to have changed its position during the afternoon and night opened sudden fire upon our positions and the Navy positions. The 1st and 2nd squads received some direct hits but there were no casualties. During the night at 1830 [hours] the TSUCHIYA Squad (15 men) was sent to the MATSUO Unit. The remaining one squad with the command and ammunition squad (Sgt MASAKI and 23 men) changed positions and were sent back to a point 800 metres in the rear'.[16]

* * *

Meanwhile, Advance NGF had moved from Popondetta to Dobodura. That night, Eichelberger wrote to Major General Sutherland that he was 'delighted' with the way Lieutenant Colonel Smith and his men of the II/128th Battalion had fought that day. The battalion was now 'high' in his favour; Smith had 'developed into quite a fighter';

and the men had 'a high morale'. 'As a matter of fact,' he added, 'the boys are coming to life all along the line'.[17]

* * *

In Port Moresby, General MacArthur was urging Eichelberger to speed up his preparations. Eichelberger could report that Warren Force would initiate 'D-Day' on 18 December, to be led by the Australian tanks. Its successive objectives were Duropa Plantation and Cape Endaiadere (including a bridgehead across the mouth of Simemi Creek), New Strip, and Old Strip. Urbana Force was to attack on 19 December (D+1). It was to storm the Triangle, cut through to the coast, and seize the track junction between Buna Mission and Giropa Point, isolating each, and exposing both to flank attacks.[18]

38

'YOU ARE EXPENDABLE, WE MUST TAKE THE OBJECTIVE AT WHATEVER COST'

At 9 am, 17 December, Brigadier Wootten, in accordance with Lieutenant General Eichelberger's direction, assumed command of Warren Force, taking over from Colonel Martin who would directly command the Americans in this sector. Wootten's objective was for his 18th Brigade Group to capture the area from Cape Endaiadere, New Strip, Old Strip, through to the Buna Government Station. Phase one's objective was for the men of the 2/9th Battalion, as laid down in the 18th Brigade's Operational Order No. 1 (17 December): 'To attack and capture the area bounded on the right by the coast to the mouth of Simemi Creek and on the left by a line through the east end of New Strip and the west end of Old Strip thence north west along Simemi Creek to its mouth'.[1]

The 2/9th Battalion would be the striking force, supported by seven tanks, aircraft, artillery, and American mortars. Meanwhile, the 128th Regiment and the 2/10th Battalion, with a single tank, along with the 17th Brigade carriers, would constitute the force reserve. At this point, the officers and men of the 2/10th Battalion were part of a convoy consisting of the Australian corvettes *Ballarat*, *Broome*, and *Colac* heading for the Buna area.[2]

The plan of attack on Warren front would concentrate on the main body of the tank squadron leading the way forward, with two companies of the 2/9th Battalion attacking the Duropa Plantation, straight up the coast to Cape Endaiadere. The III/128th Regiment was to mop up immediately to the rear. After taking the cape, the Australians would then wheel west to the line of Simemi Creek and emerge to the rear of the Japanese by securing a bridgehead across the creek near its mouth to the ocean. New Strip would simultaneously be attacked from south and east. The men of the I/126th Regiment would move on the bridge between the strips from its position immediately to the south. Meanwhile, preceded by the rest of the tanks and supported by the troops of the I/128th Regiment, another company from the 2/9th Battalion would attack the eastern end of New Strip, cut through the dispersal bays, and advance on the bridge between the strips via its northern edge.[3]

A heavy artillery and mortar bombardment was to precede the attack, which would include the American 105-mm howitzer south of Ango. The Australian 25-pounders on either flank, as well as the two 3.7-inch howitzers located just south of the western end of New Strip would provide the bulk of the barrage. One 25-pounder was to be moved up close to the dispersal bays at the eastern end of New Strip, to bring the bunkers there under direct fire.[4] The diarist of the 2/5th Field Regiment recorded the task to be performed by the Australian artillery: 'Maj. Hall took 2/1, 3.7 and 55 bty FOOs forward and pointed out on the ground the forward line for the concentration to be fired on the morning of 18 Dec. Later in the day he met the commander of the American Heavy Weapon Coy, and the 2/9 Bn Mortar Offr and tied in the mortar and arty tasks. This was done as the result of a conference with Col Cummings of the 2/9 Bn. It was decided that a concentration be fired from Z-10 to Z. The first eight minutes: 3 rds g.f. per minute, and the last 5 mins: 5 rds g.f. per min'.[5]

Meanwhile, the American troops were dug-in close to the enemy perimeter, in most cases less than 50 metres from the nearest Japanese bunker. These men would withdraw about 300 metres, just behind the Australian line of departure that was marked that night with white tape. This was to ensure that the attacking Australians and supporting

CHAPTER 38

American troops were not targeted with friendly fire from the artillery and mortar bombardments. This would also provide both the infantry and the tankers greater manoeuvring space during the initial assault.[6]

By 6 pm, the last hours of daylight, the seven attacking M3 Stuart tanks, now making up 'X' Squadron, commanded by Captain Norman Whitehead, had lumbered forward. The OC was in his tank, christened 'Capt. Kidd' and with the six other tanks, they headed for their assembly area. The squadron was divided into two troops of three tanks each, along with the OC tank. Commanding the three tanks of 5 Troop 'B' Squadron, was Lieutenant Victor McCrohon, with Corporal Evan Barnet, a 22-year-old medical student from Sydney, commanding his second tank; and Sergeant Jack Lattimore, a 23-year-old engraver from Harris Park in New South Wales, commanded the remaining tank.

Commanding the remaining troop was Lieutenant Grant Curtiss, with 10 Troop 'C' Squadron. His second tank was commanded by Sergeant John Church, a 26-year-old stock agent from Burren Junction, New South Wales, with 10 Troop, while his third was commanded by 22-year-old Corporal Phillip Smith, from Sydney, with 12 Troop, 'C' Squadron.[7]

The adjutant of the newly designated 'X' Squadron recorded in the unit war diary: 'Day spent in recce. Tanks moved up in rear of FUP at edge of plantation'.[8]

Lieutenant Colonel Charles Hodgson, commanding the 2/6th Armoured Regiment, recalled: 'That evening we arranged for 25-pounder and mortar programme to cover the sound of the tank engines and so brought them further up the beach to a lying-up area. The first tank slipped off the bridge – it was pitch dark and we used no lights, and it took two tanks two and a half hours to extricate it. Then we heard the sound of motorboats coming from Cape Endaiadere! We expected either a landing or a shooting until we identified American voices. A supply convoy had missed Hariko and found themselves at the Cape. Luckily, they had not landed'.[9]

Soon after, the men of the 2/9th Battalion made their way through the dark to their assembly point – a space near the waterline, less than a kilometre south of their jumping-off point, which had been marked with signal wire for 400 metres, bearing 240 degrees from a point on the water's edge that was east-south-east of the end of New Strip.[10] Sergeant William 'Bill' Spencer, a 23-year-old accountant from Adelaide, with the battalion intelligence section, recalled:

> On the afternoon of 17 December, Lieutenant Colonel Cummings, Major [Roy] Maloney, Sergeant [Alan] Elliot and I moved out towards the Japanese lines to mark a start-line. I carried a sandbag full of start-line lights (a small single-cell torch with a red glass). We stopped and climbed up on the stumps of coconut palms to have a better view of the terrain. We remained there for some ten minutes and neither saw nor were fired on by the enemy. After we climbed down and were talking, Cummings remarked, 'It's going to be tough over that patch tomorrow!' A decision was made that the start-line lamps would not be used, for which I was very grateful, and that evening the start-line was marked with tape and signal wire by Corporal Ron Fitzpatrick. The start-line ran in a dogleg from the end of the New Strip to the coast.[11]

Private Alexander Morris, a 29-year-old schoolteacher from Gympie in Queensland, also with the intelligence section, recalled the inability to conduct any reconnaissance, given the attack was to commence early next morning: 'Intelligence. Nil! I think they were driven that hard by the higher ups ... none of us had any idea of what we were going into. We knew it wasn't going to be easy, but I don't think that we expected the casualties that we had there that morning'.[12] Indeed, Captain Norman 'Tony' Worthington, a 28-year-old commercial artist from Brisbane, recalled: 'The O Group met in a sheltered depression and heard Cummings outline the information he had gleaned from

CHAPTER 38

his meeting with the US Commander. The opinion was that the task would be much harder than we had previously believed'.[13]

Some local hurried reconnaissance did take place, however, as recalled by Corporal Barnet, who accompanied Lieutenant William MacIntosh, a 28-year-old clerk from Townsville in Queensland, leading 17 Platoon, 'D' Company, 2/9th Battalion: 'Lieutenant MacIntosh, who was the platoon commander .... He and I crawled forward on the evening of the 17th in the dark. We found that in front there were some very heavily armed Japanese pillboxes. We veered off to the right and crawled up and found no Japanese and so we actually walked up and found that right up to nearly Cape Endaiadere we found ... no Japanese ... but there were these rows of pillboxes almost right up to the beach. They were at right angles to the beach so that when we drove up the beach next day, we were firing down their lines ... we created quite a bit of havoc by doing that'.[14]

The burnt-out and now rusting carrier, from Lieutenant Fergusson's ill-fated attack of 5 December, was used as a pointer to the course of this line, and a grim warning to the men of the 2/9th Battalion of their potential fate. Most of these men were veterans, not only of fighting the Germans and Italians, but also the Japanese, helping to repel their invasion of Milne Bay in August 1942. The men talked quietly in the night, and many were restless but did not show it, each mentally preparing himself as he lay with his own thoughts through the long cold night.[15]

It was recognised that given the terrain and vegetation, plus the faulty radio equipment, communications between the tanks and infantry would be problematic. Hodgson recalled: 'As for our approaching battle, the tanks would have to be closed down, in which case, because of our unreliable radio, it would be almost impossible for the infantry to talk to the tank crews. Inter-tank communication was possible to some degree but seldom back to the reserve or control tank. It was also extremely difficult to find and identify the enemy bunkers, so a series of signals were evolved to help the infantry to direct the tank fire but there was still a need for the tank commanders and platoon commanders to get together. Anyway, in the event, the infantry had to be literally alongside to prevent the Japs crawling under and over us. We had to use five-man crews with one man to observe visual signals and also spot the enemy'.[16]

The signals worked out between the tanks and infantry are recorded in the 18th Brigade war diary as follows:

> Tank requiring infantry assistance will fire a GREEN Verey light.
>
> Tank requiring tank assistance will fire a RED Verey light.
>
> Line of flight of Verey pistol fired by infantry will indicate resistance in that direction.
>
> Infantry desiring tank to move to them will raise steel helmet on rifle and bayonet.
>
> Targets or centre of resistance may be indicated by pointing rifle and bayonet at arm's Length.
>
> Positions of all wounded will be marked by fixing rifle vertically with bayonet into Ground.[17]

That night, 22-year-old Trooper John Wilson, from Sydney, who was the hull gunner of Lieutenant McCrohon's tank, recalled Brigadier Wootten making an appearance at their advanced position. The men were called together and Wootten addressed them: 'You men are here to save infantry casualties and to destroy the enemy. You are expendable, we must take the objective at whatever cost'. Wilson was not only concerned by the brigadier's address about their likely impending demise but was also worried whether the 'Japs could hear Wootten's speech' as they were close to their frontline positions.[18]

* * *

CHAPTER 38

That day, unnamed Japanese soldier [C], who was part of Colonel Yamamoto Hiroshi's force positioned within the coconut plantation near New Strip, recorded his last diary entry: 'Thursday. Fair. Intense mortar barrage before dawn. Can't come out of the camouflage. Very quiet after the mortar barrage ceases. We hear the motor of planes'.[19] It was likely he was killed the next day, given his almost daily entries. His diary was recovered ten days later by American troops, likely taken from his body.

Close by would have been Japanese soldier [E] with Colonel Yamamoto Hiroshi; they were now dug-in around the plantation and at the north-east end of New Strip. He recorded in his diary: 'To the right front of our positions, in the direction of the YAMAMOTO Unit, rifle firing heard most'.[20]

* * *

While Brigadier Wootten and his force of Australians, with American support, would be fighting up the coast towards Buna from the south-east, the American GIs of Urbana Force would continue their efforts of breaking into the Buna sector from the south. The Japanese still holding the Triangle, however, left the GIs awkwardly placed. They would have to advance along a north-east axis towards Buna Government Station, where the main Japanese resistance was still centred, with both flanks protected by strong positions. The Triangle was on the right; on the extreme left, the Japanese held Musita Island, framed by the broad mouth of Entrance Creek. Obviously, one or both flanking positions had to be taken if the American advance on the Buna Government Station was to succeed, and the rear had to be protected against any Japanese attempts at relief from the strongly held positions towards Sanananda just west of the Creek. The seizure of Musita Island would not only make it possible to bring Buna Mission under close range fire but would provide a jumping-off point for a direct assault against it from the south. The Triangle, in turn, would deliver an excellent line of departure for an advance through the Government Gardens to the sea, required before any attack on the mission from the south-east.[21]

Captain Manning, commanding the Australian guns of Bullforce, reported that day: 'An A/A gun in govt Gardens was observed by Lieut. Haywood. This gun had previously been registered and neutralised by air. A verified 25^X bracket obtained and ... all guns adjusted, and 15 rounds fired: three direct hits were observed. Subsequently a working party was observed among the ruins and five more rounds fired, a considerable number of casualties were reported. Later a vehicle and working party were heard by night in the area and four more rounds fired. No further activity in this area has been reported. It is interesting to note that the observed shooting revealed that a 50^X bracket had been obtained on this target by air'.[22]

Colonel Tomlinson, the Urbana Force commander, would soon have fresh troops for the forthcoming battle – the 127th Regiment would be available to conduct the operation. At the time, moving up from Ango were the men of the I/127th Regiment who had flown across from Port Moresby. And those of the III/127th Regiment were already in the Urbana sector, having relieved the men of the II/126th Regiment, while advanced elements of the II/127th Regiment had taken over Lieutenant Colonel Smith's positions, after the failure to take the Triangle. Smith and his men of the II/128th Regiment were sent back down the track for much-needed rest and reorganisation.[23]

Tomlinson now began reorganising the line with the arrival of reinforcements. The troops of 'I' Company, III/127th Regiment took the place of the II/128th Regiment, in the area between Musita Island and the Coconut Grove. The battalion, less the mortar platoon of 'H' Company, which remained behind, was ordered to Simemi for a well-earned rest. The men of the II/126th Regiment took over in the Coconut Grove and moved troops into position above and below the Triangle. The troops of 'E' and 'F' companies, II/127th Regiment had meanwhile reached the front and went into reserve. A mixed platoon of the 126th Regiment under Lieutenant Alfred Kirchenbauer moved

CHAPTER 38

towards Siwori Village to replace the troops of the 128th Regiment. Meanwhile, Captain William Boice and his men of the II/126th Regiment had been brought back into the line – some were located in the Coconut Grove, while others were positioned around the Triangle. Two patrols from this battalion were also sent out to their left rear, one under Lieutenant Paul Schwartz, who was leading 'F' Company, to Tarakena, and another under Lieutenant Kirchenbauer to Siwori Village. Held in reserve were two companies of II/127th Regiment.[24]

Tomlinson now ordered 'L' Company, III/127th Regiment to take Musita Island the following morning. However, this would be no easy task, as the footbridge to the island had been destroyed, and the creek was a tidal stream, unfordable even at low tide. The men had no bridge-building equipment, and the distance from one bank to the other was too great to be bridged by fallen trees. Therefore, swimmers would drag a cable across the stream, and two platoons and a light machine gun section of the company, commanded by Captain Roy Wentland, would make their way across just before noon the next day.[25]

Tomlinson's immediate objective was to capture Musita Island on his left flank on 18 December. He then proposed for his major assault against the Triangle to begin on 19 December, giving his men a comfortable start through the Government Gardens to the coast south-east of Buna Government Station (Buna Mission). This would be the start of an all-out attack on Buna Government Station from that direction.[26]

39

'WE KNEW THE BASTARDS WERE THERE, BUT YOU COULDN'T ACTUALLY SEE THEM'

The 18 December would witness the last of the fighting around the Gona beachhead at Haddy's Village to the west. Gona itself had fallen to the Australians on 9 December.[1] At Buna and Sanananda, however, the Japanese were still dug-in and resisting stubbornly.

At Buna, 18 December 1942 was slated for the tank-infantry attack in the Duropa Plantation – New Strip area.

During the early morning hours, the Australians of the 2/9th Battalion were already preparing for action. Most had arrived at their jumping-off position by 5.30 am, while Lieutenant Colonel MacNab had ordered his American infantrymen to fallback from the vicinity of the start-line to make way for the GIs. As the Australians passed through the American positions to the jump-off line, the Americans lit cigarettes and handed them to the Australians as they passed by. Between 6 am to 6.45 pm, the I/128th Regiment and the men of the III/128th Regiment withdrew quietly 300 metres to their appointed positions.[2]

With 18 Platoon, 'D' Company, 2/9th Battalion was 27-year-old Private Frank Rolleston, from Mackay in Queensland, a Bren gunner. He recalled the morning of the attack: 'At last, the sky began to grow light with the approach of dawn, and we rose and prepared to move

CHAPTER 39

to the frontline .... Since it is not wise to eat a meal before going into action we did not bother with breakfast, for if a man is wounded in the stomach, it is better that it be empty .... As we moved forward the Americans moved back ... did not appear to have established any type of defence works other than shallow holes dug-in the ground near the edge of the scrub'.[3]

Lieutenant Colonel Cummings, commanding the 2/9th Battalion, spoke to the men as they moved off to the start-line: 'Do not stop, keep going forward. If you stop you will die. If you want to live don't falter. Keep pressing to their bunkers'.[4] Cummings had three companies forward, aiming to first capture a strip of ground about 500 metres from the water's edge as far as Cape Endaiadere and from there continue another 500 metres until his men held the line of Simemi Creek.[5]

On the right, Captain Robert Griffin, a 24-year-old clerk from Rockhampton in Queensland, and his men of 'D' Company, would approach the cape itself on a 250-metre front, with Lieutenant Victor McCrohon and his three-tanks of 5 Troop, 'B' Squadron, supporting their advance. In the centre, Captain Robert Taylor, a 28-year-old labourer from Toowoomba in Queensland, and his men of 'A' Company would extend the front for a further 250 metres, supported by Lieutenant Grant Curtiss leading two tanks of 10 Troop and one from 12 Troop, 'C' Squadron.[6]

On the left was Captain Cecil Parbury, a 32-year-old grazier from Tenterfield in New South Wales, commanding 'C' Company. He and his men were to conduct a half-left to establish his men firmly at a point some 200 metres roughly north of the eastern end of New Strip, where a kunai patch ran up to the edge of the plantation. Here, Parbury could protect the flank and rear of the main advance against the Japanese, while at the same time holding the Japanese positions in the swamp and bush to the west.[7] Parbury recalled years later: 'As far as I know, no recce of the Japanese positions was made. If there was, I was left in ignorance about it. There was no indication of the Jap bunkers; where they were, nothing of this was given to me'.[8]

Finally, as soon as the Australians advanced, MacNab and his men of the III/128th Regiment, and Major Clarkson with his troops of the I/128th Regiment would move forward north and west in support of the attacking Australians.[9]

Captain Arthur Benson, a 34-year-old railway employee from Tiaro in Queensland, and his men of 'B' Company, 2/9th Battalion would be held back in reserve to be called upon as needed. They would be called forward, however, shortly after the initial attack was launched.[10]

The weather, unfortunately, prevented aircraft from assisting the attack, but at 6.50 am, the artillery opened with an intense barrage, with Captain Manning and his 25-pounders searching for the log barricade, which had barred the American advance for so long. Major Hall and his guns were dropping shells around the top of the eastern end of New Strip, while Captain O'Hare and his three howitzers were targeting the centre of the main Japanese positions.[11] The 2/5th Field Regimental diary records: 'The attack went in at 0700hrs, following a very accurate and effective concentration of Arty and mortar fire'.[12]

The 2i/C of the 2/9th Battalion, Major William Parry-Okeden, a 32-year-old grazier from Chinchilla in Queensland, recalled years later how the men coped with their fear on the eve of battle: 'There is the poor beggar who vomits, others become jovial and laugh. Some sing but most remain grim with set faces, determined to do their duty whatever happens and not make a fool of themselves in front of their mates. The old cigarette is a grandstand-by. I have seen chaps puffing away at their cigarette in a cloud of smoke with the Tommy gun at their hip bowling over Japs as they move forward .... I have seen chaps moving forward under heavy fire and not one of them would go to ground in fear that their mates may think they were afraid'.[13]

Private Frank Rolleston, with 18 Platoon, 'D' Company, 2/9th Battalion, was now at the jumping-off point waiting along with his mates for the order to advance: 'Our tanks took up their positions just

CHAPTER 39

in front of us with their engines running .... Nearby to where we were waiting, one of our three-inch mortar crews were putting over bombs as fast as they could drop them in the barrel .... Some of our planes roared over quite low, and our artillery opened up with a barrage. The moment for our attack was drawing close, and our platoon officer "Bluey" Sivyer said our brigadier wishes us the best of luck. If we do this job, we will be doing what a brigade should be doing .... Quite suddenly the barrage ceased falling as the tank in front of us started to move forward, and Jack Dalton said, "Now off we go".[14]

* * *

At 7 am, the Australians crossed their start-line, and the tanks dispersed in line and throttled down to the pace of the infantry, who moved beside or close behind them.[15] As described by the Australian official historian, to the observers, it was an 'unforgettable picture as the three companies walked upright with seeming nonchalance directly at a line of strongpoints which stretched like an unseen bar before them from the sea to the end of the strip. Each of these was a small fortress, cunningly concealed and camouflaged; some were protected by interlaced coconut logs covered with six feet [two metres] of earth, some were steel roofed, others were concreted'.[16] The battalion war diary records the advance: '0700 hrs: Bn crossed start-line. Bn advanced into terrific fire from line of pillboxes constructed of coconut trunks interlaced roofed in some instances with steel and covered with 6" [two metres] of earth, very well camouflaged and built to resist arty fire'.[17]

The adjutant of the 2/5th Field Regiment also recorded the initial advance: 'The tanks advanced to within 200 yds of the fall of rounds during the last two minutes of the concentration. As the task was fired into the second grove .... After the attack had gone through it could be seen that the area of the Jap line and 100 yds plus and minus of it had been covered by shells, and the grass and undergrowth had been flattened and burnt'.[18]

Private George Walpole, a 27-year-old waterside worker from Brisbane, with the Vickers Machine Gun Platoon, recalled witnessing the advance: 'You'd swear they were going in for a cup of tea! We laid down a barrage of Vickers [machinegun fire] and of course we were sitting watching as the battalion went in ... the way I explained that to my mother when I saw it, and, I was crying at the time, they went in just cool and calm as you like'.[19]

In Lieutenant McCrohon's tank was his hull gunner, Trooper John Wilson; they were supporting 'D' Company's advance on the right. Wilson recalled their advance and the techniques used to take out the Japanese bunkers:

The advance started about 0700 headed by our field artillery barrage. Many of the shells exploded in the trees. However, one shell exploded about ten feet [three metres] in front of our tank just as we moved off. Visibility was very limited. We immediately came under heavy fire by machine gun and mortars, hand grenades, etc .... Above all I remember the noise of the guns firing, the cordite fumes, the shrapnel hitting the tank and the heat. The Stuart tank had a large fan system which cleared the fighting compartment of fumes but only worked efficiently with the turret lid open. Of course, that was not possible because of the closeness of the enemy and his use of snipers in the tops of the palms.

We all wore head bands to keep the sweat out of our eyes. The infantry could not advance until each bunker had been neutralised. So, the crew commander worked out with the infantry leaders a plan as follows – the infantry leader would indicate the bunker which was holding him up by firing a Verey pistol at it, or throwing a grenade, or just pointing. We would advance within ten or 15 feet so that we could line up the 37-mm cannon at the correct angle, find the firing slits of the bunker which was most difficult because the bunkers were only about

CHAPTER 39

four to six feet [one to two metres] above ground and the firing slits about three or four inches high and two feet long. We picked most of them up from their muzzle blast. We would then use the 37-mm cannon using AP [armour piercing] and with HE [high explosive] shells to enlarge the opening. That usually took about ten rounds. An infantry volunteer would crawl forward with a container usually a cake tin about six to eight inches in diameter containing explosive, with a hand grenade strapped with adhesive tape to the side – primitive but effective. Of course, the hole in the bunker had to be of a size that this bomb would fit through. On exploding, the ground would shake, and smoke would come out of the vents etc of the bunker.

The Japs inside who survived the explosion would usually attempt to leave by the side entrance, which we would cover with our MGs. Very few escaped. This was the basic routine for a couple of hours and then we would have to pull back … to our base to refuel and replenish ammo. In the meantime, the infantry would hold their position until we could get back to them – say about 30 minutes to an hour depending on what progress we made, as most of our return journey from the front had to be done in reverse because of the ground we were working on. Infantry were running short of ammunition so we hung cloth bandoliers with .303 ammunition on the back of the tanks hanging down about two feet off the ground so they could reach up and grab same. Grenades were carried in the tank and given out through the turret ports as required. This system worked very successfully.[20]

* * *

The Australians advanced, with the men displaying a grim determination and extraordinary composure. Private Frank Rolleston recalled: 'Almost at once a great storm of fire swept at us from the

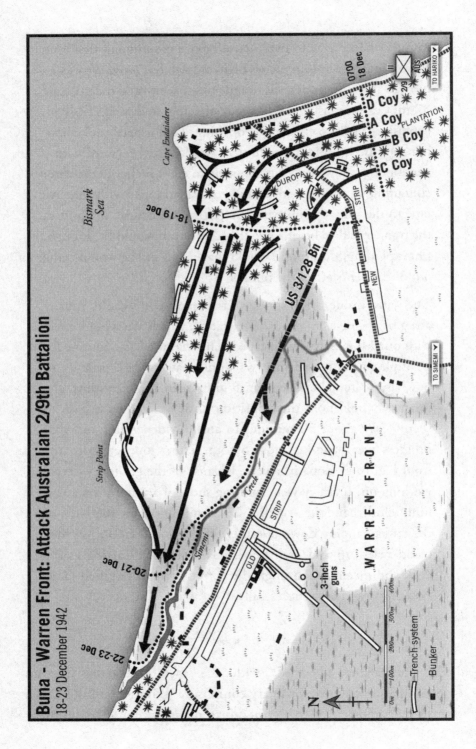

CHAPTER 39

enemy positions and the air became alive with the hiss of bullets as we moved forward. Although I did not realise it at the time, Jack Dalton only took a few steps before he was hit in the groin'.[xvii][21]

The tanks battered each post as it was encountered with the supporting infantry closing in to hurl their grenades through the small openings of the bunkers, killing their occupants to the last man. The defenders, however, refused to surrender.[22] By 8 am, the tanks were focusing on the pillboxes, with a line of bunkers stretching from the coast to the eastern end of New Strip; their presence was camouflaged by high grass and secondary growth. Lieutenant General Eichelberger recorded the advance years later:

> It was a spectacular and dramatic assault, and a brave one. From the New Strip to the sea was about half a mile [one kilometre]. American troops wheeled to the west in support, and other Americans were assigned to mopping-up duties. But behind the tanks went the fresh and jaunty Aussie veterans, tall, moustached, erect, with their blazing Tommy guns swinging before them. Concealed Japanese positions – which were even more formidable than our patrols had indicated – burst into flame. There was the greasy smell of tracer fire … and heavy machinegun fire from barricades and entrenchments. Steadily tanks and infantrymen advanced through the spare, high coconut trees, seemingly impervious to the heavy opposition.[23]

Lieutenant William MacIntosh, leading 17 Platoon, 'D' Company, as part of Captain Griffin's approach towards Cape Endaiadere, was advancing swiftly. He and his men represented the right-forward platoon along the edge of the coconuts and were moving through the scrubby bush that fringed the sand sloping gently down to the beach and the water's edge. When he crossed his start-line, he had

---

[xvii] Corporal Jack Dalton, a 35-year-old labourer from Toowoomba in Queensland would die from his wounds on 29 December 1942

Corporal Evan Barnet who was commanding one of the tanks, steer it directly for a strongly logged Japanese position on his right, which MacIntosh himself and Barnet had identified by crawling forward from the American positions the night before; two machineguns were dug-in there. The tank blasted the post, and MacIntosh's men closed in, grenading. Two of the five defenders crawled out of the smoking wreckage into the one-metre-high kunai grass surrounding the position, not before wounding Lance Corporal George Tyler, 21-year-old truck driver from Killarney in Queensland in the arm, but the NCO shot the man dead at five metres range.[24]

Barnet recalled the fighting here: 'The Japanese put up strong resistance and we supported our infantry by firing into the bunkers and periodically using the gun to chop down coconut palms containing snipers'.[25] Trooper Wilson, the hull gunner in Lieutenant McCrohon's tank, also recalled: 'The saddest memory I have of that day is seeing the infantry advancing in line into murderous machinegun fire and being shot to pieces. I saw many acts of individual bravery, particularly when they would crawl forward to bomb bunkers. One would go down and another would replace him until the job was done'.[26]

Just to the left, Corporal Robert Thomas, a 39-year-old horse trainer from Townsville in Queensland, and his infantry section were hotly engaged from a post that MacIntosh had not observed previously, with some of the Japanese there firing a captured Bren gun and grenades they had taken from the carrier commanded by Lieutenant Terence Fergusson after he had been killed and the carrier abandoned on 5 December. One of the grenades burst almost in Thomas' face as he dashed forward, and then with blood pouring over his eyes, he plunged on and killed two of the Japanese. A third fired at him with the captured Bren that had its muzzle sticking out between two logs of the machinegun nest. Seizing the muzzle of the machine gun, Thomas wrestled for its possession and dragged it through the opening and turned the gun on the Japanese gunner. Thomas then

CHAPTER 39

fought on. He remained fighting for another two days, only leaving the field on MacIntosh's orders. Corporal Robert Thomas was awarded the Distinguished Conduct Medal (DCM) for his actions during the fighting here.[27]

MacIntosh and 17 Platoon, 'D' Company, 2/9th Battalion, along with Corporal Barnet and his tankers now beat down three more entrenched Japanese positions that attempted to bar their way to the cape. On doing so, these men were the first to reach the objective: Cape Endaiadere. By 8.10 am, they had turned westward along the sea towards Strip Point. The American official historian of the campaign recorded: 'Even though the heavy artillery and mortar preparation failed to destroy the enemy bunkers, the coastal attack on Cape Endaiadere was a brilliant success. At 8.10 am., MacIntosh signalled that the cape was in Australian hands'.[28]

Meanwhile, just west of 19 Platoon's break-through, their CO, Captain Griffin, and the rest of 'D' Company were having a tougher time. Lieutenant Thomas Sivyer, a 25-year-old miner from South Johnstone in Queensland, commanding 18 Platoon, led the company advance and were the first to encounter the Japanese as they fought their way through the long lines of coconut trees and tall kunai grass that grew between them. As they approached the cape, about 200 metres south of the position, a Japanese concrete post stopped them with a well-aimed torrent of fire, which took a heavy toll on his platoon. On hearing the fire, MacIntosh and his men attempted to suppress it from the seaward side; however, Sivyer was killed, and his sergeant, Vivian Prentice, a 33-year-old farmer's assistant from Southbrook in Queensland, took over command of the platoon but was soon wounded.[29]

Private Raymond Buckley, a 35-year-old farmer from Cairns in Queensland, who was carrying one of the Bren guns, was killed with a bullet to the throat, while his Number Two on the gun, 26-year-old, Private Mervyn Osborne, from Warwick in Queensland, reached across his body to retrieve the gun but was also killed. Lance Corporal

Charles Alder, a 25-year-old painter from Brisbane, now took command of the platoon but was killed soon after.

With two-thirds of the platoon killed or wounded and no platoon headquarters remaining, the only man in the platoon with a rank higher than private was Lance Corporal Daniel Moses, a 29-year-old labourer from Rockhampton in Queensland, who had just been promoted the day before. Griffin now sent Sergeant Allen 'shorty' Walters[xviii], a 34-year-old labourer from Berkshire Park in New South Wales, to take command of 18 Platoon. But Walters, crawling forward, was shot through the head. Lance Corporal John Rudd, a 25-year-old blacksmith from Townsville in Queensland, was soon sent forward to lead the platoon.[30]

Also with 18 Platoon, Bren gunner Private Rolleston recalled his Number Two on the gun, Private Roy 'Rusty' Bains, a 25-year-old painter from Yerong Creek in New South Wales; Bains would experience his first, and last action that day. Rolleston provided a fascinating detailed account of the fighting:

> As for 'Rusty' Bain, I never set eyes on him again, but I think he had reached the Jap defences before being killed …. I suppose I had gone half the distance to the enemy positions when a blaze of machinegun bullets sent clods of dirt flying in the air hitting me in the face and chest. This occurred just as we were passing one of the Bren carriers which had been stranded out there since the ill-fated attack about two weeks before.
>
> I crossed behind the carrier to get out of the line of fire but kept moving and as I went on the other side of this carrier, I tripped over the body of what must have been a member of the ill-fated crew, for he had jungle-green shirt and trousers …. I quickly climbed to my feet and headed for what appeared to be a pillbox right ahead. As for 'Bluey' Sivyer, I never saw him

---

xviii Sergeant Allen Walters' actual surname was Armitage.

CHAPTER 39

again, and was later told that his body was found lying near the carrier ....

As soon as the second grenade burst, Charlie Alder rushed up to the hole or trench with his Thompson sub-machine gun and poured a burst of bullets into it, apparently killing the enemy occupant, for Charlie then turned and moved in on the pillbox I was engaging. He put a burst down the doorway, then moving to one side, pulled the pin out of a grenade and threw it in. The Japs must have been expecting this for although these grenades only have a four-second fuse, the grenade was hurled out of the pillbox doorway so that it exploded outside. Luckily without hitting anyone.

The Japanese must have decided to take their chances on engaging us outside, for two or three rushed out the doorway, but they were met by bursts from my Bren and Charlie's sub-machine gun and went down. I recall that one was apparently hit in the back and was trying to pull himself along by grabbing the grass, while another shot out on his hands and knees, diving around the corner of the pillbox. I got a burst at him and rushing around found him stretched out on the ground near the pillbox .... Clint Graham was near Charlie when he fell and told me later that he knew he was dead by the way he fell ....

About this time, out of 30 men who had crossed the start-line that morning, there were now only about nine of us left with no platoon headquarters ... the only man left with a rank higher than a private was Danny Moses, but he had only been promoted to lance corporal the day before and I doubt if he realised, he was now in charge ....

One of our tanks moved up behind us, and stopped a few yards away, then started to swing the short-barrelled 37 mm on to us, so fearing it might fire, we held our steel helmets up on our rifles. It did not fire on us, but began pouring machinegun fire into the pillbox, despite our desperate efforts to prevent this, for Harry Jensen was in there. 'Shorty' Walters almost stood in the doorway of the pillbox with his Thompson sub-machine gun pointing at the tank before it ceased fire.

Shortly after this, 'Shorty' was killed by a bullet between the eyes ... (having now withdrawn some 150 yards to straighten out the battalion line because advances during the day had not been as great on the left flank) .... Darkness now began to fall, and we settled into a long defence line, crouching in whatever cover by scratching holes in the soft soil with our tin helmets ... our main worry was for water for I am sure everyone had a raging thirst, and although some stew had been brought up in containers just on dark, we were too thirsty to eat much.[31]

Meanwhile, moving behind, and to the centre of 17 and 18 platoons, Warrant Officer Vince Donnelly, a 24-year-old clerk from Cairns in Queensland, and his men of 16 Platoon encountered problems of their own. As they advanced, some positions that were thought to have already been cleared by American troops previously were found to be very much alive, with enemy activity. Donnelly and his men now found themselves fully engaged with these isolated pockets of Japanese resistance.[32]

Things were also difficult on Griffin's immediate left, where Captain Taylor and 'A' Company represented the centre of the main attack. When Griffin first reached his objective at around 8.10 am, Taylor's men had at least 200 more metres to cover, but by then, they had been so badly mauled by the entrenched enemy to their front, as well as concentrated enfilade from both flanks, that they could make no further progress. Griffin's left flank in consequence remained exposed. Lieutenant Colonel Cummings now sited some machine guns, with the dual purpose of covering Griffin's open flanks and supporting Taylor and his men.[33]

CHAPTER 39

Corporal Ernie Randell, a 24-year-old labourer from Mackay in Queensland, with 7 Platoon, 'A' Company recalled the fighting here:

> The ground was strewn with old trunks of coconut palms making it difficult for the tanks to manoeuvre. I had lost a couple of my section, killed before we got to near the Jap defences. Suddenly, my mate waved me urgently to his side. Here in an open slit trench in full battle order were ten or a dozen Japs. They were watching a tank go by and hadn't noticed us. We took care of them. Now that we had reached the pillboxes, we hurled grenades down through the slits, but they were thrown back at us. Ever try holding a grenade for a few seconds? There was so much small arms [fire] around, it was not possible to tell if snipers were operating. However, during a lull in which our troops, who were totally exhausted, rested for a while, a sniper started to operate. Lyle Hicks was kneeling beside a coconut palm. I yelled, 'Did you see where that shot came from?' 'No,' he replied, 'but it was damn close to me.' As he spoke, another shot rang out and Lyle slumped forward, shot through the temple.[xix] We up and dived for the shelter of the tank. The sniper killed more men that afternoon despite our efforts to locate him. I had a tank knock out several palms that could have been hiding him. When we went forward next morning, we found his hiding spot.[34]

On the extreme left of the attack, Captain Cecil Parbury was also facing stubborn Japanese resistance at the eastern end of New Strip. His men of 'C' Company plunged into a regular hornet's nest. These men were cut to pieces by both light and medium machinegun fire from several strong posts. Even before leaving the start-line, they had suffered casualties and, as soon as they advanced, they came under a

---

[xix] Private Lyle Hicks, a 30-year-old labourer from Bangalow in New South Wales is listed as killed-in-action on 18 December 1942

hail of rifle and machinegun fire. Without tanks, they had lost 46 out of 87 men in less than ten minutes, in an advance of only about 100 metres.[35]

In this advance, Lieutenant Roy de Vantier, a 24-year-old schoolteacher from Toowong in Queensland, was killed, as was Sergeant Jack Gordon, a 35-year-old grazier from Toowoomba in Queensland, when a bullet detonated a grenade he was carrying on his belt. It was not long before the remaining NCOs, except one, had also become casualties. The surviving NCO ordered the remaining men to ground so that some at least might survive, taking up a position in the one-metre-high kunai grass. Parbury was now out of contact with 14 Platoon and feared it had been wiped out. Parbury then ordered the rest of the company to ground.[36]

At this point, Sergeant Harry Dixon, a 23-year-old salesman from Adelaide, with the Mortar Platoon, was not far behind 'C' Company. He recalled getting the order to go to ground: 'It was bloody time to do it wasn't it? There was nothing left! There was nothing left! That's all we had to do, wasn't it? I never expected to live .... But things turned out differently. Tom Parbury called out to Corporal Les Boylan. "Call the roll!" And he rolled over on his side in this grass, he got it out of his haversack and called the bloody roll. You wouldn't believe it! And some wouldn't call out, of course, and some would sing out, "I'm wounded!" And then another bloke would say, "He's dead!" And the Japs weren't any more than 50 yards in front of us! They had us pinned down and we couldn't move. We knew the bastards were there, but you couldn't actually see them'.[37]

Parbury now phoned through his situation to Cummings – years later, the young officer recalled the conversation with his CO: 'I advised Cummings by phone that we had suffered frightful losses and were unable to proceed further until tank support was furnished. He told me to try infiltration, which would not be possible, because the bunkers were close together and self-supporting, and the tree snipers had every inch of ground covered, and we had no cover to advance.

CHAPTER 39

I reluctantly sent Sgt Morey in to do this …. I still feel remorse about this'.[38] Parbury was told that he would soon be receiving tank support.[39]

Sergeant George Morey, a 31-year-old labourer from Sydney, led a section from the platoon commanded by Warrant Officer James Jesse, a 25-year-old labourer from Brisbane. As Sergeant Morey and his section, which was now one of the rapidly dwindling bands of the battalion's originals, moved forward, he was killed, along with his entire section before they had gone 15 metres. The balance of the company, some 60 metres in front of the most forward Japanese positions and about 100 metres from the main bunker line, were now stranded waiting for the tanks to come to their aid.[40]

Meanwhile, Major Gordon Clarkson with his troops of the I/128th Regiment were also trying to help in response to an appeal from Parbury to close in on his left. By crawling through the long kunai, the Americans got some distance forward unscathed but then stopped some 40 metres to the rear of the Australians, helping to bring out their wounded.[41]

* * *

Meanwhile, tank commander Captain Norman Whitehead was in the centre of the formation and just behind his two forward tank troops, intending to keep himself free as far as possible to control 'X' Squadron and to give support where needed. But almost at once, he realised that he had to leave his individual tank commanders to decide for themselves how best they could help the infantry, as visibility was limited. Whitehead was now isolated from his force, and from the beginning, he was in the thick of the fighting.[42]

Scarcely had Whitehead left the jumping-off point when he spotted a Japanese sniper high in a tall coconut three ahead of him. He called out to his gunner, Trooper Gordon Bray, a 23-year-old salesman from Balgowlah in New South Wales, 'Shoot him!' But Bray could not elevate his machine guns sufficiently. Whitehead then said, 'Shoot the tree down'.⁴³ So, Bray fired his 37-mm gun at the point where the thick butt narrowed to the tapering trunk. The first shell nicked the trunk; the second brought the tree down and the sharpshooter tumbled headlong in a neck-breaking fall. Bray then gave him a burst of his BAR for good measure as the tank pushed forward to the main Japanese defensive perimeter.⁴⁴

About an hour later, Whitehead received word from a soldier knocking on his tank that he was required to help Parbury and his men who were held up by several Japanese bunkers located northeast of the eastern end of New Strip. Whitehead immediately swung around and followed the man to the west until he found himself against three strong enemy positions, baring his way. He took on the most southerly of these and silenced it with four or five shots. However, as the tank turned against the second, Bray's sights fogged over, while Whitehead peered through the vision slit, his hands cushioning his forehead against the tank's metal wall, his face pressed to the slit. It was then that an enemy soldier leapt onto the tank and thrust the muzzle of his rifle hard against the slit and fired. The bullet and pieces of splintered metal gouged through Whitehead's face. With blood blinding one eye, dizzy and bleeding, he fell to the floor of the tank; his good eye was now puzzled by flashing circles of light that went spinning round his head. These were tracer bullets from a Japanese machine gun that was set up a bare three metres away and firing directly into the vision slit. As his good eye followed the tracers inside the tank, his 'ear registered quick new hammering notes amid the already familiar clatter of bullets on the tank. Though he did not know it then these were from the spatter of fire which killed the soldier who had shot him'.⁴⁵

Indeed, two Australian infantrymen who were just behind the tank in support now sprang into action. They saw the Japanese soldier who had initially fired into the tank only after he leaped back from his attack, flinging his arms wide in a gesture of exultation. In that moment of triumph, he was shoot dead. Soon after, the tank

CHAPTER 39

turned to take the badly wounded captain out. It was now that the tank was being targeted by an enemy soldier firing at it from behind a tree. Bray sent a 37-mm shell straight at the tree and had a clear vision of a 'pair of boots at the foot of the palm and a piece of blood-stained rag fluttering foolishly – all that remained of what had been the man'.[46]

The bleeding Whitehead was scarcely clear of his tank at the 2/9th Battalion Headquarters when, his CO, Lieutenant Colonel Charles Hodgson, commanding the 2/6th Armoured Regiment, took his place. Hodgson plunged into the fight, looking out of the open turret to get a clear view of what lay ahead. Predictably, a Japanese machine gunner had the senior officer in his sight, and on a burst of fire, Hodgson slumped back into the turret badly wounded. It was scarcely 10 am and both senior officers of the 2/6th Armoured Regiment were already out of action, with Lieutenant Grant Curtiss now in command of 'X' Squadron.[47] Hodgson, who would survive his wounds, recalled many years later:

> A message came back to say that his [Whitehead's] tank was coming back as Captain Whitehead had been wounded. A few moments later they arrived, and he was lifted out onto a stretcher bleeding from his arm and face with a dressing over his eye.
>
> Colonel Cummings said his left company, Captain Parbury, could not move without tank support so I took over Whitehead's tank and we went back to where he had been wounded. We then took on Japanese bunkers which were holding up any movement and moved slowly forward with Parbury's company. Whitehead had been wounded by a Jap jumping on his tank and firing from a few inches into the turret slit which was shattered and [it] wounded Whitehead who was observing at the time.

The observation slit was quite opaque and useless, so I had no option but to open the hatch and direct the tank with my head out – I did put on my steel helmet and for a short while all went well, and we cleared two or three bunkers. I dropped grenades straight into them but then, either a sticky bomb on the tank or machinegun rounds hitting the turret and splintering, hit me about the left temple and the blood blinded me, with the result I could not control the tank, and the driver turned and took me back to Battalion HQ. This was only about 200 yards [metres] away, which shows the scale of the operation.[48]

* * *

Meanwhile, on the right, Corporal Barnet had brought his tank into the coconut plantation in the centre of the attack, supporting 'D' Company, leaving his infantry support on the objective. He had seen Hodgson ride his tank in and got a call from his OC Lieutenant McCrohon, leading the tanks from 'B' Squadron, who had his hands full. He ordered Barnet to go to the assistance of the tank commanded by Sergeant Jack Lattimore, who was in trouble a little deeper in the plantation. He heard Lattimore calling him on the radio: 'Come on, Splinter! Come on, Splinter!' He then saw Lattimore's tank bellied on a fallen coconut tree. By now, however, Barnet was out of ammunition and radioed back to the stranded crew that he would be back. Unknown to Barnet, however, Lattimore failed to get the message, and he and his crew were anxiously wondering why they were being abandoned. Within minutes, Barnet, who was then resupplied with ammunition, returned to assist Lattimore. The Japanese had by then set fires beneath the tank, trying to roast the trapped crew who were squirting fire extinguishers through the apertures trying to scare off the Japanese.[49] Barnet recalled years later the situation at this point: 'I said to my gunner Rod Jones, who was an excellent gunner. "Take the paint off Jack's tank, and hunt those Nips back!"'[50] Within minutes,

CHAPTER 39

Lattimore and his crew were able to escape their tank, with Barnet's tank covering their retirement on foot.

Twenty-two-year-old Trooper Frank Jeavons, from Binya in New South Wales, was a member of Lattimore's crew and later wrote in his after-action report preserved in the unit war diary: 'On the morning of Dec 18 the tanks went into action. At approximately 1000 hrs Sgt Lattimore's tank of which Tpr Jeavons was a member, bellied on a log, and the Japs started to light fires around the tank, until the other two tanks drove them off and gave the tank covering fire until the crew escaped. Tank was later recovered in good order'.[51]

It was about now that it became obvious to the Australian tankers that the Japanese had turned into their radio network, as recalled by McCrohon's hull gunner, Trooper John Wilson: 'The Japs came across our radio net and in accented English came across saying "return to base, tanks return to base". We realised very quickly what was happening and put them in the picture'.[52]

Meanwhile, at around 8.15 am, while fighting with Captain Taylor commanding 'A' Company in the centre, the tank commanded by Curtiss ran onto a stump, where it remained stuck, unable to advance or withdraw. Like Lattimore's men, he and his crew narrowly escaped being roasted alive when the Japanese lit a fire beneath the stricken vehicle. Under cover of shots from the supporting infantry, the crew leapt unhurt through the hatch. By now, Sergeant John Church and his M3 were on the scene, but all his determined efforts to move the stranded tank were in vain – it was now a burnt-out wreck.[53]

Twenty-year-old, Trooper Kenneth Pulling, from Mortdale in New South Wales, and the gunner in Church's tank, recalled: 'We opened fire with machine guns, spraying bushes and coconut trees to find snipers. During this phase, a bullet hit one of the protectoscopes and broke it. We then moved forward taking our orders from the infantry and firing into the scrub even though we could not see anything .... The first Japanese I saw was in front of me with a machine gun. He appeared oblivious to the tank. I got the driver, Max Lenehan, to back the tank back so I could get the machine gunner in my sights. I then used the tank machine gun on the Japanese soldier. As we advanced onto the pillboxes, I would fire an armour-piercing shell into the pillbox followed by a high-explosive shell. We kept doing that along the row of pillboxes and used our machine gun at each end in case the Japs ran out'.[54]

At some point in the fighting, Pulling left the tank to quickly explore a shattered bunker, keen to gather anything of intelligence value: 'I jumped out of the tank into a pillbox where I gathered various equipment, Jap flags, photographs and pistols. On the way back to the tank a sniper's bullet hit me on the side of the tin hat, which knocked me to the ground. I jumped quickly back into the tank. That was witnessed by George Silk (the Department of Information photographer) who reported it to the *Sydney Sun* newspaper'.[55]

It was now that the remaining tank of 'C' Squadron, 12 Troop, commanded by Corporal Phillip Smith, also became stuck on the stump of a downed coconut tree. The squadron's turret gunner, 21-year-old, Corporal Leopold 'Leo' Gregson, from Sydney, recalled: 'In accordance with armoured drill, Phil asked the gunner to vacate the tank and undo the tow rope from the back of the tank and he had our operator call another tank for assistance. The tank arrived and pulled us clear of the stump. Throughout the operation I did not hear any gunshots'.[56] It was not long before Smith and his tanks renewed their advance in support of the infantry, with Gregson continuing his narrative:

> We then continued our advance until we were requested to halt and await further orders. I had continued to fire 37-mm high explosives and to direct Browning fire to the treetops. When we halted, I was quite disorientated, having only had a telescope to look through. I was trying to see any Japs defensive positions and I asked Phil if I could have a quick look from the turret. As soon

CHAPTER 39

as my head showed near the cupola, I was shot in the head by a tree sniper. The bullet opened up my scalp and then fragmented on the inside of the steel turret. The fragments bounced back, and numerous pieces entered the back of my head and neck. I was unconscious and the crew evacuated me to a forward CCS, having applied a field wound dressing.[57]

Here, the tank crew was replaced with another crew, although it is possible that Corporal Cecil Cambridge, a 30-year-old clerk from Sydney, the original radio operator and gun loader, joined the crew and commanded the tank as it went back into action. At around 12.30 pm, this tank was seen billowing smoke, and soon it was a burnt-out wreck, but all the crew escaped without suffering casualties. A report by the Light Aid Detachment [mechanics, fitters, armourers and electricians] of the squadron later reported it had been targeted with a magnetic mine: 'The magnetic bomb comprised four permanent magnets equally spaced round the circumference for attachment to metal surfaces. It was about three inches in diameter and wrapped in a skin-tight Hessian container. A number of strings radiated from the centre and were attached to a detonator in the bomb proper. Any of the strings, if pulled, would set the bomb off and it invariably exploded in the direction it was facing'.[58]

* * *

Sometime that day, Major Hall with the 2/5th Field Regiment was located on the right near the beach, here he witnessed the following incident, as described in the regimental war diary:

Whilst watching the advance of the tanks along the beach, three men were seen to emerge from thew undergrowth and ran into the water approximately 100 yds in front of the start-line. At first it was thought they were American, owing to the similarity of the steel helmets. Maj. Hall decided to investigate with Gnrs [Robert] Sharam and Allen H. and proceed up the beach towards the figures. By this time, one was 300 yards and another 250 from the shore, swimming. The third man was about 50 yards out, up to his armpits in water, standing with his hands in the air. Maj. Hall called to them to surrender, and the one nearest the shore started to come in. The others kept swimming, and Maj. Hall, with three rounds from a rifle, killed one of them, the other disappeared, swimming out to sea. The third man advancing towards them had both hands up. The right one was closed. When he got within ten yards of Maj. Hall, he suddenly disclosed that he had a grenade which he struck against his helmet to ignite. The grenade began to smoke, but before he could throw it, Gnr Allen fired two shots at him from his revolver. He appeared to clasp the grenade to his body and was blown up. What bastards! No further attempt will be made by 55 Bty to take prisoners. Cape Endaiadere was cleared by 2/9 Bn at approximately 1000 hrs. Maj. Hall carried out a recce of the Cape and found that excellent observation can be obtained on the Buna Mission area. This was reported to Div. Capt. Mueller, who was with 2/9 Bn HQ was shot through the knee at 1130 hrs and was replaced by Capt. Nix.[59]

* * *

Colonel Yamamoto and his men of the *144th* and *III/229th Regiment* had been completely taken by surprise. The tanks and the fresh Australian troops advancing behind them made short work of the Japanese positions in the plantation, which had so long held up the attack on the coastal flank'.[60] MacNab also recalled: 'The tanks really did that job. They apparently completely demoralised the Japs ... [who] fought like cornered rats when they were forced into the open [as a result of] having their fires masked when the tanks broke

CHAPTER 39

through their final protective line .... There were few holes knocked in the bunkers except where the tanks stood off and blasted them at short range with their 37-mm guns.[61]

* * *

Still on the extreme left, Captain Parbury was grateful for the appearance of the promised tank support. Curtiss arrived at around 1 pm, having taken over Church's tank. He also brought with him another two tanks in support of the stranded survivors of 'C' Company.[62]

While the vehicles waited behind the infantry, Parbury pointed out the Japanese positions halting his advance. By now, Parbury had re-established contact with 14 Platoon, which was being led by Private Llyod Logan, a 31-year-old station manager from Cunnamulla in Queensland. He had taken over the unit with the death of Lieutenant de Vantier. Parbury's plan was to have Warrant Officer Jesse take his men forward in line with one section on either side of the two forward tanks and one moving between them. Jesse himself would advance with the centre section, to indicate the targets for the tanks by firing Verey lights into the enemy positions. From 30 metres forward and 70 metres to his right, the 11 remaining men of 14 Platoon would give supporting fire for the renewed advance. The third platoon, commanded by Lieutenant Francis Pinwill, a 25-year-old clerk from Wolfram in Queensland, would move behind Jesse's tank-infantry line. Bren gunners would spray snipers in the trees as the men advanced. However, even as Parbury was putting the finishing touches to this plan, three enemy soldiers had sneaked forward through the kunai to set the right tank on fire with incendiary bombs, but Parbury's men riddled them with bullets before they could reach the tank.[63]

By 2 pm, the Australian advance had renewed. Jesse's Verey lights streaked into the Japanese redoubts, and tank shells quickly followed, exploding into the Japanese positions. Bren gunners sprayed the trees and kunai as the men and tanks moved out. As described by the

Australian official historian: 'Every Australian weapon was running hot. Several posts blazed high as the dried coconut logs took fire. And then the Japanese cracked. Some of them leaped in panic out of their defence s screaming in terror. Then the Australian foot soldiers were dragging out the core of the resistance, grenading right and left, behind and beside the tanks'.[64] Within 30 minutes, they had cleaned out 11 of the enemy bunkers, while the remaining five were evacuated. The fighting here had ceased by 3 pm, with the Australian line-oriented west, just above the eastern tip of New Strip. Now, American troops moved up in a mopping-up operation, occupying a position to the right and left of the Australians. Here, 85 Japanese lay dead, with a similar number of wounded who were likely interred in the shattered bunkers that the Americans destroyed.[65]

This area was later found to be made up of 20 pillboxes, several of them of concrete and steel construction. Some Japanese, less a small rearguard, withdrew along the northern edge of the strip to bunkers near the bridge. Their position, along with the engineer and anti-aircraft troops they reinforced, was now precarious. The whole bridge area and the few still intact bunkers south of the bridge had been under heavy fire during the day from the American mortar teams, along with the howitzers commanded by Captain Martin O'Hare and the lone American 105-mm howitzer south of Ango, which for the first time in the campaign had ammunition to spare.[66]

By the time Captain Parbury and his men of 'C' Company had broken through the Japanese defences on the left, Captain Benson and his 90 men of 'B' Company had already been ordered forward. They were to support 'A' and 'D' companies, as well as providing a platoon to reinforce 'C' Company. Benson and his men were now ruthlessly destroying any Japanese remnants who had remained alive in Taylor's and Griffin's wake. He and his men were targeting strongpoints close to the Australian forward position. In the fighting here, all platoon leaders of 'B' Company were killed before the surviving 20 men of the company, joined up with 'A' and 'D' companies at around 4 pm.

CHAPTER 39

With 'B' Company was 23-year-old Private Grahame Hynard, from Brisbane, who recorded in his diary later that day:

> 7 am we moved into the frontline and the Japs threw everything they had at us, they were zinging over my head like hornets. We had a few tanks and moved up behind them. In the first ten minutes my officer was killed, and my corporal was cut in the head with a grenade. The first 'deadun' I saw was a Jap, who had been that way for weeks. I surprised myself by my lack of emotion. We were pinned down by a sniper who was only a few yards away in front in a sangar.
>
> I saw Scotty our stretcher-bearer walking back with a wounded arm, he had passed me when this sniper got him in the stomach. It was terrible to hear his groans, but we had orders not to help anyone, but keep going. We disposed of the sniper with hand grenades and moved from one coconut tree to the other. The Japs had innumerable machine gun nests in concrete sangars and they had coconut and creepers growing over them so we could not see them until we were right on them.[67]

Due north of Benson was Captain Taylor and his men of 'A' Company. In the late afternoon, they were lunging forward with some of the tanks over the short but deadly space they needed to cover, finally pivoting westward around the base of Cape Endaiadere. They were now in line with Captain Griffin and his men of 'D' Company.[68]

* * *

The enemy's line in the Duropa Plantation–New Strip area had been broken, and the Japanese defences were shattered in the area east of Simemi Creek. Night found the Australians facing westward against the Japanese reserve line, on a front that ran from the sea due south to the east end of New Strip. Griffin was on the extreme right, which rested against the sea about 400 metres west of Cape Endaiadere, with a frontage of about 350 metres. Taylor held a 250-metre front to the left of Griffin, while Benson was on Taylor's left with an American platoon on his left. Parbury was anchored to the south, his left resting on the end of the track that ran north-east from New Strip to the coast.[69]

Sergeant William Spencer with the 2/9th Battalion intelligence section recalled years later: 'Moving around between the companies was a macabre and at times hair-raising task. It was sickening to see the number of mutilated, dead bodies lying everywhere, together with the torn undergrowth, blood-stained clothing and discarded utensils of war. Some of the dead lay or were slumped in natural positions, appearing to be in a deep, peaceful sleep. I thought one of our lads, Jack Hardwick, was asleep, and I had to gently push him to make sure. Poor old Jack did not wake up.[xx] Any thoughts of peace were driven from your mind when you heard the sharp crack of a sniper's bullet. Although you knew that it was not the one you could hear that claimed you, you instinctively ducked'.[70] The enemy snipers were not only in the treetops, as recalled by Sergeant Vernon Hansen, a 23-year-old farmer labourer from Laidley in Queensland, with the 2/9th Battalion: 'I remember one sniper there. He would only fire now and again. But when he shot, the man he shot, he killed him. He always shot through the heart. He might go and lay there for an hour. They [eventually] found him under a couple of palm leaves'.[71]

Communications with the Battalion Headquarters had broken down within minutes of the attack being launched. Lieutenant Edwin Beattie, a 26-year-old labourer from Atherton in Queensland, now the battalion's signals officer, recalled: 'Very, very few reports came back to rear Battalion HQ. The signal wires got destroyed as fast as they were laid. We were behind the start-line, but the air was full of bullets. The adjutant was wounded, so I went up to take his place

---

xx   Private Jack Hardwick, a 23-year-old labourer from Adelaide, is listed as dying of wounds on 22 December 1942.

CHAPTER 39

at ten o'clock. By that time seven of the 12 platoon commanders had been killed. Most of our information came from the wounded coming back, and there were plenty of them'.[72] Indeed, as dusk was falling, Lieutenant Colonel Cummings was moving forward to see the situation along his left flank, with his acting intelligence officer, Sergeant Alan Elliot, as recorded by the historian of the 2/9th Battalion:

> Picking their way cautiously through the shattered landscape they moved forward to Simemi Creek which defined the battalion's left flank. Across the creek and swamp, they could clearly see a number of Japanese calmly preparing for the night. Taking Elliot's rifle, Cummings shot one of them. When they failed to take cover, he shot two more. When Elliot asked for his rifle back so he could have a go, Cummings replied: 'No. You will only draw the crabs, let's go'. Whether another shot would have drawn the crabs any more than the previous three, and the advisability of a battalion commander being so far forward taking pot shots at the enemy are problematical points, but in fairness to Cummings, it had been a hard day for him. He had ordered his battalion forward and watched helplessly as they suffered unprecedented casualties against a ferocious and unforgiving enemy. As they walked back, he confided to Elliot that he felt better. It had felt terrible sending all those young men to their death but now at least he had done something'.[73]

Dudley McCarthy concluded in the official history: 'With dash and hardihood which boded well for the rest of Wootten's plans, the 2/9th had thus completed their first task – for the loss of 11 officers and 160 men, more than one-third of their attacking strength. But resolute though they were, they owed much to the tanks. Two of these had been burnt out'.[74]

Indeed, the area of the day's attack was the most suitable ground for tank operations in the whole Buna area. The Stuart tanks were fast moving, and their speed was part of their overall protection (since speed demands lightness), and so armour had been sacrificed to achieve it. Even so, the ground was far from perfect. In the plantation among the high, coarse kunai grass, tree stumps, through the swamp mud, over the bomb craters and shell holes, they could merely grind in their lowest gear at the pace of a walking man, even if the necessity for cooperating with the infantry required they keep their speed down to walking pace. They were not designed as supporting infantry tanks, and their crews had no training or experience for this role. Neither had the infantry been trained to work with tanks. So, both had to improvise during the fighting. Although improvised signals were developed, the extent to which they could be used was reduced, as the tanks were almost blind – their vision was restricted at the best of times, being shut off by the tropical vegetation.[75]

In Lieutenant McCrohon's tank, Trooper John Wilson, his hull gunner, recalled the end of the fighting: 'By midday the crews were feeling the extreme heat and loss of body fluid. We continued on until dark and returned using our headlights. We were helped out of the tanks by US troops – in fact I was lifted out completely exhausted after almost nine hours of combat. US troops stood guard for us all night'.[76] McCrohon estimated that about 36 bunkers and gun positions had been destroyed that day alone.[77]

The 18th Brigade war diary records the situation by the late afternoon to dusk: 'By 1500 hrs the area captured had been generally cleared of enemy and mopped up but a strong enemy centre of resistance consisting of approximately 20 pillboxes situated at the dispersal bays at East end of NEW STRIP had resisted all attempts to subdue it. At approx. 1600 hrs an attack by two coys 2/9 Aust Inf Bn and four tks [tanks] was made upon it. Hard and continued fighting ensued in this locality for approx. two hours but at 1800 hrs approx. the strong point was reduced. This eliminated the bottleneck East of

CHAPTER 39

NEW STRIP'.[78] The adjutant of the 2/9th Battalion acknowledged that the battalion had suffered over 33 per cent casualties in the day's fight:

> 1020 hrs: 12 Pl ['B' Company] with tks attacking barricade of pillboxes. C Coy reports at least six LMGs holding them up these being untouched by arty fire. One tk destroyed. Attack by C Coy and tks against steel covered pillboxes unsuccessful. Snipers very active between A & D Coys. 1100 hrs: C Coy reinforced by two tks attacked to cut off the V of the New Strip. A Coys strength now 48 estimated 50% casualties. D Coy 40 casualties. B Coy strength 1 Offr, 21 ORs. 1400 hrs: C Coy reported 14 Pl to be out of contact and believed wiped out. D Coy reported parties of Japs moving West. 1600 hrs: C Coy progressing slowly although delayed by arming of tks. B Coy now advancing against second line of pillboxes. 1700 hrs: A Coy moved forward with support of tks to strengthened line while B Coy took up defensive posns at 303245 [around New Strip area]. 1830 hrs: Bn held a line with D Coy on right flank from a point 300 yds West along beach then running South 350 yds contacting A Coy's right flank. A Coy's front 250 yds then B Coy then pl of 3/128 US Regt then C Coy whose left flank rested on track running to coast from strip .... Bn HQ moved to hut at 305249 [about 700 metres south of Cape Endaiadere, close to the beach]. 1850 hrs: C Coy reported that attack with tks, two fwd and one behind and inf in V formation, was successful against series of pillboxes .... During this day's action the Bn casualties were 5 Offs and 49 ORs KIA, and 6 Offrs and 111 ORs wounded.[79]

Brigadier Wootten that night decided to spend the following day reorganising his men. Later that night, the men of the 2/10th Battalion, less two companies, came in from Porlock Harbour. The

2/10th Battalion diary records: 'Spent entire daylight hours on sea lane between Cape VOGEL & ORO BAY'.[80] The convoy dropped anchor at their destination later that night at around 11.30 pm.[81] The incoming troops took over the bivouac area previously occupied by their mates of the 2/9th Battalion, who were now holding the frontline positions of Warren Force. The Australians of the 2/10th Battalion now represented the brigade reserve.[82]

Private John Kirkmoe, a 23-year-old bread carter from Adelaide, with 15 Platoon, 'C' Company, 2/10th Battalion recalled many years later: 'The 2/9th Battalion had already been in action there. We knew that we were going in pretty soon. We didn't know exactly when. It was all coconut groves where we first landed and where the 2/9th Battalion went in was coconut groves. We had to get across a swamp to the airstrip, because the Japanese were entrenched right up in a coconut grove on the coast at the end of the airstrip. They were really dug-in. They'd made fortifications there with coconut logs. They were well prepared. We had to get across the swamp and form across the airstrip in preparation for attack'.[83]

* * *

Japanese medical officer Lieutenant Yamamoto Kiyoshi reported incorrectly that five enemy tanks had been destroyed, but after ten hours of fighting, 'it proved impossible to hold on and the defenders were wiped out'.[84] This resulted in a significant redeployment of the Japanese positions along the strip. In 16 days of fighting, before the Australian attack, only ten men of the *III/229th Regiment* had been reported killed, and 22 wounded. It was now reported widely that the men of this battalion were 'annihilated by enemy tanks'.[85]

The official Japanese history records the day's battle along the eastern flank of the Buna position (Warren front):

> The shelling stopped at 5 am, whereupon the freshly arrived Australian troops, with tanks in the lead, began their advance.

CHAPTER 39

The concealed Japanese positions could not be destroyed despite the heavy clearing fire in front of the advance. The appearance of the tanks, however, was a great shock to the Japanese troops. This was because the tanks were not visible under heavy fire until they were right over the concealed Japanese positions. The tanks had been diverted via the coastline near the outer camp to penetrate the Japanese positions. The Japanese defended grimly and set fire to two of the tanks near the frontline. The remaining three tanks halted at pillboxes and concealments positioned some 500 metres to the rear of the outer camp.

The Japanese garrison at the Old Strip front safely defended their positions during the day. The turret of one of the two tanks that was providing direct support stopped moving, owing to damage by machinegun fire. Four further tanks arrived at the front at 4 pm, and the Japanese defensive line was finally breached. The 3rd Battalion of the 229th Infantry Regiment had been guarding the outer camp during the day's battle. It suffered heavy casualties and withdrew to a line east of the creek.

The Army troops led by Colonel Yamamoto withdrew over the bridge or by wading through the shallows near the river mouth and established a second-line camp. The fire fight over the bridge continued throughout 20 December. Meanwhile, communications had been severed between the garrison headquarters and the Buna Camp area.[86]

* * *

Sometime that day, the body of Lieutenant Terence Fergusson, who had commanded the Bren gun carrier force on 5 December, was recovered, as recalled by the adjutant of the 2/5th Field Regiment: 'The body of Lieut. Fergusson of the Inf Carrier Pl, who had been missing since 5 Dec was found today behind the Jap lines. His wallet and paybook were intact and were handed to the Coy Comdr by Maj. Hall'.[87] Years later, Lieutenant Colonel MacNab, when writing of the carrier attack for the American official historian of the campaign, recorded: 'This unit was commanded by a Lt Ferguson [sic], a courageous and altogether fine young Australian'.[88]

* * *

Meanwhile, further west at Urbana front, the plan for 18 December, developed by Lieutenant Colonel Tomlinson, had fallen apart almost from the start. Unopposed, Captain Roy Wentland, commanding 'L' Company, III/127th Regiment, had crossed Entrance Creek by noon with two platoons. These men were soon joined by a third platoon. Wentland and his men moved forward along the eastern half of Musita Island without meeting any Japanese. However, when they started moving towards the bridge connecting the island with the mission, they encountered heavy fire from concealed positions. In the fire fight that followed, five men, including Captain Wentland, where killed, and six were wounded. The heavy enemy fire continued, and the troops, under the impression that they were heavily outnumbered, pulled back to the mainland that night, leaving the island still in enemy hands.[89]

It was decided that two companies of the II/126th Regiment would attack across the bridge the following morning from the Coconut Grove, while a third company would block the position from the south. The attack would be preceded by air strikes against the mission, while the Triangle would be bombarded by Lieutenant Colonel Melvin and his seventeen 81-mm mortars, about 300 metres south of the bridge to Musita Island. Since the Triangle was narrow and inaccessible, neither air nor artillery would be used in direct support, due to the fear that their own troops would be hit by friendly fire.[90]

Around 100 men from 'E' and 'G' companies, II/126th Regiment, along with the attached weapons crews of 'H' Company would mount the attack. They crossed the bridge over Entrance Creek and

CHAPTER 39

moved into the bridgehead area at the mouth of the Triangle at 10 pm that night. Shortly thereafter, the 36-man holding force from 'F' Company, II/126th Regiment went into position in the area below the track junction.[91]

Meanwhile, Lieutenant Paul Schwartz and his patrol from 'F' Company, II/126th Regiment, west of Girua River, had clashed with Japanese patrols near Siwori Village. Within days, upon the insistence of Lieutenant General Herring that the left flank had to be better secured, Schwartz was reinforced with another 20 men of his battalion. These men had been in reserve at the time, south of Buna Village. Schwartz's force, now numbering 35 men, began moving on its objective, Tarakena, a small village on the west bank of Konombi Creek, which was about two kilometres west of Siwori Village.[92]

* * *

That night, Lieutenant General Eichelberger wrote to Major General Sutherland as the mopping-up operations continued. He now argued, with the benefit of hindsight, that their infantry with the weapons and support provided to the 32nd Division could never have penetrated the Japanese lines: 'I know General MacArthur will be glad to know, that we found concrete pillboxes with steel doors, interlocked in such a way that it would have been almost impossible for [infantry] unassisted [by tanks] to get across'.[93]

40
'... THE CAPACITY OF SEASONED AIF TROOPS'

By the morning of 19 December, the Australians were cleaning up the area they had taken the previous day, linking up with Lieutenant Colonel Alexander MacNab and his men of the III/128th Regiment's right, occupying the eastern end of New Strip. As recorded in the 18th Brigade war diary: 'The enemy [was] dislodged from strong points at the East end of NEW STRIP by 2/9 Aust Inf Bn on 18 Dec. [The enemy] abandoned his hold on the STRIP during the day and by nightfall it was in our hands'.[1]

By now, the officers and men of the 2/10th Battalion were sorting themselves out at Hariko, having arrived there during the early morning hours as recorded by the battalion war diary: '0230 hrs: First barge beached at landing point 1800 yds south of Cape ENDAIAFDERE & was met by ... Intelligence Personnel ... received instns re positions of companies as for perimeter defence. 0400 hrs: D & C [companies] arrive, we are completing landing. 0430 hrs: All companies in position prepared for immediate action in event of counterattack by enemy'.[2]

Meanwhile, two Australian 4.5-inch howitzers of Stokes Troop had flown in the previous day and would go into action behind O'Hare Troop south of the bridge between the two strips. Several concentrations were fired during the morning, on newly located Japanese bunkers in the bridge area. And Major Gordon Clarkson, with his troops of the I/128th Regiment, moved forward along the northern edge of the strip to join Major Chester Beaver and his depleted companies of the I/126th Regiment in front of the bridge.[3]

CHAPTER 40

Brigadier Wootten now planned to renew the attack with his men of the 2/9th Battalion the next day. Supporting this attack would be Captain Hugh Matheson, a 30-year-old mechanic from Port Pirie in South Australia, and his men of 'C' Company, 2/10th Battalion. The adjutant with the 2/10th Battalion recorded: '1400 hrs: CO and Coy Comdrs made recce of Cape ENDAIADERE. 1700 hrs: C Coy moved in reserve of 2/9th Bn [towards] Cape ENDAIADERE'.[4] Wootten informed Lieutenant Colonel Cummings, who was commanding the 2/9th Battalion, to complete the first phase of his previous orders, requiring him to secure the whole of the area north of the strips and enclosed by the coast and Simemi Creek. The 2/9th Battalion war diary records that day's preparations:

0700 Remainder Bn HQ moved to new HQ area. 0917: C Coy sent patrol out 200 yds; NO contact made. Second patrol sent along edge of jungle reported this, the first phase of the original objective, free of enemy and Coy moved forward to occupy this area, without opposition. Patrol from A Coy West to investigate pillboxes in coconuts at 301251 [about 600 metres north of New Strip – just west of the aircraft bays]. Slight opposition met from snipers and pillboxes which were then burned out and A & D coys moved forward to straighten the line which was now approx. the 30 Grid line [north to south] from the coast to the New Strip.1745 hrs: C Coy moved to occupy Bn HQ area at first hut [about 700 metres south of Cape Endaiadere, close to the beach] while the line vacated by them was occupied by Coy 3/128 US Regt. Bn HQ moved to area CAPE ENDAIADERE. C Coy 2/10 Bn came under command 2/9 Bn at 1900 hrs. 1750 hrs: Throughout the day burial parties search the battlefield for our dead, many were found within a few feet of pillboxes, including SBs [stretcher-bearers] who had fallen where they tended the wounded. 4 ORs evacuated, 2 wounded during the day. Reported 2 Died of wounds. Lieut. POWER P.A.G.[xxi] dies of wounds'.[5]

Once again, the Australian gunners and tankers would support the men of the 2/9th Battalion. Major Norman Moss, a 31-year-old merchant from Wahroonga in New South Wales, now in charge of the tanks, was described by the Australian official historian as: 'A dark, strongly made man of more than average height, whose thrusting approach to any problems which might beset him had earned him the nickname "Bull", was now in command of the tanks, having arrived that day from Port Moresby'.[6] As recorded in the regimental war diary, Major Moss, Lieutenant Ewan Gunn, a 30-year-old insurance agent from Orange in New South Wales, and 11 other ranks arrived at Brigade Headquarters at 11.30 am. They soon made contacted with Lieutenant Grant Curtiss at Cape Endaiadere where the tanks were harboured. Major Moss was advised by Wootten that the tanks would support the 2/9th Battalion the next morning. Later that afternoon, Moss, Curtiss and Lieutenant Victor McCrohon liaised with the 2/9th Battalion, regarding the planned attack.[7]

In addition to the guns and tanks, available aircraft would also support the assault. MacNab and his men of the III/128th Regiment would also support the attack by following up and occupying the ground covered, as part of the Australians advance. They would then attempt to advance with the support of Major Gordon Clarkson and his men of the I/128th Regiment, south of New Strip and Major Chester Beaver and his mortar teams in the bridge area.[8]

After conferring with Brigadier Wootten, Major William Hall, commanding the 2/5th Field Regiment, conducted a reconnaissance of the Japanese frontline positions, as recorded by his adjutant in

---

[xxi] Twenty-five-year-old Lieutenant Patrick Power from Brisbane is listed as dying on 19 December 1942.

CHAPTER 40

the unit war diary: 'Maj. Hall went forward with Brig. Wootten and the plan for the continuance of the attack was discussed with Col Cummings, Col Dobbs, and Col Martin, US Maj., Hall, with Col Martin, carried out a recce of the south-east and of the New Strip, which area was being taken over by 1 Bn, 126 Regt. Pillboxes and dugouts in the previous day's battlefield were [taken] out with grenades and anti-tank mines. During the process, several live Japs were discovered amongst the bodies and were promptly dealt with'.[9]

* * *

That day, Lieutenant General Herring wrote to General Blamey, having been briefed on the previous day's fighting along Warren front: 'Wootten handled his force very well yesterday .... The outstanding factors in the [operation] so far are I think three. The first is Wootten's leadership, the second the value of the tanks for which we have to thank you and the third the capacity of seasoned AIF troops'.[10]

* * *

Among the Japanese survivors from the *III/229th Regiment* from the previous day's fighting was Lance Corporal Uchiyama Seiichi, with Captain Matsuo's *No. 9 Company*. He was still missing his light machine gun. He recorded: 'Enemy planes attacked before dawn, bombing fiercely for an hour. Mortar firing for an hour. Two men wounded. 1500 [hours] Concentrated firing; retreated into the trenches. A captured automatic rifle issued in lieu of a light machine gun'.[11]

That day, Japanese soldier [E] with Colonel Yamamoto Hiroshi's force at Warren front recorded in his diary: 'Our troops which captured positions in the coconut grove were repulsed due to enemy tanks'.[12]

* * *

Further west – and following the failure of the previous day to take Musita Island – Lieutenant Colonel Tomlinson, commanding Urbana Force, turned his attention to again taking the Triangle. At 6.50 am, nine Marauder aircraft bombed the Government Station, and in less than an hour, 13 Boston bombers, dropping 475 twenty-pound cluster-fragmentation bombs, and fired more than 21,000 rounds of .30-caliber and .50-caliber ammunition. Their accuracy, however, left much to be desired, as a stick of four bombs was dropped within 50 metres of a bivouac area occupied by the men of the 127th Infantry, and a chaplain visiting the troops at Buna Village was hit by bullets meant for the Japanese at Giropa Point.[13]

As the second wave of bombers pounded the station, Captain William Boice, commanding 'E' and 'G' companies, II/126th Regiment, totalling just 107 men, prepared to advance southward against the rear of the Triangle from the bridgehead leading down from the Coconut Grove. Just before 7 am, Lieutenant Colonel McCreary's mortarmen dropped their bombs into the Triangle. Fifteen minutes later, Boice and his men attacked under cover of a rolling mortar barrage. The bombardment, however, did little good, as the Japanese were well dug-in and waiting, repulsing the American assault with intense enfilade targeting them immediately after they left the line of departure. In the lead, Captain Boice did everything he could to get things moving again, but the crossfire proved impenetrable. Every attempt by his men to reach the enemy lines only added to the toll of casualties. At 9.45 am, Captain William Boice was mortally wounded by mortar fire, dying within hours.[14]

The 126th Regimental war diary records: 'After air and mortar barrage our troops made slow advance up by strongly fortified machinegun positions. Because of heavy casualties the strength was down to 30 to 40 men per company. Capt. Boice was killed, Capt. [John] Sullivan, who had arrived with replacements from the rear base, took command'.[15] Captain Boice was awarded the DSC posthumously for his actions.

CHAPTER 40

Lieutenant General Eichelberger now ordered the mortars to lay down a concentration of white phosphorous smoke in the Triangle at 2.15 pm, and the attack was to resume under this smoke screen. The troops gained a few metres with the help of the smoke but were stopped by enemy enfilade. At 4 pm, a third attack was launched with the mortar teams lopping around 700 bombs into the enemy positions before the attack went underway, but the result was the same; the GIs found it impossible to break through the murderous enemy crossfire. When night fell and the utterly exhausted troops dug-in, they had suffered 40 casualties from their force of 107 men who had begun the attack.[16]

In no condition to continue the attack, the two companies would be relieved early next morning by 'E' Company, II/127th Regiment, and go into reserve with the rest of the II/126th Regiment now numbering just 240 men. The only exception being the men of 'F' Company, who would continue to hold the position at the southern tip of the Triangle, along with Lieutenant Paul Schwartz and his patrol who were now further west approaching Siwori Village and the Tarakena area. The main burden of operations at Urbana front now fell upon the troops of the 127th Regiment.[17]

* * *

Meanwhile, the new chief of operations from the *Imperial Headquarters*, Colonel Sanada Jōichirō, arrived in Rabaul that morning. He explained the new operational doctrine to be adopted in eastern Papua.

> When seen in the light of the rapid advance of Allied operations in New Guinea, and its overall strategic importance, Imperial Headquarters considers that if a firm foothold is not maintained for an offensive against Guadalcanal, and eastern New Guinea is not quickly secured, then there are fears that the 8th Area Army will suffer a total loss.

Consequently, there are those who feel that New Guinea should be accorded less importance. On the other hand, there are also those who feel that New Guinea should be quickly secured and stabilised.

Hence this outline. If Lae, Salamaua, and Madang are firmly secured, then there will be the opportunity to retake Buna later, even if it is now lost. We are currently facing two options: to simply discard Buna; or to support a withdrawal from Buna. If withdrawal is chosen, it must be done now. This means that the area army needs to spread itself in a manageable fashion.[18]

The next day, the *Imperial Headquarters* provided new orders: 'The current situation demands that units in the Buna area withdraw to the Salamaua area and occupy key locations'.[19]

41

'I AM GOING TO BRING TOMLINSON IN HERE FOR A DAY OR SO ...'

At 6.30 am, 20 December 1942, three Allied bombers dropped fifteen 500-pound bombs over Giropa Point. In addition, shells, mortar-bombs and machinegun fire exploded and sprayed into the area through which the Australians of the 2/9th Battalion would advance at 7 am. This attack would be supported by the M3 tanks, with Lieutenants Ewan Gunn and Victor McCrohon spacing their four tanks among the infantrymen. Captain Robert Griffin and his men of 'D' Company were now on the right, near the water's edge, with Captain Robert Taylor and his men of 'A' Company in the centre. Captain Arthur Benson and his men of 'B' Company were on the left.

Meanwhile, Captain Cecil Parbury and 'C' Company were in reserve with 12 men from the transport platoon added to make up some of their losses. The men of 'C' Company would, however, soon advance to support 'B' Company's attack.

At Cape Endaiadere, Lieutenant Colonel Cummings was holding back Captain Hugh Matheson and his fresh men of 'C' Company, 2/10th Battalion, pending developments.[1]

At first, only Japanese sniper and harassing fire disputed the Australian advance through the tangled undergrowth among the coconut trees. Supporting the advance, the tanks fired their machine guns into the treetops to take out the snipers. After almost three hours of fighting, the infantry broke out from among the regularly spaced trees into the stunted bush and kunai-covered marshland, almost due south of Strip Point, typical of the Buna area, spreading as far as Simemi Creek beyond which ordered rows of plantation trees dominated again. There, Parbury passed through Taylor and his men of 'A' Company who then fell back into reserve. It was now that Taylor himself was seriously wounded.[2]

Benson with Parbury in support pushed across 800 metres of the first of two patches of kunai and through the boggy ground, with their men spread out across the base of Strip Point. At that time, Griffin and his men of 'D' Company had skirted the water's edge along the beach, rounding the point itself and reporting that the Japanese had evacuated the position there. Soon, Parbury and his men of 'C' Company took the lead from 'B' Company and were tramping through the swampy bushland, leading towards the second kunai patch. But this precarious country had proved too much for the tanks, as the marshy terrain west of Strip Point worked against them. One tank had to be abandoned, and another could not be extricated until the following day when the attack on the Japanese in the finger at the mouth of the creek was resumed. Only the beach offered any chance of getting the tanks forward.[3]

The 2/9th Battalion war diary records that at 9.43 am, 'A' and 'D' companies had reached the edge of jungle and grassland, with 'C' Company passing through 'A' Company, taking up a position in the kunai grass. The men of 'B' Company encountered heavy going through dense jungle and Sago swamp, while 'D' Company moved round Strip Point. The men of 'C' and 'B' companies searched the grass, with 'B' Company's left flank now against the creek. Two tanks were reportedly in trouble, one bogged in a bomb crater, but it was later recovered and joined the infantry advance. However, the going was 'extremely hard through dense jungle and tall grass'.[4]

Fred Folkard, a war correspondent with the *Sunday Sun*, described to his readers the situation faced by 30-year-old Lieutenant Ewan Gunn, from Broken Hill in New South Wales, and his crew of 9 Troop,

CHAPTER 41

'C' Squadron that day: 'Trapped in a tank that had run into a creek near Buna, five Australians spent an uncomfortable hour up to their necks in water. All the time the tank was under heavy Japanese fire, which made their rescue hazardous …. The tank was operating in the Semimi [sic] Creek area, spraying the undergrowth with machinegun fire to rout out hidden Japs, when it ran into a creek. It immediately tilted to an angle of 30 degrees and water poured through to the level of the bottom of the turret. The five men had to put their heads into the narrow space of the turret to avoid drowning. There they had to remain with the Japanese firing on them, until infantrymen rescued them. The tank was [later] pulled out'.[5]

By 1.30 pm, the ill-fated men of 'C' Company were once again in trouble. The right forward platoon was close against the beach and Lieutenant Francis Pinwill and his platoon were on the left; they had temporarily lost contact with the platoon on their right. They continued to plunge further into the kunai grass, where they came unexpectedly against a Japanese defensive perimeter that ran north from the creek to the coast. Here, Sergeant Thornton MacCarthy, a 35-year-old carpenter from Mackay in Queensland, knocked out one enemy post with a grenade; however, Lieutenant Francis Pinwill was killed, along with two of his men, and four of the others (MacCarthy among them) were wounded. The remaining men fell back upon the other forward platoon near the water.[6]

Parbury recalled the fighting here: 'We came under machinegun fire from the enemy whose line ran from Simemi Creek north to the coast. Pinwill's platoon came up against the Jap positions, with one post being knocked by a grenade thrown by Sgt MacCarthy. The platoon came under flanking fire and was pushed back. Pinwill was killed along with three others and MacCarthy was wounded in the face.'[xxii] [7] The battalion war diary records the situation at

---

[xxii] Sergeant Thornton MacCarthy, a 35-year-old labourer from Childers in Queensland, would survive his wound but would soon after be honourably discharged from the Army due to his wound.

around 2 pm: 'C Coy advanced elements were fired upon by LMGs and MMGs at short range and forced to retire with heavy losses. Jap defence line appeared to run North and South across edge of grasslands from Coast to SIMEMI CREEK'.[8]

Meanwhile, Cummings arrived at Parbury's position, and they were discussing the situation. It was now that Griffin and his men, who were following the coastline after reaching Strip Point, joined them. Almost immediately, the Japanese began to drop mortar-bombs on them from 300 metres to their front, with several men becoming casualties, including Parbury who was wounded. Here, 'C' Company was amalgamated with 'D' Company, and Griffin with Benson and his men of 'B' Company in support, renewed their attack against the Japanese positions. They were soon forced to ground, suffering a further 25 casualties in the fighting there. They now formed a blunt arrowhead facing west and from a point on the coast about half-way between Strip Point and the mouth of the creek.[9]

Meanwhile, just on dusk, Lieutenant Colonel MacNab and his men of the III/128th Regiment came up on the left of the Australians, linking up with Benson. Earlier, the Americans of 'I' Company, on the far left, ran into a sizable Japanese force before it reached the bank of Simemi Creek. A heavy fire fight ensued, but the company, with the aid of a few survivors of 'C' Company, 2/9th Battalion, on their right, cleared out the enemy pocket and the GIs were able to push onto the bank of the creek. By the end of the day, only a small finger of land, extending into the mouth of the creek, remained in Japanese hands. In the New Strip area, the last pocket of Japanese resistance was mopped up by nightfall.[10] That night, the 18th Brigade war diarist recorded the advances made that day.

> Supported by tks, 2/9 Aust Inf Bn attacked at conclusion of preliminary arty concentrations. A day of hard fighting ensued. While it was found that tks were not able to move with any practicable degree of freedom after the West edge of

CHAPTER 41

the coconut [tree line] had been reached owing to difficulties of ground which consisted of marsh and jungle. By nightfall, the advance had continued west past STRIP POINT and had reached a line running ... south along Eastern edge of small grass patch where contact was made with US tps .... At midday 2/10 Aust Inf Bn less one coy ['C' Company] was moved fwd to a concentration area astride the track leading NE from the Western end of the NEW STRIP to the coast. The swampy nature of the ground bordering the SIMEMI CK made it increasingly apparent that an essential prelude to an attack on the Old Strip was to secure a crossing for the tks either at the mouth of the SIMEMI CK or over the vital bridge [between the strips]. 1/126 USA Bn were ordered to attempt the crossing of the SIMEMI CK under cover of darkness to secure this BRIDGE.[11]

The boggy terrain and the entrenched Japanese were going to make it difficult to cross Simemi Creek. The most obvious crossing was at the mouth of the creek, where the water was known to run shallow as it emptied into the sea, and at the point where the bridge spanned the creek between the two airstrips. But the creek's mouth was still in enemy hands, and as for the bridge area, the continued lack of success there by the Americans since their very first approach a month before did not bode well for success. Indeed, that morning, an attempt to cross the bridge by one of Beaver's patrols had been forced to retire almost before they advanced. During this withdrawal, Private Steve Parks turned back under intense Japanese fire, to bring back a wounded man; he was awarded the DSC for his actions.

It remained unclear how the Australians would cross the creek. Tanks could not negotiate the shallows, and any assault across the bridge – which was about 40 metres long and spanned not only the creek but heavy swamp on either side of it – would obviously result in fearsome casualties, likely with little to show for the sacrifice. The

Japanese had already blown a large gap in the middle of the bridge and were covering it with several machine guns supported by 40 to 50 riflemen.[12]

Another patrol from the I/128th Regiment attempted to cross the bridge just before noon, but intense fire drove them back. Later in the day, a few men of the Ammunition and Pioneer Platoon of the I/126th Regiment, under their commanding officer Lieutenant John Sweet, tried to put down a catwalk across the hole in the bridge, under cover of smoke shells from two 37-mm guns. With two of his men, Sweet moved out in the face of Japanese fire and started laying the catwalk, only to find that the planks were 15 centimetres too short. Lieutenant John Sweet was later awarded the DSC for his actions.[13]

With the failure to close the gap in the bridge, Colonel Martin proposed another attempt, this time with the aid of one of the Stuart tanks. While the troops were laying the catwalk, Martin suggested the tank would engage the enemy bunkers at the other end of the bridge and draw their fire. Brigadier Wootten, however, had other plans for the tanks, and so Martin's idea was dropped.[14]

Only one alternative remained: to have troops cross the creek on foot and take out the Japanese at the northern end of the bridge. This, however, would be a difficult task, as the creek, except at its mouth, was very deep, and the approaches to it were through heavy swamp, full of prickly, closely spaced sago palms around seven metres tall. The 2/5th Filed Regiment records receiving a request for artillery support: '1600 hrs – 1 Bn, 126 Regt – asked for a smoke screen across the Old Strip to cover the crossing of the bridge and the establishment of a bridgehead between the two strips. Whilst registering the points of origin, 1 Bn, 128, reported that our rounds were falling short, and [they] immediately apologised as the offenders were their own mortars. An effective screen was provided from 1700 to 1706 hrs. 1 Bn, 126 was ordered by Brig. Wootten to take and hold the bridgehead'.[15]

CHAPTER 41

The Americans of 'B' Company, I/126th Regiment were tasked with crossing the creek west of the bridge to establish the bridgehead under cover of darkness. The following day, the intelligence officer with the I/126th Regiment, Lieutenant Elliget, submitted his scribbled report on the attempts of 'B' Company to establish the bridgehead; his notes are preserved in the 18th Brigade war diary:

S2 Report

1st Bn 126 Inf

21 Dec 1942

Subject: Report of attempted bridge head nite [sic] of 20 Dec. 1942.

1. The 37m.m. gun was placed in position to left of Dobodura track south of bridge. Fired 30 rounds of canister ammunition. Fired on north bank of creek, from 2350 hrs to 2400 hrs.

2. Co. 'B' men started moving north across creek at 2400 hrs. They moved just to west of bridge. Water at first was knee to waist deep. As they approached center of creek water became overhead deep. No enemy fire up till now. Platoon leader moved west along creek in effort to find shallower crossing. But ran into heavy mossy undergrowth and deep mud. Returned to bridge and he and five men crawled onto good section on far side. Four of men ran north on bridge to northern bank. Other two men followed close behind. As four men reached bank two Jap m.guns [machineguns] opened fire .... Four men dove on bank on left side of bridge and gained some protection from riverbank. What they stated to be 18 inches high and gently sloping. Jap. m.g. fire was sweeping bridge knee high. And a few rifle shots were coming from both sides & front.

3. The two men still on bridge jumped into creek to escape m.g. fire. Ground to north of creek is very flat with no grass or other objects for concealment. The Jap m.g. fire was very heavy, and it was impossible for any man to remain on bridge. Six men returned to south side of creek by swimming. It was necessary for two of the men to help back one of others who could not swim. The officer who was in charge of group who crossed river stated that its [sic] his belief it would be impossible to make any advance movement along northern bank of creek while Jap m.gs. were firing their grazing fire. The heavy undergrowth and mud would not permit them to cross at any other point.

4. Ten minutes after men returned to southern bank of creek the Jap m.g. again opened fire down bridge with two light m.gs. and a .50 cal. m.g. which had not previously fired. Officer also stated that section still up would support a light tank, and that track on both ends of bridge was firm.

5. No casualties.
Lt Elliget
1st Bn S2.[16]

On receiving this report, Martin called the whole thing off. It was clear that there was no way of crossing in the bridge area.[17]

* * *

Here was located unnamed Japanese soldier [F], who occupied a bunker position just north of the bridge between the two strips: 'With dawn the enemy starts shooting all over. All I could do was shed tears of resentment. As soon as the sweeping fire and explosions cease a concentration of mortar fire starts and Superior Private [indecipherable] is killed. Enemy fires fiercely. ADSHITA Unit in danger. We of the 2nd Platoon hear there is to be a charge and,

CHAPTER 41

after making complete preparations, fill ourselves up with dry bread. Now we are only waiting for death. The rest of you comrades, get revenge for me. Since the great Far East War, I have come from Hong Kong to Sumatra to New Guinea. The time for my glorious death is now 12.07'.[18] However, his imminent death was to be delayed, as he concluded soon after: 'The enemy is quiet after that, and the attack is not made. Shelling again at night and I cannot sleep. Raining'.[19]

To the north-west was unknown Japanese soldier [E] with Colonel Yamamoto Hiroshi's force at Warren front. They had been in the coconut plantation area. The soldier recorded his second-last entry in his diary: 'Two or three enemy planes reconnoitred our positions and the Navy positions [the Triangle] several times. Artillery and mortar fire around our positions, following this there was rifle fire. In the afternoon motor noises resembling tanks were heard. At 1430 [hours] firing was most severe. At 1700 platoon leader, Lance Corp. MATSUME went on liaison to regimental OP'.[20]

The skilful delaying action by Colonel Yamamoto managed to get the bulk of his remaining troops, mostly from the *III/229th Regiment*, across the creek, using two principal points. Those who had fought in New Strip used the bridge, and those who had survived the Duropa Plantation–Strip Point fighting crossed the shallows at the mouth of the creek. Yamamoto took great pains to guard this crossing, as it was the only place along the entire length of the creek where troops could wade across at relative ease. A Japanese strongpoint on a tiny island at the mouth of the creek was heavily reinforced, with emplacements sited to fire across the shallows from the west bank of the creek to deal with any attempt by the enemy to cross at that point. This would be one of the last Japanese positions at Buna to fall to the Australian and American troops.[21]

* * *

Further west at Urbana front, the attack against the entrenched Japanese at the Triangle resumed. Because the attack was to be proceeded with an intense artillery barrage, safeguards were taken to ensure this barrage did not inadvertently hit the attacking troops. Captain James Alford and his men of 'E' Company, II/127th Regiment, who were to deliver the main attack, were ordered into the Coconut Grove at daybreak. These men were to remain there under cover until ordered across the creek, over which a second footbridge had been built a short distance from the first. Meanwhile, the men of 'F' Company, II/126th Regiment, still in place south of the Triangle, were ordered to pull back about 300 metres to permit the artillery to use the track junction as its registration point.[22]

After registration shots had been fire, the 25-pounder battery commanded by Captain Manning, along with the American 105-mm howitzer, both using smoke, were to fire on the Japanese positions around the track junction for five minutes at the rate of two rounds per gun per minute. A second five-minute preparation was to follow at a faster rate. As soon as the registration shoots had been fired, and the first five-minute preparation began, the troops of 'E' Company, II/127th Regiment, who were covered by smoke from the artillery and the mortars, were to dash across the two bridges, form up on the east bank of the stream at a position south of the original crossing, and wait out the artillery fire there. When it ceased, the mortars, firing a salvo every minute, would place a concentration of 40 rounds of white phosphorus on the target. When the first smoke bombs exploded, these men were to rush forward, get within close range of the bunkers under cover of the smoke and clear out the Japanese with hand grenades.[23]

The artillery began registration at 8.45 am. And as this fire commenced, the troops dashed across the creek in a cloud of smoke. Just as everything seemed to be going well, some 'trigger-happy' machine gunners on the west bank of the creek, and to the rear of the jumping-off line, spoiled everything by opening fire prematurely. This threw the attacking troops into confusion. When they finally renewed their advance at around 10 am, they found the Japanese alert and ready for them. In an hour and a half of action, 'E' Company,

CHAPTER 41

II/127th Regiment was unable to get within grenade distance of the entrenched enemy, and the attack was called off at 11.30 am.[24]

Captain Alford proposed a new attempt, requesting a reinforced platoon, led by Lieutenant Paul Whittaker, with Lieutenant Donald Feury as his 2i/C, to infiltrate the low-lying area in the centre of the Triangle, with the help of fire from the rest of his company. When the platoon was as close as it could get to the Japanese bunkers, it would charge and clean them out with hand grenades. Lieutenant Colonel Tomlinson approved the plan, but Lieutenant General Eichelberger, who was present, vetoed it immediately as reckless and likely only to cause useless casualties. On Alford's assurance that the two lieutenants and the men who were to make the attack were confident of success, Eichelberger relented.[25]

With Staff Sergeant John Rehak leading the way, the platoon managed to get within grenade distance of the bunkers and his men charged, but the Japanese had pulled out of the bunkers in anticipation of the attack. They caught the platoon with enfilade and nearly wiped it out to a man, with a few bursts of their automatic weapons. Seven men, including Lieutenant Feury, Lieutenant Whittaker, and Sergeant Rehak, were killed, and 20 others were wounded. Lieutenant Paul Whittaker and Lieutenant Donald Feury were awarded the Silver Star posthumously, while Sergeant John Rehak was awarded the DSC. The two attacks had gained nothing, and they cost 'E' Company, 39 casualties – around 40 per cent of its strength, in its first day of combat.[26]

Tomlinson then called off the attack at 1.35 pm, and a badly rattled 'E' Company spent the next few hours getting its dead and wounded out of the Triangle area; this was made perilous by the Japanese – they took full advantage of the situation, laying down heavy fire on the rescue parties. When the wounded had been evacuated, the company, less outposts in the mouth of the Triangle, withdrew back to the Coconut Grove where the men were made as comfortable as the circumstances would permit.[27]

After three days of fighting, no progress had been made towards clearing the way to the Buna Government Station (Buna Mission), and the enemy still held both the Triangle and Musita Island. At 2.10 pm, a physically exhausted Tomlinson suggested to Colonel Grose that he take over command of Urbana Force, given that his 127th Regiment now made up the bulk of the troops in the line. Grose replied he did not have the authority to assume command and informed Tomlinson that he could take over only if ordered by Eichelberger. At 3.22 pm, Tomlinson called Eichelberger and asked to be relieved of command of Urbana Force. Realising that Tomlinson had been under strain for some time, Eichelberger approved his request and ordered Grose to take over command. Eichelberger wrote to Major General Sutherland at the time that: 'I am going to bring Tomlinson in here for a day or so to rest him up'.[28] Grose would assume command of Urbana Force at 5 pm, and all elements of the 127th Regiment were immediately ordered to the front.[29]

* * *

Covering the extreme left flank of the Buna sector was Lieutenant Paul Schwartz and his 35-man platoon, 'F' Company, II/126th Regiment. The young officer and his men that morning reached Tarakena, about two kilometres west of Siwori Village, only to be thrown out of the village by a superior Japanese force. Colonel Frank Bowen, operations officer to Buna Force, immediately ordered forward another mixed unit of 32 men from the II/126th Regiment to further reinforce Schwartz. These men reached Schwartz's position that afternoon, and his force now numbering 67 men. They moved on to Tarakena Village at dusk to stage, as Schwartz recalled: 'A heckling party' for the Japanese benefit.[30] They succeeded in retaking a corner of the village during the night, but the Japanese counterattacked and forced the Americans back across Konombi Creek.

In the fighting, Schwartz suffered 15 casualties, the young officer himself being wounded. Command of the patrol fell to Lieutenant

CHAPTER 41

James Griffith, but he was himself soon wounded. Lieutenant Louis Chagnon with the Headquarters Company, 127th Regiment was now rushed forward to take over command, bring with him several men of the Headquarters and Service companies. Since he was obviously outnumbered, Chagnon took up a defensive position a few hundred metres south-east of Tarakena and awaited the next move of the Japanese.[31]

* * *

Eichelberger was now planning to bypass the Triangle, having already discussed this with Lieutenant General Herring, who agreed that if the next attack failed, they might feel for a way through the Government Gardens without first reducing this strong point.[32] Eichelberger explained the situation to Sutherland that night: 'General Herring is very anxious for me to take the track junction, and I am most willing, but the enemy is ... strong there and is able to reinforce his position at will. I am going to pour in artillery on him ... and I am going to continue that tomorrow morning. Then I am going to find a weak spot across Government Gardens'.[33]

Major General Frank Berryman, Deputy Chief of the General Staff to General Blamey, would later express concerns about the overall way the campaign had degenerated into ad-hoc ill-advised attacks, stating that Advance NGF seemed to be 'characterised by rushed, desperate, ill-conceived' attempts to 'clear things up quickly'.[34] This not only applied to Buna but also marked the fighting at Gona and the ongoing struggles to take Sanananda.

* * *

That day, the orders from the *Imperial Headquarters* in Tokyo arrived at Rabaul, stating that there was a shift in policy for the *8th Area Army*. Lieutenant General Hitoshi Imamura was now tasked with focusing on the defence of the Japanese position's further west at Lae, Salamaua and Madang. No further reinforcements would be sent to the two remaining beachheads at Buna and Sanananda. It was also stated that the forces there were permitted to be withdrawn if necessary. Indeed, it would not be long before orders would arrive from Tokyo that the Japanese forces at these beachheads be shifted further west to Lae, Salamaua and Madang.[35]

42

'THAT'S WHAT WE'RE TRYING TO DO SARGE'

On 21 December, Brigadier Wootten ordered the two battalions of the American 128th Regiment and the main part of the 2/10th Battalion (which had concentrated around the eastern end of New Strip the previous afternoon) to search Simemi Creek for a crossing. The fresh Australians set about this task with a will; they also had a score to settle with the Japanese, for their momentary setback at K.B. Mission during the fighting for Milne Bay in late August. However, they found it hard to locate the actual course of the creek in the marshy bushland, and many patrols following what they believed to be the creek found themselves stuck in reeking mud and water up to their necks. In this swampland, the Australians needed more than determination, they also needed luck to find their way through.[1]

It was now that Major Gordon Clarkson and his men of the I/128th Regiment came to the assistance of the Australians. Lieutenant Colonel James Dobbs, commanding the 2/10th Battalion, was anxiously questioning the best way forward, when Clarkson suggested it might be possible to cross the creek where it twisted into a U-bend a short distance north-east of the lower end of Old Strip. Dobbs quickly detailed Captain Roger Sanderson, a 30-year-old life assurance inspector from Glenelg in South Australia, leading 'A' Company, to examine the area. However, at first light, the next morning, Sanderson, who went out with his men of 9 Platoon, became tired and bewildered and no closer to getting across the creek.[2]

The battalion war diary records that the rest of the battalion spent the day in the Coconut Grove area around map reference number 291 255, which would place them just south of Strip Point and north of Old Strip, east of the creek. The adjutant concluded that day with: 'Few Japs killed during day while mopping up'.[3]

Meanwhile, the men of the 2/9th Battalion, north-west of the 2/10th Battalion, had been ordered to complete the capture of the tongue of land enclosed on the right by the coast and Simemi Creek on the left. Lieutenant Colonel Cummings, commanding the 2/9th Battalion, had tried to rest and reorganise his men that day, but the inevitable patrols had to be conducted and the last Japanese resistance rooted out of the area that had been taken. Warrant Officer Vincent Donnelly, leading 16 Platoon, 'D' Company, patrolling west along the creek, ran into almost point-blank machinegun fire from concealed positions. Donnelly approached a bunker and slipped a grenade through a rear entrance hole. After the explosion, he was getting ready to throw another grenade to ensure the enemy had been killed, when a grenade thrown by one of his men bounced off the top of the bunker and struck him on the head without exploding – a dud. Outraged, he leapt to his feet and shouted: 'What in the hell do you think you are doing, you're liable to kill someone doing that'. Back came a muffled reply: 'That's what we're trying to do sarge'.[4]

Soon after Donnelly and his men came across the almost lifeless body of Private William 'Jock' Milne, a 29-year-old farmer from Bowen in Queensland, with the Battalion Intelligence Section. He had been mortally wounded the day before and was now drawing his last breath. He had been hit be a Japanese sniper and had tried crawling back to reach the Battalion Headquarters' position but found himself among Japanese who bayoneted him. In his dying words, he whispered that the Japanese were close by, as he had heard them throughout the night. After giving Milne some water and organising a stretcher-bearer, Donnelly and his men moved out to continue their patrol.[5]

CHAPTER 42

Soon after, Donnelly, with revolver in hand, was struck by a bullet from a medium machinegun, several light machineguns joined-in and the patrol was now pinned down. Donnelly recalled: 'Bullets were cracking around me, and boy, when they crack, they're close! I hit the ground and still they were cracking around my ears. With my face buried in dirt I looked to my left to see where my troops were. On the right L/Cpl Ike Gill was crouched behind the stump of a tree returning fire with his Tommy gun. On my left Kenny Grant was lying prone with his Bren gun.[xxiii] I lifted my head to see if I could locate where the rest of the fire was coming from when I was hit in the forehead a glancing blow from the left which momentarily stunned me ....'[6]

Private Ronald Berry, a 23-year-old labourer from Cairns in Queensland, with 16 Platoon, recorded in his diary sometime that day the situation soon after finding Milne:

> I looked through the jungle and can see forms running towards us, the leading one disappears into what must be pits, I tell the Section leader and he yells JAPS and there are [a] volley of shots from each side (this happens about a minute after leaving Jock Milne). I jump to a fairly large stump as this is my only cover. Gill has a tree about six inches through and he stands up behind it and lets go with his Tommy gun. A machine gun opens up at my cover. Explosive bullets, for I can see the little puffs of smoke. I wonder how long my rotten stump is going to last as large pieces are falling from it. The machine gun lets up from me. I see a Jap behind a tree with what appears to be the machine gun. I raise my elbow and [on] one knee in the act of raising to have a go at this Jap. A machine gun from somewhere also has another go in my direction and wham!!! Something strikes in the vicinity of the magazine of my rifle. I feel a sharp pain at the base of my thumb. I look at it. Too trifling for a homer. Look

---

[xxiii] Private Kenneth Grant, a 23-year-old station manager from Barcaldine in Queensland, is listed as killed-in-action on 22 December 1942.

at my rifle and the butt is busted off it. An explosive bullet. How lucky was I. I look for another rifle. None in sight. I feel something warm in the vicinity of my belt and it is sticky. I look down. My shirt is all tattered at my right breast and is covered in blood. My equipment strap is only holding by a few threads. I have a slight panic and feel around my right shoulder blade, funny I cannot feel anything. I feel numb, maybe fright. I scrambled back.

During the battle I see men falling. Our Bren gunner is killed and his No. 2 is wounded. Frank Forward runs in front of me to get cover from my stump and is wounded. A couple of men to my right are wounded. Vince Donnelly drops like a stone .... Jock Milne is left in the same place and bullets fly all around him. I scramble back about 20 metres to a big tree. Blue the stretcher-bearer is crouching behind this tree, he goes to dress my wounds and I tell him to go to Jock. I go back further to HQ Company RAP orderlies, and they dress my wounds. Frank Forward goes with me. We go out to our RAP and the doctor McGregor and Noel Connors the RAP Sergeant dress our wounds and give us morphia.[7]

Lieutenant William MacIntosh and his men of 17 Platoon, 'D' Company now tried to assist Donnelly and his men, observing fire from a group of five Japanese who occupied a position under the spreading above-ground roots of nearby large trees. So determined were these Japanese, and so well they defended their position, MacIntosh could do no more than cover 16 Platoon's retirement and help bring in their wounded. Getting out one of the wounded, lying well forward and helpless, was a dangerous task made possible only by the bravery of MacIntosh himself and Private Jogn Christensen, a 38-year-old rigger from Adelaide, and the coolness of Corporal Leslie Thorne, a 26-year-old salesman from New Farm in Queensland, who stood exposed to provide covering fire.[8]

CHAPTER 42

The 2/9th Battalion adjutant recorded that day: 'One Pl D Coy patrolled West along creek for 50 yds, where heavy fire was encountered from at least one MMG and 4 LMGs, own casualties two killed, five wounded. Patrols from I/128 US Regt sent South across creek without contacting enemy. Lieut. MACINTOSH was commended for courageous action in bring in a wounded man under fire. During day Bn prepared for attack on the following day by cutting track across grass and jungle to edge of second grass patch so that tks could move'.[9]

Close by, Major Hall, commanding the guns of the 2/5th Field Regiment, had moved forward to conduct a further reconnaissance of the area held by the enemy in the area near the bridge positioned in between the two airstrips. While there, he would conduct a meeting with his CO, Lieutenant Colonel Lewis Barker, a 47-year-old professional soldier from Mulgrave in Victoria, attached to the Australian 7th Division Headquarters, who had just arrived in the area. As recorded in the unit war diary: 'During the afternoon Maj. Hall proceeded to the [captured] pillbox area to meet Brig. Barker. Whilst there several Japs were seen moving in the long grass plus [north] of the bridge. Maj. Hall shot one …. The 3.7 Bty carried out a very successful close shoot on the pillboxes, plus the bridge'.[10]

While laying a telephone cable to the FOO in the pillboxes south side of the bridge, one of his men, 25-year-old gunner, Stanley Reid, from Queanbeyan in New South Wales, was hit by a Japanese sniper. The bullet went right through, and 'may have touched his lungs, as he was haemorrhaging from the mouth a little'.[11] Barker now ordered, against Hall's advice, that a lone gun be brought forward to target the Japanese bunkers using open sights. The next day, it would be reported that no position for this gun could be found, and the order would be rescinded.[12]

Meanwhile, near Cape Endaiadere, the Australian tankers spent the day conducting urgent maintenance on their Stuart tanks, as recorded in the unit war diary: 'Tanks overhauled, and men rested. A recce was made by Major Moss, Lts Curtiss and McCrohon and 2i/C of 2/9 Bn, of forward area, over which attack was to take place'.[13]

*　*　*

That day, unknown Japanese soldier [E] with Colonel Yamamoto Hiroshi's force at Warren front recorded his final entry in his diary: 'Concentrated mortar fire around our positions. The observation planes [RAAF] reconnoitred about ten times over our position. Seems as if it were coordinating with artillery fire. At 1200 [hours] 30–40 enemy appeared in right front near jungle. 12 rounds of amm. fired today'.[14] It was likely that this soldier was killed later that day or the next; his diary was recovered by American troops on 29 December.

Just south-west of this position was unnamed Japanese soldier [F], who occupied a bunker position near the road junction just north of the bridge between the two strips. He recorded his second-last entry in his diary:

> Stopped raining. First of all, we fill up our stomachs at 5 AM. Now we are ready for shelling and bombing. The news that reinforcements had come turned out to be a bad rumour. No hope at all. Only thing to do is to wait for the final moment though we can't tell when that will be. Enemy explosions coming nearer. Will it start again? Starting at 0700 there is a heavy mortar concentration fire, and Superior Privates TSUTSUI and OKAMOTO killed. What's left are the squad leader and four men. Cpl HATTORI, HASEGAWA, and TAJIMI have minor wounds too. The only ones not wounded at all are Superior Private KOJIMA and myself. All day long we stay in the bunker and let the enemy do as they will. We are filled with vexation. If only we had troops and guns.
>
> Comrades, are you going to just stand by and watch us die. Even the invincible Imperial Army is at a loss. Can't anything be done. Please God. Day fades away during the firing and night

CHAPTER 42

falls again. Must be about the 13th or 15th night of the moon but when she is completely round, I suppose something will be done. The end seems to be near. Shelling ceases so we start fixing the bunker. Is all this so that we may live. Three reinforcements come to the Ind. Squad tonight. One is ADACHI who had been at the field train and the other two are temporarily assigned from other units. Now we are eight with the squad leader. But we have no light MG and feel sad. After work we bury the two dead.[15]

* * *

Further west at Urbana front, Lieutenant General Eichelberger ordered Captain James Alford and his men of 'E' Company, II/127th Regiment to contain the Japanese in the Triangle from the north, while the men of 'F' Company, II/126th Regiment were to continue blocking it from the south. Eichelberger tried a ruse to lead the Japanese into believing that another infantry attack against the Triangle was imminent.[16]

The programme of artillery and mortar fire executed the day before was repeated, with the same five-minute intervals of artillery fire, with smoke from the mortars. The men of 'E' Company dashed across the bridge, as they had done the day before, and were followed by smoke shells. With this, the men cheered loudly for two minutes. The Japanese pulled out of their bunkers in the Triangle, bracing for the expected infantry attack. This time, however, there was no charge; instead, the artillery and mortars now poured everything they had into the smoke-enveloped track junction.[17]

Eichelberger would now bypass the position, advancing along a more promising axis of attack across Entrance Creek in the area north of the Coconut Grove and the Triangle. The main task now was to establish the initial bridgehead on the other side of the creek. After studying available maps, Eichelberger concluded that the best place was in a fringe of woods just off the north-west end of the gardens where there appeared to be good cover and less Japanese fire. He issued orders that the bridgehead was to be established there the following day by the men of the III/127th Regiment.

That afternoon, Colonel Grose ordered 'L' Company to move from its position south of Musita Island to the right of 'I' Company, which was deployed in the area immediately north of the Coconut Grove. The men of 'K' Company, which had previously been to the rear of 'I' Company, were ordered to go in on 'L' Company's left and to extend along the west bank of the creek almost to its mouth.[18]

From the beginning, Grose realised that the crossing of the creek by 'K' Company would be more difficult than that of 'I' Company. The swift tidal creek was less than 25 metres wide in 'I' Company's sector, and the engineers that morning finished building a small footbridge improvised from a few saplings and a captured enemy boat anchored in the centre of the stream. In 'K' Company's sector, however, the creek was at least 50 metres wide at the point of crossing and about two metres deep.

When Grose went down to reconnoitrer 'K' Company's position before they crossed, he did not like what he saw. Thinking that there was a possibility that 'K' Company, crossing in 'I' Company's sector, might be able to work its way under the bank to the bridgehead area and establish itself there, he telephoned Eichelberger and asked for more time. In the heat of the moment, he failed to make clear to Eichelberger the reason for his request, and so the general was impatient of any suggestion for postponement. He therefore refused to give him more time, and Grose at once was forced to call Captain Alfred Meyer, commanding 'K' Company, and order him to proceed with the crossing.[19]

At 4 pm, Meyer sent troops into the creek to see if it could be forded. Not only could they find no crossing, but they were nearly 'blown out of the water' by Japanese fire from the opposite bank. Greatly concerned, he considered it suicide to order his men to cross from the there. Meyer therefore pleaded with Grose to let him cross

CHAPTER 42

over the bridge in 'I' Company's area. And if that was not possible, Meyer requested that he be allowed to cross at night with the aid of ropes, pontoons, or whatever equipment was available. Grose, who had already asked for more time without being able to get it, told Meyer that he was to start crossing immediately, even if the men had to swim across.[20]

Meyer then returned to his company and made several attempts to get men across, but the fire from the other side of the creek proved too heavy. By nightfall, the company had finally located a heavy rope, and they renewed their attempts to cross Entrance Creek to the east bank. Lieutenant Edward Greene picked up one end of the rope, and with several enlisted men, they all started swimming for the opposite shore. The young lieutenant was killed almost immediately on entering the water, and his body was swept away by the current. A few minutes later, one of the enlisted men lost his hold on the rope and he too was swept away. Another, however, got the rope across the river just as darkness fell, and the rest of the night was spent in getting the heavily weighted troops over in the face of the continuing enemy fire. By 2 am, 47 men were on the other side of the creek, and when daylight came, the total was 75. The men of 'K' Company suffered 54 casualties that night – six killed or drowned in the crossing, with eight killed and 40 wounded in the fighting at the bridgehead.[21]

43

'I WON'T SEND MY MEN OVER THAT CREEK ...'

At first light, 22 December, Lieutenant Colonel Dobbs, commanding the 2/10th Battalion, had made his way to Captain Roger Sanderson's position, who had tried to find a crossing over Simemi Creek. The unhappy captain said: 'My platoons have patrolled all night, Sir, and found nothing'. Dobbs replied angrily: 'You know what to do when your platoon commanders can't manage a job!'[1] The 2/10th Battalion war diary records: '0630 [hours] Patrol from A Coy (No. 9 Pln.) ordered to recce swamp for crossing to NE side of Old Strip at M/R approx. 28002575'.[2] This reference indicates they were near the mouth of Simemi Creek.

Sanderson and his men of 9 Platoon, 'A' Company then turned towards the marsh and creek. Twenty-one-year-old Private Gordon 'Peter' Bowden, from Brisbane, with 8 Platoon, recalled that while Sanderson was a brave and determined officer, he was not well known for his sense of direction. Sanderson requested that Private Timothy Hughes, a 23-year-old indigenous labourer from Stenhouse in South Australia, scout out ahead. Bowden recalled: 'Captain Sanderson asked him to go and have a recce ... and we knew that if anyone could find a way across it, it was Tim. And he came back within a few hours I think ... and we went across one by one. I had to hold the Bren gun over my head, up to my neck in water .... I've never been so hot in my life, it was like walking into a bloody great oven, going through that mud and shit and then the sun beating down on that bloody great high kunai and I can remember digging into that sandy ground and making a little place for my Bren gun'.[3]

CHAPTER 43

As recorded in the brigade war diary: 'A crossing was discovered by a patrol of 2/10 Aust Inf Bn at the creek bend [about 300 metres north-west from the eastern end of Old Strip] .... The Bn Comdr ordered immediate exploitation of this possibility by utilising it to move 2/10 Aust Inf Bn across [the] creek to the area at SE end of OLD STRIP. The crossing had only been discovered [by] ... vigorous patrolling for it involved men moving at times neck-deep in water through jungle and swamp, for, at this point, there was no defined creek but an area of dense marshy jungle'.[4]

Within 15 minutes, the rest of 9 Platoon, less one section, had established a beachhead on the other side of the creek. By 1.40 pm, Sanderson reported that most of 'A' Company had crossed over. Sanderson and his men had seen no enemy troops except for two fleeting figures that disappeared into the bush ahead of them. Dobbs now had his beachhead, and by 2.30 pm, he had relocated his headquarters to M/R 282258, indicating just east of the creek crossing.[5]

By 6 pm, Major James Trevivian, a 29-year-old electrical engineer from Adelaide, and his men of 'D' Company had followed, also settling on the far bank for the night. Corporal Frank Rolleston, with 18 Platoon, 'D' Company recalled:

> We were steadily losing men and I recall Alan Schy was hit (in the leg I think) and Joe Smith was badly wounded near the knee. As we moved close in to the spot where Vince Donnelly and his patrol had been shot up, a machine gun opened up from a distance of about 20 metres killing Fred Pashen outright, mortally wounding Owen Davis[xxiv], and also wounding about five others. Fred Pashen appeared to be shot through the heart and must have died at once, while Owen Davis fell only about

---

xxiv Twenty-seven-year-old Private Frederick Pashen from Brisbane is listed as killed-in-action on 23 December 1942; Private Owen Davis, a 24-year-old farm labourer from Nobby in Queensland, is listed as dying on 22 December 1942.

four feet from me, and he had been shot clean through the body, for I could see that the bullet had come out through the haversack he had on his back, the spot being marked by some blood which must have been carried through with the bullet.

Among the wounded was Scotty Wright, for a bullet had wounded him in the wrist, luckily without breaking any bones. One very lucky man was Tom Franks, a Bren gunner who came from Cairns in North Queensland, for his haversack containing among other things, some Bren magazines was almost cut off his back, for it appeared to have been hit by a whole burst of bullets ….

In the face of this fire we flattened in the grass, and Owen Davis was lying almost on my right hand side with his feet moving in a restless fashion. It was then that I noticed that the hole marked with blood was through his pack. A stretcher-bearer crawled up and said, 'Are you both hit?' and I said, 'No, only one of us', so by keeping well down they got Owen on a stretcher and got him out.[6]

The battalion adjutant recorded at 11 pm: 'D Coy in position forward of A Coy both coys form perimeter defence for night. CP 28102575 approx. 100 yds in swamp from Strip'.[7] At first light the next morning, Captain Austen Ifould, a 25-year-old mining engineer from Adelaide, and his men of 'B' Company, 2/10th Battalion would cross over to help consolidate the newly established beachhead west of the creek.[8]

* * *

Meanwhile, by 7.50 am, shells began to fall ahead of Lieutenant Colonel Cummings and his men of the 2/9th Battalion as they waited on their start-line, which was running almost due south from the coast and nearly spanning the wedge of swampland and vegetation,

CHAPTER 43

little more than a kilometre ahead, that then narrowed to a point at the mouth of Simemi Creek.

Ten minutes after the barrage opened, the Australians advanced. Captain Robert Griffin and his composite 'D'/'C' company was on the right, while Lieutenant Victor Thomas, a 25-year-old salesman from Gympie in Queensland, now commanding 'A' Company, was on the left, and Benson and his men of 'B' Company were in reserve, slightly to the rear. Vickers machinegun fire from their flanks whipped through the leaves of the trees and tore into the long grass ahead of the advance. The Australian infantry moved slowly, searching the long grass as they pushed forward, killing any Japanese who hid there, waiting until the Australians were almost on top of them before they fired into the advancing enemy.[9]

At first, only sporadic small arms fire met the Australian advance until just before 9 am, when machinegun enfilade from the right targeted the men of 'A' Company. This checked the advance while the dangerous and deadly business of hunting down and killing the enemy got under way. Worse, however, was to come, as within 30 minutes, shells from a Japanese anti-aircraft gun began to target with disconcerting effect in the vicinity of the Australian jumping-off point; it was here that the headquarters elements were located, and within a very short time, 20 of these men were casualties.[10]

It was now that tank support was provided.

In one of the tanks was Trooper John Wilson, the hull gunner of Lieutenant McCrohon's tank leading 'B' Squadron. He recalled the situation just after 9 am: 'We advanced with the infantry, some small arms fire was received. We could not see anything because of the grass, likewise the Japs were in the same position. A couple of MG posts were overcome. It was very hard to observe in which direction the fire was coming from. We continued on as before at times coming under heavy MG fire and kept getting bogged, until we could make no further progress because of the soft ground. During this time some of our tank crews not engaged in tank work volunteered to act as stretcher-bearers and form small parties, and did anti-sniping patrols'.[11]

Even so, the advancing Australians were still less than halfway to their objective. Close by was Lieutenant Colonel MacNab and his men of the III/128th Regiment, who were moving up the line of the creek, closing on their left, with two tanks engaging the strong posts on the right. By noon, however, the tanks were forced to retire to their refuelling point, and the infantry – still behind the barrier thrown out by the Japanese machine guns and with the kunai ahead of them on fire – withdrew to the shelter of scrub, while the shells of the well-placed Japanese anti-aircraft guns exploded in the rear areas.[12]

Trooper John Wilson recalled: 'We advanced with the infantry and some small arms fire was received. We could not see anything because of the grass – likewise the Japs were in the same position. A couple of machine gun posts were overcome. It was very hard to observe in which direction the machine gun fire was coming from. We continued on as before at times coming under heavy machine gun fire and kept getting bogged, until we could make no further progress because of the soft ground. During that time some of our tank crews not engaged in tank work volunteered to act as stretcher-bearers or formed small parties and did anti-sniper patrols'.[13]

It was now that Captain Lionel Nix conducted fire against the Japanese anti-aircraft guns with his battery. The 2/5th Field Regiment recorded that soon after targeting this gun, it was silenced. It was also now that one of the Wirraways of the RAAF spotting for the gunners was shot down by Japanese fighters – both pilot and spotter were killed, crashing to the ground in flames just 500 metres from the forward artillery observation post.[14]

Meanwhile, by 1.30 pm, the tanks, having refuelled, were back in action. Soon afterwards, Griffin and his composite 'D'/'C' Company was reportedly progressing on the right. Even so, the renewal of the advance was difficult, less than 30 minutes after the resumption of assault, as both components of the composite company had lost all officers to the Japanese fire. Lieutenant William MacIntosh was badly

CHAPTER 43

wounded by a shell burst; Captain Robert Griffin, a fine leader and athlete, was killed as he bravely rushed forward and began hammering on the side of the supporting tank to direct its fire against a Japanese machinegun post that was holding up their advance. His 2i/C, Captain Percy Roberts, a 28-year-old stock agent from Charleville in Queensland, had an eye blown out by a shell fragment. This left Sergeant Stephen McCready, a 25-year-old bank clerk from Brisbane, in charge of 'D'/'C' Company.[15]

Later in the afternoon, Major William Parry-Okeden gathered the few survivors of the three attacking companies into one and, with one tank remaining to assist – the other was temporarily bogged – attacked the enemy pillboxes that were still holding out. So spirited was this assault that by 5 pm, Parry-Okeden was able to report that the point area up to the mouth of the creek was in Australian hands. Even so, one strong point remained unsubdued located on the island in the centre of the creek mouth. The men of the 2/9th Battalion now settled to hold the ground gained. And by the end of the day, the fighting had cost the battalion eight officers and 50 men as casualties.[16]

Major Parry-Okeden soon after reported to his CO: 'The point up to the false mouth of the creek in our hands'.[17] The battalion adjutant concluded that night in the unit war diary: 'Bn dug-in along creek and beach; Bde Command issued instructions that this area must be held at all costs as command of it was essential for future ops. Own casualties: Offrs 1 killed, 7 wounded. ORs 7 killed, 39 wounded, 4 died of wounds Capt. R.R. GRIFFIN was killed'.[18]

At 7.30 pm that night, Cummings advised Brigade that he did not believe it was possible to cross Simemi Creek and directly assault the dug-in position on the island. He said he planned to drive the Japanese off the island during the night, using Vickers machinegun and mortar fire. Later, with this fire failing to drive the Japanese out, he suggested that no purpose would be served by a direct assault, other than the loss of more men's lives for little if any gain. Another man who stood close by his CO as he discussed the matter with brigade remembers it a little differently from the brigade report. Sergeant Edward Palmer recalled his CO stating decidedly: 'I won't send my men over that creek, even if I lose my command over it'.[19] It was agreed, for now at least, this Japanese position would be bypassed.

* * *

The official Japanese history succinctly records of the day's fight here: 'A superior force of Allied tanks and accompanying infantry, under heavy artillery cover, assaulted the frontline of the Japanese garrison headquarters for 30 minutes from 5.50 am on 22 December. Most of the important documents of the [Yamamoto's] unit were destroyed at this time'.[20]

At Buna was medic Yokoyama Yoriichi, who recalled years later the Australian spotter aircraft: 'Every day at Buna we were bombarded by 60 to 80 rounds of artillery, at the same time every morning and late every afternoon …. We didn't have proper weapons, but just kept digging holes to hide ourselves in. Moreover, during the daytime Australian observation planes were flying over us. If they saw us, they would soon contact artillery units and tell them where to shot. We said to each other, "Here they are again! Put out the fire and don't make any smoke"'.[21]

Close by was Lance Corporal Uchiyama Seiichi, with the *No. 9 Company, 229th Regiment*. His second-last diary entry records: 'No thoughts of returning home alive. Want to die like a soldier and go to Yasukuni Shrine. Writing in this diary word by word, not knowing when a shell may strike and I will be killed. 35 days since we started to fight. 17.30. Artillery firing, shells dropping all around the trenches. Full moon shining through the trees in the jungle, hearing the cries of birds and insects, the breeze blowing gently and peacefully …. Good news – friendly troops are near in the rear and friendly planes will fly tomorrow. How far is this true and how far an unfounded rumour? Whatever it is, it is happy news'.[22]

Still manning a bunker, just north of the bridge between the two

CHAPTER 43

airstrips, was unnamed Japanese soldier [F]. That day, he recorded his last entry in his diary:

> As usual, shelling at dawn. At 0600 [hours] concentrated shelling but in a different direction and we are somewhat safe. Last night Sgt Major OGAWA said that our troops had come as far as Rock 14 [?] and that this was just a matter of two or three days more of hardship. Cannot be thought of as any other than to cheer us up with rumours. At 1300 heavy bombing and mortar fire. Enemy planes fly overhead all the time and we can only watch crouched down in our bunkers. Night falls. The enemy finally seems to be using tanks and smashing our frontlines. Headed this way. Conditions take a turn for the worse. KAMADA was standing guard and said he saw two enemy troops. Wanted to throw a grenade, but I told him to make sure and it turned out to be a bird or rat. Runner WAKAMATSU and Sgt Major OGAWA came and told of guards becoming completely afraid of the enemy and running back as soon as a shot was fired. Said that was unbecoming to a Japanese soldier who had the Great Work of establishing peace in the Far East'.[23]

This unknown Japanese soldier was likely killed sometime the next day, and his diary was recovered by American troops from his bunker about a week later.

* * *

At Urbana front, during the early morning hours, the 127th Regiment were attacking the Japanese positions. The men of 'K' Company, III/127th Regiment engaged the enemy on the eastern side of Entrance Creek, having established a narrow beachhead. Now the heavy weapons teams of 'M' Company, III/127th Regiment were supporting them with fire from the west bank, while the men of 'I' Company, III/127th Regiment, under Captain Michael Ustruck, crossed the footbridge. Finding, as Colonel Grose had surmised, that there was a safe and easy approach to the bridgehead under the bank, the men of 'I' Company went into position on 'K' Company's right by 12.35 pm, without losing a man.[24]

As the men consolidated their positions, the bodies of the men from 'K' Company who had drowned in the crossing were now observed bobbing in the creek, but the crossing had been accomplished, and there was a strong bridgehead on the other side of the creek. It had been a difficult and frustrating operation. Lieutenant General Eichelberger recalled two days later: 'When we put K Company across an unfordable stream in the dark against heavy fire the other night, we did something that would be a Leavenworth nightmare'.[25]

Meanwhile, the engineers remained unmolested by the Japanese as they worked on repairing a bridge that had previously linked the mainland with the western end of the southern side of Musita Island near the creek mouth. By the afternoon, the work was completed and a strong patrol from 'L' Company, III/127th Regiment had crossed to the island without interference. Still unopposed, having traversed the island from west to east, it approached the second bridge, which connected the island to the Government Station area. Only then did they come under fire.

Now, two platoons of 'F' Company, II/127th Regiment and a machinegun section of 'M' Company, III/127th Regiment under Lieutenant Colonel Benjamin Farrar, then serving as the regimental Operations Officer, moved in to take command of the situation. It would not be until around noon the next day that the Americans would be in possession of the whole island and in a position to harass the Government Station with fire, which included a 37-mm gun that they brought up. With this, the men of 'F' Company pulled back to the mainland, with their position on the island taken over by those of 'H' Company, II/127th Regiment.[26]

Meanwhile, Eichelberger was deciding whether to establish a bridgehead from the island or persist with his plan to attack through

CHAPTER 43

the more southerly bridgehead, which was already firm. Wisely, in view of the proximity of the main Government Station defences to the island, he would decide to continue with the southern bridgehead option.[27]

44

'MAYBE I CAN GET A TOEHOLD THERE'

By 23 December, after six days of desperate fighting, phase one of Brigadier George Wootten's plan had been completed. It was now time to launch phase two: the clearing of the bridge between the strips and occupation of Old Strip.

It began when Captain Austen Ifould and his men of 'B' Company, 2/10th Battalion, who had been with the 2/9th Battalion, crossed over Simemi Creek south of Old Strip during the dawn hours to reach 'A' and 'D' companies of the 2/10th Battalion, who had established their beachhead west of Simemi Creek. Lieutenant Colonel Dobbs positioned 'B' Company to cover the left flank, just north of Old Strip. The Australian crossing of the creek had completely surprised the Japanese.[1]

Dobbs' men were now to the rear of the Japanese in the bridge area, and at once sent two companies south to clear out the remaining Japanese. The enemy troops here had considered the swamps impassable, and to their consternation, they were now forced to abandon, without further struggle, the sites that had defied the Americans for so long. This was the first time that they had been forced to evacuate any of their coastal positions in such haste.[2] By noon, the few Japanese remaining there had been killed, and the Australians were able to report 'the bridge and 300 yards north neutralised'.[3]

The bridge, however, was still under fire from emplacements on the south-west side of Old Strip, but these pockets of resistance would be dealt with later when the repairs to the bridge were completed, and the American GIs and the M3 tanks crossed over to the opposite

CHAPTER 44

side. Indeed, the American engineers, under the courageous and tireless leadership of Lieutenant James Doughtie, 3rd Platoon, 'C' Company, 114th Engineer Battalion, set to work repairing the bridge for the passage of both foot soldiers and tanks. They had gathered and hauled the needed timbers and other materials to the bridge site, mostly coconut logs. They were put in place, and the bridge was secured across Simemi Creek. Wootten then ordered Major Chester Beaver and his men of 'B' Company, I/126th Regiment across, to keep in contact with 'B' Company, 2/10th Battalion covering the battalion's left flank, just north of Old Strip.[4] As described by the American official historian of the campaign, Samuel Milner: 'Doughtie was everywhere, directing, encouraging, and steadying his men. By noon the repair of the bridge was well advanced. Half an hour later Doughtie had a catwalk down, and in ten minutes the leading platoon of Company B, 126th Infantry was on the other side of the creek'.[5]

As soon as they crossed the bridge, Beaver and his men moved towards the eastern end of Old Strip. Japanese fire from flat-trajectory weapons and mortars was heavy, and progress was slow. Colonel Martin joined the troops at 3.30 pm. They had moved in on Dobbs' left by 5.45 pm and took up a position along the southern edge of the strip. Now, Major Clarkson and his men of the I/128th Regiment crossed the creek and were on Beaver's left by 7.20 pm.

The plan then was to have the tanks cross the bridge and join the infantry early the next morning. Upon their arrival, the 2/10th Battalion, with the Americans in support, would attack straight up the strip. The force would jump off from a line drawn perpendicularly across the strip from the galvanised iron hut or control tower to where the Australians had established their first bridgehead two days before.[6]

By nightfall, the men of 'B' Company, 2/10th Battalion were 400 metres up on the right of Old Strip, while Beaver and his men of 'B' Company, 126th Regiment were on his left but angled back to the south-east with Clarkson and his men of the I/128th Regiment on Beaver's left, barely across the bridge.[7]

Meanwhile, just north along the coastal area, the men of the 2/9th Battalion continued attacking the area to the west, supported by tanks that were greatly restricted due to the nature of the terrain, which was largely swamp. Even so, the battalion had by nightfall captured the whole area bounded by Simemi Creek to the west and by the coast to the north and east.[8] The adjutant of the 2/9th Battalion recorded the situation at around 1 pm: 'Bn assumed responsibility for protection of area North of SIMEMI CREEK under command 3/128 US Bn. During morning enemy mortars on the point caused casualties to fwd coys. An attempt by the enemy to push a party across the sand spit at the mouth of the creek was repulsed'.[9]

As recorded in the 18th Brigade war diary, the Japanese continued to hold the small island at the mouth of the creek, 'which was to prove a degree of annoyance until the end of the action. It was decided not to attempt to attack this island as to do so would only result in heavy casualties without due reward for it had been found that no practicable tank crossing existed along the whole length of SIMEMI C'.[10]

* * *

Colonel Yamamoto Hiroshi had time to man the prepared positions in the Old Strip area and was now holding them in strength. The area was a warren of trenches and bunkers. His troops had dug several lines of trenches across the width of the strip and their trench system extended from the swamp to Simemi Creek. There were bunkers in the dispersal bays north of the strip, in the area south of it on the strip itself, and in a plantation of coconut trees off its north-western end.[11]

Yamamoto was also not lacking weapons – he was well provided with machine guns and mortars, and he had at least two 75-mm guns, two 37-mm guns, and, at the north-west end of the strip, several 25-mm dual and triple pom-poms, as well as multiple barrel

CHAPTER 44

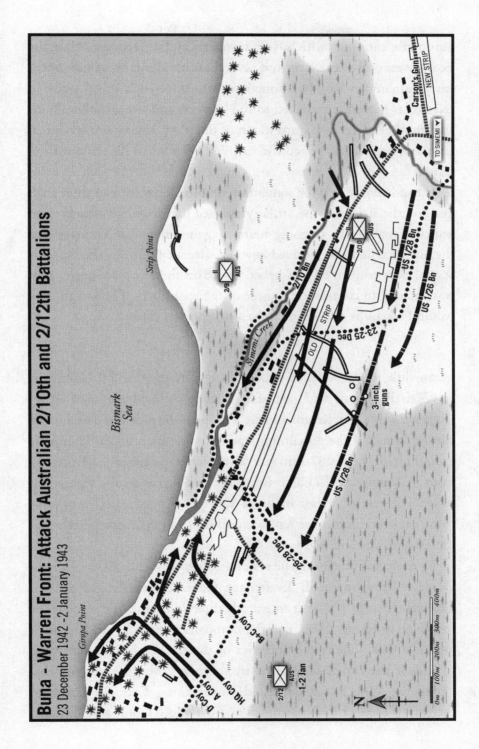

Buna - Warren Front: Attack Australian 2/10th and 2/12th Battalions
23 December 1942 - 2 January 1943

automatic cannons, which were favoured by the Japanese. Near the north-west end of the strip and several hundred metres to the south-east, Yamamoto had positioned several three-inch naval guns in triangular pattern connected to the bunkers and fire trenches. With still another three-inch guns north of the strip, Yamamoto was in an excellent position to sweep the strip with fire while his ammunition lasted.[12]

It had been known for some time that the Japanese had three-inch guns on the strip, but the artillery assessed that they had already been knocked out by the ongoing barrage against the area. The fact that the air force had not received any anti-aircraft fire from the strip for several days confirmed this belief. To be on the safe side, however, it was decided to commit only three of the four tanks. The fourth tank would be kept in reserve until the situation was clarified.[13]

* * *

Meanwhile to the west, at Urbana front, the men of 'H' Company, II/127th Regiment had just after midday relieved the men of 'F' Company, II/127th Regiment who had spent the previous day clearing Musita Island of the remaining Japanese. The men of 'H' Company brought with them a 37-mm gun with 'plenty of canister'.[14] A platoon from 'E' Company, II/127th Regiment, who were on the village spit (the small peninsula east of Buna Village), also had a 37-mm gun-firing canister. From their separate points of vantage, each gun shelled the mission day and night.

By dusk, with the bridgehead at the north-west end of Government Gardens firmly secured, Lieutenant General Eichelberger ordered Colonel Grose to attack in an easterly direction across the gardens the following morning. Grose had five companies of the 127th Regiment for the attack. The rifle companies of the III/127th Regiment were to launch the attack, supported by the heavy-weapon crews of 'M' Company, III/127th Regiment disposed along Entrance Creek to the rear of the line of departure. The men of 'G' Company, II/127th

CHAPTER 44

Regiment would be in reserve and be prepared to go into action at short notice when ordered by Grose.[15]

There would be no direct air support, as the troops were now too close to the Japanese positions. The Australian 25-pounders, along with the lone American 105-mm howitzer positioned south of Ango, along with Lieutenant Colonel McCreary and his massed mortars south of Musita Island would, however, lay down a heavy preparation before the troops jumped off, to be followed with a rolling barrage when the advance got under way. The men of 'H' Company, II/127th Regiment on the island, and those on the village spit would also saturate the mission with fire, to help deceive the Japanese as to the direction of the attack and to prevent reinforcements reaching the positions in the garden area.[16]

The GIs on the island and those on the village spit, that night, laid down heavy fire on the mission, as did the Australian artillery and American howitzer around Ango. The Japanese, in turn, kept the bridgehead under continual harassment, using mountain guns, heavy mortars, and anti-aircraft guns depressed for flat-trajectory fire. All along the line of departure, the American infantry remained on the alert throughout the night, but the Japanese made no move to counterattack or to infiltrate their lines.[17] Eichelberger informed Major General Sutherland: 'Maybe I can get a toehold there. It might prove easier, than where I now plan to go across'.[18]

* * *

Later that night, at around 10 pm, two fast-moving boats were reported offshore, thought to be Japanese. Observers near Old Strip saw tracers reaching out from the shore and 37-mm guns targeted the vessels. Flames leaped from the water at Hariko as one of the Allied supply crafts took fire – the barge *Eva*, which was laden with artillery, mortar, and small-arms ammunition, was then being unloaded by the troops of the Service Company, 128th Regiment.[19] The 2/5th Field Regiment diary records this incident: 'At 2245hrs

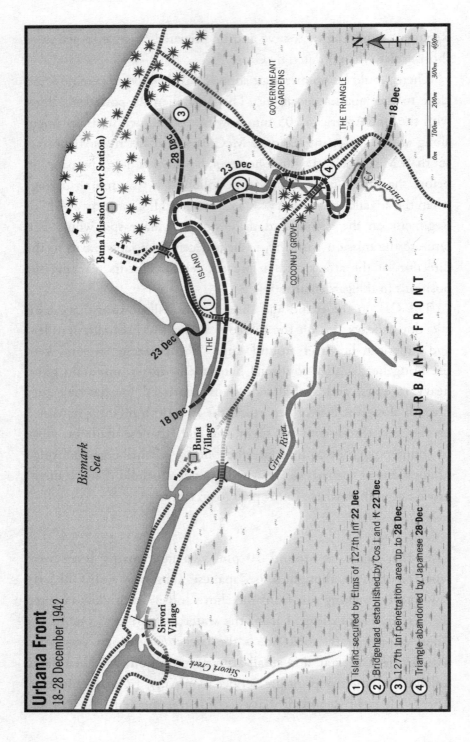

CHAPTER 44

the general Stand-To was called, as two unidentified ships were sighted off-shore. They proved to be enemy ships, and attacked a ship unloading at Hariko, and machine gunned the village and surrounding areas. The ship was set on fire and sunk. Its main cargo was 25 Pdr ammunition and stores belonging to 55 Bty .... Owing to the loss of the ammunition the HF tasks were cut down to 500 rounds'.[20]

The Service Company answered with small arms fire from positions just off the beach, but the boats got away before heavier weapons could be brought to bear upon them. These 'enemy' boats were not long gone before suspicion began to grow in the minds of some of the officers and men ashore, as reports were coming in that the attacking craft resembled American torpedo boats. Six of these boasts had just been based at Milne Bay under American naval command, with their forward headquarters at Tufi. Their task was to prevent Japanese reinforcements landing in the area Buna–Mambare River and to assist in protecting Allied shipping.[21]

It was now believed that these torpedo boats, new to this theatre of operations, had mistaken their own vessels for Japanese; this would soon prove to be the case.

Next day, Major General Frank Berryman, Deputy Chief of the General Staff to General Blamey in Port Moresby wrote back to Australia: 'Some motor torpedo boats attacked our small craft at Hariko last night and set one of them on fire which blew up. We strongly suspect that this was the first successful action of the PT boats which were operating, or supposed to be operating, in an adjacent area last night. However, keep this well under your hat and mention it to no one other than the CGS as it may not be true; even if it is we may never be able to prove it'. To this he added a little later: 'It is true and admitted'.[22]

Meanwhile, further down the coast at Oro Bay, the *Bantam*, a KPM ship of the same class as the *Karsik* and the *Japara*, arrived and anchored in the bay with two more precious Stuart tanks, and 420 tons of supplies. The ship was quickly unloaded and returned safely to Porlock Harbour before daybreak.[23]

*　*　*

In Rabaul, the *18th Army Headquarters* were forced to realise just how desperate the situation was at the beachheads. Staff officer Lieutenant Colonel Sugiyama Shigeru approached the *8th Area Army* for an offensive against Buna by Army air units. Reinforcements to the area had previously been unsuccessful by sea, due to Allied sorties against their shipping. Only Japanese airmen could counter these attacks. Subsequently, Naval aircraft launched an attack that night against the Allied positions around Buna, focusing on the airstrip at Dobodura. The attack consisted of four waves, each consisting of eight land-based attack aircraft from 6.55 pm to 8.45 pm. On their return, the airmen reported signs of 'damage to Allied positions at several locations'.[24]

45

'... CIRCLED AROUND THE TURRET LIKE A TIN OPENER'

The following morning, 24 December 1942, Brigadier George Wootten had no intentions of losing the initiative he had gained over the last week of fighting. He ordered Lieutenant Colonel Dobbs, commanding the 2/10th Battalion, to continue his advance along Old Strip, with the assistance of three M3s with a fourth in reserve. These were the last serviceable tanks at hand, the balance of the original eight. Only now had another two arrived at Oro Bay with seven more tanks leaving Milne Bay for Buna.[1] The 2/10 Battalion war diary records at 4.30 pm, the operation group held a conference, the result being that the advance was to continue, but only two tanks would be in direct support: 'Advance along strip with four tanks, two in support, two in reserve'.[2]

Wootten was concerned about endangering the last of his tanks, particularly because he knew that the Japanese had anti-aircraft guns capable of an anti-tank role in the area. But these guns, in the face of air attack, and artillery bombardments were believed to have been destroyed days before. It was also judged, even if these guns were still serviceable, they were likely out of ammunition; or worryingly, their silence was a ruse, and the Japanese gunners were waiting for the appearance of the Australian tanks. Whatever Wootten's misgivings, he did not communicate them to Lieutenant Victor McCrohon, who was commanding the tanks.

Wootten and his intelligence officer, when briefing McCrohon, told him that he could disregard any threat from these guns. Looking north-west along the strip, a worrying stretch of open ground covered in kunai grass and unevenly bush-fringed on either side waited the advance of the Australian tankers. McCrohon requested that he advance with all four tanks in his initial movement, stating that the front was too wide for just three tanks. Wootten was initially reluctant but relented to McCrohon's request.[3]

At first, everything seemed to be going to plan. At 7 am, the tanks moved to the bridge area and by 9 am the tank commanders were in conference with Dobbs, commanding the 2/10th Battalion. At 9.30 am, after a ten-minute barrage with 12 guns, which included smoke, the tanks went up Old Strip in a line, 50 metres apart. On the left was McCrohon (5 Troop, 'B' Squadron), to his right was Sergeant Jack Lattimore (5 Troop, 'B' Squadron), followed by Corporal Evan Barnet (5 Troop, 'B' Squadron), and on the extreme right was Sergeant John Church (10 Troop, 'C' Squadron). The infantrymen were close behind with Major James Trevivian and his men of 'D' Company, 2/10th Battalion to the right of the strip. And Captain Austen Ifould and his men of 'B' Company, 2/10th Battalion were moving up the strip on their left in the centre, while the Americans were covering the left flank. Captain Roger Sanderson and his men of 'A' Company, 2/10th Battalion were in reserve.[4]

It was not long before a lone Japanese sniper was targeting Ifould's men in the centre of the advance. From the start, Captain Ifould stood upright and engaged the marksman himself, but he lost the exchange; he is listed as killed that day. The battalion historian recorded: 'He had been with the battalion since Tobruk and had proved a cool and courageous leader'.[5]

Lieutenant Murray Brown, a 23-year-old draughtsman from Adelaide, now led the company. He recalled: 'I heard the orders for the attack along the airstrip, and it seemed to me to be the craziest orders I'd ever heard, for troops to advance against dug-in machine guns on either side. I ran over and there was Justin Ifould with a bullet through

CHAPTER 45

the forehead … it was not possible to evacuate the wounded because we were on open bullet-swept ground, it was kunai grass about waist-high. As soon as you stood up you were under crossfire'.[6] Brown and his men, however, had crossed the line as part of a steady advance, which continued for 30 minutes with tanks and infantry combining to sweep the Japanese before them along the strip.[7]

It was around 10 am when the tankers' worst fears became a reality. While, McCrohon's tanks were concentrating on their front, searching for the pom-pom guns known to be located towards the end of the strip, McCrohon saw a flash to his left front and then another; an explosion followed, and the whole of the left side of his tank seemed to split open. He told his wireless operator to warn the other tanks: 'Get out! The ack-ack gun's operating'. But the wireless was not working, and the driver swung the tank round. McCrohon yelled above the sound of the engine, and firing: 'You're headed straight for a crater!' The driver replied 'There's nothing you can do about it! I can't steer!'[8] Then the tank fell into the crater. McCrohon's hull gunner, Trooper John Wilson also recalled:

> We moved down the strip at about five miles per hour, with the infantry following. Heavy machinegun and mortar fire was received, and we had only proceeded a short distance when McCrohon … ordered the driver to swing left in the direction of where we knew the ack-ack gun was situated. The turret gunner opened fire with the 37 and only got away a couple of shots when he had a misfire, in that the round failed to go off …. Next thing we knew there was a loud explosion, the tank shook, and we knew we had been hit. This happened as the tank was making a circle to the left and the shell stuck the centre side of the tank near the track about level with my head and the radio equipment. Radio and other stores were blown out of the compartment, the radio struck me on the head, and I was knocked out for a few seconds. The next thing I knew the crew

commander had me by the hair shaking my head to see if I was all right .... As my eyes came into focus, I saw that the side of the tank hull had opened up and I could see up along the strip we were supposed to be advancing.⁹

Wilson and the rest of the crew were able to deactivate the tanks guns and vacated the vehicle, eventually making it back to safety, recalling: 'Whilst crawling along under fire and passing different slit trenches, the morale of the infantry was still high and a few ribald remarks were called out and one character wanted to bet us ten shillings that we would never make it'.¹⁰

The Japanese gunner now targeted and took out Barnet's tank. This shot crashed through the turret, killing Corporal Thomas Jones, a 33-year-old bank clerk from Forbes in New South Wales, and mangling Barnet's arm. Barnet recalled years later:

The missile sort of hit the turret, circled around the turret like a tin opener, killing my gunner, Jones, who was standing immediately in front of me and thus protecting me ... instructions had been given to my driver that if we were hit at any time ... to turn and go for hell out of it, which he did do, but at the same time when the tank was hit, the top, the lid of the tank was thrown open, and I was thrown halfway out of the tank ... when the tank turned I was thrown out onto the ground .... I had difficulty deciding which direction was the enemy and which direction was our own troops .... I took potluck and turned around and headed in a direction. Because of the kunai grass ... they couldn't see me ... my arm was shattered, and I carried my arm .... Kevin Kennedy, my hull gunner, and my whole crew had come looking for me.¹¹

Next it was Lattimore's turn, with a 75-mm shell exploding into the hull gunner's flap, killing Trooper Frank Forster, a 26-year-old salesman from Sydney, as well as mortally wounding Corporal

CHAPTER 45

Reginald Leggatt, a 22-year-old clerk from Coolabah in New South Wales, while blowing off one of Lattimore's legs.[12] Twenty-four-year-old driver Trooper Norman Nye, a 24-year-old, from Sydney, recalled the situation:

> The crew commander called 'Bale out' and I dived through the hole and seeing a tank coming behind and about 20 yards [Church's tank] away I ran to them and yelled, 'Go back – get out.' The commander of that tank started to get out and called out, 'What about the rest of your crew?' I told him I was going back to see what I could do – which I did. At that time the other tank was hit also …. I ran back to my tank and pulled the commander out and left him on the ground and then went into the tank and got Reggie Leggatt out. Reggie had lost both legs and he was bleeding very badly although conscious. I put him on the ground and looked for a dugout and found one with an infantry crew. I got my mates into the dugout and borrowed a shell dressing to put around his wounds and burrowed morphine in a type of capsule to give Reggie – actually an infantryman put the morphine in. It took several hours for stretcher-bearers to get him because the Jap's mortar-bombs were picking our boys off. I helped carry the stretcher back to first aid.[13]

Lastly, in this quick and very ordered process of destruction, Church's tank had also been knocked out. His turret was hit from a shell on the right, wrecking the gun, but inflicting no casualties. With damage also done to the driving hub, the crew bailed out and were able to make it back to the Australian lines.[14]

The 2/10th Battalion adjutant recorded the situation at 10 am: 'Advance held up by heavy MG fire. Heavy casualties. Two supporting tanks put out of action. Reserve tanks come into operation and very shortly [also] put out of action, about 30 yds [metres] from tin hut area'.[15]

Meanwhile, the forward artillery observer assigned to the 2/10th Battalion, Lieutenant Arthur Outridge, located one of the Japanese anti-aircraft guns on the left shortly after it had fired on the tanks, and the artillery promptly knocked it out. They were, however, unable to locate the remaining guns. Now, with all four tanks out of action, the infantry was left alone to the destructive fire from the well-concealed and strongly defended bunkers. As recorded in the 2/5th Field Regiment war diary: 'Steady progress was made by our troops, and by 1130hrs were 800 yards up the Old Strip. F Troop reported one tank on fire. One bogged soon after, and two were knocked out'.[16]

The official Japanese history records the action of their anti-aircraft guns: 'Fighting resumed in the area of Old Strip on 24 December. Australian troops, as usual with preparatory covering fire, departed from the offensive line 180 metres from the northern end of the strip at 7.55 am. The Japanese defenders withstood the assault, then aimed the two Navy anti-aircraft guns at the tanks, three of which were instantly destroyed. The Japanese then turned their firepower towards the airstrip'.[17]

The Japanese guns and pom-poms were now firing down the centre of the strip at the advancing infantrymen. The men of 'A' Company, 2/10th Battalion had to move from its position on the strip in the centre of the Allied line to the Australian side of the runway. Indeed, Brown and his men of 'B' Company were the focus of the Japanese response, facing a redoubt about the centre of the strip, as his men were falling rapidly. Uncertain as to the whereabouts of the Americans on his left, he was asking them to fire flares so he could locate their flanks. It soon became apparent that the Americans on the left had again not systematically moped up the positions as they passed through. The American officers and NCOs were now losing men to sweeping enfilade fire from their rear and from trees.[18]

The 2/10th Battalion war diary records at 1 pm: 'Bn advance slowly pos, A Coy level with tin hut astride strip. B Coy 300 yds forward of A. D stretched along NE side of strip from T.H. [tin hut] to approx.

CHAPTER 45

M/R 27652600 [about 500 metres east of Giropa Point]'.[19] An hour later, the diary reports: 'B Coy unable to advance further owing to E [enemy] posn. immediately front and left'.[20]

The advance slackened with the loss of the tanks. In the early afternoon, however, Major Trevivian, leading 'D' Company, 2/10th Battalion, had advanced on the right until he approached the outskirts of the large coconut plantation, which followed the coastline around from Buna Government Station and past Giropa Point. He had deployed 16 Platoon from the edge of the swamp up to and slightly over the bank leading onto the strip; 17 Platoon was spread from that embankment to the right flank of 'B' Company; and 18 Platoon was in reserve. It was now that Trevivian and his men came to a halt, and the rest of the day was given over to minor infiltrations and encirclement in the face of determined opposition, with the Australians having gained around 700 metres for the day and lying in a backward-sweeping curve across the strip linking up with 'B' and 'A' companies.[21]

During the afternoon, 18 Platoon was sent to plug a serious gap in the diminishing 'B' Company front. Lance Corporal William Moroney, a 24-year-old labourer from Wayville in South Australia, was among them, recalling: 'I was going up then to find the gap in the line, crawling through the grass and I struck Frank Duffy, who was a bloke I knew extra well, he was the Mortar Sergeant. And he's trying to get a pit settled up so he could put a mortar in it …. He said, "You got a match on you?" So, I gave him my lighter, and he lit his smoke and put the lighter in his pocket. He said, "You're going up there aren't you?" I said, "Yeah." He said, "You won't bloody well need this then!" …. I struck Wally Cramey of B Company … there weren't many of his platoon left in the pits. The rest had been left behind dead or wounded'.[22]

To the Australian left, Major Beaver and his men of the I/126th Regiment were covering the flank farther forward than the two centre Australian companies but not as far advanced as Trevivian. Supporting

Beaver's men were those of Major Gordon Clarkson and his men of the I/128th Regiment who had been combing the swamp on the extreme left during the morning but had bogged down there and been pulled out to give Beaver depth. Fighting patrols were out in the darkness but made no gains.[23]

With 'D' Company, 2/10th Battalion was Corporal William McAuliffe, a 32-year-old labourer from Berri in South Australia, who was later awarded a Military Medal for his actions during the day's fighting. The battalion historian recorded:

> During the afternoon 'D' Company attacked strong enemy positions. The attack was repulsed with heavy loss. Corporal McAuliffe was wounded in the head. As the remnants of two platoons fell back, despite his painful wound, Corporal McAuliffe took control, organised them into one platoon and established a line. His prompt action and the example of his courage held the line against enemy attacks. But for him, it was most probable that the line would have been broken, at least temporarily. Corporal McAuliffe then saved many lives by organising and bringing in the wounded lying in front of our line, whilst under heavy fire. He refused to be evacuated and led the platoon until almost the end of Sanananda, showing the same qualities of courage, determination and leadership throughout, particularly in two attacks he led.[24]

Later that night, Lieutenant Walter Wissell, a 26-year-old bank official from Adelaide, leading 12 Platoon, 'B' Company, 2/10th Battalion, took out a fighting patrol to take out the entrenched enemy position blocking the company's advance, but they were unsuccessful. It was now that 'B' Company was relieved and placed in reserve, with the men of 'A' Company occupying their forward position on Old Strip, to continue the fight the next morning.[25]

Meanwhile, the men of the 2/9th Battalion and III/128th Regiment

CHAPTER 45

improved their positions around Cape Endaiadere. The Australians occupied the east bank of the creek and the shore from its mouth to Strip Point, while the Americans took over the defensive line from the coastline from Strip Point around Cape Endaiadere and south to Boreo. With fighting here having ceased, the Americans took time to clean up. Those along the coast were permitted to swim, with some even amusing themselves by catching fish, using grenades.[26]

It was now, however, that the battalion CO was now wounded by Japanese shell fire. The battalion war diary records: '1625 hrs – Bn area again shelled and the CO Lieut. Col C.J. CUMMINGS was wounded. Maj. W.N. PARRY-OKEDEN assumed comd of Bn. 3.77 mm guns from 3/126 US Bn were brought up to engage Jap gun. 1815 – Heavy concentration of arty on posn of Jap gun. Direct hit believed on gun posn as large fire was started near pit. Owing to evacuation of Lieut. Col CUMMINGS responsibility for protection of area North of SIMEMI CREEK passed to Lieut. Col MACNAB of 3/128 US Bn'.[27] Lieutenant Colonel MacNab, whose CP was just south of Cape Endaiadere, with the wounding of Cummings, was now placed in command of the sector. As Captain Hugh Matheson and his men of 'C' Company, 2/10th Battalion were no longer needed in the area, it was detached from the 2/9th Battalion and ordered across Simemi Creek, using the bridge between the strips to rejoin the 2/10th Battalion.[28]

Australian photographic journalist George Silk was in the thick of the fighting and would take some of the most evocative images of the fighting in the Pacific. He had already risked death several times while at Buna. He recalled that day: 'After I did Cape Endaiadere, and the mass of casualties, and I came out of there pretty shot up emotionally and everything else, I took a couple of days at Battalion Headquarters or Regimental Headquarters, and then I went back into the fighting at Giropa Point'.[29]

* * *

Lance Corporal Uchiyama Seiichi, with *No. 9 Company, 229th Regiment*, located at Warren front recorded his last brief diary entry: 'Dawn, concentrated artillery fire. 10.00 [hours]. Enemy firing in front of us'.[30]

* * *

Further west, after a night of harassing and searching fire by both the Americans of Urbana Force and the Japanese, Colonel Grose that morning sent the rifle companies of the III/127th Regiment into the Government Gardens, less than a kilometre from the beach, but they occupied a precarious position.[31]

At dawn, the men of 'L' Company, replaced 'I' Company on the left. The men of 'I' Company now extended to the right, and 'K' Company, shaken by its experience of the night before, now went into reserve. Soon after, the two main assault companies of 'I' and 'L' companies, each reinforced with weapons crews from 'M' Company, moved into position along the line of departure. At 6 am, the artillery and mortars began firing their preparation, and 'H' Company on Musita Island opened on the mission with all its weapons. Covered by the rolling barrage, the troops jumped off 15 minutes later, on a 400-metre front. Meanwhile, the men of 'G' Company, II/127th Regiment crossed Entrance Creek, as the reserve for the attack, while the remaining men of the heavy-weapons crew of 'M' Company, 127th Regiment took up a supporting position along its bank.[32]

The drive across the gardens to the sea had about 800 metres to cover. Not more than 500 metres south-west, the Triangle was still occupied in strength by the Japanese against that flank. Neglected and overgrown with thick clumps of shoulder-high kunai, the gardens extended for some 400 metres to a swamp about 100 metres wide. Japanese entrenchments, including concealed bunkers and strongpoints, dominated this area. On the other side of the swamp, looking out on the sea, was a coconut plantation, about 300 metres across, through which ran the coastal track between Buna Mission

CHAPTER 45

and Giropa Point. On the higher and drier ground was the Buna Government Station.[33]

Here, Captain Yasuda Yoshitatsu, commanding the surviving marines of the *5th Yokosuka*, *5th Sasebo*, *SNLP* and the supporting naval pioneer troops, had the area well prepared for defence. His men covered nearly every metre of ground, with both observed and unobserved fire. The track through the gardens was also covered by bunkers, and on either side of it, echeloned in depth to the rear and hidden by the kunai, were numerous individual foxholes and firing pits, most of them with overhead cover. In the surrounding swamp, north and east of the gardens, were strong bunker positions, and even stronger fortifications were to be found in the plantation and along the shoreline.[34]

Lieutenant Robert McCampbell, with 'C' Company, I/127th Regiment, recalled the situation: 'There was very little cover on the eastward side of Entrance Creek which forced troops to be heavily bunched during the staging period of an attack. The gardens themselves were very flat, covered by a substantial growth of kunai grass, and accordingly provided excellent cover for the Japanese as well as a good field of fire. The surrounding swamp areas were infested with snipers in trees. All of which made operations across the Government Gardens a very difficult manoeuvre'.[35]

As the men of 'I' and 'L' companies, III/127th Regiment, started their advance through the kunai, they were met with streams of bullets, and both companies were forced to the ground. The fire was particularly heavy to the front of 'I' Company. These men soon after began to clean out an isolated bunker just forward of their line of departure, but the men's attempts to infiltrate and knock out a main Japanese strong point immediately to the rear of the bunker met with no success. Making full use of the many hidden positions, the Japanese successfully countered 'I' Company's advance. While the company was pinned down in front of the strongpoint, Sergeant Elmer Burr saw an enemy grenade land close to Captain Michael Ustruck, who was out in front with his men. Burr threw himself on the grenade and smothered the explosion with his body. Burr was posthumously awarded the Medal of Honour; he was the first man to receive this award during the campaign.[36]

Another member of the 'I' Company, the wounded Private Albert Fisher, was being evacuated to an aid station just behind the frontlines, when he saw two wounded men from his unit lying in an area swept with Japanese fire. Disregarding his wound and the ongoing enemy fire, he dragged both men to safety. Private Albert Fisher was awarded the DSC for his actions.[37]

Grose's temporary forward CP was close to the jumping-off line, so close that Lieutenant Colonel Benjamin Farrar, the regimental Operations Officer, was wounded that morning by small arms fire while at the post. Grose could not see why 'I' Company was not moving forward. Major Harold Hootman, the regimental Supply Officer, who was in the CP with him, asked permission to go to 'I' Company to assess the situation. Grose recalled that he was 'a bit flabbergasted [at the request] because it seemed to be the desire of so many to find a good reason for going to the rear'.[38] He gave Hootman permission to go, asking him to report his findings to him when he got back. That was the last time this officer was seen alive by his CO. Major Harold Hootman's body was later recovered, rifle in hand, not far from a Japanese bunker under circumstances which suggested he was killed while singlehandedly trying to destroy the enemy position.[39]

Major Hootman had scarcely left the CP when news came back that 'I' Company had suffered heavy casualties and were disorganised. Grose went out to the company himself and what he saw confirmed the report. Grose pulled back the company at 9.50 am to reorganise, and he now replaced it with Captain William Dames and his men of 'G' Company, II/127th Regiment. At first, it seemed that Dames might regain the impetus of the advance. Inspired by Sergeant Francis Vondracek – who had been acting as a platoon commander with 'I' Company, III/127th Regiment, who had remained in the line – the

CHAPTER 45

newcomers took out the most forward of the Japanese positions. Covered by rifle fire from 'G' Company, Vondracek knocked out the three bunkers in quick succession by flinging hand grenades through their firing slits. Sergeant Francis Vondracek was later awarded the DSC for his actions that day. Within the hour, 'G' Company reported that the Japanese had been cleared out of a three-bunker strongpoint, which had held up the advance. Despite this promising start, the men of 'G' Company did not get much farther that day.[40]

Setting up his CP in the most forward of the captured bunkers, Dames continued with the task of rooting out the enemy from his remaining bunker positions. Under this aggressive commander, the fresh company cut through to the track and straddled it; however, try as these men could, they were unable to move forward from there because the Japanese fire was too intense from Japanese hidden bunker positions.[41]

Disappointing though the day was on the right flank and centre, the most bitter frustration was on the left. There, 'L' Company, III/127th Regiment was strongly supported by the heavy weapons spread along the creek, and the mortar teams commanded by Lieutenant Colonel McCreary; he was directing the fire of his mortars personally most of the day from a coconut tree about 50 metres from the Japanese lines – the only good observation post he could find. Though wounded in the back by a shell fragment, he strapped himself to the tree and continued to direct fire, until he lapsed into unconsciousness from loss of blood and was evacuated. Lieutenant Colonel Melvin McCreary was later awarded the DSC for his actions.[42]

Colonel Horace Harding, Lieutenant General Eichelberger's artillery commander, who was then inspecting the frontlines, now took over. Additional supporting fire was provided by the troops on Musita Island and adjacent positions to the north. Aware of the situation, Grose – at 10.28 am – ordered a platoon of 20 men from 'A' Company, I/127th Regiment to cross over to the mission from the island by way of the north bridge and hold there if possible. The

Japanese were so busy in the gardens, enabling these men to get across the bridge, which though rickety was still standing, but they were now observed, and the Japanese immediately attacked; the Americans suffered eight men killed and fell back across the bridge.[43]

At the time, Colonel Grose was unaware of their initial success, but Brigadier Spencer Akin, General MacArthur's signal officer, was briefly on the island during the afternoon and saw American troops walking about the mission area. General Eichelberger soon after began receiving congratulations on having taken the mission. Eichelberger, however, not only refused to accept the congratulations but demanded an immediate explanation. Grose was at a loss to understand what Eichelberger was talking about until he later came across Akin.[44]

The fighting here also resulted in some confusion among the Japanese. The defence of Captain Yasuda Yoshitatsu was spread thin, and he was now forced to transfer troops from the strongpoint at the north-west end of the gardens to the mission. Near the garden and now feeling the pressure upon his front ease, 'L' Company's left platoon, with lieutenants Fred Matz and Charles Middendorf, began pushing forward. Meeting little opposition, the platoon pushed on alone through the kunai, unnoticed by the rest of the company. Within a short time, the platoon was through the gardens and on the outskirts of the Coconut Plantation. They had broken right through to the beach by 9.35 am. There, two enemy bunkers brought the advance to a halt, with the men now forced to dig-in.[45]

Sergeant Kenneth Gruennert refused, however, to be stopped and single-handed, he threw grenades at the defenders of the first post, killing the Japanese manning the position. Although severely wounded in the shoulder while doing so, he refused to return to the rear. He bandaged the wound himself and moved out against the second bunker. Hurling his grenades with precision despite his shoulder wound, Gruennert forced the Japanese out of the second bunker as well. The gallant NCO then fell dead to a nearby rifle shot. The rest of the platoon advanced, no doubt inspired by the actions of

CHAPTER 45

their sergeant, and by noon had reached the sea. Sergeant Kenneth Gruennert was posthumously awarded the Medal of Honour, the second to be conferred on a soldier of the 127th Infantry Regiment during the day's fighting.[46]

The Japanese, however, now surrounded the stranded platoon, and to make matters worse, shells from Australian gunners, who had no way of knowing that the Americans had broken through, began to explode around them. Middendorf was now killed, while Matz was wounded. Finally, Matz, with only eight survivors, fell back, ordering his men out after an afternoon of bitter resistance and with darkness descending. One of the eight survivors was, however, badly wounded and unable to be taken out, so Matz remained behind with him. The six men of the platoon made it back to their lines two days later after a difficult march, most of it through hip-deep swamp. Matz and his wounded man, who would have died if his officer had not remained with him, hid behind the Japanese lines until the position here was overrun eight days later by American troops. For his actions, Lieutenant Fred Matz was awarded the DSC.[47]

Grose remained ignorant of the platoon's break-through until just before noon when a runner arrived with the news. He ordered 'I' Company, III/127th Regiment back into the line to the right of 'G' Company II/127th Regiment and sent 'K' Company, III/127th Regiment to the far left, with orders to break through to 'L' Company's isolated platoon near the beach. The men of 'K' Company attacked in the direction they judged to be where the stranded platoon was located. Captain Yasuda had meanwhile plugged the hole in his line here, and it was only after heavy fighting that Lieutenant Paul Krasne and eight men of 'K' Company finally broke through. They raced to the beach, found no trace of the Matz or his men and promptly withdrew lest they be cut off.[48]

Seeing that the line had barely advanced, Grose now ordered Captain Byron Bradford and his men of 'F' Company, II/127th Regiment to attack on 'L' Company's right at 3.11 pm. The result was the same. The line remained unchanged, and by the evening, it was no more than 150 metres from the start-line. Grose therefore asked Eichelberger for time to reorganise but the request was refused, and he was ordered instead to resume the attack early Christmas morning. Eichelberger, who had been at the front all day, reported the failure to MacArthur the next day, adding in words charged with emotion that seeing the attack fail had been the 'all time low' of his life.[49]

46

'... GET ON WITH YOUR JOB, MY BOY'

On Christmas Day, 1942, Lieutenant Colonel Dobbs, commanding the 2/10th Battalion, renewed his advance. It was now that Brigadier Wootten emphasised to Dobbs that he use 'soft-spot' tactics and directed his attention to the Japanese right, which, he thought, seemed most likely to yield to pressure.

Dobbs, at the time, planned to use Captain Hugh Matheson and his men of 'C' Company, 2/10th Battalion, to attack the Japanese, for these men had just rejoined the battalion at first light, having previously been brought over from the 2/9th Battalion area to guard the bridge between the strips spanning Simemi Creek. Therefore, Matheson was sent around to the left of the Americans, but it was not until late in the day that Matheson found himself angled against the strong Japanese positions, which had stopped Major Chester Beaver and his men of 'C' Company, I/126th Regiment soon after 7 am when these men led the American advance that morning.[1]

The 2/9th Battalion war diary records that some of the exhausted men of the battalion were finally getting some much-needed rest: 'Two pls A Coy moved to Bde area to become Bde reserve, B Echelon personnel were pressed into service as Inf. to fill gaps in line caused by removal of A Coy. Snipers were very active from across river, one casualty being caused, but our snipers retaliated with the odds in our favour. During the afternoon the arty registered harassing tasks'.[2]

The efforts of Colonel Martin, commanding the American infantry, had attempted a wide deployment of both the I/126th and the I/128th regiments, but they had achieved little, and these men were now forced to dig-in against several Japanese strongpoints. Martin, who was commanding from the frontlines, ordered a patrol of the I/128th Regiment into the swamp with orders to come in behind the Japanese. The patrol returned with a report that the swamp was impenetrable. Convinced, however, that troops could get through if they had the will to do so, Martin asked Clarkson, commanding the I/128th Regiment, or an officer with 'guts' to take the assignment. Clarkson picked Lieutenant George Hess of 'A' Company for the task.

Hess then left the battalion CP at about 9 am with 15 men. Swinging to the left, he and his section worked their way through the swamp, sometimes sinking waist-deep in mud. Martin had gone about halfway with them, giving his final orders before returning to the American line. By early afternoon, the patrol had cut its way around the Japanese right flank and established itself on dry ground on the Japanese left rear without being observed by the enemy.[3]

Meanwhile, Martin spent the rest of the day back in the frontlines trying to get troops through to the position held by Hess but was not able to do so because heavy fighting developed all along the front. However, there was little change in dispositions except for the flanking movement. Indeed, Martin at one point climbed a tall tree that overlooked the Japanese positions to get a better 'bead on enemy troops lurking in the tall grass immediately to his front'.[4] From this vantage spot, and using a rifle, he accounted for several Japanese, and he would be awarded the DSC for his ongoing actions during the fighting at Buna.[5]

By late afternoon, the Allied line was a shallow V, with Old Strip being the point of the V east of the area where Colonel Yamamoto Hiroshi had most of his three-inch guns emplaced. In the afternoon, however, through the dense undergrowth, the American GIs started providing mortar and small arms fire in the support of Hess and his section. The men of 'C' Company, I/128th Regiment, under Lieutenant Donald Foss, reached Hess and his men before nightfall. Except for intermittent area fire, these men encountered no opposition

CHAPTER 46

from the Japanese. Martin now ordered Foss to launch an attack the next morning on the nearest enemy emplacement about 100 metres to the north-east.[6]

The Australians had achieved very little that day. Major James Trevivian and his men of 'D' Company, 2/10th Battalion had only gained a few metres, held up by one of the most outflung of the Japanese bunkers on the edge of the coconut plantation. Lieutenant Murray Brown and the remnants of 'B' Company were behind him, while the night before, Captain Roger Sanderson and his men of 'A' Company had taken their place on the left of the strip covering the right of the Americans. His men, like those of Trevivian, had gained only a few metres. Dobbs therefore now proposed that his three companies on Old Strip drive ahead the following morning, while Matheson and his fresh men of 'C' Company were to sweep across from the left. The Americans would move forward on their flank against the positions that had been holding them up.[7]

As this fighting raged, the battalion CO had been anxiously waiting for information of his men's progress, as recorded in the battalion published history: 'Battalion HQ was well up on the right and the CO and adjutant moved about, almost regardless of danger, in the constant efforts needed. At one stage a digger was dashing past the CO with a message when a burst of fire immediately overhead caused the digger to crash in an exhausted state at the CO's feet. "Are you hurt?" the CO asked him. "No, sir," was the reply, to which the CO answered, "Well, get up and get on with your job, my boy". It was tough going and no relenting if they were to win through'.[8] Indeed, throughout the fighting, both Cummings and Dobbs were observed to move about the battlefield at Buna 'almost regardless of danger' – the former 'standing up with his felt hat on with enemy snipers all round swearing like a trooper'.[9]

Not far behind the frontline troops of the 2/10th Battalion was their Regimental Aid Posts, as recalled by the historian of the 2/10th Battalion: 'Most of the wounded were evacuated during the night, and the MO, Captain [Geoffrey] Verco, with the stretcher-bearers, had been on their legs during the previous day and night without pause. They were heedless of danger in attending to, and bringing back, the casualties. The RAP, situated as the eastern end of the strip, caught lots of overthrows from the battle, and the shells from the naval guns of the enemy at the top of the strip and on the flank screamed low over the top of their shelter'.[10]

Meanwhile, FOO Lieutenant Arthur Outridge was wounded and brought into a field dressing station, while the Australian gunners managed that night to bring a lone 25-pounder gun forward to target the Japanese positions over open sights, as recorded in the 2/5th Field Regiment war diary:

> Sgt [Roderick] Carson was ordered forward with his gun at 1800 hrs. The gun was towed by a jeep to the Lagoon at Burie, but it was found that the bridge was too narrow to take the gun. At approximately 2100 hrs a Bren carrier was obtained, and as the tide was running out, and the moon coming up, the gun was towed through the lagoon mouth. The gun was hitched to the carrier by a tow rope 30 yards long. The carrier was on the plus side of the lagoon, and had a straight run along firm, wet sand. By this means, and with the help of some 30 men, the gun was got safely across. The Jeep then took over and towed the gun up to the pillboxes. No small credit is due to Sgt Schurr for his excellent driving along the jungle track, and the swampy new strip. While the gun was being got up another party was working on the emplacement, using material salvaged from the Jap pillboxes. By the morning the gun was in place, 1000 yards from the enemy lines. The camouflage is excellent, and many troops passed by within five yards of the gun and were not aware of its presence.[11]

* * *

CHAPTER 46

Further west, at Urbana front, Lieutenant General Eichelberger summed up the situation for 25 December: 'I was awakened on Christmas morning by heavy Japanese bombing from the air, and my Christmas dinner was a cup of soup given me by a thoughtful doctor at a trailside hospital. For the projected American advance had not proceeded as expected. Troops of Urbana Force bogged down in the kunai grass of Government Gardens and their commander lost contact with his forward units'.[12]

Distressed and off balance, Colonel Grose again asked for a pause to reorganise. Eichelberger told him to press on with the attack and gave him, in addition to the other two battalions of the 127th Regiment, elements of the I/127th Regiment, which were just arriving at the front. Grose would now have eight companies of the regiment involved in directly attacking the Japanese positions: 'A', 'C', 'F', 'G', 'I', 'K', 'L', and 'M' companies.

His plan was to have the men of 'A' Company, I/127th Regiment and 'F' Company, II/127th Regiment attack on the far left and push through to the coast, while 'K' and 'L' companies, III/127th Regiment, in the centre of the line, would push forward in their sector in concert with the companies on the left. Meanwhile, the officers and men of 'G' and 'I' companies, III/127th Regiment would focus on reducing the bunkers covering the track through the gardens, aided by a diversionary attack in the afternoon on the Japanese positions in the Triangle. The men of 'C' Company, I/127th Regiment would be held in reserve.[13]

Captain Horace Harger, with his men of 'A' Company, along with Captain Byron Bradford and 'F' Company would launch their attack on the far left without mortar or artillery support. Their attack would, however, be supported by a demonstration of a full-scale attack against the mission by 'H' Company, II/127th Regiment from Musita Island, to draw Japanese troops from the gardens. As soon as it became evident that the enemy had taken the bait, 'A' and 'F' companies would attack the gardens.[14]

As the mortars and artillery opened an intense bombardment against the mission station, 'H' Company, on the island, made a great show of being about to attack the mission across the north makeshift bridge. At 11.35 am, while the commotion on the island was at its height, 'A' and 'F' companies attacked across the gardens. Captain Horace Harger and his men of 'A' Company (less two platoons, which had yet to arrive) were held up, but Captain Byron Bradford and 'F' Company, which had found it impossible to move forward the day before, now found the going relatively easy. These men cut their way through the gardens and the swamp and reached the Coconut Plantation by 1.45 pm. While the Japanese were initially caught off balance, they quickly rallied and surrounded the company, and then they began a counterattack. While this attack was repulsed, the GIs suffered heavy casualties in the fighting. Bradford and his men had established an all-around perimeter in a triangular cluster of shell holes just outside the plantation. The position was about 200 metres west of the track junction, about 250 metres from the sea, and around 600 metres from the mission station.[15]

Meanwhile, an advance by a detachment from 'A' Company, led by Captain Harger, broke through to 'F' Company's position at around 4.20 pm, but its weapons platoon was ambushed and destroyed by the Japanese just as it was on the point of also breaking through. The remaining two platoons of 'A' Company reached the front late in the afternoon but were unable to get through to their commanding officer. As night fell, its leading elements and those of 'K' and 'L' companies were at least 350 metres from the beleaguered American garrison near the coast.[16]

The officers and men of 'A' and 'F' companies were now totally isolated, their radios were wet and failed to work. Three men of 127th Regimental Headquarters Company, privates Gordon Eoff and William Balza, along with Sergeant William Fale, distinguished themselves in attempting to get a telephone cable through to the stranded garrison, but they were unable to break through to them. Both men were later awarded the DSC for their actions.[17]

CHAPTER 46

The attack by 'G' and 'I' companies against the three bunkers in the garden area by day's end had made only slight gains. The Japanese bunkers were too well defended and too cleverly concealed. Captain William Dames, commanding 'G' Company, and Lieutenant Marcelles Fahres, now leading 'L' Company with the death of Captain Roy Wentland days before, tried digging saps towards them, but at the end of the day, the Japanese bunkers remained intact, impregnable.[18]

The diversionary attack against the Japanese bunker positions in the Triangle to assist the attacks by the men of 'G' and 'I' companies on the right was mounted late in the afternoon. A platoon of 'E' Company, II/127th Regiment was to advance into the mouth of the Triangle and engage the enemy with fire, while a platoon of 'C' Company, supported with heavy weapons from 'D' Company, would launch the main attack from the south. Although the attack, led by Captain James Workman, commanding 'C' Company, was carefully planned and prepared, it failed, like all others before it. The attack was called off towards evening after Captain James Workman was killed while charging an enemy bunker at the head of his troops. He was awarded the DSC posthumously.[19]

Late in the afternoon, Grose was reorganising his companies, rotating 'the units so that they could get out of the line and have a few days rest'.[20] He pulled 'I' and 'K' companies out of the line, while ordering the rest of 'C' Company (less one platoon, which was holding the area below the Triangle) to take over the position on the far left. Grose issued orders to 'C' Company that these men the next day were to break through to 'A' and 'F' companies near the coast and link up with them to form a corridor from Entrance Creek to the sea. Major Edmund Schroeder, commander of I/127th Regiment, who reported to Grose that evening, would take command of the attempt to break through. Meanwhile, the men of 'L' Company, extended to the right in support of 'G' Company in the Government Garden area, just north and east of the Triangle.[21]

Grose later recalled at this point that there were no facilities for resting the troops: 'It was difficult to find a dry spot for this purpose, and since there were no tents or other shelter, the men were quite often wet from rain even when resting. The relief from the tensions of the front was a help. I found that this system worked, and continued to use it all the way through, despite the fact that there were those in the higher echelons who insisted that all the men needed was proper leadership'.[22]

* * *

Meanwhile, at Rabaul, Japanese Lieutenant Colonel Imoto recorded in his diary the chaotic situation at the *18th Army Headquarters*, regarding Buna:

25 December

Sugiyama (Lieutenant Colonel Sugiyama Shigeru, 18th [Area] Army staff officer): 'I would like to see orders and instructions for the Army issued at the discretion of the Army commander'. Imoto: 'Was there some issue related to area Army orders and the like?' Sugiyama: 'We had no alternative but to make a furious dash into Buna when orders were issued to secure the area'. Imoto: 'This was contained in a great Army order issued by Imperial Headquarters. The area Army cannot issue such an order. Imperial Headquarters cancelled the order to secure Buna based on the Army–Navy central agreement'.[23]

* * *

Tank commander Corporal Evan Barnet, who had been seriously wounded in the arm and thrown out of his turret while advancing down Old Strip the previous day, now had his arm amputated. Barnet recalled years later:

I was severely wounded, resulting in an amputation in a field hospital under a tree, actually a tarpaulin, the next day –

CHAPTER 46

Christmas Day. I was carried by 'Fuzzy Wuzzy Angels' 14 miles [21 kilometres] to Popondetta airstrip .... I had seven men in my team – one Boss Boy, four carrying me and two supporting. Periodically along the 14-mile track, the Boss Boy used to send one of the spare boys up a tree to pick a coconut and give me a drink. I can assure you, along that track those drinks of coconut juice were wonderful.

On arrival at the airstrip, I was met by an American medical orderly who asked me if I would like a drink. He looked at me with both arms bandaged and went away. He came back with a bowl and put it down beside me and a plastic tube which he placed in my mouth ... and I had my first drink of real American coffee, which I have never forgotten and ... it is not nearly as good these days. I was then flown over the Owen Stanleys to Port Moresby and hospital.[24]

47

'I NOMINATE THAT BLOKE FOR THE NEXT ROUND'

The day of 26 December did not begin well for the Allies. The main Australian attack on Warren front began at 7 am, 15 minutes after the first smoke shell exploded to help cover their advance. The attack would be launched by Lieutenant Colonel Dobbs and his men of the 2/10th Battalion. On the right, Major James Trevivian and his men of 'D' Company had some success by driving into one of the dispersal bays near the western end of the airstrip. To his left, in the centre, Captain Roger Sanderson with his men of 'A' Company also advanced for a time and disappeared into a confused fight as they tried to draw level with 'D' Company. Dobbs, however, temporarily lost touch with them, due to a fire to the rear caused by American GIs. Captain Hugh Matheson and his men of 'C' Company on the left would have the greatest success that day, advancing well forward of the battalion.[1]

The battalion history records the bush fire incident: 'During the day battalion HQ staff were close up behind "D" Company. About midday they were crouching low behind a little cover and having a brief but hard-earned rest as they snatched a bite of bully. A short distance away to their rear, a party [of] Americans lit a fire causing smoke to rise in a cloud. The CO 2/10th Battalion was dashing off to investigate them, but the adjutant restrained him. The latter got the American party on the phone and the CO spoke to one of their officers. He devastatingly told those fellows something about their ancestry, their sons, and the folly of their sins. Result: no more smoke, Americans still alive'.[2]

CHAPTER 47

On the right of the strip, Trevivian, leading 'D' Company, at zero hour, moved forward cautiously, inching forward. He had sent Lieutenant Francis Leonard, a 23-year-old salesman from Coonamble in New South Wales and his men of 18 Platoon to swing around the extreme right in an attempt to flank the Japanese. This platoon suffered heavy casualties but helped the company advance. By nightfall, however, Lieutenant Francis Leonard was dead and his platoon 'virtually ceased to exist'.[3] With 18 Platoon was Private Reginald Brandon, a 26-year-old farm labourer from Murat Bay in South Australia, who rushed a Japanese pillbox, firing his Bren, taking out the position, but in doing so he was seriously wounded; he was awarded the Military Medal for his actions.[4]

Meanwhile, Sanderson and his men of 'A' Company had broken into the Japanese position that had defended the centre of Old Strip. Here, Private Timothy Hughes, with 9 Platoon, who had just days before found a creek crossing, distinguished himself again with outstanding courage even judged against the fierce fighting by his mates, shooting and grenading the enemy out of their trenches and foxholes. Private Hughes was awarded the Military Medal for his actions. His platoon commander, 23-year-old Lieutenant Leslie Redden, from Greenwich in New South Wales, was seriously wounded in the fighting, enemy fire was targeting their right which now slowed down their advance. The Japanese here were entrenched around the north-western corner of the strip. Sergeant Frank Duff, a 29-year-old labourer from Broken Hill in New South Wales (likely still with Lance Corporal William Moroney's cigarette lighter), and Private Donald Crutchett, a 33-year-old clerk from Monta in South Australia, were now detailed to conduct a reconnaissance of the enemy position.[5] The historian of the battalion recorded:

> 'Duff', lean and freckled, was quite a boy. No stranger to the stringent procedure inflicted for playing up in and around camps. He was in battle, and whenever necessary, a brave,

reckless Irish Australian. His stripes were off as often as on. But 'Duff' was mighty when needed. This occasion again revealed the man. Carefully, accurately, and at great personal risk he crawled forward under great difficulty. The two danger points were pin-pointed and the details relayed to the mortars, and this particular enemy fire was silenced. This enabled our troops to move forward. For this work which had quite an influence on the attack, Sergeant Duffy was awarded the Military Medal.[6]

The battalion historian was correct regarding Sergeant Duffy's rebellious streak, as when later discharged honourably from the Army, his service record has him listed as Private Frank Duff.

Soon after, 'A' Company's advance was again targeted by enemy fire, but now to their left. Lieutenant Oswald Gray, a 28-year-old butcher from Clare in South Australia, leading 8 Platoon, attempted to pushed forward against the entrenched Japanese on the company's left front. Gray, however, was wounded, as were most of his men – only three from the platoon emerged unscathed. One of the three was 24-year-old Private Frank Gray from Adelaide. He recalled years later: 'We got about 30 feet [10 metres], a little closer maybe, from that post and that's when we got all the casualties. But that's where we reckon they were firing a gun without any shells in it, it was killing blokes outright, but there were no wounds anywhere on 'em. The blast was killing them'.[7]

Captain Hugh Matheson and 'C' Company to their left soon silenced the Japanese machinegun nest. Private Arthur Evans, a 23-year-old labourer from Hilton in South Australia, with 14 Platoon, watched 13 and 15 platoons attack the position: 'We flanked the billbox. Then we cut in until we found a track that had been used from the pillbox ... they attacked the pillbox, and they raced out to the pillbox all right and they started feeding grenades in. But the Japs were pretty smart – they chucked them back again. And that cost us a lot .... So our people were holding the grenades for a couple

CHAPTER 47

of seconds before feeding them in. It went on for quite a while, but eventually they were successful'.[8]

The battalion historian recorded soon after renewing their advance, that Sanderson's men came across, '15 Americans looking very lonely as their command post was some 300 yards away on the left flank. They were loaded with automatics and ammunition and without a leader. Not having been given any orders, they were delighted to join the diggers and thicken-up the line. They were a great asset, and "A" Company now had the strongest fire power in the battalion'.[9] Even so, the advance here was soon forced to ground with a strong Japanese blocking force baring further progress.[10]

Meanwhile, Matheson was advancing with 13 and 15 platoons up front with 14 Platoon in support. These men conducted another spirited assault, this time against an enemy anti-aircraft gun holding up their advance along with those of 'A' Company. He planned to smother the Japanese weapon with a sudden attack by 13 and 15 platoons under cover of two-inch mortar smoke. The other anti-aircraft gun, which had been a constant threat located about 200 metres east of the gun currently holding up the advance, now ceased to be a problem. Major Chester Beaver and his men of 'C' Company, I/126th Regiment, with one of Major Gordon Clarkson's companies, I/128th Regiment in support, had overran this gun position. It was silent as they closed in on it because it had run out of ammunition.[11] The Japanese official history records the loss of this gun: 'The Allies closed in on the flank of the anti-aircraft gun emplacement at 7.02 am on 26 December. The emplacement was overrun after an hour of close combat'.[12]

Matheson's mortar teams put down their smoke barrage to cover the attack by 13 and 15 platoons, but instead of thick smoke covering their advance, only wisps of smoke emerged, leaving his men exposed. Even so, Lieutenants Alan McDougall, a 22-year-old cabinet maker from Fullarton in South Australia, commanding 15 Platoon, and Reginald Maclean, a 24-year-old grocery carter from Sydney, leading

13 Platoon, led their men against the entrenched Japanese. These men were targeted with concentrated fire, the core of it coming from a captured World War One vintage Lewis gun. Maclean, McDougall, and several of their men were immediately hit, though McDougall, who had previously been wounded while earlier attached to the 2/9th Battalion (and concealed the fact), courageously held to the last of his strength to remain with his platoon during the fighting to capture the enemy position. Some withdrew about 40 metres to assault the positions from the long kunai while others with Sergeant George Spencer, a 33-year-old labourer from Maggea in South Australia, directing them. Lieutenant Alan McDougall was awarded the Military Cross (MC) for his actions.[13]

As described by the Australian official historian: 'Something very like a particularly murderous brawl then developed. The Australians pounded grenades into the posts, but several times Japanese hurled them back before they could explode within the defences. Wild-eyed but purposeful, one Japanese was firing blank rounds from the anti-aircraft gun as he tried to set fire to the grass and add flames to the confusion. Japanese riflemen kept popping stiffly up from the depths of the defences like marionettes and, as stiffly, sinking back into them again. The Australians called for petrol bombs but could get only one – which they splashed against the barriers. And then, almost suddenly, it was ended. The defenders were dead, with many dead and wounded Australians out of the 50 or 60 who had made the assault lying near them'.[14] Corporal Peter Heron, a 24-year-old bank clerk from Mt Gambier in South Australia, leading his section here, was killed as he directed the final movements to capture the position.[15]

Matheson now handed the gun in its concrete casement over to the Americans (much to Dobbs' subsequent annoyance) and advanced a further 300 metres north-west along the fringes of the strip before these men dug-in for the night – well forward of the rest of the battalion. To their right rear, however, in the last of the light, the Japanese fell upon Major Trevivian's leading platoon of 'D' Company on the right of Old

CHAPTER 47

Strip so 'savagely that the platoon had to give up the ground it had won and emerged with only four of its number left'.[16]

By the end of the day, the men of 'A' Company, 2/10th Battalion had crossed the runway and taken up a position on the left centre in line with 'C' Company, I/126th Regiment's right, leaving 'D' and 'B' companies, 2/10th Battalion to deal with the Japanese to the right of the strip. The men of 'C' Company, 2/10 Battalion had flanked farther to the left and dealt with the formidable concentration of bunkers on the strip.[17]

Except for the movement on the left flank, little progress was made, with the centre of the line still about 650 metres up the strip. The line itself had the appearance of a sickle: the Australian troops on the far right formed the handle; the Australian and American troops in the centre and left centre, the blade; and 'C' Company, 2/10th Battalion, on the far left and thrusting northward, the hook. The Japanese, however, still firmly held the end of the strip proper, and later that day, they launched an unsuccessful counterattack against the Australian positions. Even so, it was clear that a considerable effort would be required before the Japanese could finally be finally dislodged.[18]

The 2/5th Field Regiment war diary records that several of the FOOs had been wounded performing their roles: 'FOOs are not having much luck in 55 Bty, but they are doing a good job. Such a job as cannot be done without incurring risk. Maj. Hall has repeatedly warned them all about undue exposure, but observation is so difficult that the job cannot be done without incurring danger. The B.C. has decided to send up another FOO on the left flank. Marr is on the right .... Earlier, [John] Mackay-Sim, [Arthur] Outridge, [Peter] Gibson are all out of this fight, but thank God are all certain to be back soon'.[19] That said, Hall himself was in the thick of the action, and the still sick and wounded FOO, Captain Lionel Nix, attached to the 2/9th Battalion, remained on duty.[20]

Meanwhile, the Australian 3.7-inch howitzers of the O'Hare Troop below the bridge had run out of ammunition and could take no further part in the fighting until resupplied. Sergeant Roderick Carson, a 40-year-old wool expert from Sydney, with his lone 25-pounder from Hall's Troop was at the south-east end of Old Strip and would finally help break the Japanese defence of Old Strip. The gunners had excellent observation of the Japanese positions on the strip, bringing observed direct fire upon them. Using armour-piercing shells with supercharge at about one-kilometre range, the 25-pounder not only knocked out one of the remaining enemy pom-poms, but together with the 4.5-inch howitzers of the recently arrived Stokes Troop, they forced Japanese troops out of their bunkers by fire alone, a feat that only the American 105-mm howitzer had previously been able to do.[21]

The 4.5-inch howitzers of the Australian militia 13th Field Regiment were commanded by Captain Norman Stokes, a 24-year-old clerk from Unley in South Australia. Two of these guns had been flown to Dobodura on 20 December and moved up the track to a position about 500 metres south of O'Hare. The other two had arrived from Port Moresby by sea, landing at Hariko on 23 December and dragged inland to complete the troop. Stokes instructed his gunners to leave in place the small brass-protecting caps that came with the fuses, giving the shells a slightly delayed action, which increased their effectiveness in penetrating the dug-in Japanese positions before exploding.[22]

Sergeant Roderick Carson and his gunners throughout their time at Buna proved spectacularly successful and would become famous throughout Buna as 'Carson's Gun'. The battery commander, Major William Hall, at one point arrived at the gun, to target a Japanese pillbox, using armour-piercing shells in preference to high explosive to lessen the danger to the Allied infantry spread close by. His first shell disappeared through the 30-centimetre square embrasure of his target with the flash of its tracer flame bursting brightly as it penetrated the aperture. It was later found that this shot carried away the breech mechanism of a 75-mm gun that was housed in the bunker. Soon after, the gun settled down to a two-day duel with a Japanese triple-

CHAPTER 47

barrelled 25-mm piece which, at first, gave back more than it took. However, the next day, after the personal war between the gunners, the enemy gun was completely silenced. This was merely a beginning, for Carson and his gunners would claim more sniping successes as the days went on.[23]

It was said that Carson and his gunners disputed any assertions that you could not snipe with a 25-pounder, as recalled by the regimental historian:

> The deadly accuracy of the laying gave the OPO [Observation Post Officer] the power of life and death over any individual Jap seen in the target area. Lieut. [Thomas] Handran-Smith, the OPO, would sometimes nominate his targets [to Carson] .... When the Japs were withdrawing from the pillboxes on the far side of the strip, Handran-Smith spied a Japanese giving orders to a couple of his men. The officer, or NCO, stopped momentarily in a short shallow trench near the 'Wireless Mast'. This trench had been accurately registered, and many Japs had been killed in its locality by direct hits. Said the OPO: 'I nominate that bloke for the next round'. Orders were quickly passed to the gun; all eyes were on the Jap. When the 25-pounder fired, the Jap appeared to sense that that round was meant for him. He jumped on to the parapet with the idea of making a dash. Foolish move! The onlookers assert that the shell hit him in the pit of the stomach. At all events he disappeared in instant disintegration.[24]

Such stories as these were borne out by the infantry. Major Trevivian recalled that when he and his men were fighting from the dispersal bays at the end of Old Strip, shells from Carson's gun were clearing the tops of the bays by centimetres: 'The draught wore a track across the top of the bays'.[25] Far behind the vivid flash of this 25-pounder, the other gunners were going about their critical tasks of support, before almost every infantry and tank attack, and their shells poured into the Japanese defences, helping to wear down the Japanese will to fight.[26]

* * *

Meanwhile, at Urbana front further west, the men of 'G' Company, II/127th Regiment, assisted by 'I' Company, III/127th Regiment took out several bunkers on the right along the track during the morning and began working on those that remained. On the far left, however, the Japanese stubbornly held on with the Americans of 'C' Company, I/127th Regiment making little progress in their attempt to reach the stranded American garrison further north near the coast at the plantation. There, Captain Byron Bradford and his men of 'F' Company, II/127th Regiment, and Captain Horace Harger and his two platoons of 'A' Company, I/127th Regiment, were still holding out. The Japanese had obviously reinforced their positions north of the gardens directly from the mission to repulse any such attempt, even though the Allied artillery had put down a ten-minute barrage on the south-west corner of the mission to stop such a movement. Major Edmund Schroeder now ordered an element of 'C' Company, split into patrols, into the swamp north of the gardens to attack the Japanese there. The rest of the company, joined during the afternoon by Lieutenant John Lewis and his men of 'B' Company, continued to attack frontally. The attack, however, made little progress, and it became apparent during the early afternoon that 'C' Company was not going to break through.[27]

Colonel Grose ordered Colonel Sladen Bradley, now chief of staff of the 32nd Division, to go to the beleaguered companies and report back on their situation. Bradley, who was also acting as executive officer of the 127th Regiment, was to be accompanied by Major Schroeder, Lieutenant Robert McCampbell, the intelligence officer of the II/127th Regiment, and a platoon of 'C' Company, led by Lieutenant Ted Johnson. These men set out carrying with them a telephone line,

CHAPTER 47

ammunition, and food. After some sharp skirmishing with the enemy, the patrol reached Bradford, Harger and their survivors still holding their precarious position near the coast in the Coconut Plantation at 5.45 pm.[28]

Lieutenant McCampbell recalled: 'The condition of the companies on our arrival was deplorable. The dead had not been buried. Wounded, bunched together, [the men] had been given only a modicum of care, and the troops were demoralised. Major Schroeder did a wonderful job of reorganising the position and helping the wounded. The dead were covered with earth . . . the entire tactical position of the companies were reorganised and [they were] placed in a strong defensive position'.[29] That evening, Bradley, accompanied by a small patrol, returned from the perimeter with his report. Major Schroeder and Lieutenant McCampbell remained behind to continue organising the garrison's defence.[30]

Grose later admitted that Eichelberger wrote a letter that night to Major General Sutherland, but he decided not to send it. Grose recalled that his CO wrote of the situation as Bradley reported it to him. It was to the effect that 'F' Company had been 'practically wiped out', and that the detachment of 'A' Company had received, 'numerous casualties. I must be frank, however, and tell you that the first two companies have taken tremendous losses, and everyone on the Urbana front has recommended that we reorganise and substitute two fresh companies. I believe that the greater part of the Japanese strength has been on our two forward companies'.[31]

Major Edmund Schroeder and Lieutenant Robert McCampbell would later be awarded the DSC for their actions, while Colonel Sladen Bradley would be awarded the Silver Star.[32]

* * *

At Rabaul, the impending collapse at Buna was causing the headquarters of the Japanese *18th Army* great concern. Lieutenant General Adachi Hatazo issued an order to Major General Yamagata Tsuyuo, whose

BLOODY BUNA

headquarters was then at Danawatu, west of Gona: 'Quickly mobilise your available strength by sea to an area to the north of Giruwa and attack the flank of the Allied force to the west of Buna. Bring aid to the Army and Navy units in the Buna area, and secure north Giruwa, regardless of how desperate the situation becomes'.[33]

48
'THE SHIT HIT THE FAN AS USUAL'

By the morning of 27 December, the fighting to finally take Old Strip was in its final stages. The Australian artillery fire, plus the pressure on the right flank forced Colonel Yamamoto Hiroshi to begin withdrawing to the plantation area around Giropa Point, though a fighting rearguard tried to keep the fact of the withdrawal from the Australians and Americans for as long as possible. And so, the Australian companies moving on the Japanese positions at the head of the strip from either flank met appreciably less resistance. In the centre, the Australian and American troops who, up to this time, had been meeting the most fanatical Japanese opposition noted a similar weakening.[1]

During the morning, Major James Trevivian and his men of 'D' Company, 2/10th Battalion, with Lieutenant Murray Brown and the remnants of 'B' Company, numbering just 20 men, and a group from the Headquarters Company swept away a Japanese position just off the end of Old Strip proper to the right. Corporal Bill Neate, a 33-year-old clerk from Kent Town in South Australia, recalled: 'They had a pillbox at the end of the strip and another one on the right. The ocean was only about 500 yards away, and a lot of 18 Platoon had been killed there earlier. I was there when the Japs broke cover. We got the lot, about 11 or 12'.[2]

On the edge of the coconut tree line, however, remained the hardest core of the Japanese resistance. By the early afternoon, Captain Roger Sanderson and 'A' Company, having struggled all the previous day to take their forward position, only to then be forced to abandoned it during the night, had reoccupied the position, with the Americans strengthening both his flanks.[3]

On the extreme left, Captain Hugh Matheson and his men of 'C' Company had also been roused, feeling their way along the edge of the coconut plantation so far to the north-west that the strip lay well behind them. They were now more than a kilometre ahead of the main body. Matheson was concerned about a southward running track, which he had scouted the previous night and down which, he assessed, was a strong Japanese position. And although some American troops had arrived as a blocking force on this track, he remained concerned.[4]

By 4.15 pm, Colonel Martin, commanding the Americans, reported that the Japanese were on the run. The Australians of 'A' and 'D' companies, 2/10th Battalion, along with Major Clarkson and his men of the I/128th Regiment, aided by elements of 'C' Company, 2/10th Battalion, squeezed the Japanese out of the last line of trenches across the strip. They were then cleaning out a large bunker close to the dispersal bay. At nightfall, the troops in the centre 'A' Company, 2/10th Battalion, and 'A' Company, I/128th Infantry, were said to be working on a main enemy bunker behind the dispersal bay – this was the last organised enemy position on the runway.[5]

The war diary of the 126th Regiment records: 'Following an artillery barrage, a heavy smoke screen is laid down through which our attack begins. Enemy pillbox positions halfway up the strip held up our advance, but these are captured in the afternoon fighting. Then follows a general push along all lines. The enemy is routed. Our troops begin mopping-up operations. Lt Thomas Burns killed leading an attack with Company "A"'.[6]

By nightfall, a company from the 2/9th Battalion, in brigade reserve, had been ordered across the bridge to be available on Old Strip in case they were needed. By nightfall, the Australian and American frontline extended from the edge of the swamp on the left with Simemi Creek on their right. Miller reported that the line was now held from left to right by the men of 'C' Company, 2/10th Battalion, 'B' Company,

CHAPTER 48

I/128th Regiment, and 'D' and 'B' companies, 2/10th Battalion, with other tired and depleted units in close support.[7]

* * *

The Japanese official history records the day's events briefly: 'The battle around the airstrips finally moved into the final stages on 27 December. Colonel Yamamoto withdrew his main strength to the plantations near Giropa Point and mounted a second counter-offensive against the Australians' right flank with troops in the strip's aircraft concealments. However, their strength was not effectively applied, and they were repelled with heavy casualties'.[8]

* * *

Indeed, later that night, the Japanese launched a vigorous local assault against the right flank of the Australians. With 'D' Company, 2/10th Battalion close to the edge of the coconut plantation, the Japanese launched a counterattack to the right of the company's flank anchored against Simemi Creek at around 9 pm. The Japanese overran the right forward perimeter. There, the already wounded and dependable Corporal William McAuliffe, who refused to leave the line, was on the left flank. He telephoned Trevivian to say that he thought the Japanese had overrun the right front. Trevivian at once hurried Lieutenant Murray Brown and his 20 or so men of 'B' Company (who were nearby in reserve) towards the threatened part of the line. Brown found the line here staggering in some confusion and gathered the men to drive out the enemy. Brown was wounded; indeed, of all the company's officers and NCOs, only Sergeant Stanley Harrington, a 24-year-old labourer from Barmera in South Australia, remained. Brown's counterattack was launched before the enemy could setup their machine guns, otherwise the position likely could not have been restored that night.[9]

Brown recalled years later: 'A man come running back and flung himself down and said, "The Japs have counterattacked and taken the forward positions! So, there was no time for differing. One couldn't see far. I came across a couple of Japs with a light machine gun. I attacked them with a machete and shot a couple of others with a pistol and then someone shot me through the left lung. And then some of the stretcher-bearers came who were wonderful'.[10] Private Joseph Coombe, a 23-year-old truck driver from Monta in South Australia, also recalled: 'The shit hit the fan as usual. I was a Bren gunner. And when we got to this place, I remember Browny getting hit and he said, "Get these bastards out of here and I'm with you, and if you don't, I'm stuffed!"'[11]

Coombs also recalled the plight of one of his mates – Private Bernie 'Mayor' Wright, a 32-year-old labourer from Wayville in South Australia – just after the fighting: 'I remember afterwards I was lying down and you could hear the Japs yabbering away and they were just over a bit of a bank ... and I said, "Are you down a hole, Mayor?" And he said "Yes." So I tossed a grenade over there, and it shook the Japs up. And Mayor said, "You bloody beauty, I'm hit in the foot!" I said, "You said you were down a hole!" He said, "Oh yes, but only a little hole, me feet were sticking up!"'[12]

The battalion historian recorded: 'On reaching the area where the fighting was going on in the semi-darkness [Brown] swept round the Japs, and, waving a bare bayonet in his hand, led his men into the attack. They followed literally fighting tooth and nail. Such was the ferocity of their attack with rifle and bayonet, and backed by "D" Company men, that not a Jap was left alive, and a dangerous situation was averted'.[13] Lieutenant Brown was awarded an MC for his leadership that night. The remaining few men of 'B' Company were now absorbed in 'D' Company, with a full strength of just 30 men, effectively a platoon. Indeed, that battalion itself now numbered around 170 officers and men – a large company.[14]

Heavy Japanese fire still originated from the dispersal bays at the head of the strip, and there was still heavier fire from the positions in the Government Plantation immediately to the rear. In the area

CHAPTER 48

through which Old Strip ran and on the strip itself, however, there was little but sporadic rifle fire. Organised enemy resistance in this area would completely collapse by noon the next day.[15]

* * *

That night, the Australian freighter *Mulcra* anchored in Oro Bay with a troop of Stuart tanks and 400 tons of cargo. Although Brigadier Wootten still had four tanks on hand, and 11 more were on their way from Oro Bay, he no longer needed tanks for the reduction of Old Strip. Some of tanks would be sent into the swamps of Sanananda to the west, with disastrous results for all involved.[16]

* * *

That morning, to the west at Urbana front, Captain Millard Gray, Lieutenant General Eichelberger' aide-de-camp who had taken over 'C' Company, I/127th Regiment, spent the day attacking the Japanese swamp positions on the American extreme left, while Lieutenant John Lewis, leading 'B' Company, I/127th Regiment, took advantage of the Japanese focus on Gray to edge closer to Major Edmund Schroeder, who was still commanding the stranded garrison in the plantation further north, with captains Byron Bradford leading 'F' Company, II/127th Regiment and Horace Harger, commanding 'A' Company, I/127th Regiment; and by 5 pm, he had broken through.[17]

Eichelberger later wrote: 'I was to explore the depths of depression … on the night of 27 December …. At two am a conference took place in my tent. We heard the reports, and they were grave all right. Our troops, if the reports were to be credited, were suffering from battle shock and had become incapable of advance. A number of my senior officers were convinced the situation was desperate. I think I said, as I had said before: "Let us not take counsel of our fears". Nevertheless, I was thoroughly alarmed'.[18]

A few hours later, however, the Americans finally took the Triangle – without a shot being fired. The II/126th Regiment war diary records: "Occupied defence positions the "Triangle" area after it had been cleaned of enemy by the 127th Infantry. Little resistance was encountered in this move'.[19] The American Official History of the Battle for Buna also records: 'A volunteer group from E Company led by S/Sgt Charles E. Wagner and Pfc. James J. Greene, attacked this position in the evening. They found that the enemy had at last evacuated it'.[20]

Squad leader, Ernest Gerber, with the II/128th Regiment, recalled the nature of the fighting at and around the Triangle:

> The thing that eventually worked the best was sheer guts. You waited and waited until you knew where the fire was coming from. Then, some brave souls, or a brave squad, would sneak up as well as they could and try to lob a hand grenade into their slot. Usually, we tried to get up from the rear. There were openings in the front. In many cases, to be blunt, the Japanese were forced to evacuate. They were getting killed too. And they were dying of disease by the dozens. Once in a while we were fortunate. There was some damned place that we attacked day after day after day, got shot and killed, and just couldn't get at it. Then one morning we'd walk up to it and there wasn't a goddamn soul there. Once in a while that was it. More often, it was slug it out. One by one. Take one, and try another, do this, get a few guys killed and wounded, get the next one. The combination of that and the Japanese just finally getting tired was what made the operation successful.[21]

* * *

Meanwhile, Major General Tsuyuo Yamagata had lost no time in complying with the orders sent to him by the commander of the *18th Army*, Lieutenant General Adachi Hatazo, the previous day. Yamagata ordered Colonel Yazawa Kiyoshi, who had led the *41st Infantry*

CHAPTER 48

Regiment, across the Owen Stanley Range and back, who was his most experienced and resourceful commander to take a force to Giruwa to relieve the men at Buna and secure Giruwa – an impossible task, with the numbers at hand. He would command a force of around 430 men from the *I/170th Regiment* (minus its *No. 3* and *No. 4 companies*), *No. 9 Company, III/170th Regiment*, the *Regimental Artillery Company*, the *Brigade Signals Unit*, the *25th Machine-cannon Company*, elements of the *Brigade Engineer Unit*, and whatever troops from the *South Seas Force* he could muster. During the day, advanced elements were to be mobilised by barge to a staging point near north Giruwa.[22]

Meanwhile, in Rabaul, Lieutenant Colonel Imoto with the *18th Army Headquarters* recorded in his diary the plight of the troops at Buna:

27 December

Yoshihara (Major General Yoshihara Kane, 18th Army chief of staff): 'I would like clarification concerning the future use of the 51st Division. Pouring military strength into Buna is problematic from a strategic point of view, but it is not possible for the Army just to abandon the area. It is essential to retake Buna [positions] by gradually deploying the 51st Division from the coast. If the Navy is not willing to cooperate, the operation will have to be conducted with our Army barges. The distance between Salamaua and Buna can be divided into five 50-kilometres stages. Four barges can make 40 round trips over each stage. This can be accomplished with one shipping engineer regiment'.

Katō [Lieutenant General Katō Rinpei, *8th Area Army* chief of staff]: 'As I have explained, advancing troops to Buna is problematic. It is only possible to indicate the first stage of our plan at this time'.

Yoshihara [Major General, *18th Army* chief of staff]: 'Even if we attempted to withdraw from Buna, it would not be possible. To do nothing would also be a disaster. Staff officer Aotsu's battalion entered north Giruwa last night carrying some provisions. It will be possible to retore the situation at Buna if military strength can be applied to key battlefields. If we now attempt to bring relief to Buna, it must be an infantry regiment that is first disembarked. We would have withdrawn from Buna if this had not been possible'.

Katō: 'Even if the Navy could supply assistance and key areas were reinforced, this would, on the contrary, increase our troubles. Resupply is simply not possible'.

Yoshihara: 'Well, what do you propose?'

Katō: 'There is no alternative at this point but to adopt a policy to strengthen our position to the west of Lae and Salamaua'.

Yoshihara: 'The Army commander may have visited commander Imamura [commander of the Japanese *8th Area Army*], but if not, he should go and speak to him immediately. It is not satisfactory that Adachi speaks only to his staff officers'.[23]

49
'WITHDRAW FOR BUNA, ASSEMBLE AT NORTH GIRUWA'

By 28 December, despite the support of the Australian artillery – notably Sergeant Roderick and his 25-pounder, which targeted Japanese positions at close range along Old Strip, including enemy positions within the coconut planation – the Allies were still finding the going along the western end of Old Strip extremely hard.[1]

Captain Hugh Matheson and his surviving 46 men of 'C' Company were to advance through open kunai grass into the coconut plantation and then onto the coast. On his right, Captain Roger Sanderson and 'A' Company was to do likewise. Matheson, from experience, was concerned about the planned attack. Lieutenant Andrews, the Signals Officers of the battalion, recalled the conversation between the Matheson and his CO: 'Dobbs was told he had to do it. When Matheson got his orders, I was there at the O Group conference when Matheson actually got his orders, and Matheson actually had tears in his eyes, knowing what was going to happen. And Dobbs said something to the effect, "Well, it's got to be done, you've got to do it." And Matheson said, "We can't Sir, we can't do it!" And Dobbs repeated, "We've got to do it!"'[2]

Major James Trevivian and his men of 'D' Company, 2/10th Battalion, with his surviving 30 or 40 men, 2/10th Battalion, were still in the right pivot among the coconut trees off the upper end of the strip and the lower end of the dispersal bays. In their attempts to finally clear out the defenders from these bays and his men, a gap had developed between them and Captain Sanderson and 'A' Company during their joint advance. A company from Major Gordon Clarkson's I/128th Regiment, however, filled this hole in the line from the left of the strip, coming in on Sanderson's right.[3]

Sanderson's men were soon approaching the north-west to a point about halfway up the line of the aircraft bays. Another gap soon opened, this time between his left and Matheson with 'C' Company, which was some hundreds of metres to the north-west. Corporal Jim Ellis, 26-year-old labourer from Adelaide, with 14 Platoon, 'C' Company recalled: 'On the left flank as we advanced there was foxholes. The left flank of my section was pretty slow in going through the foxholes. And I kept singing out to them, "Keep the line up!" The section coming behind me, we'd flush 'em and they'd deal with them whatever was left behind us. The next thing I know, we get a shower of grenades thrown at us and that's when I copped it'.[4]

As the morning advanced, more Americans GIs filled this gap between 'A' and 'C' companies. The battalion war diary records the situation just after 7 am: 'Overnight A Coy reformed & advanced …. US troops mop up in rear & take up psns between A & C coys'.[5] Not long after, however, Lieutenant Colonel Dobbs, commanding the 2/10th Battalion, complained to Brigadier Wootten, commanding Warren Force, that the Americans were not keeping up with Matheson in his efforts to close more firmly on the Japanese. At around 8 am, Wootten informed Colonel Clarence Martin that isolated pockets of Japanese resistance were being passed through by his men and that the employment of 'soft-spot tactics did not mean leaving centres of resistance of unknown strength behind'.[6]

Matheson and his men of 'C' Company were to pivot north towards the coast, representing the left flank of the line, while 'A' Company and the Americans in the centre were to conform and support their advance, with Trevivian and 'D' Company covering the right flank. They were to push forward through the coconut plantation to the coast between the mouth of Simemi Creek and Giropa Point. The

CHAPTER 49

battalion adjutant recorded at 9.25 am: 'D Coy advanced closer to coconuts. Heavy E fire … hampers operations on right flank. HE on Giropa Point'.[7] An hour later, the war diary records: 'A Coy right flank move up in line with D Coy. B Coy move up behind D Coy …. Posn of coys obscure, IO & CO go out to locate FDLs'.[8] It was reported at dusk that 'C' Company was trying to drive a wedge into the Japanese perimeter in the coconut grove but had to withdraw in the 'face of very heavy SA fire'.[9]

This plan resulted in a day of bloody skirmishing and local assaults, with several Japanese appearing in American and Australian uniforms attempting to mislead their opponents. The American official historian Samuel Milner wrote of the fighting here: 'The remaining Japanese, cornered and hopeless, fought to the end. Hand grenades tossed into their holes would be tossed back, and the Allied troops always had to be on the alert for frenzied suicide rushes with sword or bayonet. Some of the bypassed enemy troops had taken refuge in trees. In at least one instance, three Japanese were shot out of a single tree. In another case half-a-dozen Japanese troops were cut down carrying M1s and wearing American helmets and fatigues. A few Japanese on the far left tried to escape by taking to the swamp; they were picked off one by one by troops ordered by Major Clarkson into the swamp for that purpose'.[10]

As the Allies strained to tighten their grip, the Japanese remained steadfast in defending their positions. Matheson had ventured far to the north-west, crossing Giropa Creek. Enemy fire coming from the south began to fall near these men, and Matheson believed he was now positioned in the path of the Urbana Force advance, an assumption which was soon confirmed by meeting Americans troops. He informed these Americans that the way to the coast south of Buna on that axis was now open. Matheson, however, was now dangerously detached from Warren Force and was forced to return across the creek. He was then ordered to get astride the track that ran north-west across his front to Giropa Point. Though he had doubt about the wisdom and necessity of this given its exposed position, he tasked Lieutenant John Rudall, a 22-year-old university student from Gawler in South Australia, and the men of 14 Platoon to cover the approach.[11]

Rudall and his men quickly occupied the position, but soon after, the enemy closed in on them. He was losing men at an alarming rate; he himself was shot through the hip. Matheson then realised it was not feasible to send his other two platoons to reinforce Rudall, so he ordered him to withdraw. Rudall, a courageous officer, insisted on staying with Matheson until the last of his wounded had been evacuated to an American medical post located in the position occupied by 'C' Company, I/128th Regiment. Only after that did he make his own way for medical help at the American dressing station.[12]

The Japanese were by now on full alert, and at 11 pm, those still in the dispersal bays at the head of the strip unleashed their third counterattack over the next three nights, falling once more on Trevivian's long-suffering few men of 'D' Company, 2/10th Battalion on the right. Nonetheless, Trevivian, with one of Sanderson's platoons temporarily assigned to reinforce his depleted company, repulsed the enemy attack. However, roving bands of Japanese attempted to fight their way through the Allied lines under cover of darkness.[13]

One of these attacks was launched near the end of Old Strip; the Japanese here were supposed to have been cleared out the day before by American troops. That night, they broke into the headquarters area of Clarkson's company, which lay near Matheson's position, attacking in the dark with grenades and bayonets, some yelling, 'Medic, Medic', which was the call used by American wounded. Several men who were asleep in the CP area were bayoneted, and other Americans, mostly without weapons, were killed in hand-to-hand encounters. By the time the Japanese were driven out, they had killed 15 men and wounded 12, including Lieutenant Foss from 'C' Company. This was the company's fifth commander in five weeks since the fighting began. Because Foss was the company's only remaining officer, Lieutenant Sheldon Dannelly, commanding officer of 'A' Company, I/128th Regiment,

CHAPTER 49

which was on their right, took over command of 'C' Company. Only five of the raiding Japanese were killed. In this attack, the Japanese also killed Lieutenant John Rudall and several of his wounded men at the American medical post.[14]

During this incident, FOO Lieutenant William Marr received a request for artillery support to suppress what was thought to be a Japanese counterattack, as recorded in the 2/5th Field Regiment war diary: 'Counterattacks were put in by the enemy. Mr Marr called for DF tasks. After firing 13 rounds the order to stop was received. This order came through an American liaison officer, but the source of its origin could not be traced. During the night, infiltration was done by the Japs in the part of the line held by American troops. Several casualties were caused but no deep penetration was made. All communications with C Coy 2/10 Bn on the extreme left failed during the night. Several more tanks arrived'.[15]

* * *

Meanwhile, Major Norman Moss commanding 'X' Squadron, 2/6th Armoured Regiment, attended a conference at 18th Brigade Headquarters that day where the plan of the next day's attack was outlined. Soon after, he sent some of his officers from the Cape Endaiadere area to the area south of Old Strip. Here they conducted a reconnaissance of the terrain and vegetation, reporting back that the area was suitable for tank operations.[16]

By now, Old Strip was firmly in Allied hands; with Warren Force within easy striking distance of Giropa Point. This position now represented the last enemy stronghold on Warren front. The next stage was to take the point and swing back east to clear the area between it and Simemi Creek. Once this phase was accomplished, it would put the entire shore between Giropa Point and Cape Endaiadere in Allied hands – Brigadier Wootten was keen to finish the job.[17]

* * *

BLOODY BUNA

Japanese medic Yokoyama Yoriichi, at Warren front, distinctly recalled the events of 28 December, as he was seriously wounded by an Australian soldier, but he would ultimately admit that it saved his life:

> The next event I remember was on 28 December 1942. Since I had nothing to do, I was just sitting down, wondering about food and my home town. I felt there was something in front of my hole, so I looked around. Then I realised there was an Australian soldier peeking from behind a tree.
>
> I was surprised. If I hadn't sensed something was up, I would have died there. I took the rifle next to me and tried to shoot him, even though I knew I was, being a medic, not very capable with a rifle. When I put the gun to my shoulder and shot, he hid behind the tree. We both fired at each other at least three times, then I saw a red flame from his gun flash towards me. I had previously thought I could easily sacrifice my life, but now I was scared. What you think before the event, and when it actually happens, are two totally different things.
>
> I felt like someone from the back punched me in the head, and I put my hand onto my cheek. Nothing was there and four of my fingers went into my mouth. Then I realised I'd been shot in the face. I lay there vacantly thinking my life was going to end there at Buna. The wound kept bleeding and I had nothing to stop it. Odd thoughts came to me. I wondered if it was payday back home at my old work, or if I should shout banzai, and other silly stuff.
>
> I didn't know it then, but that Australian soldier who shot me was sniped and killed by my friend. A soldier from another position came to see if I was all right and I heard his voice from a distance saying, 'Yokoyama is dead, shot in the face.' It made me want to say, 'I'm still alive!' but I couldn't. The blood was flowing fast, and I had to patch up the wound as soon as

CHAPTER 49

possible, but I couldn't find anything. Fortunately, I found a bandage from the dead enemy soldier and was able to treat my injury with it. That stopped the bleeding and saved my life.

I was supposed to have hatred towards the Australian who shot me, but I felt rather thankful to him for leaving me the bandage.

Some maggots started to crawl in the wound because I didn't have anything to clean it with. I tried to get rid of the maggots until a veteran told me the maggots would actually cure my wound without suppurating. He said to me, 'Because of the maggots and the dead Australian soldier, you are still alive and talking to us now.'[18]

* * *

Meanwhile, to the west at the Urbana front, Lieutenant General Eichelberger, had a rough sleep:

At 2 am a conference took place in my tent. We heard the reports, and they were grave all right. Our troops, if the reports were to be credited, were suffering badly from battle shock and had become incapable of advance. A number of my senior officers were convinced the situation was desperate .... There was no way to evacuate our units. Could I get reinforcements? I decided to sleep an hour or so and then go forward to discover the truth for myself. Tossing on my cot, there in the tropical darkness, I remembered my conversation with General MacArthur three weeks before on the veranda at Port Moresby. At one point he had turned to me with the memory of Bataan in his eyes and a bitter query on his lips.

'Must I always,' he demanded, 'lead a forlorn hope?'

Was Buna, I asked myself, to be an American military disaster? Were the sacrifices represented by the rude crosses in Buna

Cemetery to have been made in vain?

Daylight is good medicine for the fears of darkness. When I reached the Urbana command post, Bill Bowen was already receiving telephone messages from such line commanders as Colonel Howe and Major Schroeder. The tenor of all messages was the same: the military situation was not desperate; it was encouraging. The field commanders were confident of attaining the beach – and a little more than 24 hours later they did. Buna Mission was isolated, and final victory became a certainty.[19]

Later that morning, Eichelberger – accompanied by Major General Sutherland, Colonel Frank Bowen, Colonel Gordon Rogers, and Colonel Horace Harding – arrived at Colonel Grose's Buna Force headquarters at around 1.30 pm. Grose gave them a report of the situation, informing them that he had just taken the III/127th Regiment out of the line for a much-needed rest. An hour later, without discussing the matter with Grose, Eichelberger ordered this battalion to be split into two elements, with each to launch an immediate attack against Buna Mission (Government Station). One element was to advance on the mission from the Musita Island by way of the north bridge. The other, starting from the southern side of the island, was to move upon it in five assault boats, which had reached the front the day before.[20]

Eichelberger and Grose had previously discussed this plan days before, but Grose had failed to work out any details. Grose recalled that he was startled by the sudden order to commit the exhausted men of this battalion to the attack. Aside from the weariness of his troops, there was another even greater difficulty. The Japanese had a line of bunkers just off the northern end of the bridge, and the bridge itself, a narrow, makeshift structure 12 metres long and less than a metre wide, had a five-metre gap at its northern end, the result of a recent barrage. Grose also recalled: 'As soon as I had my thoughts collected, I called for volunteers among the officers present to do certain things.

CHAPTER 49

Colonel Bowen volunteered to get the engineers and collect the necessary timbers to fix the bridge, Colonel Rogers to reconnoitre the position on the island and see that the troops were conducted thereto, and Harding to co-ordinate and control the mortar and artillery fire. I ordered Captain Stephen Hewitt, my S-2 [intelligence officer], to make the reconnaissance of the route the boats were to take … and Captain Leonard Garret, my S-3 [operations officer], to arrange for and co-ordinate the fires of Company H from the island and the troops on the finger, both of which were to fire on the mission preceding the attack'.[21] This 'village finger' was a narrow spit of land projecting from the vicinity of Buna Village to the mouth of Entrance Creek.

Grose quickly worked out the details. To suppress the Japanese positions covering the crossing, a 15-minute artillery and mortar barrage was arranged. Under cover of the barrage, the five assault boats would round the eastern side of the island, with the troops storming ashore at the northern end of the bridge. Once landed, these men were to establish a beachhead while the main assault crossed the bridge itself. In their wake would be a volunteer party tasked to span the bridge with stout planks across the gap in the bridge decking.[22]

Guided by directions given from Hewitt from his reconnaissance, 40 men of 'K' Company, III/127th Regiment were ordered to round the eastern end of the island under the cover of the barrage, in the five assault boats. They were to land east of the bridge and establish a bridgehead. Supported by fire from 'H' Company, II/127th Regiment on the island, and from a platoon of 'E' Company, II/127th Regiment at the tip of the village finger, they were to assault the Japanese with fire as a decoy, while the bridge was repaired. As soon as the planks were down, the rest of 'K' Company would rush across in single file, followed by the men of 'I' and 'L' companies, III/127th Regiment. When all three companies were across, they would attack north, in concert with Major Edmund Schroeder and his men on the coast, who would attack from the south-east.[23]

However, all did not go to plan.

At 5.20 pm, the barrage began to fall. With this, Lieutenant Clarence Riggs of the III/127th Regiment's Ammunition and Pioneer Platoon, commanding the assault boats, quickly moved them into position in some heavy foliage off the southern side of the island. The rest of the battalion, guided by Rogers, began moving forward to the bridge area from the centre of Musita Island. These men, having only just been told that they were to be given a rest, were now ordered to support the assault. Rogers, unfortunately, was unable to get them into position south of the bridge until the first salvo of the artillery preparation hit the mission.[24]

It was now 5.20 pm as the barrage commenced, and the boats pushed into the creek. The troops had been misdirected by Hewitt, however, and instead of going around the island and landing on the east side of Entrance Creek, they tried to land on what was soon called the 'mission finger' spit. The platoon of 'E' Company on the village finger mistook them for the Japanese and opened fire on them, as did the Japanese. Lieutenant Riggs' boat was up front and was swamped and quickly sank, and although Riggs could not swim, he reached shore and managed to stop the friendly fire. Staff Sergeant Milan Miljativich now took command of the boats and tried to drive the attack home, but the remaining boats were in mid-stream when the barrage lifted, and they were caught in the open. Miljativich's boat was sunk, and the other four boats washed back to the American side. Staff Sergeant Milan Miljativich was later awarded the DSC for his actions that day.[25]

Meanwhile, the assault from the bridge was underway. Amid heavy fire from the opposite shore, the six men who had volunteered to repair the bridge successfully dropped the three timbers in place. These men were privates Arthur Melanson and Karl Wittelberger, Technicians Fifth Grade Charles Gray and Bart McDonough of 'A' Company, 114th Engineer Battalion, and privates Elmer Hangartner and Edward Squires of 'H' Company, 127th Infantry. As soon as the timbers were in place, the men of 'K' Company started crossing. Scarcely had the

CHAPTER 49

first two men reached the northern end of the bridge, when the newly laid planks fell into the stream. Now, Private Wittelberger was hit and killed by Japanese fire; the other five volunteers managed to escape. Of the two men who had had been thrown into the water when the bridge partially collapsed, one was wounded, and neither could swim – both were now stranded on the opposite bank. They were, however, rescued the next night by Lieutenant William Bragg and three of his men who swam across the creek and brought them in, under cover of darkness.[26]

* * *

Captain Yasuda Yoshitatsu, whose *5th Yokosuka*, *5th Sasebo* (*SNLP*), and supporting naval pioneer troops had held the critical position at the Triangle, sent his final telegram to Rabaul from Buna: 'The garrison is being gradually destroyed by concentrated enemy fire. Our troops repeatedly mount counterattacks, often inflicting heavy casualties on the Allies in hand-to-hand combat. Our assessment of the overall situation is that we will be able to hold the garrison until tomorrow morning. On reflection, in over 40 days of battle, all the men, whether Navy personnel or labourers, have given all that could be asked of them. Our gratitude to our commanders and the support of Navy air and surface forces is boundless. We pray for the prosperity of our imperial land far away, and for lasting success in battle for all'.[27] After sending this message, the telegraph machine was destroyed, and the codebook burned.[28]

Meanwhile, Lieutenant General Hatazo Adachi, commanding the *18th Army*, ordered Buna to be evacuated: 'Withdraw from Buna, assemble at north Giruwa, and hold that position'.[29] Its defenders were to fight their way to Giruwa at Sanananda with the help of the special force being gathered by Colonel Yazawa Kiyoshi, commander of the *41st Infantry Regiment*. This force was now tasked with a rescue mission to reach Buna Mission from Giruwa by way of the beach and attack the Allied left flank. After cutting his way through to the beleaguered Japanese Army and Navy troops holding the mission, he was to withdraw with them to Giruwa.[30]

It was a desperate plan, but not necessarily an impracticable one. The Japanese must have known – from clashing with Lieutenant Louis Chagnon, and his 52 men positioned south-east of Tarakena – that the American flank covering Buna was mostly undefended. They may have thought that Yazawa and his men might still save the defenders of Buna Mission, only three kilometres from Tarakena by beach, by launching a sudden surprise attack, advancing swiftly, and making a quick withdrawal.[31]

* * *

Further inland and along the coast west of Buna, reports were coming in from the Australian officers and Australian and Papuans NCOs commanding the Papuan Infantry Battalion (PIB), who were patrolling the outer beachhead sectors, that small groups of Japanese were using inland tracks and rivers to escape from the Buna area. The PIB patrols and attachments scattered throughout the area were advised by the only means of communication – runners – to be prepared to encounter and decimate these parties of escapees.[32]

PART 4
BUNA BEACHHEAD FALLS

50

'... FAIRLY TRAUMATIC EXPERIENCE TO SEE THE DEAD AND DECAYING BODIES'

On 29 December, Warren Force was now ready to conduct phase three of Wootten's plan: the capture of the coastal area from the western bank of the mouth of Simemi Creek through to Giropa Point itself, and their surrounding defences. Urbana Force was already enveloping Buna Mission (Government Station)along the newly established corridor from Entrance Creek to the coast the reduction of the Japanese positions on the Buna side of Girua River was finally about to commence. The enemy at Buna was heavily outnumbered and almost surrounded, but they were fighting stubbornly. The Japanese would be cleared from their remaining positions at Buna, only after some of the bitterest fighting of the campaign.[1]

* * *

Brigadier George Wootten devoted the morning to regrouping and reorganising his force. The men of 'A' Company, 2/10th Battalion moved to the left flank and took up a position on the right of 'C' Company, representing the far left as the main assault company. The men of 'B/D' Company were on the far right, covering the flank. The Americans of 'A' and 'C' companies, I/128th Regiment, and 'C' Company, I/126th Regiment, with 'A' Company, I/126th Regiment in support, were in the centre of the line. In reserve were the men of

'B' Company, I/126th Regiment, 'B' Company, I/128th Regiment, and a composite company of the 2/9th Battalion.[2]

Major William Hall was informed by Lieutenant Colonel Keith O'Connell that he and the exhausted and battle-weary Australian gunners of the 2/1st and 2/5th field regiments would soon be transferred to support the fighting raging around Sanananda, as there were now few viable targets for them at Buna. Indeed, many of the guns, including Carson's gun, were in serious need of maintenance, with many leaking oil – this would see many of the guns remain out of action for the next few days.[3]

That morning, Wootten met with Lieutenant Colonel James Dobbs, commanding the 2/10th Battalion, along with Major Norman Moss, commanding 'X' Squadron, 2/6th Armoured Regiment, on New Strip. Wootten was critical of the efforts of Dobbs and his battalion. As recorded by the Australian official historian, Dobbs was 'sick, worn with the strain, heartbroken over the loss of so many of his men, only his courage sustaining him. There was heat in some of their exchanges until Dobbs finally received Wootten's orders for the afternoon'.[4] The adjutant of the battalion, 27-year-old Captain Theodore Schmedje, from Wonthaggi in Victoria, recalled the encounter: 'Poor old Dobbsy! I kept saying, "Colonel, I can't take this!' And I can remember saying to him, "Brigade's running our operation." I admired him with his illness, the old bugger, and he was standing up to the Brigadier and standing up to the BM [Brigade Major] … he was aggressive towards them. He'd lost too many lives … he knew it. He was happy with the way we'd started but bloody miserable with the way we'd finished'.[5]

Years later, Schmedje also admitted the effect that Buna had on him: 'You've got no idea what it's like to lose blokes like Ifould and Bunny Wilson [Trooper John Wilson] because of these terrible tactical blunders; and this is what I can never forgive brigade for. Nobody's got any idea of tactics … alright, we'll hold the line there but we'll go around their flanks! But get behind them! Then you've got them! It's our operation! I never knew him [Wootten] to interfere like this

CHAPTER 50

.... From then onwards, you'll appreciate that our companies were reduced to platoons. And this broke my heart, I've hated Buna. To think of it ever since ... all those blokes that died. It's tragic, I've never got over it'.[6]

Wootten's plans focused on the use of the balance of the tanks from 'B' Squadron commanded by Major Kenneth Tye, a 36-year-old meter inspector from Sydney. He had arrived with 11 Stuart tanks from Milne Bay over the last few days. Having been warned by Wootten the previous night, Tye now had four of his tanks waiting near the bridge between the strips at 7.30 am that morning. Another seven newly arrived tanks were at New Strip, led by his 2i/C, Captain Roderick May, a 27-year-old engineer from Bathurst in New South Wales.[7]

Wootten informed Dobbs that, Tye's four leading tanks, along with Lieutenant Robert Emson, a 37-year-old insurance agent from Sale in Victoria, commanding 'A' Company, 2/9th Battalion, who had moved around to the bridge area a few days before to protect this area and to act as brigade reserve, were to support his attack. Dobbs was to push north to clear the coconut plantation to the coast between the mouth of Simemi Creek and Giropa Point. The left of the attack would be from the position held by Captain Hugh Matheson and his men of 'C' Company, 2/10th Battalion, with a frontage sufficient to enable the attackers to mass for their attack and to consolidate the newly captured position to repel any attack from either the south-east or the north-west. The guns would lay down shells along the beach running south-east from Giropa Point for ten minutes before the infantry assault. The gunners, would then switch to concentrate on covering the left of the attack. Major Gordon Clarkson and his men of the I/128th Regiment would maintain a rearwards guard as the Australians advanced, facing west, south-west, and south.[8]

As Captain Roger Sanderson and 'A' Company, 2/10th Battalion had moved across to Matheson's right in the early morning hours, Dobbs was going to use these two companies as the spearhead for his attack. To them, he added one of Emson's platoons as a reserve to be used only as a last resort. The murder of the wounded Lieutenant John Rudall and several of his men at the American aid post by marauding Japanese was still fresh, and Matheson had sent out patrols to the wide left to ensure this incident was not repeated. From these reports, he now had a good assessment of the Japanese strength and positions. With 46 men, Matheson waited in the early afternoon for the tanks to come up, while Sanderson, also with 46 men, waited on his right. These men were ready by 2 pm in the stunted bush and kunai, looking towards the remains of the coconut trees, which were now a belt of stumps some 40 metres wide and incorporated into the Japanese strongpoints. However, no tanks arrived. Then the start-time was set for 4 pm.[9]

That hour came and went without the tanks making an appearance. So, it was difficult for the infantry to know what to do, and with his men now targeted with Japanese fire, Dobbs set out to find the tanks. Soon after, one appeared in front of Matheson's position, but even as his men rose to support it, the tank advanced into the belt of stumps and became stuck fast. Not surprisingly, indecision gripped the infantry, and they remained at their jumping offline. It was around 5.30 pm when the remaining three tanks appeared.

Major Norman Moss, having been informed of the situation (possibly from Dobbs), sent out an officer to direct the tanks to their assigned position, at the denuded area in front of, and slightly to the left of Sanderson's position. To make up for lost time, the tanks moved at high speed and came in obliquely across the line of departure. Without waiting for the slower-moving infantry to close in behind them, the tanks moved north without moderating their speed. The infantry now advanced, but because of the speeding tanks, they had to attack independent of them, and the tanks, far in front of the infantry, had to move on the enemy bunkers without infantry support.[10]

On the right, the tanks came to a halt on the edge of the coconut trees, and as they approached the first line of bunkers, the Japanese, with no enemy infantrymen to stop them, were free to retire to their

CHAPTER 50

second bunker line. When the tanks finally discovered what had happened and began working on the second line, the Japanese filtered back into the first line, in plenty of time to fire into the Australian infantrymen who had by then fought their way into the grove.[11]

It was now that the tank commanded by Sergeant John Gollan, a 35-year-old school teacher from Sydney, with 6 Troop, 'B' Squadron, was hit, as recalled by his driver, 21-year-old Trooper Cecil Ganderton from Sydney:

> We were close enough to see the first line of bunkers, that is the crew commander and turret gunner, all I could see was this grass and here the Jap bullets hitting the tank. Our gunner Wal Roberts started plastering the bunkers with the 37 and .30 Browning machine gun.
>
> Keith Baird began mowing the grass with the hull gun and at last I could see the bunkers in front of us. We were going well for about 15 minutes and John [Gollan] told me to move up; at that very moment there was this bang on the turret and bits flying around inside. John fell and landed on top of me with a fatal wound to the forehead.[xxv] I was very lucky to have my tin hat on as the cover on the vision slit John was looking through knocked it off. The reason I had the hat on was to deflect the hot shell cases which were hot enough to blister the skin even though our battle jackets were buttoned to the collar they could get down one's back.
>
> Having nobody to guide me as the turret crew were trying to help John, I immediately started to go in a circle to find the track in the grass where I came in, which I found fairly quickly. After I got away down the track a bit I stopped and opened the driver's flap to let some fresh air in, as I had John's head on my left shoulder, I drove back to the start-line with one hand. I told

---

xxv Sergeant John Gollan died from his wounds on 12 January 1943.

John 'Jack' Mullins [loader and radio operator] to get on the radio and warn the other tanks we had been hit with something heavier than a machine gun, but the hit had put the radio out.

On talking to the other crews that night, Norm Rowland, who was the gunner in the tank to our right, said he saw a flash in the bushes to his left, so he traversed around and let go a couple of 37s. When the area was overrun … we found a 37-mm anti-tank gun with a hole in the shield, a round in the breech and two dead Japs nearby. To this day I feel Norm saved us from getting hit again.[12]

Sanderson and his men of 'A' Company now found themselves stopped while they tried to cross the cleared area, as they encountered strong positions located not more than five metres from the first line of standing palms. To their left, advancing against weaker opposition, Matheson and his men of 'C' Company were still advancing.

Sergeant John Mitchell, a 24-year-old salesman from Wayville in South Australia, leading 13 Platoon, pushed through to the coast, with Sergeant Robert Fee, a 29-year-old labourer from Semaphore in South Australia, who was commanding Rudall's 14 Platoon, covering his right rear and Sergeant George Spencer (who would be awarded the DCM for his actions that day) leading 15 Platoon to his left rear. And yet it was now with Mitchell on his objective; with Fee backing him strongly; with Spencer and his men engaging a Japanese element to Mitchell's left; and with Spencer himself, 'his tall, square figure planted firmly in the open, his square face unafraid, deluging converging Japanese with two-inch mortar fire – the last error was played out'.[13]

Confused tankers now turned their guns against these Australians, forcing them to evacuate the position just captured. Matheson recalled that the tanks 'practically wiped them [Mitchell's men] out'.[14] The tanks also struck down some of Fee's men. Private 'Snowy' Arthur Evans, with 14 Platoon, raced across to one of the tanks and, 'springing

CHAPTER 50

on top of it with fire bursting all round him, hammered against the armour to attract the attention of the crew. But apparently, they did not hear him and went on firing'.[15] It is possible the message below preserved in the 2/6th Armoured Regiment war diary relates to this then unknown friendly fire incident: '1800: Major Tye reports. Tanks in need of ammunition. Tanks appear to have swung too far to right, enemy retreating to South and being shot up. Urgently requires two reserve tanks'.[16]

Private Evans recalled: 'And we moved into the coconut grove, which I was very happy about because we got the protection of the trees, and we sort of came to a halt. The attack stopped. The tanks were still shooting and a chap alongside of me yelled out, "Snow!" he said, "They're shooting our own blokes!" So, I raced out, without thinking of course, and I belted with my Tommy gun on the side of the tank and yelled out to them. It went on … and then I realised that the pinging I could hear was the Jap bullets flying off the tank, they were trying to nail me, so I got the hell out of there fast!'[17]

By 6.30 pm, Matheson shot green Verey lights (the signal for withdrawal) into the darkening sky and brought what remained of his company back to their original positions, with only three men left of the 13 who had started off with Mitchell, and the company was down to 22 men, having started off that morning with 46 men. His 2i/C, Captain Colin Mackie, a 31-year-old nurseryman from Kensington Park in South Australia, was among the killed, while Lieutenant Robert Emson, with 'A' Company, 2/9th Battalion, who was keen to support the attack, had also been killed. Matheson, therefore, now joined forces with Sanderson, who was himself wounded, though he refused to acknowledge it. And by now, darkness had descended.[18]

Private John Kirkmoe, with 15 Platoon, 'C' Company, 2/10th Battalion, who was in this battle, recalled many years later:

> The battle of Buna finally knocked all ideas of religion out of me because I determined in my own mind that if there was a

supreme being that had these great powers that are attributed to that supreme being, how on earth could he allow men to go in and slaughter each other like that? It didn't add up. Nothing added up to me. I thought, 'That's it. That's the finish.' That finished me with religion. [I lost many] mates ... at Buna. My old friend Fred Atkinson. Right at the start of the battle of Buna he got badly hit in the arm and lost his arm. That was very, very upsetting. We lost lots of men there. One of the chaps in the I Section, that's the Intelligence Section, used to come past on a daily basis. He'd be gathering in names of chaps that had been killed. Every time he came and told me someone from 15 Platoon ... had been killed and so many of them were killed from 15 Platoon.[19]

Major Kenneth Tye had gone out ahead of his tanks and was not available to direct operations. Two of his junior officers, Lieutenant Victor McCrohon and Lieutenant Des Heap, a 22-year-old regular soldier from Sydney, who were not suppose to participate in the fighting that day now stepped up and moved forward to help. McCrohon – a veteran of the desert war, and the fighting around the two airstrips at Buna just weeks before – saw the trouble begin and moved on from the replacement area. Heap was described as a 'slim, deceptively mild in normal times, not yet tried in action', and later in the day, he took over a returning tank and rushed it back into the fight.[20] Still on the battleground was the tank that had first appeared before Matheson's company, which remained stuck on the felled timber. Heap failed in salvaging the vehicle but got the crew out and left the field only when it was so dark that he had to walk ahead of his tank to bring it back to Old Strip.[21]

The reason for the late appearance of the tanks was that one or more of them had moved out from the bridge area and become bogged almost immediately, and by 4 pm, no one appeared able to say with certainty where they were in regard to the 11 tanks of 'B' Squadron,

CHAPTER 50

which were then churning around both strips. Major Norman Moss (from the tank replacement area near the bridge) also reported at 3.45 pm that two tanks were at the rendezvous, which had been fixed – two were still somewhere on the way up to that point; two were bogged on the lower end of Old Strip; two were in reserve at the bridge; while three were still at New Strip. A later report from Moss, at 6.25 pm, stated that one tank was in action; two were out of ammunition; one was knocked out; one was unserviceable; one was on its way to the front; two were still bogged down; two others were trying to help them out; while one was still in the reserve area. The chaotic situation was largely due to the inexperience of the tankers, and faulty and insufficient reconnaissance that resulted in the tanks becoming lost.[22]

Another deciding factor in the failure of the attack was the fighting ability of the Japanese. They were too strong for two weak and tired companies, each below half strength. More difficult to explain was the decision to go ahead with the attack after the tanks first failed to arrive, and darkness was fast approaching.

That night, the Japanese – still full of spirit, and true to what they had established as an almost nightly practice during the fighting for Old Strip fighting – launched an attack against the Australian right flank. But Major James Trevivian and his men of 'B/D' Company, 2/10th Battalion, using their two-inch mortar fired flares, bathed the battlefield in a soft light that flooded the startled Japanese when they were only 20 metres from the Australian perimeter. Four Vickers machine guns sited to the left of the company (near the Americans) poured enfilade into the Japanese, blowing 'them into a twisting heap'.[23] The Australian infantrymen also pitched grenades into the mass of dead and dying, while the flares slowly sailed to the ground. The next morning, Trevivian and his men counted 42 dead Japanese.[24]

Meanwhile, Dobbs' battalion was spent, and it was timely that new forces were arriving. Earlier that day, the men of the 2/12th Battalion had left Goodenough Island (replaced there by men of the 7th Brigade from Milne Bay) and had arrived at Oro Bay that night.

Their CO, Lieutenant Colonel Arthur Arnold, a 36-year-old public servant from Kensington Gardens in South Australia, hurried ahead while his officers and men made their way up the coast to Duropa Plantation. At this point, the battalion consisted of 33 officers and 582 men. Arnold, originally an officer of the 2/10th Battalion would arrive at Dobbs' headquarters the next morning, anxious to survey the task he was about to undertake. By 8 pm that night, however, he issued orders to his battalion for their take-over, the following day, of the area around the western end of Old Strip where Sanderson, Matheson and their men of 'A' and 'C' companies, 2/10th Battalion would be relieved.[25] As recorded in the brigade war diary that night: 'It was decided by Bde Comd that 2/10 Aust Inf Bn should now hold the ground already gained and that the fresh Bn – 2/12 Aust Inf Bn – should make a further attack supported by tks'.[26]

* * *

A recent reinforcement to the 2/9th Battalion was 21-year-old Private Bryan Wells, from Ipswich in Queensland, who was sent into the line that day. He recalled years later:

> We arrived in the area of the battalion, and this was my first experience of battle I suppose and maybe it's different in a Unit that goes together into battle but when you come as a reinforcement to a unit that's already in action and you come into a battlefield it's a fairly traumatic experience to see the dead and decaying bodies. Fortunately, most of them were Japanese. They had removed for burial all of our own troops, but the stench is probably something never forgotten in your lifetime coming on it in that situation you know the smell of decaying human flesh is a different smell than other smells that you might experience in your lifetime, however, it was something that we'd volunteered for and something we had to accept. So, we were taken to an area where there was a cookhouse. We were given

CHAPTER 50

a meal of bully beef and carrots and mashed potato I think it was and somebody said to me Corporal Randel will take you to your position.

We were taken up to an area in Giropa Plantation where the battle was taking place and it was a separation between an old airstrip and a new airstrip at Buna and there was a putrid swampy creek that ran up one side of it called Simemi Creek and the part of it where I was taken to was at the mouth of Simemi Creek at the top end of the Giropa Plantation and I was introduced to a couple of fellows there and Tony Randell said these blokes will look after you just do what they tell you. By this time, it was just about dark and over the other side of Simemi Creek was quite a lot of activity with small arms fire and grenades and mortar bursts because the 2/10th Battalion was attacking what they called the Old Buna Strip which was just across this Simemi Creek. However, it settled down through the night and we had a rotation of an hour on and an hour off with your foxhole mate to be on the alert and I don't think I slept much that night.[27]

*　*　*

Meanwhile, at Urbana front, during the dark hours of 28–29 December, the ammunition and pioneer troops of the 127th Regiment had finished digging a one-metre-deep trench across the north-west end of the gardens. Early on 29 December, it went into use as a route by which supplies were brought forward and the wounded were carried back.[28]

During the morning of 29 December, the men who had originally constituted Urbana Force, II/126th Regiment, and the II/128th Regiment went back into the line. The II/126th Regiment, less the GIs at Tarakena and Siwori Village, took up a holding position at the south-east end of the Government Gardens. The regiment war diary records: 'The battalion moved forward into defence positions 500 yards south of Buna Village protecting a front of 400 yards. Their total strength at this time was about 80 men'.[29] Those men of the II/128th Regiment moved into the Triangle to take over its defence. Just after these battalions began moving forward, Lieutenant John Lewis leading 'B' Company, I/127th Regiment moved out from their position just south-east of the mission and pushed forward to the sea in order to establish a 70-metre frontage along the shore.[30]

Close by, Major Edmund Schroeder, still commanding 'A' and 'F' companies, 127th Regiment, had now extended his line from Entrance Creek to the sea, but the troops on Musita Island were still held up by fire from the northern end of the bridge. Just before midnight, a patrol from 'H' Company, II/127th Regiment, however, under Lieutenant Allan Simms, waded across from the village sandspit to the spit projecting from the mission. The patrol remained on the mission side of the creek for 30 minutes – the Japanese had evacuated the position. A plan, therefore, was quickly developed to envelop the mission at dawn on the 30 December.[31]

* * *

That day, Major General Yamagata Tsuyuo arrived at Giruwa and ordered Colonel Yazawa Kiyoshi, commander of the *41st Infantry Regiment*, to push through to Buna, even though his force was still being assembled. At this point, he had around 230 men, most from his Regimental Headquarters, and the *I/170th Regiment*, and *No. 9 Company, III/170th Regiment*. Yazawa anxiously awaited the arrival of the barges, which would ferry his men to Buna Mission.[32]

51

'ENEMY TANKS HAVE ALREADY PENETRATED NEAR UNIT HEADQUARTERS'

Next morning, 30 December, Brigadier Wootten, commanding Warren Force, informed his officers that the area of the coconut plantation that lay between the mouth of Simemi Creek on the right and Giropa Point on the left was to be taken on the first day of 1943. On his right, the Australians of the 2/10th Battalion and Americans of the and III/128th Regiment (Lieutenant Colonel MacNab had brought his men around from the eastern bank of Simemi Creek that day, changing places with elements of the 126th Regiment) were to push through to the coconut plantation in conjunction with the main attack.

After Lieutenant Colonel Arnold, commanding the 2/12th Battalion, had consolidated along the coast covering the extreme left flank, he was to turn south-east through the plantation and exploit back towards Old Strip and the coast. Keen to avoid the confusion of the previous day, Wootten issued detailed orders for Captain Roderick May, who was now commanding 'X' Squadron, 2/6th Armour Regiment; he would command six M3 tanks during the planned attack for the first day of 1943.[1]

There would be full artillery support for the attack, with Major Hall and his battery, 2/5th Field Regiment, firing on registered targets on the beach for ten minutes before the attack, and Sergeant Roderick Carson and his 25-pounder targeting observed targets in the plantation area from first light until the attacking companies crossed their start-line. Lieutenant Colonel James Dobbs and his mortarmen from the 2/10th Battalion would also lay smoke at Arnold's request, and the 2/9th Battalion, from their positions on the eastern end of Simemi Creek, would support the attack with fire along the beach east of Giropa Point.[2]

In reserve would be three additional tanks, along with Lieutenant Victor Thomas, who had taken over 'A' Company, 2/9th Battalion after the death of Lieutenant Robert Emson. This company had just been strengthened with a platoon, commanded by Lieutenant Christopher Tippetts, a 31-year-old truck driver from Boronia in Victoria. Also making up the brigade reserve was a recently arrived company of the 2/10th Battalion consisting of four officers and 74 men who had just arrived. The 2/9th Battalion adjutant recorded some time that day in the unit war diary: 'Received Instn. 087 18 Bde. A Coy under comd 2/10 Bn moved to 285245 [just south of Old Strip]. One Pl under comd. Lieut. Tippetts joined them and with 2 Pls A Coy reorganised as A Coy under Comd Lieut. Thomas and reverted to Bde reserve. Message from 18 Bde MMG, mortar, and arty fire will be restricted to an area south through STRIP PT'.[3]

* * *

Further west, at the Urbana front, Colonel Grose was keen to take advantage of the situation discovered by the men of 'H' Company, II/127th Regiment when hours before they had crossed the shallows from the narrow finger-like spit projecting eastward from Buna Village to the Government Station shore, finding the position empty of Japanese. Grose planned to throw a force across the shallows, simultaneously forcing the passage of the bridge and massing to the south for an attack where Major Edmund Schroeder was now in strength.[4]

Schroeder had by now gathered most of his men of I/127th Regiment at this position, reinforced with elements of II and III

CHAPTER 51

battalions just north of the junction of the coastal and Gardens' tracks, and with Lieutenant John Lewis and his men of 'B' Company, I/127th Regiment, they were closing the gap between the right flank and the sea. In the gardens south of the track, other elements were still clearing out the remaining Japanese isolated among the kunai and on the fringes of the Triangle. Schroeder had been attacking towards the mission, but the Japanese were in strength along the coast, and he had made little progress. There was no cause for concern, however, for Schroeder's position was secure.[5]

Directly opposing Buna Mission were Schroeder and his command consisting of 'A' and 'F' companies 127th Regiment, along with 'K' and 'L' companies (III/127th Regiment). Elements of 'M' Company (III/127th Regiment) and 'B' Company (I/127th Regiment) in platoon strength were in place in the gardens on both sides of the corridor, while 'C' Company (I/127th Regiment) and 'I' Company (III/127th Regiment) were in the centre of the corridor, and 'D' Company (I/127th Regiment) was to the east of it facing Giropa Point. It was clear that the Japanese would not be able to hold onto the coast when the attacks from the village and the Musita Island were launched.[6]

Meanwhile, the main attacking force was preparing to launch their assault. The plan was for 'E' Company (I/127th Regiment) to attack across the shallows. The morale of this company was low after its struggles at the Triangle, and it was now led by Lieutenant William Bragg, who had previously been with 'H' Company (II/127th Regiment). Bragg, with three of his men, had just days before rescued the two stranded men when the bridge at Musita Island partially collapsed. Bragg now volunteered to lead 'E' Company in the attack.

In close support was 'F' Company (II/128th Regiment), commanded by Captain Jefferson Cronk, who would also cross the shallows between the village and the mission. Bragg and the men of 'E' Company would then turn right and establish a bridgehead. While those of 'F' Company, in support, would follow closely behind and then move north-east along the coast directly on the mission, as soon as 'E' Company had knocked out the bunkers and the bridge was repaired. Meanwhile, 'H' and 'G' companies (both with the II/128th Regiment) would cross over from the island to the right of 'F' Company (II/127th Regiment) along the coast and attack.

At this time, Major Edmund Schroeder and his force of 'A' and 'F' companies (127th Regiment) would move on the mission from the south-east. This would result in a double envelopment of the mission, with separate columns converging upon it simultaneously from the front and both flanks. This final, multi-pronged attack was to begin at dawn the following morning.[7]

* * *

At the Japanese Giruwa position at the Sanananda beachhead west of Buna, the commanders there were still unaware of the desperate situation playing itself out at Buna. The first information they had of its imminent fall was from two swimmers who each carried with them messages from the Buna sector headquarters. The message stated: 'Enemy tanks have already penetrated near unit headquarters, and fierce fighting has developed. Numbers are down to around 250 and food is scarce. They will be able to hold out for only a short time longer'.[8]

52

'TODAY, WE ARE MOVING ON BUNA MISSION FROM BOTH DIRECTIONS ...'

During the morning of 31 December 1942, the two left companies of the 2/10th Battalion fell back as Lieutenant Colonel Arnold and his men of the 2/12th Battalion came forward. Japanese snipers picked off five of the fresh troops who exposed themselves as they moved into position. Intermittently, clusters of Japanese light mortar-bombs also fell among them. In Arnold's right forward position, the CO had Captain Colin Kirk, a 27-year-old clerk from Toowoomba in Queensland, and his men of 'B' Company, along with Major Keith Gategood, a 37-year-old salesman from New Farm in Queensland, and his men of 'C' Company in support. On the left of the 400-metre line, Captain Alexander Murray, a 35-year-old farmer from Kew in Victoria, leading 'A' Company, was forward with Captain Charles Ivey, a 29-year-old orchardist from Cygnet in Tasmania, and 'D' Company supporting. The objective of the support companies was to kill small Japanese parties screening the strongpoints from isolated defensive positions.[1]

By evening, the battalions were in position with the 2/12th Battalion on the left, the III/128th Regiment in the centre, and the 2/10th Battalion on the right. The 2/12th Battalion and the III/128th Regiment were on an 1100-metre east-west front facing the coast. The 2/10th Battalion, tasked with a holding action, was drawn across the head of Old Strip on a 500-metre front at right angles to them; the battalion's left was against the III/128th Regiment, and its right on Simemi Creek. Major Gordon Clarkson and his men of the I/128th Regiment were in support of the 2/12th Battalion to their left rear, while 'A' Company, 2/9th Battalion was held in reserve.[2]

Sergeant Reginald Spinks, a 28-year-old transport driver from Hobart, with the 2/12th Battalion, recalled the anxious wait for the next day's attack:

> We were briefed by 2/10th lads never to expose ourselves, always crouch as low as possible when moving around. Several of our men were wounded or KIA before the take-over was complete. Lt Hugh Geizendanner contacted me on dusk and advised me that the CO had notified him that he was to join BHQ for the attack and I was given charge of the [headquarters] commandos. Watchers were set as we settled down for Zero Hour. We were in the BHQ area with our orders coming directly from the CO. During the long wait men spoke in whispers. One could feel togetherness, mateship and fellowship that existed between each of the men. Animosity, ill-feeling and other petty trivial things had disappeared from their minds. Many of us were married on arriving back from the Middle East and naturally our thoughts were of our wives and relations.[3]

With the Battalion Headquarters Company was Private Roland 'Slim' Irwin, a 21-year-old labourer from Toowoomba in Queensland. He recalled that afternoon: 'As we were taking our positions a red-headed Yank said, "Stay with it guys, it will be all over in a fortnight". He didn't know what was to take place [the] next day. The airstrip was overgrown with kunai grass about three feet high [one metre] and as we were to take over without the Japanese being aware of our presence, we couldn't get much of a view of their position except a

CHAPTER 52

lot of shaggy torn-about coconut palms'.[4] Corporal Joseph 'Jinny' Williams[xxvi] with the headquarters commandos also had a chat with one of the American troops that afternoon: 'We took up positions. I was talking to a Yank who told me they had been there for 40 days and still could not take the position. I just said, "Don't worry, we will"'.[5] Williams would be true to his word.

Final orders arrived at the 2/12th Battalion Headquarters at 5 pm: 'Attack to be carried out from present line on bearing of 45 degrees on 400-yard front to beach, with the second phase area GIROPA POINT – SIMEMI CREEK. Attack to be supported by six 13-ton tanks, with three tanks in reserve. Zero, 0800 hours 1 Jan 43'.[6] It was also recorded during the night that harassing fire by the Australian 25-pounders commenced, otherwise it was a quiet night.[7]

The 2/9th Battalion war diary records: 'Quiet day. Sniping only. Several unaccounted-for fires broke out among the coconuts in Jap hands'.[8] The adjutant of the 2/10th Battalion recorded after dark at around 7 pm: 'A & C Coys relieved by 2/12 Bn. C Coy moved to position 200 yards rear of Tin Hut. A Coy moved to rear of D & B coys'.[9]

That day, Sergeant Roderick Carson, still commanding his 25-pounder gun, fired 278 shells into identified Japanese pillbox positions in the coconut plantation area north-west of Old Strip.[10]

* * *

At 3.35 pm, Brigadier Wootten issued his final plans for the next day's attack to capture Giropa Point and the area between it and the mouth of Simemi Creek. The attack would be supported by the mortars of the 2/10th Battalion, the 25-pounders of the Manning and Hall

---

xxvi   Two soldiers with the 2/12th Battalion with the surname Williams are listed as wounded at Buna on 1 January 1943; both are listed as privates. It appears, however, that the likely candidate for 'Jinny' Williams is 26-year-old Private Joseph Williams, from Sydney, because his wounds as listed in his service record closely reflect those suffered by Corporal 'Jinny' Williams, and his Christian name also indicates his nickname could have been 'Jinny'.

troops, and the 4.5-inch howitzers of the Stokes Troop. Of the 11 Stuart tanks now at Buna, six commanded by Captain Roderick May, commanding 'X' Squadron, would be committed to the attack, with another three tanks in reserve to be committed as required.[11]

At dust, Lieutenant Victor McCrohon went out with Sergeant Kenneth McGill, a 24-year-old bank clerk from Sydney, and 27-year-old Corporal Norm Russell, from Merriwa in New South Wales, to take note of the area they would be fighting for the next day. Russell recalled:

> It was fairly dark and suddenly a shell passed overhead and before he [McGill] had time to say 'that was bloody close' it landed fifty yards or so in front of us. The next thing we were confronted by the OP officer of 2/5th Field Regiment who had just begun to range his guns on a huge bunker he'd found. He gave us the choice to stay and lay with him or get out quick. Digger McCrohon, who seemingly and obviously had more faith in 25-pounders than I would at that time, said that we would stay a while and, 'watch just how good you boys are'. The first round had passed over the bunker – he said something back to his guns and then another round came over, missing the bunker but level with it. Then he spoke to the guns again and told us to lie flat down and stay down as three shells arrived in quick succession. When the ground stopped shaking and the dirt and smoke cleared, one end of the bunker and its roof had disappeared. Digger McCrohon calmly thanked him for the exhibition and asked him was he going to do anymore as he still had some more of the area to show us …. We found out later we had witnessed the famous Carson's Gun in action.

> Both Digger McGill and I had known Digger McCrohon since he joined us after serving in the Middle East but after that night and to the end of Giropa Point we agreed he was certainly a cool

CHAPTER 52

customer – very exact in what he wanted and just a bloody good leader.[12]

The next day's fighting would be in two stages. Stage one would see the men of the 2/12th Battalion and the six tanks of 'X' Squadron, with the I/128th Regiment in support attacking north-east to break through to the coast. They were to then turn south-east, completing the encirclement of the Japanese. Stage two would see the men of the 2/12th Battalion herd the encircled Japanese towards the companies advancing on the right and, with their help, destroy them.[13]

That night, while the troops snatched what rest they could, the KPM ship *Bath* and the Australian freighter *Comara* came into Oro Bay with 350 and 500 tons of cargo, respectively, unloaded and then departed before daybreak. The arrival of these ships marked a logistical milestone in the campaign. Since the night of 11–12 December, when the *Karsik* made the first trip to Oro Bay, six freighters making nine individual trips had brought in roughly 4000 tons of cargo. This was more than three times the 1252 tons that the transport aircraft had flown into the 32nd Division during the same period, and 1550 more than the 2450 tons that it was to fly in for the 32nd Division during the entire campaign. Between the freighters and the luggers, an average of 200 tons of cargo was coming into Oro Bay daily and had been since 20 December. The tonnage brought in by the freighters during the 20-day period included 3100 tons of general cargo and an estimated 900 tons of tanks, vehicles, and road building equipment. Supply at Buna had ceased to be a problem, just as the fighting for this beachhead was concluding.[14]

* * *

Meanwhile, at Urbana front, the planned pincer attack against Buna Mission was underway. At 4.30 am, the men of 'E' Company, II/127th Regiment, and 'F' Company, II/128th Regiment, started moving out in single file under the cover of darkness across the shallows between the finger and the mission station. The men of 'E' Company were in the lead, with Lieutenant William Bragg at the head of the column. They were to launch a surprise attack against the Japanese who were opposite the bridge at daybreak. Bragg and 'E' Company gained the spit on the mission side without alerting the enemy and turned right and began to move inland. Just as the leading elements of the company reached the spit, however, some of the men to the rear, unable to resist the temptation, threw grenades into a couple of landing barges stranded on the beach. At once, the whole area broke into an uproar – the beach lit up with Japanese flares, and the Americans were targeted with hand grenades, as well as machinegun and rifle fire.[15]

As described in the American official history: 'The Japanese reaction threw the troops into a panic. Their plight became even worse when Lieutenant Bragg, who in General Eichelberger's words was to have been "the spark plug of the whole affair", was shot in the legs during the first few moments of the firing and, in the confusion of the moment, was reported missing'.[16]

Meanwhile, Colonel Grose was waiting on the village spit to hear news of the attack. He had organised for a telephone to follow behind the attackers to report on their progress. The first information Grose heard on the phone was when the lieutenant, who had taken command after Bragg was wounded, with this the men were 'running to the rear'.[17] Grose recalled: 'I told the man to stop them and send them back. He replied that he couldn't because they were already past him. Then the man said: "The whole company is following them". So, I placed myself on the trail over which I knew they would have to come, and pistol in hand, I stopped the lieutenant and all those following him. I directed the lieutenant to return, and he said he couldn't. I then asked him if he knew what that meant, and he said he did. The first sergeant was wounded, and I therefore let him proceed to the dressing station. I designated a sergeant nearby to take the men back and he did so. I then sent the lieutenant to the rear in arrest and under guard'.[18]

Although 'E' Company passed through the men of 'F' Company,

CHAPTER 52

Captain Jefferson Cronk and his men were not affected by the disorganisation of 'E' Company. Cronk recalled Grose was as 'calm and collected as if he were on the drill field'.[19] Cronk and his men moved forward steadily and, by the time they were finally rejoined by 'E' Company, 'F' Company had established a strong position on the spit and were holding their own. Grose now ordered Cronk to take command of 'E' Company, and the two companies began fighting their way towards the bunkers in the area north of the bridge. They then met stiff resistance, and Cronk could report only a small advance, as darkness had set in. However, he hoped to do better the next day.[20] The American official historian, Samuel Milner, recorded: 'The steadiness under fire of Captain Cronk's company had saved the day. General Eichelberger finally had his long-sought toehold on the mission, and Captain Yasuda's troops, under attack for the first time from two directions, faced annihilation'.[21]

Indeed, while Captain Yasuda Yoshitatsu had received some rations and ammunition by submarine on the night of 25 December and continued to fight stoutly for the mission with his remaining troops, he must have known the writing was on the wall. The fighting was particularly bitter along the coast south-east of the mission and in the swamp north of the gardens, where elements of 'C' Company were cleaning out pockets of Japanese resistance. Meanwhile, 'E', 'F' and 'H' companies, II/126th Infantry, under Captain John Sullivan, had advanced 300 metres in the area east of the right fork of the Triangle, capturing the gardens. The day's gains along the coast and in the swamp north of the gardens were, however, overall disappointing in relation to expectations.[22]

During the fighting that day, privates Earl Johnson and Herman Bender, 'M' Company, III/127th Regiment, distinguished themselves in the fighting along the coast. Johnson was killed while covering the withdrawal of his squad from a dangerously advanced and exposed position where it had been pinned. Close by, Bender was also killed when dashing across open ground swept with Japanese fire to find the

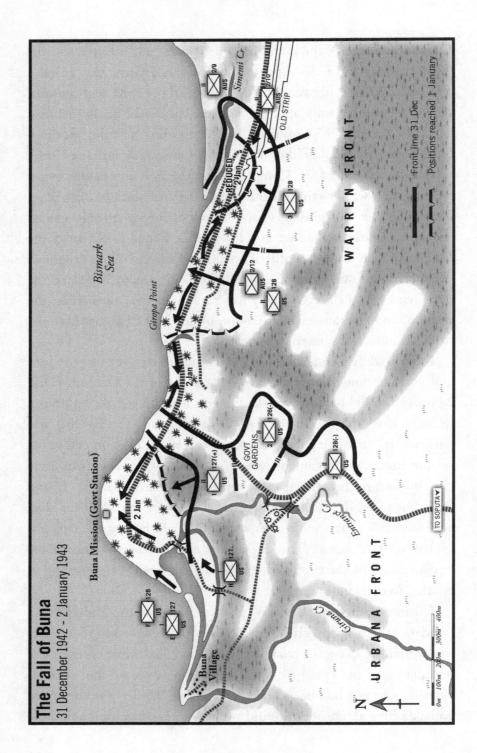

CHAPTER 52

flank of a neighbouring unit with which all contact had been lost. Both privates were posthumously awarded the DSC.[23]

The Japanese were resisting stubbornly, but they were nearing the end of their ability to defend their positions with any strength. The men of Urbana and Warren forces were increasing converging. Not only were the two forces moving closer together, but a patrol of the II/126th Regiment made contact that morning with a patrol of Warren Force at the south-west end of the gardens.[24]

As the men of Warren Force were to mount their final attack against Giropa Point the next morning, 'B' Company, I/127th Regiment was ordered to attack eastward in support to link up with Warren Force and assist it in the expected mopping-up operations. Eichelberger wrote to Major General Sutherland that night that he hoped the attack would 'go through in fine shape. If it did, it will then be just a matter of cleaning up Buna Mission'.[25] Eichelberger also described the situation at this point:

> On the right, the Australians with their tanks have moved up to the mouth of Simemi Creek, [and] the entire area of the two strips is in our hands. Martin's men have extended to the left from the Old Strip for several hundred yards so that the forces of the Urbana and Warren fronts are now only about 600 yards apart. On the left, we have established a corridor between Giropa Point and Buna Mission and have moved enough men in there to make it hold. The famous Triangle, which held us up so long, was finally taken, and our men also occupy the island south of Buna Village. Today, we are moving on Buna Mission from both directions, and I sincerely hope we will be able to knock it off.[26]

53

'... EASY PICKING WITH MY TOMMY GUN AND HAND GRENADES'

At Buna, New Year's Day 1943 was clear and fine with an oblique wind blowing, which ruled out the use of smoke to help cover the attack set for 8 am. Prior to the assault, a heavy artillery and mortar bombardment would commence. On the left at the Warren front, the Australians of the 2/12th Battalion, and six of the ten tanks still serviceable at Buna, were preparing to cut north-east through the plantation towards the coast near Giropa Point. Two tank troops would lead the attack, each consisting of three Stuart tanks: one led by Lieutenant Grant Curtiss, and the other by 26-year-old Lieutenant Max Schoeffel, from Liverpool in New South Wales. The Americans of the I/128th Regiment were preparing to support the Australian attack. Facing north, 'I', 'K' and 'L' companies, III/128th Regiment, were to take the isolated pockets of resistance located in parts of the dispersal bays at the north-west end of Old Strip from the south, and the 2/10 Battalion, facing west, would remain in position on Old Strip.[1]

Lieutenant Colonel Arnold, commanding the 2/12th Battalion, ordered the advance as the zero hour ticked over. One man in each section was carrying a prepared demolition charge made of one kilogram of ammonal, a grenade, and a piece of instantaneous fuse. Captain Roderick May, in the command tank could communicate with the other tanks using a wireless, was with Arnold at the Battalion Headquarters. As planned, Arnold deployed his six tanks in front of

CHAPTER 53

the infantry with the three others kept under Arnold's command. This would enable him to keep the momentum with any vehicle coming back for ammunition or fuel replenishment, replaced immediately by another going forward in its place. The artillery had already prepared the way forward, and machine gunners were firing into the top of the palms to take out the Japanese snipers.[2]

The 2/12th Battalion adjutant recorded the situation just before the men advanced: 'Weather fine & clear & Bn ready to attack with strength of 33 officers, 610 O/Rs. All tks were in position on SL [start-line] by 0730 hrs. Initial barrage of 25 pdrs firing point blank, 3" mortars and 12 MMGs fired at 0745 hrs. Bn attacked 0800 hrs close support of tks'.[3] A mortar man with the battalion recalled: 'The firing we did do was at a dangerous low range, 250 yards [metres] which is the laid down minimum range, but our bombs were landing much shorter than that. I think it was one hundred yards'.[4]

The tanks were the first to cross the open ground. When they reached the still-standing palm trees, the infantry closed on them, protecting the rear and flanks of the armour, which were moving at walking pace. Captain May had his tanks moving with controlled precision as they first took on the Japanese who, from pits, screened the strong posts, and then they battered at the loopholes and doors before the attacking infantrymen rushed them with their ammonal charges.[5] Private Roland Irwin with the battalion recalled: 'Anyone who was there knows what a hell the first 20 minutes were. Men were falling even before they had got halfway across the airstrip. But the attack went on with heavy casualties.[6]

Lieutenant Colonel MacNab recalled the demolition of the Japanese bunkers: 'A tank would knock a corner off the enemy bunker, and while this hole was "buttoned up" by automatic or rifle fire, a volunteer would creep up to the side of the bunker, heave in the bomb, and duck. The explosion would rock the bunker and stupefy the Japanese inside. Then a can of Jap aviation gasoline would be tossed in, ignited by tracers, and the bunker would be burned out'.[7] The 'bomb' consisted of a mixture of ammonium, powdered aluminium, and charcoal, and was noted for its powerful explosive force.[8]

* * *

On the left flank of the attack, Captain Alexander Murray, leading 'A' Company, and Captain Charles Ivey, commanding 'D' Company, had gone forward. With 'A' Company, was Corporal Athol Summers, a 25-year-old labourer from Newtown in Tasmania. He recalled:

> Because of Major Boucher's illness Captain Alec Murray was our Company Commander. Lieutenant Tim Logan our 9 Platoon Commander, Sgt Hosier 9 Pl Sgt, myself 9 Section … Leader.
>
> The tank 9 Pl was following on the left flank broke down, so the platoon just kept going. Enemy fire was hot, causing casualties. Micky Phillips was calling for me, I got to him to find he had been wounded and was unable to make his way back to the RAP.[xxvii] I dressed his wounds, and stuck his rifle in the ground, so that the stretcher-bearers could find him, then set out again.
>
> I now ran across George Ling, wounded and leaning up against a tree. Had a look at his wound and cheered him up by telling him his wound was a clean one. It had gone clean through his shoulder. He was able to make his own way back to the RAP. Sergeant Hosier had been wounded, and Sergeant Cocky Mayne had taken his place.
>
> We reached the beachfront but had suffered heavy casualties …. 8 Platoon had suffered terribly.[9]

Private Kevin Hill, a 23-year-old orchardist from Hobart in Tasmania, was a member of 8 Platoon; he recalled the fighting on this flank: '8 Platoon under Lieut. [Louis] Jim Smith, and Sgt Harry Clayton was

---

[xxvii] Private Michael Phillips, a 28-year-old clerk from Newtown in Tasmania, is listed as dying from his wounds on 7 January 1943.

CHAPTER 53

wounded after ten minutes.[xxviii] Corporal Don McCulloch ran to him to help. Captain Alec Murray said, "Keep pushing forward and tell Tim to take over (meaning Lieut. Tim Logan). Private Hill and his No 2, Jaynes[xxix], were also wounded before much longer. Many great mates and soldiers were killed before the objective was taken. Some being: D Noble. C Rothall, E Dennis, Harris, Thompson[xxx], so the list goes on'.[10]

It was now that Captain Alexander Murray was killed, while two platoon commanders, lieutenants Louis Smith, a 22-year-old accountant from Hobart, with 8 Platoon, and Duncan Clarke, a 27-year-old insurance manager from Cairns in Queensland, with 7 Platoon were wounded. Even so, Clarke took over 'A' Company on Murray's death.[11] Lieutenant Clarke recalled: 'Captain Murray didn't last long. He was killed soon after we started. The enemy fire was sustained and quite heavy, but what I did notice was that it was damn accurate, as though they were experienced troops, and they weren't wasting ammunition. It soon became apparent that there were a lot of snipers around the trees ... they had a magnificent field of fire'.[12]

Meanwhile, to the left, Captain Ivey and his men of 'D' Company were also taking casualties. His 2i/C, Lieutenant Colin Elphinstone, a 35-year-old farmer from Myalla in Tasmania, and Lieutenant Silcock, a 30-year-old regular soldier from Gymea Bay in New South Wales, a platoon commander, were both wounded along with several of their men.[13]

Vickers machine gunner with the battalion, Private Geoff Lowe, a 23-year-old shop assistant from Launceston in Tasmania, was

---

[xxviii] Sergeant Harry Clayton, a 31-year-old labourer from Dover in Tasmania, is listed as dying from his wounds on 25 January 1943.

[xxix] Thirty-year-old, Private Leslie Jaynes, from North Tamborine in Queensland, is listed as killed-in-action on 1 January 1943.

[xxx] Private Douglas Noble, a 27-year-old tramway employee from Hobart; Corporal Clement Rothall, a 29-year-old labourer from Burns Creek; Private Eldon Dennis, a 24-year-old labourer from Hobart; Private John Harris, a 29-year-old labourer from Launceston – all in Tasmania; and Corporal Bruce Thompson, a 34-year-old manager from Sydney, are all listed as killed-in-action on 1 January 1943.

supporting the advance of 'A' and 'D' companies and recalled the deadly effect of the Japanese snipers, one of who killed Captain Murray:

> I was in Lieutenant Mike Steddy's machinegun platoon. On that morning, six of the Vickers guns were supporting the left flank, and six were supporting the right flank. We had a sergeant responsible for each set of three guns.
>
> Mike was with the six guns supporting the left flank of the advance which was the responsibility of A and D companies. Once A Company had got across [Old Strip], Mike ordered us to go too, with three guns going first, whilst the others covered [them], and then the second group to cross, being covered by the group already across.
>
> I was responsible for one of the guns in the first set, and Charlie Knight was responsible for the second gun. Mike had come across with us. We were beside one of the bunker mounds just inside the plantation, when Charlie went on to the mound to check out where best to place his gun to provide a clear field of fire in support of the advancing sections. Charlie slumped back dead, having been shot in the centre of the forehead by a sniper's bullet.[xxxi]
>
> Mike then ordered me to move my gun down to the left edge of the bunker. His wish was for me to give fire support to our men, whilst he would move to the right edge of the bunker and see if he could locate where the enemy sniper fire was coming from.
>
> No sooner had he done this, then he too succumbed to a sniper's bullet in the centre of the forehead. He fell down and lay sort of propped up on the edge of the bunker near Charlies [sic] partly

---

[xxxi] Private Charles Knight, a 25-year-old truck driver from Brighton in Tasmania, is listed as killed-in-action on 1 January 1943.

CHAPTER 53

assembled gun.[xxxii] His head was facing back towards the strip, in the direction from which we had advanced. A great man and a great leader had been lost to us.

Shortly afterwards, Private Brian Shone, a tall man from New Norfolk in Tasmania, was coming back with Private Bluey Sawford from delivering a message to the A Company commander Alex Murray. They also passed through the general area in which the sniper was operating and Shone was killed.[xxxiii]

This further incident worried Captain Murray, who came back to where we were and asked us to concentrate again on raking the palms above to see if we could get this elusive sniper. A short time after this, Captain Murray was also killed by presumably this self-same sniper operating in our area.

That was not the end of it, by a long shot. One of the 3" mortar crews came across to provide further impetus to the assault, and mortarmen Tom Davis and Dick Green were also killed by presumably our unknown sniper.[xxxiv] He seemed to be very close to us, because his shots seemed very accurate.[14]

Again, in the thick of the action here, was war photographer George Silk. He captured an imagine of these machine gunners in action that day. Silk recalled:

I'd never seen pictures of a machine gun surrounded by dead gunners, so I just stood quickly up with the open Rolleiflex, with the open finder [and] shot only one picture and [then sat] down again …. That's the one that caused all the fuss. The arm

---

[xxxii] Lieutenant Edwin 'Mike' Steddy, a 28-year-old grazier from Richmond in Queensland, is listed as killed-in-action on 1 January 1943.

[xxxiii] Private Henric Brian Shone, a 26-year-old farmer from New Norfolk in Tasmania, is listed as killed-in-action on 1 January 1943.

[xxxiv] Twenty-four-year-old Private Thomas Davis, from Brighton in Tasmania, is listed as dying from wounds on 3 January 1943; Sergeant Vernon 'Dick' Green, a 23-year-old labourer from Oatlands in Tasmania, is listed as killed-in-action on 1 January 1943.

> is a dead soldier, and they didn't want the picture to be used at all so …. I just got a pair of scissors and cut it off …. I understood that you couldn't use dead bodies, and so I tried to get part of the dead body in, but not the whole thing. I could argue with them that it was only half a dead body; something like that …. Instead of that they [Department of Information] carefully sat there and censored the pictures! …. Said, 'They're not fit and proper pictures! This guy has a mother. You can't publish his picture, what will his mother say? What will she think?' Well, you know, that's what the war was about.[15]

An unknown soldier taking part in the fighting here recalled the continued advance after the death of the company CO, Captain Murray, and a lucky escape by his replacement:

> What struck everybody was the way Lieutenant Clarke led the company. He had to take over when the company commander was killed. There was a whole series of pillboxes in front of us and the Jap fire was pretty hot, but Lieutenant Clarke pulled the company together and led us from one pillbox to another.

> Just before we got to our first objective, I was to the side of him and a little behind him, when I saw a bullet go through his tin hat. Luckily the bullet sort of swerved and only hit him on the side of the head but all the same it dazed him a bit. However, he pulled himself together and went on.

> He was in front all the time and led our attacks on about two dozen pillboxes one after the other. This was one of the toughest spots in the whole show and we found out later that it was the Jap Headquarters. There were about 150 Japs there. I reckon Mr Clarke did a marvellous job.[16]

Lieutenant Clarke recalled the heavy price his men paid in gaining their objective: 'We got to the beach and there I lost the last officer

CHAPTER 53

that I had, Tim Logan ... I had the phone, and I was talking to the old man, when Tim suddenly stood up. And I yelled out, "For Christ's sake get down!" And as I did so, to this day I'm quite convinced that I could actually see the discolouration on the side of his neck as the bullet either hit him or was coming out the other side'.[17] Corporal Athol Summers also recalled the death of Lieutenant Logan:[xxxv] 'We were inspecting a Jap tent when Lieutenant Logan was instantly killed, with a shot through the head'.[18]

The battalion war diary records that soon after the left flank reached the beach, breaking into the Japanese administrative area, their success flair was fired from the beach and was observed exploding in the sky at 8.51 am – Giropa Point had been taken. These men now commenced the next phase by attacking just west towards Giropa Creek, with 'A' Company on the right on the beach and 'D' Company to their left.[19]

With 'D' Company was Platoon Sergeant Frank Millett, a 29-year-old schoolteacher from Charters Towers in Queensland. He also recalled the fighting that day: 'The sight of the 2/12th advancing across that airstrip on New Year's Day on a two-company front was something I will never forget. In spite of the hail of lead thrown at us (88 men went down on the way across) the battalion kept moving and got in close enough to rapidly alter the situation. The morale, skill and teamwork of officers and men were such that it was inevitable the success signal would go up, [and] as soon [as] it did, Giropa Point was ours'.[20]

* * *

Meanwhile, on the right, the enemy strong posts were thickly spread and well manned so that Captain Colin Kirk, commanding 'B' Company, and Major Keith Gategood, leading 'C' Company, struck serious trouble early. Just as they advanced, Gategood was wounded, and his 2i/C, Captain Owen Curtis, a 30-year-old bank official from

---

[xxxv] Lieutenant Talbot 'Tim' Logan, a 29-year-old stockman from Hughenden in Queensland, is listed as killed-in-action on 1 January 1943.

Hobert, took command of the company.[xxxvi] Machinegun fire tore into the attackers, and snipers picked them off. By 9 am, the two companies were out of communication with the rest of the battalion, and for some time, intense fire frustrated all attempts to restore communications. Messages could only be passed to and from by tanks. Arnold sent forward a three-inch mortar team, but well-directed fire also brought this attempt to nothing, with most of the team killed in the advance.[21]

Company Sergeant Major George Harper, a 34-year-old farmer from Home Hill in Queensland, with 'B' Company, recalled:

> We went forward with two platoons and Coy HQ in line, with one platoon coming up in reserve. B Coy men were SUPERB, they kept going forward, and dropping like ninepins. The signaller who was a few yards away from me, was hit in the leg. He shouted to me, 'Take this coil of wire on, or you won't be able to phone back to HQ'. I bent down and picked it up and went to go forward.
>
> There wasn't a soul in sight. Only Captain Kirk trying to get his two-way radio to work. Then he was hit again and killed. It was only then I saw the bunker, which was at least 15 yards long and five feet high. It was made of palm logs and dirt, with grass growing on it. TALK ABOUT CAMOUFLAGE, it was only 100 yards in front of me, and it just merged into the landscape. The hole which they were shooting from was so small, I could hardly see it.
>
> It then started to have a go at me. I was lucky. There was a palm tree handy, and I got behind it. He fired at least a dozen rounds, one hit my boot, the rest were too close for comfort. As I said, I was lucky, he could not quite see me.

[xxxvi] Note the battalion history records that the Australian official history incorrectly states Captain Gategood was wounded later that morning while making efforts to gather the remnants of both companies.

CHAPTER 53

A young lad, I do not think he was more than 18 years, and in his first action was a few yards from me. He sang out, 'Sergeant Major I'm hit. What will I do?' I said, 'You lucky so and so get back out of it.' He said, 'It's my leg.' I said, 'Crawl out then!' But he didn't. Then a few minutes later he said, 'I'm hit through the heart.' I said, 'Don't be silly, you would be dead. GET OUT OF HERE.' He then got up and ran out on two legs (it appeared only the small bone was broken).

That young lad did have a hole in his heart, he lived until eleven o'clock that night. The doctors could not do anything for him.

In the meantime, one of our tanks came along and stood at one end of the bunker. After some time, it turned and started to go away and outran a Jap. I fired a shot at him but missed. He had some sort of bomb which he threw on the back of the tank. The engine caught fire but there was enough power in it to turn back before it went dead. When the tank swung back, it fired many rounds into the bunker. After that there was no more firing from [there] ….

I fired a few rounds at what I thought were Japs sitting on the top of the trench. They didn't move. Then a sniper got to me, and I put my arm out to drag the wire in for more protection, when I got it in the arm.

When I was getting out, I had lost so much blood that it was like a bad fog. I couldn't see very far. Whilst going out luck was with me again. There was a shower of lead passing over my head. If they were firing at me, they should have put their sights down. It made a whispering noise.

However, when I got as far as the bomb crater, where we had spent the night, I was met by two Transport men who were acting as stretcher-bearers. They were Tasmanians; one of them was Alf Clark.[22]

BLOODY BUNA

Stretcher-bearer Private Alfred Clark, a 25-year-old labourer from Hobart, recalled bringing in the wounded sergeant major:

> To get the men back we had to cross a marshy piece of ground, and right in the middle of it was one big clump of bullrushes. What we used to do was, with our casualty, move very quickly to this clump of rushes, by which time we were generally knocked up, rest there, and then tempt fate for the second time [and then] move off at speed across the balance of this comparatively open ground, to the safety of our reserve lines.
>
> George was not exactly a light man to carry, and as the explosive bullet had made a real mess of his wrist, I sought to stabilise his limb for the journey [by] using a stick which immobilised the arm from the shoulder down. Apart from the complication of George wanting to get off the stretcher mid-way (and insisting that we were risking our lives unnecessarily for him), Brian Gill and I managed to get him back to the RAP, without further incident.
>
> At the RAP, Doc Sampson listened to my report as to how I had treated the wound, and [he] indicated that I had done a fairly good job in the circumstances, but said, 'It would have helped if you had chosen a straight [stick], as against [*sic*] [a] bent stick.' My answer was. 'I'm afraid, positioned, as we were in a shell crater, and [with] snipers all around, we didn't have much of a selection from which to choose!'[23]

Close to where Major Harper had been wounded was 34-year-old Lance Corporal Bertie 'Grubby' Allen, from Toowoomba in Queensland, with 'C' Company. He recalled:

> Sergeant Poet Armstrong was rolling a smoke behind a coconut tree when he called, 'Grubby KEEP DOWN that pillbox is lined up on you all'. As he spoke, Cliff Hoskins fell in front of

CHAPTER 53

me as did others.[xxxvii] Next a bullet [hitting] … my helmet broke my rifle butt and grazed my left hand.

I was shocked and stood up and the bullet [went] through my right shoulder [and] put me down, paralysing my right arm. I decided to go back to Dr Sampson so turned on the enemy and was shot in the back which kept me down to 2 pm.

Stretcher-bearers took me back and during my deliriums all I could think of was how could I tell them why I was shot in the back. Good soldiers don't do that.

When I was lying wounded, all my strength deserted me and I was unable to move. My fear was what if the boys had to withdraw, I could not defend myself. But, oddly enough, I could not forget that Poet Armstrong was between me and the Japs. All would be well. He had risked his life in Tobruk going back to enemy lines (which he had raided) to find me. I had between times taken a short route back to the post and he told me what he thought when he eventually found me safe, and here I was now confident he could hold them.[24]

The battalion adjutant recorded the situation at around 9 am: 'B and C coys on the RIGHT flank met very hvy [heavy] opposition (LMG & snipers) – suffered very hvy casualties. By 0900 hrs line comms with this flank were cut. It was impossible to communicate by runners owing to hvy sniping. One tk on this flank was knocked out by a Molotov Cocktail. Attempts were made to re-establish comms with this flank by sending a 108 set … through but … found it impossible to get through owing to sniping. Information was only available through the tks'.[25] The battalion war diary also records: 'Tps followed tanks at 25/35 yds over the open ground but in the close timber were immediately in rear and on flanks of tanks. Tank knocked out by

---

xxxvii Lieutenant Clifford Hoskins, a 33-year-old bank official from Townsville in Queensland, is listed as killed-in-action on 1 January 1943.

Molotov Cocktail occurred when tps were 25 yds away, although fired at by tps the Japanese soldier responsible was able to throw it before being hit. Tanks engaged enemy inf who occupied posns around the pillboxes with MGs and blasted the loopholes and doors with 37-mm cannon'.[26]

By 10.20 am, Kirk had been killed, and all his officers in 'B' Company had been wounded, with several of their men also as casualties. Captain Owen Curtis, now commanding 'C' Company, was the only officer remaining. Indeed, Corporal Alfred Dyne, a 22-year-old labourer from Yandina in Queensland, leading a section from 'C' Company, had advanced with ten men, and in a short time, he was the only one left standing. Later that day, he would take command of the remaining members of the company, finally taking their objective. There were by then just 20 survivors remaining in the whole company. Corporal Dyne was awarded the Military Medal for his actions that day.[27]

Also with 'C' Company was 23-year-old Lance Corporal Frederick 'Tojo' Etchells, from Sydney, who recalled men falling all around him as they pushed forward. He was soon shot in the knee, and each time he tried to move, he would be targeted by a sniper in a tree. Eventually, a tank came along and took out the tree. He then managed to take cover behind a tree where he found one of his men also taking cover, unwounded. The man asked: 'Where's the rest of them, Tojo?' Indignantly, Etchells replied, 'Up the bloody front, where you should be'. The soldier poked his head around the tree and was immediately killed with a shot to the head. He was the sixth man from his section to be killed that day.[28]

Curtis later recalled how grateful the Australians were for the treatment and care supplied to their wounded by American medical units in the field, but he and his mates were not impressed with the American GIs: 'The ancillary caring support provided by the American medical units to our battle casualties were fantastic. Many of our men alive today would not be, had it not been for

CHAPTER 53

their presence in close proximity to the battle area. The fact remains; however, we saw no "combative" American infantry working in close proximity with us for the duration of both the Buna and Sanananda campaigns'.[29]

54

'"... OH, THOSE TWO," SAID THE CO AND SEEMED QUITE AMUSED'

After taking Giropa Point, 'A' Company, commanded by Corporal Athol Summers, renewed their advance west: 'From the beach front we turned left and attacked up the beach towards Buna Mission Station clearing out pillboxes and bunkers as we advanced. Late afternoon found us at a creek [Giropa Creek]. With Buna Mission in sight. The last pillbox for the day was blasted by a tank, with a few Japs still around. Cpl Bill Burey was hit and received a serious wound and was evacuated. We were pulled back a few yards and prepared defensive positions for the night'.[1]

Lieutenant Neil Russell, a 25-year-old clerk from Townsville in Queensland, with 'A' Company, described Sergeant Millett's interaction with an American officer that afternoon: 'Late in the day before Buna Mission was cleared, Frank Millett, the platoon sergeant at the time, said he had been approached by a senior NCO from a US Infantry Regiment which was in reserve nearby. He was wanting to know if they could be given a task. I suggested they take up a protective position on our flank. The American said he would have to confirm with his company officers who were a mile in the rear! They did take up this role and proceeded to blast off with their weapons all night at nothing in particular'.[2]

Australian stretcher-bearer, Private Alfred Clerk – who had earlier brought in among many others that day, the wounded Sergeant Major George Harper – recalled an American GI coming to his

CHAPTER 54

assistance that afternoon: 'The American went to the front end of the stretcher, and then changed his mind, and started to come back along the stretcher, saying that it would be best if I took the front, since I knew where we needed to go to. As he then stooped over the rear ends of the stretcher to pick it up, he collapsed over the wounded occupant, having at that moment been shot in the back by a Japanese sniper. The least I could do later in the day, when I buried [Private Brian] Shone at the base of a small tree, was to bury this GI beside him; in remembrance for his spontaneous assistance in wishing to assist us evacuate our wounded'.[3]

The men of 'D' Company were still to the left of 'A' Company, and here with 17 Platoon was Corporal Roy Rodgers, a 21-year-old shop assistant from Brisbane, who recalled the advance just after 'A' company had taken the key objective:

> After we had advanced about 150 yards [metres] through kunai grass, we turned partly left and advanced approximately in a NW direction towards Giropa Point (we did NOT follow A Coy through towards the beach). We moved towards the lines of Japanese Pillboxes which defined Giropa Point in great depth. We were caught continually under enemy fire from this point on for some hours, however, it was pretty difficult to ascertain what fire was being directed at us, due to the constant noise of the battle, which was concentrated into a relatively small area. The noise of course was coming from our own tanks, and our two-inch and three-inch mortar fire and grenade explosions, plus machine gun, submachine gun and rifle fire, not forgetting the enemy fire ....
>
> I received information from Captain Ivey at D Company Headquarters that accurate enemy fire from Pillboxes slightly to the left of my section's axis of advance was seriously holding up some elements of the Company ....

BLOODY BUNA

Captain Ivey directed me to attempt to make contact with tank commander with a view to having this tank engage the enemy elements with both gun and machinegun fire. I approached the tank from the rear and attempted to draw the attention of the crew by hitting the rear and side of the tank with the butt of my submachine gun. This was unsuccessful ....

With some caution and difficulty, I was able to climb the rear of the tank and was able to make contact with the commander (or gunner) through a small opening (or shutter) in the turret. Because of the noise of battle plus the engine noise of the tank we found voice communication very difficult and at times impossible. I therefore decided to use a combination of hand signals, voice and finally and most importantly, some rough sketches which I hurriedly made on pieces of note pad paper from my note pad which in a section commander I always carried .... I do recall one of the more unpleasant aspects of the operation was that the metal of the tank was pretty bloody hot on hands & body .... I was pretty happy to get the 'thumbs up' from the tank commander and apparently my messages had been received and understood. The tank redirected its fire – both accurate gun and machinegun fire – with most unfavourable results for the enemy. Those elements of the Company that had been held up now continued to move forward.[4]

Still in the thick of the action was photographer George Silk, who at this point took a photograph of Corporal Rodgers on the back of the tank. He recalled: 'It's a pretty little scene! Someone's just been hit here; someone's been hit there; and here's another guy behind a tank shooting .... I mean I was very much aware that this was an amazing position to be in, where you could stand up and take pictures and not get immediately shot! I expected to be shot, because look what's going on'.[5]

CHAPTER 54

One of Silk's colleagues, Fred Folkard, a war correspondent with the *Sunday Sun*, was close by and described to his readers Schoeffel's tank in action at around 11.30 am: 'Lieutenant Max Schoeffel ... said his gunner saw about 30 Japs lying on the top of a "plane dispersal bay". The turret slewed around and from less than 30 yards spouted high explosive shells straight at the enemy. They didn't see those Japs again, especially as a tank coming up on the other side also had a shot at them. When one pillbox became troublesome another tank went around behind and put the spout of its cannon less than five feet [two metres] from the deep entrance hole. Nobody inside could have survived that blast'.[6]

* * *

Earlier, at around noon, Captain Angus Suthers, a 24-year-old engineer from Dover Heights in New South Wales, with elements of the Headquarters Company, had been ordered to advance with a mixed party of men because communications with the forward companies had broken down. He and his men were to assist the right flank attack by following in the wake of the two left-flanking units of 'A' and 'D' companies. An unknow soldier, likely with the Headquarters Company, recalled: 'Just before midday on the first day, two companies were held up by the enemy's fierce resistance and we lost communication with them. All the men in reserve were mustered, including transport drivers etc and pioneers, and they were sent in under Captain Suthers. He immediately took command of the situation, reorganised the companies, whose officers had suffered casualties – then led an assault on large pillboxes that enabled the men to advance. He was wounded slightly but pushed on'.[7]

Suthers also recalled: 'The assault wire broke, and we were out of contact. And Arnold said to me, "Look, [collect] all the odds and sods, get in there and straighten it out!" So I got in there ... with perhaps 50 men, cooks, transport drivers, batmen ... anyone who could carry a rifle'.[8] These men pushed on across the strip and through the gap created by 'A' and 'C' company's advance, attacking the bunkers there, which were slowing 'B' and 'C' companies advance. Not only had transport and pioneers been called to go forward with Suthers, but also administrative staff, including pay clerks, such as Sergeant Jack Lennell, a 34-year-old labourer from Monta Ponds in South Australia, as recalled by the same unknown soldiers: 'Although Johnnie's proper job was pay clerk in Company Headquarters, he couldn't have been put into a worse fight. He was one of the bravest in the show. He was cheerful and cool the whole time. I saw him lead his section on to a couple of pillboxes and finish [them] off and nobody could have done a better job'.[9]

Suthers recalled: 'Their snipers were bloody good! .... There was one bastard who laid doggo during the whole of New Year's Day, and on the second, he shot one of our blokes ... he let the whole of the bloody fight go on for a day! We knew bloody well that it was only a matter of time before we got it too! They went in [an] extended line and just took it!'[10]

Corporal 'Jinny' Williams, with the headquarters commandos, was leading his section in as part of Suthers' advance; he also recalled:

> We moved across in arrowhead formation and just about reached the beach. It was here that a tank was bogged near a bunker. I spoke to the occupants from the rear of the tank. They told me they had been there for two hours and could do nothing. They wanted to get out, so I placed the section in position and told them that when I hit the tank they were to come out, one at a time. I told the boys to put up covering fire. Gordon Gleadow with the Vickers gun gave us support. We got them all out without casualties.
>
> After the tank incident, I was told to go along the beach, which I did, expecting the section to follow me. But when I looked around there was no one in sight. One officer had told them

CHAPTER 54

different. I was not too happy about it but managed to get back .... I soon ordered them down and to take up a defensive position behind the palm trees.

I could see Lieut. [William] Bowerman in the rear and Captain Suthers who were saying or indicating, to move forward. I was near the beach and some of the Japs were starting to break, easy picking with my Tommy gun and hand grenades.

The Japs decided to get rid of me. I copped one across my left cheek and a piece out of my ear. I turned around and heard the boys say, 'Jinny's hit'. I asked Geoff Holmes for covering fire and as I got near him, I copped one through the chest near my heart. It came out under my arm, an explosive bullet. That finished me. There were no stretcher-bearers allowed in owing to the high casualty rate.

I lay there for hours. Finally, I saw a barrage of smoke bombs along the Jap defences and two stretcher-bearers, Jack Kavanagh (Tassie), Ring Dwyer and a covering section. The bearers picked me up and got me to the MO.

On the way out I saw the Yank who had said [the day before] that they were there 40 days, and I said, 'I told you we would do them'.

Then things began to get dark in my eyes.[11]

Private Geoff Holmes, a 22-year-old labourer from Bernie in Tasmania, recalled providing covering fire for Williams: 'Jinny was slightly in front and to the left when he was hit. He called out to me first, "Can you see him?" I said, "No." He then said he was hit and asked for covering fire. I responded, by firing a long burst off with the Bren into the bushes where I thought the enemy soldier lurked. As Jinny ran back, he dropped his knapsack as he came. Just opposite my position, Jinny was hit for the second time but managed to keep going. Those explosive bullets the Japanese were using, made a real mess of a man's body'.[12]

The Japanese continued to put up stubborn resistance, still holding several strong posts fringing the beachline between Giropa Point and Simemi Creek to the east. Here, the scrub, lawyer vines, and swampland made movement problematic Meanwhile, Captain Suthers, with elements of the Headquarters Company, had penetrated to the coast and turned south-east to face towards the mouth of Simemi Creek to help secure the area down to the creek. Suthers recalled:

> We swung right and there was this large bloody pillbox holding us up. So, I just said, 'Come on fellas, I want a couple of volunteers to come with me, and we'll take this bloody thing out!' I don't know who the blokes were to this day. They got up and I had one of these blast grenades, and I told the blokes to give us covering fire, and they beat up the front of it, and as we got near they stopped firing. And we went in and down the smoke hole! They had the door shut and it blew the door out! You imagine the equivalent of four sticks of gelignite going off in a confined space! I took one through the side about 20 minutes before that …. Just a flesh wound … you couldn't pull out because we were losing too many NCOs and too many officers. You had to stop there. But the blokes were good, by Christ they were good![13]

Where the tanks could manoeuvre, the infantrymen fired Verey lights to guide the tank fire, and then they followed this up with grenades and sweeping rushes. In many places, the tanks could not operate due to the boggy ground, and here the foot soldiers had to attack the entrenched Japanese, without tank support. Lieutenant William Bowerman, a 27-year-old clerk from Hobert, with Suthers' company, was noted by many as he led a 'platoon' of transport drivers in a series of spirited attacks. By the end of the day, the Australians had captured

CHAPTER 54

a large network of posts over an area scored by radiating crawl trenches. Some of the strong defensive positions were found to contain as few as ten men, most averaging around 30 defenders, but one was observed to contain about 70 Japanese, as testified by the dead men strewn across the position.[14] Captain Suthers recalled the fight here:

> As our attack developed, we encountered a continuous hardening in the ferocity of the resistance from the Japanese positions and at 1300 hours I spoke to the CO and requested reinforcements.
>
> At approximately 1500 hours a depleted company of the 2/9th Australian Infantry Battalion under Lieut. Chris Tippetts reported to me, and I gave him his objectives – a large pillbox that was enfilading our positions and told him he had the use of one of the M3 Stuart Light tanks.
>
> Lieut. Chris Tippetts was a quietly spoken man who showed no emotion under fire and his calm deliberate manner was an inspiration to everyone privileged to serve with him.
>
> On receiving his orders, he calmly ran forward and climbed onto the rear of the tank, spoke to the tank commander and then led his men in an assault whilst the tank put the muzzle of its 37-mm cannon into a rifle slit and fired HE shells into the bunker. This enabled the 2/9th Battalion company to push blast grenades – Buna Specials – into the strong point through the rifle slits.
>
> During the attack by the 2/9th Company, Lieut. Tippetts received a massive wound from shrapnel and I had to order him back to the Regimental Aid Post.
>
> After the battle I recommended him, amongst others, for a bravery award but like so many other citations of officers, NCOs and men that day, the 'powers that be' chose to ignore the recommendations.[15]

Towards the end of the day, Suther's and his mixed party – now including the two platoons from 'A' Company, 2/9th Battalion under lieutenants Victor Thomas and Christopher Tippetts – were exhausted after making a significant advance in support of 'B' and 'C' companies. Thomas recalled years later: 'Captain Angus Suthers required thickening on the right flank of the action. His eastern drive was a sticky one contested by bunkers and pillboxes supported by strong earth works and myriads of fanatical Japs eager to do and be done. The fighting was very severe, but [the] ground was slowly being won and casualties inevitable'.[16]

With the 2/9th Battalion reinforcements was Private Bryan Wells, who recalled the fighting here years later:

> On the afternoon of the 1st of January 43 [we] moved into a position in front of two bunkers on the Japanese left at the end of the old Buna strip and the mouth of Simemi Creek. And we were moved into position so that we would take them on the morning of 2 January. So, we took up positions during the night or the late afternoon and there were some sniper operations because one fellow was killed shot through the head and two other chappies who were fairly adjacent to me Bernie Graham and a fellow named George Hassell were both shot in the face but not seriously, they didn't leave the lines actually.
>
> We took up position during the late afternoon, settled down for the night with instructions not to move out of our positions during the hours of darkness and anything that moved would be [the] ... enemy and we were to eliminate them. And this was my really first encounter at close quarters with the enemy and I suppose you've got to give him an 'A' for courage in the position that they were in because there was no way in the world that they were going – they played gramophone music in those bunkers during the night. And on occasions whether they were outside the bunkers or talking through the firing slots or not

CHAPTER 54

they yell out 'Aussie bastard no fight'. We didn't do anything about it because we knew that if we fired the muzzle flash would reveal our positions and some of them were out moving around during the night and we did fire some shots [but] whether we killed any during the night I'm not sure.[17]

Meanwhile, Major Hall, commanding the guns of the 2/5th Field Regiment, was again out moving forward, as recorded by his adjutant in the unit war diary: 'The B.C. has been ordered to examine the pillboxes and Pom-Pom gun engaged by Carson's gun and to endeavour to differentiate and report on the difference in damage done by 119 cap and 231 [instantaneous and delayed fuses]. The B.C. today did a recce for new positions further up the strip for Carson's gun. Whilst in … Handren-Smith's OP report was received from 128 US Regt that Buna Mission was surrounded. The day was spent in 2/10 Bn fwd Coy HQ. The attack was watched from Handren-Smith's OP, and the tanks were seen to move in, followed by 2/12 Bn, and were seen to move down through the coconut grove'.[18]

The adjutant of the 2/12th Battalion recorded the situation from around 4 pm, with three-inch mortars being used in close infantry support, and by 4.20 pm, 'D' Company on the left had reached 200 metres south of Giropa Creek's entrance to the ocean. At around 5 pm, the supporting company from the 2/9th Battalion moved into the reserve area at the Battalion Headquarters position. Meanwhile, the advance of the right continued slowly, and by 6 pm, these men had consolidated on a line from the coast 175 metres west of Simemi Creek to a point at map reference 277 256, indicating a few hundred metres west of the Simemi Creek mouth. This line also included the remains of 'B' and 'C' companies, who were now under the command of Captain Suthers. On the left flank, 'A' Company had consolidated 80 metres east of Giropa Point after one of the tanks had become bogged in this area.[19]

BLOODY BUNA

It was not only around Giropa Point and Simemi Creek that the Australians were conducting mopping-up operations. Some isolated pockets of Japanese resistance still remained in the vicinity of Old Strip, as recalled by stretcher-bearer Private Roland 'Slim' Irwin:

About five o'clock in the afternoon hot food for the troops arrived at BHQ and had to be delivered by stretcher. Dad[xxxviii] and I rolled up our stretcher and poked it through the handles of a four-gallon [18 litres] dixie of stew and a four-gallon dixie of tea and trotted them out to D Coy's 15 Platoon.

Now just over from their position there was a Jap pillbox that hadn't been cleaned out and the Japs could be heard talking in it. Bert Mealing and Digger Dixon were section leaders in 18 Platoon and just as Dad and I arrived with the stew Bert said to Digger, 'There are a few Nips in there. Let's stir the bastards up'.

They went over and took up positions on either side and bowled a hand grenade into the entrance. Nips came out of every opening and Bert and Digger were using their Tommy guns to good effect, but Japs seemed to be everywhere. 'Watch the one on your right, Digger,' said Bert. 'I'll take care of him. You look after your own,' replied Digger.

Bullets were flying everywhere, and Dad and I had only our stretcher to defend ourselves with and as things were starting to get warm, I said to Dad, 'I'm getting out of here.' He said, 'So am I!'

So, we took off across the strip with bullets singing through the kunai grass all around us.

When we got back to BHQ the CO asked us what was going on and we told him. 'Mealing and Dixon are having some

---

xxxviii Private Bill Gill, a 26-year-old labourer from Launceston in Tasmania.

CHAPTER 54

shooting practice.' 'Oh, those two,' said the CO and seemed quite amused.[20]

By nightfall, reports confirmed that on the right flank only disconnected fragments of the defences held out. These were in a pocket contained by 100 to 200 metres of beach running northwest from the mouth of Simemi Creek. The Japanese, however, still stubbornly held parts of the dispersal bays of Old Strip. Along the eastern end of this pocket along the creek, lieutenant colonels Dobbs and MacNab were positioned. Close by, Suthers had established a line running southward to a point just north of the dispersal bays. Farther up the coast, the other two companies had made a line of Giropa Creek, except for the strong post that was still holding out at the mouth of Simemi Creek.

Darkness brought thunder, lightning and rain, through it scattered Japanese groups, and individuals tried to break out of the Simemi pocket. One such band came upon Captain Victor Sampson, a 27-year-old medical practitioner from Corinth in Queensland, and his medical post. Sampson and his men repulsed the Japanese marauders. Captain Victor Sampson was awarded the MC for his actions.[21]

The remaining Australians and Americans, whose part in the day's fighting was to mop-up behind the advance, conducted several hard-fought clashes in the dark and rain, shooting the Japanese in the flashes of lightning.[22] The fighting here included both lieutenant colonels Arthur Arnold, the CO of the 2/12th Battalion, and Alexander MacNab, CO of the III/128th Regiment. The American officer later recalled:

> Arnold and I took our outfits in with a sort of old-time flourish .... Arnold and I had been in view of each other almost continuously during this period, each in the front of his troops .... When he had gotten fairly close to the line of bunkers (we were coming in on their rear and flank) he yelled to my troops,

'Where is the American commander?' I replied ... 'You know damn well where I am, you've been trying to get abreast for an hour.' He yelled, 'Lets [sic] get the bastards,' and I yelled at my Company L and one platoon of Company K in the front wave, 'Come on you grease balls (never before or since have I ever called a man that).' We all, Aussies and Yanks, went in on the run. There were not many Japs left. We killed them in the grass with bayonets, and ... when we couldn't reach them [with fire].[23]

The 2/12th war diary lists its casualty figures for the days fighting: 62 men killed and 128 wounded, while another 16 men were evacuated sick. The Japanese on the Warren front, however, were finished. All that remained was to deliver the coup de grâce.[24]

* * *

Sometime that day, George Silk – who had been in the thick of the action capturing for posterity some of the most graphic images of fighting in the Pacific, and who had been at Buna for weeks, and was lucky to still be alive – had hit a physical and emotional brick wall. That day, he had been in the thick of the fighting and had witnessed and documented some of the bitterest fighting to take place at Buna. He recalled: 'I turned around and wanted to go back. I'd had enough. I only went a short distance, and I passed out'.[25] George Silk was soon after shipped back to Australia due to illness – his war, however, was far from over.

55

'... HERE WE WERE, THOROUGHLY DEFEATED'

Further west, Urbana Force launched what was expected to be the final assault on Buna Mission. That morning, several Allied sorties targeted the mission station. An unnamed witnessed recalled: 'Smoke, flame, fountains of sand and flying earth and logs belched from the labyrinth of defences around Buna Mission. Flying Fortresses dropped 500-pound demolition and fragmentation bombs. Beaufighters and Havocs (modified Bostons) fired many thousands of rounds of machinegun fire and Kittyhawks dive-bombed the positions'.[1]

Soon after these attacks, while 'B' Company, I/127th Regiment attacked eastward towards Giropa Point, the artillery and mortars laid down a heavy barrage on the mission, and the rest of Urbana Force struck at the Japanese positions around the mission. Captain Jefferson Cronk attacked from the mission spit, and Major Edmund Schroeder and his men, pivoting on Entrance Creek, moved on the mission from the south-east. Some men of 'B' Company could already see the tanks on Giropa Point, but the company was still held up by strong enemy resistance.[2]

The men of 'F' Company (II/128th Regiment) were now alone on the spit after Colonel Grose had withdrawn 'E' Company (II/127th Regiment) for reorganisation. Cronk and his men also found themselves unable to advance. In the swamp, 'C' Company (I/127th Regiment), supported on the right by 'M' Company (III/127th Regiment), moved forward 150 metres. The remaining companies to the right of 'M' Company – 'F' Company (II/127th Regiment), 'A' Company (I/127th Regiment), and 'L' Company (III/127th Regiment) – made some progress, with the men of 'I' Company (III/127th Regiment) and 'D' Company (I/127th Regiment) behind in support. In the fighting here, Private Robert Campbell, with 'M' Company, crawled out to rescue a wounded member of his unit who was lying in the open under direct line of Japanese machinegun fire – he was later awarded the DSC for his actions.[3]

The Japanese fought with the great tenacity, but evidence of their disintegration was becoming obvious. That afternoon, while Lieutenant Colonel Smith, commanding II/128th Regiment, and Major Gordon Clarkson, commanding the I/128th Regiment, established a joint Urbana–Warren force outpost in the no-man's land between their two fronts. Japanese troops were then sighted for the first-time swimming from the mission, trying to reach the Sanananda beachhead to the west – an unmistakable sign that the mission's defence was on the point of collapse.[4]

Meanwhile, careful preparations were being made for the next day's attack. The main attack was to be along the coast, spearheaded by two relatively rested units – 'G' Company (II/127th Regiment) and 'G' Company (II/128th Regiment) – which had gone into reserve when the troops on the mission spit failed to knock out the bunkers facing the north bridge. The men of 'H' Company (II/127th Infantry) would cross from Musita Island as soon as either 'F' Company (II/128th Regiment) advanced from the mission spit, or 'C' Company (I/127th Regiment) moved up through the swamp north of the gardens and took over the area north of the bridge, to then make repairs to the bridge.[5]

* * *

The wounded Japanese medic, Yokoyama Yoriichi, who had been shot in the face by an Australian, was now ordered, along with others,

CHAPTER 55

to cut their way through to Sanananda. He recalled many years after the war:

> It was strange that we started withdrawing without any notice from high command. The orderly came back from Battalion Headquarters and said, 'We've got to get out of here quickly! Other units are leaving'.
>
> We casually left grenades for the wounded. After spending a lot of time together, it was easy to understand each other, like some kind of tacit agreement. The ones who were willing to kill themselves received the grenades without a word and the other ones who couldn't decide to kill themselves grovelled and tried to follow us. It was hell, for real. I felt shocked and furious at the same time. I didn't know any other appropriate expressions to describe my feelings. It was so hard leaving my wounded comrades behind to run away. I'm so sorry about that.
>
> There were soldiers crawling and following us in the jungle for the first half hour. They knew we were running away. When leaving them behind, some soldiers even lied to the wounded saying, 'We are going to attack the enemy now'. The wounded men asked us to help them kill themselves. After the war I heard about a man who annually held a memorial service for the dead whom he shot and helped to their deaths.
>
> A couple of mornings later I was walking with just one friend. We were taking a rest when I said I wanted to catch up with our company as soon as possible. He said there was no rush, that I was spoiling the rest break. I could not get rid of this strange feeling and decided to go without him. No sooner had I caught up than there was shooting back the way I came and we all scattered again into the jungle. I never saw my friend again and blamed myself because I let him stay behind. I don't know how many times I have blamed myself for not taking him with me,

but it couldn't be helped, because he chose to stay. I guess that was his destiny. The hardest part of the war is to be separated from your friends.

Around that time, I came across a few soldiers dying on the ground, surrounded by flies and crawling with maggots. One was still holding onto a cooking pot as if he wouldn't let it go until he died.

Later I found another familiar face. He was a lieutenant from my neighbouring village, such a dignified man. But at that time, he was lying down, seeming to be unable to move, and holding his sword closely to his chest. I just could not leave him alone so I went up to him saying, 'I am Yokoyama from the next village. Would you walk with me, sir? I could help you out.' He replied, 'No, just go without me. I am tired. Besides it feels good lying on the warm grass like this, so I don't mind dying here.' I had no choice but to leave him. I suppose there was no other option, but it was terribly hard.

Once we had escaped the danger it occurred to me that we were supposed to be a brave regiment, full of valour, but here we were, thoroughly defeated.[6]

56

'ENSIGN SUZUKI ENTERED THE SEA AT 2.30 AM'

The end of the fighting for the men of Warren Force came the next morning, 2 January 1943. At dawn, these men were in the thick of the action, with two Australian tanks each reporting to the Simemi and Giropa flanks and the Australians of the 2/9th Battalion clearing the east bank of the Simemi. Most of the day was taken up in swift but brutal encounters.

It was at this point that the battalion received its first fatality for the day, as recalled by Corporal Athol Summers with 'A' Company:

> The night passed quietly enough, except for Oscar Grindle's dixies rattling every time he moved! He was told in no uncertain terms, to repack his so-and-so dixies.
>
> During the night, a white flag had been hoisted on a Jap pillbox to our front, and in trying to get a better look, one of the Sigs attached to A Company, who was standing beside me, was killed instantly.[xxxix] It was a bad start for the day.
>
> Mopping up was the order of the day, and we saw the Americans in action on Buna Mission. We could see the Japs fleeing, and swimming out into the bay, trying to get away.
>
> So far, we had taken no prisoners. We had found some drums

[xxxix] Private Sidney Duckett, a 24-year-old saw miller from Brighton in Tasmania, is listed as killed on 2 January 1943.

of petrol and were using it to smoke out the pillboxes, and with some success too. During the day I trod on a live Jap who had covered himself with palm leaves, well hidden, but he joined his forefathers promptly.[1]

On the left, the men of this battalion encountered stubborn Japanese resistance around Giropa Point in the few remaining pillboxes still in enemy hands. The battalion was reinforced with a company from the 2/9th Battalion, temporarily led by Lieutenant Hugh Geizendanner, a 26-year-old miner from Townsville in Queensland, who commanded the commando unit with the 2/12th Battalion. The last strong defensive position had been reduced by 9.55 am; it had taken these men until the afternoon to hunt down the remnants of the defenders.[2]

Lieutenant Colonel Arthur Arnold, CO of the battalion, witnessed one of these encounters. Two Japanese officers emerged from an isolated post, which had held out against the 2/9th Battalion since 22 December. The official Australian historian of the campaign, Dudley McCarthy, recorded that Arnold, sick of the killing, called to two officers to surrender: 'They gave no sign of understanding or even of hearing. One leisurely turned away. The other washed himself in the brackish water and drank some. Then, quite regardless of the silent watchers, he bowed very low three times into the sun. As he then stood erect and faced the Australians, Arnold called "I'll give you until I count ten to surrender". With no word the officer took a small Japanese flag and tied one end to his upraised sword and held the other end in his left hand so that it covered his breast. And so, he faced his enemies still silent. Arnold counted deliberately. As he reached "Nine" the Japanese shouted in a loud, clear voice "Out!" Then the Australians riddled him. The other they found hanging by the neck, dead'.[3]

Suthers also recalled this incident slightly differently, but essentially the same: 'We got through to Simemi Creek. And across the other side, there's a bloody officer, all done out in his finery ... obviously a

CHAPTER 56

Staff Officer from Headquarters ... and he came out with a big sword, and he made a sign that he wanted to have a fight. He went whoosh with the sword, and he carved all the bits off the side of the palm fonds. Now, at this time the old man arrived up ... Arnold, and I said, "Bugger 'im we'll give him ten to surrender!" There was one other Jap behind him, and I had a Vickers gun brought forward. And I said to them, "Righto, one, two, three, four ... nine, ten!" And this Jap said "Out!" And we just opened up and that was it'.[4]

With the 2/9th Battalion was Private Wells, who had the night before been positioned in front of a couple of Japanese bunkers the night before, listening to the Japanese play a gramophone. He recalled many years later:

When daylight came, we had to advance on the two bunkers. They were fairly big ones. We had an officer with us from the 2/12th Battalion. I think it was Angus Suthers, he had a brother in the 2/9th Battalion too, Captain Suthers. And Angus said to me ... well the method of disposing of these bunkers at that stage was to – they had a tin which they filled with [explosive] and tied a strapped a hand grenade on the top of them with a four second fuse and somebody had to go up and toss it through the slot into the bunker and the explosion of course would concuss anybody that was inside. I was handed one of these and Angus Suthers said, 'Here Wells you take this we'll give you covering fire and you throw it through the slot'. It was something I wasn't expecting, and I didn't envy the job but anyway I managed to get there and get it in the slot and achieved the objective and survived. I don't know who did the other one but that was literally the end of the action at Buna in respect of the 2/9th Battalion. We stayed there until the 5th of January.[5]

The war diary of the 2/6th Armoured Regiment records at zero hour, 8.15 am, the tanks and infantry crossed the start-line.

At 9.10 am, another tank was made available to help clean up Giropa Point. A reconnaissance was made of the Giropa Creek bridge and the ground to determine whether the tanks could use the bridge and traverse the terrain.

At noon, it is recorded that 23 Japanese were captured, almost certainly Korean indentured workers. By 1.30 pm, the tanks were moving south-east down Simemi Creek, closely supported by infantry, and five minutes later, a Japanese prisoner was taken, with maps.

At 2.15 pm, Major Kenneth Tye reported the bridge on Giropa Creek was crossable and tanks could also cross at the creek at its mouth. Just before 3 pm, the captured Japanese soldier confirmed that Giropa Point was the headquarters for Buna sector, and that about 190 enemy were still positioned south-east, with elements in the Coconut Grove. By 3.15 pm, the fighting on Simemi Creek had been concluded, although a few snipers were still active. One tank remained at the Regimental Headquarters, while all other tanks were to be now withdrawn to the harbour area for urgent maintenance.[6]

Meanwhile, the Australians of 'C' and 'D' companies, 2/12th Battalion, and the Americans of the III/128th Regiment, with tank support, attacked and finally took the Japanese dispersal bay of Old Strip and the nearby bunkers. By noon, these men had made steadily progress and were now reinforced with a company from the 2/9th Battalion. Supporting the fighting here was Sergeant Roderick Carson and his 25-pounder gunners, as recalled by the 2/5th Field Regiment diarist: 'None of the pillboxes was occupied and praise was heard everywhere for the job done by Carson's gun. The area had actually been sniped by a 25 Pr'.[7]

Later that afternoon, Major William Hall, commanding these guns, moved across the Girua River to begin locating positions for his guns to target the Japanese still dug-in around the Sanananda Beachhead.[8]

Just after 2 pm, the right flank contacted the men of the 2/10th Battalion, and mopping-up operations here continued until around 5 pm. Soon after, the men of the 2/12th Battalion were all gathered at

CHAPTER 56

Giropa Point. The day before, only eight Japanese allowed themselves to be taken prisoner and six of these were labourers. By the end of the day, only one Japanese soldier was taken prisoner.[9]

Platoon Sergeant Frank Millett, with 'D' Company, 2/12th Battalion, recalled the sudden appearance of a senior American officer as they were still conducting mopping-up operations: 'A group of us were moving across our area on our way to continue with the task of forcing the Japanese out of their bunkers, when an American jeep, loaded six feet [two metres] high with cartons of cigarettes drove into the lines. The jeep contained a Master Sergeant as driver and a high-ranking US officer. I like to think it was General Eichelberger (it was). He certainly wore three stars. Just as we were going past, he ordered the M-Sergeant to start throwing out the cartons of cigarettes, saying quite clearly, "Nothing is too good for these men"'.[10]

In the day's fighting, the 2/12th Battalion suffered another 12 officers and 179 men as casualties. The total loss in the three 18th Brigade battalions was recorded as 55 officers and 808 men for the period 18 December 1942 to 2 January 1943, inclusive – a casualty rate of around 60 per cent. It was a heavy cost by any standards. It was estimated that Japanese casualties were between 800 to 1200.[11] It was recorded in the 18th Brigade war diary, however: 'Accurate figures cannot be given as enemy dead were largely found and buried in pillboxes and a detailed count was not possible'.[12]

McCarthy recorded the strength of the Japanese forces during the fighting to take the Buna Beachhead:

> The Australians had ... been fighting strong, well-entrenched and well-armed foes .... on 17th November with the *III/229th Regiment*, Colonel Yamamoto, [who] had disposed in the whole Buna area probably a little over 2500 men; that, of these, Captain Yasuda deployed about 500 marines and probably several hundred other men (mainly construction round the Buna Government Station–Triangle–Buna Village area. Of the

balance of the force, Yamamoto sited more than 1000 (including the fresh infantry) in Duropa Plantation, at Cape Endaiadere, and along the edge of New Strip, while, at the bridge between the strips and round the southern end of Old Strip, odds and ends of various Army units were dug-in with a strength of several hundred.

When, therefore, the 2/9th Battalion attacked on 18th December it is possible that they fronted up to twice their numbers, and the Japanese were in very strong and well-prepared defensive positions. When Yamamoto was forced to yield to the pressure of their amazing feat of arms, he pulled his men back by degrees across the shallow mouth of the creek and across the bridge between the strips, having been holding firmly at the bridge for some time. He was then determined to prevent any crossing of the shallows at the creek mouth and commanded them from an island set there and from the western bank. Although it is not known how many men remained to him after he had made the crossing it seems likely that he still had a substantial part of his force intact. With these, he manned the defences which had been prepared on and about the Old Strip – a warren of trenches and bunkers, with several lines of bunkers across the strip, extending in one case to Simemi Creek on the right and in another to the swamp on the left: with bunkers in the dispersal bays above the strip, in the area below the strip, on the strip itself and in the coconut grove off its western end.

Integrated with these defences, Yamamoto had machine guns and mortars, at least two 75-mm mountain guns, two 37-mm guns, several 25-mm pom-poms mounted dual and triple at the far end of the strip. About three-quarters of the way up the strip, and about 200 yards to the south, he had in position several three-inch naval guns. To the north of the strip, he had another three-inch gun.[13]

CHAPTER 56

Despite the formidable Japanese defensive works, the Japanese forces east of Giropa Point alone were almost destroyed, with around 900 known to have been buried there and, as always, there were many others unrecorded. This was the last organised attack delivered by the men of Warren Force. After taking Giropa Point and the area immediately to the east, the troops had little left to do but mop up. Orders were issued that day to the 2/12 Battalion and the III/128th Regiment, to begin moving westward towards Buna Mission in the morning. The orders were revoked a few hours later, when it was found that contact had been made with Urbana Force, and these men were already about to take Buna Mission.[14]

It was now that the small Japanese force occupying the island at the river mouth were attacked by the exhausted and battle-weary men of the 2/9th Battalion, as recorded in the unit war diary: 1500 hrs – Area reported clear of enemy except mouth of SIMEMI CREEK. US tps pushing N.W. reported to have contacted 2/12 Bn .... Patrol from B Coy sent forward to investigate false mouth SIMEMI CREEK and were fired on. 1815 hrs – Pl of B Coy attacked posn on island formed by false mouth of creek. 19 Japs killed'.[15]

* * *

Indeed, at Urbana front, the Japanese continued their desperate attempts to escape. Just before dawn, 20 Japanese carrying heavy packs and led by a lieutenant made a break for the beached landing barges on the mission spit. They had three machine guns with them, and their packs were later found to be loaded with food, medicine, and personal effects. Captain Jefferson Cronk's men turned their machine guns and rifles on them and cut them down to a man. American troops all the way from Buna Village to Tarakena caught sight of large numbers of Japanese in the water. Some were swimming, others were clinging to boxes, rafts, and logs, while others were trying to escape in small boats. They were targeted with artillery and machinegun fire, and at 10 am, Allied airmen systematically strafed them with sorties of B25s, P39s, and Wirraways.[16]

Even though the Buna Mission Station was already partly evacuated, there were still enough Japanese there and along its approaches to give Urbana Force, as later recorded by Lieutenant General Eichelberger: 'the darndest fight' all day.[17] At 10 am, just as the attack was about to begin, the gallant Major Edmund Schroeder, who was in a forward observation post, was struck and mortally wounded by a Japanese sniper who shot him in the head. Captain Donald Runnoe, a member of Schroeder's staff, at once took over command of the I/127th Regiment, and Colonel Grose came up and took personal charge of the coastal drive.[18]

Captain Dames and his men of 'G' Company, II/127th Regiment moved out at 10.15 am. They then advanced up the shoreline from the south-east through the coconut trees, with 'G' Company (II/128th Regiment) close by in support. In the centre were the men of 'C' Company, (I/127th Regiment), led by Captain Millard Gray. They all heaved themselves out of the swamp, where they had been working tirelessly for days, to clear the positions commanding the bridge and allow the long-sought passage from the island to open. From the spit, Captain Cronk and his men of 'F' Company (II/128th Regiment) were held up, as was 'B' Company (I/127th Regiment), which had resumed its attack eastward. By 2 pm, 'C' Company was in sight of the bunkers covering the north bridge.[19]

Ninety minutes later, 'G' Company (II/127th Regiment) reached the point of the mission, with 'G' Company (II/128th Regiment) hard on its heels. Only scattered rifle fire met the troops, and it was here that they took their first prisoners – a dozen indentured Chinese laborers. At this point, 'C' Company (I/127th Regiment) came up, followed by 'M' Company (III/127th Regiment), and within minutes, they were joined by the men of 'I', 'L', and 'A' companies (127th regiment). Meanwhile, the engineers had been repairing the north bridge, and by 4.30 pm, 'H' Company (II/127th Regiment) was across, finally completing the pincer attack.[20]

CHAPTER 56

The mission was finally overrun at 4.32 pm. The remaining Japanese in the area were either flushed out of their hiding places and killed or entombed in them. Most fought to the last man, with the enemy having to be 'rooted out of each dugout and bunker by grenade, machinegun, and submachine gun fire'.[21] The mission was a scene of utter desolation. All through the area, the ground was pitted with shell holes, and trees were smashed. Abandoned weapons and derelict landing craft littered the beach, and Japanese dead were everywhere. By 5 pm, the fighting was over, except in a few pockets of resistance near the beach, where a handful of Japanese held out stubbornly and were left to be dealt with the next day.[22]

The attack went smoothly from the first. The smoke shells set fire to the grass and trees in the mission area and, in one instance, exposed a whole line of Japanese bunkers to Allied artillery fire. Attempts by the Japanese to flee these exposed positions were met by machinegun fire from the troops on Musita Island and on the mission spit. As the smoke shells exploded in trees, they also set fire to several of the huts in the mission. When Japanese in dugouts beneath the burning huts tried to escape, they were targeted with bursts of machinegun fire.[23]

Meanwhile, in their attack to the west of Giropa Point, the men of 'B' Company (I/127th Regiment) were held up by a line of Japanese bunkers at the track junction near the coast, which had been bypassed in the coastal advance. As soon as he could, Lieutenant General Eichelberger pulled 'C' Company (I/127th Regiment) out of the mission area and sent it to the assistance of 'B' Company. The two companies launched an attack late in the afternoon, clearing out the bunkers, and by 7.30 pm, they had contacted the Australians of the 2/12th Battalion. With the 2/10th Battalion and the I/128th and II/128th regiments, the 2/12th Battalion had finished clearing out the area between Giropa Point and the west bank of Simemi Creek earlier in the day.

After more than six weeks of fighting, the Buna area was finally in Allied hands.[24]

The exhausted and battle-weary 80 or so survivors of the II/126th Regiment were still located just south of Buna Village, and the regimental war diary records that day: 'Enemy patrols filtered through our lines aided by rain, but our patrols cleared them out'.

The adjutant of the 2/10th Battalion recorded that day of the men of the 2/12th Battalion mopping up the area in the Coconut Grove, with the men of the 2/10th Battalion occupying the position at 4.15 pm. And about an hour later, the men of 'C' Company were mopping up the area at the mouth of Simemi Creek.[25] The diary concludes on 2 January 1943, with the casualties suffered by the battalion in its contribution to take Buna: 'Bn battle casualties Buna 22 Dec 1942/ 2 Jan 1943. 21 officers, 298 ORs'.[26] Of these, eight officers and 105 other ranks had been killed outright.[27]

The war diary of the 2/5th Field Regiment records the situation at the end of the day: 'Today the USA troops took the Buna Mission area, and at night fall, only a small pocket of Japs between the Mission and Giropa area remained to be cleared up. One MG in the swamp at Sememi Creek was still in action. These two points will receive appropriate attention in the morning. Maj. Hall has sent Capt. Nix to Oro Bay tonight to check on Bty stores there, and to endeavour to trace mail., none of which has been received for weeks. Separate reports have been made to Div. on guns captured. Maintenance on guns has been done during today and all are in first class condition. A prisoner was taken today by sigs of 2/1 Regt, but he died of wounds'.[28]

* * *

The official Japanese history of the campaign concludes for the final 24 hours of fighting at Buna between 1 and 2 January 1943:

> A general withdrawal was decided on during the night. A total of 70–80 Army and Navy staff from garrison headquarters, including 30–40 walking wounded, left their air raid shelters

CHAPTER 56

and joined soldiers holed up at Buna Village [*sic* Giropa Point] to break through the Australian lines and head for north Giruwa.

The night assault party, led by the commander of the mountain artillery company, Lieutenant Shiiki Kazuo, suffered almost complete losses of its 70 men when it attempted to break through the Allied lines. The members of the garrison returned to the air-raid shelters, recognising the low probability of successfully penetrating the lines. At this time, a total of barely ten Army and Navy personnel were fit to fight.

The surviving Army and Navy commanders, adjutants, doctors, and probationary officers huddled around the last candle and discussed the coming of their final day. Just before the arrival of the tanks early in the morning two days previously, the commanders had led an assault that penetrated the Allied camp. Now, the unit's place of death had been chosen and the final stage of the Buna Garrison headquarters was determined.

Having foreseen this situation, it had been established that able-bodied swimmers would provide a last report to those at Giruwa [Sanananda]. However, none who could swim became available in the frantic continuing battle. Consequently, Captain Yasuda ordered Ensign Suzuki Kiyotaka from the Yokosuka 5th Special Naval Landing Party to steal through the heavy Allied encirclement and head for Giruwa by sea. Captain Yasuda entrusted Suzuki with his final report to his superiors as follows: 'It is deeply regrettable that we have not been able to hold out for the arrival of the relief party'.

Ensign Suzuki entered the sea at 2.30 am. The distant shore was approximately 1000 metres away in the dark. It seemed from the glimpses between the swell that the battle on land had started early. Leaving his unit behind was unbearable. However, he kept swimming. He finally arrived on the beach at Giruwa around 9.30 am.[29]

The final details regarding the fate of remining Japanese officers and men at Buna remain largely undocumented, as almost all were killed, and no records were recovered relating to their final hours. Even so, it is known that the two top Japanese commanders at Buna had chosen to die at their posts. Realising that the end was near, Captain Yasuda Yoshitatsu and Colonel Yamamoto Hiroshi met at a central point that day and killed themselves in the traditional Japanese fashion by Harakiri.[30] Japanese historian Tanaka Kengoro wrote: 'Captain Yasuda of the Imperial Japanese Navy and Colonel Yamamoto of the Imperial Japanese Army were honourably killed together with the remnants of the units on 2 January 1943, early in the morning'.[31]

57

'NOW THAT THE BATTLE FOR BUNA IS OVER AND WON ...'

Mopping-up operations contributed into the next day – 3 December 1943. A heavy rain had fallen throughout the night and early morning. The men of Warren and Urbana forces had by now linked up. The 2/12th Battalion adjutant recorded the situation that morning: 'A plan was made to continue our advance WEST, and beyond the GIROPA area, but this became unnecessary in view of the USA forces obtaining their objective. Offers of assistance from mortars to enable the Americans to clean up their final objective, were turned down by the Americans'.[1]

At first light, the Japanese machinegun position in the swamp was targeted by Australian tanks; however, they could not get close enough to silence it, given the conditions. A recently arrived American 37-mm anti-tank gun was brought forward, which quickly silenced the machinegun nest. Fifteen more Japanese were hunted down and killed in the Coconut Grove.[2]

Isolated pockets of Japanese resistance on both Warren and Urbana fronts continued for several days until the last of the enemy troops were accounted for. On 8 January, a reporter with the *New York Times* published his description of the scene as witnessed on 3 January:

[By] Sunday, the . . . front from the shattered palms of Buna Village to Cape Endaiadere was almost peaceful. It was possible to walk its entire length and hear only a few scattered shots and occasional bursts of mortar fire. In the ... swamp ... a few Japanese snipers still held out, in a patch of jungle ... a bunker or two still resisted, but great stretches of the front were scenes of quiet desolation .... The only considerable fighting during the day occurred in the jungle area south-west of Giropa Point, where a small group of laborers, estimated as high as a hundred, fled when the point was captured. Their intention perhaps was to try to escape through the swamps and jungles, and scatter into the interior ....

Americans and Australians, however, drew a line around them from all sides and made contact along the beach between Buna Mission and Giropa Point, and methodically mopped up the enemy pocket.

Americans quelled the last resistance to Buna Mission by Sunday noon in a little thicket on the beach where a few Japanese held out in bunkers. Routed from the bunkers, some scurried behind a wrecked barge on the beach and continued to fire. They were finally killed by a high explosive charge that blew the barge and the Japanese to bits.

By noon, the Americans had counted roughly 150 Japanese dead in the Buna Mission area.

Small squads finished the job of eliminating the last fighting Japanese. Some Americans [went swimming in] the sea. Some washed out their clothing for the first time in weeks, some simply slept the deep sleep of exhaustion, curled up under shell-shattered trees or in sandy foxholes. By Tuesday, the only Japanese left in the area extending from Buna Village through Cape Endaiadere were roving groups and individuals ... who were hiding out in jungle and sago swamp, and who by now had become desperately hungry. These Japanese were trying to keep under cover during the day [to prowl] at night through

CHAPTER 57

moonless blackness in American–Australian lines seeking something to eat.³

The total Japanese casualties defending Buna was estimated at around 3000 killed, wounded, and missing. On the Warren front, much equipment was captured. Including the three-inch naval guns and the pompoms, rifles, machine guns, radio equipment, several 37-mm guns, two 75-mm mountain guns, nine unserviceable trucks, some of American make, and several smashed fighter aircraft, two of them, Zero fighters, were found on Old Strip and looked as if they could be repaired. At Urbana Force, equipment captured included the weapons taken in the Triangle and several anti-aircraft guns taken in the Government Gardens, including a 75-mm gun and miscellaneous items of equipment. Hardly any food or ammunition was found on either front.⁴

* * *

By 3 January, it was obvious that all organised resistance on the Buna side of the Girua River was over. In a special memorandum issued at noon that day, Lieutenant General Eichelberger told American troops who had taken part in the fighting that they had had their baptism of fire and were now veterans. The lessons they had learned at Buna, he added, would serve to reduce losses in the future and bring further victories.⁵

Later that day, General Blamey sent a message of congratulations to Brigadier Wootten and the troops serving under him, on the successful conclusion of the fighting at Buna:

CONGRADULATORY MESSAGE FROM C-in-C.

The GOC, NGF, has pleasure in forwarding the appended signal from the C-in-C, Allied Forces:

'Please accept yourself and convey to your staff and command hearty congratulations on the successful conclusion of operations on BUNA front. They have been thoroughly planned and valorously executed'.[6]

Lieutenant General Herring, commanding Advance NGF in turn, issued a special order of the day:

ORDER OF THE DAY

by

Lt Gen E. F. HERRING C.B.E., D.S.O., MC., E.D.

General Officer Commanding New Guinea Force

3rd January 1943

Now that the battle for BUNA is over and won, I desire to express to all ranks who have engaged in the battle, whether on the ground, or in the air; American and Australian alike, my heartfelt appreciation of your magnificent and prolonged effort. The enemy's defences were exceedingly strong, and he fought the battle with a selfless devotion to duty that was worthy of a better cause. He had to defend an area that lent itself to defence: the going has been hard; you have performed great feats of endurance, you have overcome and borne hardships with cheerfulness and with a determination to prevail so steadfast, that your efforts have been crowned with victory.

You have done a job of which both our countries should indeed be proud.

The battle for BUNA is but a step on the way, we have now to clear the enemy out of SANANANDA Area. You know what the going will be like, it will not be any easier than BUNA, but I know that you will tackle it with the same determination, and, I believe, with the same result.

Good luck to you all.[7]

CHAPTER 57

General George Marshall in Washington DC sent General MacArthur his congratulations the next day. MacArthur thanked him for his message, and ever the 'victim', added: 'However unwarranted it may be, the impression prevailed that this area's efforts were belittled and disparaged at home, and despite all my efforts to the contrary, the effect was depressing. Your tributes have had a tonic effect'.[8]

* * *

Private Edward Beechy, a 28-year-old labourer from Cradoc in Tasmania, with 'A' Company, 2/12th Battalion, years later wrote what was likely in the minds of many of the officers and men who fought at the beachheads: 'No doubt the worst job for a soldier after a battle is being on a burial party. Jim Parcell, myself and others were detailed on one section for this horrible job. Putting our mates in shallow graves. The smell of death was sickening. I remarked to a mate, "It's a pity some of these cursed bastards that cause wars are not here to be placed in these"'.[9]

* * *

Meanwhile, having been ordered to rescue the troops at Buna Mission, Colonel Yazawa Kiyoshi had been unable to leave Giruwa due to a shortage of petrol for the motor launchers. Major General Yamagata Tsuyuo had ordered him on 2 January to advance on to Buna on foot. That night, Yazawa, with around 250 men, crossed the first arm of Girua River and advanced into the jungle. Two days later, they encountered Lieutenant Louis Chagnon and his 52 men positioned south-east of Tarakena. After conducting a hasty reconnaissance of the American position, Yazawa ordered an attack at dusk with the bulk of his force.[10]

That afternoon (4 January), Chagnon had been reinforced with 21 men of 'E' Company, II/126th Regiment. When attacked, he had under his command 73 men from seven different companies, including men from the Headquarters and Service Companies of the

127th Regiment, a 60-mm mortar, and three light machine guns. The force was short of ammunition and grenades, and the attack came as a complete surprise. Hit from the front, rear, and left, Chagnon and his men fought as best they could until all their ammunition was gone, and they were forced to withdraw, most having to swim across the river. Chagnon continued pouring fire into the attacking Japanese, until his machine gun jammed; he was the last man out. Members of Chagnon's party kept straggling into Siwori Village all that night. By the following day, all but four had come in – a small loss, given Yazawa's attack had been made in overwhelming strength.[11]

After clearing Chagnon's position on the spit and mainland, Yazawa was able to report that he had picked up some 180 Army and 190 Navy survivors of the Buna garrison. Most of them had swum from the mission and had had the good sense to keep out of sight during the day. By the early morning hours of 5 January, Colonel John Grose had part of 'F' Company, I/127th Regiment across Siwori Creek. The crossing was unopposed, as Yazawa and his force, now numbering around 600 men, fell back towards the Sanananda Beachhead on being informed that Buna had already fallen. The Americans therefore quickly re-established themselves on the other side of the creek and began moving north-west.[12]

Buna had fallen, and the bridgehead across Siwori Creek had been re-established.

However, west of the Girua River on the Sanananda front, things were at a stalemate, and had been for some time. As Colonel Leslie Skerry, a senior officer to Eichelberger's staff, stated: 'While we were engaged in the Buna area, we did not have much opportunity to think about what was going on elsewhere. But after getting rid of the Japanese here, we awoke to the fact that there was another most difficult situation existing in the Sanananda area next door [there] ... a state of semi-siege has been going on ... with little progress being made'.[13]

With the Americans of the 127th Regiment in position to move

CHAPTER 57

on Tarakena, and the men of the Australian 18th Brigade along with Australian tanks, and most of their artillery in use at Buna now available for use on the other side of the river, the time had come to throw all Allied resources against the sole remaining Japanese beachhead at Sanananda.

EPILOGUE

At Buna, the whole of the American 32nd Infantry Division, except for the small parts of the 126th Regiment on the Sanananda Track, had been committed. Also involved in heavy fighting here were the Australians of the 18th Infantry Brigade, commandos of the 2/6th Independent company, two squadrons of armour from the 2/6th Armoured Regiment, Bren gun carriers from the 18th Brigade carrier group crewed by men of the 17th Brigade, artillery from the 13th (militia), 2/1st and 2/5th field regiments, and engineers from the 2/4th Field Company. Also, the operation included the use of Allied airmen and the build-up of an elaborate system of air-sea supply.[1]

Lieutenant General Robert Eichelberger would later write disingenuously in his memoir: 'Buna was the first Allied Ground Force victory in the Pacific (the Buna campaign was ended before the fall of Guadalcanal)[xl] .... A great deal has been said and whispered about the 32nd Division, and much of it makes no sense. The 32nd which "failed" at Buna was the same 32nd that won the victory there. No one else did'.[2]

These claims are also regurgitated word for word in the published history of the 32nd Division. Indeed, the later publication, as well as the American official history of the Battle for Buna by Marshall, barely even mentions the role of the Australians at Buna, which was truly significant. A more recent American history perpetuates this myth by again repeating Eichelberger's claim that the 32nd Division alone took Buna – 'No one else did'.[3]

Tell that to the Australian commandos of the 2/6th Independent

---

[xl] It is universally recognised (at the time and later) that the first significant defeat of Jaspanese land forces was by the Australian 18th Brigade at Milne Bay in late August and early September 1942 when they repulsed a Japanese invasion force supported by Japanese artillery, tanks, aircraft, and naval gun fire.

EPILOGUE

Company, who were continually in the frontlines November to mid-December 1942, taking out Japanese bunkers and conducting deep reconnaissance.

Tell that to the men of the Australian 18th Brigade, along with Bren gun carrier crews, artillerymen and tankers who spearheaded the attacks at Warren front, who fought and died, finally taking New Strip, Old Strip, Cape Endaiadere, the mouth of Simemi Creek, Giropa Point, and other heavily defended Japanese positions at Buna during mid-December 1942 and early January 1943. Indeed, the fact that Warren Force was commanded by an Australian during the critical period when enemy positions at Buna were finally captured is usually also completely ignored by American historians of the Papua campaign.

However, American military historian, Eric Bergerud, in his ground-breaking history: *Touched with Fire: the land war in the South Pacific*, concluded succinctly: 'The war in the South Pacific was not a general's war. The essence of combat in the theatre was found at a much lower level of command. We know now that Australia had the best Army in the South Pacific ... it never lost a battle after the Japanese withdrew first from Milne Bay and soon after from positions near the Imita Ridge outside Port Moresby. When brought up to strength and given the flexibility and firepower that modern sea and airpower provided, the invincible Australian killing machine of 1943 developed smoothly from the AIF of late 1942. Few armies in modern times have combined steadiness, savvy, and ferocity the way Australians did. It was an extraordinary performance'.[4]

Allied casualties at Buna amounted to 2817 men. The American 32nd Division sustained 1954 of these casualties, 353 killed (18 per cent), 1508 wounded, and 93 missing. The overall casualty rate for the division stands at around round 40 per cent, suffered over a six-week period. The Australian 18th Infantry Brigade and supporting elements suffered 863 casualties, 267 killed (31 per cent), 557 wounded, and 39 missing, amounting to around 60 per cent casualties over just three weeks of fighting.[5] Not only does the fact that most positions at Warren front were taken by the Australians, but the higher casualty rate (especially in those killed) attests to the vigour of this brigade and the significance of their contribution in helping to take the Buna beachhead.[6]

The Japanese are known to have lost a minimum of 1390 men killed at Buna. These were 900 counted dead east of Giropa Point, 490 west of that point, including the 190 buried at the Government Station itself. How many more, buried alive or dead in their strongpoints or uncounted, must be added to that minimum – the ultimate number of Japanese dead is now lost to history, but an estimate of 3000 is likely conservative. Fifty prisoners were taken on the Warren Force front, 21 workers and one soldier. On Urbana Force front, 28 men, most workers were captured, but a few soldiers were dragged naked and defenceless from the sea after they had come to exhaustion in attempting to escape to the Sanananda Beachhead.[7]

Indeed, the overall Japanese casualties associated with the battles for the three beachheads has been estimated by Japanese historian Tanaka Kengoro at around 8000 men, approaching a casualty rate of 70 per cent – most killed. Until around mid-December, Japanese sick and wounded could be evacuated from the beachhead positions back to Rabaul on the empty ships heading back to Rabaul after having delivered reinforcements and supplies to the beachheads. If not for this, the Japanese casualty would have been significantly higher.[8]

With the Japanese Buna positions captured by Australian and American troops, and the threat from Gona and westward now removed, with the Australian victories there by 18 December, the Allies could now focus entirely on Sanananda. The fighting at this beachhead was desperate and bloody, and another three weeks would be required before it was also finally in Allied hands, marking the end of the Japanese Campaign to take Port Moresby.[9]

END NOTES

Chapter 1
1. Cameron, 2020b, 2020c; McCarthy, 1959; Milner, 1957.
2. McCarthy, 1959; Milner, 1957.
3. McCarthy, 1959; Milner, 1957.
4. Cameron, 2020; McCarthy, 1959; Milner, 1957; Powell, 2003; Smith 2020.
5. Austin, 2007, p.12.
6. Austin, 2007, p.55.
7. Cameron, 2020, 2022a, 2022b, 2022c.
8. McCarthy, 1959; Milner, 1957.
9. Quoted from Milner, 1957, p.133.
10. Quotes from Campbell, 2007, p.67.
11. Milner, 1957, p.132.
12. Milner, 1957.
13. Eichelberger, 1950, p.39.
14. Milner, 1957.
15. NARA – RG 319, Box 7.
16. Milner, 1957.
17. Quoted from McCarthy, 1959, p.352.
18. Quoted from McCarthy, 1959, p.352.
19. Quoted from Milner, 1957, p.138.
20. McCarthy, 1959; Milner, 1957.
21. Bergerud, 1996; Borneman, 2016; Bullard, 2007; Dean, 2011; Duffy, 2016; Edgerton,
22. 1977; Frank, 1990; Friedman, 2007; Horner, 1978, 1992; McAulay, 1992; McCarthy, 1959; Milner, 1957; Nash, 2022.
23. Quoted from Milner, 1957, p.138.

Chapter 2
1. Quoted from McCarthy, 1959, p.278.
2. Cameron, 2022a, 2022b, 2022c.
3. Bergerud, 1996; Campbell, 2007; Duffy, 2016; Gailey, 2000; Keogh, 1965; McAulay, 1992; McCarthy, 1959; Shaw, 2017.
4. Corrective Notes on 126th Combat Team, Buna Campaign; Marshall, 1945; Milner, 1957.
5. Quoted from Milner, 1957, p.112.
6. Campbell, 2007; Milner, 1957.
7. McCarthy, 1959; Milner, 1957.
8. Quoted from Milner, 1957, p.114.
9. Quoted from McCarthy, 1959, p.279.
10. Campbell, 2007; McCarthy, 1959; Mayo, 1975; Milner, 1957.
11. Bergerud, 1996; Blake, 2019; Campbell, 2007; Duffy, 2016; McAulay, 1992;
12. McCarthy, 1959; Milner, 1957; Trigellis-Smith, 1992.

13. Quoted from Trigellis-Smith, 1992, p.82.
14. McAulay, 1992.
15. Trigellis-Smith, 1992.
16. Quoted from Milner, 1957, p.107.
17. Blake, 2019; Milner, 1957; Trigellis-Smith, 1992.
18. Milner, 1957.
19. McCarthy, 1959; Milner, 1957; Shaw, 2017.
20. Milner, 1957.
21. Corrective Notes on 126th Combat Team, Buna Campaign.
22. Quoted from Milner, 1957, p.121.
23. Milner, 1957.
24. Milner, 1957.
25. Milner, 1957.
26. Milner, 1957.
27. Milner, 1957.
28. AWM 52 25/3/6/4; Byrnes, 1989; Cameron, 2020; Hooper, 1994.
29. AWM 52 4/2/5/16.
30. Cameron, 2022c; McCarthy, 1959; Milner, 1957.
31. Dean, 2011; Horner, 1992; McCarthy, 1959; Milner, 1957.
32. AWM 52 8/2/18.

Chapter 3
1. Cameron, 2023; Horner, 1992; McCarthy, 1959; Milner, 1957.
2. Milner, 1957.
3. Milner, 1957.
4. AWM 52 25/3/6/4; Milner, 1957; *History of the 32nd Division*, Eisenhower Library.
5. AWM 52 25/3/6/4; Milner, 1957; *History of the 32nd Division*, Eisenhower Library.
6. Milner, 1957.
7. NARA – RG 319, Box 7.
8. NARA – RG 319, Box 7.
9. Milner, 1957.
10. Quoted from Milner, 1957, p.137.
11. Quoted from Milner, 1957, p.136.
12. Quoted from Milner, 1957, p.137.
13. Quotes from Milner, 1957, p.137.
14. Quoted from Milner, 1957, p.139.
15. Horner, 1992; McCarthy, 1959; Milner, 1957.
16. Quoted from Milner, 1957, p.139.
17. Quoted from Milner, 1957, p.139.
18. McCarthy, 1959; Milner, 1957.
19. Quoted from Bergerud, 1996, pp.217–18.

Chapter 4
1. Cameron, 2023a, 2023b; Milner, 1957.
2. Milner, 1957.
3. Milner, 1957.

END NOTES

4. Milner, 1957.
5. Milner, 1957.
6. Milner, 1957.
7. Cameron, 2020; McCarthy, 1959; Milner, 1957.
8. Allchin, 1958, pp.283–84.
9. Eichelberger Buna Report, Eisenhower Library.
10. Correspondence Eichelberger to Floyd, dated 27 February 1943, Eisenhower Library.
11. Milner, 1957.
12. Cameron, 2022c, 2023a; McCarthy, 1959; Milner, 1957; Nash, 2022.
13. Milner, 1957; McCarthy, 1959.
14. Milner, 1957; McCarthy, 1959.
15. Bullard, 2007; Collie & Marutani, 2009; McAulay, 1992; Milner, 1957; McCarthy, 1959.
16. Borneman, 2016; Frank, 1990; Friedman, 2007; Milner, 1957; Tanaka, 1980.
17. Cameron, 2022c, 2023a; McCarthy, 1959; Milner, 1957.
18. Milner, 1957.
19. Milner, 1957.
20. Milner, 1957.

Chapter 5
1. McCarthy, 1959; Milner, 1957.
2. McCarthy, 1959.
3. McCarthy, 1959; Milner, 1957.
4. Horner, 1995; McCarthy, 1959; Milner, 1957.
5. Milner, 1957.
6. Bullard, 2007, p.205.
7. Bullard, 2007; Claringbould & Ingman, 2022.
8. Horner, 1995; Milner, 1957.
9. Claringbould & Ingman, 2022; McCarthy, 1959; Milner, 1957.
10. Claringbould & Ingman, 2022; McCarthy, 1959; Milner, 1957.
11. O'Brien, 1950, p.171.
12. Bullard, 2007.
13. Borneman, 2016; Bullard, 2007; Collie & Marutani, 2009; Edgerton, 1997; Frank, 1990; Friedman, 2007; Nash, 2022; Tanaka, 1980.
14. Hayashi & Coox, 1959, p.64.
15. Bullard, 2007; Collie & Marutani, 2009; Tanaka, 1980.
16. Quoted from Claringbould & Ingman, 2022, p.153.
17. Bullard, 2007; Hayashi & Coox, 1959; Long, 1973; McAulay, 1992; Tanaka, 1980.

Chapter 6
1. Horner, 1992; McCarthy, 1959; O'Brien, 1950.
2. Horner, 1992; McCarthy, 1959; O'Brien, 1950.
3. McCarthy, 1959; Milner, 1957; Shaw, 2017.
4. Milner, 1957.
5. McCarthy, 1959; Milner, 1957.
6. AWM 52 25/3/6/4.
7. Quoted from Horner, 1978, p.225.
8. Bullard, 2007; Hayashi & Coox, 1959; Long, 1973; McAulay, 1992; Tanaka, 1980.

Chapter 7

1. NARA – RG 319, Box 7.
2. Blakeley, 1957; Keogh, 1965; McCarthy, 1959; Marshall, 1945.
3. NARA – RG 319, Box 7.
4. Blakeley, 1957; McCarthy, 1959; Marshall, 1945; Milner, 1957.
5. AWM 52 25/3/6/4.
6. AWM 52 8/2/18.
7. Quoted from Bullard, 2007, p.208.
8. Quoted from Bullard, 2007, p.208.
9. Borneman, 2016; Bullard, 2007; Edgerton, 1997; Frank, 1990; Friedman, 2007; Nash, 2022; Tanaka, 1980.
10. Quoted from Tanaka, 1980, p.37.
11. Bullard, 2007; Collie & Marutani, 2009; Hayashi & Coox, 1959; Long, 1973; McAulay, 1992; Tanaka, 1980.
12. AWM 52 8/2/18.
13. AWM 52 8/1/18.

Chapter 8

1. Horner, 1992; McCarthy, 1959; Marshall, 1945.
2. Horner, 1992; McCarthy, 1959.
3. NARA – RG 319, Box 7.
4. *History of the 32nd Division*, Eisenhower Library; Milner, 1957.
5. Keogh, 1965; Marshall, 1945; Milner, 1957.
6. McCarthy, 1959; Milner, 1957.
7. NARA – RG 319, Box 7.
8. Bullard, 2007; Collie & Marutani, 2009; McAulay, 1992; Milner, 1957.
9. NARA – RG 319, Box 7.
10. McCarthy, 1959; Marshall, 1945; Miller, 1957.
11. NARA – RG 319, Box 7.
12. Milner, 1957, p.175.
13. Milner, 1957.
14. Quoted from Milner, p.175.
15. Milner, 1957, p.175.
16. McCarthy, 1959, p.359.
17. Quoted from McCarthy, 1959, p.359.
18. NARA – RG 319, Box 7.
19. Marshall, 1945; Milner, 1957.
20. Milner, 1957, p.176.
21. Milner, 1957.
22. Milner, 1957.
23. NARA – RG 319, Box 7.
24. Quoted from McAulay, 1992, p.30.
25. AWM 52 8/2/18.
26. Quoted from McAulay, 1992, p.30.
27. AWM 52 8/2/18.
28. Quoted from McCarthy, 1959, p.359.
29. Cameron, 2023a, 2023b; McCarthy, 1959.

END NOTES

Chapter 9
1. Bullard, 2007; McCarthy, 1957; Milner, 1959.
2. Milner, 1957, p.176.
3. Milner, 1957.
4. AWM 52 8/2/18.
5. McCarthy, 1959; Milner, 1957.
6. Quoted from Bullard, 2007, p.207.
7. Bullard, 2007; Hayashi & Coox, 1959; Cameron, 2023.

Chapter 10
1. Quoted from Mayo, 1975, p.102.
2. Blakeley, 1957; Marshall, 1945; Milner, 1957.
3. AWM 52 25/3/6/4; Blake, 2019; McCarthy, 1959; Trigellis-Smith, 1992.
4. Milner, 1957.
5. McCarthy, 1959; Milner, 1957.
6. McCarthy, 1959; Milner, 1957.
7. Cameron, 2022a, 2022b, 2022c, 2023a, 2023b; McCarthy, 1959; Milner, 1957.
8. McCarthy, 1959; Milner, 1957.
9. Corrective Notes on 126th Combat Team, Buna Campaign.
10. AWM 52 25/3/6/4; Trigellis-Smith, 1992.
11. AWM 52 25/3/6/4.
12. AWM 52 25/3/6/4; Trigellis-Smith, 1992.
13. AWM 52 25/3/6/4.
14. AWM 52 25/3/6/4.
15. AWM 52 25/3/6/4; Trigellis-Smith, 1992.
16. AWM 52 25/3/6/4.
17. AWM 52 25/3/6/4.
18. AWM 52 25/3/6/4; McCarthy, 1959.
19. Quoted from Trigellis-Smith, 1992, p.100.
20. AWM 52 25/3/6/4.
21. Quoted from Trigellis-Smith, 1990, p.104.
22. AWM 52 25/3/6/4.
23. McCarthy, 1959; Milner, 1957.
24. McCarthy, 1959.
25. Quoted from Bergerud, 1996, pp.216–17.
26. McCarthy, 1959.
27. Quoted from Campbell, 2007, p.174.
28. Quoted from Campbell, 2007, p.174.
29. NARA – RG 319, Box 4 – Colonel A. Herbert Smith to Samuel Milner, 20 January 1950; Milner, 1957.
30. NARA – RG 319, Box 7.
31. Horner, 1992; McCarthy, 1959; *History of the 32nd Division*, Eisenhower Library.
32. McCarthy, 1959.
33. McCarthy, 1959; Milner, 1957.
34. Milner, 1959.
35. AWM 52 4/2/5/16; McCarthy, 1959; O'Brien, 1950.

36. AWM 52 4/2/5/16; McCarthy, 1959; O'Brien, 1950.
37. AWM 52 4/2/1/19; Horner, 1992, 1995; McCarthy, 1959.
38. McCarthy, 1959.
39. Keogh, 1965; McCarthy, 1959.
40. AWM 52 8/2/18.

Chapter 11
1. Keogh, 1965; McCarthy, 1959; Marshall, 1945; Milner, 1957.
2. McCarthy, 1959; Milner, 1957.
3. NARA – RG 319, Box 7.
4. AWM 52 25/3/6/4; McCarthy, 1959.
5. AWM 52 25/3/6/4.
6. AWM 52 25/3/6/4.
7. AWM 52 25/3/6/4.
8. AWM 52 25/3/6/4.
9. AWM 52 25/3/6/4.
10. Quoted from Blake, 2019, p.122.
11. Blake, 2019.
12. NARA – RG 319, Box 7.
13. Dickens, 2005; McCarthy, 1959; Milner, 1967; Spencer, 1999.
14. Corrective Notes on 126th Combat Team, Buna Campaign.
15. AWM 52 8/2/18.
16. Milner, 1957.
17. Milner, 1957.
18. Milner, 1957.
19. Bullard, 2007; Collie & Marutani, 2009; McAulay, 1992; Milner, 1957.

Chapter 12
1. McCarthy, 1959; Milner, 1957.
2. AWM 52 25/3/6/4.
3. AWM 52 25/3/6/4.
4. Quoted from Trigellis-Smith, 1992, p.104.
5. NARA – RG 319, Box 7.
6. AWM 52 25/3/6/4.
7. Quoted from Trigellis-Smith, 1992, p.98.
8. AWFA interview 1319.
9. Milner, 1957.
10. NARA – RG 319, Box 7.
11. Milner, 1957.
12. Quoted from Campbell, 2007, p.192.
13. Milner, 1957.
14. NARA – RG 319, Box 7.
15. NARA – RG 319, Box 4 – Colonel Herbert A. Smith to Samuel Milner, 20 January 1950.
16. NARA – RG 319, Box 4 – Colonel Herbert A. Smith to Samuel Milner, 20 January 1950; McCarthy, 1959.

END NOTES

17. Horner, 1995; McCarthy, 1959; Milner, 1957.
18. Milner, 1959.
19. AWM 52 8/2/18.
20. Quoted from Horner, 1992, pp.219–20.

Chapter 13
1. NARA – RG 319, Box 4 – Colonel Herbert A. Smith to Samuel Milner, 20 January 1957.
2. McCarthy, 1959; Milner, 1957; *History of the 32nd Division*, Eisenhower Library.
3. Marshall, 1945; Milner, 1957.
4. Quoted from Campbell, 2007, p.193.
5. Quoted from Campbell, 2007, pp.194–95.
6. Milner, 1957.
7. Marshall, 1945; Milner, 1957.
8. NARA – RG 319, Box 4 – Colonel Herbert A. Smith to Samuel Milner, 20 January 1950.
9. Milner, 1957.
10. NARA – RG 319, Box 4 – Colonel Herbert A. Smith to Samuel Milner, 20 January 1950.
11. Milner, 1957.
12. NARA – RG 319, Box 4 – Colonel Herbert A. Smith to Samuel Milner, 20 January 1950.
13. NARA – RG 319, Box 4 – Colonel Herbert A. Smith to Samuel Milner, 20 January 1950; Milner, 1957.
14. Milner, 1957.
15. NARA – RG 319, Box 4 – Colonel Herbert A. Smith to Samuel Milner, 20 January 1950; Milner, 1957.
16. NARA – RG 319, Box 4 – Colonel Herbert A. Smith to Samuel Milner, 20 January 1957.
17. Milner, 1957.
18. Milner, 1957.
19. AWM 52 25/3/6/4.
20. Quoted from Trigellis-Smith, 1992, p.105.
21. Quoted from Trigellis-Smith, 1992, p.105.
22. AWM 52 25/3/6/4.
23. McCarthy, 1959; Marshall, 1945; Milner, 1957.
24. NARA – RG 319, Box 7.
25. Quoted from McCarthy, 1959, p.368.
26. AWM 52 8/2/18.

Chapter 14
1. NARA – RG 319, Box 7.
2. McCarthy, 1959.
3. AWM 52 25/3/6/4.
4. AWM 52 25/3/6/4.
5. Quoted from Bergerud, 1996, pp.221–22.
6. Quoted from Williams, 2021, pp.54–55.
7. NARA – RG 319, Box 4 – Colonel Herbert A. Smith to Samuel Milner.
8. Quoted from Milner, 1957, pp.187–88.
9. NARA – RG 319, Box 4 – Colonel Herbert A. Smith to Samuel Milner.

10. Milner, 1957.
11. AWM 52 8/2/18.
12. Quoted from McAulay, 1992, p.235.

Chapter 15
1. NARA – RG 319, Box 7.
2. Bullard, 2007; McCarthy, 1959.
3. Horner, 1995; McCarthy, 1959.
4. AWM 52 25/3/6/4; Milner, 1957.
5. Milner, 1957.
6. McCarthy, 1959; Milner, 1957.
7. McCarthy, 1959; Milner, 1957.
8. Corrective Notes on 126th Combat Team, Buna Campaign.
9. Milner, 1957, p.181.
10. AWM 52 25/3/6/4.
11. McCarthy, 1959; Milner, 1957.
12. AWM 52 25/3/6/4.
13. AWM 52 25/3/6/4.
14. AWM 52 25/3/6/4.
15. AWM 52 25/3/6/4.
16. Milner, 1957.
17. NARA – RG 319, Box 3 – Harding Diary.
18. Bullard, 2007.
19. AWM 52 8/2/18.
20. Quoted from Bullard, 2007, p.208.
21. Bullard, 2007.

Chapter 16
1. NARA – RG 319, Box 7.
2. Milner, 1957.
3. AWM 52 25/3/6/4.
4. AWM 52 25/3/6/4.
5. NARA – RG 319, Box 4 – Colonel Herbert A. Smith to Samuel Milner, 20 January 1950; Blakeley, 1957; McCarthy, 1959; Milner, 1957.
6. NARA – RG 319, Box 4 – Colonel Herbert A. Smith to Samuel Milner, 20 January 1950.
7. NARA – RG 319, Box 4 – Colonel Herbert A. Smith to Samuel Milner, 20 January 1950.
8. Milner, 1957.
9. NARA – RG 319, Box 3 – Harding Diary.
10. Bradbury, 2012; Brune, 1994, 2003; Claringbould & Ingman, 2022; McCarthy, 1959; McLeod, 2019; Reading, 1946; Walker, 1957.
11. Sweeting unpublished, pp.12–14.
12. Reading, 1946, pp.171–72.
13. Bullard, 2007; Cameron, 2023a.

Chapter 17
1. NARA – RG 319, Box 7; Milner, 1957; McCarthy, 1959.
2. NARA – RG 319, Box 7.

END NOTES

3. NARA – RG 319, Box 7.
4. AWM 52 25/3/6/4.
5. McCarthy, 1959.
6. Quoted from McCarthy, 1959, p.367.
7. McCarthy, 1959; Marshall, 1945; *History of the 32nd Division*, Eisenhower Library.
8. McCarthy, 1959.
9. Milner, 1957, pp.196–97.
10. Milner, 1957.
11. Quoted from Blakeley, 1957, p.77.
12. McCarthy, 1959; O'Brien, 1950.
13. Quoted from McCarthy, 1959, p.368.
14. Claringbould & Ingman, 2022, p.206.
15. Claringbould & Ingman, 2022.
16. McCarthy, 1959; O'Brien, 1950.
17. O'Brien, 1950, pp.180–81.
18. Bullard, 2007.
19. Bullard, 2007; Cameron, 2023a; Claringbould & Ingman, 2022.
20. AWM 52 8/2/18.
21. AWM 52 8/2/18.
22. AWM 52 8/2/18.

Chapter 18
1. Milner, 1957.
2. Milner, 1957.
3. NARA – RG 319, Box 4 – Colonel Herbert A. Smith to Samuel Milner, 20 January 1950; Milner, 1957.
4. Campbell, 2007.
5. Quoted from Campbell, 2007, pp.205–06.
6. AWM 52 25/3/6/4.
7. AWM 52 25/3/6/4.
8. AWM 52 8/2/18.
9. Eichelberger, 1950; Gallaway, 2000; McCarthy, 1959; Milner, 1957.
10. Bullard, 2007; Cameron, 2023a; Claringbould & Ingman, 2022.

Chapter 19
1. McCarthy, 1959; Milner, 1957.
2. McCarthy, 1959; Milner, 1957.
3. AWM 52 4/2/1/19.
4. Quoted from Milner, 1957, p.191.
5. Quoted from Milner, 1957, pp.191–92.
6. Milner, 1957.
7. Quoted from Campbell, 2007, p.211.
8. Milner, 1957.
9. Milner, 1957.
10. Milner, 1957.
11. Milner, 1957.

12. Milner, 1957.
13. AWM 52 8/2/18.
14. McCarthy, 1959; Milner, 1957.
15. Milner, 1957.
16. McCarthy, 1959; Milner, 1957.
17. McCarthy, 1959; Milner, 1957.
18. McCarthy, 1959; Milner, 1957.
19. McCarthy, 1959; Milner, 1957.
20. AWM 52 25/3/6/4.
21. AWM 52 25/3/6/4.
22. AWM 52 25/3/6/4.
23. Quoted from Trigellis-Smith, 1992, p.97.
24. Milner, 1957.
25. NARA – RG 319, Box 3 – Harding Diary.
26. Quoted from McAulay, 1992, p.83.
27. AWM 52 8/2/18.
28. Bullard, 2007; McCarthy, 1959; Milner, 1957.
29. Quoted from Bullard, 2007, pp.210–11.

Chapter 20
1. McCarthy, 1959; Milner, 1957.
2. McCarthy, 1959; Milner, 1957.
3. McCarthy, 1959; Mayo, 1975; Milner, 1957.
4. NARA – RG 319, Box 3 – Harding Diary.
5. McCarthy, 1959; Milner, 1957.
6. NARA – RG 319, Box 3 – Harding Diary.
7. NARA – RG 319, Box 3 – Harding Diary.
8. Cameron, 2022a, 2022b, 2022c; Horner, 1978; McCarthy, 1959.
9. Quoted from Milner, 1957, p.202.
10. Quoted from Milner, 1957, p.202.
11. Quoted from Milner, 1957, p.202.
12. Milner, 1957.
13. Quotes from Milner, 1957, p.203.
14. Milner, 1957, p.203.
15. Quoted from Horner, 1978, p.232.
16. Brune, 2003; McCarthy, 1959; Milner, 1957.
17. Brune, 2003; McCarthy, 1959; Milner, 1957.
18. Milner, 1957.
19. Blakeley, 1957; Milner, 1957.
20. Eichelberger, 1950, pp.20–21.
21. Eichelberger Buna Report, Eisenhower Library.
22. Blakeley, 1957; Milner, 1957.

Chapter 21
1. Eichelberger, 1950, p.22.
2. NARA – RG 319, Box 3 – Harding Diary.

END NOTES

3. Milner, 1957.
4. Quoted from Milner, 1957, p.205.
5. McCarthy, 1959.
6. Quoted from Milner, 1957, p.207.
7. Milner, 1957.
8. AWM 52 25/3/6/5.
9. AWM 52 25/3/6/5.
10. AWM 52 4/2/1/19.
11. Bradley, 2012; Eichelberger, 1950.
12. AWM 52 8/2/18.
13. Quoted from McAulay, 1992, p.95.
14. AWM 52 8/2/18.
15. Milner, 1957.
16. Milner, 1957, p.206.
17. AWM 52 8/2/18.

Chapter 22
1. McCarthy, 1959.
2. Corrective Notes on 126th Combat Team, Buna Campaign; McCarthy, 1959.
3. McCarthy, 1959; Milner, 1957.
4. Milner, 1957.
5. Corrective Notes on 126th Combat Team, Buna Campaign.
6. AWM 52 25/3/6/5.
7. AWM 52 25/3/6/5.
8. AWM 52 25/3/6/5.
9. Quoted from Milner, 1957, p.210.
10. Quotes from Milner, 1957, p.210.
11. Milner, 1957.
12. Milner, 1957.
13. AWM 52 8/2/18.
14. AWM 52 8/2/18.
15. NARA – RG 319, Box 3 – Harding Diary.
16. Milner, 1957, p.209.
17. Milner, 1957, p.209.
18. NARA – RG 319, Box 4 – Colonel Herbert A. Smith to Samuel Milner, 20 January 1950).
19. NARA – RG 319, Box 4 – Colonel Herbert A. Smith to Samuel Milner, 20 January 1950.
20. NARA – RG 319, Box 3 – Harding Diary.
21. Eichelberger, 1950; Milner, 1957.
22. Quoted from Milner, 1957, p.207.
23. Quoted from Milner, 1957, p.207.
24. Milner, 1957.
25. Eichelberger, 1950; Milner, 1957.
26. Eichelberger, 1950; Eichelberger, 1950; Milner, 1957.
27. NARA – RG 319, Box 3 – Harding Diary.
28. NARA – RG 319, Box 3 – Harding Diary; Eichelberger, 1950; Milner, 1957.
29. Quoted from Milner, 1957, p.207.

30. Quoted from Milner, 1957, p.207.
31. Milner, 1957, p.207.
32. Quoted from Milner, 1957, p.207.
33. NARA – RG 319, Box 3 – Harding Diary.
34. Eichelberger, 1950, pp.24–7.
35. NARA – RG 319, Box 4 – Colonel Herbert A. Smith to Samuel Milner, 20 January 1950.
36. Eichelberger, 1950; Gallaway, 2000; Mayo, 1975; Milner, 1957.
37. NARA – RG 319, Box 3 – Harding Diary.
38. Quoted from Milner, 1957, pp.211–12.
39. Bergerud, 1996; Borneman, 2016; Duffy, 2016; Eichelberger Buna Report, Eisenhower Library; Eichelberger, 1950; Gailey, 2000; McCarthy, 1959; Marshall, 1945; Milner, 1957.
40. Quoted from Blakeley, 1957, p.84.
41. AWM 52 8/2/18.

Chapter 23
1. McCarthy, 1959; Milner, 1957.
2. Quoted from Horner, 1978, p.234.
3. Milner, 1957.
4. Quoted from Milner, 1957, p.235.
5. Quoted from Milner, 1957, p.235.
6. Quoted from Milner, 1957, p.235.
7. Quoted from Milner, 1957, p.235.
8. Quoted from Milner, 1957, p.235.
9. Quoted from Milner, 1947, p.235.
10. Quoted from Milner, 1947, p.235.
11. McCarthy, 1959; Milner, 1957.
12. AWM 52 25/3/6/5; Milner, 1957.
13. AWM 52 25/3/6/5.
14. AWM 52 25/3/6/5.
15. Quoted from Trigellis-Smith, 1992, p.112.
16. Johnston, 1944, p.230.
17. Quoted from McAulay, 1992, p.181.
18. AWM 52 8/2/18.
19. AWM 52 8/2/18.
20. AWM 52 8/2/18.
21. Milner, 1957.
22. Milner, 1957.
23. NARA – RG 319, Box 4 – Colonel Herbert A. Smith to Samuel Milner, 20 January 1950.
24. AWM 52 4/2/1/19; McCarthy, 1959.
25. McCarthy, 1959, p.375.
26. McCarthy, 1959.
27. McCarthy, 1959.
28. Milner, 1957.

Chapter 24
1. Eichelberger Buna Report, Eisenhower Library; Milner, 1957.
2. Milner, 1957.

END NOTES

3. McCarthy, 1959, p.376.
4. NARA – GR 319, Box 4 – letter of MacNab to Milner, 15 August 1950.
5. NARA – GR 319, Box 4 – letter of MacNab to Milner, 15 August 1950; Milner, 1957.
6. Hopkins, 1978, p.112.
7. Quoted from Milner, 1957, p.237.
8. Trigellis-Smith, 1992.
9. AWM 52 25/3/6/5.
10. Quoted from Trigellis-Smith, 1992, p.115.
11. AWM 52 25/3/6/5.
12. AWM 52 25/3/6/5.
13. AWM 52 25/3/6/5.
14. Bullard, 2007; Collie & Marutani, 2009; McCarthy, 1959; Milner, 1957.
15. AWM 52 8/2/18.
16. AWM 52 8/2/18.
17. Milner, 1957; *History of the 32nd Division*, Eisenhower Library.
18. Quoted from Bergerud, 1996, p.288.
19. Bullard, 2007; Collie & Marutani, 2009; McAulay, 1992; McCarthy, 1959; Milner, 1957.
20. Brune, 1997.
21. Quoted from Brune, 1997, pp.228–29.

Chapter 25
1. McCarthy, 1959.
2. AWM 52 25/3/6/5; McCarthy, 1959.
3. McCarthy, 1959; Marshall, 1945; Milner, 1957.
4. McCarthy, 1959; Milner, 1957; Threlfall, 2014.
5. McCarthy, 1959.
6. McCarthy, 1959.
7. McCarthy, 1959.
8. McCarthy, 1959.
9. NARA – GR 319, Box 4 – letter of MacNab to Milner, 15 August 1950.
10. McCarthy, 1959; Milner, 1957.
11. Eichelberger Buna Report, Eisenhower Library; McCarthy, 1959; Milner, 1957.
12. Eichelberger Buna Report, Eisenhower Library; McCarthy, 1959; Milner, 1957.
13. NARA – GR 319, Box 4 – letter of MacNab to Milner, 15 August 1950.
14. AWM 52 4/2/5/16.
15. AWM 52 8/2/18.
16. AWM 52 8/2/18.
17. AWM 52 8/2/18.
18. Quoted from Bullard, 2007, p.223.
19. McCarthy, 1959; Marshall, 1945; Milner, 1957.
20. McCarthy, 1959; Marshall, 1945; Milner, 1957.
21. Marshall, 1945; Milner, 1957.
22. Corrective Notes on 126th Combat Team, Buna Campaign; Marshall, 1945; Milner, 1957.
23. Corrective Notes on 126th Combat Team, Buna Campaign.
24. McCarthy, 1959.

25. AWM 52 25/3/6/5.
26. AWM 52 25/3/6/5.
27. AWM 52 8/3/7.
28. AWM 52 8/3/7.
29. Quoted from Milner, 1987, p.241.

Chapter 26
1. McCarthy, 1959; Milner, 1957.
2. Blakeley, 1957; Marshall, 1945; Milner, 1957.
3. McCarthy, 1959; Marshall, 1945; Milner, 1957.
4. Bullard, 2007; Collie & Marutani, 2009; McAulay, 1992; Milner, 1957.
5. Eichelberger Buna Report, Eisenhower Library; Blakeley, 1957; Eichelberger, 1950; McCarthy, 1959; Marshall, 1945; Milner, 1957.
6. Campbell, 2007, p.236.
7. Blakeley, 1957; Campbell, 2007; McCarthy, 1959; Milner, 1957.
8. Milner, 1957.
9. Quoted from Milner, 1957, p.243.
10. Quoted from Milner, 1957, p.243.
11. Eichelberger Buna Report, Eisenhower Library; Blakeley, 1957; Eichelberger, 1950; Milner, 1957.
12. Quoted from Bullard, 2007, p.223.
13. Blakeley, 1957; McCarthy, 1959; Milner, 1957.
14. Blakeley, 1957; McCarthy, 1959; Milner, 1957.
15. Eichelberger, 1950, p.32.
16. Eichelberger, 1950, pp.28–29.
17. Milner, 1957.
18. Quoted from Milner, 1957, pp.244–45.
19. Correspondence Eichelberger to Floyd, dated 1 February 1943, Eisenhower Library.
20. Quoted from Milner, 1957, p.245.
21. Milner, 1957.
22. AWM 52 8/2/18.

Chapter 27
1. AWM 52 25/3/6/5; Milner, 1957.
2. AWM 52 25/3/6/5.
3. AWM 52 25/3/6/5; Milner, 1957.
4. AWM 52 25/3/6/5.
5. AWM 52 25/3/6/5.
6. AWM 52 25/3/6/5.
7. AWM 52 8/2/18.
8. AWM 52 8/2/18.
9. Milner, 957, p.248.
10. Milner, 1957.
11. Quoted from Milner, 1957, p.249.
12. AWM 52 4/2/5/16.
13. Blakeley, 1957; McCarthy, 1959; Marshall, 1945; Milner, 1957.

END NOTES

14. AWM 52 8/2/18.
15. Milner, 1957.
16. Milner, 1957.
17. Milner, 1957.
18. Bullard, 2007; Cameron, 2023; Hayashi & Coox, 1959; Tanaka, 1980.
19. Bullard, 2007; Cameron, 2023a; Hayashi & Coox, 1959; Tanaka, 1980.

Chapter 28
1. McCarthy, 1959; Milner, 1957.
2. McCarthy, 1959; Milner, 1957.
3. Quoted from Milner, 1957, p.249.
4. Blakeley, 1957; Milner, 1957.
5. Blakeley, 1957; Milner, 1957.
6. Collie & Marutani, 2009; McCarthy, 1959; McAulay, 1992; Milner, 1957.
7. Quoted from Milner, 1957, p.246.
8. Milner, 1957.
9. Quoted from Milner, 1957, p.247.
10. Milner, 1957.
11. Milner, 1957.
12. Quoted from Archer, 1985, pp.112–13.
13. Quoted by Milner, 1957, p.247.
14. Milner, 1957.
15. AWM 52 25/3/6/5.
16. AWM 52 25/3/6/5.
17. AWM 52 8/2/16.
18. AWM 52 8/2/16.
19. McCarthy, 1959.
20. Cameron, 2023a; McCarthy, 1959.
21. Brune, 1997; Milner, 1957.
22. Keogh, 1965; Milner, 1957.

Chapter 29
1. Milner, 1957.
2. McCarthy, 1959; Milner, 1957.
3. Quoted from Milner, 1957, p.250.
4. Quoted from Bullard, 2007, p.223.
5. AWM 52 8/2/18.
6. Quoted from McAulay, 1992, p.190.
7. AWM 52 4/2/5/16; McCarthy, 1959.
8. AWM 52 4/2/5/16.
9. O'Brien, Guns and Gunners, pp.174–76.
10. McCarthy, 1959; Milner, 1957.
11. AWM 52 4/2/1/19.
12. AWM 52 25/3/6/5.
13. AWM 52 25/3/6/5.
14. AWM 52 8/2/18.

15. Quoted from Williams, 2021, pp.53–54.
16. AWM 52 8/3/10; AWM 52 8/3/12; Allchin, 1958; Brune, 1997; Dickens, 2005; McCarthy, 1959.
17. Anderson, 2018; Bergerud, 1996; Borneman, 2016; Brune, 2003; Gailey, 2000; McCarthy, 1959; Henderson, 1992.
18. Slim, 1956, pp.187–88.

Chapter 30
1. Cameron, 2023a; Milner, 1957.
2. AWM 52 25/3/6/5; McCarthy, 1959; Milner, 1957; Trigellis-Smith, 1992.
3. AWM 52 25/3/6/5.
4. AWM 52 25/3/6/5.
5. AWM 52 25/3/6/5.
6. AWM 52 25/3/6/5.
7. AWM 52 25/3/6/5.
8. AWM 52 4/2/5/16; O'Brien, 1950.
9. AWM 52 4/2/5/16; O'Brien, 1950.
10. AWM 52 25/3/6/5.
11. AWM 52 25/3/6/5.
12. AWN 52 8/2/18.
13. AWM 52 8/2/18.
14. Quoted from Bullard, 2007, p.224.
15. Milner, 1957.
16. AWM 52 4/2/1/19.
17. Keogh, 1965; Milner, 1957.
18. AWM 52 8/2/18.

Chapter 31
1. Quoted from Milner, 1957, p.248.
2. Blakeley, 1957; McCarthy, 1959; Milner, 1957.
3. Milner, 1957.
4. AWM 52 4/2/5/16.
5. Claringbould & Ingman, 2022; McCarthy, 1959; Milner, 1957.
6. AWM 52 4/2/5/16.
7. AWM 52 4/2/5/16.
8. AWM 52 8/2/18.
9. AWM 52 8/2/18.
10. AWM 52 8/2/18.
11. AWM 52 25/3/6/5.
12. Quoted from Trigellis, 1992, p.118.
13. Trigellis-Smith, 1992, p.118.
14. McCarthy, 1959.
15. AWM 52 3/1/12/2.
16. Quoted from Handel, 2004, p.128.
17. AWM 52 8/2/18.
18. AWM 52 3/1/12/2; AWM 52 8/3/10; Allchin, 1958; Brune, 1997; McCarthy, 1959; Milner, 1957.

END NOTES

19. Dickens, 2005; McCarthy, 1959; Milner, 1957; Shaw, 2017.
20. McCarthy, 1959; Milner, 1957.
21. Bullard, 2007; Cameron, 2023; Collie & Marutani, 2009.

Chapter 32
1. Cameron, 2023a; Milner, 1957; McCarthy, 1959.
2. Milner, 1957.
3. Milner, 1957.
4. AWM 52 4/2/5/16.
5. AWM 52 4/2/5/16.
6. AWM 52 8/2/18.
7. McCarthy, 1957; Milner, 1957.
8. McCarthy, 1959; Milner, 1957.
9. AWM 52 8/2/18.
10. AWM 52 8/2/18; Milner, 1957; Shaw, 2017.
11. Dickens, 2005; Milner, 1957; Shaw, 2017.

Chapter 33
1. McCarthy, 1959.
2. AWM 52 8/2/18.
3. Keogh, 1965; McCarthy, 1959; Milner, 1957; Nicoll, 1982.
4. Corrective Notes on 126th Combat Team, Buna Campaign.
5. AWM 52 8/2/18; AWM 52 8/3/9; AWM 52 8/3/10; AWM 52 8/3/12; Allchin, 1958; Dickens, 2005; McCarthy, 1959; Milner, 1957.
6. Quoted from Hendel, 2004, p.130.
7. Quoted from Handel, 2004, pp.132–33.
8. AWM 52 4/2/5/16.
9. AWM 52 4/2/5/16.
10. AWM 52 8/3/9; AWM 52 8/3/10; Allchin, 1958; Dickens, 2005; Milner, 1957; Shaw, 2017.
11. AWM 52 8/2/16.
12. Quoted from Bullard, 2007, p.212.
13. Quoted from Bullard, 2007, p.212.
14. Quoted from Bullard, 2007, p.211.

Chapter 34
1. Milner, 1957.
2. Quotes from McCarthy, 1959, p.453.
3. AWM 52 3/1/12/2; AWM 52 8/2/18; Dickens, 2005; Handel, 2004; McCarthy, 1959; Shaw, 2017.
4. McCarthy, 1959, p.453.
5. McCarthy, 1959.
6. McCarthy, 1959.
7. AWM 52 8/2/18.
8. AWM 52 8/2/18.

Chapter 35
1. AWM 52 8/2/18.
2. Quoted from Spencer, 1999, pp.120–121.
3. Spencer, 1999.
4. AWM 52 4/2/5/17 – Appendix A.
5. AWM 52 4/2/5/17 – Appendix A.
6. AWM 52 8/2/18 – Appendices.
7. AWM 52 8/2/18.
8. Milner, 1957.
9. Milner, 1957, p.252.
10. Milner, 1957.
11. Brune, 1994, 2003; Bullard, 2007; Cameron, 2023a; McAulay, 1992; McCarthy, 1959; Marshall, 1945; Nash, 2022; Tanaka, 1980.
12. Quoted from McAulay, 1992, p.141.
13. Quoted from Claringbould & Ingman, 2022, p.190.
14. Cameron, 2023a; Collie & Marutani, 2009; Marshall, 1945; Milner, 1957; Tanaka, 1980.
15. AWM 52 8/2/18.

Chapter 36
1. Milner, 1957.
2. Milner, 1957.
3. Quoted from Bergerud, 1996, pp.72–73.
4. Quoted from Milner, 1957, p.253.
5. Milner, 1957.
6. AWM 52 4/2/5/17 – Appendix A.
7. AWM 52 4/2/5/17 – Appendix A.
8. AWM 52 3/1/12/2; Milner, 1957; Shaw, 2017.
9. Quoted from McAulay, 1992, p.204.
10. AWM 52 8/2/18.

Chapter 37
1. Quoted from Milner, 1957, p.253.
2. Milner, 1957.
3. Quoted from Milner, 1957, p.253.
4. Marshall, 1945; Milner, 1957.
5. Milner, 1957.
6. Milner, 1957.
7. Milner, 1957.
8. AWM 52 8/3/10.
9. AWM 52 4/2/5/17 – Appendix A; AWM 52 8/2/18; Allchin, 1958; Brune, 1997; McCarthy, 1959.
10. AWM 52 8/2/18.
11. AWM 52 4/2/5/17 – Appendix A; AWM 52 8/2/18.
12. McCarthy, 1959; Milner, 1957.
13. NARA – GR 319, Box 4 – letter of MacNab to Milner, 15 August 1950.

END NOTES

14. Collie & Marutani, 2009; McAulay, 1992; Milner, 1957.
15. AWM 52 8/2/18.
16. AWM 52 8/2/18.
17. Quoted from Milner, 1957, p.254.
18. Milner, 1947.

Chapter 38
1. Quoted from Dickens, 2005, p.195.
2. AWM 52 3/1/12/2; AWM 52 8/2/18; AWM 52 8/3/10; Allchin, 1958; McCarthy, 1959.
3. AWM 52 3/1/12/2; AWM 52 8/2/18; Milner, 1957; Shaw, 2017.
4. Milner, 1957.
5. AWM 52 4/2/5/17 – Appendix A.
6. Milner, 1957.
7. AWM 52 3/1/12/2; Handel, 2004.
8. AWM 52 3/1/12/2.
9. Quoted from Handel, 2004, p.131.
10. McCarthy, 1959; Spencer, 1999.
11. Spencer, 1999, pp124–25.
12. Quoted from Brune, 1997, p.165.
13. Brune, 1997, p.165.
14. Quoted from Brune, 2003, p.504.
15. McCarthy, 1959.
16. Quoted from Handel, 2004, pp.135–36.
17. AWM 52 8/2/18/39.
18. Quotes from Handel, 2004, p.137.
19. AWM 52 8/2/18.
20. AWM 52 8/2/18.
21. McCarthy, 1959; Milner, 1957.
22. AWM 52 4/2/5/17 – Appendix A.
23. McCarthy, 1959; Milner, 1957.
24. Blakeley, 1957; McCarthy, 1959; Milner, 1957.
25. Milner, 1957.
26. McCarthy, 1959.

Chapter 39
1. Brune, 1994, 2003; Cameron, 2023.
2. AWM 52 8/2/18; Dickens, 2005; McCarthy, 1959; Milner, 1957.
3. Quoted from Graeme-Evans, 1990, p.240.
4. Quoted from Dickens, 2005, p.197.
5. AWM 52 8/2/18; Dickens, 2005; McCarthy, 1959; Milner, 1957.
6. AWM 52 8/2/18; McCarthy, 1959; Milner, 1957; Spencer, 1999.
7. AWM 52 8/2/18; McCarthy, 1959; Milner, 1957; Spencer, 1999.
8. Quoted from Brune, 1997, p.164.
9. AWM 52 8/2/18; McCarthy, 1959; Milner, 1957; Spencer, 1999.
10. AWM 52 8/2/18; McCarthy, 1959; Milner, 1957; Spencer, 1999.

11. McCarthy, 1959.
12. AWM 52 4/2/5/17 – Appendix A.
13. Quoted from Dickens, 2005, p.196.
14. Quoted from Graeme-Evans, 1990, pp.240–41.
15. AWM 52 3/1/12/2; AWM 52 8/2/18; McCarthy, 1959.
16. McCarthy, 1959, p.456.
17. AWM 52 8/3/9.
18. AWM 52 4/2/5/17 – Appendix A.
19. Quoted from Brune, 1997, p.168.
20. Quoted from Handel, 2004, pp.139–141.
21. Quoted from Graeme-Evans, 1990, p.241.
22. AWM 52 8/2/18; McCarthy, 1959.
23. Eichelberger, 1950, pp.44–45.
24. AWM 52 3/1/12/2; AWM 52 8/2/18; McCarthy, 1959.
25. Quoted from Handel, 2004, p.142.
26. Quoted from Brune, 1997, p.168.
27. AWM 52 8/2/18; McCarthy, 1959.
28. AWM 52 3/1/12/2; AWM 52 8/2/18; McCarthy, 1959.
29. AWM 52 8/2/18; Dickens, 2005; McCarthy, 1959.
30. AWM 52 8/2/18; Dickens, 2005; McCarthy, 1959.
31. Quoted from Graeme-Evans, 1990, p.241.
32. Spencer, 1999.
33. AWM 52 8/2/18; McCarthy, 1959.
34. Quoted from Spencer, 1999, p.129.
35. McCarthy, 1959.
36. AWM 52 8/2/18; Dickens, 2005; McCarthy, 1959; Spencer, 1999.
37. Quoted from Brune, 1997, p.174.
38. Quoted from Brune, 1997, p.174.
39. McCarthy, 1959.
40. AWM 52 8/2/18; Dickens, 2005; McCarthy, 1959; Spencer, 1999.
41. AWM 52 8/2/18; McCarthy, 1959.
42. AWM 52 8/2/18; McCarthy, 1959.
43. Quotes from McCarthy, 1959, p.459.
44. AWM 52 8/2/18; McCarthy, 1959.
45. Quoted from McCarthy, 1959, p.459.
46. McCarthy, 1959, p.459.
47. AWM 52 3/1/12/2; AWM 52 8/2/18; Handel, 2004; McCarthy, 1959.
48. Quoted from Handel, 2004, pp.150–51.
49. Brune, 1997; Handel, 2004; McCarthy, 1959.
50. Quoted from Brune, 1997, p.172.
51. AWM 52 3/1/12/2.
52. Quoted from Handel, 2004, p.152.
53. AWM 52 8/2/18; Handel, 2004; McCarthy, 1959.
54. Quoted from Handel, 2004, p.144.
55. Quoted from Handel, 2004, p.148.
56. Quoted from Handel, 2004, p.145.

END NOTES

57. Quoted from Handel, 2004, p.146.
58. Quoted from Handel, 2004, p.148.
59. AWM 52 4/2/5/17 – Appendix A.
60. Milner, 1957, p.262.
61. Quoted from Milner, 1957, p.263.
62. AWM 52 8/2/18; McCarthy, 1959.
63. AWM 52 8/2/18; McCarthy, 1959.
64. McCarthy, 1959, p.461.
65. AWM 52 8/2/18; McCarthy, 1959.
66. Milner, 1957, p.264.
67. Quoted from Brune, 2003, p.510.
68. AWM 52 8/2/18; McCarthy, 1959; Spencer, 1999.
69. AWM 52 8/2/18; McCarthy, 1959; Milner, 1957.
70. Spencer, 1999, p.132.
71. Quoted from MacDonald & Brune, 1998, p.129.
72. Quoted from Brune, 1997, pp.176–77.
73. Quoted from Dickens, 2005, pp.203–04.
74. McCarthy, 1959, p.462.
75. AWM 52 8/2/18; McCarthy, 1959.
76. Quoted from Handel, 2004, p.152
77. Handel, 2004.
78. AWM 52 8/2/18.
79. AWM 52 8/3/9.
80. AWM 52 8/3/10.
81. AWM 52 8/3/10.
82. AWM 52 8/2/18; AWM 52 8/3/10; Allchin, 1958; Milner, 1957.
83. AWFA interview 1814.
84. Quoted from McAulay, 1992, p.215.
85. Quoted from McAulay, 1992, p.215.
86. Quoted from Bullard, 2007, p.224.
87. AWM 52 4/2/5/17 – Appendix A.
88. NARA – GR 319, Box 4 – letter of MacNab to Milner, 15 August 1950.
89. Blakeley, 1957; Milner, 1957; McCarthy, 1959.
90. Blakeley, 1957; Milner, 1957.
91. Milner, 1957.
92. Blakeley, 1957; Milner, 1957.
93. Quoted from Milner, 1957, p.264.

Chapter 40
1. AWM 52 8/2/18.
2. AWM 52 8/3/10.
3. AWM 52 4/2/5/16; Milner, 1957.
4. AWM 52 8/3/10.
5. AWM 52 8/3/9.
6. McCarthy, 1959, p.462.
7. AWM 52 3/1/12/2.

8. McCarthy, 1959.
9. AWM 52 4/2/5/17 – Appendix A.
10. Quoted from Horner, 1978, p.246.
11. Quoted from McAulay, 1992, p.217.
12. AWM 52 8/2/18.
13. McCarthy, 1959; Milner, 1957.
14. Milner, 1957.
15. Corrective Notes on 126th Combat Team, Buna Campaign.
16. Milner, 1957.
17. Blakeley, 1957; Milner, 1957.
18. Quoted from Bullard, 2007, p.212.
19. Quoted from Bullard, 2007, p.212.

Chapter 41
1. AWM 52 8/3/9; Allchin, 1958; McCarthy, 1959.
2. AWM 52 3/1/12/2; AWM 52 8/2/18; McCarthy, 1959.
3. AWM 52 3/1/12/2; McCarthy, 1959; Milner, 1957.
4. AWM 52 8/3/9.
5. Quoted from Handel, 2004, pp.156–57.
6. McCarthy, 1959.
7. Quoted from Brune, 1997, p.180.
8. AWM 52 8/3/9.
9. McCarthy, 1959.
10. AWM 52 8/2/18; McCarthy, 1959; Milner, 1957.
11. AWM 52 8/2/19.
12. Blakeley, 1957; McCarthy, 1959; Milner, 1957.
13. Milner, 1957.
14. Milner, 1957.
15. AWM 52 4/2/5/17 – Appendix A.
16. AWM 52 8/2/19.
17. Milner, 1957; McCarthy, 1959.
18. AWM 52 8/2/18.
19. AWM 52 8/2/18.
20. AWM 52 8/2/18.
21. Collie & Marutani, 2009; Milner, 1957.
22. Marshall, 1945; Milner, 1957.
23. Milner, 1957.
24. Milner, 1957.
25. Milner, 1957.
26. Milner, 1957.
27. Milner, 1957.
28. Quoted from Milner, 1957, p.288.
29. McCarthy, 1959; Milner, 1957.
30. Quoted from Milner, 1957, p.291.
31. Milner, 1957.
32. McCarthy, 1959; Milner, 1957.

END NOTES

33. Quoted from Milner, 1957, p.288.
34. Quote from Dean, 2011, p.192.
35. Tanaka, 1980.

Chapter 42
1. AWM 52 8/2/18; Allchin, 1958; Brune, 2003; Keogh, 1965; McCarthy, 1959; Marshall, 1945.
2. AWM 52 8/2/18; Allchin, 1958; Keogh, 1965; McCarthy, 1959.
3. AWM 52 8/3/10.
4. Quoted from Dickens, 2005, p.200.
5. AWM 52 8/2/18; McCarthy, 1959.
6. Quoted from Spencer, 1999, p.136.
7. Dickens, 2005, p.210.
8. AWM 52 8/2/18; McCarthy, 1959.
9. AWM 52 8/3/9.
10. AWM 52 4/2/5/17 – Appendix A.
11. AWM 52 4/2/5/17 – Appendix A.
12. AWM 52 4/2/5/17 – Appendix A.
13. AWM 52 3/1/12/2.
14. AWM 52 8/2/18.
15. AWM 52 8/2/18.
16. Milner, 1957.
17. Milner, 1957.
18. McCarthy, 1959; Milner, 1957.
19. Blakeley, 1957; Milner, 1957.
20. Blakeley, 1957; Milner, 1957.
21. Blakeley, 1957; Milner, 1957.

Chapter 43
1. Quoted from McCarthy, 1958, p.465.
2. AWM 52 8/3/10.
3. Quoted from Brune, 1997, pp.189–91.
4. AWM 52 8/2/18.
5. AWM 52 8/3/10.
6. Quoted from Dickens, 2005, p.211.
7. AWM 52 8/3/10.
8. AWM 52 8/3/10; Allchin, 1958; McCarthy, 1959.
9. AWM 52 8/3/9; McCarthy, 1959.
10. AWM 52 8/3/9; McCarthy, 1959.
11. Quoted from Brune, 1997, p.184.
12. McCarthy, 1959.
13. Quoted from Handel, 2004, p.159.
14. AWM 52 4/2/5/17 – Appendix A.
15. AWM 52 3/1/12/2; McCarthy, 1959.
16. AWM 52 3/1/12/2; AWM 52 8/3/9; McCarthy, 1959.
17. AWM 52 8/3/9.

18. AWM 52 8/3/9.
19. Quoted from Dickens, 2005, p.213.
20. Quoted from Bullard, 2007, p.224.
21. Quoted from Williams, 2021, p.52.
22. Quoted from Collie & Marutani, 2009, p.246 and from McAulay, 1992, pp.230–31.
23. AWM 52 8/2/16.
24. Milner, 1957.
25. Quoted from Milner, 1957, p.291.
26. Milner, 1957.
27. McCarthy, 1959.

Chapter 44
1. AWM 52 8/3/10; Allchin, 1958; McCarthy, 1959.
2. AWM 52 8/2/18; McCarthy, 1959.
3. Quoted from Milner, 1957, p.271.
4. AWM 52 8/3/10; Blakeley, 1957; McCarthy, 1959; Milner, 1957.
5. Milner, 1957, p.271.
6. Milner, 1957.
7. McCarthy, 1959; Milner, 1957.
8. AWM 52 8/2/18.
9. AWM 52 8/3/9.
10. AWM 52 8/2/18.
11. Milner, 1957.
12. Milner, 1957.
13. Milner, 1957.
14. Quoted from Milner, 1957, p.292.
15. Milner, 1957.
16. Milner, 1957.
17. Milner, 1957.
18. Quoted from Milner, 1957, pp.292–93.
19. McCarthy, 1959; Milner, 1957.
20. AWM 52 4/2/5/17 – Appendix A.
21. McCarthy, 1959; Milner, 1957.
22. Quotes from McCarthy, 1959, p.469.
23. Milner, 1957; Shaw, 2017.
24. Bullard, 2007, p.220.

Chapter 45
1. McCarthy, 1959.
2. AWM 52 8/3/10.
3. McCarthy, 1959.
4. AWM 52 4/2/5/17 – Appendix A; AWM 52 8/2/18; AWM 52 8/3/10; Handel, 2004; McCarthy, 1959.
5. Allchin, 1958, p.288.
6. Quoted from Brune, 1997, p.194.

END NOTES

7. Allchin, 1958; McCarthy, 1959.
8. Quotes from McCarthy, 1959, p.470.
9. Quoted from Brune, 1997, pp.194–95.
10. Quoted from Brune, 1997, p.195.
11. Quoted from Brune, 1997, p.195.
12. Handel, 2004.
13. Quoted from Handel, 2004, pp.167–68.
14. Handel, 2004.
15. AWM 52 8/3/10.
16. AWM 52 4/2/5/17 – Appendix A.
17. Quoted from Bullard, 2007, p.225.
18. McCarthy, 1959; Milner, 1957.
19. AWM 52 8/3/10.
20. AWM 52 8/3/10.
21. AWM 52 8/3/10; McCarthy, 1959.
22. Quoted from Brune, 1997, p.196.
23. AWM 52 8/3/10; McCarthy, 1959.
24. Allchin, 1958, pp.290–91.
25. AWM 52 8/3/10; Allchin, 1958.
26. Allchin, 1958; Milner, 1957.
27. AWM 52 8/3/9.
28. Allchin, 1958; AWM 52 8/3/9.
29. McDonald & Brune, 1998, p.135.
30. Quoted from McAulay, 1992, p.234.
31. Milner, 1957; McCarthy, 1959.
32. Milner, 1957.
33. McCarthy, 1957; Milner, 1957.
34. Collie & Marutani, 2009; McAulay, 1992; Milner, 1957.
35. Quoted from Milner, 1957, p.294.
36. Blakeley, 1957; Marshall, 1945; Milner, 1957.
37. Blakeley, 1957; Milner, 1957.
38. Quoted from Milner, 1957, p.294.
39. Milner, 1957.
40. Blakeley, 1957; Marshall, 1945; Milner, 1957.
41. McCarthy, 1959; Marshall, 1945; Milner, 1957.
42. Milner, 1957.
43. McCarthy, 1959; Milner, 1957.
44. Milner, 1957.
45. Blakeley, 1957; McCarthy, 1959; Marshall, 1945; Milner, 1957.
46. Blakeley, 1957; McCarthy, 1959; Marshall, 1945; Milner, 1957.
47. Blakeley, 1957; McCarthy, 1959; Milner, 1957.
48. Blakeley, 1957; Milner, 1957.
49. Quoted from Milner, 1957, p.298.

Chapter 46
1. AWM 52 8/2/18; Keogh, 1965; McCarthy, 1959; Milner, 1957.

2. AWM 52 8/3/9.
3. Milner, 1957.
4. Milner, 1957, p.276.
5. Milner, 1957.
6. Milner, 1957.
7. AWM 52 8/3/10; McCarthy, 1959.
8. Allchin, 1958, p.293.
9. Quoted from Patten, 2009, p.193.
10. Allchin, 1958, p.291.
11. AWM 52 4/2/5/17 – Appendix A.
12. Eichelberger, 1950, p.47.
13. McCarthy, 1959; Milner, 1957.
14. McCarthy, 1959; Marshall, 1945; Milner, 1957.
15. McCarthy, 1959; Marshall, 1945; Milner, 1957.
16. McCarthy, 1959; Milner, 1957.
17. Blakeley, 1957; Milner, 1957.
18. Blakeley, 1957; McCarthy, 1959; Marshall, 1945; Milner, 1957.
19. McCarthy, 1959; Milner, 1957.
20. Quoted from Milner, 1957, p.299.
21. McCarthy, 1959; Marshall, 1945; Milner, 1957.
22. Quoted from Milner, 1957, p.299.
23. Quoted from Bullard, 2007, p.213.
24. Quoted from Handel, 2004, p.172.

Chapter 47
1. Allchin, 1958; McCarthy, 1959.
2. Allchin, 1958, p.296.
3. Allchin, 1958, p.295.
4. Allchin, 1958; McCarthy, 1959.
5. AWM 52 8/2/18; AWM 52 8/3/10; Allchin, 1958; McCarthy, 1959.
6. Allchin, 1958, pp.294–95.
7. Quoted from Brune, 1997, p.199.
8. Quoted from Brune, 1997, p.199.
9. Allchin, 1958, p.296.
10. Allchin, 1958; McCarthy, 1959.
11. AWM 52 8/2/18; Allchin, 1958; McCarthy, 1959.
12. Quoted from Bullard, 2007, p.225.
13. Allchin, 1958; McCarthy, 1959.
14. McCarthy, 1959, p.472.
15. McCarthy, 1959.
16. McCarthy, 1959, p.473.
17. Bullard, 2007; McCarthy, 1959; Milner, 1957.
18. Bullard, 2007; McCarthy, 1959; Milner, 1957.
19. AWM 52 4/2/5/17 – Appendix A.
20. AWM 52 4/2/5/17 – Appendix A.
21. O'Brien, 1950; McCarthy, 1959.

END NOTES

22. Milner, 1957.
23. McCarthy, 1959; O'Brien, 1950.
24. O'Brien, 1950, pp.189–90.
25. Quoted from McCarthy, 1959, p.475.
26. O'Brien, 1950; McCarthy, 1959.
27. Blakeley, 1957; McCarthy, 1959; Marshall, 1945; Milner, 1957.
28. McCarthy, 1959; Marshall, 1945; Milner, 1957.
29. Quoted from Milner, 1957, p.300.
30. Marshall, 1945; Milner, 1957.
31. Quoted from Milner, 1957, p.301.
32. Milner, 1957.
33. Quoted from Bullard, 2007, p.214.

Chapter 48
1. Milner, 1957.
2. Quoted from Brune, 1997, p.200.
3. AWM 52 8/3/10; McCarthy, 1959.
4. AWM 52 8/3/10; McCarthy, 1959.
5. Milner, 1957.
6. Corrective Notes on 126th Combat Team, Buna Campaign.
7. AWM 52 8/3/10; Milner, 1957.
8. Quoted from Bullard, 2007, p.225.
9. Allchin, 1958; Brune, 1997; McCarthy, 1959.
10. Quoted from Brune, 1997, p.210.
11. Quoted from Brune, 1997, p.201.
12. Quoted from Brune, 1997, p.202.
13. Allchin, 1958, p.297.
14. Allchin, 1958.
15. McCarthy, 1959, Milner, 1957.
16. Handel, 2004; McCarthy, 1959; Milner, 1957.
17. Blakeley, 1957; McCarthy, 1959; Milner, 1957.
18. Eichelberger, 1950, pp.47–48.
19. Corrective Notes on 126th Combat Team, Buna Campaign.
20. Marshall, 1945, p.56.
21. Quoted from Bergerud, 1996, p.375.
22. Bullard, 2007; Collie & Marutani, 2009.
23. Quoted from Bullard, 2007, pp.213–14.

Chapter 49
1. AWM 52 4/2/5/17 – Appendix A; AWM 52 8/3/19; McCarthy, 1959.
2. Quoted from Brune, 1997, p.206.
3. AWM 52 4/2/5/17 – Appendix A; AWM 52 8/3/19; McCarthy, 1959.
4. Quoted from Brune, 1997, p.204.
5. AWM 52 8/3/10.
6. McCarthy, 1959, p.476.
7. AWM 52 8/3/10.

8. AWM 52 8/3/10.
9. AWM 52 8/3/10.
10. Milner, 1957, p.279.
11. McCarthy, 1959.
12. McCarthy, 1959.
13. McCarthy, 1959.
14. McCarthy, 1959; Milner, 1957.
15. AWM 52 4/2/5/17 – Appendix A.
16. AWM 52 3/1/12/2; AWM 52 8/2/18.
17. Milner, 1957.
18. Quoted from Williams, 2021, pp.55–56.
19. Eichelberger, 1950, p.48.
20. Milner, 1957.
21. Milner, 1957, p.310.
22. McCarthy, 1959.
23. Marshall, 1945; Milner, 1957.
24. Marshall, 1945; Milner, 1957.
25. Milner, 1957.
26. Blakeley, 1957; McCarthy, 1959; Milner, 1957.
27. Quoted from Bullard, 2007, p.225.
28. Bullard, 2007; Collie & Marutani, 2009; McAulay, 1992.
29. Quoted from Bullard, 2007, p.214.
30. Bullard, 2007; Cameron, 2023; Collie & Marutani, 2009; McCarthy, 1959; Milner, 1957.
31. Cameron, 2023; McCarthy, 1959; Milner, 1957.
32. Byrnes, 1989; Sinclair, 1990.

Chapter 50
1. Keogh, 1965; Milner, 1957; McCarthy, 1959.
2. AWM 52 8/2/18; Milner, 1957; McCarthy, 1959.
3. AWM 52 4/2/5/17 – Appendix A.
4. McCarthy, 1959, p.477.
5. Quoted from Brune, 1997, p.205.
6. Quoted from Brune, 2003, p.526.
7. AWM 52 3/1/12/2; McCarthy, 1959; Milner, 1957.
8. McCarthy, 1959.
9. McCarthy, 1959.
10. AWM 52 3/1/12/2; McCarthy, 1959; Milner, 1957.
11. AWM 52 3/1/12/2; McCarthy, 1959; Milner, 1957.
12. Quoted from Handel, 2004, pp.180–81.
13. McCarthy, 1959, p.478.
14. Quoted from McCarthy, 1959, p.478.
15. McCarthy, 1959, pp.478–79.
16. AWM 52 3/1/12/3.
17. Quoted from Brune, 1997, p.208.
18. AWM 52 3/1/12/2; Allchin, 1958; McCarthy, 1959.

END NOTES

19. AWFA interview 1814.
20. McCarthy, 1959, p.479.
21. AWM 52 3/1/12/2; McCarthy, 1959.
22. AWM 52 3/1/12/2; McCarthy, 1959.
23. McCarthy, 1959, p.480.
24. McCarthy, 1959.
25. AWM 52 8/2/18; AWM 52 8/3/12; Allchin, 1958; McCarthy, 1959.
26. AWM 52 8/2/18.
27. AWFA interview 696.
28. Milner, 1957.
29. Corrective Notes on 126th Combat Team, Buna Campaign.
30. Milner, 1957.
31. Marshall, 1945; Milner, 1957.
32. Bullard, 2007; Cameron, 2023a; McCarthy, 1959; Milner, 1957.

Chapter 51
1. AWM 52 3/1/12/2; AWM 52 8/2/18; Allchin, 1958; McCarthy, 1959.
2. McCarthy, 1959; Marshall, 1945.
3. AWM 52 8/3/9.
4. McCarthy, 1959.
5. Milner, 1957.
6. Milner, 1957.
7. Blakeley, 1957; Milner, 1957.
8. Quoted from Bullard, 2007, p.226.

Chapter 52
1. AWM 52 8/2/18; McCarthy, 1959.
2. Milner, 1957.
3. Quoted from Graeme-Evans, 1990, p.252.
4. Quoted from Graeme-Evans, 1990, p.255.
5. Quoted from Graeme-Evans, 1990, p.255.
6. Quoted from Graeme-Evans, 1990, p.252.
7. Graeme-Evans, 1990.
8. AWM 52 8/3/9.
9. AWM 52 8/3/10.
10. AWM 52 4/2/5/17 – Appendix A.
11. McCarthy, 1959.
12. Quoted from Handel, 2004, pp.185–86.
13. Milner, 1957.
14. Milner, 1957; Shaw, 2017.
15. McCarthy, 1959; Milner, 1957.
16. Milner, 1957, p.313.
17. Quoted from Milner, 1957, p.313.
18. Quoted from Milner, 1957, p.313.
19. Quoted from Milner, 1957, pp.313–14.
20. McCarthy, 1959; Milner, 1957.

21. Milner, 1957, p.314.
22. McCarthy, 1959; Milner, 1957.
23. Blakeley, 1957; Milner, 1957.
24. McCarthy, 1959; Milner, 1957.
25. Quoted from Milner, 1957, p.314.
26. Quoted from Milner, 1957, p.315.

Chapter 53
1. AWM 52 3/1/12/3; AWM 52 8/2/18; AWM 52 8/3/12; McCarthy, 1959; Milner, 1957.
2. AWM 52 3/1/12/3; AWM 52 8/2/18; McCarthy, 1959.
3. AWM 52 8/3/12.
4. Quoted from Graeme-Evans, 1990, p.260.
5. McCarthy, 1959; Milner, 1957.
6. Quoted from Graeme-Evans, 1990, p.260.
7. Quoted from Milner, 1957, p.308.
8. McCarthy, 1959; Milner, 1957.
9. Quoted from Graeme-Evans, 1990, p.263.
10. Quoted from Graeme-Evans, 1990, p.263.
11. AWM 52 8/2/18; AWM 52 8/3/12; McCarthy, 1959.
12. Quoted from Brune, 1997, p.215.
13. AWM 52 8/2/18; AWM 52 8/3/12; McCarthy, 1959.
14. Quoted from Graeme-Evans, 1990, p.265.
15. Quoted from McDonald & Brune, 1998, p.149.
16. Quoted from Graeme-Evans, 1990, p.268.
17. Quoted from Brune, 1997, p.215.
18. Quoted from Graeme-Evans, 1990, p.268.
19. AWM 52 8/2/18; AWM 52 8/3/12; Graeme-Evans, 1991; McCarthy, 1959.
20. Quoted from Graeme-Evans, 1990, p.264.
21. AWM 52 8/2/18; AWM 52 8/3/12; Graeme-Evans, 1991; McCarthy, 1959.
22. Quoted from Graeme-Evans, 1990, p.272.
23. Quoted from Graeme-Evans, 1990, p.272.
24. Quoted from Graeme-Evans, 1990, p.272.
25. AWM 52 8/3/12.
26. AWM 52 8/3/12.
27. Graeme-Evans, 1990.
28. Quotes from Bradbury, 2012, p.154.
29. Quoted from Graeme-Evans, 1990, p.271.

Chapter 54
1. Quoted from Graeme-Evans, 1990, p.269.
2. Quoted from Graeme-Evans, 1990, p.270.
3. Quoted from Graeme-Evans, 1990, p.277.
4. Quoted from Brune, 1997, pp.215–16.
5. Quoted from McDonald & Brune, 1998, p.145.
6. Quoted from Handel, 2004, p.189.
7. Quoted from Graeme-Evans, 1990, p.273.

END NOTES

8. Quoted from Brune, 1967, pp.218–19.
9. Quoted from Graeme-Evans, 1990, p.273.
10. Quoted from Brune, 1997, p.215.
11. Quoted from Graeme-Evans, 1990, pp.273–74.
12. Quoted from Graeme-Evans, 1990, p.274.
13. Quoted from Brune, 1997, p.219.
14. AWM 52 8/2/18; McCarthy, 1959.
15. Quoted from Dickens, 2005, p.218.
16. Quoted from Brune, 1967, p.220.
17. AWFA interview 696.
18. AWM 52 4/2/5/17 – Appendix A.
19. AWM 52 8/3/12.
20. Quoted from Graeme-Evans, 1990, p.279.
21. AWM 52 8/2/18; McCarthy, 1959.
22. AWM 52 8/2/18; McCarthy, 1959.
23. Quoted from Milner, 1957, p.309.
24. AWM 52 8/3/12; Milner, 1957.
25. McDonald & Brune, 1998, p.154

Chapter 55
1. Quoted from Graeme-Evans, 1990, p.284.
2. Blakeley, 1957; McCarthy, 1959; Milner, 1957.
3. Blakeley, 1957; McCarthy, 1959; Milner, 1957.
4. McCarthy, 1959; Milner, 1957.
5. McCarthy, 1959; Milner, 1957.
6. Quoted from Williams, 2021, pp.61–62.

Chapter 56
1. Quoted from Graeme-Evans, 1990, p.285.
2. AWM 52 8/2/18; AWM 52 8/3/12; Graeme-Evans, 1991; McCarthy, 1959.
3. Quotes from McCarthy, 1959, p.484.
4. Quoted from Brune, 1997, p.221.
5. AWFA interview 696.
6. AWM 52 3/1/12/3.
7. AWM 52 4/2/5/17 – Appendix A.
8. AWM 52 4/2/5/17 – Appendix A.
9. AWM 52 8/2/18; AWM 52 8/3/12; Graeme-Evans, 1991; McCarthy, 1959.
10. Quoted from Graeme-Evans, 1990, p.286.
11. AWM 52 8/2/18; McCarthy, 1959.
12. AWM 52 8/2/18.
13. Quoted from McCarthy, 1959, pp.484–85.
14. McCarthy, 1959; Milner, 1957.
15. AWM 52 8/3/9.
16. McCarthy, 1959; Milner, 1957.
17. Quoted from Milner, 1957, p.317.
18. Blakeley, 1957; Milner, 1957.

19. Marshall, 1945; Milner, 1957.
20. Milner, 1957.
21. Milner, 1957, p.317.
22. Milner, 1957.
23. Milner, 1957.
24. McCarthy, 1959; Milner, 1957.
25. AWM 52 8/3/10.
26. AWM 52 8/3/10.
27. Allchin, 1958.
28. AWM 52 4/2/5/17 – Appendix A.
29. Bullard, 2007, p.226.
30. McCarthy, 1959; Milner, 1957.
31. Tanka, 1980, p.39.

Chapter 57
1. AWM 52 8/3/12.
2. AWM 52 4/2/5/17 – Appendix A.
3. Quoted from Milner, 1957, p.319.
4. Milner, 1957.
5. Milner, 1957.
6. AWM 52 8/2/19.
7. AWM 52 8/2/19.
8. Quoted from Milner, 1957, pp.322–323.
9. Quoted from Graeme-Evans, 1990, p.287.
10. Blakeley, 1957; Bullard, 2007; Milner, 1957.
11. Blakeley, 1957; Milner, 1957.
12. Blakeley, 1957; Bullard, 2007; Milner, 1957.
13. Quoted from Milner, 1957, pp.325–26.

Epilogue
1. McCarthy, 1959; Nicoll, 1982.
2. Eichelberger, 1950, p.17 and p.22.
3. Duffy, 2016, p.179.
4. Bergerud, 1996, p.50 and pp.267–68.
5. McCarthy, 1959; Milner, 1957.
6. McCarthy, 1959.
7. McCarthy, 1959.
8. Tanaka, 1980.
9. McCarthy, 1959.

BIBLIOGRAPHY

Australian War Memorial, Canberra
Unit War Diaries

AWM 52 3/1/12/2 – 2/6th Armoured Regiment: July to December 1942.
AWM 52 3/1/12/3 – 2/6th Armoured Regiment: January 1943.
AWM 52 4/2/1/19 – 2/1st Australian Field Regiment: September to December 1942.
AWM 52 4/2/5/16 – 2/5th Australian Field Regiment: July to December 1942.
AWM 52 4/2/5/17 – 2/5th Australian Field Regiment: January to February 1942.
AWM 52 8/2/18/32 – 18th Infantry Brigade: December 1942.
AWM 52 8/2/18/34 – 18th Infantry Brigade: December 1942 – Appendices.
AWM 52 8/2/18/39 – 18th Infantry Brigade: January 1943.
AWM 52 8/3/7 – 2/7th Battalion: December 1942.
AWM 52 8/3/9 – 2/9th Battalion: December 1942.
AWM 52 8/3/9 – 2/9th Battalion: January 1943.
AWM 52 8/3/10 – 2/10th Battalion: July to December 1942.
AWM 52 8/3/10 – 2/10th Battalion: January to June 1943.
AWM 52 8/3/12 – 2/12th Battalion: January to July 12943.
AWM 52 25/3/6/4 – 2/6th Independent Company: November 1942
AWM 52 25/3/6/5 – 2/6th Independent Company: December 1942

Dwight D. Eisenhower Library, Abilene Kansas, USA
(Kindly supplied by Dr Gregory Blake)

Corrective Notes on 126th Combat Team, Buna Campaign, 126th Regiment, After Action Report, Box 1342.
Correspondence (1941–43) Parks, Floyd. L., Military Associate Papers, 1913–65, Box 5.
Eichelberger Report of Buna Forces on the Buna Campaign 1 Dec 1942 to 25 January 1943,
File #1, Collection of 20th Century Military Records, 1918–50, Series II, Box 21.
History of the 32nd Division, Box 885.

National Archives and Records Administration, Washington, D.C., USA

(Kindly supplied by Dr Gregory Blake)
RG 319, Records of the Army Staff – Center of Military History – Victory in Papua

Box 3: Warren Letters – Bulk Package #1, Box 3: Major General Edwin Harding Diary.

Box 4: Intelligence and Supply – Bulk Package #3, Box 4: Various correspondence with US

Official Historian, Samuel Milner, and participants of the campaign (see Endnotes for individual details).

Box 7: G-3 Reports – December 1942, Box 4: Various contemporary handwritten messages, orders, and typed reports generated during the fighting for Buna (see Endnotes for individual details).

University of New South Wales (UNSW)
Australians at War Film Archive (AWFA)

Kirkmoe, John: Archive number 1814, interviewed 16 April 2004.

Osborne, Allan: Archive number 1319, interviewed 3 February 2004.

Wells, Bryan: Archive number 696, interviewed 21st August 2003.

Department of Veterans Affairs / National Archives Australia

Most basic biographical details of Australian military personnel discussed are checked against the on-line electronic files of the DVA Nominal Roll and the NAA, using identified army serial numbers. Most serial numbers taken from McCarthy, 1959 and battalion-published histories or names searched through database.

Official Histories

Bullard, S. (2007) *Japanese Army Operations in the South Pacific Area: New Britain and Papua Campaigns, 1942–43*, Australian War Memorial (English translation of the Japanese Official History).

Gillison, D. (1962) *Royal Australian Air Force 1939–1942, Australia in the War of 1939–1945*, (Air Force Series) Australian War Memorial, Canberra.

BIBLIOGRAPHY

McCarthy, D. (1959) *South-West Pacific Area First Year, Kokoda to Wau, Australia in the War of 1939–1945*, (Army Series) Australian War Memorial, Canberra.

Milner, S. (1955) *The War in the Pacific: Victory in Papua, United States Army in World War II*, Center of Military History United States Army, Washington, D.C.

Tanaka, K. (1980) *Operations of the Imperial Japanese Armed Forces in the Papua New Guinea Theatre during World War II*, Japan Papua New Guinea Goodwill Society, Japan.

Walker, A.S. (1957) *The Island Campaigns, Australia in the War of 1939–1945*, (Medical Series) Australian War Memorial, Canberra.

Published Unit History

Allchin, K. (1958) *Purple and Blue: The History of the 2/10 Battalion, AIF (The Adelaide Rifles), 1939–1945*, Battalion Association, Adelaide.

Blakeley, H.W. (1957) *The 32nd Infantry Division in World War II*, Thirty-Second Infantry Division History Commission, State of Wisconsin.

Byrnes, G.M. (1989) *Green Shadows: A War History of the Papuan Infantry Battalion*, Queensland Corrective Services Commission, Queensland.

Dickson, G. (2005) *Never Late: The 2/9th Australian Infantry Battalion, 1939–1945*, Australian Military History Publications, Loftus, New South Wales.

Graeme-Evans, A. (1991) *Of Storms and Rainbows: The Story of the men of the 2/12th Battalion A.I.F. Volume Two: March 1942 – January 1946*, 12th Battalion Association, Tasmania.

Handel, P. (2004) *The Vital Factor: A History of 2/6th Australian Armoured Regiment 1941–1946*, Australian Military History Publications, Loftus, New South Wales.

Hopkins, R.N.L. (1978) *Australian Armour: A History of the Royal Australian Armoured Corps 1927–1972*, Australian War Memorial, Canberra.

McNicoll, R.R. (1982) *The Royal Australian Engineers 1919 to 1945: Teeth and Tail* (Volume 3), Corps Committee of The Royal Australian Engineers, Canberra.

O'Brien, J. (1950) *Guns and Gunners: The Story of the 2/5th Australian Field Regiment in World War II*, Angus and Robertson, Australia.

Powell, A. (2003) *The Third Force: ANGAU's New Guinea War, 1942–46*, Oxford University Press, Melbourne.

Sinclair, J. (1990) *To Find a Path: The Life and Times of the Royal Pacific Islands Regiment, Volume 1 – Yesterday's Heroes 1885–1950*, Boolarong Publications, Brisbane.

Smith, N.C. (2020) *Men of ANGAU: A History of the Australian New Guinea Administrative Unit*, Mostly Unsung Military History Research and Publications, Victoria.

Trigellis-Smith, S. (1992) *The Purple Devils: A History of the 2/6 Australian Commando Squadron formerly the 2/6 Australian Independent Company 1942–1946*, 2/6 Commando Squadron Association, Melbourne.

Books/Book Chapters

Anderson, N. (2018) The Battle of Milne Bay, 1942, *Australian Army Campaign Series No. 24*, Australian Army History Unit, Canberra.

Archer, J. (1985) *Jungle Fighters: A GI Correspondent's experiences in the New Guina Campaign*, Julian Messner, New York.

Bergerud, E. (1996) *Touched with Fire: the land war in the South Pacific*, Penguin Books, New York.

Blake, G. (2019) *Jungle Cavalry: Australian Independent Companies and Commandos 1941–1945*, Helion & Company, Warwick UK.

Borneman, W.R. (2016) *MacArthur at War: World War II in the Pacific*, Little Brown and Company, New York.

Bradley, P. (2012) *Hell's Battlefield: the Australians in New Guinea in World War II*, Allen & Unwin, Sydney.

Brune, P. (1991) *Those Rugged Bloody Heroes: from the Kokoda Trail to Gona Beach, 1942*, Allen & Unwin, Sydney.

Brune, P. (1994) *Gona's Gone! The Battle for the beachhead 1942*, Allen & Unwin, Sydney.

Brune, P. (1997) *The Spell Broken: Exploding the Myth of Japanese Invincibility*, Allen & Unwin, Sydney.

Brune, P. (2003) *A Bastard of a Place: The Australians in Papua: Kokoda, Milne Bay, Gona, Buna and Sanananda*, Allen & Unwin, Sydney.

Cameron, D.W. (2020) *The Battles for Kokoda Plateau: Three weeks of hell defending the gateway to the Owen Stanleys*, Allen & Unwin, Sydney.

Cameron, D.W. (2022a) *The Battle of Isurava: Fighting in the Clouds of the Owen Stanleys*, Big Sky Publishing, Sydney.

Cameron, D.W. (2022b) *Saving Port Moresby: Fighting at the end of the Kokoda Track*, Big Sky Publishing, Sydney.

Cameron, D.W. (2022c) *Retaking Kokoda: The Battles for Templeton's Crossing, Eora Creek and the Oivi-Gorari positions*, Big Sky Publishing, Sydney.

BIBLIOGRAPHY

Cameron, D.W. (2023) *Gona's Gone: The Battle for the Beachhead, New Guinea 1942*, Big Sky Publishing, Sydney.

Campbell, J. (2007) *The Ghost Mountain Boys: Their Epic March and the Terrifying Battle for New Guinea – The Forgotten War of the South Pacific*, Crown Publishers, New York.

Claringbould, M. & Ingman, P. (2022) *South Pacific Air War Volume 5: Crisis in Papua September–December 1942*, Avonmore Books, Kent Town, South Australia.

Collie, C & Marutani, H. (2009) *The Path of Infinite Sorrow: the Japanese on the Kokoda Track*, Allen & Unwin, Sydney.

Day, D. (2003) *The Politics of War: Australia at War, 1939–45: From Churchill to MacArthur*, HarperCollins Publishers, Sydney.

Dean, P.J. (2011) *The Architect of Victory: The military career of Lieutenant General Sir Frank Horton Berryman*, Cambridge University Press, Melbourne.

Duffy, J.P. (2016) *War at the End of the World: Douglas MacArthur and the Forgotten Fight for New Guinea, 1942–1945*, Nal Caliber, New York.

Edgerton, R.B. (1977) *Warriors of the Rising Sun: A History of the Japanese Military*, Westview Press, USA.

Eichelberger, R.L. (1950) *Our Jungle Road to Tokyo*, The Viking Press, New York.

Frank, R.B. (1990) *Guadalcanal: the definitive account of the landmark battle*, Penguin Books, USA.

Friedman, K.I. (2007) *Morning of the Rising Sun: the heroic story of the battle for Guadalcanal*, Friedman, USA.

Gailey, H. (2000) *MacArthur Strikes Back: Decision at Buna: New Guinea, 1942–43*, Presidio, USA.

Gallaway, J. (2000) *The Odd Couple: Blamey and MacArthur at War*, University of Queensland Press, Brisbane.

Hayashi, S. & Coox, A.D. (1959) *KŌGUN: The Japanese Army in the Pacific War*, The Marine Corps Association, Quantico, USA.

Henderson, J. (1992) *Onward Boy Soldiers: The Battle for Milne Bay, 1942*, University of Western Australia Press, Perth.

Hooper, A.E. (1994) *Love, War & Letters: PNG 1940–45*, Robert Brown & Associates Pty Ltd, Queensland.

Horner, D.M. (1978) *Crisis of Command: Australian Generalship and the Japanese Threat, 1941–1943*, Australian National University Press, Canberra.

Horner, D.M. (1992) *General Vesay's War*, Melbourne University Press, Victoria.

Horner, D.M. (1995) *The Gunners: A History of Australian Artillery*, Allen & Unwin, Sydney.

Horner, D.M. (1996) *Inside the War Cabinet: Directing Australia's War Effort 1939–45*, Allen & Unwin, Sydney.

Horner, D.M. (1998) *Blamey: Commander-in-Chief*, Allen & Unwin, Sydney.

Johnston, G.H. (1944) *New Guinea Diary*, Angus & Robertson, Sydney.

Keogh, E.G. (1965) *South-West Pacific 1941–45*, Grayflower Productions, Melbourne.

Marshall, G.C. (1945) *Papuan Campaign: The Buna-Sanananda Operations, 16 November 1942 – 23 January 1943*, Centre of Military History, United States Army, Washington, D.C. (1990 edition).

Mayo, L. (1975) *Bloody Buna: the campaign that halted the Japanese invasion of Australia*, Australian National University Press, Canberra.

McAulay, L. (1992) *To the Bitter End: The Japanese Defeat at Buna and Gona 1942–43*, Random House, Australia.

McDonald, N. & Brune, P. (1998) *200 Shots: Damien Parer, George Silk, and the Australians at War in New Guina*, Allen & Unwin, Sydney.

McLeod, J. (2019) *Shadows on the Track: Australia's Medical War in Papua 1942–43 (Kokoda – Milne Bay – The Beachhead Battles)*, Big Sky Publishing, Sydney.

Nash, N.S. (2022) *In the Service of the Emperor: The Rise and Fall of the Japanese Empire 1931–1945*, Pen & Sword, Yorkshire, UK.

Powell, A. (2003) *The Third Force: ANGAU's New Guinea War, 1942–46*, Oxford University Press, Melbourne.

Pratten, G. (2009) *Australian Battalion Commanders in the Second World War*, Cambridge University Press, Melbourne.

Reading, G. (1946) *Papuan Story*, Angus & Robertson, Sydney.

Schon, A. (2004) *The Eagle and the Rising Sun: The Japanese – American War 1941–1943*, W.W. Norton & Company, New York.

Shaw, I.W. (2017) *The Rag Tag Fleet: The unknown story of the Australian men and boats that helped win the war in the Pacific*, Hachette, Australia.

Slim, W. (1956) *Defeat into Victory*, Cassell, London.

Smith, N.C. (2020) *Men of ANGAU: A History of the Australian New Guinea Administrative Unit*, Mostly Unsung Military History Research and Publications, Victoria.

Spencer, B. (1999) *In the Footsteps of Ghosts: With the 2/9th Battalion in the African desert and the jungles of the Pacific*, Allen & Unwin, Sydney.

BIBLIOGRAPHY

Threlfall, A. (2014) *Jungle Warriors: From Tobruk to Kokoda and beyond, how the Australian Army became the world's most deadly jungle fighting force*, Allen & Unwin, Sydney.

Williams, P. (2021) *Japan's Pacific War: Personal accounts of the Emperor's warriors*, Pen & Sword, Yorkshire, UK.

Unpublished manuscript

Sweeting, A.J. (undated) *The 2/4th Field Ambulance A.I.F. during the Owen Stanleys Campaign 1942 Memories of Sgt. A.J. (Bill) Sweeting M.B.E.*

INDEX

2/6th Independent Company (2 AIF) 2, 17, 19, 40, 44, 51, 53, 66, 120–1, 233, 249–50, 512
  intelligence gathering 72–5, 89–90
  Warren front 102–4, 115, 135, 145–6, 162–3, 183, 216–17, 238–41
2/9th Battalion (2 AIF) 228, 236, 251–2, 261, 264, 336, 394, 449, 454, 497
  Buna area, arrival in 270–1, 281
  Cape Endaiadere 386
  Giropa Point 483, 492–8
  Simemi Creek 361–5
  Strip Point assault 336–340
  Warren front 286–91, 295–325, 330–2, 351–5, 445–6
2/10th Battalion (2 AIF) 286, 324, 329, 336, 449
  coastal area, capture of 436–45, 448
  Giropa Point 452–6, 495, 500
  Old Strip, consolidating 369–71, 378–86, 394–7, 408, 414–18, 422–6
  Simemi Creek, crossing 350–1, 359–61
32nd Infantry Division (US Army) 2, 6, 7–11, 24–5, 32, 40, 53, 79, 81, 130, 155, 456, 511
126th Infantry Regiment (US Army) 2, 7, 15–17, 22–3, 28, 181–2, 193
  advance on Buna 44, 49–50, 52–3, 56–7, 173–4
  Buna Mission 456–60
  Buna Village 133–4, 139–40, 165, 186, 208–9, 212, 219, 229, 244–5, 501
  Cape Endaiadere 114–15
  Coconut Grove 293–4, 327–8, 333–4
  Government Gardens 446–7
  New Strip 162, 283
  Old Strip 408, 415
  Sanananda 83–6, 511
  Simemi Creek 204–5, 287, 370–1, 448
  Triangle 97–9, 345, 356, 418–19
  Urbana front 95, 117, 256, 456–60
  Vasey, under 78, 125, 151
  Warren front 102–4, 225

127th Infantry Regiment (US Army) 125, 126, 152, 245, 250, 254, 293–4, 327, 509
  Buna Mission 456–60, 488–9, 499–500
  condition of soldiers 401, 411–12, 418, 429
  Urbana front 347–8, 366–7, 373–4, 387–93, 398–400, 411–12, 429–31, 446–7, 449–51, 456–60
128th Infantry Regiment (US Army) 2, 7, 14, 17, 19, 21, 23, 24, 84, 193, 275, 286–7, 394
  advance on Buna 43, 49–53, 57–62, 65–72, 76, 84–6
  Buna Mission 456–7, 489, 498–500
  Buna Village 186, 208–9, 212
  Cape Endaiadere 113, 143, 385–6
  Coconut Grove 134, 140–1, 272, 280–1, 293
  Duropa Plantation 196
  Entrance Creek 122, 212
  Government Gardens 446
  Musita Island 219, 293, 450–1
  New Strip 102, 106, 113–15, 120, 162–3, 167–8, 182–3, 196, 202, 238–9, 283, 329–31, 350
  Old Strip 415–16, 452–3, 461, 495
  Simemi Creek 363, 370–1, 448
  Siwori Creek 133–4, 140, 186
  Triangle 97–9, 122, 134, 276, 419, 447
  Urbana front 95, 279
  Warren front 179, 226

A

Abau 14
Abel's Field 23
Abuari 14
Adachi, Lieutenant General Hatazo 46–7, 252–3, 265, 412, 432–3
aerial assaults 25
  air spotting 105, 233
  Allied 65, 69, 71, 83–4, 97, 113, 130–1, 136, 167–8, 196, 208–9, 273–4, 331, 333, 336, 488
  friendly fire, casualties 21, 71, 120
  Japanese 44–6, 50, 80, 114, 118, 123, 238, 377
air transport 17, 19, 22

INDEX

airdrops 22, 31, 44, 50, 58, 188, 220, 252, 254
   medical supplies 32
Akin, Brigadier Spencer 391
Alacrity 45
Alder, Lance Corporal Charles 304–5, 306
Alford, Captain James 345–6, 356
Allen, Lance Corporal Bertie 'Grubby' 471
ALMA Force 188
Anderson, Lieutenant David 189
Anderson, NCO John 'Bill' 90, 103
Andrews, Lieutenant 422
Ango 28, 50, 52, 69, 95, 97, 133, 266
Ango Corner 28
Archer, Pilot Officer John 130
Armstrong, Sergeant Poet 471, 472
Arnold, Lieutenant Colonel Arthur 445, 448–9, 452, 461–2, 469, 478–9, 486, 493–4
artillery 2, 49, 89, 127–8, 138, 224, 254–5, 263, 271, 282–3, 287, 345, 365, 374, 409–11, 448–9
   maintenance 437
   Observation Post Officer (OPO) 410
Asashio 51
Atkins, Lance Corporal Victor 'Toby' 103
Atkinson, Fred 443
Austin, Sergeant Victor 6
Australian Army 512–13
   1st Australian Imperial Force (1st AIF) 6
   2nd Australian Imperial Force (2nd AIF) 6–7
   2/1st Battalion 1
   2/2nd Battalion 1
   2/5th Field Regiment 24, 45, 200, 219, 231, 240, 247, 255, 261, 263, 282, 287, 297–8, 363, 374–5, 383, 397, 408, 426, 437, 448, 495, 501, 511
   2/6th Armoured Regiment 146, 228, 251, 260, 266–8, 277, 281
   2/6th Independent Company *see* 2/6th Independent Company (2 AIF)
   2/9th Battalion *see* 2/9th Battalion (2 AIF)
   2/10th Battalion *see* 2/10th Battalion (2 AIF)
   2/12th Battalion 234, 444–5, 452–6, 461–8, 484–7, 494–8, 500
   2/14th Battalion 1
   2/16th Battalion 1
   2/25th Battalion 1
   2/27th Battalion 1
   2/31st Battalion 1
   2/33rd Battalion 1
   3rd Battalion 1, 2, 7, 227
   3/3rd Battalion 1
   7th Division 2, 24–5, 47, 56, 78, 81, 130, 151, 249
   16th Brigade 1, 2, 14, 24, 31–2, 56–7, 78, 83, 227
   17th Brigade 206, 227, 281, 511
   18th Brigade 3, 227, 228, 236, 260, 270, 276, 286, 323, 339, 510, 511–12
   21st Brigade 1, 2, 27, 31, 227
   25th Brigade 1, 2, 14, 24, 27, 31–2, 227
   39th Battalion 1, 2, 7, 227
   supplies *see* supplies
Australian militia (Citizen Military Force – CMF) 6–7, 17, 227
Australian New Guinea Administrative Unit (ANGAU) 6, 16
Awala 2

B

Baetcke, Major Bernd 181
Bailey, Lieutenant Cladie 139, 209, 211
Bains, Private Roy 'Rusty' 305
Baird, Keith 440
Bajdek, Private Walter 256
Bakken, Captain 99–101, 121
Ballarat 252, 264
Balza, Private William 399
Bantam 376
Barker, Lieutenant Colonel Lewis 354
Barnet, Corporal Evan 288–9, 303–4, 313–14, 379, 381, 401–2
Bath 456
Beattie, Lieutenant Edwin 321
Beaver, Major Chester 212, 246, 329, 331, 340, 370–1, 384–5, 394, 406
Beechy, Private Edward 508
Bell, Lieutenant 99, 101
Belmer, Captain Rossall 72–4, 84–5, 89–90, 102–3, 106, 115, 120, 127, 163, 168–9
Bender, Private Herman 458
Benson, Captain Arthur 297, 319–21, 336–9, 362, 362
Berry, Private Ronald 352–3
Berryman, Major General Frank 348, 376
Birkness, Major Ralph 50, 79
Blainey, Lieutenant Gordon 121, 127, 167, 169, 205, 239

BLOODY BUNA

Blamey, Major General Sir Thomas 2, 5, 51, 64, 194, 227–8, 234, 251, 332, 348
   American troops, on 152–3, 194–5
   message of congratulations 506–7
Bloecher, Lieutenant Milan 203
Boerem, Major Richard 22–3, 83
Bofu 11, 17, 22, 23
Boice, Captain William 15, 223, 229, 294, 333
Bond, Major George 22, 56, 83
Bonwin 45
Boreo 43, 50, 52, 57, 144, 276, 386
Borio 23
Bottcher, Sergeant Herman 211, 212–213, 222–3
Bottcher's Corner 211, 213, 219, 222–4, 256
Boucher, Major 463
Bougainville 6
Bowden, Private Gordon 'Peter' 359
Bowen, Colonel Frank 'Bill' 347, 429–30
Bowerman, Lieutenant William 480, 481
Boylan, Corporal Les 309
Bradford, Captain Byron 392, 398–9, 411–12, 418
Bradley, Colonel Sladen 411–12
Bragg, Lieutenant William 432, 450, 457
Brandon, Private Reginald 404
Bray, Trooper Gordon 310–12
Bren gun carriers 190–1, 197–202, 247, 247, 255, 281, 397
Brigade Hill 1
Broome 252, 264
Brown, Lieutenant Murray 379–80, 396, 414, 416–17
Buckley, Private Raymond 304
Buna 3, 5, 64
   Australian reinforcements 228
   Japanese defence 29–30, 35–42, 81, 88, 264–5
   Japanese invasion of 1
   Japanese reinforcements 48, 51, 54
   Japanese withdrawal 335, 432–3, 501–3
   mopping up operations 504–6
   plan to retake 10–1
Buna Force 347, 429
Buna Government Station 76, 209, 224, 252, 260, 286, 292, 294, 333, 347, 367–8, 384, 429, 436, 449
Buna Mission 28, 35, 37–41, 53, 58, 84, 110, 194, 292, 294, 450, 498, 505
   assaults on 112, 208–12, 244, 429–36, 456–60, 475, 484, 488–9, 498–501

Buna Village 27–8, 34, 35, 39, 53, 58, 76, 110, 175–7, 194, 430, 447, 449, 498, 501
   assaults on 112, 133–4, 139–40, 146, 148, 161–2, 165, 167, 186, 189, 208–16, 218–20, 229–34, 244–5, 266–9
   Australian entry into 272–3
Burey, Corporal Bill 475
Burns, Lieutenant Thomas 415
Burr, Sergeant Elmer 388–9
Byers, Brigadier Clovis 136, 156, 157, 178, 214, 218, 260, 275
   Coconut Grove assault 279–81

C

Cambridge, Corporal Cecil 316
Cameron, Private Angus 198
Campbell, Private Robert 489
Cape Endaiadere 23, 28, 36, 39, 44, 51, 58–9, 66, 68, 79, 86, 252, 296, 354, 426, 497, 504, 505, 512
   American assaults on 106, 113–15, 135, 143–6, 162, 196, 260, 261, 286
   Australian assaults on 302–20, 385–6
   reconnaissance 289–90
Cape Killerton 35
Cape Sudest 23, 24, 28, 45, 264
Carew, Colonel John 31, 45
Carrier, Lieutenant Colonel Edmund 22–3, 44, 66, 68–9, 117, 246
   advance on Buna 196, 203–4, 205
   coastal drive 89
   Warren front 102, 113–15, 143–4, 162–3, 167–8, 182–3, 225–6
Carson, Sergeant Roderick 397, 409–10, 437, 448, 454, 484, 495
casualties 321, 437–8, 512–13
   American 77, 85, 100, 114, 146, 155, 200, 250, 280, 346, 358, 392, 425, 458, 501
   Australian 45–6, 303–10, 322, 324, 362, 407, 442–3, 464, 487, 496
   burial of 508
   evacuation of 123, 396–7, 401–2
   Japanese 1, 33, 63, 243, 248, 273–4, 319, 325, 407, 482, 496, 506, 513
   sick, evacuation of 11, 513
Chaforce 2
Chagnon, Lieutenant Louis 348, 433, 508–9
Chamberlain, Brigadier Stephen 154
Chandler, Lieutenant Harold 15
Charles, Major Thomas 136

INDEX

'chockos' 6–7
Christensen, Private Jogn 353
Church, Sergeant John 288, 314, 379, 382
Clark, Private Alfred 470–1, 475–6
Clarke, Lieutenant Duncan 464, 467
Clarkson, Major Gordon 246, 297, 310, 329, 331, 350, 370–1, 385, 395, 406, 423, 424, 438, 453, 489
Clayton, Sergeant Harry 463, 464
Clowes, Major General Cyril 81–2, 120, 128, 187
Coconut Grove 35, 37, 38, 41, 64, 66, 76, 88, 90, 164, 171, 192, 201, 212, 217, 226, 239, 271, 351, 391, 501, 504
   assaults on 134, 140–2, 272–3, 275, 279–81, 293–4, 327–8, 333–4, 345
Coconut Plantation 399, 412
Colac 252, 264
Comara 456
Combined Operational Service Command (COSC) 21
communication
   Japanese interception of 314
   problems 31, 50, 109–10, 138, 150–1, 290–1, 321–2, 472
Connors, Noel 353
Coombe, Private Joseph 417
Cotteral, Corporal Maurice 'Mervyn' 270–1
Coulston, Sergeant James 130
Cramey, Wally 384
Cramp, Captain Septimus 207
Cronk, Captain Jefferson 450, 458, 488, 498
Crow, Lieutenant John 65
Crutchett, Private Donald 404
Cummings, Lieutenant Colonel Clement 261, 263, 277, 287, 289, 296, 307, 312, 322, 330, 336, 339, 361, 364, 386, 396
Curtin, John 194
Curtis, Captain Owen 468, 473
Curtiss, Lieutenant Grant 266, 288, 296, 318, 331, 355, 461

D

Dalton, Jack 298, 302
Dames, Captain William 389–90, 400, 499
Daniels, Sergeant Delmar 168
Dannelly, Lieutenant Sheldon 425
Darnton, Byron 21
Davies, Corporal Frank 198
Davis, Private Owen 360–1

Davis, Private Thomas 466
De Graaf, Colonel George 179, 188, 250
De Rosier, Edwin 60
de Vantier, Lieutenant Roy 309, 318
dengue fever 32, 172, 184
Deniki 1, 14
Dennis, Private Eldon 464
Dexter, Commando Barrie 17
diarrhea 10
Dixon, Sergeant Harry 309, 485–6
Dobbs, Lieutenant Colonel James 264, 276–7, 403, 407, 422–3, 437–9, 449
   Old Strip 369–70, 378–9, 394, 396, 486
   Simemi Creek, crossing 350, 359–60, 369
   Wootten, conflict with 437–8
Dobodura 28, 31, 39, 43, 44, 50–3, 86, 95, 112, 152, 160, 252, 284
   airstrip 79, 118, 130, 150, 188, 224, 254
Donnelly, Warrant Officer Vincent 307, 351–3, 360
Doughtie, Lieutenant James 370
Downer, Lieutenant James 15, 243–4
Duckett, Private Sidney 492
Duffy, Sergeant Frank 384, 404–5
Duropa Plantation 28, 37, 40, 58, 137, 189, 196–200, 286, 295, 445, 497
   conditions 107
Dwyer, Ring 480
Dyne, Corporal Alfred 473
dysentery 10, 16, 32, 42, 184

E

Eastwood, Private Howard 115
Edwards, Captain Daniel 171, 175, 208, 214
Egan, Lieutenant Richard 72, 73
Eichelberger, Lieutenant General Robert 7–10, 22, 31, 39, 136, 154, 163, 181, 186, 195, 223, 228, 246, 257, 281, 284, 412
   Buna, on 511
   Dobodura 160–1, 252
   Giropa Point assault 457–60, 496
   Japanese defences, on 328
   message to troops 506
   plans to take Buna 250–1, 260, 271, 285, 302, 348, 367–8
   Port Moresby, visit to 155–7, 160
   Urbana front 167, 171–80, 208, 210, 213–15, 220, 346–7, 356–8, 367–8, 391, 393, 398, 418, 428–9

Elliget, Lieutenant 342
Elliot, Sergeant Alan 289, 322
Ellis, Corporal Jim 423
Elphinstone, Lieutenant Colin 464
Embi 23, 43
Embogo 23, 28, 43, 50, 51, 118
Emson, Lieutenant Robert 438, 442, 449
Entrance Creek 27, 37, 96, 97, 117, 186, 208, 212, 281, 292, 327–8, 356, 387, 430–1, 436, 447, 488
Eoff, Private Gordon 399
Eora Creek 1, 14, 41
equipment
    Australian forces 9–10
    captured 506
    Japanese forces 41–2
    US forces 9–10
Eroro Mission 23
Estrada, Private Bernardino 279–80
Etchells, Lance Corporal Frederick 'Tojo' 473
Eva 374
Evans, Private Arthur 'Snowy' 405, 441–2
explosive bullets 104, 480–1

F

Fahnestock, Lieutenant Bruce 21
Fahres, Lieutenant Marcelles 400
Farrar, Lieutenant Colonel Benjamin 367, 389
Fee, Sergeant Robert 441
Ferguson, Lieutenant 99, 102
Fergusson, Lieutenant Terence 187, 189–90, 196–200, 206, 290, 303, 326
Feury, Lieutenant Donald 346
Fielding, Lieutenant Geoffrey 73, 169, 191, 196, 205, 216, 239
First World War 6
Fisher, Private Albert 389
Fitzpatrick, Corporal Ron 289
Florey, Lieutenant Theodore 78, 99–102
Folkard, Fred 337, 478
Folland, Lieutenant Owen 73
Forster, Trooper Frank 381
Forward, Frank 353
Foss, Lieutenant Donald 395–6, 425
Franks, Tom 361
Fryday, Lieutenant Carl 79, 102, 115, 120, 162, 182
Fuzzy Wuzzy Angels *see* Papuan carriers

G

Ganderton, Trooper Cecil 440
Garret, Captain Leonard 430
Gategood, Major Keith 452, 468, 469
Geerds, Lieutenant Colonel Henry 15, 21
Geizendanner, Lieutenant Hugh 453, 493
Gerber, Ernest 34, 76, 193, 276, 419
Gerua 50, 76
Gibson, Peter 408
Gill, Brian 471
Gill, Lance Corporal Ike 352
Gill, Private Bill 485
Giropa Creek 261, 495
Giropa Point 333, 336, 384, 414, 416, 423–4, 426, 436, 438, 448–9, 505, 512
    Allied assault on 452–6, 461–8, 475–87, 492–8
    Japanese defence 450, 493, 498
Girua River 25, 27, 35, 43, 52, 56–7, 69, 83, 140, 152, 208, 212, 249, 436, 508
Giruwa 63, 248, 266, 413, 420–1, 432–3, 447, 451, 502–3
Gleadow, Gordon 479
Gollan, Sergeant John 440
Gona 2, 5, 7, 12–13, 47, 64, 96, 124, 218, 295, 348, 513
    Australian advance on 24, 126, 227
    Australian capture of 238
    Japanese defence of 35, 221
    Japanese reinforcements 136
Gona Creek 13
Goodenough Island 234, 261, 444
Gorari 1, 5, 33, 41
Gordan, Sergeant Jack 309
Gosden, Private Les 191
Government Gardens 35, 37, 76, 88, 100, 281, 293, 294, 348, 374, 387, 398–401, 411–12, 446–7, 449–51
Government Plantation 417
Graber, Sergeant Harold 210
Graham, Bernie 483
Graham, Clint 306
Grant, Kenny 352
Gray, Captain Millard 418, 499
Gray, Charles 431
Gray, Lieutenant Oswald 405
Green, Private Gordon 92
Green, Sergeant Vernon 'Dick' 466
Greene, Lieutenant Edward 358
Greene, Private James J 419

INDEX

Gregson, Corporal Leopold 'Leo' 315–16
Griffin, Captain Robert 296, 302, 304, 305–7, 319–21, 336–9, 362–4
Griffith, Lieutenant James 347–8
Grindle, Oscar 492
Grose, Colonel John 179, 185, 208, 214, 218, 245, 509
   Buna Force 429–31
   Buna Mission assault 457–8, 488, 499
   Urbana Force 347, 357–8, 367, 387, 389–93, 398–401, 411–12
Gruennert, Sergeant Kenneth 391–2
Guadalcanal 1, 10, 13, 41, 46–7, 53–4, 118, 334
Gunn, Lieutenant Ewan 331, 336–8
Guri Guri 19

H

Haddy's Village 2, 221, 274, 295
Haggestad, Captain 121
Hale, Colonel Tracy 17, 79, 94, 102, 113, 117, 146, 154, 162, 169–70, 179
Hall, Major William 80, 127, 131, 231–2, 240, 247, 255, 263, 271, 282, 287, 297, 408, 409, 437, 448
   reconnaissance 276–7, 316–17, 331–2, 354, 484, 495
Hall, Sergeant Irving 87
Handran-Smith, Lieutenant Thomas 410, 484
Handy, Colonel 11
Hangartner Private Elmer 431
Hansen, Sergeant Vernon 321
Hanson, Major Arthur 80
Hantlemann, Captain Harold 140, 165, 173
Harbert, Lieutenant John 45
Harcourt, Major Harry 19, 23–4, 44, 66, 104, 116, 146, 163, 167, 190, 241, 249
   Buna Village assault 191
   coastal drive 68–9, 167–8, 183
   New Strip 84–5, 90, 106, 135, 162, 216, 238
Harding, Colonel Horace 240, 390, 429–30
Harding, Eleanor 8
Harding, Major General Edwin 2, 7–8, 10–11, 15, 22, 57, 64, 68, 78, 85
   air support 104–5
   communication issues 31, 50, 94–5, 150–1
   Eichelberger, and 160–1
   Minnemura, attack on 45
   plan of attack 28, 32–3, 49–51, 52, 69, 79, 128–9, 178

supply situation 32, 58
Sutherland, and 150–5
tanks 120, 128, 137, 146
Urbana front 117–18, 122–3, 167, 171–9
Warren front 104–5, 110, 114, 125–9
Hardwick, Jack 321
Harger, Captain Horace 398–9, 411–12, 418
Hariko 23, 43–4, 80, 93, 113, 169–70, 186, 231, 251, 329, 374
   friendly fire attack 374, 376
   tanks, arrival of 267–8
Harper, Sergeant Major George 469–71, 475
Harrington, Sergeant Stanley 416
Harris, Private John 464
Hartt, Private Lawrence 103
Haruyoshi, Lieutenant General Hyakutake 46
Hassel, George 483
Hawkins, Major 12
Hayward, Lieutenant 293
Heap, Lieutenant Des 443
Heishichi, Major Kenmotsu 47, 119
Henahamburi 228
Heron, Corporal Peter 407
Herring, Lieutenant General Edmund 27, 51, 56, 78, 96, 112, 125–6, 161, 181, 215, 220, 228, 252, 257, 328, 332
   Harding, meeting with 150–2, 154–5
   plan of attack 260, 348
   special order of the day 507
Hess, Lieutenant George 395
Hewitt, Captain Stephen 430–1
Hicks, Lyle 308
Hihonda 25
Hill, Private Kevin 463–4
Hiroichi, Fuji'i 130
Hodgson, Lieutenant Colonel Charles 251, 260, 261, 263
   tanks 266, 288, 290, 312–13
Holmes, Private Geoff 480–1
Holnicote Bay 24
Hootman, Major Harold 289
Hopkins, Brigadier Ronald 161, 190, 228, 260
Horanda 50, 56
Horii, Major General Tomitarô 2, 13, 40, 273
Horton, Captain Samuel 196, 199
Hosier, Sergeant 463
Hoskins, Lieutenant Clifford 472
Howe, Lieutenant Colonel Merle 214

Hughes, Private Timothy 359, 404
Hunt, Lieutenant James 173
Hynard, Private Grahame 320
I
Ichiji, Colonel Suigita 118
Ifould, Captain Austen 361, 369, 379, 437
Imamura, Lieutenant General Hitoshi 46, 53, 118, 252, 348
Imoto, Lieutenant Colonel 265, 401, 420
Imperial Japanese Army 66
    8th Area Army 53, 118, 252, 334, 348, 377, 420–1
    15th Independent Engineer Regiment 40, 192, 283
    17th Army 46
    18th Army 46–7, 118, 148, 221, 412, 419–21
    21st Independent Mixed Brigade 118, 124, 131, 221
    38th Mountain Artillery Regiment 47, 119
    41st Infantry Regiment 1, 221, 419–20, 432
    47th Field Anti-aircraft Artillery Battalion 41, 119, 192, 284
    51st Division 54
    55th Cavalry Regiment 41
    65th Brigade 54
    144th Infantry Regiment 1, 40, 41, 47, 54, 58, 62, 118, 171, 192, 283, 317
    170th Infantry Regiment 67, 124, 131, 221, 273, 420
    229th Regiment 41, 47, 54, 58, 62, 119, 171, 192, 283, 317, 325, 332, 496
    conditions for soldiers 66, 86, 110–11, 132, 142, 164–6, 180, 192, 201–2, 215, 242–3, 248–9, 343–4
    fighting ability 10, 424, 444
    South Seas Force 1, 13, 33, 40, 47, 107, 149, 273, 420
Imperial Japanese Navy 54, 66, 252
    5th Yokosuka, 5th Sasebo SNLP 41, 58, 88, 119, 194, 209, 224, 283, 388, 432
    14th Naval Pioneer Unit 41
    15th Naval Pioneer Unit 41
Inonda 25, 28, 50, 52
intelligence 38
    gathering 19, 72–3, 289–90
    Japanese forces, regarding 12–13, 33–4
    local Papuan 33

Ioribaiwa Ridge 1, 5, 7, 14, 41, 153
Irwin, Private Roland 'Slim' 453, 462, 485
Isurava 1, 14
Ivey, Captain Charles 452, 463, 464, 476–7
J
Japanese Army *see Imperial Japanese Army*
Japara 376
Jaure 14, 15–17, 21, 223
Jaynes, Private Leslie 464
Jeavons, Trooper Frank 314
Jensen, Harry 307
Jesse, Warrant Officer 318
Johns, Brigadier Dwight 21, 137, 254
Johnson, Lieutenant Ted 411
Johnson, Private Earl 458
Jōichirō, Colonel Sanada 334
Jones, Corporal Thomas 381
Jones, Rod 313
Jumbora 2
jungle warfare 10–11, 34, 177
    equipment and clothing 9–10
K
Kagiroi 48
Kalikodobu 15
Karsik 252, 257, 267, 277, 376, 456
Kasahar, Sergeant Hiroshi 273
Katō, Lieutenant General Rinpei 420–1
Kavanagh, Jack 480
Kawakaze 51, 54
Kazuo, Lieutenant Shiiki 47, 119, 502
Kazagumo 48, 136
Kelton 50, 51, 79–80
Kennedy, Kevin 381
Kenney, Major General George 153, 156
Kent, Private Jim 75
King, Captain Gordon 121
King, Gunner Alan 46
King John 21
Kirchenbauer, Lieutenant Alfred 293–4
Kirk, Captain Colin 452, 468, 469, 473
Kirkmoe, Private John 325, 442–3
Kiyoshi, Colonel Yazawa 419–20, 432–3, 447, 508–9
Kiyoshi, Lieutenant Yamamoto 325
Kiyotaka, Ensign Suzuki 502
Knight, Charlie 465
Knight, Colonel Harry 11
Knode, Lieutenant Thomas 210

INDEX

Kokoda Campaign 1, 5
Kokoda Plateau 1, 5
Kokoda Track 1, 7, 14, 33, 107, 155, 227
Konombi Creek 328, 347
Kooraki (SS) 24
Krasne, Lieutenant Paul 392
Kumusi River 1, 5, 6, 24, 41
Kuri Marau (SS) 231–2
Kusunose, Colonel Masao 47, 58

L

Lae 47, 53, 114, 219, 238, 335, 348–9, 421
Larr, Colonel David 154, 156
Lattimore, Sergeant Jack 313–14, 379, 381–2
Leggatt, Corporal Reginald 382
Lenehan, Max 315
Lennell, Sergeant Jack 479
Leonard, Lieutenant Francis 404
Lewis, Lieutenant John 411, 418, 447, 450
Lincoln, Sergeant Boyd 139
Ling, George 463
Locke, Private Leslie 198
Logan, Lieutenant Talbot 'Tim' 463–4, 468
Logan, Private Llyod 318
Lowe, Private Geoff 464
Lucas, Corporal Norman 189, 197
Lutjens, Sergeant Paul 16, 98, 139, 210
  letter to a girl 134–5

M

M1 carbine 9
MacArthur, General Douglas 2, 5–6, 64, 68, 150, 194–5, 215, 228, 285, 393, 428, 508
  frustration with progress 152–7, 160–1, 178
  Order of the Day 250
McAuliffe, Corporal William 385, 416
McCampbell, Lieutenant Robert 388, 411–12
McCarthy, Dudley 267, 322, 493, 496
MacCarthy, Sergeant Thornton 338
McCoy, Lieutenant Colonel Robert 43, 51, 79, 106, 246
  advance on Buna 57–9, 61, 65, 68–71, 196, 202–3, 205
  coastal drive 89
  Warren front 102, 113, 143–4, 162–3, 167–8, 182–3, 226
McCready, Sergeant Stephen 364
McCreary, Lieutenant Colonel Melvin 44, 179, 186, 218–19, 229, 243, 276, 333, 355, 374, 390

McCrohon, Lieutenant Victor 267, 288, 291, 296, 299, 313, 336, 443
  Giropa Point 455
  Old Strip, consolidation of 378–80
McCulloch, Corporal Don 464
McDonald, Major Hew 123
McDonough, Bart 431
McDougall, Lieutenant Alan 406–7
McGill, Sergeant Kenneth 455
MacIntosh, Lieutenant William 290, 302–4, 353–4, 363
Mackay-Sim, John 408
McKenny, Lieutenant Colonel Lawrence 23, 44, 50
Mackie, Captain Colin 442
McKitterick, Corporal John 116
McKittrick, NCO Frederick 190–1
Maclean, Lieutenant Reginald 406–7
MacNab, Lieutenant Colonel Alexander 10, 65, 154, 170, 199, 246, 317, 327, 386, 448, 462
  coastal drive 79, 83, 89, 113, 283
  Giropa Point 486–7
  reconnaissance 189
  supporting Australian troops 295, 297, 329, 339, 363
MacNider, Brigadier Hanford 14, 23, 28, 43, 51, 52, 59, 62, 66, 79, 83, 90
Madang 47, 336, 348–9
Makigumo 48, 13
malaria 32, 42, 184
Malony, Major Roy 289
Mambare River 12, 273
Manning, Captain Herbert 81, 95–6, 113, 127–8, 138, 244, 282, 297, 345
Marauder aircraft 333
Marr, Lieutenant William 80, 240, 263, 426
Marshall, General George 508
Martin, Colonel Clarence 161, 167, 169–70, 179, 189, 203, 220, 225, 231, 255, 271, 286, 341, 370, 394–6, 415, 423
Martin, Private Stanley 74
Matheson, Captain Hugh 330, 336, 386, 394, 396, 403, 405–7, 415, 422–5, 438–43, 445
Matsuo, Captain 277
Matz, Lieutenant Fred 391, 392
May, Captain Roderick 438, 448, 455, 461–2
Mayne, Sergeant Cocky 463
Mealing, Bert 485

BLOODY BUNA

Medendorp, Captain Alfred 15
medical treatment 396–7
    Papuan carriers *see* Papuan carriers
    supplies 32
    US Army 473–4
Melanson, Private Arthur 431
Melvin, Lieutenant Colonel 327
Mendaropu 11, 50, 53
Meyer, Captain Alfred 357–8
Middendorf, Lieutenant Charles 391, 392
Middlebrook, Lieutenant Garrett 274
Miljativich, Staff Sergeant Milan 431
Miller, Lieutenant Colonel Kelsie 19, 23, 43, 52, 106, 196, 246
    advance on Buna 57–61, 68–9, 76, 79
    Warren front 113–15, 143, 226
Millett, Sergeant Frank 468, 475, 496
Milne Bay 3, 5, 21, 24, 187, 206, 228, 232, 234, 251, 350, 376, 512
    Japanese invasion 234, 290
Milne, Private William 'Jock' 351–3
Minnemura 45
Mission Ridge 14
Mitchell, Corporal Harold 222–3
Mitchell, Sergeant John 441–2
Mitsu Island 230
Moffatt, Major Carroll 257, 264
Morey, Sergeant George 310
Moroney, Lance Corporal William 384, 404
Morris, Private Alexander 289
Moses, Lance Corporal Daniel 305, 306
Moss, Major Norman 'Bull' 331, 355, 426, 437, 439, 444
Moten, Brigadier Murray 187
Mott, Colonel John 52, 117, 121–3, 127, 138, 154
    Buna Village 133, 140, 146, 148, 161
    Urbana front 167, 171–80
Mueller, Captain Charles 44–5, 80, 240, 247, 263, 271, 317
Mulcra 418
Mullins, John 'Jack' 441
Murray, Captain Alexander 452, 463–7
Musa River 14, 19
Musita Island 219, 275, 292–4, 327, 333, 347, 357, 367, 373–4, 387–91, 398, 429, 431, 447, 450–1, 489

N

native carriers *see* Papuan carriers

Natunga 17, 21, 22–3
Neate, Corporal Bill 414
New Britain 6
New Guinea 6
New Guinea Force (NGF) 5–6, 14, 137, 155, 215, 228
    Advance NGF 284–5, 348
New Ireland 6
New Strip 36, 37–9, 41, 58, 61, 68–9, 84–5, 102, 118, 127, 171, 192, 217, 252, 260, 512
    allied occupation of 329
    American assaults on 102, 106, 113–15, 120, 135, 162–3, 167–8, 182–3, 196, 202–3, 238–41, 255, 283, 286, 329–31, 350
    Australian assaults on 295–325
    Japanese defences 282, 497
    reconnaissance 72–4, 89–90, 92–3
Nix, Captain Lionel 80, 231–2, 240, 247, 271, 363, 408
Noble, Private Douglas 464
Nojiri, Major 273
Nummer, Lieutenant Erwin 140
Nye, Trooper Norman 382

O

O'Brien, Lieutenant Colonel John 46, 231–2
O'Connell, Lieutenant Colonel Keith 80, 186, 233, 437
Oda, Major General Kensaku 273–4
Odell, Lieutenant Robert 138–9, 211, 223–4
O'Hare, Captain Martin 49, 59, 113, 127, 219, 231–2, 282, 297, 319
Oivi 1, 5, 7, 33, 41, 155
Old Strip 35–9, 61, 196, 238, 252, 260, 286, 351, 443–4, 512
    assaults on 408, 415–16, 452–3, 461, 495, 497–8
    Japanese counterattack 416–18, 425–6, 444–5
occupation and consolidation of 369, 378–86, 394–7, 403–11, 414–18, 422–6, 452–4, 461, 485–7, 495
Oro Bay 17, 24, 31, 44, 80, 251, 252, 267, 270, 277, 444, 456
    tanks, arrival of 376, 418
Orpwood, Corporal James 197–9
Osborne, Private Allen 74, 92, 103, 183
Osborne, Private Mervyn 304
Outridge, Lieutenant Arthur 240, 247, 383, 397, 408

INDEX

Owen Stanley Range 1, 5, 227, 420
    conditions 15–16
Oyashio 48

P

Palmer, Sergeant Edward 365
Papua New Guinea 6
Papuan Army
    Papuan Infantry Battalion (PIB) 1, 433
Papuan carriers 16, 49, 123, 402
Parbury, Captain Cecil 296, 308–10, 311, 312, 318–19, 321, 336–9
Parcell, Jim 508
Parker, Major David 59–60
Parks, Brigadier Floyd 39, 214
Parks, Private Steve 340
Parry-Okeden, Major William 297, 364, 386
Pashen, Private Frederick 360
Peabody, Lieutenant Herbert 45
Phillips, Francis 'Lorraine' 134
Phillips, Micky 463
Pinwill, Lieutenant Francis 318, 338
Pongani 14, 17, 19, 21–4, 43, 51, 66
Popondetta 2, 25, 52, 56, 81, 86, 125, 130, 252, 257, 284
    airstrip 188, 254
Porlock Harbour 44, 137, 187, 232, 252, 264, 324, 377
Port Moresby 1, 47, 148–9, 228, 512, 513
porters *see* Papuan carriers
Pravda, Sergeant George 211
Prentice, Sergeant Vivian 304
prisoners of war 281, 317, 495–6, 499, 513
    execution of 62
Pulling, Trooper Kenneth 314–15

Q

Quinn, Colonel Lawrence 22

R

Rabaul 13, 44, 47–8, 53–4, 264, 334, 348, 401, 412
    reinforcements and supplies from 33–4, 40–2, 148–9, 238, 252–3, 269, 348–9, 377
Randell, Corporal Ernie 308
Randell, Corporal Tony 308
Randle, Dick 107
Reading, Geoffrey 124
Redden, Lieutenant Leslie 404
Regimental Aid Posts (RAPs) 396–7, 471
Rehak, Staff Sergeant John 346

Reid, Gunner Stanley 354
rifle grenades 225
Riggs, Lieutenant Clarence 431
Rigo 14
Rini, Corporal Daniel 279–80
Roberts, Captain Percy 364
Roberts, Gunner Wal 440
Robertson, Lieutenant Colonel William 150–1
Roderick, Sergeant 422
Rodgers, Corporal Roy 476–7
Rogers, Colonel Gordon 161, 167, 169–70, 176, 179, 429–31
Rolleston, Private Frank 295, 297, 305–7, 360
Rothall, Corporal Clement 464
Rowell, Lieutenant General Sydney 27
Rowland, Norm 440
Rudall, Lieutenant John 425–6, 439
Rudd, Lance Corporal John 305
Runnoe, Captain Donald 499
Russell, Corporal Norm 455
Russell, Lieutenant Neil 475

S

Sadahide, Lieutenant Colonel Fuchiyama 192
Salamaua 47, 53, 335, 348–9, 420–1
Samboga River 43, 44, 270
Sampson, Captain Victor 471–2, 486
Sanananda 2, 5, 7, 12–13, 24, 27, 42, 47, 54, 64, 96, 181, 193, 238, 266, 348, 418, 432, 507, 509–10
    Japanese defence of 35, 221, 509
    Japanese retreat to 489–91
Sanderson, Captain Roger 350, 359–60, 379, 396, 403–4, 406, 414, 422–3, 438–42, 445
Satonao, Kuba 142, 165, 180, 215, 219–20, 230, 245, 251, 255, 269, 274
Sawford, Private Bluey 466
Schmedje, Captain Theodore 437
Schmidt, Colonel Edwin 245
Schoeffel, Lieutenant Max 461, 478
Schroeder, Major Edmund 400, 411–12, 418, 429, 430, 447, 449–51, 488, 499
Schultz, Captain Melvin 210
Schwartz, Lieutenant Paul 212, 294, 328, 334, 347
Schy, Alan 360
Scott, Lieutenant Robert 72–3, 169, 202–3, 205, 239
scrub-typhus 184

Secombe, Brigadier Victor 21
Seiichi, Lance Corporal Uchiyama 63, 277, 332, 365, 387
Sharam, Gunner Robert 317
Sherney, Sergeant Paul 65
Shigeru, Lieutenant Colonel Sugiyama 401
Shiratsuyu 136
Shone, Private Henric Brian 466, 476
Silcock, Lieutenant 464
Silk, George 315, 386, 466–7, 477–8, 487
Simemi 12, 28, 43, 49, 52, 57, 61, 79, 186
Simemi Creek 27, 38, 61, 204, 261, 296, 320, 322, 330, 415, 423, 426, 436, 438, 448–9, 486, 512
   assaults 204–5, 286–7, 338–40, 361–5, 370–1, 448, 494–8, 500
   crossing 340–1, 350, 359–60, 369, 386
   Japanese defences 371, 373
Simemi Village 28, 57, 61
Simms, Lieutenant Allan 447
Sivyer, Lieutenant Thomas 'Bluey' 298, 304, 305
Siwori Creek 133–4, 140, 186, 509
Siwori Village 140, 275, 294, 328, 334, 347, 447, 509
Skerry, Colonel Leslie 509
Sledge Hammer Force 281–2
Slim, Lord 234
Smith, Corporal Phillip 288, 315
Smith, Joe 360
Smith, Lieutenant Colonel Herbert A. 23, 43, 57, 69, 76–8, 83, 284, 489
   Buna Village 112, 186, 212–13, 218, 272–3
   Coconut Grove 275–6, 279–81
   Urbana front 86–8, 94–7, 99–102, 104, 109–10, 121, 172–3
Smith, Lieutenant Louis 'Jim' 463–4
Smith, Major Herbert M. 21, 94–6, 122, 133, 174, 186
   Buna Village 208, 218, 222–3, 244–5
Smith, Sergeant Russell 16
snipers 59–60, 85, 308, 310, 321, 336, 354, 379, 394, 452, 465–6
Solomon Islands 1, 13, 33
Soputa 2, 28, 52, 56, 56–7, 78, 112
   airstrip 123
South West Pacific Area (SWPA) 5
Spencer, Sergeant George 407, 441
Spencer, Sergeant William 'Bill' 289, 321

Spinks, Sergeant Reginald 453
Spraetz, Captain 121
Squires, Private Edward 431
Steddy, Lieutenant Edwin 'Mike' 465, 466
Stehling, Captain Joseph 280
Stokes, Captain Norman 409
Strip Point 114, 189, 260, 261, 304, 337–40, 351
Stuart, Private Albert 191
Suganuma, Lieutenant 55, 63, 66, 164, 171, 185, 192, 201, 217, 226, 234–5, 242, 248–9
Sullivan, Captain John 333, 458
Summers, Corporal Athol 463, 468, 475, 492–2
Sumpit Village 131
supplies 11, 21, 187, 188, 254
   airdrops 22, 31, 44, 50, 58, 184, 188, 220, 252, 254
   ammunition 130–1, 137, 186–7, 224–5, 254
   boat, by 45, 50, 79–80, 129, 231, 252, 257, 288, 374, 376–7, 456
   Japanese 41–2, 110–11, 252–3, 273–4
   problems with 52, 106, 129
Sutherland, Major General Richard 10, 150–6, 214, 284, 328, 347, 374, 412, 429, 460
Suthers, Captain Angus 478–84, 486, 493–4
Sweet, Lieutenant John 341
Sweeting, Sergeant Bill 123

T

Tanaka, Corporal 148, 164
tanks 81–2, 120, 128, 137, 146, 220, 246, 251–2, 256, 266–9, 376, 378, 451, 478, 510
   communication issues 290–1
   crossing creeks 340–3
   friendly fire 441–2
   Giropa Point 461–2, 484, 494–5
   importance of 331–2, 462
   M3 Stuart tanks 256, 257, 261, 263, 268–9, 277, 288, 299, 323, 336, 354–5, 376, 438
   maintenance 354–5
   New Strip assault 296–326
   Old Strip, consolidation of 378–86
   Simemi Creek 362–5, 370–1
   Strip Point 337–8
   Wootten's use of 438–44, 448–9, 454–5, 461–2, 469–70, 472–3
Tarakena 294, 328, 334, 347–8, 433, 447, 498, 508, 510
Taylor, Captain Robert 296, 307, 314, 319–21, 336–7

INDEX

Taylor, Sergeant Douglas 'Jock' 189, 197–8
Templeton's Crossing 1, 14, 41
Thomas, Corporal Robert 303–4
Thomas, Lieutenant Victor 362, 449, 483
Thompson, Corporal Bruce 464
Thompson submachine guns 10
Thorne, Corporal Leslie 353
Timoshenko 21
Tippetts, Lieutenant Christopher 449, 482–3
Tomita, Lieutenant Colonel Yoshinobu 42
Tomlinson, Colonel Clarence 22, 28, 31, 49, 52, 56, 152, 193, 210, 218
    Sanananda 83, 126, 181
    Urbana front 222, 280, 293–4, 327, 333, 346–7
training
    carriers and tanks 190
    US forces 8–9
Tregarthen, Lieutenant Arthur 72–5, 84–5, 92, 116, 145, 168–9, 205–6, 216, 240–1
Trevivian, Major James 360, 379, 384, 396, 403–4, 407, 410, 414, 416, 422–3, 425, 444
Triangle 28, 35–7, 39–40, 41, 58, 76, 86–8, 95, 98–101, 109–10, 122, 137, 142, 172, 194, 292, 327–8, 432, 447, 450
    attempts to take 333–4, 344–8, 418–19, 460
    containment actions 356–8, 398, 400
    terrain 276, 387
Tsukamoto, Lieutenant Colonel Hatsuo 142
Tufi 376
Two Freddies 50
Tye, Major Kenneth 438, 443, 495
Tyler, Lance Corporal George 303

U

Umikaze 51, 54
United States Forces
    32nd Infantry Division *see* 32nd Infantry Division (US Army)
    41st Infantry Division 136
    126th Infantry Regiment *see* 126th Infantry Regiment (US Army)
    127th Infantry Regiment *see* 127th Infantry Regiment (US Army)
    128th Infantry Regiment *see* 128th Infantry Regiment (US Army)
    American I Corps 7
    equipment 9–10
    Third Army (Krueger) 7
    training 8–9

Urbana Force 31, 40, 94, 109, 129, 137, 165, 179, 223, 250, 292–4, 333, 346–7, 436, 488
    reorganisation 188–9
    Warren Force, contact with 424, 460, 498, 504
Urbana front 76, 86–8, 94–7, 99–102, 104, 117–18, 121–2, 127–9, 161, 171–80, 185–6, 193, 255, 260–1, 272–3, 428–32
    Buna Mission 456–60, 488–9, 498–501
    Buna Village 208–16, 218–20, 229–30, 243–5, 266–9
    Coconut Grove 275–6, 279–80, 327–8
    containment actions 356–8
    Entrance Creek 366–7
    Government Gardens 398–401, 411–12, 446–7, 449–51
    Japanese withdrawal 498–9
    night assault 133–4
    Triangle, attempts to take 333–4, 344–8, 418–19
Ustruck, Captain Michael 366, 388

V

Val dive bombers 44, 123
Vasey, Major General George 'Bloody' 2, 27, 31, 33, 56–7, 78, 81, 96, 112, 125–6, 151
Verco, Captain Geoffrey 397
Verey lights 291, 318, 442, 481
Vickery, Major Ian 123, 124
Vondracek, Sergeant Francis 389–90

W

Wada, Private Noburo 184
Wagner, Sergeant Charles E 419
Wairopi 27
Waldron, Brigadier Albert 44, 45, 95, 127, 167, 171, 173–4, 179, 214, 224
    plan of attack 188–9
Walker, Lieutenant Ian 187, 199, 200, 206
Walpole, Private George 299
Walters, Sergeant Allen 'Shorty' 305, 307
Wanigela 14, 17, 19, 21, 24, 80, 234, 264
Warisota Plantation 43
Warren Force 28, 31, 43, 57, 83, 93, 104, 113, 127–9, 137, 142–6, 167–70, 179, 207, 250, 286–91, 436, 492, 512
    reorganisation 188–9, 228, 246, 260
    Urbana Force, contact with 424, 460, 498, 504
Warren front 12, 79, 83, 86, 96, 102–16, 129, 135, 179, 220, 231–4, 256, 269, 271–2, 461, 487
    coastal areas, capture of 436–45
    conditions 225–7

New Strip 162–4
Old Strip 403–11, 414–18, 422–6
patrolling and reconnaissance 224–5, 238–43, 276–8, 351–5
reorganisation 181–3
war of attrition 246
Wootten's objectives 260–4, 286–91, 295–325, 330–2
Wau 5
Wells, Private Bryan 445–6, 494
Wentland, Captain Roy 294, 327, 400
Whitehead, Brigadier Ennis 32, 83, 104
Whitehead, Captain Norman 261, 266–7, 288, 310–12
Whittaker, Lieutenant Paul 346
Williams, Corporal 'Jinny' 479–80
Williams, Corporal Joseph 'Joey' 454
Willoughby, Major General Charles 12–13, 33
Willyama 50
Wilson, Trooper John 'Bunny' 291, 299, 303, 314, 323, 362–3, 380–1, 437
Wilton, Corporal Cecil 197, 199
Winzenreid, Sergeant Samuel 266
Wirraways 105, 130–1, 143, 224, 363
Wissell, Lieutenant Walter 385
Wittelberger, Private Karl 431–2
Wootten, Brigadier George 228, 234, 251–2, 257, 418, 423, 426
  message of congratulations 506–7
  plan of attack 260–1, 281–3, 330–2, 369, 436–8, 448, 454–5
  tanks, use of 438–44, 454–5
  Warren Force 286, 291, 324, 350, 378–9
Workman, Captain James 400
Worthington, Captain Norman 'Tony' 289
Wright, Private Bernie 'Mayor' 417
Wright, Scotty 361

Y

Yamagata, Major General Tsuyuo 67, 124, 132, 136, 221, 264, 274, 412, 419–20, 508
Yamamoto, Colonel Hiroshi 47–8, 51, 54–5, 58, 62, 66, 118, 148, 163, 168, 171, 192, 221, 344, 371, 373, 395, 414, 416, 496–7, 503
Yasuda, Captain Yoshitatsu 40, 58, 88, 119, 194, 209, 211, 224, 230, 283–4, 388, 391, 392, 432, 458, 496, 502–3
Yoriichi, Yokoyama 107–9, 365, 427–8, 489–91
Yoshihara, Major General Kane 420–1

Yosuke, Colonel Yokoyama 40, 42, 192
Yūgumo 48, 136

Z

Zeros 44, 46, 50, 80, 114, 123, 130, 184, 238
Ziebell, Major Milton 182
Zinser, Major Roy 272–3, 275, 279